FREEDOM FROM ADDICTIONS

Errata

1. Note that there is a Tables 21 in the text and a different Table 21 in Appendix M. The latter is identified as such.
2. On page 359, ignore "Appendix J" since Table 8 is still part of Appendix I.
3. Insert "program" after Clinical Psychology in R. Reynolds biography.

FREEDOM FROM ADDICTIONS[1]

A PSYCHOLOGICAL DETECTIVE STORY

Douglas A. Quirk, MA, CPsych[2]
and
Reg M. Reynolds, PhD, CPsych (Retired)[3]
Ontario Correctional Institute

---

[1] Acknowledgement is gratefully made of the impressive work done on this project by Nicole Pekmezaris.

[2] The opinions offered in this book are those of the authors, mainly the senior author, Douglas Quirk (1931–1997). They do not necessarily represent the views of the Ontario Correctional Institute (where data used in the studies referenced were collected) or the Ontario Ministry of the Solicitor General and Correctional Services.

[3] Reg Reynolds considers himself to be the junior author in this project, since his main roles have been as cotherapist and editor (most often trying to catch up to and clarify the senior author's prolific productions).

To order additional copies of this book, contact:
Xlibris
1-888-795-4274
www.Xlibris.com
Orders@Xlibris.com
787637

CONTENTS

INTRODUCTION
    Purpose And Preliminary Tasks Overview ix
Chapter 1: Objectification 1
    Overview of Purpose and Preliminary Tasks 3
Chapter 2: A Theory of Addiction 6
    Causality 6
    Causes and Personality 10
    Some Effects of Some Chemicals 17
Chapter 3: Creating the Test 20
    Selection of Need and Reinforcement Items 20
    Dimensional Concepts 23
    Sentences...25
    Statements 26
    Other Communication Variables.......................................27
    Item Numbers...28
    Response Alternatives...28
    Summary..29
Chapter 4: Item Construction 30
Chapter 5: Scale Selection for Addictions...................................33
    Main Causal Functions 35
    Secondary Causal Functions...37
    Source of Dependent Measures..38
Chapter 6: Context of the Study 40
    Subjects and Setting...40
    Commentary on Subject Characteristics...........................43
    "Treatment of Addictions" 45
    Informants as Sources of Information 46

Negative Format ('Don't Drink') Statements 48
Chapter 7: Approach to Measurement 50
    Scales and Measures 51
    Raw Dependent Variables 55
    Computed Dependent Variables 57
Chapter 8: Psychometrics I (Item Analysis) 59
    The Addicause Scales 59
    Data Reduction 60
    Reliability 62
Chapter 9: Psychometrics II (Scale Characteristics) 66
Chapter 10: Psychometrics III (Validity) 70
    Concurrent Validity 71
    Predictive Validity 73
    Cautionary Notes 77
    Contributions of Various Test Variables 78
    Validation of S and N Total Scores 80
    Additional Observations 81
    Summary 82
Chapter 11: Construct Validation 83
    Introduction 83
    Task Reduction 84
    Scale Reduction 84
    Reduction to Simple Structure 87
Chapter 12: Design of the Treatment Programs 91
    Choosing Targets for the Proposed Treatments 91
    Design of the Treatment Programmes 93
    Format for treatment 93
    Scheduling treatments and their components 94
    A brief overview of each of the nine treatment
    programmes. 96
Chapter 13: Experimental Design 106
    Subjects 106
    Processing of Dependent Measures 108
Chapter 14: Experimental Results 109

Probabilities associated with the effects of the treatments 109

Construct Validity and Precision 111

Addictions and Criminality: Are They Confounded? 114

Summary and Conclusions 116

Chapter 15: Effect Of Addicure On Criminal Recidivism 117

Designing a Series of Preliminary Experiments 117

Short-Term Effects 121

Medium-Term Post-Release Effects 131

Results 132

Conclusions 135

Chapter 16: Addictions and Criminality: Are They Confounded? 136

Chapter 17: Prevention of Addictions 144

Not Holding Out Much Hope of Scientifically-Derived Knowledge Being Used 144

Conventional Approaches to Addictions 147

An Example of Thinking 151

Where to Target Prevention Efforts 152

Barriers to Implementation 154

REFERENCES

APPENDICES

APPENDIX A: Dimensional Addicause Questionnaire (DAQ): Long Form 157

APPENDIX B: Dimensional Addicause Questionnaire (DAQ): Short Form 197

APPENDIX C: Factor Structure of Substances Use(Table 1) 213

APPENDIX D: Addicause Item Analysis: Factor Loadings (Table 2) 219

APPENDIX E: Addicause Reliabilities (Table 3) 239

APPENDIX F: Addicause Stability (Table 4) 241

APPENDIX G: Total Score: S and N Factor Loadings (Table 5) 243

APPENDIX H: Addicause and MMPI Correlation
Matrix (Table 6) 249
APPENDIX I: Discriminant Function % Correct
Classifications and Correlation Coefficients
between the Addicause axes and ninety-one MMPI
Scales (Table 7) and Summary of Table 7 for
Alcohol and Drug Abuse (Table 8) 289
APPENDIX J: Expanded Specifications of Addicure
Treatments..359
APPENDIX K: Probabilities of Treatment Effects
on S Scores (Table 9)..373
APPENDIX K: Probabilities of Treatment Effects
on S Scores (Table 9)..509
    Probabilities of Treatment Effects on N Scores
    (Table 10)..510
    Treatment Effects on Most Relevant S Scores
    (Table 11)..512
    Treatment Effects on Most Relevant N Scores
    (Table 12)..513
    Single-Treatment Effects on S Scores (Table 13) 514
    Single-Treatment Effects on N Scores (Table 14).......515
    Single-Treatment Effects on Relevant S Scores
    (Table 15) 517
    Single-Treatment Effects on Relevant N Scores
    (Table 16)..518
    Treatment Effects on Regrouped Axes (Table 17) 519
    Treatment Effects on Selected Axes (Table 18)..........523
APPENDIX L: Addicause and STFB Correlation
Matrix (Table 19)..525
    Probabilities of Treatment Effects on STFB
    (Table 20) 526
APPENDIX M: DAQ and MMPI Predictions of
Substance Factors (Table 21) 527

INTRODUCTION

Purpose And Preliminary Tasks Overview

The purpose of this work is to present a model to account for addictive behaviour in such a way that it can be modified, to detail a treatment based on this model, and to report on how well that works in practice. At times, the presentation might sound too theoretical and abstract. At times, it might sound too empirical and perhaps concrete. Sometimes, the reader may wonder about the sources of the evidence for the statements made. A word of explanation is needed to pull these scattering statements together.

This work reports a scientific study of addictions. However, the authors are clinicians rather than academics, and our interests do not lie in academic advancement, merely in solving a very mundane everyday problem. We have not had the advantages of either research grants or student assistants. The materials described here are not presented in their historical context. We have not undertaken the scholarly task of reviewing the literature. There are plenty of good reviews of the literature from any perspective one might wish to adopt (Baker, 1988; Davis, 1989; Lowinson et al., 1992).[4] Rather, we have addressed the task as an empirical one and have been concerned with specifically relevant theory only.

It is a truism that the solution of the problem of addictions is one of the most urgent and important tasks facing contemporary society. The consequences of addictive behaviour affect almost everybody

---

[4] Unfortunately, I don't have access to the complete references for these three papers. – RR

in one way or another. Most people have been victims of crime arising from addiction or have experienced interference with their community or family life due to disturbing events associated with addictions. Most communities' social and economic lives have been impaired by addiction-related events. The functioning of most of society's institutions has been disrupted due to problems associated with addictions, affecting student dropouts from the educational system; addiction-related crimes, which burden the justice system; and addiction-produced illnesses as well as addiction to some medications, which strain health system resources. Given the size and the generality of the problem, it is not surprising that priorities in political and governmental action are increasingly targeted on the issue of addictions.

However, it needs to be recognized that being addicted is not unlawful, even if possession and/or use of some addictive substances is. Thus, treatment of being addicted cannot be enforced. This means that treatment of an addiction remains voluntary. Unfortunately, many addicted people do not recognize that they are addicted, so they do not seek treatment. Thus, tests of 'degree of addictiveness' might be helpful to us as a criterion for research selection into addiction programmes. This treatise, however, is not primarily concerned with whether or not a person is addicted or the degree of addictiveness. Instead, it seeks to identify and modify the motivational causes that initiate and perpetuate addictions, assuming the person's own willingness or ability to recognize addictive behaviour.

The material described here comes from a very particular, and quite wide-ranging, source: two large projects conducted with sentenced adult male offenders at the Ontario Correctional Institute (OCI), a modern 220-bed correctional facility where psychosocial treatment is one of the main correctional programs. Several fairly specific criteria serve as the basis on which adult male offenders serving sentences of less than two years are classified to be sent to the OCI. These criteria include

- court recommendation for treatment during incarceration;
- sexual offence, arson, and/or escalating assault or violence;
- moderate degrees of psychological disorder;
- difficulties in inmate classification, most often involving addictive behaviour; and
- voluntary application for treatment. Even if only after a time on the intake unit, transfer to one of the five treatment units requires voluntary application for treatment.

As a result of these selection criterion, about 75% of the admissions to the intake unit exhibit significant degrees of addiction.

For many years, the authors were, respectively, the Senior Psychologist and Chief Psychologist at that facility. The subjects of these studies were, in effect, a "captive audience", albeit having volunteered for treatment, whose treatment just happened to allow for the investigation of their addictions, as well as addiction in general.

The addiction-related projects conducted were designated as the ADDICAUSE and the ADDICURE studies. These studies were undertaken to identify the modifiable causes of addictions. It is not yet complete. Time will have to pass and further research be done before follow-up can meaningfully determine the amount of treatment required to effect lasting therapeutic effects. However, enough has been learned already about the nature and modifiability of addictions that it seems appropriate to report the methods employed and the results achieved in the seven years during which work on this project was in progress.

What appears to have been achieved is nothing less than a fairly comprehensive grasp of the main treatable, and perhaps preventable, causative factors affecting certain kinds of addictive behaviour and the development of measures of each of these factors. Some of the discoveries made represent a major divergence from traditional views about addictions, and new approaches had to be adopted or invented to deal with some of the problems encountered. Consequently, some unexpected explanatory digressions will be required. However, patience will be rewarded with a fairly clear understanding of

addictions and with the means by which addictions can potentially be cured without an insupportable burden on either the addicted person or the resources of the community.

Any scientific research report is like a detective story. Science starts with a mystery to be solved. The problem to be investigated has to be characterized so that it can be observed and so that the tasks to be performed can be clarified. The available bits of information have to be located and subjected to careful measurement and detailed examination. Evidence has to be assembled in such a way that it is capable of being communicated to others in a definitive way. Then all the information has to be presented clearly enough that readers, serving as jurors, can evaluate whether or not there is adequate proof of the conclusions reached.

To do justice to this very complicated and difficult problem, it will be both necessary and entertaining to follow the rather elaborate and convoluted process through which a scientific exploration of a major area of investigation must progress. Science requires that a phenomenon under investigation be made (1) observable (objectification and measurement), (2) understandable (characterization and simplification), (3) controllable (alterable causes identified), (4) modifiable (shown to be subject to technical control), and (5) possibly preventable.

The effort needed to explain why some of the decisions and directions were taken in this research was increased appreciably both by the attempt to create a means by which to objectify a wide sphere of human suffering and by the range of levels of conceptual abstraction demanded in the pursuit of the task. There is no point in seeking to apologize for the resulting difficulty. It must be expected. Still, an attempt will be made to break the task down into meaningful steps and to minimize problems of understanding without entirely removing the challenge and mystery that will be encountered along the way.

CHAPTER 1

Objectification

The first step of any scientific investigation is to make the subject matter studied observable. Can you imagine trying to study the behaviour in an electron without being able to observe it or its behaviour (e.g., by means of an electron microscope)? Or can you imagine setting out to understand and treat an organ illness, such as appendicitis, without being able to observe an inflamed appendix? There are several steps involved in the process of making any event or thing observable. And the result of these steps ought to be the ability to examine the thing being studied in various ways, as it were, to be able to 'diagnose' the state of the event or thing.

A proper 'diagnosis' involves all the elements that will be addressed in this volume, and more. It includes a means by which to observe and record the elements or 'symptoms' of the event and tools or tests as means by which to verify the presence and state of the event and to measure it. Within that context, we have also chosen to explore (i) knowledge of the 'causes' or the aetiology of the event; (ii) knowledge of what, if anything, has gone wrong (its pathology); (iii) knowledge of the means by which its causes can be controlled or modified (its treatment or cure); and (iv) knowledge of how to create or prevent it, depending on whether people view it as an desirable or undesirable event. If any of these elements is missing from knowledge about the event, the event is imperfectly understood,

its understanding is in the realm of conjecture and personal belief, and no complete or proper diagnosis can be attempted.

In order to be clear about the task to be undertaken in this volume, the components of a diagnosis need to be listed, and then those parts that will be addressed in this work need to be identified. A proper diagnosis requires <u>all</u> of the following:

(a) A <u>complaint</u> or presenting problem demanding attention and cure
(b) Recognition of a complex of symptoms called a <u>syndrome</u>
(c) Determination of the 'cost' in pain or <u>inconvenience</u> suffered (which determines whether the costs of a cure are worthwhile)
(d) Defining the <u>limits</u> of the person's acceptance of services
(e) Pursuing various options of diagnoses (<u>differential diagnoses</u>)
(f) Selecting a particular <u>class</u> of symptoms to be addressed (diagnostic label)
(g) Discovery of the causes initially creating it (<u>aetiology</u>)
(h) Determining its biological consequences (<u>organic pathology</u>)
(i) Determining psychological consequences (<u>functional pathology</u>)
(j) Determining its social/other consequences (<u>social pathology</u>)
(k) Knowing what will happen if treated or not treated (<u>course</u>)
(l) Knowing about the person's pre-existing and '<u>normal</u>' states
(m) If chronic, discovering what gains keep it going (<u>perpetuators</u>)
(n) If chronic, discovering what needs it fulfils (<u>final causes</u>)
(o) Knowing what the person can do on his/her own (<u>prescriptions</u>)
(p) Knowing treatments which will control or cure it (<u>treatments</u>)
(q) Knowing the <u>process</u> or course through which treatment will go
(r) Knowing the <u>side effects or complications</u> of each treatment
(s) Knowing <u>how to fix</u> side effects or complications that occur
(t) Knowing how to <u>create</u> it <u>or</u> to <u>prevent</u> it from occurring

In what follows here, attention will be directed solely at those components of diagnosis from step e to step t. Steps a to d do not require attention here. The complaint (a) and the limitations beyond which the person is unwilling to go in accepting a service (d) are determined

by the individuals involved. Addiction (b) is well recognized in the community and in the literature, although some forms of addictive behaviour have not received extensive attention <u>as</u> addictions. The means to determine the 'costs' (c) of alcohol and drug addictions in pain and inconvenience, and thus to measure the *degree* of addiction, are already available as widely used standard instruments such as the Michigan Alcoholism Screening Test (MAST) and the Drug Abuse Screening Test (DAST). This work is <u>not</u> concerned with any attempt to measure the degree of addiction, preferring instead to employ the MAST and DAST for that purpose. That is, the instrument developed here is intended for purposes other than the determination of the presence or strength of alcoholism or drug abuse.

Although this treatise is concerned with steps e to t, it excludes attention to steps h to j, since they are the main focus of the existing literature on addictions. Steps q and t are yet to be undertaken and will be reported when completed.

Overview of Purpose and Preliminary Tasks

The primary purpose of the ADDICAUSE project is to find the main operating causes that control alcohol and drug addictions and to develop measures of each of them. A cursory review of the literature – a complete review of the literature is a scholarly task that has not been undertaken here – did not reveal the kinds of knowledge being sought. Certainly, there were suggestions of some possible causes, and there were tentative indications of promising ways to treat addictions. For example, a great deal of work has been dedicated to single but common addictions such as that to tobacco (Dunn, 1973; Hunt, 1970). But in this area of addictions, as in others, the causes identified were single causative agents with limited evidence to support them, and/or were selected inferentially to justify a particular type of understanding of addictions, and/or were not meaningfully or demonstrably associated with effective means for treatment. Most of what was encountered in the literature was not considered to be

particularly helpful in the search for modifiable measures (and, by inference, modifiable cause of addictive behaviour).

It seemed necessary to use the resources at hand to determine how to proceed. The gleanings from the literature had been applied in many years of clinical treatment work, during which addicts of all sorts were encountered in various settings and circumstances. From these gleanings, and from experimental attempts to address the particular problems presented by clients, a beginning sense of the underlying nature of several types of addictions seemed to have been developed. But no organized idea had emerged about how to identify the causes that would be the targets of any treatment that it might be worthwhile to evaluate.

Since the aim was to identify the causes of addictions in order to be able to treat them, it seemed best to begin by trying out in an experimental treatment program the beginnings of ideas about what might control addictions. A questionnaire was drawn up comprised of nineteen fourteen-item scales to estimate things like anxiety, depression, stimulus hunger, need for disinhibition, and the like. It was administered to a fairly large group of inmates who attended a treatment program aimed at addictions. The questionnaires were scored for each participant, and the substances that he might have been presumed to use on the basis of his answers were listed.

The logic used to predict each individual's preferred substance(s) was a primitive one. If the anxiety score was relatively high, then tranquillizing substances would be listed; if the depression score was relatively high, then excitant substances (psycho-activators) would be listed; if inhibitive trends seemed particularly strong, then disinhibiting substances were listed. When the participants were then asked to list their most commonly used substances and their lists were compared impressionistically with the predictions, the match seemed almost perfect at the level of classes of substances.

These results were encouraging enough to try again. Based on the mismatches and what had emerged during the ensuing discussion, the questionnaire was extended to twenty-six fourteen-item scales. A new group of fifty inmates was assembled for a second trial of the

questionnaire and treatment for addictions. There were, if anything, fewer mismatches in the new group using the new questionnaire. Thus, it seemed safe to assume that the original (impressionistic) results were at least not merely due to sample bias in the original group. However, it was not clear that the group therapy format did not somehow create a 'priming' effect such that participants were reporting substance uses suggested by something in the group interaction.

It was time to find out just which reportable factors might really account for various types of addictions. Considerable effort was expended to construct a set of sixty-eight twelve-item scales to cover the types of variables that this group experience and other psychotherapy experience suggested as underlying addictions. The purpose of this exercise was to identify, among inmate clientele, the causes that controlled their addictions to substances, or Addicause.

CHAPTER 2

A Theory of Addiction

The approach adopted in the elucidation of any problem emerges from a particular point of view or theory concerning the issue under investigation, and as any review of the literature on addictions will quickly reveal, a host of different points of view have been adopted in research in this field. Before developing the logic by which the causes of addictions are to be made observable, therefore, it seems necessary to explain the view of addictions adopted in this project. A very particular, but not especially novel, point of view was adopted. It is comprised of a number of elements, some of which may be quite unexpected.

Causality

The first element that needs to be addressed concerns the nature of causality itself. This element is necessary because the aim is to find the causes of addictions and because of the apparently 'chronic' nature of addictions. The contention will be advanced that 'chronicity' of any human condition is largely a by-product of the approach adopted to its causality.

If one asks almost anybody to define the concept of *cause*, the response is apt to be that a cause is any event that regularly precedes the occurrence of another event. Indeed, not only is this the common

view of the entire range of the concept, it is also the view that is conventionally adopted in all science. Modelled after the physical sciences, all sciences seem to have restricted themselves to the pursuit of antecedent or initial (iota or *i*) causes in their spheres of investigation. And the pursuit of these types of causes has proved to be highly effective, particularly in the physical sciences (physics, chemistry).

The physical universe is spatially distributed. This means that if we look for a <u>thing</u> in the wrong <u>place,</u> we will not find it. It also directs attention to causal concepts such as energy and force by which physical things move or remain fixed in space. Two kinds of causes seem to operate in the physical universe. The main one of these is initial (iota) cause in which energy acts on a thing to change it in specifiable ways, with the cause preceding its effect(s). A secondary one is the kind of perpetuating (nu) cause, which is recognized in phenomena such as inertia. This latter kind of cause, whereby a thing remains in its state unless and until another force or energy acts upon it, seems to operate at the same time as its effects, going along with them and neither preceding nor following them.

The behavioural universe, by way of contrast, is temporally distributed, which means that if we look for an <u>action</u> or event in the wrong <u>time,</u> we will not find it. It also draws attention to the ephemeral nature of behaviour and to the direction or goal of the action over time. Three kinds of causes seem to operate in the behavioural universe. In addition to any initial (iota, *i*) and perpetuating (nu, *v*) causes that may act on behaviour, final (omega, *w*) causes or purposes – the intended goal – affect any behavioural event.

Consider a person performing the action of throwing a ball. The initial cause of the motion of the physical object (the ball) is the force applied to it by the person's arm and hand. That application of force itself has initial causes arising from the energy provided by the ingestion of food and the intake of oxygen that preceded the throw. Moreover, the ball continues to be still or to move (inertia) until another force is applied to it. All these things are aspects of the spatially distributed physical universe. But by themselves, they are not

interesting enough to spectators to warrant any attention – until the events of the psychological or behavioural universe are considered. The interesting properties of an event involve its motivation and 'life' (existing only when there is action), which are related to the psychological universe.

If the ball is perceived to be a basketball, for example, the purpose to which it is likely to be used would commonly involve an overhand throw, generally in an upwards direction, towards a hoop. If, however, it is perceived to be a bowling ball, the purpose to which it is likely to be turned would ordinarily involve an underhand throw, generally in a horizontal plane, towards some other object. The purpose (final, <u>omega</u>, $\underline{w}$ cause) determines <u>whether</u> or not the ball will be thrown at all and <u>how</u> and <u>where</u> it will be thrown. And achieving that goal (getting the ball through the hoop or striking the other object), the purpose (or final cause) of the action, is not achieved until <u>after</u> the consequences that it causes. That is, final causes occur simultaneously with or <u>after</u> their effects in time.

Moreover, whether or not the throw of the ball achieves its purpose is determined by another kind of cause acting in the behavioural universe. The skill of the thrower will determine, or at least have an effect on, whether or not the basketball enters the hoop or the bowling ball strikes its intended object. The thrower's skill is comprised of such elements as his/her sensitivity to the cybernetic feedback experienced during the first parts of the act of throwing and the habit strength (or practised ease) with which the throw is accomplished. And the elements involved in the thrower's skill occur <u>at the time</u> of the behaviour of throwing. That is, the skill elements are perpetuating (<u>nu</u>, $\underline{v}$) causes involved in the behavioural universe.

Of course, there are initial (<u>iota</u>, $\underline{i}$) causes acting in the behavioural universe as well. Prior experience with balls on the part of the thrower will likely determine in large part how he/she perceives the ball that is at hand. And prior practice in throwing each type of ball, as well as the success he/she has encountered in that sort of activity, will determine in a measure the skill he/she manifests in achieving the purpose of the throw. These last comments may seem so obvious that

they might almost better be left unsaid. However, it is important to note that once the perceptions and/or the skills have been laid down through the initial causes of experience and practice, they are well-nigh immutable. That is to say, although not commonly true in the physical universe, in the behavioural universe, initial causes, once having had their effects, cannot thereafter conveniently be changed or their effects removed.

Try thinking of it this way. The behavioural universe (personality) can be thought of as a rather amorphous or amoeba-shaped entity comprised of many arrows representing motivational vectors. The arrows are of varying lengths and go in different directions, pulling the person to do many things at once. The resolution of this force field determines what the person will do at any given moment. An initial cause occurs and the force field is changed, some of the arrows change length or direction a bit. Then the whole system adjusts itself to accommodate to the effects of that initial cause. Then another initial cause occurs, and the force field's changes and adjustments occur again. Now, try to remove the first initial cause and its effects. It cannot be done because the effects have become part of the whole system and because the initial cause has happened and is a thing of the past.

Indeed, in the behavioural or functional universe, analyses or treatments aimed at initial causes are likely to fail. Obvious illustrations of this notion are to be found in retrospectively directed initial cause treatment methods, such as psychoanalysis, which have been unable to demonstrate a difference in outcomes from the effects of no treatment and in the concept of chronic illness in medicine – a field devoted almost exclusively to initial cause analyses or ways of understanding things.

It needs to be said again: in the behavioural universe, initial (iota, i) causes do play a small part in the initial formation of habits, but they are then essentially immutable or intractable, like the proverbial 'water which has passed under the bridge'. The causes that most control events in the behavioural universe are perpetuating (nu, v) causes of habit strength and reinforcers and final (omega, w) causes

10 Douglas A. Quirk and Reg M. Reynolds

or purposes and goals. Moreover, and almost most importantly, since these types of causes are not made kinetic, at least until the target behaviour is being performed, they are modifiable as means by which to alter the behavioural or functional effects represented, for example, in the subject's presenting problem(s).

Indeed, there is some justification to state as a principle that all effective treatment of behavioural or functional presenting problems depends on the modification of perpetuating causes and/or final causes and possibly on nothing else. It may even be true that at least one reason why cognitive therapies seem to be relatively more effective than most other forms of psychotherapy is that many (though not all) final causes (purposes, goals) are strongly represented in the cognitive system where they are also fairly readily modifiable.

But what has all this to do with the advertised topic of addictions? First, addictions are considered to be 'chronic' and relatively 'intractable' disorders. This may be due to the fact that addictive behaviour has traditionally been viewed almost exclusively through points of view solely seeking its initial causes, which may well result in no capability to effect change in such behaviour or its causes. Second, it is contended that any attempt to construct a model for observation and/or modification of addictions ought to be focused most specifically on means by which to observe, measure, and alter perpetuating and final causes while perhaps also examining any initial causes that can be identified. As will be seen later, the present project makes this latter contention a central theme throughout – in observation, measurement, and treatment.

Causes and Personality

Traditionally, we have asked, What causes addictions? This question may have been put rather poorly. It seems to direct attention to initial or antecedent causes, the weakness of which has just been remarked. And it seems to place the addict and his/her addiction as if he/she and it were effects of some external cause(s). A fairly

modern approach to treatment of addictions (Relapse Prevention) has implicitly asked, What does the addict notice or find? One of the answers to this question has been that he/she finds addictive triggers and immediate gratification. At least this question and answer seek some of the reinforcers or perpetuating causes of addictions, and they include the addict as part of the causal process.

Another even better way to formulate the question might be, What is the addict (as the active, causal subject) seeking to achieve with addictive behaviour? Possible answers to this question might include definable kinds of effects on the way he/she feels (reinforcements or perpetuating causes) or gratification or relief of a motivation or a felt need (final causes). A brief digression is required at this juncture.

When the author has talked to others about the notions being put forwards here, the almost-automatic rejoinder at this point has been, But what causes the needs (final causes) or the effects (perpetuating causes)? So deeply entrenched by our training is our reliance on initial cause thinking that it is almost impossible for us to put it aside even for a moment. Having said that, however, the question leads in an important other direction.

Indeed, what causes or creates any need or any element of personality? The answer is probably relatively simple. The body comes equipped with very few systems that can create lasting (or chronic) problems or states. As Selye (1976) and many others have shown at the level of problem generation and as Wolpe (1958) and others have shown at the level of treatment, the main available bodily system implicated in most human suffering and presenting problems is the autonomic nervous system (ANS). It is a hardwired system feeding all the organ systems of the body directly or indirectly. It is a survival system, which means that its messages achieve predominance over all others. It is an adaptable system that can be modified in any direction of its responses and thus can regulate other adaptive behaviours. And it is comprised of nervous tissue, so it learns. And it can learn extremely quickly. Its effects are so versatile and pervasive that it is contended here that the ANS and the stress, immune, and anxiety responses it stimulates and orchestrates underlie most (although not

quite all) lasting human suffering (the presenting symptoms that the patient wishes to have addressed).

The <u>first level</u> at which the ANS can produce suffering or problems involves direct arousal of its anxiety/anger/stress branch (known as the Sympathetic Nervous System). The experience created is commonly uncomfortable, and the response to such arousal – the fight or flight response – tends to motivate attack or avoidance. The arousal-anxiety response of the ANS can be uncomfortable or unpleasant, escape or avoidance behaviour can be maladaptive in some circumstances, and both the arousal and the avoidance actions may evoke uncomfortable or unpleasant derivative responses such as muscle tension and its many consequences. Also, any of these responses can themselves become habitual (learned), so their unpleasant consequences can become relatively chronic.

The <u>second level</u> at which suffering can be produced by ANS activation is built on the first as a higher-order conditioned response. Learned escape can be conditioned to predictive cues to create conditioned anticipatory avoidance. Almost anything can be avoided in an anticipatory fashion. 'I never get angry', 'I don't know what love feels like', 'I am always clear in my mind about everything', 'I am never confused', and a host of other expressions of anticipatory avoidance illustrate this level of human subjective experience. Anticipatory avoidance habits are clearly learned, and they tend to be represented in many of the characteristics or traits by which people describe themselves and in many of their problems.

The <u>third level</u> at which the ANS can produce suffering is built on the second by still higher-order conditioning. Traits or characteristics generated by anticipatory avoidance, if they create comfort in the person, can be generalized, or if they feel uncomfortable can serve as cues for further avoidance. If clear or rational thinking diminishes confusion and its discomfort, the person may become increasingly introverted and rational, which, however, can itself become an unrecognized source of confusion and/or dissatisfaction. If an absence of felt anger is valued or feels good, anticipatory avoidance of all energy use may develop, which can to lead to depression

or anhedonia. If a lack of awareness of love feelings results in an uncomfortable emptiness and the presence of internal bodily sensations feels reassuring, the latter may be magnified, perhaps to eventuate in hypochondriasis. Since the avoidances involved often go unnoticed, the resulting state of the person may become habitual and may become even more clearly a source of self-definition or of presenting problem.

A fourth level can then emerge derived through the above chain of higher-order conditioned sequences. And here the progression at last may result in addictive behaviour. Introversion and its consequences may feel oppressive; depression and its associated consequences, or hypochondriasis, may feel awful or create desperation; and weak positive emotions may feel unfulfilling. Such consequences of this stage in higher-order conditioning tend to become lasting and pervasive temperamental states of the person, setting him/her up to demand repeated relief from them. In the attempt to relieve these unpleasant feelings, the person may seek and find rapid means by which to relieve his/her distress. Such means include the use of chemical substances (or of actions that perform equivalent functions). Using such means to create relief from the distress of higher-order conditioned or derived feelings tends to have two effects. First, if relief is achieved, however temporarily, the means for its relief (perpetuating reinforcement) may be learned rapidly as addictive behaviour. Second, the accomplishment of the state (purpose or final cause) achieved as a result of the relief (e.g., feelings of omnipotence or euphoria) may itself become a learned need, pursued as though it were a positive goal.

According to the present point of view or model then, addictive behaviour is seen as a habit, rewarded repeatedly by immediate relief of an uncomfortable and relatively continuous higher-order conditioned habit or trait. And achievement of the polar opposite of the uncomfortable habit can itself become a learned need pursued in addictive behaviour. That is, **according to the present view, a substance is addictive if it relatively and rapidly effects changes in the subjective state of a person, either reducing an**

uncomfortable state or creating, however temporarily, a desired or pleasant state. And each substance, by virtue of its potential to alter specific kinds of subjective states, is only addictive for those people who experience and are uncomfortable with those specific habitual states that the substance alters. That is, addictive behaviour amounts to self-medication (Khantzian, 1975). The particular subjective states that may be learned and that, modified by substances, create addiction to them will be developed later in the section on the derivation of the scales to measure causes of addictions.

Recognizing that addictive substances are chemicals, and given the contemporary preoccupation with chemical explanations for events in human life, it is hardly surprising that the predominant 'common sense' view concerning substance abuses is that addictions must be due to some chemical cause in the body. Although it is clear that all sorts of chemical interactions occur within the body associated with ingestion of addictive (or any other) substances, many of which can be measured, there is not a scrap of satisfactory evidence for chemical causation of addictions beyond the already remarked irrelevant issues. This is not to state that some addictive chemicals do not store cognates of themselves in the body, which can recreate the addictive state easily with lesser than usual quantities of the substances (e.g., heroin), nor is it to say that addictive chemicals do not have profound, if temporary, effects on the body. Instead, it is intended to state that it is the <u>subjective</u> effects it has on pre-existing states in the body that determine whether or not the chemical will be addictive for any given individual.

If an analgesic is effective in relieving an individual's pain and if it is taken frequently <u>at the time</u> when the person is experiencing pain, the frequency and intensity of the type of pain experienced will be reinforced and, hence, increase over time, and addictive reliance on the analgesic can develop. If a poison (e.g., nicotine) is introduced into the body, the body reacts each time with the protective stress-immune response. This alone does not ensure addiction to cigarettes. If, however, the person's conditioned <u>pre-existing</u> subjective state

feels, say, a trifle lethargic and if relief of that lethargy feels good or is welcome, then an addiction to nicotine can develop as a means to enhance arousal. It is the repeated <u>subjective effects</u> of addictive substances <u>on pre-existing habitual states</u> of people that creates addictions.

Chemical addictions are not the only forms of manifestly addicted behaviour. Compulsions of all types (such as handwashing, cross-dressing, checking doors, and even some arsons) are probably created and respond exactly as chemical addictions. If a person has a learned fear of contamination by dirt, washing relieves the fear temporarily, thus increasing the habit strength to washing – perhaps, eventually, compulsively. If a person has developed a tendency to enjoy soft tactile sensations, he may find the sensations of contact over his body from silky material pleasurable enough that he seeks that contact compulsively in cross-dressing (especially in silks and satins). If a person, fearing insecurity, values security, he/she may find relief of fear in confirming that a door is locked, resulting in increased habit strength for checking doors, maybe to eventuate in a compulsion to do so. The list is endless.

Moreover, addictive behaviour often does not continue as it began. Adolescents frequently start smoking tobacco products under the pleasant illusion that it makes them look or feel 'grown up' (a final cause). Over time, either the nicotine habit (described above) takes over or else the tobacco addiction does not develop and the person stops smoking. Other reinforcers, however, often take over from the original one(s). That is, the original causes frequently fade, and new causal factors take over to maintain the addiction.

The new causes that take over, like the original cause, are not the kinds of causes commonly understood to serve as causes. Once more, the contemporary materialistic preoccupation with physical and chemical events has shaped people's thinking to believe that the (only) kind of cause is that (antecedent) event that is regularly <u>followed</u> by its effect(s) – initial (<u>iota</u>, i) cause. In adult human life, however, 'initial' causes are neither the only kind of operating causes, nor even the most important ones. Also, as mentioned above, in

human living, initial causes are very nearly intractable. That is, they do not lend themselves well through modification via treatment.

Perpetuating (habit strength, nu, v) and Final (purpose, omega, w) causes, in contrast, participate richly in human living; and since they are either ongoing at the time of the events that they cause (perpetuating causes) or happen after the events they cause (final causes or purposes), they are much more easy to alter.

Workers in the field of addictions have long sought the elusive touchstone of 'the addictive personality'. It has not been discovered for the simple reason that there is not just one kind of addictive personality, but many of them. Nor do these personality characteristics represent the whole of an individual's personality. Instead, they are merely learned traits or habit patterns that create their own 'needs' or are themselves learned needs.

If a person learns to be depressed, the needs associated with the depression include the needs to be a nice person, to be dependent on others, and to experience a lift in his/her mood. If a person learns to be fearful, the needs arising from the fear include the needs to avoid feared events, to protect him/herself, and to experience relief from fear. These needs serve as motives to drive the person to do (depend, avoid, etc.) and to experience (lift in mood, relief from fear) particular states. These motives (to achieve something not yet in evidence) serve as the final causes that pull the person to actions now in the hope of achieving the desired state in the future. Each of these needs or purposes, if it can be achieved by means of a substance, may form another element of the addictive personality.

If a learned need (an element of personality) drives a person to achieve a desired state that can temporarily be achieved by use of a substance (chemical) or by an action (behavioural), then that substance or action is potentially addictive. The addictive behaviour is thus caused (final cause) by satisfaction of the need state that motivates it or that drives the person from the future to pursue the addiction and to achieve some relief or 'feeling better' with respect to the disturbance that is experienced as a need.

But the substance or action will not be addictive unless it, however temporarily, does appear to relieve the need state or make the person 'feel better'. To be addictive, a substance or action must have some desired subjective <u>effect</u>. If the substance or action does have that effect of appearing to make the person feel better, it is rewarding and reinforcing. These reinforcing effects serve as the perpetuating causes that maintain the habit strength or the addiction. In this sense, the reinforcing effects, occurring <u>with</u> the use of the substance or action and maintaining the habit strength to continue use of the substance or action, also serve as (perpetuating) causes of the addictive behaviour.

The Addicause project seeks to identify the personality elements that serve as needs (final, <u>omega,</u> or w causes), relief of which reinforces (perpetuating, <u>nu,</u> or v causes) the habit strength or addictive use of given substances. The Addicure project seeks to address the identified learned needs and their associated reinforcers in order to modify the habit strength of relief-seeking addictive behaviour and thereby modify the addictive response.

Some Effects of Some Chemicals

Some chemicals seem to have addictive properties, and some do not. What effects do the addictive substances have that others do not? There is an extensive literature on this matter, which is not reviewed here. Instead, a couple of examples may serve to illustrate the manner in which the thinking underlying the present project developed.

<u>Alcohols</u> are soporifics. The basic effect of their ingestion is to decorticate. In effect, it functions as a temporary lobotomy. Most effects of alcohol ingestion follow from this decorticating effect, due to its soporific effect on the cerebral cortex. The consequence of this decorticating effect is twofold.

The first group of consequences does <u>not</u> have major addictive properties for most people, but they provide the main reason why the community is wary about alcohol ingestion. Decortication results in impairment of functions crucial to efficient action, such as those

required in driving a car. Distance perception, perceptual acuity, muscle coordination, reaction time and judgement, as well as other cortical efficiency functions, are impaired roughly in proportion to the amount of alcohol ingested. This results in increased risk of traffic accidents following alcohol ingestion and in the clumsy and unbalanced gait and speech often associated with excessive drinking. A few imbibers enjoy the image created by these effects, and for them, these effects are addictive.

A second group of consequences are inclined to be addictive for those who feel troubled or oppressed by the states altered by these decorticating effects. Decortication does not greatly diminish the ANS anxiety response, but it does reduce awareness of it, as well as reducing the clarity of thought associated with evoking anticipatory anxiety. It does not remove depressive affect, but it does relieve worries, inhibitions, and the pressure of thought that often underlie depression. It does not take away habitual inhibitions, but it does diminish the reasoning that maintains them. And it does foster impulsiveness by removing cortical controls temporarily. These are only some of the effects of decortication, but they do illustrate the reinforcing effect on some people of alcohol ingestion. If the person feels (and only if he/she feels) uncomfortable due to habitual anxiety or despairs due to habitual depression or experiences learned inhibition and/or controls as oppressive, then relief of the discomfort, despair, or oppressive feelings is inherently rewarding; and the habit or addiction to use alcohol is apt to develop rapidly.

Street drugs may have a calming or mellowing effect on the person, which may secondarily enhance sexual appetite; they may have excitant or activating effects, which may secondarily enhance the person's sense of power or importance (ego expansion); or they may have the effect of increasing acuity and/or restricting the breadth of sensory or perceptual awareness, which may create the illusion of brightened colours, shimmering surface qualities, and/or a mixture of perception and fantasy that changes the appearance of the self or surroundings. These are only some of the possible effects of street drugs, but they suffice for illustrative purposes. For those who are

(but not for those who are not) uncomfortably tense, who experience relatively weak sexual appetites, who feel the joylessness of apathy, who feel weak and unimportant, who despair about the boredom of life, or who seek enjoyment from external sensory experience, the effects of street drugs may afford reinforcements and thus create habitual or addictive involvement with the relevant kinds of drugs.

In light of the foregoing, it might be possible to develop measures of the causes of addiction to various kinds of substances by taking account of (1) the varieties of uncomfortable human conditions that the substances might relieve, (2) the definable subjective effects of addictive substances, and (3) the kinds of derived or learned needs that might be gratified temporarily by such substances. This idea was the basis on which the Addicause scales were created.

CHAPTER 3

Creating the Test

Selection of Need and Reinforcement Items

How would you go about finding the necessary elements of the addictive personality, the needs, and the reinforcers that may cause addictions? You might sift through the needs proposed by McDougall (1923) or later elaborated in Murray's (1938) Need-Press theory, as Jackson (1974) has done. You might examine the literature on addictions to decide which reinforcing triggers, if modified in treatment, might have therapeutic effects, as Marlatt and Gordon (1985) have done. You might plod through the extensive writings in clinical psychology and psychiatry to guess which learned or pathological needs might seem likely nominees as final or perpetuating causes of addictions, as many of the efforts at psychotherapy in addictions have done. You might explore the literature on conditioning and other forms or therapy in order to find which motivations, once altered, seem to reduce some addictive behaviour, as Peniston and Kulkosky (1990) and studies on the effects of behaviour therapy have done (e.g., Quirk, 1976). Or you might use all of these and other sources of classes of motivations and listen carefully to what addicted people say about the needs and rewards operating in them. Given the rather limited therapeutic effects reported in the addictions literature and some success in the treatment of various types of clients exhibiting addictions, the writer adopted the latter approach, if in a rather strange way.

Identifying needs and reinforcers is one issue. How the person who is to be studied may provide information about himself or herself concerning the needs and reinforcers acting in him/her is another issue. For example, if, as in the final part of the test (the Dimensional Addicause Questionnaire **or** DAQ) where utilization of substances is the focus of inquiry, the respondent were asked to state the cause(s) of his substance use, the response typically given would be well-nigh meaningless. Respondents tend to give answers like 'peer pressure' or 'being addicted'. If, however, the question is posed in terms of the effects of substance use, the answers given seem to be generally more meaningful. The answers tend to express underlying motivations, such as 'felt important', 'more relaxed', 'felt accepted', and the like.

In most psychological scale construction, the two issues of needs and reinforcers and how they are reported tend to be muddled together and to be treated in an empirical way. Regardless of its 'real' meaning, if people exhibiting a target behaviour tend to respond to a statement in one direction and those not displaying that behaviour tend to respond in the other direction, that statement can be adopted as a part of a measure of that behaviour. When this approach to scale construction has been used, a great deal of effort is then required to tease out the meanings of the statements employed in the measure. And thereby lies another problem.

The enormous variety of types of addictions suggested that the usual empirical approach would be far too cumbersome. Indeed, if, as was intended, one sets out to find the causes of more than one or many kinds of addictions, the empirical approach would likely not even be practical. This is because, during scale development, it would be necessary to test very large numbers of people *for each revision* in order to obtain analysable data in which the expected amount of any given substance's use was not an absolute zero. Accordingly, another approach to statement creation was sought. And the initial part of the approach adopted was, again, based more on theory than empirical data.

Words employed in self-descriptive statements involve cognitive and/or motivational aspects, in addition to behavioural and habitual

elements (characteristics of the person's behaviour). Needs ($\underline{w}$ causes) and reinforcers ($\underline{v}$ causes) operate in and on the person's motivational system. It seemed necessary, in order to access the motivational attributes of respondents, to find the kinds of words that carry motivational properties. The implications or connotations of such words should include a kind of 'pull' towards or 'push' away from something in order to represent their motivational properties.

If a cause or an effect has had power or importance in a person's life sufficient to create major and relatively intractable consequences (such as addiction or other psychological maladies), then the concepts used in the statements to express that cause or effect ought to represent 'power' or 'importance' in some way. That is, the concepts employed in motivation-relevant self-descriptive statements represent (or ought to represent) power or importance to the respondent. But what sorts of words or concepts carry the meaning of *power* or *importance* to any respondent? At first, it was thought that *power* and *importance* statements would necessarily have to represent strong negative affects or feelings. Then it was noticed that many addicts present extremely positive feelings as being associated with use of addictive substances.

Words that carry an implication of power or a motivated pull or push in one direction or another should be polar words or concepts implying two poles such that the concept for one pole seems automatically to imply contrast against the other pole. This kind of thinking is similar to that underlying that used by Osgood (1953) in the development of the Semantic Differential, except that the focus here was less on the motivational nature of the respondent's conceptual universe and more on the use of the conceptual universe to extract information about motivation. Still, if carefully selected polar concepts were used, it seemed possible to create partially orthogonal dimensions such that, although to a degree of orthogonality less than that found in the Semantic Differential, the polar concepts might be construed as independent of one another. That is, without undertaking a factor analysis of 'conceptual space', it was hoped that it would be possible, using polar concepts, to create conceptual dimensions with which to

measure relatively independent types of motivations to estimate needs and reinforcers operating in and on addicts.

It was not yet entirely clear how to establish the relationship between specific needs and reinforcers relating to addictions and the polar conceptual dimensions with which they might be measured. A leap of faith was taken.

Dimensional Concepts

Two valued colleagues accompanied the writer (DQ) to lunch, and the request was made that the time be devoted to the task of identifying every imaginable 'dimensionalized concept'. Large numbers of polar concepts were found. These served as a basis for an extended list of polar words, some of which are displayed below. Some of the concepts are followed by an indicator of the class of human suffering with which they were thought to be associated (unless the class was addictions). The list below is presented for illustrative purposes, with those concepts that were chosen as the bases for the Dimensional Addicause Questionnaire (DAQ) in bold.

Used Mainly as Verbs	Used Mainly as Nouns
Facilitate-Impede	**Satisfied-Dissatisfied**
Change-Persist	**Facilitate-Impede**
Fail-Succeed	**Self-Other**
Lose-Gain	**Beauty-Ugliness**
Approach-Avoid	**Alone-Group**
Sensitive-Insensitive	**Bad-Good**
Integrate-Disintegrate	**Forwards-Backwards**
Rigid-Change/Learn	**Real-Unreal**
Purpose-Random	**Up-Down**
Separate-Together	**Isolated-Social**
Sleep-Awaken	**Pain-Pleasure**
Power-Impotence	**Active-Passive**
Anxious-Depressed	**Mind-Body**

Tense-Relax	**Error-Precise**
Grow-Regress (schizophrenic)	Forwards-Backwards (schizophrenic)
Receive-Give (criminal)	Introvert-Extrovert (obsessive)
Begin-End (obsessive)	Cause-Effect (depressive)
Accept-Reject (criminal)	Huge-Tiny (depressive)
Hope-Do (depressive)	Light-Dark (schizophrenic)
Dislike-Enjoy (depressive)	Close-Distant (paranoid)
Push-Pull (paranoid)	Birth-Death (depressive)
Believe-Doubt (paranoid)	Evidence-Inference (paranoid)
Know-Feel-Imagine (obsessive)	Strong-Weak (schizophrenia)
Think-Act (obsessive)	Independent-Dependent (depressive)
Break-Mend (schizophrenic)	Prosocial-Antisocial (criminal)
Loud-Quiet (depressive)	Kind-Mean (paranoid)
Prevent-Allow (criminal)	Comfort-Pain (depressive)
Resist-Yield (criminal)	Joyless-Joyful (depressive)
Stop-Help (depressive)	Anger-Coolness (paranoid)
Love-Reject (paranoid)	Clean-Dirty (obsessive)
Attend-Ignore (paranoid)	Sadness-Happiness (depressive)
Find-Lose (depressive)	Fear-Calmness (anxious)
Fight-Surrender (criminal)	Orderly-Grotesque (schizophrenic)
Penetrate-Protect (schizophrenic)	Rough-Smooth (criminal)
Excite-Soothe (anxious)	Humility-Greatness (criminal)
Mix-Separate (schizophrenic)	Tough-Gentle (obsessive)
Show-Hide (schizophrenic)	Constant-Periodic (epil.)
Forgive-Revenge (paranoid)	Deformed-Normal (schizophrenic)
Live-Inert (depressive)	Superior-Inferior (criminal)
Do-Think (obsessive)	Certain-Uncertain (schizophrenic)
Happen-Create (depressive)	Definite-Ambiguous (schizophrenic)
Sink-Rise (schizophrenic)	Fate-Planned (schizophrenic)
Twist-Straighten (schizophrenic)	Keep-Exchange-Give (paranoid)
Drift-Stay (schizophrenic)	Fresh-Exhausted (depressive)
Close-Open (schizophrenic)	Clean-Dirty (obsessive)

The list goes on, including Tall-Short, Singular-Plural, Fast-Slow, Talkative-Silent, Sick-Well, Wide-Narrow, Deep-Shallow, Clever-Dumb, Many-Few, Careful-Carefree, Hazy-Clear, Tender-Tough, Bland-Bitter, Hot-Cold, Below-Above, Tight-Loose, Coordinated-Awkward, Clear-Vague, Rude-Polite, Unique-Common, Stiff-Limp, Sweet-Sour, Lustful-Platonic, Actual-Virtual, Direct-Circuitous, Damaged-Intact, Solid-Yielding, Part-Whole, Ally-Enemy, Inside-Outside, Hard-Soft, Be-Become, Stay-Go, Big-Small, Incline-Decline, High-Low, and so on. It was thought that any of these polar concepts might prove useful in creating scales to estimate various kinds of human psychological conditions.

There are two reasons for the extensive list above. The first reason is that consideration was given to writing scales to measure variables underlying many other types of human suffering in addition to addictions. However, that task is beyond the scope of the present work. The second reason is to point out the possible relevance of various polar concepts to different kinds of human conditions. The designations in parentheses following some of the concepts in the two lists above reflect a guess about conditions to which the polar concepts might be relevant.

A series of polar concepts were now available to serve as dimensions along which respondents might be able to express their participation in various types of motivations. How would these polar concepts be used in statements to form test item contents?

Sentences

As in all language, test item statements are expressed in sentences. Sentences are comprised of a subject, a verb, and an object. In all self-descriptive statements, the subject of the sentence is a constant, the personal pronoun. That leaves unselected only the verb and the object of each self-descriptive sentence that might be used as a test item. This means that the verb and the object of the sentence remain as variables to carry the essences of the meaning in the statement. The

next question was, Are there any constraints acting on the verb and/ or object variables that might help in the construction of appropriate and useful statements?

In order to select the verbs and objects of the statements to be used in the *Dimensional Addicause Questionnaire*, the list of polar concepts was reduced to those to which 'it seemed likely' that addicted clients might refer in talking about their addictive behaviour. Note the ambiguity in the last statement's reference to addicted clients' utterances. The ambiguity is intentional. It is not affirmed that any addicted client ever actually used any of the polar concepts highlighted above. The intention is to make a kind of clinical statement in which the long-since-forgotten statements of former clients were reviewed in a kind of analogical memory to try to reconstruct 'the fit' between each of the polar concepts and the clinician's 'sense of who the person was'. When a sense of fit was found between this admittedly inexact analogical memory of several addicted patients' self-descriptions and a polar concept, the concept was accepted as one 'bearing promise' for use and evaluation in the test.

This rather subjective and conceptual kind of analysis led to the selection of the certain dimensional concepts to provide the verbs and the objects in the sentences that would serve as the items for the *Dimensional Addicause Questionnaire* (DAQ). It might seem that it would be fairly easy to write statements in which the subject, the verb, and the object were predetermined. However, there was another matter yet to be considered.

There were actually a number of other considerations that were taken into account when writing test items to include in the planned scales. Each merits brief discussion as an introduction to the actual scales.

Statements

Whether or not he/she knows it, the one who knows most about the characteristics of any given respondent is usually the person him/

herself. The person describes him/herself in statements. Recognizing that some self-knowledge is explicit and a great deal of it is implicit, if the right statement is found that cues or communicates in just the right way with the person's conceptual system, it ought to be possible to obtain meaningful information from the person. But what are the characteristics of statements that can be expected to communicate effectively with the person?

Other Communication Variables

In addition to the elements of its sentence structure, the form of a statement references or cues various kinds of memories in people in order to provide meaning and understanding for the bare parts of speech. People vary in the ways in which they reference memory images and thus create meaning out of cuing stimuli. Some people are practised most thoroughly in verbal-conceptual handling of material, and others are most practised in processing material emotionally or in terms of the feelings evoked. Again, some people tend to reference their memory images through the sensory modality of sight, others through hearing, and still others through feelings represented by experience internal to the body.

That is, there appear to be 'cognitive processors' and 'emotional or affective processors', and there appear to those who rely mainly on the visual sense, others who rely mainly on the auditory sense, and others who rely mainly on the kinaesthetic sense to reference memories and self-relevant images. These statements about people have a long history in the psychological literature so that they hardly require references to offer support for their consideration in this context. Besides, the intention was to evaluate the usefulness of these concepts in item development rather than to assume a meaningful role for them in verbal cuing.

If it is true that people process and reference information in the above ways, it would seem prudent to ensure that no particular type of processing and referencing is afforded special advantage in responding to the test undergoing development. To allow such

advantage to one or other type of respondent would obviously create the risk that any results obtained with the test would be biased from the start. In order to avoid a 'built-in' risk of bias, it was decided that each scale constructed would have cognitive and emotional, as well as visual, auditory, and kinaesthetic, elements counterbalanced within its item composition.

Item Numbers

The next question that needed to be addressed was the number of items to be written to provide scales to measure each variable. Psychometric lore, which seemed repeatedly to have been verified in personal research in both dependent measure development and design of treatments, suggested that the 'ideal' (maximizing predictive/ outcome efficiency) number of correlated items in a scale would be sixteen, with a range of acceptability from 12 to 20. A great number of variables was to be scaled, which might suggest that minimizing the number of items per scale would be appropriate. However, it was planned to counterbalance two processing (cognitive and emotional) and three sensory (visual, auditory, and kinaesthetic) variables in each scale, and this might suggest that the number of items per scale would have to be a multiple of 6 and should favour larger numbers. Considering the uncertain value of the processing and sensory subscales, the anticipated length of the whole test recommended that twelve items be used in each scale, even if that would risk some imprecision in any subscales to be evaluated. Means were explored to compensate for the risk to subscale reliabilities, given that subscales of only four items each were being planned to measure the relative roles of visual, auditory, and kinaesthetic factors in test respondents.

Response Alternatives

The next question considered was the range of response alternatives to be made available to respondents. It was recognized

that Likert-type scaling would have an advantage over binary (True/False) responding by extending the range of variability within each scale and subscale; and extending the response range might compensate for any impairment of reliability that might derive from the limited numbers of items in the subscales. Moreover, the polar nature of the concepts to be used recommended the idea of providing for distribution of responses along a scale. It was decided to employ Likert scaling for the response options offered.

But how many positions should the Likert response scales afford? The possibilities seemed restricted to three, five, or seven positions as response options. On one hand, the larger the number of options, the wider and more discriminating should be the response distributions for each scale. On the other hand, many of the respondents to whom the test might be expected to be administered might well be incapable of highly refined discriminations within their experiences, so a smaller number of options might be most appropriate. These two competing considerations suggested the selection of five response options: extremes, a middle, and somewhere in between. The response scale of 0 to 4 was selected as the most likely to be an appropriate range for responding.

Summary

A variety of dimensions were selected for scaling items in each of the scales planned for the *Dimensional Addicause Questionnaire* (DAQ). Provision would be made for responses to range between extremes represented by 0 and 4. Half of the items would permit cognitive habits, and half would permit emotional habits of response to exhibit their effects separately in the scales. A tripartite division of items would permit visual, auditory, and kinaesthetic imagery to have their effects separately analysed. And dimensional or polar concepts would be employed in the verbs and objects of scale items to evoke in respondents associations accessing the power/importance of various types of effects (the different scales) on and in them.

CHAPTER 4

Item Construction

A format or formula was constructed for each axis of the scale as follows.

Item Number	Verb: First Polar Concept	Object: Second Polar Concept	Processing	Sense Modality	Response
1	Dimension X+	Dimension Y−	Cognitive	Visual	0 1 2 3 4
2	Dimension X+	Dimension Y−	Cognitive	Auditory	0 1 2 3 4
3	Dimension X+	Dimension Y−	Cognitive	Kinesthetic	0 1 2 3 4
4	Dimension X−	Dimension Y+	Cognitive	Visual	0 1 2 3 4
5	Dimension X−	Dimension Y+	Cognitive	Auditory	0 1 2 3 4
6	Dimension X−	Dimension Y+	Cognitive	Kinesthetic	0 1 2 3 4
7	Dimension X−	Dimension Y+	Affective	Visual	0 1 2 3 4
8	Dimension X−	Dimension Y+	Affective	Auditory	0 1 2 3 4
9	Dimension X−	Dimension Y+	Affective	Kinesthetic	0 1 2 3 4
10	Dimension X+	Dimension Y−	Affective	Visual	0 1 2 3 4
11	Dimension X+	Dimension Y−	Affective	Auditory	0 1 2 3 4
12	Dimension X+	Dimension Y−	Affective	Kinesthetic	0 1 2 3 4

Each of the twelve items for each scale or variable would start with the personal pronoun, continue with a verb based on the one pole of each polar concept to be used for the scale, and conclude with an object based on the object to be used for that variable. The two poles of each dimension (represented by the '+' or '−' following

the *X* or *Y*) would be counterbalanced in groups of three, but always tending in opposite directions with respect to each other to represent the probability that 'conflict' would be part of addiction-relevant variables. The first six items of each scale would be expressed in cognitive terms, while the last six would be expressed in affective or emotional terms. In addition, visual, auditory, and kinaesthetic imagery would be woven into item contents in rotating order. Finally, the response options 0 to 4 would be used for every item.

For example, consider the items chosen for the second axis of the ADDICAUSE questionnaire, Group Enjoyment. The first six items of the second axis are cognitive (for example, "I *avoid* intimate groups when I can be in <u>large groups</u>" and "I *seek* the excitement and fun of <u>being with others</u>") while the final six items are affective: "I *keep from* feeling <u>isolated</u> as much as I can" and "I *enjoy seeing* friends and <u>going to parties</u>". Note that italics are added here (but not in the test itself) to emphasize the approach/avoidance dimension of this axis, and the underlining (also not in the test itself) is to highlight the object of the approach or avoidance. The other items in this axis follow a similar pattern but attempt to be phrased in auditory or kinaesthetic terms. For example, for the auditory sensory modality, items are "I *spend* as much time as I can <u>talking with others</u>" and "I *am most at ease* when I am <u>talking with friends</u>"; and for the kinaesthetic sensory modality, items are "I *try to avoid* working at tasks I have to <u>do alone</u>" and "I *feel* least uptight when I am <u>doing social things</u>".

With this much constraint imposed on the writing of each item, it is hardly surprising that the items almost 'wrote themselves'. Obviously, items written to a formula in this fashion would run the risk of being boring and repetitive. Some variation was afforded by the use of the two poles of each dimension, which were also employed in a counterbalanced fashion (see the + and − signs). In addition, for the sake of maintaining interest, an attempt was made to vary the apparent nature and content of each item slightly without putting aside the 'formula'.

Yet another constraint was imposed on the writing of items for the scales. The optimism or pessimism of the author of scales such as these could easily affect the nature of the scales written. Moreover, it seemed very likely that respondents would differ both in their own optimism or pessimism and in the effect of each variable upon their addictive behaviours. In order to address these possible sources of respondent variability, two scales were constructed for most pairs of dimensional concepts. The items for one scale (odd-numbered axes) of each pair adopted a generally negative emotional tone, while the items for the other (even-numbered axes) employed a generally positive emotional tone. Aside from the fact that experience suggested that both kinds of emotional tone would be needed, it turned out to be fortunate that positive emotional tone scales were also used.

The constraints to be employed in writing items were assembled in the format as shown at the beginning of this chapter. Little by way of creativity was possible given the limitations imposed by the format. Where possible, no reference was made to uses of addictive substances, in order to minimize specific referencing to addictive contexts on the part of respondents while answering the questionnaire. That is, the attempt was made to obtain responses bearing on the general personality of the respondent regardless of whether or not he/ she had used any substance or considered the issue in the question relevant to his/her addictive behaviour.

CHAPTER 5

Scale Selection for Addictions

The actual scales developed are shown in Appendix A. At this point, however, it seems appropriate to list the dimensional concepts selected to be employed in the sixty-eight scales, along with the emotional tone (axis number's sign) adopted in each scale's items and the primary causal function (final cause/need [*Nd* or *sD*] and perpetuating cause/reinforcer [*Rf* or *rf*]) intended for each scale. Each scale is called an axis to express its dimensional nature.

Axis and Tone	Addicause Scale Title	Main Causal Function	Final Cause of the Behaviour (Purpose, Need)[5]	Perpetuating Cause (Habit Strength or Reinforcer)[6]
01–	Social Anxiety	*rf*	Avoid/Approach	Social/Self
02+	Group Enjoyment	*RF*	Approach/Avoid	Social/Self
03–	Reactive Depression	*sD*	Passive/Active	Integration/Disintegration
04+	Stimulus Hunger	*Nd*	Active/Passive	Integration/Disintegration
05–	Rigid Self-Image	*sD*	Unchanging/Learn	Purposive/Random Self
06+	Social Influence	*Nd*	Learn/Unchanging	Social/Self
07–	Aggression Inhibition	*Nd*	Avoid/Approach	Active/Passive
08+	Guilt Intolerance	*Rf*	Avoid/Approach	Passive/Active
09–	Loneliness	*rf*	Passive/Active	Social/Alone
10+	Social Contact Need	*Nd*	Active/Passive	Social/Alone
11–	Reality Denial	*Rf*	Avoid/Approach	Real/Unreal

---

[5] Mostly the verb employing Dimension 1 (X)

[6] Mostly the object employing Dimension 2 (Y)

12+	Authority Rebellion	*Nd*	Approach/Avoid	Unreal/Real
13−	Joyless Depression	*sD*	Impotency/Power	Forwards/Backwards
14+	Vivid Imagery	*Nd*	Power/Impotency	Forwards/Backwards
15−	Control Effort	*Rf*	Power/Impotency	Mind/Body
16+	Control of Others	*Rf*	Power/Impotency	Mind/Body
17−	Grief Reaction	*sD*	Power/Impotency	Loss/Gain
18+	Event Self-Enhancement	*Nd*	Power/Impotency	Loss/Gain
19−	Pain Sensitivity	*sD*	Sensitive/Insensitive	Pain/Pleasure
20+	Hedonism	*Rf*	Sensitive/Insensitive	Pain/Pleasure
21−	Social Withdrawal	*Rf*	Bad/Good	Social/Alone
22−	Subcultural Values	*sD*	Good/Bad	Social/Alone
23−	Dependency Inhibition	*Nd*	Power/Impotency	Change/Persistence
24+	PIG Effect	*Rf*	Power/Impotency	Change/Persistence
25−	Paranoid Sensitivity	*Rf*	Sensitive/Insensitive	Social/Alone
26+	Rationality Defence	*Rf*	Sensitive/Insensitive	Social/Alone
27−	Oppressive Inhibition	*Rf*	Precise/Error	Good/Bad
28+	Comfortable Inhibition	Rf	Precise/Error	Good/Bad
29−	Disturbed Feelings	*rf*	Anxious/Depressed	Mind/Body
30+	Affect Denial	*rf*	Avoid/Approach	Body/Mind
31−	Put Down Others	*Nd*	Dissatisfy/Satisfy	Other/Self
32+	Group Satisfaction	*Rf*	Satisfy/Dissatisfy	Group/Self
33−	Dogmatism	*Rf*	Good/Bad	Persistence/Change
34+	Need to Be Different	*Nd*	Bad/Good	Persistence/Change
35−	Self-Depreciation	*rf*	Bad/Good	Self/Other
36+	Rigid Moralization	*sD*	Good/Bad	Self/Other
37−	Paroxysmal Energy	*sD*	Impotency/Power	Facilitate/Impede
38+	Rules Intolerance	*rf*	Impotency/Power	Facilitate/Impede
39−	Effort Strain	*rf*	Power/Impotency	Facilitate/Impede
40+	Pep-Up Effect	*Rf*	Power/Impotency	Facilitate/Impede
41−	Rigid Habits	*sD*	Persist/Change	Habit/Learning
42+	Easy-Going Enjoyment	*Rf*	Change/Persist	Learning/Rigidity
43−	Metabolic Disorder	*sD*	Avoid/Approach	Power/Impotency
44+	Fast-Lane Living	*Nd*	Approach/Avoid	Power/Impotency
45−	Hypoglycaemia	*rf*	Insensitive/Sensitive	Body/Mind
46+	Allergy Stress	*rf*	Sensitive/Insensitive	Body/Mind
47−	Physiological Anxiety	*rf*	Power/Impotency	Body/Mind
48+	Punitive Rewards	*Rf*	Bad/Good	Learning/Rigidity

49−	Affect Avoidance	*Nd*	Sensitive/Insensitive	Ugly/Beauty
50+	Sensitivity Control	*Rf*	Sensitive/Insensitive	Beauty/Ugly
51−	Guilt Proneness	*sD*	Passive/Active	Power/Impotence
52−	Anger, Hostility	*Rf*	Power/Impotency	Active/Passive
53−	Somatic Depression	*Rf*	Passive/Active	Body/Mind
54+	Hungry Heart	*Nd*	Active/Passive	Mind/Body
55−	Impaired Self-Esteem	*rf*	Lose/Gain	Other/Self
56+	Masked Disappointment	*sD*	Lose/Gain	Other/Self
57−	Felt Rejection	*rf*	Separate/Together	Other/Self
58+	Communication Need	*Nd*	Together/Separate	Other/Self
59−	Calm-Nerves Need	*Nd*	Avoid/Approach	Pain/Pleasure
60+	Substance Excitement	*Nd*	Approach/Avoid	Up/Down
61−	Forget Failures	*Nd*	Lose/Gain	Failure/Success
62+	Different Experience	*Nd*	Gain/Lose	Change/Persist
63−	Avoid Depression	*Rf*	Avoid/Approach	Passive/Active
64+	Assert Confidence	*Nd*	Approach/Avoid	Active/Passive
65−	Avoid Attractiveness	*Rf*	Avoid/Approach	Beauty/Ugliness
66+	Impaired Sleep	*sD*	Impair/Facilitate	Asleep/Awake
67−	Relaxation Need	*Nd*	Facilitate/Impair	Calmness/Tension
68+	Substance Dependency	*Nd*	Passive/Active	Self/Other

Intended Purpose of the Axis, i.e., Hypothetical Function Only

Nd = A need that one might actively pursue

sD = A derived need or drive stimulus

Rf = Reinforcement (obvious)

rf = Reinforcement (derived or implicit)

Main Causal Functions

The middle column of the above listing has been included to express the importance assigned in construction of this instrument to final (purpose, need) and perpetuating (habit strength, reinforcement) causes. This column is headed Main Causal Function to represent the attempt to illustrate this other (causal) aspect, which was 'built into' each Addicause axis or scale. Four types of designations are used, each of which expresses how the axis in question was viewed and

the function it was intended to fulfil. Half of the axes were intended primarily to access needs (final, $\underline{w}$, omega causes), and they are designated as either *Nd* or *sD* in the middle column. The other half of the axes were intended primarily to access reinforcers (perpetuating, $\underline{v}$, nu causes), and they are designated as either *Rf* or *rf* in the middle column. These designations require brief explanation.

The 'need' components of some of the axes are obvious. Stimulus Hunger (04), reliance on Social Influence (06), Inhibiting Aggression (07), Social Contact (10), and Self-Enhancement by means of Substances (18) seem fairly clearly to represent needs (*Nd*) that a person might pursue actively. The need components of other axes are implicit. Authority Rebellion (12) and Vivid Imagery (14) are needs for means by which to achieve their purposes, i.e., rebellion or bright images, respectively. In these ways, both kinds of drives may be thought of as needs in and of themselves. Still other human initiatives or actions create needs implicitly. Reactive Depression (03) creates uncomfortable sensations that are likely to drive the person to actively seek a happier or more comfortable kind of state; and Rigid Self-Images (05) may limit the range of personal experience or perpetuate an unpleasant view of the self, which would be likely to drive the person to actively seek varied experiences or to escape from awareness of a negative self-image. In these ways, some of the needs involved in these dimensions form derived needs or create drive stimuli (*sD*).

The 'reinforcement' components of some of the axes are obvious. Social Enjoyment (02), inhibiting Intolerable Guilt (08), Denying painful Reality (11), and successful Effort at Control (15) or Control of Others (16), if achieved, are fairly obviously likely to be experienced as rewarding (reinforcing, *Rf*). Other reinforcement elements of some axes are implicit. Although Hedonism (20) sounds like an actively pursued need (and probably is), it seems possible that the achievement of hedonistic pleasure would be rewarding whether or not hedonism was pursued actively, and the pleasure aspect of hedonism may be more important to the person or more generally applicable than the pursuit of a hedonistic lifestyle. Still others of the dimensions

may create their own derived reinforcers (rf). Social Anxiety (01) creates the need for avoidance of upsetting social situations, which, accomplished, feels better or rewarding; Loneliness (09) creates an unpleasant set of sensations whose purpose seems to be to drive the person to become more sociable and thereby to obtain the rewarding state of affairs of relief from the loneliness; and Social Withdrawal (21) creates the reward of relief from oppressive sensations experienced in social contact. In these ways, some of the reinforcers involved in these dimensions form derived reinforcers (rf) rather than primary ones.

Having said all this, it must be remarked that the above observations are intended only as hypotheses. So far in our exploration, there is no basis for stating definitively either that there are primary and derived needs or reinforcers or that the axes designated as relating to final (Nd, sD) or perpetuating (Rf, rf) causes really do relate as specified. All that can be said at this time is that the sixty-eight dimensions or axes were designed with the intention that half (thirty-four) of them mainly function to identify final (need – Nd, sD) causes, and the other half (thirty-four) mainly function to identify perpetuating (reinforcement – Rf, rf) causes.

Secondary Causal Functions

Part of the reason for listing the axes here bears on the next provision made in the test being constructed. It was felt that it might be a good idea not to rely totally on the responses to the scales to provide information about the variables that control an individual's addictive behaviour, at least at first. Thus, it was decided to obtain from respondents their own views about the factors that controlled their addictive acts.

It was recognized that the manner in which the questions were asked of respondents would likely affect greatly how they responded. For example, merely asking a respondent to indicate the causes of or reasons for his addictions would likely evoke responses reflecting

the contemporary (or their own) views about causality generally and about the causation of addictions, history of rationalizations used, and/or their personal notions about the purpose of the question being asked (i.e., response sets) – although it would certainly be nice if the responses obtained were thoughtful or meaningful.

Three pages (see Appendix A) were added to the end of the *Dimensional Addicause Questionnaire* (DAQ). The first of these pages provides separate sections for Foods, Tobaccos, Medications, Alcohol, and Street Drugs. It asks respondents to indicate, first, the causes or reasons for using and, second, the effects on them from use of each class of addictive substances. It was planned that the responses obtained would be classified and coded to the above list of sixty-eight variables comprising the full-length Addicause test.

Source of Dependent Measures

The last page of the questionnaire was designed to be used as the source of information about actual use of addictive substances. It asked respondents to indicate Years of use (Y), Strength of use (U), Months since terminated use (O), and Present want (W) for each of five types of foodstuffs, three types of tobaccos, ten types of medications, ten types of alcohol, thirteen types of street drugs, and three types of solvents. The Strength of use and Present want estimates were in the form of ratings, and these ratings were provided with definitional anchors to standardize the ratings made. These anchoring definitions were provided on the second to last page of the questionnaire.

The reliability with which respondents might report their uses of addictive substances on the last page of the questionnaire was unclear. It was somewhat reassuring to watch respondents completing the questionnaire. They appeared to be about as bored in answering the questions in the Addicause Axes as they appeared to be in responding to the items in the many other psychological tests they were asked to complete. However, when they reached the last page of the Addicause

questionnaire, many of the respondents brightened up visibly as though they were getting vicarious pleasure from reviewing their memories of addictive behaviours, which seemed to suggest that they were likely to respond fairly honestly. But since these records of use would be employed as the dependent measures in the Addicause part of the project, some further attention to these records' reliability seemed warranted.

To confirm the reliability of these records of substance use, a 'spot check' was undertaken with a number of the respondents. Without reference to his responses, the author picked every twentieth or so respondent completing the questionnaire. The respondent was approached from one to two weeks after completing the questionnaire. He was told that his responses were not entirely clear or had been lost, and he was asked to complete the substance use page again. Only two respondents were encountered who gave even one variant from the original responses. One of these respondents, while completing the page for the second time, expressed some surprise as he offered a different number of years of use for one kind of alcohol from the original value to one that was two years longer. While doing so, he said that he forgot that he had started using that kind of alcohol while in an earlier life setting. The spot checks were stopped after about twenty respondents' responses had been evaluated in this way because of the almost perfect fit between first and second ratings. No further attempt was made to confirm the reports made by respondents on the last page of the questionnaire.

CHAPTER 6

Context of the Study

Subjects and Setting

A basic question that needs to be addressed concerns the subjects involved in the study. In dealing with aberrant behaviour, the most important issue needing to be addressed is the nature of the subjects to justify the contention that the study has real meaning with respect to the subject matter under investigation. Indeed, it is necessary to describe both the subject group and the setting in which the subjects were obtained in order to recognize this source of strengths and weaknesses of any study.

The Ontario Correctional Institute (OCI) is a modern 220-bed correctional facility, receiving sentenced adult male offenders serving 'provincial' sentences (i.e., less than two years). The designated correctional program at the OCI is treatment. All inmates admitted to the Institute are assessed and classified on its 54-bed intake unit before being selected (or not) for treatment on one of its five 30- or 34-bed treatment units.

Once admitted to a treatment unit, all residents become involved in the core program of that unit and, based on the assessments conducted, are invited to attend off-unit 'specialized' (or individualized) programmes. The core program includes relationship counselling with an assigned Case Manager (a correctional officer), peer reviews, case conferences, milieu therapy, on-unit group programmes, and democratic house meetings. Specialized programs may include

academic or vocational pursuits, but the main specialized treatment programs are offered by the Psychology Department and are organized in a number of different ways. The latter include some individual psychotherapy, behaviour therapy and biofeedback treatments, some small-group therapy and group training programmes, and a variety of large-group treatment workshops, such as the series of treatment workshops to be referred to later in this report. The assessment program (Addicause) and the treatment program (Addicure) described here were part of the specialized services provided at the OCI.

Inmates are admitted from jails and detention centres to OCI's intake unit based on the following criteria:

(a) Voluntary application for treatment as their correctional programme. (In order to be admitted to treatment at the OCI, any resident must apply voluntarily for treatment, if only after he has been on the intake unit for a while.)

(b) Court recommendation for assessment or treatment (e.g., drug or alcohol, psychiatric or psychological assessment or treatment).

(c) 'Criterion' offences, which include all sex offenders, arsonists, and offenders whose histories exhibit a pattern of escalating aggression or violence. (Substance abusers are often included as if they were criterion offenders.)

(d) Mental or emotional disorder, as this is understood and recognized by Ministry classification personnel (usually recognized in sex offence, violence, and substance abuse histories), health centre staff (usually referring to psychiatric conditions), or superintendents (usually noted from adjustment or behavioural difficulties observed in offenders while incarcerated).

(e) Unusual or complex inmate circumstances encountered by classification personnel during inmate classification (commonly encountered with addicted inmates).

As a result of these admission criteria, a wide variety of inmates are transferred to the OCI for consideration for treatment. The resident population admitted to the five treatment units tends to be comprised roughly as follows:

(1) Substance abusers (distributed across the range of person and property offences) comprise about 75% of the residents on the treatment units.
(2) Sex offenders (at present, mostly incest offenders) comprise between 35% to 45% of the residents on treatment units.
(3) Violent offenders (including domestic violence, assaults, and robbery with violence) comprise about 25% of the residents on the treatment units.
(4) Property offenders (including arson, breaking and entering, and theft) comprise about 25% of the residents on the treatment units.
(5) Mildly to moderately mentally/emotionally disordered offenders (convicted of various types of offences) comprise about 15% of the residents on the treatment units and tend to be housed together on one of the five treatment units.

You will note that many offenders meet more than one of these categories.

The first phase of the present study (Addicause) considered all successive admissions to the intake unit at the OCI (see criteria a to e above), regardless of whether or not they were later selected for admission to treatment. The intake unit residents employed as subjects in this first (Addicause) phase included all those admitted during 1989 and most of 1990. There were about 650 inmates in the Addicause analyses. In addition, about forty-five nonincarcerated mostly female volunteers were obtained to complete the Addicause procedure from among correctional volunteers, AA groups, and members of a fitness club. The total subject group for the Addicause phase of this project was 695.

The second phase of the present study (Addicure) employed all the residents on the treatment units from mid-1993 to early 1994

whose Michigan Alcoholism Screening Test (MAST) and/or Drug Abuse Screening Test (DAST) scores revealed significant personal 'costs' in inconvenience or distress due to alcohol or drug abuse in their histories. Some residents with relatively low MAST and/or DAST scores (5 to 9) were included if they claimed particular difficulties with substance abuse. Of course, some of the residents with high MAST and/or DAST scores denied having any problems with substance abuse. They were nevertheless included and invited to attend the programs for which their randomly assigned experimental groups qualified (see Design, later). The 193 subjects for the Addicure phase of the project included about 75% of the residents on the treatment units (all the addicted inmates) at the time.

Commentary on Subject Characteristics

There will be at least three main limitations or complexities involved in the present study due to the nature of the subject groups used for its purposes. First, and most obviously, the fact that nearly all the subjects were offenders' results in a high degree of selection among addicts, restricting the study to those addicts whose addictions occurred within the context of criminal behaviour and may have contributed to criminal conduct, either by motivating them to obtain addictive substances or by impairing judgement and normal controls. This means that, strictly speaking, the results ought *not* to be generalized to all addicts. But it also means that the addicts to which they might be generalized represent those about whom society and its institutions are most likely to be most deeply concerned.

Second, there is a consequence to the fact that most of the addicted subjects were offenders. There is apt to be a confounder in these data associated with the criminality of the subjects, which might well be construed to represent an independent dimension affecting how they respond. While the possibility of confounded results may seem to be a disadvantage, there is a positive consequence of their offender status. Since most of these people's offences were in some way affected

by their addictions, it becomes fairly easy to conduct extended, if indirect, follow-up about their addictive status. Confidentiality constraints limit access to continuing information about addicts following treatment in most settings. Offence information, however, is relatively public. It was intended to obtain follow-up justice system records on the subjects from the Addicure part of this project after they have been released for two years.

Moreover, any criminality confounder can be extracted from the data in this study. A set of measures of criminality have been developed, which predict very well to criminal conduct and which also lend themselves to modification through treatment (Reynolds and Quirk, *Transforming the Criminal Mind*, 1994). Although the measures of criminality may be confounded with addictiveness, in the same way as the measures of addictiveness may be confounded with criminality, each set of measures can be used to partial out its phenomena from the other set of measures.

Third, for the most part, the addicted offenders serving as subjects in the Addicure phase of the present project were mainly from the younger adult group, ages eighteen through forty. Although there are many older adults in the OCI population, they tend to be nonaddicted sex offenders. The main consequence of this limitation of the present data seems to be that the addicts are either long-term or high-intensity substance abusers but typically not both. It is unclear how this fact may affect the extent to which the results of these studies can properly by generalized to the full range of addicts.

From a practical perspective, however, for want of clear information about the effects of long-term and intensive alcohol and drug abuse, it seems possible that with these latter types of offenders, it may be necessary to supplement the present type of treatment program with some others. For example, in some cases, it may be necessary to supplement their programs with biofeedback procedures such as Peniston's (1990) alpha-theta EEG training procedure or, in some cases, Sterman's (1974) SMR-EEG training procedure. These particular supplementary needs are receiving pilot investigation as part of a part stage of this project.

"Treatment of Addictions"

The intention to assess and treat addictions in a correctional centre presents some important associated issues that need to be mentioned, in order to provide some of the conceptual framework within which the present task acquires meaning. The concept of addictions is one of those issues.

Addictions, like high temperature and headache, are presenting problems or symptoms rather than their causes, which are the proper targets of treatment. That does not mean to say that symptoms ought not to be targeted and relieved, sometimes for the sake of bodily health (e.g., risk to brain cells from prolonged high body temperature), sometimes for the sake of the sufferer's comfort (e.g., pain relief), and sometimes for the sake of other people (e.g., families of addicts). That also does not mean to say that addressing the symptoms directly, in order to prevent them, is not appropriate. The function of AA and NA is to foster suppression of the symptom of addictive behaviour using any procedures (the twelve steps, social support groups, personal counsellor/sponsor) that might work for the purpose. Indeed, the present program is <u>NOT</u> and never was intended to compete with AA and/or NA. If an addicted person can use these groups, then the present series of studies will be of little interest to him/her. The present observations and results are aimed at those people who either are unable to use/work with AA and/or NA or are potential future addicts.

The caution expressed in the last paragraph is particularly relevant to the treatment of addictions among inmates. Certainly at the OCI, but also in many other correctional centres, inmates do not have ready access to addictive substances. This means that the symptom of addiction is artificially suppressed during some periods of incarceration, so the addictive response can be seen only in altered form and the target addictive behaviour cannot be observed at all. Treatment cannot effectively be undertaken when changes in its target(s) cannot be observed. Even AA and NA utilization has to function in a different way during incarceration where addictive

substances are unavailable. The latter programs can be useful under such circumstances as opportunities to establish connectedness and group reliance on the part of the person to permit him/her to use the suppressive program when he/she is once more at liberty on the street. Under the conditions of incarceration described above, other programs concerned with addictions can address those phenomena that continue to operate within the person and in which changes can be observed and recorded in spite of artificial suppression of the addictive behaviour. These phenomena that continue to operate within the person are the elements in him/her of the addictive personality – the very issues that Addicause seeks to address.

If addictions are to be 'cured', rather than relieved, it will be important to place them in a workable context. That context would be that addictive behaviours are 'symptoms' caused by something else. While ameliorative measures and problem management do address undesired symptoms, the term *treatment* refers here to the attempt to locate and to modify the causes underlying the symptoms. The present work addresses treatment viewed in this way.

Informants as Sources of Information

A number of causes of addictive behaviour have been suggested over the many years that addictions have been studied. Physicians, being trained exclusively in the anatomy and chemistry of the body, have tended to look for interactions between addictive substances and body chemicals and to seek both a chemical basis for understanding addictive behaviour and chemical antidotes for substance use or 'replacement' substances (e.g., other psychotropic chemicals, methadone, and the nicotine patches) or punitive methods for addictive behaviour (e.g., Antabuse). Psychiatrists, being trained largely in the diagnosis and chemical treatment of mental disorders, have tended to look for interactions between psychiatric diagnoses and addictive behaviour and to seek both the addictive personality and chemical substitutes for used addictive substances (which often maintain the addiction, even if transferred to

another substance). Psychologists, being trained in how the living body functions and acquires habitual behaviours, tend to labour to identify in more and more refined detail the mechanisms by which to account for addictive behaviour and to seek to provide educational programs (e.g., relapse prevention) by which to address addictions. Finally, the untrained member of the community, who is most directly concerned in the matter, brings his/her personal (and probably unrelated) experience and pre-existing suppositions and beliefs to bear on the understanding of addictions and thereby muddies the already murky waters even more. This latter source of confusion is best represented in the well-intentioned but naive efforts of media personnel to address the issues involved in addiction. The kinds of evaluations and judgements they commonly bring to obscure understanding is frequently counterproductive, breeding the appearance of authority and understanding to mislead others while propagating sheer common (non)sense.

Addicted clients are not able to provide workers with much useful help in understanding addictions either. The addict, like any other sufferer, is able to describe how he/she feels, what substances he/she uses, some of the things he/she was aware of early in the addictive process, and a host of other (probably irrelevant) details about his/her life and history. Too often, the addict experiences too much confusion to be much help to the inquirer, if only because of the effects of the addictive substances on him/her or because of the turmoil of competing thoughts, explanations, and beliefs that buzz in his/her head with no means by which to sort them out into meaningful components. In fact, relying on the addicted person to help in the task of directly unravelling the causes underlying addictions is largely a futile task, equivalent to the prescientific efforts at understanding behaviour with which Freud laboured – a case of 'the blind leading the blind'.

A major part of the difficulty that has been encountered in discovering the causes of addictive behaviour, in addition to that afforded by the point of view of the student (professional, researcher, addict or affected others), lies in confusion concerning the nature of causality as it applies to human behaviour. This issue has already been addressed in a general way.

Negative Format ('Don't Drink') Statements

Given that a solution to the causes underlying addictions has not emerged as quickly as workers in the field might wish, premature programs have been mounted seeking to deal with it by exhortation and appeals to fears, conscience, or morality. Some of these programs have worked quite well, and some appear to be counterproductive, if anything.

Among those programs that have worked quite well, one would surely include social support programs such as those used by AA and NA, community integration and support programs such as the one implemented in Toronto years ago by Dr. Gordon Bell, and the 'designated driver' programs that are now commonly encountered in developed societies. These programs have in common the fact that they have managed, for the most part, to avoid the pitfall of 'negative format' or prohibitive instructions and advertising and to employ 'positive format' statements and positive initiatives in order to achieve their effect.

There is considerable reason to believe, however, that the many advertising schemes (e.g., 'If You Drink, Don't Drive', 'Only You Can Stop Drunk Driving', or 'Mothers Against Drunk Driving') aimed at public awareness, with the hope that increased consciousness of the problem will help to impede or prevent it, have in common a reliance on prohibitive instructions. Unfortunately, prohibitive instructions seem mainly to remind the receiver about the act which is to be inhibited and, far from fostering inhibition of the undesired behaviour (particularly among addicts and offenders), seem to foster the prohibited conduct. It is kind of like the prohibition 'Don't think of a pink elephant'. In order to not think about it, you have to think about it.

This idea can be illustrated with an example. The most likely time in the day during which a targeted alcoholic is likely to encounter and notice one of the 'don't drink' advertisements is when he/she is in motion, such as when driving home while stone-cold sober. He/she may see the 'don't' part of the instruction, but he/she is most

likely to <u>notice</u> and respond to the 'drink' part of the sign. The result is potentially an enhanced likelihood of stopping off on his/her way for one or more drinks.

The difficulties with prohibitive or 'negative format' statements are that they (a) remind the person to think about the very act they seek to inhibit, (b) instruct the person to do the prohibited act (e.g., '. . . drink'), (c) do not suggest any alternative conduct with which to distract the person from the evoked thought, and (d) employ a sentence format that many people must either challenge or react to by both doing and then seeking to undo the act in question. Permissive statements such as 'Arrive alive' are essentially always superior ways to achieve desired conduct in oneself or another. They (a) offer the person an alternative kind of conduct to that which is to be impeded, (b) instruct the person to perform the desired act, (c) distract the person from thinking about the act which is to be impeded, and (d) offer the person three, instead of two, options of conduct (i.e., they contribute to freedom of choice, namely, the suggested action) – the unmentioned but prohibited action and in-between actions that are neither suggested nor prohibited.

The above way of thinking was adopted in a host of ways as part of the planning, implementation, and communications involved in both the Addicause and Addicure phases of the present project. Wherever possible, all the way from exhortations employed in the treatment programs through item selection for the assessment instrument to statements of program titles, the attempt was made to avoid negative format statements and to employ positive format and permissive statements. This apparently isolated element of procedure employed is mentioned here because of its relevance to the topic addressed in the preceding section. Addictions as such were not treated. The attempt was made to create conditions under which the causes of addictions could be identified and modified so that addictive behaviour might become irrelevant.

CHAPTER 7

Approach to Measurement

Observation, assessment, or measurement can be undertaken in many different ways. It can be done by 'ecological' observation of the event's 'natural' occurrences under free conditions in its environment. While this is the best way to determine the 'real' occurrences of the event (e.g., addictive behaviour), it is also a relatively inefficient time- and labour-intensive method of assessment. Moreover, ecological observation is apt to shift towards epidemiological study, which tends to lose predictive capabilities with respect to the individual. It can be done by experimental observation of the event's occurrences under controlled conditions in the laboratory. While this approach tends to yield precise observations, it also creates artificial conditions for responding and somewhat distorted responses, and it is both labour-intensive and costly (in creating the conditions for control and recording of observations). It can also be done with human behaviour by relying on self-observation and self-report as with the use of tests. While this approach is time efficient, labour efficient, and cost efficient, if great care is not taken, it can easily produce a host of distortions, false leads, and errors (imprecisions) that can render its results useless and possibly even counterproductive.

The present study adopts the test approach to its assessment task, and it therefore demands careful preliminary attention to the details of <u>how</u> the assessment task is to be undertaken and how the measures

achieved behave. This means that thoughtful consideration has had to be devoted to the methods used to construct the observation/ assessment instrument. And there remain some steps to be reported concerning the development of the instrument.

Scales and Measures

The sixty-eight twelve-item scales that comprise the whole Addicause test are presented in Appendix A. Appendix A also contains the last three pages of the questionnaire, asking for information about the respondents' opinions about the causes and effects of his/ her use of classes of addictive substances and about the Years, Use, Time-Off, and present Want of various specific kinds of addictive substances. The development of each of these parts of Appendix A has already been described in the foregoing.

Before analyses could be undertaken and reported, however, it was necessary to decide how the Addicause axes would be approached in order to isolate the various types of information contained in them. This is the task of the present chapter, and it is based on the thinking that has been discussed and reviewed previously.

Some of the scores to be isolated were built directly into the axes before the items for each were written. These included the following:

C *(Cognitive Processing)*. The first six items of each axis were intended to represent cognitive or thoughtful ways of processing experience. The circled numbers (response values) for the first six items of each scale were <u>summed</u> to create the C score for that axis (Maximum = 24).

E *(Emotional Processing)*. The last six items of each axis were intended to represent emotional or affective ways of processing experience. The circled numbers (response values) for the last six items of each scale were <u>summed</u> to create the E score (Maximum = 24).

V *(Visual Modality)*. The first, fourth, seventh, and tenth items of each axis were intended to represent experience in the visual sense modality. The circled numbers (response values) for these four items of each scale were <u>summed</u> to create the *V* score (Maximum = 16).

A *(Auditory Modality)*. The second, fifth, eighth, and eleventh items of each axis were intended to represent experience in the auditory sense modality. The circled numbers (response values) for these four items of each scale were <u>summed</u> to create the *A* score (Maximum = 16).

K *(Kinaesthetic Modality)*. The third, sixth, ninth, and twelfth items of each axis were intended to represent experience in the kinaesthetic sense modality. The circled numbers (response values) for these four items of each scale were <u>summed</u> to create the *K* score (Maximum = 16).

p *(Dimensional Axis p)*. With accidental errors of execution on some of the axes (sometimes the *C* score is the same as the *p* score), for the most part, either the first, second, third, seventh, eighth, and ninth items or the first, second, third, tenth, eleventh, and twelfth items carried the intended polarity expressed as the <u>primary</u> dimension for the axis (e.g., Axis 1: Social Anxiety: Avoid-Social). The circled numbers (response values) for the six items involved were <u>summed</u> to create the *p* score for each axis (Maximum = 24).

s *(Dimensional Axis s)*. With unintentional errors (sometimes the *E* score is identical to the *s* score), for the most part, either the fourth, fifth, sixth, seventh, eighth, and ninth items or the ninth, fifth, sixth, tenth, eleventh, and twelfth items carried the intended <u>secondary</u> or mirror image of the polarity expressed as the primary dimension for the axis (e.g., Axis 1: Social Anxiety: Approach-Self). The circled numbers (response values) for the six items involved were <u>summed</u> to create the *s* score for each axis (Maximum = 24).

Axis− (Axis Mood−). For the most part, the axes with <u>odd</u> numbers (i.e., 01, 03, 05, etc.) express a rather negative or unpleasant mood

or feeling (e.g., Social Anxiety, Reactive Depression, etc.). For high scores on these axes, it seems likely that addictive properties of substances would require relief of the feeling involved to serve as a reinforcer (v cause) and the need (w cause) would involve pursuit of avoidance of a learned negative state.

Axis+ (Axis Mood+). For the most part, axes with even numbers (i.e., 02, 04, 06, etc.) express a rather pleasant or desirable mood or feeling (e.g., Social Enjoyment, Stimulus Hunger, etc.). For high scores on these axes, it seems likely that addictive properties of substances would have to foster pleasant experiences to serve as a reinforcer (v cause) and the need (w cause) would involve creation of a positive state to replace a learned negative state.

The last two axis-related sets of measures might seem to offer another approach to an answer to the often-stated requirement that indicators of the various types of causes affecting behaviour be found – in addition to the 'built-in' need and reinforcement functions of the dimensions (the Main Causal Functions). While they might offer another means to access the sought causes, the Axis Mood measures seem a bit weak as measures of final (w) and perpetuating (v) causes. But another hypothesis was formulated that, if it could be verified in some way, might offer another means by which to find measures of these two kinds of causes.

In addition to the above ways of scoring each axis, there were two other possible ways to generate total scores from each. One way would be to sum (S) all the values (circled answers) to the twelve items of each scale. This should represent a 'power' measure associated with each axis. Another way would be to count (N) the number out of the twelve items of each axis for which the response exceeded a certain value, say 1. This should represent an 'extensivity' measure for each scale.

These two ways of handling each axis's **total** score were considered carefully. It seemed just remotely possible that the 'power' (sum or S) measure might represent the importance of that axis's variable in terms of its 'meaning' to the respondent. If so, it might permit the

'pull' or 'need' or 'final cause' aspect of the variable to be represented or measured by it. Similarly, it seemed just remotely possible that the 'extensivity' (count or N) measure might represent the variety of settings in which the person might respond to alterations of the state represented by the axis or variable. If so, it might represent the susceptibility of the person to be reinforced or perpetuated by modification of the variable. Stating this last comment differently, the extensivity (N) score might represent the generality of application of the variable in the person's life, which, in turn, should provide some information about the position of the variable in the person's habit family hierarchy or of the variable's habit strength.

These hypothetical possibilities, remote though they might seem, made it seem appropriate not to select between these two possible ways of expressing the total score for each axis, but rather to retain both at least tentatively. But even if the S and N scores did afford means by which to approach final (w) and perpetuating (v) causes, respectively, that would leave out initial (i) causes.

The third to the last page of the questionnaire had been designed to identify possible initial (i) causes by asking respondents to state their opinions about the causes and the effects of their uses of classes of substances. The 'cause' responses acquired were mostly rather vague (e.g., 'I wanted to try it') or repetitive with respect to the effects reported or else were omitted. In order to obtain any information, the causes and the effects reported were combined as if (as they appeared to be) they were interchangeable. In order to make the resulting initial cause scores generally comparable with the other scores, initial (i) causes (or Z) scores were created by counting the number of times across substances that the respondent claimed a cause or an effect that could be classified and coded as related to (designated as) the sixty-eight Addicause axes. Thus the initial cause (Z) score for each axis was the number of references to that axis among the respondent's claimed causes and effects of use of any of the listed classes of substances.

This thinking resulted in three more scores for each axis:

S *(Sum of Responses)*. The circled numbers (response values) for all twelve items of each scale were <u>summed</u> together to form a total S score (Maximum = 48).

N *(Number of Responses > 1)*. The <u>number</u> of the twelve response values that reached 2 or more for each scale was <u>counted</u> to form a total N score (Maximum = 12).

Z *(Number of Initial Causes)*. The number of times the respondent claimed any given axis as a cause or an effect of his/her use of any of the five substance classes was <u>counted</u> to form a total Z score (Maximum = 10).

The intention to include all these scores, plus the specific response value given by each subject for each and every item of the Addicause test will seem excessive to some. There will be those who would suggest that the attempt was made to milk the data to death. Without wishing to contradict any such contention, it should be recalled that the Addicause instrument was undergoing development and evaluation at this point. There was yet no way of knowing just how each of the variables (items, scores of various types) would behave and whether or which variables would offer useful information. At this point, the earlier comments about the impracticability of pretesting items and scales as an empirical exercise in instrument development might usefully be recalled.

Raw Dependent Variables

As if the above was not sufficiently complicated, there were yet other measures to be considered. The Addicause instrument was to be used to identify the several types of causes of addictions. To do this, it would be necessary to have measures to represent each respondent's addictions or lack of addiction. Two measures, external to the Addicause test, were selected:

MAST (Michigan Alcoholism Screening Test). The MAST was administered routinely to all admissions to the OCI and was available as a 'cost of addiction' measure for alcoholism.

DAST (Drug Abuse Screening Test). The DAST was administered routinely to all admissions to the OCI, and it too was available as a 'cost of addiction' measure for drug abuse.

The final page of the Dimensional Addicause Questionnaire (DAQ, see Appendix A) requested respondents to indicate all the following for each of five categories of foods, three categories of tobacco products, ten categories of medications, ten categories of alcoholic beverages, thirteen categories of street drugs, and three categories of solvents:

Y *(Years of Use).* The respondent was asked to show the number of Years of use of each substance as the Y score.

U *(Strength of Use).* On an anchored scale from 0 to 7, for which each position was predefined for the respondent, he/she was asked to show the strength of Use of each substance as the U score.

O *(Time Off).* The respondent was asked to show the number of months since he/she used each substance as the O score. It quickly became clear that this score was meaningless. The fact that the respondents were incarcerated at the time introduced an unmanageable element into responses in this category. For example, some of the respondents estimated time off from the point of their incarceration, while others gave the length of time they had been in prison.

W *(Present Want).* On an anchored scale from 0 to 7, for which each position was predefined for the respondent, he/she was asked to show the strength of his/her present Want/desire to use each substance as the W score. This score was intended to get at the addictive feeling of the incarcerated person removed from access to substances (other than foods and tobaccos and limited access to some medications). Once more, it soon became clear that this score was less than ideally useful. Most addicts removed from

access to their substances tend to experience a major decline in their addictive want, which may be reinstated as soon as access is again possible. Many incarcerated people, in order to create the image of having achieved major changes in their lives, simply deny wanting substances. This reduced the numbers of subjects acknowledging wants.

Computed Dependent Variables

The Years estimates, of course, would have to be and were greatly affected by age ($\underline{r}$ = .567). In order to extract the effect of age on the estimates of Years of use, the regression of Age on Years of use for each substance was computed, and a new weighted score calculated for each subject. This new score is designated as Age-Corrected Years (*YCA*). Since all derived scores are a step removed from 'reality', it was intended to perform some analyses on Years of use (*Y*) and some on the Age-Corrected Years (*YCA*) score. It was intended to determine the utility of the Addicause axes in predicting (1) estimates of uses of specific substances, (2) estimates of uses of classes of substances, and (3) addictiveness as a generic phenomenon. In order to create use estimates for the classes of substances, the Age-Corrected Years (*YCA*) and amount of Use (*U*) scores were factored and the factor scores saved as new variables. This created the following new dependent variables, not all of which would in fact be needed:

YAF1-2. Two factor scores for Years of Alcohol use.
YDF1-4. Four factor scores for Years of street Drug use.
UAF1-3. Three factor scores for strength of Alcohol use.
UDF1-3. Three factor scores for strength of Drug use.
YADF1-6. Six factor scores for Years of Alcohol and Drugs.
UADF1-5. Five factor scores for Use of Alcohol and Drugs.
UYAF1-5. Five factor scores for Alcohol Use and Years.
UYDF1-8. Eight factor scores for Drug Use and Years.

UYADF1-13. Thirteen factor scores for Alcohol <u>and</u> Drug use <u>and</u> Years (to help represent generic addictiveness).

In each of the above factor analyses, the factor compositions are interesting but not unexpected. For the most part, the alcohols and street drugs appear in different factors, and the substances loading on the various factors appear to be meaningfully related to one another. The substances falling under each factor, along with their loadings, are presented in Table 1 (Appendix C). In Table 1 (Appendix C), an attempt has been made to suggest a common meaning or identity for the cluster of substances loading with each factor. Although an interpretation of each factor is offered in Table 1 (Appendix C), it must be emphasized that the 'meaning' suggested is in no important way relevant to the present uses of the factor scores. The factor scores have been generated solely for the purpose of data reduction to permit an empirical approach to generalization to <u>classes</u> of substances.

Finally, it must be acknowledged that the enormous number of independent and dependent variables included in the foregoing will inevitably create much confusion. That is the downside. The upside is that the results will lend themselves in many ways to answering questions that occur to readers. Indeed, it is intended to present large amounts of data so that the results can be employed by others in ways that have not occurred to the writer.

CHAPTER 8

Psychometrics I (Item Analysis)

As stated earlier, the Subjects for the Addicause phase of the present project were 650 successive adult male offender admissions to the OCI supplemented with 45 nonoffenders, mostly female, who served as volunteers at the OCI or were members of an AA group or were members of a fitness club. A few (twenty) of the inmate subjects completed an early version of the DAQ that contained only sixty-five axes/scales. Also, a few of the subjects failed to complete some or all the final pages (initial causes page and substance uses page). Consequently, there are slightly different numbers (as low as 580) of subjects in some of the statistical analyses undertaken. However, careful examination of the cases involved did not reveal any meaningful or systematic elements that might bias results reported.

The Addicause Scales

The whole Addicause test contained 68×12, or 816, items. The first question of importance had to do with the extent to which item writing had succeeded in creating items related to one another and to the sixty-eight scales to which they had been assigned. This question was addressed in two ways, namely, factor analysis and item-scale reliabilities.

Data Reduction

Factor analysis of the items in the 695 subjects of the Addicause sample tended to group the items of each of the axes together in the same factor. Many of the scales contained items that did not fall in the same factor; however, in most of these instances, the variant items tended to fall in factors representing either axes with the same axis 'tone' (with an odd or even axis number) or factors from the pair of axes using the same polar dimensions (see Chapter 5). This suggested that, for the most part, the items had been written in scale groupings such that they were accessing the same types of personal experiences. Table 2 (Appendix D) presents the item groupings under different factors, along with their loadings on the factors into which they fall.

The above observations might suggest orthogonality between the Addicause axes (scales). This would not be an entirely justified conclusion, in spite of the usual rotation effect of between-factors zero values in the covariance matrix for the factor scores. The correlation matrix for the items showed a considerable amount of relationship among most items regardless of the axes to which they had been assigned but tending to higher intercorrelations among items assigned to any given axis. Moreover, as is common among items and scales of a composite test, the axes' (scales') scores also displayed correlation coefficients of moderate sizes, depending to some extent on the scale scores being correlated. These characteristics of most multivariable tests do not, by themselves, mean that the test variables are undiscriminating. It only means that the test's items are drawn from the same conceptual universe and that its parts have a similar cuing effect on the respondents.

Regardless, the item and/or scale correlations and factor structures are useful sources of information for both the test constructor and the test user. In particular, at the point of item analysis, intercorrelations varying from the expected, such as those involving items that load with axes other than the one to which each was assigned, do identify items that were imperfectly written to communicate what was intended. In effect, the factor structure of the items represents respondents'

indications of the meaning communicated by the items as written. For this reason, Table 2 (Appendix D) presents factor loadings for all the Addicause items, rather than displaying an illustrative sample. Indeed, the items' factor loadings and their intercorrelation matrix was used to identify faulty items for reconsideration.

The number of faulty items was not excessive. Still, in the usual test construction exercise, they would be rewritten and tried again. In this case, however, it was decided to wait to see whether all sixty-eight axes or scales would need to be used in order to identify the causes of addictions. Although this statement may be a bit premature, it is appropriate at this point to state that not all the Addicause axes turned out to be required for the main task it was assumed the test would have to perform. Indeed, it was concluded at a later stage that a short-form of the test, comprised of twenty to twenty-five axes, was sufficient to identify the main causal variables in alcohol and drug abuse. When this short-form Addicause was being prepared, the variant items (from the twenty axes) identified in this item analysis were reviewed and modified slightly for the sake of clarification.

Ordinarily, item analysis would be also used to permit scales to be developed or restructured to create empirical scales. The matter was given some thought. The advantages should be that, at least in the present sample, the reliabilities of the scales should be enhanced somewhat. The disadvantages of reformulating the scales to create empirical scales would be that the resulting scales would (1) be of different lengths, (2) have mixed conceptual contents and thus be difficult to understand, and (3) be potentially subject to sample biases. Since there was some advantage to retaining the conceptually organized scales rather than moving immediately to restructure the items into empirical scales, it was decided to see how the reliability of the existing axis structure tested out.

Reliability

Several types of reliability are recognized. The most commonly used variety is a measure of *internal consistency*, or item-scale reliability, which should provide the main kind of information required to determine whether it is necessary to move from conceptual to empirical scales. It is also necessary to determine the *stability*, or test-retest reliability, of the measures, if only to determine how modifiable they may be. Finally, the real test of reliability is concerned with the *precision* of the measures to be used.

Internal consistency. Item-scale alphas[7] were run for all sixty-eight axes, each containing its original twelve items. Table 3 (Appendix E) presents the alphas obtained in these analyses using the entire 695 subjects of the Addicause sample. It will be observed from Table 3 (Appendix E) that the alphas range from 0.67 to 0.94 (Mean alpha = 0.84). The maximum variation between the scale alpha and the standardized item alpha was 0.02 (Axes 28 and 45). Consequently, only the scale alphas are shown, along with the axes' means, in Table 3 (Appendix E). Axis 03, Reactive Depression, is the only scale whose alpha is worrisome, since it is one of the twenty axes to be included in the short-form of the Addicause test. While its relatively lower alpha suggests it will have to be watched carefully, it is noteworthy that six of its twelve items fall in one factor and five in the next factor (in five), so it does seem to have some internally consistent elements. For the most part, the *internal consistencies* (as indicated by their alphas) of the axes were deemed by the author to be satisfactory for the purposes for which the scales were constructed.

Response Sets. By inspection, the *mean scores* shown in Table 3 (Appendix E) are neither too low nor too variable, which suggests that response sets are not operating to such a degree that they impair measurement. One factor that might affect the reliability of the instrument in clinical application could be the lack of negatively

---

[7]   *Alpha* is a statistic useful in deciding whether or not two variables in a statistical analysis are related. Most researchers typically use an alpha level of 0.05 as the cut-off.

phrased questions in the test. This fact might make the instrument seem prone to influence from response sets such as the Social Desirability variable. No attempt was made to compensate for the operation of response sets, nor to test for their effects. The intention of the test was to record (positive in their effect) purposes or needs and reinforcers or habits in respondents' personalities. If, for example, social desirability is a need operating in the individual, it is assumed that this fact will be manifested, to the extent that it needs to be identified, in the pattern of elevated and depressed axis scores. The point is that, as stated earlier, the test is not conceived to be one aiming at verifying the presence or absence of addictions (a task for which the MAST and DAST are used here) but rather one of recognizing causes of addictions in the person that he/she is willing in some way to acknowledge.

Nevertheless, some will wish at least some recognition to be paid to the question of response sets acting in this test. In this connection, attention is drawn to the mean scores reported in Table 3 (Appendix E) for axes 22 (Subcultural Values), 31 (Demean Others), 55 (Impaired Self Esteem), and 68 (Substance Dependency), probably among the axes carrying pejorative implications from the perspective of others. Their means vary around the grand mean for all sixty-eight axes (20.4). Also, it may be recalled that the odd-numbered axes were designed to access pessimism and 'negative' mood and emotional tone, whereas the even-numbered axes were designed to measure optimism and 'positive' mood and emotional tone. The mean of the means for the odd-numbered axes is 19.4, whereas that for the even-numbered axes is 21.4. The difference might suggest the operation of some social desirability in respondents' test responses, but not enough to erase either 'desirable' or 'undesirable' responding.

Stability. In addition to his appalling lack of appreciation about the importance of response sets, the senior author is wickedly unconcerned that this instrument should possess adequate stability. Not only did he not consider the question of retest stability during test design, he would now admit to insufficient temerity to have asked his subjects to accept a second testing with the whole Addicause

test, which would have tested the patience of a saint, let alone the population being studied. In addition, however, it should be remembered that stability is not a particularly desirable quality in the test designed to measure personality qualities that it is hoped will change with treatment.

Split-half reliability might have been used as a substitute for test/ retest reliability, except that the scales were designed so tightly with respect to their infrastructures that it would be hard to know how to split axes or the test in meaningful ways.

Nevertheless, a minor exercise was undertaken with the first two axes (01 and 02). The split-half alphas for axis 01 were, for part 1, 0.83 and, for part 2, 0.81. For axis 02, which had the lower internal consistency of the two, the split-half alphas were, for part 1, 0.068 and, for part 2, 0.73. The split-half method was then used for both scales together. The split-half alphas were, for part 1 (02), 0.82 and, for part 2 (01), 0.90. These, of course, are precisely the internal consistency alphas we already had. So the first four axes' items were combined for split-half analysis. The alphas were, for part 1 (01 and 02), 0.76 and, for part 2 (03 and 04), 0.83. It would appear that the split-half method does essentially the same task as the item-scale method.

In spite of the difficulty of obtaining test/retest measures, as mentioned above, a group of inmate subjects, referred to earlier as the Addicure subjects, were administered the twenty-axis short-form of the Addicause twice. The problem here was that, except for the control group, a treatment program aimed at the Addicause variables was applied between the two administrations. Nevertheless, the relative stability of the test might be assessed in this sample of 143 inmates. Although all the test-retest Pearson correlations for all the axes of the short-form test (except the relatively low internal consistency axis 03 where the probability is 0.01) are associated with 0.000 probabilities, thankfully, the impression is that the coefficients are relatively low. That is, providentially, the axes are found to have only modest stabilities with a mix of treatment-interpolated and no-treatment control subjects. Table 4 (Appendix F) displays the correlation coefficients obtained.

It may be recalled that no decision was made earlier about which of the two total axis scores (sum of values or number of values greater than 1) would be used. In order to illustrate the idea that the two scores might be measuring slightly different aspects of each axis, the intercorrelations among the axes' S (sum of values) and the axes' N (number of values > 1) scores are displayed separately in Table 4 (Appendix F) for the entire Addicure sample (N = 143). In addition, for the sake of comparison, Table 4 (Appendix F) presents the S (sum of values) scores' retest correlations for the no-treatment Control group (N = 19) and for those Experimental subjects receiving a single (N = 81) and a plurality (N = 32) of Addicure treatment programmes.

In Table 4 (Appendix F), the only meaningful but limited data concerning stability is to be found in the column reporting retest correlations for the no-treatment Control group. The problem with this column of figures is that it is based on a small number of subjects (N = 19). And even these data, as indications of the stability of the Addicause measures, are flawed. All the subjects involved in the Addicure study (Controls and Experimentals) received some treatment between the test and the retest since all were resident on the treatment units at the OCI. The only difference between the Controls and the Experimentals is that the latter (but not the former) received some treatment related to the Addicause axes (i.e., Addicure treatment). The contrast afforded by the other columns of Table 4 (Appendix F) ends to suggest that the Addicure treatments between the test and the retest had effects on the test scores. But this is getting a bit ahead of the story. For now, it would appear from the results with the Control subjects presented in Table 4 that most of the Addicause axes (except 03, 02, 36 and 53) are adequately stable. The other columns of Table 4 (Appendix F) suggest that the test scores may also be modifiable.

Precision. For the present, the question of the precision of the Addicause test must be begged. Table 4 (Appendix F) does suggest that the test is sufficiently precise that it can be modified by treatments interpolated between test and retest. However, the degree of the precision of the scales must await confirmation in a later part of this volume.

CHAPTER 9

Psychometrics II (Scale Characteristics)

The foregoing has been concerned with the items, their assignments to axes or scales, and the reliability of the scales. It is now necessary to turn to an examination of the several characteristics of the scales and the measures derived from them.

It will be recalled that, at the point of item writing, two processing (cognitive and affective) and three sensory (visual, auditory, and kinaesthetic) dimensions were counterbalanced in the items of each scale. Moreover, two total scores were proposed, namely, the S (sum of values) and the N (number of values > 1) scores. It would be important to determine at this point which of these scales should be retained as providing potentially useful information about respondents.

Processing and sensory measures. Quite apart from whether or not response bias was balanced out by ensuring equal representation of processing styles and preferred sensory modalities, it is important to determine whether these classes of respondent attributes contribute any kind of information. Of course, if they can be shown to provide some information about respondents, it would then be necessary to discover whether the information provided is meaningful or useful. One way to find out whether the processing and sensory scores provide any information (useful or not) would be to determine whether they affected subjects' responses. This can be evaluated by means of a factor analysis of the processing and sensory scores. If factors emerge that seem to cluster one or other processing or sensory

scales together, then it could be concluded that the clustering scales provide some information.

Two factor analyses were run, including all the C, E, V, A, and K scores for each half of the Addicause axes (01 to 34 and 35 to 68). With one exception, the factors that emerged were all formed from the axes, each factor (as in the analysis shown in Table 2 (Appendix D) being comprised essentially of the subscale scores for one axis. Of the factors that emerged, only factor #2 from the first half of the test (01 to 34) displayed anything but equal inclusions of C, E, V, A, and K scores. Factor #2 for the first thirty-four axes was exclusively a V-score factor, and its V scores were fairly equally split between the negatively toned odd-numbered axes (twelve V scores) and the positively toned even-numbered axes (nine V scores).

These observations would seem to suggest that the V (visual) scores for the first half of the test alone, among the processing and sensory subscales, may contain information. However, it should be noted that this applied only for the first half of the test. Thus, even if there is some meaningful information contained in these V scores, the information contained applies inconsistently and is therefore undependable. This means that for the purpose of future analyses of these data, the C, E, V, A, and K scores can safely by ignored. From here on, they are abandoned.

Total scores (S, N, and Z). But what of the total scores for each scale? Factor analysis of these two scales was, at first, rather disappointing in that the factors that emerged were axis related, as with the C, E, V, A, and K scores. But there was a subtle difference. The first factor that emerged, as in most analyses, included a large variety of those variables that most affect the variance of the test. Interestingly, these higher-power variables mostly involved the odd-numbered axes – the axes with a pessimistic and negative emotional tone.

However, there was a difference in the order in which the variables contributed to the first factor in the S and N analyses. When the S (sum of values) scores were analysed, the axes that appeared first (higher correlations with the first factor) were the more 'active' or

energized of the negatively toned axes. When the N (<u>number</u> of values > 1) scores were analysed, the axes that appeared first were the more 'passive' or de-energized of the negatively toned axes. It looked as though the S scores referred to active pursuit of 'feeling better' or as if the S scores might reflect the pressure in the person of needs or purposes (final causes). In contrast, it looked as though the N scores referred to passive states in which, as it were, the person was waiting for something to happen or as if the N scores might reflect passivity driven by existing habit strength or possibly reinforcing states of affairs (perpetuating causes?). Parenthetically, there was more information on this issue that was yet to emerge. Table 5 (Appendix G) seeks to illustrate this subtle difference between the S and N scores. Table 5 (Appendix G) displays the factor loadings for the S and N score analyses and the title assigned to each axis.

The relatively subtle differences in the ordering of the axes in the first factor for the S and N scores, even though there are also shifts in the location of the factors other than the first, may seem weak as a basis for drawing the inference that the S and N scores refer to different aspects of causality. However, two other remarks might be made in support of this inference.

First, the weakness of the argument did not go unnoticed. The Addicause and the Addicure samples were completely independent of each other. So the factor analyses were replicated in the Addicure sample. The order of the S axes was exactly the same, and the factor loadings were either identical or varied by a maximum of 0.01. The maximum variation in the N axes' first factor loadings was 0.02, and the order of four sequences of three N axes was changed but not in a way that altered the impression noted above.

Second, it should be recalled that very little difference would be expected among indicators of needs ($\underline{w}$ causes) and reinforcers ($\underline{v}$ causes) since a reinforcer acts on a need and a need has to be present for a reinforcer to be effective. The difference between indications of the two ought, in principle, to be only that needs are actively pursued, while reinforcers can have effects while the person is (1) actively pursuing gratification <u>or</u> (2) passively waiting. Having

said that, however, it is certainly acknowledged that the difference between the referents of the S and N scores remains no more than a hypothesis. Moreover, aside from the importance attached to final and perpetuating causes in the early remarks about causality and addictions, the main other purpose for the hypothesis at this point is to justify retention of both types of total axis scores.

No meaning at all could be found to be associated with the Z scores (respondents' claimed causes and effects of substance uses). Even when the Z scores were factored along with the MAST (alcohol addiction) and DAST (drug addiction) scores, the only axis that shifted (from the first factor) to cluster in a separate factor with the MAST and DAST scores was axis 14 (Vivid Imagery). The absence of (useful) information afforded by the Z scores corresponded to the impressions of the author while entering the Z score data.

Summary. Although a large variety of scores were initially devised to represent different aspects of each of the sixty-eight Addicause axes, none but the total axis scores emerged from analysis of the scales' characteristics as contributing appreciable useful information. Accordingly, no further attention will be paid to the C, E, V, A, K scores; and limited attention will be paid to the Z scores. However, the subtle differences between the S and N scores warrant continuing separate use of both of them.

CHAPTER 10

Psychometrics III (Validity)

Several varieties of validity have to be considered in the validation of an instrument. *Face validity*, which recognizes the <u>apparent</u> relationship between test items and the variables it seeks to address, is not considered here. It is impossible at this stage to determine what the causal variables in addictions are, so it is impossible to say what items purporting to identify them 'ought' to look like. *Concurrent validity* seeks to determine whether the instrument in question behaves like other instruments addressing the same issues. With the exception of a limited range of tests, such as the Alcadd Test and the Manson (1965a, 1965b) Evaluation Form, there are no other satisfactory tests with which to compare the Addicause. Of course, it is necessary to determine whether the Addicause scales relate in meaningful ways to other tests of personality-related variables. Its relation to addictiveness as measured by other tests (e.g., MAST and DAST) is really a matter of predictive validation since these other tests are measures of something the Addicause seeks to predict. *Predictive validity* sets out to assess the capacity of an instrument to predict other issues not identified by the test undergoing evaluation. To the extent that the instrument being assessed can be shown to predict the other issues, its variables may be inferred to control, and thus to cause, the other issues. In this case, the 'other issues' to be predicted are various measures of addictive behaviour. This is a central part of the evaluation of the Addicause test, and this matter

is addressed in this chapter. *Construct validity* is perhaps the most essential form of validation. It seeks to evaluate the extent to which the instrument is related meaningfully to the theory and constructs underlying it (see next chapter).

Concurrent Validity

Since, like all other tests, the Addicause addresses a particular band of personality variables, approached in a specific way, it seems quite likely that it will be difficult to demonstrate a high degree of relationship between its axes and other personality test scores. This last statement was quickly verified in the first attempt to create simple structure from the Addicause and the Minnesota Multiphasic Personality Inventory (MMPI). When the sixty-eight Addicause axes and ninety MMPI scales (i.e., the basic clinical scales and a host of experimental scales – Dahlstrom et al. [1975]) were factored together, the expected happened. The MMPI scales clustered together in MMPI factors, and the Addicause axes clustered together in Addicause factors. This statement sounds as though there was little relationship between the scales from the two tests. Actually, there were many strong relationships among their scales. However, the similarities within the tests tended to overwhelm the similarities between the tests, probably due to the conceptual homogeneity of their respective item compositions. That is, the focus of inquiry is mainly directed at psychopathology in the MMPI items and into motivation and experience in the Addicause items and scales.

Table 6 (Appendix H) illustrates the meaningfulness of the concurrent relationships between the MMPI and the Addicause scales. Table 6 (Appendix H) presents the correlations obtained in the Addicause sample ($N = 650$) between the Addicause axes and the ninety MMPI scales that were scored. The purposes of presenting the data in this way are (a) to ensure that the reader has wide access to the more familiar MMPI variables, (b) to permit the behaviour of the Addicause scales to be tracked, and (c) specifically, to make it

possible to create some operational meaning for the manner in which the Addicause axes were constructed.

This last purpose requires brief explanation. It will be recalled that the Addicause axes were created in pairs such that, for the most part, the mood or emotional tone of the two axes of a pair (odd- and even-numbered) would be in opposite directions. A quick scan across the Table 6 (Appendix H) columns for axes 01, 02, and 03 will reveal that the direction of mood is consistently the same for axes 01 and 03 and that their direction of mood is consistently the opposite from that for axis 02. That is, either the sign is the same for axes 01 and 03 and the opposite for axis 02 or the magnitude of the coefficient approaches zero. Thus, given the mood and meaning of any MMPI scale, the Addicause axes behave in relation to it as they should, if one considers the way the latter were written.

At the same time, there are noteworthy variations from the last statement. For example, axis 04, which 'should' behave in opposite ways from axes 03, 05, and 01 does not appear to do so. Although this fact may appear to invalidate axis 04, careful consideration needs to be given before 'the baby is thrown out with the bath water'. On the one hand, axis 04 was written to represent the opposite poles from those used in axis 03, and so it should behave in the opposite direction conceptually. On the other hand, the items of both of these axes are largely concerned with stress. 03 represents the debilitating effects of stress, and 04 represents the activating or exhilarating effects of stress. What meaning is likely to be taken by respondents from the items of these two axes?

Is it possible that the respondents are reacting to the items of these two scales (and others carrying negative 'tone') more in terms of the stress component than the tone of the reaction to it? Some indications that this might be what happened may be found in Table 6 (Appendix H) in the variant (from 01, 02, 05) correlations found with 04 on the MMPI scales of *D* (02), *M* (09), Si (00), Ego Strength, Self-Control, Alcoholism, Spy, Anhedonia, Displacement, Reaction Formation, Paedophilia, Phobia, Poor Health, Social Adjustment, and Social Presence (Dahlstrom et al., 1972, 1975).

The attempt was made to permit some degree of overlap of MMPI and Addicause scales in factors by reducing the number of variables entered into the analysis. There was no change in the tendency for the MMPI scales to factor together and for the Addicause axes to factor together, regardless of numbers and types of variables used. Although these data might have been used to reduce the number of Addicause variables from sixty-eight to a more manageable number, it still seemed premature to do so. It is true that some of the Addicause scales did not perform quite as they 'should' when their performance was evaluated through their relationships to other test scales. However, the critical test of the <u>usefulness</u> of the variables, regardless of whether their 'meaning' had been correctly identified, would come from the predictive and construct validity analyses. It is time to get on with predictive validation.

Predictive Validity

In the causal thinking involved in most science, that which regularly antedates something else is said to be the cause of something else. That is, causes predict their effects. If the Addicause test does contain some of the real causes of addictive behaviour, then its variables or axes ought to predict to addictive behaviour. Although recognizing that there are some errors in the way in which some of the Addicause items were written (identified in the item analysis above), the scales appear to be have been written appropriately enough to be used to test their purpose.

It remains to consider how addictive behaviour is to be represented in order to be predicted. Two kinds of dependent measures were listed in Chapter 7, namely, the MAST and DAST (cost of addictive behaviour) measures and the Years (Y) and Strength of Use (U) measures reported by respondents on the last page of the Addicause questionnaire. In addition, one might think it appropriate to employ the MMPI scales of Alcoholism and Drug Abuse. However, both of these scales are derived scales whose items are somewhat confounded

and which anyway display only modest correlations with the MAST and DAST scores (see Table 6.5, Appendix H).

Although the MAST and DAST scales pose no immediate problem from the point of view of analysis, the Y and U ratings do pose a particular kind of problem. The Y and U ratings do have many zero values, which, on the upside, allows for nonaddiction to be well represented. At the same time, the ratings are extremely complex, having been obtained separately for a host of different specific substances in each class of addictive substances. While there are ways to reduce the complexity in data, these methods tend to result in fabricated variables that do not really represent any respondent's reality. So for predictive validation purpose, the Y and U scores were handled as given by respondents.

Two methods of analysis were adopted, namely, analysis of variance (anova) and discriminant function analysis. Table 7 (Appendix I) presents the results of these analyses. Table 7 (Appendix I) shows the significance of the prediction of the substance use indicator (columns) by each of the available predictor indices (rows). Asterisks mark those variables that entered into the discriminant analysis of the substance use indicator (columns). The percentage of correct discriminant function predictions of each substance category by group of variables is shown in Table 7 (Appendix I) in the first row of each subtable for the Addicause predictions and in the last row of each subtable for the predictions based on the MMPI, MAST, DAST, and the Survey of Thoughts, Feelings, and Behaviours (STFB) factors (Reynolds, 1994).

The absolute size of Table 7 (Appendix I) is apt to be intimidating. But have courage. The table is intended to provide information of any kind that might be of interest. In it, one can examine the behaviour of the Years and/or Use of any substance or of any personality variable (Addicause, MMPI, Criminality) that may be querried.

The first observation that will occur to the reader looking at the immense number of cells in Table 7.1 to 7.4 (Appendix I), each presenting a probability of F, will be that a great many of the probabilities will reach significance by chance alone. Indeed, at the

5% level of confidence, 5% of the cells should present significant findings by chance alone. To respond to this observation, a subtable has been appended to each part of Table 7 (Appendix I) that shows the percentage of cells for each group of variables (Addicause $\underline{S}$ and $\underline{N}$, MMPI, and STFB/Criminality) in each column that reach the 5% level of confidence. In any given column, if the percentage shown in the subtable for a group of variables approximates 5% (probably $\pm$ 5%) then it should be concluded that the group of variables in question does not provide any information about the type of substance use represented by that column (even if discriminant function seems to show that it does).

At first glance, the results presented in the several subtables of Table 7 (Appendix I) may seem disappointing. An established test (the MMPI) seems to do as well as the Addicause in predicting Years and Use of most of the addictive substances considered. After all this work, perhaps the Addicause is unnecessary. Perhaps the existing MMPI offers all the information needed about the causes of addictive behaviour. By itself, that idea would not be unwelcome. Although it might obviate the need for the Addicause test, it would suggest that the commonly used MMPI would afford useful information about the personality variables that drive alcohol and drug addictions. But Table 7 (Appendix I) may offer more information than just that.

Perhaps because the subjects are offenders, it is frequently the criminality-related variables, both from the MMPI and from the STFB (a test of criminality), that are significantly related to the substance use dependent variables and that enter the discriminant function predictions of substance use. To a lesser extent, the same might be said of the Addicause variables, in that Subcultural Values (22) and Guilt Intolerance (08), for example, commonly enter the discriminant predictions. These observations can be verified by tracking across the rows for the criminality-relevant variables in the several tables of Table 7 (Appendix I).

Perhaps partly because the offender subjects were admitted to the OCI on the strength of someone's notion that they might require treatment, the indicators of disturbed affects or feelings in both the

MMPI and the Addicause seem also to provide a strong source of variables significantly driving substance uses and contributing to the discriminant predictions of these uses. This observation can also be verified by tracking across the rows representing disturbing affects such as anxiety, depression, anger, and the like. In a similar vein, to the extent that the main clinical scales from the MMPI contain items representing strong feelings, they too tend to exhibit a disproportionate rate of significant Fs and of contributions to discriminant predictions. That is, there may be subject-selection factors that account, in some measure, for some of the significant findings in Table 7 (Appendix I). Indeed, the above observations do suggest that it is factors from the individual's motivational life that may drive addictions. That is, needs and personally effective reinforcers may well be the factors that most control addictive behaviour.

A kind of indirect verification of this idea can be seen in the last two short tables of Table 7 (Appendix I). In these two short tables, the correct prediction rates for rated Want for a variety of substances (while the person is in jail) are displayed. Although in some cases the number of subjects' rated Want is relative low, the successful predictions of these Want categories tend to be slightly higher than the equivalent predictions of strength of Use and Years of use. It would seem likely that the Want ratings would represent both motivational states and disturbed feelings to a greater extent than either Years or strength of Use.

But what of the instrument of particular interest here, the Addicause? There are at least two initial observations that need to be made about this instrument. First, since this chapter also addresses concurrent validation, it should be observed that the Addicause behaves in much the same ways as the MMPI and the STFB in predicting uses of addictive substances. Although it sometimes predicts substance uses that the MMPI does not predict quite as well (and it should be noted that the reverse is also true), like the MMPI, it does predict uses of many types of substances quite well. Second, since this section has to do with predictive validation, it is worthy of note that the Addicause does account for a major part of the variance

of use of many addictive substances. Moreover, as the percentages presented in the following subtables of Table 7 (Appendix I) reveal, in most cases, a very high proportion of the Addicause variables are significantly related to the uses of many addictive substances.

Parenthetically, the high percentages of Addicause variables that are significantly related to uses of many kinds of substances may suggest that the Addicause variables are highly redundant or highly intercorrelated. To beg the question, it might be pointed out that the same type of redundancy can be seen among the MMPI variables in their relationships to some substance uses.

But there are at least two other observations that bear on this apparent redundancy. First, there is a modest negative relationship between the percentages of correct discriminant function classifications and the percentages of significant Fs in most columns. This should mean that the Addicause (and to a lesser extent the MMPI) variables interact in fairly complicated ways in their relationships to substance uses. That is, the redundancy may be more apparent than real. Second, although some variables contribute very frequently to the discriminant predictions (e.g., 37, 22), a considerable variety of different Addicause variables contributes to control and prediction of the different types of substances. This should mean that different types of Addicause variables account for uses of different types of substances and, once more, that the redundancy may be more apparent than real.

Cautionary Notes

The real essence of predictive validity is concerned with the ability of the Addicause (and the MMPI and STFB) to predict Years and Use (none, some, much) of the various kinds of substances. But discriminant analysis has some peculiarities that need to be recalled in evaluating the data (asterisks and percentage correct classifications) presented in Table 7 (Appendix I).

If the groups (none, some, much) are not of roughly equal sizes, the classification results tend to become distorted. For this reason, in each discriminant function result reported, the numbers of subjects is roughly equal. Since three groups are used (with only a few exceptions where there were not enough users for three groups), the expected (chance) percentage of correct classifications is 33%. That is, percentage correct classifications approaching 33% are likely due to chance. The larger the number of subjects in each class to be predicted, the greater the difficulty of discriminant function to classify the subjects due to increased between-subjects variability. A glance across the correct classifications percentages in Table 7 (Appendix I) will tend to verify this fact. Those substances that tend to be relatively rarely used (low Ns) tend to be predicted at higher rates than those that are more commonly used. This does not necessarily mean that the commonly used substances are not predicted fairly well by the scales. In most studies employing discriminant function analysis, the numbers of subjects in each group tend to be fairly small. Consequently, to compare the percentages presented in Table 7 (Appendix I) with those reported in other discriminant function studies is apt to be misleading. Predictions reported for the infrequently used substances can probably be compared fairly meaningfully with those reported in other research reports. However, there are few studies using subject numbers as large as those used for Table 7 (Appendix I) with commonly used substances such as beer, rye, cocaine, hashish, marijuana, coffee, and cigarettes.

Given the above observations, the percentages of correct prediction shown in Table 7 (Appendix I) for alcohols and street drugs probably represent a very good level of discrimination of substance uses by the scales reported.

Contributions of Various Test Variables

Nevertheless, some readers might wish to remark that the MMPI seems to do as good (or better) a job than the Addicause in predicting

most substance uses. In response, it should be stated, first, that there is no intention that the Addicause should be able to 'compete' with the MMPI in predicting substance uses. Both contribute their own kinds of information about the causation of addictions – which is why both are reported fully in Table 7 (Appendix I).

Second, it should be noted that (to limit costs of analyses) the MMPI variables are combined with the MAST and DAST and the STFB variables in the predictions (note the '+' following the MMPI heading for the MMPI+ prediction rows [used to denote the fact of inclusion of the other sources of variables]). Many of the significant Fs in the various substance use columns are derived from the MAST, DAST, and STFB variables; and many of the variables contributing to the discriminant classifications (*) are from these other MAST, DAST, and STFB test sources. Moreover, it is noteworthy that, as stated earlier, many of the MMPI variables that tend to contribute significant Fs and discriminant predictions are apparently criminality-related variables (like the STFB). That is, there may be a confounding variable between their addictions and their criminality in the predictions of substance uses among the offender subjects employed in this study.

Third, that the Addicause does appear to contribute its own additional information that can be seen (at least initially) from the number/percentage of significant Fs shown in the subtables following each of the parts of Table 7 (Appendix I). A high proportion of the Addicause scales are commonly significantly related to the substance use indicators. This impression is enhanced in Table 21 (Appendix M) where a limited number of Addicause scales (short-form) is combined with the MMPI scales in discriminant function analyses of the derived factors of substance use (from Table 1). In Table 21 (Appendix M) it will be noticed that Addicause variables, as well as MMPI variables, are selected in the discriminant function classifications in most instances.

Validation of S and N Total Scores

Although the S (<u>sum</u> or values) and N (<u>number</u> of values > 1) scores are presented separately in the various subtables of Table 7 (Appendix I), the complexity of the tables makes it well-nigh impossible to 'see' the differential behaviour (if any) of these two types of scores. For this reason, Table 8 (Appendix I) has been constructed to distil the relevant information from Table 7 (Appendix I).

In Table 8 (Appendix I), for each test variable, the number of significant probabilities of $\underline{F}$ and the number of times the variable entered the discriminant function predictions is assembled (from Table 7) separately for the uses of alcohols and street drugs. Whether each axis contributes primarily to the prediction of uses of alcohol (A), drugs (D), or both (b) is shown in the second last column of Table 8 (Appendix I). And the last column seeks to recognize the fact that there may be different respondent characteristics based on the nature of the subject group used, including offenders (Cr), addicts (Ad), and people seeking treatment (Tx), which might affect the role of each variable in predicting substance uses.

In addition, a postscript (s or n) is added to the number of inclusions in the discriminant analysis for those Addicause variables where there is a noteworthy predominance of S or N score inclusions. Finally, the notation concerning its main causal function (see Chapter 5) follows the axis name indicating whether the axis mainly represents a need (Nd), a derived need creating drive stimuli (sD), a source of reinforcement (Rf), or a derived source of reinforcement (rf).

In particular, Table 8 (Appendix I) is included as a suggestive (but not definitive) support for the earlier-stated hypothesis about the difference between the S and N scores. The predominances of S or N scores (postscripts following the number of inclusions of the variables) in the discriminant analyses correspond quite well to the need (Nd, sD) or reinforcer (Rf, rf) qualities associated with the Addicause axes (main causal functions). The information contained in Table 8 (extracted from Table 7) does seem to suggest quite strongly that the S and N scores exert slightly different causal effects on the

uses of addictive substances. It is true that the differences between these two scores are subtle, but Table 8 (Appendix I) does seem to justify their continued separate use. Seventeen of the sixty-eight Addicause variables do <u>not</u> display any predominance of S or N scores among the discriminating variables. Three of the sixty-eight axes show a predominance of S for one class of substance (alcohol <u>or</u> drugs) and of N for the other class of substances. The S scores are found to predominate in twenty-five discriminants, while N scores (which mathematically ought to be less discriminating) are found to predominate in twenty-three discriminants. And each is found to predominate for axes designed mainly to reference the type of cause (final/need or perpetuating/reinforcement) hypothesized to be represented by the S and N scores.

These observations from Table 8 (Appendix I) afford the clearest evidence yet found to verify the hypothesis that the S scores best represent the 'need' (final cause) aspects of variables and that the N scores best represent the 'reinforcement' (perpetuating cause) aspects of the Addicause variables.

Additional Observations

Finally, it needs to be said that Table 8 (Appendix I) contained some surprises. It had been thought that the secondary tranquillizing effect of alcohol, arising from its soporific effect on the cerebral cortex, would mean that alcohol should have an antianxiety effect, and thus a reinforcing effect, on addicts. While Physiological Anxiety (<u>47</u>) and, to a lesser extent, Phobias (MMPI) do seem to help in discriminating alcoholics, the other indicators of anxiety (<u>01</u> – Social Anxiety and MMPI – Anxiety, for example) do not. Also it had been thought that the arousing/excitant effects of some street drugs ('rush', 'buzz') should afford reinforcement, and thus addiction to drugs, in depressed people. It does seem to work that way with Flat Depression (<u>13</u>), perhaps with Somatic Depression (<u>53</u>) and Depression (MMPI – 02 D) and to a lesser extent with Reactive Depression (<u>03</u>), but it

does not seem to work that way with the MMPI scales of Depressive Affect or Anhedonia. There remains much to be learned from these data.

Summary

There are subtle differences within the S and N scores, and between the Addicause and the MMPI and STFB scores in predicting uses of various types of addictive substances and the MAST and DAST ('cost' of addictive behaviour) scores. However, all three sources of variables (Addicause, MMPI, and STFB) do appear to provide information about what drives addictions of various kinds. It may be true that some of the power of the MMPI and STFB in predicting addictive behaviour in this sample is due to the fact that all the subjects studied were offenders (offender-relevant variables participate heavily among the significant $\underline{F}$s) and/or people seeking treatment (emotional distress variables also participate among the significant $\underline{F}$s). Still, at least in this sample, all three test sources of variables (Addicause, MMPI, and STFB) seem to afford useful information about factors predicting, and thus controlling or causing, addictive behaviour. Although possibly to a degree no greater than the MMPI and STFB scales, the Addicause axes and their two kinds of total scores (S and N) do appear to possess sufficient predictive validity with respect to addictive behaviour to warrant their use in identifying some of the causes of addiction.

CHAPTER 11

Construct Validation

Introduction

$\mathbf{A}$ kind of a theory was advanced to account for addictive behaviour. Then the Addicause test was designed to conform to the requirements of that theory. The fact that the Addicause scales/axes do predict fairly well to various kinds of addictive behaviour affords a kind of validation for the theory from which the test was developed. In that sense, it may already be claimed that construct validation of the Addicause test has been demonstrated.

However, the demands of construct validation of the original purpose have not yet been fulfilled. The MMPI and STFB provide predictions of addictive behaviour that are quite similar to that afforded by the Addicause instrument. Moreover, although labels have been proposed for each of the Addicause axes, the relevance of the conceptual system employed to addictive behaviour has not really been evaluated. The task of the present chapter is to provide a relatively complete test of the construct validity of the Addicause instrument.

But how would one go about such a task? There is explicit and implicit theory underlying the development of the instrument, and both types of theory ought to be evaluated. One common way to explore the construct validity of a test such as this would be to derive an application of the theory employed, based on both explicit and

implicit elements in the test, and then evaluating the application. Specifically, a treatment program was devised to modify the Addicause axes and evaluate the changes (if any) observed. There are several steps involved in this process. Each one will be described below.

Task Reduction

The Addicause scales were designed and evaluated as measures of a wide range of addictions. To address food, tobacco, medication, alcohol, drug, and solvent abuse in one treatment study would seem both foolhardy and excessive. From the perspective of the community at large, the most troublesome forms of addiction are those to alcohol and street drugs. Besides, the author had access to a population (incarcerated people) in which alcohol and drug abuse were relatively commonplace. Moreover, follow-up among the available subjects could be undertaken only with respect to criminal recidivism, and it seemed likely that criminal recidivism would depend more on alcohol and drug abuse than on food, tobacco, or medication addictions. Accordingly, it seemed appropriate to select alcohol and drug abuse as the specific targets of the construct validation study.

Scale Reduction

It is clear from Table 7 (Appendix I) that not all the Addicause axes contribute equally usefully to the prediction (i.e., causal control) of alcohol and drug abuse. And to ask subjects to complete all sixty-eight scales of the test two or more times would seem a bit excessive. It seemed appropriate, therefore, to construct and employ a short-form of the Addicause. Essentially, the Addicause might be viewed as a source pool of scales from which samples might be selected for different purposes.

In selecting axes for the short-form of the test, the approach adopted involved several considerations. Each one of which requires brief comment.

How many axes was the first question addressed. For want of any rational basis on which to make this decision, it was arbitrarily decided to select twenty axes for the short-form Addicause. Although this decision appears to have been satisfactory for the present purposes, a caveat needs to be added for anyone making such a selection in the future. Once one makes a selection for any purpose and then collects data based on that selection, it becomes difficult at a later date to make another selection. For example, when axes were being selected at a later date for another (unrelated) purpose, the author could not bring himself to make a new independent selection. Instead he found himself committed to the same twenty scales, adding three more to address another aspect of the problem under investigation.

Which ones of the axes was the obvious next question. Of the several approaches to axis selection that might have been used, it was decided to choose axes based on their generality, i.e., the extent to which they seemed to represent generic addictiveness to alcohol and drugs. The simplest way to do this seemed to be to count the number of times each axis contributed to discriminant function predictions of the various uses and kinds of alcohols and street drugs.

This selection could have been accomplished from Table 7 (Appendix I) if it had been completed at the time. Since it was not yet completed when it became necessary to make decisions about the composition of the short-form, the choices were made somewhat more subjectively.

It was clear, by this selection method, that axes 37 (contributing to fifty-two alcohol and drug years and uses discriminants), 22 (contributing to twenty-nine discriminations), 48 (contributing to twenty-one), 53 (contributing to twenty), 36 (contributing to twenty), 08 (contributing to eighteen), and 24 (contributing to eighteen discriminations) would have to be included in the short-form. However, from this point onward, there were reasons for excluding axes even if they contributed to many discriminants.

Axis 18 (Substance Self-Enhancement) (seventeen discriminants) seemed too direct, possibly suggesting the purpose of the test. Axis 17 (Grief Reaction) (twelve discriminants) seemed too specific with respect to the subjects who might respond to it. Axis 29 (Affect Disturbance) (twelve discriminants) would be addressed in several other treatment programs into which the available subjects might be selected. The same would be true for 09 (Loneliness) for which other treatment programs were available at the OCI. And there were other considerations to be taken into account in axis selection for the short-form.

Balance of causal functions was the next question considered. It seemed desirable to include in the short-form approximately equal numbers of axes presumed to access final (S/needs) and perpetuating (N/reinforcements) causes. The importance of this issue lay partly in the intention to design treatments addressing both the final (need) and perpetuating (reinforcement) aspects of addictiveness. Although this balancing of main causal functions was performed in lockstep with the next issue, the result was gratifying. Ten axes were selected from each of the need (*Nd, sD*) and reinforcement (*Rf, rf*) scales (see table of axes, Chapter 5).

Specificity with respect to the 'simple structure' (see next section) being generated was the final issue considered. The argument involved here is entirely too convoluted to be committed to paper. The author remained at home for almost two months contemplating the data he had at hand – from item analyses, factor analyses, analyses of variance, to discriminant function analyses. The purpose of this intense period of analogical analysis was to attempt to create 'simple structure' from the mass of data about alcohol and drug addictions, in order to generate conceptually discrete (i.e., differential) and specific targets for treatment and from that, to devise a targeted treatment programme, which would then be evaluated. Part of the spin-off from this exercise would be the selection of specific test axes that might be expected to represent the selected treatment targets.

The Addicause axes finally selected for the short-form of the test are reproduced in Appendix B. They are also marked with an

asterisk (*) following the axis numbers in Table 8 (Appendix I), where their rates of contribution to alcohol and drug discriminants and of significant anovas, as well as their main causal functions, can be seen by the interested reader.

Reduction to Simple Structure

It did not seem possible to design a treatment program to address the determinants of addictions without some conceptual simplification of the plethora of information that has been presented. But how to accomplish such simplification? Statistical methods, such as factor analysis, are available to assist in data reduction. However, the computer cannot include issues such as conceptual meaning and purpose in its computations. The task reduces to one of sorting, shuffling, and thinking.

Factor analysis of the S and N scores for the sixty-eight axes produced a large first factor concerned with arousal of a stressful and uncomfortable kind. A second factor was comprised of many of the axes from 58 to 67 – axes introduced partly from discussions of causes and effects of substance use in offender groups. A third factor was interpreted as related to sensation seeking. A fourth factor involved social contact variables. A fifth and a sixth factor suggested criminality from a self-centred perspective and from the perspective of values, respectively. A seventh factor was concerned with felt inhibitions. An eighth was comprised of 01 (Social Anxiety). A ninth reflected positive feelings, and a tenth was concerned with rigid attitudes. The eleventh to fourteenth were comprised of single axes: Hedonism, Social Enjoyment, Control of Others, and Affect Denial. The task now reduced to one of exclusion and selection of axes.

Based on the frequencies of entry into the discriminant analyses, one variable had already been selected to represent each of the fifth (08), sixth (22), ninth (24), and tenth (36) factors; and three variables had been selected for the first factor (53, 48, and 37). It seemed reasonable to exclude variables from the seventh and eighth factors

since it seemed likely that MMPI scales would account adequately for them. And the thirteenth factor was omitted since it seemed to bear mainly on drug traffickers rather than drug users. The single variables from each of the eleventh (20), twelfth (02), and fourteenth (30) factors were included. That would leave ten more variables to be chosen. Factor 3 seemed best represented by Pep-Up Effect (40), and factor 4 by Social Contact Need (10). And one variable (44) was included because it appeared on factor 1 (44N) and on factor 5 (44S).

The above fifteen axes were factored with various combinations of five other axes from the first and second factors. The factors derived in this way were considered for their meaningfulness and for the extent to which they might lend themselves to conceptual simplicity and to design of treatments. In these repeated analyses, Substance Excitement (60) seemed to maintain its position with the other variables in the second factor, and so it was selected to represent that factor. The remaining variables that held together apparently meaningfully were from the first factor, which accounted for 44% of the variance. They were Physiological Anxiety (47), Authority Rebellion (12), Need to be Different (34), Allergy Stress (46), Flat Depression (13), and Reactive Depression (03). That seemed to satisfy the requirement for a short-form Addicause. But it did not yet permit the variables selected to be reduced to simple structure.

Factor analysis of the twenty selected axes yielded eight factors. However, the first of these factors, accounting for 42% of the variance, seemed to be comprised of two conceptually different elements, namely, a behavioural (rebellious) and a cognitive (values) element. This suggested that the overall treatment program to be developed might usefully be comprised of nine different parts.

Given the views expressed earlier about the importance of final and perpetuating causes and the sense that these two kinds of causes were fairly well represented in the axes and in the S and N scores (see Table 8), it is to be expected that each type of cause would be richly represented in any treatment program to be developed. Accordingly,

it was decided that five of the nine parts of the treatment program would be devoted primarily to final cause modification and four to perpetuating cause modification. Moreover, it was concluded that the four parts relating to perpetuating causes should come first in the series of treatments to modify the effect of reinforcers in (possibly) perpetuating needs (final causes).

It was now time to focus specifically on the nature of the nine component parts of the treatment programme. And, in doing so, it would be important to organize each component around a particular variable (axis) in order to permit evaluation of the effects of treatment to be targeted on a specific variable rather than a composite one.

Nine general variables were identified that, it was felt, represented the factors adequately and that should lend themselves well to treatment intervention. These nine variables are listed below, along with the axes that were construed to be related to them. It will be noted that there is a plurality of axes associated with each concept. This is due to the facts that (i) most of the axes selected were generic predictors of abuses of various types of alcohols and drugs and (ii) the attempt to achieve simple structure was made inclusively rather than exclusively to ensure the widest possible coverage of treatments to be designed for the experimental addictions programme.

For purposes of ease of differentiation among the several DAQ axes under each concept, those axes construed to be particularly relevant to each concept are presented in **bold**, and the single most representative DAQ axis is also **<u>underlined</u>**.

In addition to seeking to address as many addictive issues as possible in each treatment programme, each program was also designed to focus on a specific issue that could be represented simply as related to a single DAQ axis (<u>underlined</u> <u>axis</u> in the above list of general concepts and axes).

Naming the Treatment Programs. Finally, a title was assigned for the treatment program to be designed for each of the simple structure variables identified below.

No.	General Concept	Treatment Name	Conceptual Contents and Related Axes
1.	Failure	Creating . . . SUCCESS	Failure/Punishment History/Expectation 03, **12**, 13, 20, **24**, **37**, 47, <u>**48**</u>
2.	Inflexibility	Creating . . . FLEXIBILITY	Rigid/Inflexible Habits/Adjustment 08, **12**, <u>**36**</u>, **37**, 47
3.	Excitement-Seeking	Creating . . . EXCITEMENT	Apathy/Inhibition –> Stimulus-Hunger **12**, **20**, 24, 30, <u>**37s**</u>, 40, <u>**60n**</u>
4.	Gratification Need	Creating . . . SATISFACTION	Immediate Satisfaction/Relief Need 10, **12**, **13**, 20, **24**, 36, **37**, **40**, 44, <u>**47**</u>, 48, 53
5.	Conflicted Values	Creating . . . VALUES	Subcultural/Primitive/Regressive Values **08**, 12, **13**, <u>**22**</u>, **34**, 36, **37**, 40, 44, 47, **48**
6.	Guilt Intolerance	Creating . . . INNOCENCE	Guilt Proneness or Guilt Intolerance **02**, <u>**08**</u>, 12, **30**, 36, 37, 48, 60
7.	Distress	Creating . . . HEALTH	Ill Health/Stress/Distress/Anxiety 03, 08, **13**, 34, 37, <u>**44**</u>, **47**, 53
8.	Joylessness	Creating . . . HAPPINESS	Depression/Joylessness/Unfulfilment **02**, 03, **08**, 10, 12, **13**, 30, **36**, <u>**40**</u>, 44, 48, **53**
9.	Weak Integration	Creating . . . INTEGRATION	A/Antisocial Adjustment/Integration **02**, **03**, 10, **12**, 20, **22**, <u>**30**</u>, 34, **36**, 40, **44**, 48

CHAPTER 12

Design of the Treatment Programs

Choosing Targets for the Proposed Treatments

The logic involved in treatment design begins to be illustrated by the explanations below of the axes selected to represent each of the proposed treatments.

Treatment 1 (Creating Success) was designed most specifically to affect DAQ axis 48 (History of Punitive Reinforcements, i.e., failure expectations).

Treatment 2 (Creating Flexibility) was designed most specifically to affect DAQ axis 36 (Rigid Moralizations or fixed attitudes/ beliefs).

Treatment 3 (Creating Excitement) was designed most specifically to affect the S aspect of DAQ axis 37 (need pressure of 'grown up ADDs'/paroxysmals to pursue excitement) and the N aspect of DAQ axis 60 (the reinforcing effect of excitement achieved from use of exogenous events).

Treatment 4 (Creating Satisfaction) was designed most specifically to affect DAQ axis 47 (Physiological Anxiety, by turning the subject's attention to external sources of gratification, thus distracting the person from preoccupation with internal distress).

Treatment 5 (Creating Values) was designed most specifically to affect DAQ axis 22 (Subcultural Values, in order to foster the

development of values that might support a prosocial adjustment and lifestyle).

Treatment 6 (Creating Innocence) was designed most specifically to affect DAQ axis 08 (Guilt Intolerance or the poignant sense of guilt that the subject seeks to deny in defensive intolerance).

Treatment 7 (Creating Health) was designed most specifically to affect DAQ axis 44 (desire for Fast-Lane Living, by altering the implicit motto 'I will live fast, die young' with a focus of attention on health and its maintenance).

Treatment 8 (Creating Happiness) was designed most specifically to affect DAQ axis 40 (Pep-Up Need, by countering the depressive undertones beneath this need with a continuous happy adjustment).

Treatment 9 (Creating Integration) was designed most specifically to affect DAQ axis 30 (Affect Denial). The generality of affect denial underlying several of the variables (including Guilt Intolerance, Rebelliousness in the Face of Authority, Flat Depression, Hedonism, etc.) recommended this axis or variable as the one most likely to represent the generality or inclusiveness of Treatment 9.

It is acknowledged that the derivation method for the above variables and the treatments for them is imperfectly explained. There is an element of analogical thinking involved that the author finds impossible to recreate in words. And for the particular experiences in psychotherapy that the author has had participated strongly in in the selection process, these varied experiences also defy description. Still, an attempt will be made below to describe some of the treatment elements that were included in each of the above treatment programmes.

Design of the Treatment Programmes8

Having developed a set of manageable concepts ('simple structure') around which to design treatments, the next task was to select the treatment components that would be used for the evaluation of construct validity. There were several issues to be considered in this task.

Format for treatment

The experimental design would certainly require a relatively large number of subjects. If treatment was offered individually or in small groups, the time involved in the whole task would be hard to manage, and the treatments afforded the different individuals or small groups could be expected to differ considerably due to the individuals involved and the various therapists that would be required. Consequently, conventional treatment formats were excluded at the outset.

Large-group (forty to seventy inmates at a time), day-long (four hours, allowing for meals, security checks, etc.) treatment workshops of certain kinds had been shown to have treatment effects of at least as great magnitude as equivalent programs run individually (Quirk and Reynolds, 1991). Of course, anybody exposed to such a statement is bound to ask how that could possibly happen. A major part of the answer seems to lie in a kind of priming or mobilizing or contagion ('riot') effect when peers are together in large groups. Another part of the answer is that treatment effects in any given format seem to depend on the kind of material or treatment programs selected and on the manner in which the program is executed. Regardless of the

---

8 Having followed my friend Doug's spiderweb mind through to a particular understanding of the final and perpetuating causes of addictions, the real fun part of the process begins. This is where we test whether or not this understanding provides an insight into how to cure and possibly prevent addictions. – RR

explanation given, however, these writers were able to demonstrate repeatedly, in this kind of large group, effects easily comparable to those achieved by others in individual therapy. For this reason, it was decided to employ the large-group, day-long treatment workshop format as the means by which the present treatments would be implemented.

Scheduling treatments and their components

Thursday was the Psychology Department's large-group treatment workshop day at the Ontario Correctional Institute (OCI). Several types of treatment workshops were conducted by various members of the Psychology Department. In order to minimize the disruption of this ongoing programme, the present series of treatments were scheduled every second Thursday. But there would be a two-month break somewhere in the middle of the present series of treatments due to a protracted leave planned by the author. It was decided that the first four treatments (concerned with reinforcements/perpetuating causes) would be implemented prior to this break, and the remaining five (concerned with needs/final causes) would be implemented following the break.

With a brashness that some might think exceeds folly, but which was based on previous large-group treatment experiences, it was decided that each of the nine treatment components would be addressed in a separate single-day (four-hour) treatment workshop. That is, only a single four-hour day was set aside in which to provide the treatment for each of the nine variables listed above. This would mean that there would be a total of nine Thursdays set aside for the present evaluation study, with four preceding the break and five following it.

Each treatment day began at 9:00 AM and ended at 4:30 PM. Due to institutional counts, coffee breaks and lunch periods on each treatment day would have to be composed of four roughly one-hour blocks of time: 9:00 to 10:00, 10:30 to 11:30, 1:30 to 2:30, and

3:30 to 4:30. These time ranges are a bit inaccurate, and the actual time available each day was approximately four hours and forty minutes. However, as in past treatment workshop studies, the first and last twenty minutes of each treatment day were devoted to the administration of repeating monitoring tests of motivations, affects, and cognitive activity not related to the main dependent measures of the study.

Because the day seemed to fall fairly naturally into four hour-long time periods with ample rest between, the four time blocks were used in the following way in all the treatment workshop programmes:

First block (Orientation). The attempt was made during this time interval to direct participants' thoughts and points of view into areas and towards ideas that might foster therapeutic involvement with the methods to be used in the remaining time.

Second block (Tools). The attempt was made during this time to provide participants with relevant psychological tools that they might use on their own to foster therapeutic change – self-help methods.

Third block (Therapeutics). Here the attempt was made to get all participants involved in performing specific therapeutic or 'healing' tasks in order to provide specific in-session treatments aimed at the targets of treatment for that day.

Fourth block (Summary and Integration). The attempt was made in this interval to repeat and summarize the preceding day's activities, to introduce means by which participants might be able to integrate what they had learned in their daily lives and to consolidate their learning, and if time permitted, to undertake other brief therapeutic procedures.

By any conventional treatment standards, the above plan was at the very least ambitious, and it will be conceived by some as presumptuous and close to preposterous. Even to hope for any therapeutic benefit from such brief and necessarily sketchy treatment would be viewed by many as at least overly optimistic and perhaps

even arrogant. These remarks are made to let it be known that the author is not unaware of what others might think of what was being proposed. To attempt to placate anyone who might feel offended by this proposal, it might be pointed out that the attempt was being made to determine whether <u>test scores</u> could be modified by minimal treatments.

A brief overview of each of the nine treatment programmes.

More detail concerning the treatments that were designed and implemented is provided in Appendix J. Only a brief overview of each of the nine treatment programs is given here.

Treatment 1: *Creating SUCCESS*. The main target of this treatment program is the sense of failure experienced by many addicts both throughout their histories (as seen in their proneness to report and expect punishment and failure) and in their attempts to stop their addictive behaviours. Failure is a punishing experience for them, and they often seek to forget it. It is difficult to set out to reduce their sense of failure as it is often denied, and focusing on it seems mainly to impair their involvement or participation. To seek to enhance their unrealistic view of their success and importance, however, can be equally inappropriate. It affords more practice for them in avoiding reality. The solution seemed to be to help participants to succeed in various ways.

Block 1: *Orientation*. Failure as acceptance of another's judgement. Judgements are based on individuals' values, which differ from person to person. If I am attempting to do one thing (with which I succeed to a degree), I will be failing to do something else that someone else may fail to understand I was trying to accomplish. Humans are the world's most magnificent and perfect learning machines. You are incredibly good at learning, at figuring out what YOU want to do, and at accomplishing that. But we

sometimes don't know quite how to go about accomplishing something we want to do. Problems in the way of success may come from weak attention to the task (ADD) or concentration (distractions). The learning circle's (Knowledge<–Learning<–Effort<–Interest<–Knowledge) point of entry is effort. The role of attitude (failure expectations, self-image, willingness to try, concepts of external causation/locus of control, habits of waiting for others to initiate) and of simply 'doing'.

Block 2: Tools. Simple tools for learning: Estimate the Number of Dots task, Perceptual Discrimination tasks, Precision Learning, Self-Reward and Graphing Successes. Simple tools for success: Relaxation (Programming) and Planning (Goal-Finding). Introduction to the Goal-Finding programme, and handing out its materials. How always to succeed: (1) Set goals with which you can succeed and (2) Use the Personal Development goals procedure from the Goal-Finding programme. Explanation and practice exercise. Note: The Goal-Finding programme's Trainer's Manual and Materials used here are available.

Block 3: Therapeutics. Change History of Failures (with Timeline). Undo Effects of Failure (with Rapid Phobia Treatment). Convert Failure to Success, and change Disapproval to Approval (Visual Squash using these polarities). List the day's achievements.

Block 4: Consolidation. Design your Future (for positive experiences). Goal-Finding Personal Development Goals' Method for self-reward/running your own life and destiny. Summary of program and cuing observations.

Treatment 2: Creating FLEXIBILITY. The main target of this program is the resistance of addictions to modification, which is to be seen both in their apparently intractable nature and in the fixity of attitudes frequently encountered among addicts. Of course, such inflexibility tends to be denied, with addicts typically preferring to assign their intractability to addictive properties of their preferred chemicals. At the same time, flexibility tends to be devalued and

routines followed. However, it was felt that setting flexibility as a target would not serve as an impediment to treatment in this setting.

Block 1: Orientation. The nature of the human learning machine. Sources of rigidity: in habit strength and ongoing reinforcers, in general adaptation of the system to continuous stressors, in group/clique-founding involvements, in used of language (especially action-stultifying nouns). Ways to allow greater adaptability, variety of experience, and fun.

Block 2: Tools. Self-Reward (Goal-Finding Personal Development goals method). Finding the good and adaptable in yourself, everything, and everybody else (Respect Training and Estimating percentage of time of goodness and achievement). Here-and-Now living (Zen principles and illustrations) and Divergent Thinking (*Dictionary for Divergent Thinkers*).

Block 3: Therapeutics. Anti-Introversion Training (Transcendental Meditation, Task Focus, Outgoing as Personal Development Goal) and Finding the Good in self and others (Respect Training and Assertive Training).

Block 4: Consolidation. Creating Response Alternatives (Assertive Training and Divergent Thinking). Expanding chosen Alternatives (Dream Image; if there are two of anything, then there are three). Letting go of Control (Freedom Training). Laugh, then find a reason for doing so. Summary and cuing observations.

Treatment 3: Creating EXCITEMENT. The main focus of this program is reinforcing consequences of chemicals in perpetuating addictive behaviour. Excitement is rewarding; it is sometimes a need to be pursued, and it is considered by many addicts to be achievable only through use of excitant chemicals. There is no point trying to reduce the need or pleasure in excitement. There is some point in reducing the joylessness of depression and/or introversion in order to make excitement-seeking less necessary (see Treatment 8). However, it at least seems appropriate to provide ideas about other kinds of

excitement and reinforcement that might work to replace excitant chemicals.

Block 1: Orientation. The role of buzz/rush and immediate gratification (PIG) in addictions. The expanded and the anticipated Present (consequences/what will follow are present perceived events). The sources of joylessness (the 'Love Test Tube'). Taking control over one's own life and contingencies. The nature of the Unconscious as the realm of the Possible.

Block 2: Tools. Use of Verbs in place of Nouns. Being 'at cause'. A Book of Natural Highs (e.g., Concentration, Arousal, Now-Events Focus, Sexual Enhancement, Excitement Acts, Spiritual Experiences, Divergent Thinking/Humour, Creativity, Joy Experiences, Problem-Solving/Discovery, Falling, Mastery, Self-Reinforcement, Showing Off, Achievement, Self-Actualization).

Block 3: Therapeutics. Means to enhance possibilities and excitement (Preliminary exposure to Values package and 'Book of Natural Highs' exercises). Treatment for the Love Test Tube (Affect Training exercises and Taking Risks). Enhancing Future Experience (Timeline Future Pacing exercises).

Block 4: Consolidation. How to Achieve Joy (Respect, Trust, Love) and exercises in each. Personal Development Goal-Finding Method (to achieve qualities of joy and excitement). Summary of program and cuing observations.

Treatment 4: Creating SATISFACTION. The main focus of this program is on the achievement of full satisfaction of needs to replace immediate gratification needs that reinforce addictive conduct. Seeking for Satisfaction/Feelings in bodily experiences in order to supplant physiological discomforts – which themselves are enhanced by attention to the body in seeking (absent) feelings. Create pleasant/comfortable/healthy bodily experiences by simple exercises (long out-breaths, good posture and movements, activity/exercise). Immediate reinforcements do drive habit development, so there is no point denying it. Delayed reinforcements do not influence habits

very strongly. It seemed necessary to alter perception and concepts of time as well as the degree of fulfilment in reinforcers.

> *Block 1: Orientation.* The nature and sources of satisfaction. The roles of expectations, attitudes, and beliefs. The way that self-talk works and how it can be changed (using pragmatism in place of absolute truth concepts). The role of the media in establishing unrealistic expectations and in supporting the notion that satisfactions come from external sources (especially sudden and capricious/luck events), wealth, and passivity.
> *Block 2: Tools.* Beliefs Training materials. Attitudes Training materials. Finding and Using positive feelings and attitudes (Find three Things you Like; Affective Responses Training). Practicing Delay to enhance enjoyment. Self-hypnosis to enhance experience.
> *Block 3: Therapeutics.* Beliefs and Self-Talk (Rational-Emotive Therapy). Sending Communications (Assertive Training: 'I' sentences, three-part statements). Listening Skills Training. Energy Use Training (Posture; Volume of speech; Enunciation crispness; Expansive Gestures). In vivo Desensitization (for lack of gratification/satisfaction).
> *Block 4: Consolidation.* Self-Reinforcement with Positive Feelings. Exercise in self-hypnotic experience enhancement. Acquiring Satisfactions to support Happiness. Various types of Self-Actualization. Summary and cuing observations.

Treatment 5: Creating VALUES. The focus of this program is on adaptive and mature values development. Years of investment in values of childhood and then the addictive subculture need to be countered. Some of the common attitudes and values of the subculture (e.g., 'rat', 'solid', substance use values) need to be challenged, and any void created thereby filled with other values. James and Woodsmall's (1988 work in this area is drawn on heavily.

> *Block 1: Orientation.* Nature, sources, and persistence of values. What are they? What do they do in your life? Sample of values and

values predictions (re: Precision, Reliability, Effectiveness, Power, Cleverness, Thoughtfulness – as residual evaluators from childhood).

Block 2: *Tools*. Values, materials, and exercises in working through them. The evolution of values, personal and cultural. Prioritizing personal values. Media Proofing.

Block 3: *Therapeutics.* Examine subsumed beliefs. Swish for any particularly persistent values. Imagery for common subcultural values' polarities. Visual Squash (bad versus Good; Follow versus Lead; and other found subcultural values).

Block 4: *Consolidation.* Reordering values as desired (Submodalities to shift values orders). Failures of Subcultural values and Reflexive values. Value of Values. Peace as an overarching value. Living a constructive lifestyle. Summary and cuing observations.

Treatment 6: *Creating INNOCENCE.* The focus of this program is on guilt feelings and the complications that can develop surrounding them, including criminality and addictions. The paradoxical manner in which treatment of conflict must be developed is nowhere more clear than in the treatment of guilt intolerance. Increasing guilt feelings tend to increase defensive denial (intolerance) of guilt, and thus increase the risk of crime (Reynolds and Quirk, 1994). Decreasing guilt feelings directly is essentially impossible as they are denied or unacknowledged. Decreasing innocence feelings is tantamount to increasing guilt with its consequences (above). And increasing innocence feelings, if incautiously done, feeds directly into the strategy offenders already tend to adopt, namely the denial of guilt. Paradoxical means need to be adopted to 'get around' this series of paradoxes.

Block 1: *Orientation.* The nature and sources of guilt and bad feelings in guilt trips. Review of the reasons why adults punish or guilt trip – for the survival and happiness of the child (though the child cannot understand it at the time). The error of guilt (in other people's judgements concerned with different intentions and

purposes). The function of guilt (anger inhibition). Letting guilt experiences persist and go (Enjoying Guilt trips). Paradoxical intent strategies.

Block 2: Tools. Finding the Good in yourself (Positive-Events Focus, Estimates of Percentage of life in 'good' conduct, and demonstrations of the errors of estimate). Assertive Training (Using Bodily Energy and Playing the Game of Anger). Helping others to find the Good in all (Creating Peace). Making a solid and worthwhile community contribution – or how we all 'make up' for our mistakes and misdeeds.

Block 3: Therapeutics. Changing History – guilt experiences (Timeline exercises). Defanging Guilt versus Innocence (Visual Squash exercises). Swish for guilt trips. Finding the Good in All (Hot Seat).

Block 4: Consolidation. Enjoying life: Finding the Good in everyone and trusting all (Beliefs Training and Anticriticism Training). Creating Peace (Goal and Purpose finding for self and strategies to achieve peacefulness). Positive-Events Focus (Perceptual Discrimination/Fair-Witness Training). Summary and cuing observations.

Treatment 7: Creating HEALTH. The focus of this program is on valuing and maintaining health. Psychological and physical health are most commonly impaired by (1) stress and (2) expectations and personal beliefs. If chronic stress can be relieved and personal health beliefs modified, future health is likely to be improved radically. Since many of the discriminants controlling addictions relate to distress and to general physical malaise, improvement of health should serve to diminish addictive behaviours or self-medications as well as improving the quality of life.

Block 1: Orientation. Stress and Health. The ANS and anxiety stress. Basic body-focused stress management (Long out-breaths, Bowel-frequency regulation, and Activity/Exercise). Antianxiety methods and their purposes and uses. Consumerism in health

– take full responsibility for own health, only using 'professionals' for information (not advice), and help with some procedures you select.

Block 2: *Tools*. Graphing self-observations for improvement. Self-reward (Lion Training of the self). Muscle use reregulation and posture. Relaxation Training. Designing healthy futures (Health Beliefs).

Block 3: *Therapeutics.* Formal Systematic Desensitization for (selected) standard anxiety stimuli.

Block 4: *Consolidation*. Health Beliefs Training. Additional Systematic Desensitization. Summary and cuing observations.

Treatment 8: *Creating HAPPINESS.* The focus in this program is on countering the various types of depressions that underlie much addictive behaviour. Depression may lead to desperation and increased impulsiveness (not governing present behaviour by future contingencies), and this may enhance the need for immediate gratification or relief and the risk of relapse. If joy springs from within, it prevents depression.

Block 1: *Orientation*. The role of depression in addictions. The nature and variations of depressions and their sources in the body. The Love Test Tube and the Energy Test Tube. The nature of happiness. Ways to achieve happy lifestyles.

Block 2: *Tools.* Methods to remove 'test tube corks': unlearn anxiety (Desensitization), practice cork reattribution/ removal (Cognitive Therapies), practice with little drilled holes (Assertive/ Affective Training). Introduction to Goal-Finding Method (Personal Development and Achievement goals). Assertive Training references. Rational-Emotive Therapy methods. Practicing Trust exercises. Desensitization in vivo – principles of 'do what you can comfortably' (Agoraphobia example). Rapid Phobia Treatment methods.

Block 3: *Therapeutics*. Practice in in vivo Desensitization. Practice exercise in Assertive/Affective Training. Perform Rapid

Phobia Treatment (for injections and surgery). Perform Swish for negative feelings (especially Depressive responses).

Block 4: Consolidation. Use bodily energy (review Assertive Training and Personal Development goals). How to achieve Joy (Respect, Trust, Love). Summary and recapitulation and cuing observations.

Treatment 9: Creating INTEGRATION. This is the most complex of the programmes. It seeks to address integration with others in social support networks, integration of parts within the self, integration and consolidation of the learning from the programmes, and stabilizing future learnings. It addresses another (avoidance of affects/emotions) aspect of addictive behaviour while also trying to assemble elements from other programmes.

Block 1: Orientation. Change and Stress. Learning and Behaviour and Self-Change. Stability-producing factors: words, experimentation, acceptance, social systems, rewards and secondary gains, locus of control, consolidation. Creating stability without boredom. Management of Life by Objectives and Results: the nature of science and its uses in finding strategies in living (Experimentation, Evidence Proneness, Delayed Gratification).

Block 2: Tools. Graphing self-observations. Self-reward. Selecting your own 'gains' in living. Tolerating/Enjoying unpleasant events: Psychological First Aid (Long out-breaths, Sleep induction, Reducing Thought Pressure, Swish). Lifestyle reformulation methods. Developing personal social support systems/taking social chances.

Block 3: Therapeutics. Exercise in living and enjoying Enjoyable Lifestyles. Patience and Acceptance Training. Delayed Gratification Training. Self-Importance/Self-Definition Training (through Values instead of Differences). Structuring life to achieve group recognition through Attitude Formation and Socialization Skills. Self-Image remodelling (Swish).

Block 4: _Consolidation_. Psychological First Aid. Developing personal support systems. Lifestyle enjoyments. Tolerating Uncertainty, and Enjoying it. Creating Your Future. Summary and cuing observations.

Each of the methods used is a fairly specific procedure that is either available in the psychological literature or can be learned/used fairly easily with some training and demonstration. All methods lend themselves to large-group applications. Some may find the last statement hard to swallow, for example, for Wolpe's (1958) systematic desensitization method or James and Woodsmall's (1987) Squash method. However, each method has been used, and many have been used successfully, in other large-group format settings (Quirk and Reynolds, 1991).

CHAPTER 13

Experimental Design

Given the minimal amount of treatment to be provided in each of the nine treatment components and the reasonable probability that a single-treatment component might not have major effects on participants, it seemed desirable to determine the effects of both the single-treatment components and a plurality of treatments. Accordingly, several groups of subjects receiving different kinds and amounts of treatment were assembled.

Subjects

All qualifying inmates who were residents of any of the five OCI treatment units during the time when the experimental treatment program was being conducted were considered for inclusion as described in Chapter 6 under Addicure subjects. To qualify for inclusion as a subject for this study, inmates had MAST (Michigan Alcoholism Screening Test) or DAST (Drug Abuse Screening Test) scores greater than nine, suggesting significant 'cost' in inconvenience from involvement with alcohol and/or drugs. Some inmates with slightly lower scores were included if they had complained of major problems with alcohol and/or drugs. The total subject pool for this (Addicure) study included 75% of the residents on treatment units over the study period (1993–1994).

OCI residents were <u>invited to attend,</u> and were admitted at, only and all those day-long treatment programs to which they were assigned according to their experimental group membership, as described below.

Since residents are admitted from the intake unit to treatment units as beds become available, it was concluded that, on any given date, residents' release dates would not be subject to any study-relevant systematic effects. Consequently, discharge dates might serve as convenient and satisfactory <u>means</u> by which <u>to randomize</u> assignment of subjects to groups. Subjects were therefore assigned to experimental conditions strictly based on their discharge dates.

Five levels of <u>amount of treatment</u> were selected, namely, no addictions-specific treatment (Control subjects – c), one (only) addictions-specific treatment, four addictions-specific treatments (Treatments 1 to 4 – primarily focused on reinforcement effects), five addictions-specific treatments (Treatments 5 to 9 – primarily addressing needs/final causes), and (all) nine addictions-specific treatments. A total of 169 residents were invited to attend one or more of the treatment programmes, distributed as follows:

- a – Invited to attend the first four treatment programs ($N = 20$)
- b – Invited to attend the last five treatment programs ($N = 20$)
- c – Invited to attend no (zero) treatment programs ($N = 30$)[9]
- d – Invited to attend all nine treatment programs ($N = 24$) and
- e–m – Nine groups, each invited to attend a single different treatment program ($N = 11$ for each of treatment groups e–m)

Again, it was recognized that four hours of treatment time would be minimal time in which to achieve therapeutic benefits. Therefore,

---

[9] In the follow-up results reported later, this number is shown as 32. I don't know how the additional two subjects got to be included in the control group. – RR

The reported number of subjects attending the treatment workshops are given in the results section of this study as:

Treatment 'Amount'	0	1	2	3	4	5	6+
Subject Numbers	32	86	7	9	12	15	9

it was decided that, in order to be included in the data analyses as having 'received a treatment programme', a resident should have attended at least a majority of the time for that programme. Consequently, the <u>independent variable</u> for the experiment was set at three or four hours as compared to zero hours of attendance at each separate treatment programme.

Pretest. All residents, regardless of whether or not they would remain for treatment at the OCI, were administered a series of <u>tests</u> at the point of their <u>admission to the OCI</u> intake unit. The test battery included the short-form (twenty axes) Addicause (<u>DAQ</u>), a test of criminality (<u>STFB</u>), Minnesota Multiphasic Personality Inventory (MMPI), Ravens Progressive Matrices (RPM), ABLE reading ability (ABLE), IPAT Anxiety Form (CAS), Michigan Alcoholism Screening Test (MAST), and Drug Abuse Screening Test (DAST).

Post-test. Depending on their availability, the short-form (twenty axes) Addicause (<u>DAQ</u>) and the <u>STFB</u> were administered again to all research subjects about a month (or more) following their last treatment (experimental groups) or their pretest (control group). Also a midterm retest was administered to the 'nine-treatments' (d) group of subjects a month after the fourth treatment program (prior to the fifth).

Processing of Dependent Measures

The regression of each post-treatment measure on its pretreatment measure was computed for all the <u>DAQ</u> S and N scores for all twenty axes and <u>STFB</u> scores, and standardized residual gain scores were calculated. The residual gain scores for the twenty <u>DAQ</u> S, the twenty <u>DAQ</u> N, and (secondarily) the nine <u>STFB</u> scales served as the dependent measures in this study.

CHAPTER 14

Experimental Results

Probabilities associated with the effects of the treatments

In Tables 9 and 10 (Appendix K), the nine treatment programs are represented in the columns, and the twenty DAQ axes are represented in the rows. The cells present the two-tailed probabilities of t-tests of mean differences of residual gain scores for subjects receiving three to four hours or zero hours of each treatment. For ease of recognition, significant probabilities are presented in **bold**, and probabilities associated with predicted or expected treatment effects are displayed with a leading asterisk (*) in Tables 9 and 10 (Appendix K). Specifically predicted relationships are emphasized by underlining their asterisks (*) in Tables 9 and 10 (Appendix K) and their probabilities in Tables 11 and 12 (Appendix K). The tables address the S (Tables 9, 11) and N (Tables 10, 12) scores separately.

Tables 9 and 10 (Appendix K) present the probabilities associated with the effects of all nine treatments on all twenty DAQ axes. It will be noted that, of the eighty-eight 'main' predicted effects of treatments on DAQ axes (see **bold** in earlier listing of general treatment concepts and axes), seventy-one (81%) were confirmed. Of the seventy-eight secondary predictions, twenty-seven (35%) were confirmed; and of the 194 tests where no relationship was predicted (no leading asterisks), only 5 (3%) achieve statistical significance

(shown in **bold** in the tables). Reminder: 5% of statistical tests will be significant by chance alone.

In Table 9 (table of S scores), prediction of effects was made for eighty-three of the cells (marked with *), of which forty-four predictions were considered to be clearly related to the treatment issue (marked with *). Of the eighty-three predictions, fifty-two (63%) were confirmed. Of the forty-four main predictions, thirty-seven (84%) were confirmed. By way of contrast, of the ninety-seven relationships where no prediction was made, only one (1%) yielded a statistically significant finding.

In Table 10 (Table of N scores), prediction of effects was made for eighty-three of the cells (marked with *), of which forty-four predictions were considered to be clearly related to the treatment issue (marked with *). Of the eighty-three predictions, forty-six (55%) were confirmed. Of the forty-four main predictions, thirty-four (77%) were confirmed. By way of contrast, of the ninety-seven relationships where no prediction was made, only four (4%) yielded a statistically significant finding.

The findings from Tables 9 and 10 (Appendix K) provide strong support for the experimental hypotheses that:

1. the Addicause (<u>DAQ</u>) scores are <u>modifiable</u> by suitably designed treatment interventions,
2. the Addicure treatments did address the <u>addiction-related variables</u> that they were selected to modify, and
3. to the extent that the <u>DAQ</u> axes represent causes underlying addictive behaviour, these <u>causes were modified</u>, thus offering some justification for proceeding with the planned two-year follow-up on all the research subjects to determine what (threshold) amount of treatment is required to modify addictive behaviour in addicts.

Tables 9 and 10 (Appendix K) are rather confusing due to the large number of apparently scattered experimental hypotheses being tested. Although this confusing complexity is a natural

result of the attempt to address as many as possible of the issues related to addictions in the design of the treatments, the resulting complexity was anticipated, and means to permit simplification had been devised.

Of course, no rational psychotherapist would expect to be able in treatment to modify any one variable and not a host of other variables. Indeed, it will seem irrational to most practitioners to expect to obtain any significant therapeutic effects at all in four hours of treatment. Nevertheless, in the face of all odds and reason, the experimental hypotheses were advanced that treatment effects would be accomplished and that differential treatment effects would be achieved. Tables 11 and 12 (Appendix K) are intended to test these hypotheses.

Construct Validity and Precision

Construct validation requires that an application (the Addicure treatments) from the theory underlying the instrument being validated (Addicause) can be shown to behave as the theory would predict. Tables 9 and 10 (Appendix K) begin to provide the required information, and Tables 11 and 12 (Appendix K) extend the demonstration of the construct validity of the test.

Precision, as the most basic feature of reliability of an instrument, was not demonstrated earlier in the section on reliability. Precision of an instrument would be demonstrated most directly and convincingly if the various parts of the instrument (a) respond to changes of relevant and specific kinds and (b) respond differentially to discriminably different treatments. That is, (a) if Addicause can record treatment effects in meaningful ways (see Tables 9 and 10), it can be said to possess considerable precision; and (b) if Addicause can be shown to record treatment effects in a differential way, it can be said to possess a high degree of precision.

Tables 11 and 12 (Appendix K) are structured so that the specific DAQ axes, on which particular effects were expected, are presented

in the same order as the treatment programs devised to treat them. Consequently, under the experimental hypothesis of 'differential treatment', ideally, the only significant probabilities (displayed in **bold** type) should be found on the diagonal of cells from upper left to lower right – underlined in the tables to mark cells expected to display significant findings.

Tables 11 (S scores) and Table 12 (N scores) indicate that significant treatment effects were achieved and that differential treatment was also achieved. Significant probabilities were found for all (100%) of the single-treatment effects on their most relevant single axes – upper-left to lower-right diagonal of each table's cells. It is true that differential treatment effects did not achieve an absolutely perfect match with the 'ideal'. Of the 144 cells in which statistical significance would not have been predicted under a strict application of the differential treatment hypothesis, 26 (18%) display statistical significance.

The above results were obtained using as subjects all inmates who received each particular treatment and the controls who received none. One might be justified to ask whether the effects observed are due to a catalytic or general treatment effect from subjects receiving a plurality of treatments. The problem encountered in seeking to provide a definitive answer to this question resides in the relatively small numbers of subjects who received only one treatment program and completed the post-tests. Nevertheless, recognizing that the small numbers involved will produce a severe attrition in the number of significant findings and that they might distort the results to some extent, t-tests were computed using only those subjects who received only one treatment compared with the no-treatment controls. The results appear in Tables 13 through 16 (Appendix K), which are structured in the same way as Tables 9 through 12 (Appendix K). In Tables 13 through 16 (Appendix K), the numbers of experimental subjects per group are as follows:

Treatment 1: Creating Success $EN = 8$
Treatment 2: Creating Flexibility $EN = 4$
Treatment 3: Creating Enjoyment $EN = 9$
Treatment 4: Creating Satisfaction $EN = 8$
Treatment 5: Creating Values $EN = 10$
Treatment 6: Creating Innocence $EN = 10$
Treatment 7: Creating Health $EN = 9$
Treatment 8: Creating Happiness $EN = 5$
Treatment 9: Creating Integration $EN = 8$
No-Treatment Control subjects $CN = 19$

Tables 13 and 14 (Appendix K) reveal the expected attrition in numbers and magnitude of significant findings. Most of the statistically significant values are meaningfully related to the treatment methods employed. And although many predicted relationships are not confirmed in these data, there remains a preponderance of significant findings among the predicted relationships over those not predicted. Tables 15 and 16 (Appendix K) display the attrition in the significance of the results under the differential treatment hypothesis.

In spite of the small numbers of subjects, the value of the data from the analyses with single treatments lies in the picture they provide of the kinds of psychological effects produced by the treatment methods employed in each programme. In order to examine in greater detail the impact of each treatment on the Addicause axes, Tables 17 and 18 (Appendix K) group the apparently most affected axes together under each treatment heading (Table 17) and one or two axes under each treatment heading (Table 18). Brief notes are made for each treatment heading in Table 15 (Appendix K) to express the nature of the findings that appear to emerge.

Addictions and Criminality: Are They Confounded?

A secondary part of this study was to examine the effects of the experimental addictions treatment program on criminality. This intention was expressed in noting that the dependent measures in the treatment study included those from the Survey of Thoughts, Feelings, and Behaviours (STFB: Reynolds, 1994). However, there is another matter that needs to be addressed before turning to the effects of the treatments on the criminality measures.

Since the present addictions project was conducted using addicted offenders and since our criminality project (Reynolds and Quirk, "Transforming the Criminal Mind," 1994) was conducted using (an independent sample of) offenders, many (75%) of whom were also substance abusers, it seems possible that at least some of the scales of both addictions (DAQ) and criminality (STFB) may be assaying criminality or addictions or both or some feature they have in common. Moreover, since it is intended to use the addictions (DAQ) and criminality (STFB) measures in future studies to extract confounding effects statistically from responses of individual subjects, it seemed prudent to determine in advance the extent to which the two types of scales are confounded with one another. This question was addressed in two ways.

The intercorrelation matrix between DAQ Axes and STFB Factors is displayed in Table 19 (Appendix L). It is true that the magnitudes of some of the correlations were high enough to indicate significant relationships between Axes and Factors. However, the higher relationships tended to be restricted to DAQ Axes, which are manifestly relevant to criminality, especially Axes 12 (Authority (Rebellion), 48 (Punitive Reinforcements/ Expectations) and 22 (Subcultural Values). The noteworthy and meaningful variants from this principle are shown in **bold** in Table 19 (Appendix L). Two Axes related negatively to the STFB Factors, and some displayed relationships barely varying from 0.00.

Table 19 (Appendix L) reveals a striking similarity among the correlation coefficients for the six STFB Factors within each DAQ

Axis (rows). It would appear that the STFB Factors do not differ appreciably from one another in their relationships with the DAQ Axes. If one ignores the correlations with the maverick STFB Factor 4, shown elsewhere to vary independently from the other STFB Factors (Reynolds, 1994), the consistency of relationships within DAQ Axes is even more striking. Given that the STFB Factors were derived empirically as relatively independent variables (see Reynolds, 1994), this limited variability within Axes, especially where the relationships are stronger, means that the Axes are not controlling (not interacting with) the variability of the STFB scales (and thus the correlations with the Factors) in this sample, which was limited to addicts among offenders. Offenders who differ in amount of addictiveness should exhibit Axis variations, and they do. That is, the Factors and the Axes are not interacting. This, in turn, should mean that the two sets of measures vary independently of one another (unless controlled by sample selection) and that they are minimally confounded.

The same question was addressed in another way. Pre- and post-treatment DAQ and STFB measures were available for the addictions-treatment programme. Given that the DAQ Axes had already been shown to reveal differential treatment effects (Tables 9 to 11), if any approximation to differential treatment with the STFB Factors can be shown, the treatments would have applied differentially the STFB variables as well as to the DAQ. If this finding were to be demonstrated, the two sets of measures would have been found to be conceptually indistinguishable, and thus measuring equivalent constructs. To the extent that differential treatment is not found on the STFB Factors as a result of these addiction-focused treatments, to that extent the DAQ and the STFB variables represent different constructs. Table 18 (Appendix L) presents the probabilities of t-tests of residual gain scores' mean differences for each of the nine STFB scales (Total, Social Desirability Neutral, and Social Undesirability, and six Factor scales) on each of the nine addictions treatments. Since the effects that the addictions' treatments might have on the criminality measures were a matter of interest rather than specific

prediction, there are no hypotheses to test in Table 20. For ease of recognition, the statistically significant probabilities displayed in this table are again presented in **bold**.

These results suggest (although they do not prove) that (1) both the tests of and treatments for criminality and addictions are relatively independent of one another, (2) criminality (total score) may be modified by treatment for addictions (among offenders), (3) STFB Factor 2 (grown-up ADDs) may be particularly related to addictiveness and thus affected by its treatment, and (4) the Values programme, ineffective in modifying criminality alone (Reynolds and Quirk, 1994), might be more relevant to criminality as it is mediated by addictiveness, although this question was not specifically tested since the DAQ was not used with the criminality project subjects (Reynolds and Quirk, 1994). The second (2nd) of these observations offers some encouragement for the intention to follow-up on the effects of the addictions treatments through criminal recidivism records. The STFB Total score is the best estimate we have of criminality (Reynolds, 1994), other than incarceration itself. Since it appears to have been modified by the addictions treatments, it seems reasonable to hope that criminal recidivism will also have been affected.

Summary and Conclusions

What seems to have been achieved in the Addicause phase of the project reported is nothing less than the development of an instrument (DAQ) that appears to identify many of the need (final) and reinforcement (perpetuating) causes underlying addictions to alcohol and street drugs. These types of causes are both the main operative causes in the behavioural universe (see Chapter 1) and the causes that are most readily and effectively modifiable in treatment in that universe. Accordingly, the Addicause instrument may well provide some of the information required concerning individuals with which effective treatment can be designed and undertaken.

CHAPTER 15

Effect Of Addicure On Criminal Recidivism

Designing a Series of Preliminary Experiments

As a preliminary evaluation of the last statement, an experiment was undertaken to employ the Addicause axes most relevant to the causation of alcohol and drug abuse to design and evaluate a series of treatments. The twenty DAQ (short-form) axes were conceptually reduced to simple structure, and treatments were designed to modify the nine variables derived. The somewhat-optimistic hypotheses were advanced that (1) the DAQ axes are modifiable by suitably designed treatments (construct validity), (2) the DAQ axes' scores can meaningfully be modified in treatment interventions of four hours duration in cost-efficient large-group treatment workshops[10], and (3) differential treatment directed at the substrate of the DAQ axes can be accomplished (precision). All three of these hypotheses were confirmed in the data.

These findings would seem to offer the clearest possible test confirming the construct validity of the Addicause instrument. The treatments were selected/designed based on the explicit and implicit theory underlying the development of the test. The fact that the treatments did affect the test scores almost exactly as predicted

---

[10]   This is not to say that these treatments would not be equally effective with either individuals or small groups, merely that large-group treatment is more cost-effective. – RR

should mean that the Addicause test, at the very least, represents its intended theory well.

The almost 'surgical precision' with which the treatments were successful in modifying the Addicause axes provides some additional information about the <u>DAQ</u> test. First, the fact that specific effects were achieved where intended (and mostly did not occur where they were not intended) strongly suggests that the Addicause scales are highly <u>precise</u> (the most important aspect of instrument reliability) psychometrically. Second, the fact that treatments, designed conceptually from the Addicause axes, modified the very <u>DAQ</u> axes at which they were targeted, strongly suggests that the Addicause axes have a high degree of <u>construct validity</u> (the most general and important aspect of validity) psychometrically. Third, the fact that the treatments modified <u>DAQ</u> axes already shown to be predictive of addictive behaviour suggests (although it does not prove) that the treatment programs employed may very well serve to modify future addictive behaviour significantly.

The results of the present experimental treatment also provide some additional information about the Addicure initiative. First, it seems clear that differential treatment was reliably achieved. This means not only that the <u>DAQ</u> scales are modifiable but also that it is possible to target and modify a particular aspect of a person's presenting problem (which he/she wants to have modified) <u>and,</u> at the same time, not interfere with other aspects of the person (which he/she may want not to have modified). Second, like all demonstrations of effective 'directive' treatment, the present results again demonstrate that therapy is not (or need not be) directed and instituted solely by the individual client. It seems clear that, when appropriate, <u>directive treatment</u> can be effective. Third, it seems clear that significant therapeutic effects can be achieved in interventions as brief as four hours in duration and in groups as large as fifty-five participants. One importance of this observation is concerned with the need to find and use cost-effective procedures in an increasingly difficult economic climate for clients of treatment services.

Finally, although it is true that some statistically significant treatment effects were encountered on <u>DAQ</u> axes that were not specifically targeted for treatment (see Tables 11 and 12) and that the conclusion to be drawn from this might seem to be that differential treatment was imperfectly achieved, an additional relevant comment might be made. Of the twenty-six significant probabilities in Tables 11 and 12 that were not specifically predicted under the differential treatment hypothesis, thirteen (50%) occurred on the two 'summary' or most inclusive programs (Treatment 4 [Creating Satisfaction] and Treatment 9 [Creating Integration]). In effect, it is precisely with these programs that one might expect differential treatment effects from other programs to have meaningful additional effects. Moreover, at least eleven of the remaining thirteen statistically significant findings were on <u>DAQ</u> axes modification of which would reasonably be expected (post hoc) on the basis of the kinds of interventions undertaken. The two leftover cells displaying statistical significance, although probably meaningful, are fewer than would be expected to occur by chance alone at the 5% level of confidence in the 162 <u>t-tests</u> performed. That is, it can be argued that an even better degree of differential treatment was achieved than a cursory examination of the results might suggest.

It remains for future <u>follow-up</u> information to determine just how well (or if) the treatment interventions undertaken modified the subjects' addictive behaviour and, if some modification was achieved, how much treatment was sufficient to affect future addictive conduct. Since some of the subjects from the experiment reported here will not be released for another year, it will be at least three years before this last part of the present study can be completed. When the results from that future time have been analysed, it should be possible to determine the feasibility of mounting a program to <u>prevent</u> addictions by applying educational programs designed to address the relevant variables (axes).

At this point in our investigation of addictions, all but the last two planned steps of the project have been completed. The remaining two steps include (1) two-year follow-up of the Addicure research

subjects in order to determine the 'threshold' amount of therapeutic change that may be needed to alter addictive behaviour and (2) if the follow-up can demonstrate significant reduction in criminal recidivism among addicted inmates (and thus implicitly of addictive behaviour), further development and evaluation of a program to prevent addictions. While the remaining tasks demand interest, the results achieved already in the project seem sufficient to warrant interest.

So far, we've tried to suggest a way to understand addictions, to talk about how their causes might be measured, to show some of the characteristics of various kinds of addictive behaviour, and to describe some treatments designed to treat some causes of addiction. The next question is, Does it work, and if so, how well? However, before we can consider that question meaningfully, we have to ask you to think through with us just what 'does it work' means.

In this case, the final question about whether it works comes down to, Do the treatments result in getting rid of addictions? and What shall we use as an indicator of that? To find a complete answer to that question could require continuing, intimate contact over many years with all those treated, which has not been practical. The individual person alone, at a ripe old age, can look back over his/her life and decide (a) whether his/her addictions changed or vanished and (b) the turning point at which that happened, if it did. But to do that, he/she would have to wait until the rest of us are dead and gone, and we would have to come back to haunt large numbers of people's lives and to read their minds. Frankly, we expect to be way too busy greeting our fellow sinners to worry about doing that. So bear with us while we try to be a bit more practical than that.

You might recall that the ADDICAUSE instrument was not only created to help us to understand addictions and to find relevant variables to treat. Its other purpose was to provide a means to measure changes in the identified causes. It's true that neither you nor we would be satisfied at this stage of our understanding to restrict ourselves to findings about treatment effects limited to test scores. Neither you nor we would trust the ADDICAUSE test results yet for

the leap of faith required to assume that test measure changes are adequate assurance that addiction has been modified – although it would be nice to think so. Still, in the hope of reaching that position at some time in the future, our first step should certainly be to discover whether the implementation of these kinds of treatments has any effect on the ADDICAUSE test measures. At least we might consider retest results from the ADDICAUSE as one way to get at a short-term answer to the question of 'Does it work?'

If it is possible to show some short-term effects on the ADDICAUSE test scores, it would then be worthwhile to go to the trouble to see if the treatments have any medium-term effects on criminal recidivism. We pointed out earlier that one way to discover whether addictive behaviour has been modified, albeit indirectly, might be to examine subsequent criminal recidivism among addicted offenders. You might want to review that argument at this point. Certainly, if the tests scores change and if criminal recidivism rates change among those treated, we would be in a reasonable position to argue that addictions were affected.

It is true that neither of the above ways to discover whether these treatments 'work' is definitive. Earlier in this chapter, we argued that a proper answer to the question would be impossible, or at least impractical. The only other possibly practical way we have been able to figure out is that, if the test scores and criminal recidivism can be shown to change following treatment, we might then be in a position to experiment with prevention to see if that results in adequate reductions in subsequent addiction rates. As far as we can see, that sort of demonstration would be as far as we could go to discover whether ADDICAUSE does modify addictive behaviour.

Short-Term Effects

Subjects. All OCI inmates who were residents on any of the treatment units (see criteria, Chapter 2) during the period of time from July to December 1993 were considered for inclusion in this

experiment. All those residents whose MAST (Michigan Alcoholism Screening Test) and/or DAST (Drug Abuse Screening Test) scores revealed substance use at significant costs to them in discomfort and inconvenience were <u>accepted</u> as research subjects. About 75% ($N = 193$) of the residents on treatment units over that time interval qualified for inclusion in this way.

Experimental Design. Since inmates are admitted to treatment units as beds become available, it was concluded that, at any given time, treatment unit residents' release dates would not be subject to any systematic effects and thus could serve as convenient and satisfactory means by which to <u>randomize</u> assignment of subjects to groups. Accordingly, subjects were assigned to experimental conditions strictly on the basis of their discharge possible dates.

It was recognized that four hours of treatment time would, at best, serve as minimal time in which to achieve any therapeutic benefits, although it seemed likely that greater amounts of treatment might result in greater therapeutic effects. Since it was intended to undertake follow-up of all research subjects to determine their criminal recidivism status (and implicitly their addictive status) two years following release, provisions were made to enhance the chance of 'success' at the medium-term follow-up point. For this purpose, in addition to the <u>no</u>-treatment control group subjects, it was decided to assign experimental groups to varying 'amounts' of treatment. Five levels of 'amount of treatment' were adopted, resulting in 163 inmates (55 per programme), in the following numbers, being assigned to the following experimental groups:

- c – One control group invited to attend <u>no</u> programs ($cN = 30$)
- e–m – Nine groups, each invited to attend <u>one</u> program (e–$mN = 11$)
- a – Invited to attend the first <u>four</u> treatment programs ($aN = 20$)
- b – Invited to attend the last <u>five</u> treatment programs ($bN = 20$)
- d – Invited to attend all <u>nine</u> treatment programs ($dN = 24$)

Again, it was recognized that four hours of treatment would be minimal time in which to achieve any therapeutic benefits. It was decided, therefore, that in order to be included in the data analyses as having 'received a treatment programme', an inmate should have attended at least a majority of the time for that programme. Consequently, the cut-off for considering that any inmate had taken any particular treatment workshop was set at three or four hours, to be compared with the control group's zero (0) hours of attendance at each separate treatment programme.

Testing. All inmates, regardless of whether or not they would remain for treatment at the OCI, were administered a series of tests at the point of their admission to the OCI intake unit. The test battery included a short-form (twenty axes) ADDICAUSE (DAQ), a test of criminality (STFB), the Minnesota Multiphasic Personality Inventory (MMPI), Ravens Progressive Matrices (RPM), ABLE reading test, IPAT Self-Analysis Form, Michigan Alcoholism Screening Test (MAST), and Drug Abuse Screening Test (DAST).

Pre/Post-Testing. All Experimental and Control group subjects were tested again twice following admission to a treatment unit. The tests used at these second and third administrations were the short-form (twenty axes) ADDICAUSE (DAQ) and the STFB (Reynolds, 1996). The first retests were administered after transfer to a treatment unit and about a month prior to participation in the experimental programme. The second retests were done about a month after completion of participation in the program (or a month or more following the first retest for the Control group). A midterm retest was also administered a month after the fourth treatment program (prior to the fifth) to the 'all treatments' (d) group, partly to bridge the two-month treatment hiatus between the fourth and fifth treatments. Because of early release on parole or transfer to other institutions, not all subjects attended all their assigned treatments and/or the second retesting.

Measures. The regression of each post-treatment measure on its pretreatment counterpart was computed, and standardized residual gain scores calculated, for all the DAQ (*S* and *N* scores for all twenty)

axes and <u>STFB</u> factor scores. The residual gain scores for the twenty <u>DAQ</u> *S*, the twenty <u>DAQ</u> *N* and (secondarily) the nine <u>STFB</u> scales served as the <u>dependent measures</u> in this study.

Test Scores as an Indicator of the Effect of Treatment. In the following tables, the nine treatment programs are represented in the columns, and the <u>DAQ</u> axes are represented in the rows. The cells present the two-tailed probabilities of <u>t-tests</u> of mean differences of residual gain scores for subjects receiving three to four hours or zero hours of each treatment. For ease of recognition, significant probabilities are presented in **bold**, and probabilities associated with predicted or expected treatment effects are displayed with a leading asterisk (*) in Tables 21 and 22. Specifically predicted relationships are emphasized by <u>underlining</u> their asterisks (<u>*</u>) in Tables 21 and 22 and their <u>probabilities</u> in Tables 23 and 24. The tables address the *S* (Tables 21 and 23) and *N* (Tables 22 and 24) scores separately.

Tables 21 and 22 present the probabilities associated with the effects of all nine treatments on all twenty <u>DAQ</u> axes. It will be noted that of the seventeen *S* and eighteen *N* specific hypotheses (underlined <u>*</u>), sixteen *S* and sixteen *N* (91%) were confirmed; of the twenty-four *S* and twenty-four *N* main predicted effects (* and **bold** type in listing the general treatment concepts and axes, Chapter 7), eighteen *S* and fourteen *N* (67%) were confirmed; of the forty-two *S* and forty-two *N* lesser predictions (*), fifteen *S* and thirteen *N* (33%) were confirmed; and of the ninety-six *S* and ninety-six *N* tests where no treatment effect was expected (no leading asterisks), seven *S* and five *N* (6%), or just about exactly the 5% rate expected by chance alone, achieved statistical significance.

Table 21: <u>t-test</u> probabilities of treatment effects
on the twenty <u>DAQ</u> *S* axes: *S* score results

CREATING... .DAQ AXES	SUCC. Tx1	FLEXI Tx2	EXCIT Tx3	SATIS Tx4	VALUE Tx5	INNOC Tx6	HEALT Tx7	HAPPY Tx8	INTEG Tx9
EnjSoc S02	0.85	.28	.41	.68	.52	*.33	.45	.42	.26
RctDpr S03	*0.66	.44	.18	.64	.98	.99	*.98	*.78	.17

	Tx1	Tx2	Tx3	Tx4	Tx5	Tx6	Tx7	Tx8	Tx9
GuiInt S08	.18	*.10	.06	.02	*.01	*.01	*.00	*.01	*.00
SocCnt S10	.89	.43	.68	*.32	.75	.57	.59	*.45	*.40
AutReb S12	*.03	*.08	*.03	*.00	*.02	*.12	.03	*.02	*.01
FltDpr S13	*.20	.57	.39	*.05	*.03	.15	*.04	*.15	*.18
Hedoni S20	*.04	.38	*.19	*.08	.19	.58	.92	.95	*.99
SubCul S22	.90	.71	.22	.27	*.03	.22	*.10	*.11	*.05
PIGRes S24	*.03	.10	*.23	*.01	.52	.96	.50	.99	.94
AffDen S30	.66	.27	*.42	.50	.39	*.91	.91	*.69	*.08
DiffNd S34	.10	.72	.09	.04	*.21	.15	*.05	.08	*.01
RgdMor S36	.71	*.01	.58	*.35	*.40	*.36	.23	*.13	*.02
Paroxy S37	*.01	*.03	*.01	*.00	*.02	*.12	*.12	.12	*.05
PepUNd S40	.59	.62	*.31	*.60	*.60	.61	.57	*.04	*.15
FstLan S44	.43	.85	.43	*.05	*.18	.30	*.04	.11	*.09
AllStr S46	.60	.81	.57	.23	.20	.20	.26	.09	.11
PhyAnx S47	*.00	*.04	.07	*.00	*.01	.11	*.01	.05	.04
PunRfs S48	*.04	.21	.22	*.10	*.09	*.36	.24	*.19	.55
SomDpr S53	.02	.40	.24	*.03	.20	.53	*.17	*.63	.38
SubExc S60	.54	.48	*.72	.32	.10	*.04	.06	*.05	.03

Two-tailed tests
Ratios of: Significant Predicted to Non-Signif. Predicted to Signif. Unpredicted in the Nine Tx Columns:| 6:2:1 | 5:0:0 | 2:5:0| 9:3:2 | 7:4:0| 2:6:0 | 6:3:1| 4:8:1 |8:4:2|

Table 22: t-test probabilities of treatment effects
on the twenty DAQ N axes: N score results

CREATING.. .DAQ AXES	SUCC. Tx1	FLEXI Tx2	EXCIT Tx3	SATIS Tx4	VALUE Tx5	INNOC Tx6	HEALT Tx7	HAPPY Tx8	INTEG Tx9
EnjSoc N02	.72	.83	.90	.90	.33	*.17	.38	.30	.23
RctDpr N03	*.77	.83	.52	.65	.53	.65	*.59	*.53	.10
GuiInt N08	.08	*.03	.04	.00	*.00	*.01	*.00	*.00	*.00
SocCnt N10	.68	.99	.94	*.92	.24	.25	.15	*.13	*.10
AutReb N12	*.04	*.11	*.04	*.00	*.02	*.12	.02	*.02	*.00
FltDpr N13	*.16	.48	.32	*.08	*.02	.07	*.02	*.05	*.09
Hedoni N20	*.03	.42	*.24	*.10	.28	.43	.97	.95	*.82
SubCul N22	.92	.87	.34	.48	*.02	.16	*.06	*.08	*.06
PIGRes N24	*.35	.19	*.44	*.12	.99	.73	.98	.55	.54
AffDen N30	.79	.37	*.48	.75	.32	*.71	.54	*.52	*.06

DiffNd N34	.14	.97	.31	.36	*.36	.37	*.20	.26	***.05**
RgdMor N36	.95	*.04	.72	*.32	*.42	*.79	.54	*.43	***.10**
Paroxy N37	***.01**	*.12	***.08**	***.01**	***.05**	*.27	*.17	.16	*.11
PepUNd N40	.85	.90	*.49	*.85	*.29	.57	.34	***.04**	***.08**
FstLan N44	.29	.82	.63	*.15	*.19	.31	***.04**	.19	***.09**
AllStr N46	.69	.76	.90	.52	.30	.43	.59	.32	.27
PhyAnx N47	***.03**	*.18	.27	***.03**	***.03**	.31	***.02**	.09	.09
PunRfs N48	***.10**	.94	.66	*.33	*.14	*.56	.23	*.33	.49
SomDpr N53	**.03**	.66	.58	*.13	.18	.62	*.21	*.76	.40
SubExc N60	.33	.74	***.75**	.48	.16	***.06**	.12	***.10**	**.05**

Two-tailed tests
Ratios of: Significant Predicted to Non-Signif. Predicted to Signif. Unpredicted in the Nine Tx Columns:| 5:3:1 | 2:3:0 | 2:5:1| 5:7:1 | 6:5:0| 2:6:0 | 5:4:1| 6:6:0 |10:2:1|

These findings (see Tables 21 and 22) provide strong support for the experimental hypotheses that

1. the ADDICAUSE (DAQ) scores are meaningfully modifiable by suitably designed interventions (construct validity),
2. the ADDICURE treatments did address the addiction-related variables they were selected to modify (precision), and
3. to the extent that the DAQ axes represent causes underlying addictive behaviour, these causes were modified, justifying the planned two-year follow-up on all the research subjects.

Tables 21 and 22 are rather confusing due to the large number of apparently scattered experimental hypotheses being tested. This confusing complexity is a natural result of the attempt to address as many of the issues related to addictions in the design of the treatments as possible. However, the resulting complexity was anticipated, and means to permit simplification were devised. In addition to seeking to address as many addictive issues as possible in each treatment programme, each program was also designed to focus on a primary and a secondary specific issue that could be represented simply as

related to single <u>DAQ</u> axes (<u>underlined</u> <u>axes</u> in the earlier list of general concepts and axes and <u>probabilities</u> in Tables 23 and 24). This selection of single axes as the core issue in each treatment was discussed earlier (Chapter 7).

The effects of each treatment on its most specific primary and secondary target <u>DAQ</u> axes are shown in Tables 23 and 24. Tables 23 (S scores) and 24 (N scores) present the results associated with the experimental hypothesis that differential treatment can be demonstrated on the <u>DAQ</u> axes – differential treatment being achieved when a treatment programme, devised to address one variable and not others, can be shown to affect that variable but not any others.

Tables 23 and 24 display the effects of each of the nine treatment programs on each of nine <u>DAQ</u> axes, for each of which a different treatment was designed, with the additional axes involved in the secondary targets appended. Tables 23 and 24 are structured so that the <u>DAQ</u> axes on which primary effects were expected are presented in the same descending order as the treatment programs devised to treat them. Consequently, under the experimental hypothesis of differential treatment, ideally, the significant probabilities (displayed in **bold** type) should be found mainly on the diagonal of cells from upper left to lower right – <u>underlined</u> in the tables to mark those cells expected to display significant findings.

Tables 23 (S scores) and 24 (N scores) indicate that significant treatment effects were achieved and that differential treatment was also achieved. Significant effects were found for all (100%) of the single-treatment effects on their most relevant single axes – upper-left to lower-right diagonal of each table's cells. Differential treatment effects did not quite achieve an absolutely perfect match with the 'ideal' since, of the nine secondary main predictions in each table, 1 S and 2 N were not confirmed (i.e., only 83% were confirmed). Of the 180 cells in which statistical significance should not have been observed under a strict application of the differential treatment hypothesis, thirty-one S and twenty-seven N (32%) display statistical significance, although of those, twenty-six S and twenty-three N (27%) were predicted under the extended hypotheses (Table of

Treatments and Axes, Chapter 7), leaving five S and four N (5%) of the statistically significant findings in Tables 3 and 4 unpredicted.

Tables 23 and 24 cannot be passed over without emphasis and some further comment. The degree of differential treatment effects demonstrated in these tables has rarely been paralleled in research in psychotherapy. We know of no other work reflecting equivalent amounts of precision, whether in test measurement or in treatment design, other than that achieved in our work with criminality (see Reynolds and Quirk, 1996). Indeed, most psychotherapists would deny that such degrees of accuracy are possible. Of course, we would disagree with that contention on both empirical and theoretical grounds.

Table 23: Probabilities of Treatment Effects on Most Relevant DAQ S Axes

TREATMENTS: CREATING...DAQ AXES: NAME, NUMBER, SN	Tx1 SUCCES	Tx2 FLEXIB	Tx3 EXCITE	Tx4 SATISF	Tx5 VALUES	Tx6 INNOCE	Tx7 HEALTH	Tx8 HAPPIN	Tx9 INTEGR
Punitive Rewards Hx 48 S	**.04p**	.21	.22	**.10p**	**.09p**	.36p	.24	.19p	.55
Rigid Moralization 36 S	.71	**.01p**	.58	.35p	.40p	.36p	.23	.13p	**.02p**
Paroxysmal Energy 37 S	**(.01)p**	**.03p**	**.01p**	**.00p**	**.02p**	.12p	.12p	.12	**.05p**
Physiologic Anxiety 47 S	**.00p**	**.04p**	.07	**.00p**	**.01p**	.11	**(.01)p**	**.05**	**.04**
Subcultural Values 22 S	.90	.71	.22	.27	**.03p**	.22	**.10p**	.11p	**(.05)p**
Guilt Intolerance 08 S	.18	.10p	.06	.02	**(.01)p**	**.01p**	.00p	**.01p**	**.00p**
Fast-Lane Living 44 S	.43	.85	.43	**.05p**	.18p	.30	**.04p**	.11	**.09p**
Pep-Up Need 40 S	.59	.62	.31p	.60p	.60p	.61	.57	**.04p**	.15p
Affect Denial 30 S	.66	.27	.42p	.50	.39	.91p	.91	.69p	**.08p**
Authority Rebellion 12 S	**.03p**	(.08)p	**.03p**	**.00p**	**.02p**	.12p	.03	**.02p**	**.01p**
Flat Depression 13 S	.20p	.57	.39	**(.05)p**	**.03p**	.15	**.04p**	(.15)p	.18p
Substance Excitement 60 S	.54	.48	.72p	.32	.10	**(.04)p**	.06	**.05p**	.03

Two-tailed tests

bold = significant; underlined = main predictions; p = predicted (whether or not significant)

Table 24: Probabilities of Treatment Effects on Most Relevant DAQ N Axes

TREATMENTS: CREATING DAQ AXES: NAME, NUMBER, SN	Tx1 SUCCES	Tx2 FLEXIB	Tx3 EXCITE	Tx4 SATISF	Tx5 VALUES	Tx6 INNOCE	Tx7 HEALTH	Tx8 HAPPIN	Tx9 INTEGR
Punitive Rewards Hx 48 N	**.10p**	.94	.66	.33p	.14p	.56p	.23	.33p	.49
Rigid Moralization 36 N	.95	**.04p**	.72	.32p	.42p	.79p	.54	.43p	**.10p**
Substance Excitement 37 N	**(.01)p**	.12p	**.08p**	**.01p**	**.05p**	.27p	.17p	.16	.11p
Physiologic Anxiety 47 N	**.03p**	.18p	.27	**.03p**	**.03p**	.31	**(.02)p**	.09	.09
Subcultural Values 22 N	.92	.87	.34	.48	**.02p**	.16	**.06p**	**.08p**	**(.06)p**
Guilt Intolerance 08 N	.08	**.03p**	**.04**	**.00**	**(.00)p**	**.01p**	**.00p**	**.00p**	**.00p**
Fast-Lane Living 44 N	.29	.82	.63	.15p	.19p	.31	**.04p**	.19	.09p
Pep-Up Need 40 N	.85	.90	.49p	.85p	.29p	.57	.34	**.04p**	**.08p**
Affect Denial 30 N	.79	.37	.48p	.75	.32	.71p	.54	.52p	**.06p**
Authority Rebellion 12 N	**.04p**	**(.11)p**	**.04p**	**.00p**	**.02p**	.12p	.02	**.02p**	**.00p**
Flat Depression 13 N	.16p	.48	.32	**(.08)p**	**.02p**	.07	.02p	**(.05)p**	.09p
Substance Excitement 60 N	.33	.74	**(.75)p**	.48	.16	**(.06)p**	.12	**.10p**	**.05**

Two-tailed tests

bold = significant; <u>underlined</u> = main predictions; p = predicted (whether or not significant)

The results obtained in this study were sufficiently arresting that we undertook a second study exploring what would happen if we increased the amount of treatment (from four to twelve hours) for each separate treatment issue (target). Besides, we had achieved similar differential treatment effects in our criminality project (Reynolds and Quirk, 1996), and that work also demanded further exploration. To undertake two complete treatment studies to address fifteen different treatment issues (nine DAQ plus six STFB treatment targets) would be impractical, if only because one of us had already retired and the other was about to retire; so we decided to try to kill two birds with one stone, as it were, designing a study to explore both addictions and criminality together. That approach also reduced recidivism but, otherwise, turned out to be not as interpretable as we might have wished. Nevertheless, it is included as Appendix ?? for those who may be interested in it.

Medium-Term Post-Release Effects

Two years after all the inmates involved in the ADDICURE study had been released from the sentences during which they were treated, Justice system records were examined to see if the treatments had any effect on subsequent criminal recidivism. This medium-term effects study include the following:

Recidivism. Criminal recidivism subsequent to the sentence in which they were treated:
0 = None; 1 = Convicted recidivist.
Counts. Number of Counts of any subsequent offences: 0 = None.
Survival. Number of months on the street from release to the point of criminal recidivism: 24 = Nonrecidivist.
Log Severity of criminal recidivism. Aggregate sentence days (shown to be a good estimate of criminal seriousness (Quirk, Nutbrown, and Reynolds, 1991) imposed for subsequent offences: 0 = Nonrecidivist. Severity scores were

logarithmically transformed to deal with the problem of extreme seriousness scores obtained by some recidivists who perform very serious crimes, in contrast to the zero scores of nonrecidivists.

Offences. Categories of subsequent offences (recorded but not used here because of the difficulty of processing these data).

Results

Table 25 presents the results of the medium-term (two-year) follow-up for the subjects of this study. It displays the results of the several treatments on four measures of subsequent criminal conduct, namely, reconviction and, if reconvicted, number of offence counts and (log.) severity of offences (from sentence length) and duration of survival on the street without further offences. The results are not quite as clear as we might wish. However, Recidivism is significantly affected by all the treatments except the most general one (Treatment 9), and four of the nine treatments appear to have affected the offence Severity score to a significant degree.

Table 25: F-Test probabilities for Medium-term (two-year) follow-up results on criminal recidivism from the ADDICURE study

TREATMENTS/ OUTCOME	RECIDIV.	COUNTS	SURVIVAL	LOGSEVER
Tx 1: SUCCESS	.03	.35	.92	.38
Tx 2: FLEXIBILITY	.00	.08	.27	.04
Tx 3: EXCITEMENT	.03	.28	.95	.31
Tx 4: SATISFACTION	.02	.53	.87	.17
Tx 5: VALUES	.01	.05	.28	.09
Tx 6: INNOCENCE	.03	.20	.55	.19
Tx 7: HEALTH	.01	.13	.39	.09
Tx 8: HAPPINESS	.00	.17	.26	.02
Tx 9: INTEGRATION	.42	.47	.55	.98

Two-tailed tests

In principle, <u>predictions</u> of effects apply to all the cells in Table 25. Out of thirty-six predictions, fourteen (39%) were confirmed – to be compared with the 5% expected if chance factors alone were involved. Note, however, that eight of the nine workshops resulted in less chance of the inmate being reincarcerated, and several of them resulted in any offences being of lesser severity!

We are not yet in position to be able to examine the real numbers of human beings represented by these statistics. On the other hand, we know the following:

(1) We do know that about 95% of the types of incarcerates we see at the OCI who will be convicted of further offences tend to become recidivists within about <u>two years</u> of their releases.

(2) We do know that about 60% to 65% of the types of inmates treated at the OCI tend to be convicted of further offences within two years of their release if they serve their time at <u>settings other</u> than the OCI.

(3) We do know that, if these types of offenders <u>remain at the OCI</u> and receive the <u>basic</u> treatment program there, about 45% tend to be convicted of further offences within two years of their release (Wolfus and Stasiak, 1991), although it is 38% in this study sample ($N = 32$).

(4) We do know that recidivism rates (percentages) found in the ADDICURE study for control group (zero hours) and for experimental group members who attended three or more hours of treatment at varying numbers of the treatment workshops (one or more, two or more, three or more, etc.) – see Table 26 – are as follows:

(a) Attendance at one ($N = 86$) or more ($N = 138$) of the ADDICURE treatment workshops brings that recidivism percentage, as indicated by the number of inmates reconvicted within the approximately two-year postrelease time frame, down to 30%.

(b) Attendance at two ($N = 7$) or more ($N = 52$) of the ADDICURE treatment workshops brings that recidivism percentage down to 23%.

(c) Attendance at three ($N = 9$) or more ($N = 45$) of the ADDICURE treatment workshops brings that recidivism percentage down to 20%.

(d) Attendance at four ($N = 12$) or more ($N = 36$) of the ADDICURE treatment workshops brings that recidivism percentage down to 19%.

(e) Attendance at five ($N = 15$) or more ($N = 24$) of the ADDICURE treatment workshops brings that recidivism percentage down to 21%.

(f) Attendance at six or more ($N = 9$) of the ADDICURE treatment workshops brings that recidivism percentage down to 0%.

Of course, the chi-square is significant ($p < 0.02$). However, the percentages seem more 'telling'. It would seem that a plurality of ADDICURE specific treatments adds appreciably to the overall OCI (nonspecific) treatment effect, at least among addicted offenders, if we can rely on these results, given the relatively small numbers of subjects receiving two to six-plus workshops (Ns ranging from seven to fifteen).

Table 26: <u>Percentages</u> of ADDICURE #1 subjects convicted
of further offences and Numbers of subjects in each group
(by 'amount' of ADDICURE treatment received)

Treatment 'Amount'	Tx = 0	Tx > 0	Tx > 1	Tx > 2	Tx > 3	Tx > 4	Tx > 5
Subject Numbers	32	138	52	45	36	24	9
Recidivism Percentage	38%	30%	23%	20%	19%	21%	0%

Tx > 0 means one or more treatments; Tx > 1 means two or more treatments; etc.

Conclusions

Much more needs to be discovered about these treatment effects on individual people. For the present, it seems fair to remark that, considering the minimal amounts of treatment afforded to the inmates in this study, it seems almost a miracle that any recidivism effects at all were observable after two years on the street.

Obviously, a single study can be misleading. Any experiment needs to be replicated if conclusions and action are to be based on it. Hopefully, others will undertake that task.

CHAPTER 16

Addictions and Criminality: Are They Confounded?

A secondary purpose of these studies was to discover whether there were any confounding effects in the DAQ measures of addiction and the STFB measures of criminality in this sample of incarcerated alcohol and drug abusers. This intention was expressed when we noted that the dependent measures in ADDICAUSE study included those from the STFB, our test of criminality (Reynolds, 1996). This part of the study was necessitated since we were planning (above) to use criminal recidivism as our medium-term indicator of any treatment modification of addictive behaviour.

Even though treatment effects were demonstrated on the ADDICAUSE scores, since the ADDICAUSE was validated on criminal offenders, it was possible that both the ADDICAUSE changes and the effects of the treatments designed to produce those changes were simply results of modifying criminality. If so, any subsequent effects on criminal recidivism could be interpreted as reflecting modifications of criminality only and not modification of any addictive elements or causes. This can be stated another way. The ADDICURE studies employed addicted offenders. Our criminality project (Reynolds and Quirk, 1996) employed (an independent sample of) offenders, many (75%) of whom were also substance abusers. It is possible that our measures of both addictiveness (DAQ)

and criminality (STFB) might be assaying criminality or addictions or both or some feature they have in common.

This question was addressed in two ways. First, the intercorrelation matrix between DAQ axes and STFB factors was examined (Table 27). It is true that the magnitudes of some correlations are high enough to indicate quite strong relationships between the DAQ axes and STFB factors. However, the higher relationships tend to be found with DAQ axes that seem obviously related to criminality, such as axes 08 (Guilt Intolerance), 12 (Authority Rebellion), 48 and 37 (Punitive Reinforcements/Expectations), and 22 (Subcultural Values). Some axes are unexpectedly related to criminality (common drivers?), such as 13 (Flat Depression) and 47 (Physiological Anxiety). Two axes are negatively related to the STFB factors, and some display relationships barely varying from 0.00.

Table 8 reveals a striking similarity among the correlation coefficients for the six STFB Factors within each DAQ Axis (rows). It appears that the DAQ axes differ appreciably from one another in their relationships with the STFB factors, but rarely the reverse. If one ignores the correlations with the maverick STFB Factor 4, shown elsewhere to vary independently from the other Factors (Reynolds, 1996), the consistency of relationships within DAQ Axes is even more striking. The STFB factors were derived empirically by factor analysis using Varimax rotation to maximize independence from one another (Reynolds, 1996). This should mean that they should display considerable variability in their relationships to other external variables. The limited variability of the correlations within axes means that the axes are controlling (not interacting with) the STFB factors. Perhaps the fact that the ADDICURE sample was limited to addicts among offenders may have created the observed picture by revealing the extent to which each ADDICAUSE axis is related to criminality, even though it does not reveal the extent to which the criminality factors differentiate the ADDICAUSE addiction axes.

Table 27: Correlation matrix for DAQ Axes and STFB Factors in the ADDICURE sample ($N = 193$)

STFB Factor Scores . . . DAQ Axis NAMES and Numbers	STFB OF1	STFB OF2	STFB OF3	STFB OF4	STFB OF5	STFB OF6
Social Enjoyment 02S	.03	.07	.10	.12	−.03	.09
Reactive Depression 03S	.14	.18	**.28**	.12	.20	.18
Guilt Intolerance **08S**	.37	.38	**.43**	.19	**.42**	.29
Social Contact Need 10S	.05	.13	.19	.11	.09	.20
Authority Rebellion **12S**	.54	.56	.58	.15	.56	.51
Flat Depression **13S**	.29	.38	**.55**	.12	.43	.32
Hedonic Enjoyment 20S	.15	.10	.04	.10	.01	.16
Subcultural Values **22S**	.39	.36	.39	.35	.36	.38
PIG/Resiliency 24S	.01	−.08	−.07	−.08	−.02	.10
Affect Denial 30S	.17	.13	.10	.08	.09	**.26**
Need to Be Different **34S**	.38	.37	.36	.18	.40	.32
Rigid Moralizations 36S	**−.27**	−.16	−.18	−.05	−.15	−.16
Paroxysmality **37S**	.27	.36	.39	.27	.35	.32
Pep-Up Need 40S	.17	.03	.04	.10	.02	.17
Fast-Lane Living **44S**	**.47**	.38	.38	.17	.40	.41
Allergy Stress 46S	.16	.28	.28	.01	.16	.30
Physiological Anxiety **47S**	.23	.36	**.45**	.07	.40	.31
Punitive Rewards **48S**	.43	.47	**.52**	.25	.47	.47
Somatic Depression 53S	.17	.29	**.36**	.18	.28	.24
Substance Excitement 60S	.26	.25	.30	.07	.24	**.37**

Correlation coefficients. **High** in **bold**; Lows underlined.

The STFB was also administered to a subset ($N = 392$) of the inmates in the ADDICAUSE sample. In this sample, there was less restriction on the variability of addictions, although about 75% of the sample were addicted to alcohol and/or street drugs. Table 8 displays the correlation matrix between the STFB factors and the DAQ axes in the ADDICAUSE sample. The same controlling effect of the DAQ axes over the STFB factors is visible in Table 9, although the correlations tend to be a bit larger than in Table 8. Once more, we are seeing the relationships between DAQ axes and STFB factors as measures of criminality. It would be nice to see what the correlation

matrix would look like in noncriminal addicts and in noncriminal nonaddicts. We would guess that the correlations would be lower across the board in such samples. Unfortunately, we do not have access to such samples where both the DAQ and the STFB tests were administered.

Still, Table 28 does offer some interesting information. The axes that relate in a relatively undifferentiated way to the STFB factors (**bold and** underlined axis numbers) seem to be axes that are fairly closely related to criminality, perhaps predicated on the criminality in our samples. Some axes do not relate to criminality (no emphasis on axis numbers) and may be 'pure' addictions scales. Some STFB factors seem to 'control' the DAQ scores (columns of **bold** or underlined cell entries), and these may help us to 'define' the meanings of the STFB factors. It is mainly for these purposes that the extended information in Table 9 is presented.

Table 28: Correlation matrix for all DAQ Axes (Long-form axes appended) and STFB Factors in the ADDICAUSE sample who were administered the STFB ($N = 392$)

STFB Factors: DAQ Axis and No.	TFB OF1	TFB OF2	TFB OF3	TFB OF4	TFB OF5	TFB OF6	TFB NF1	TFB NF2	TFB NF3	TFB NF4	TFB NF5
Soc.Enjoy 02*S*	.01	.02	.06	**.18**	−01	.07	.09	−09	.02	.08	.10
React.Dpr 03*S*	.14	.28	**.33**	.12	.24	.25	.20	**.31**	.25	.22	.20
Guilt Int **08***S*	.45	.50	.56	.23	.48	.51	**.54**	.48	**.53**	.44	.31
Soc.Cntct 10*S*	.03	.09	.17	.15	.08	.16	.10	.11	.11	.08	.14
Rebellion **12***S*	.49	.58	.62	.17	.57	.51	.58	.60	.56	.45	.34
Flat Dpr. **13***S*	.28	.42	**.53**	.22	.41	.33	.35	**.53**	.41	.32	.28
Hedonism 20*S*	**.20**	.12	.04	.07	.01	.15	.17	−04	.13	.12	.08
SubCult.V **22***S*	.36	**.46**	**.48**	.29	.41	.42	.46	.38	.43	.42	.33
PIG/Resil 24*S*	−12	−17	−19	.04	−17	−00	−11	−18	−13	−12	−07
Affect Dn 30*S*	.12	.19	.18	.22	.18	.23	.18	.19	.17	.17	.21
Different **34***S*	.36	.40	.43	.22	.45	.36	.39	**.45**	**.43**	.31	.31
Rig.Moral 36*S*	**−28**	−18	−18	.10	−11	−18	**−32**	.00	−17	−16	−08
Failures **37***S*	.39	**.50**	**.55**	.21	.48	.49	.49	.45	**.54**	.44	.31
Pep-Up Nd 40*S*	.15	.17	.18	.20	.15	.18	.15	.17	.15	.19	.17

Fast-Lane **44S**	.45	.46	.49	.20	.46	.41	**.53**	.41	.48	.40	.27
Aller.Str **46S**	.24	.33	.36	.11	.30	.36	.31	.38	.31	.24	.21
Phys.Anx. **47S**	.23	.38	**.52**	.15	.45	.38	.35	**.51**	.39	.30	.24
Punish Rf **48S**	.43	**.56**	**.64**	.28	.53	.49	.52	**.58**	**.55**	.48	.34
Somat.Dpr **53S**	.21	.33	**.41**	.17	**.38**	.25	.26	**.42**	.32	.28	.24
Subs.Enh. **60S**	.33	.38	.37	.19	.36	.33	**.42**	.33	.37	.30	.20
Soc.Anx. 01S	.19	.30	**.41**	.07	.34	.22	.21	**.48**	.29	.22	.13
Stim.Hung **04S**	.45	.41	.43	.12	.38	.39	**.57**	.23	.42	.38	.21
Rigid Slf **05S**	.40	.52	**.59**	.19	.50	.40	.44	**.55**	**.53**	.44	.30
Soc.Influ 06S	.21	.19	.27	.17	.14	.21	.26	.14	.24	.20	.10
Aggr.Inh. **07S**	.25	.33	**.45**	.21	.36	.30	.31	**.44**	.37	.28	21
Lonliness **09S**	.21	.26	**.45**	.13	.36	.30	.27	**.46**	.32	.18	.24
Real.Den. **11S**	.41	.49	**.57**	.19	.46	.42	.49	.48	**.52**	.42	.23
Vivid Img 14S	−12	−16	−16	−01	−16	−08	−15	−10	−15	−15	−07
Cntrl Eff **15S**	.21	.34	**.45**	.21	.40	.32	.27	**.48**	.34	.29	.28
Slf Enh.C 16S	.09	.11	.01	.10	−00	.11	.12	.03	.07	.06	−00
Grief **17S**	.23	.38	**.47**	.13	.40	.36	.32	**.49**	.38	.29	.24
Subs.S.Enh **18S**	.42	.49	.47	.18	.45	.43	**.51**	.39	.48	.40	.28
Pain Sens 19S	.12	.25	.29	.22	.27	.22	.17	**.35**	.25	.19	.19
Soc.Withd **21S**	.26	.37	**.44**	.17	**.42**	.28	.28	**.52**	.39	.29	.19
Dpnd Inh. **23S**	.24	.36	**.49**	.17	.39	.33	.31	**.48**	.36	.29	.25
Par.Sensi **25S**	.21	.31	**.42**	.12	.31	.31	.27	**.46**	.31	.19	.21
Ratn.Def. 26S	.07	.12	.10	.00	.13	.17	.10	**.20**	.09	.04	.07
Oppres.Inh **27S**	.10	.22	**.31**	.15	.24	.21	.17	**.35**	.18	.18	.15
Cmfrt Inh 28S	.02	−00	−01	.05	−01	.05	.01	.01	−02	.01	.05
Disurb Aff **29S**	.18	.32	**.47**	.18	.39	.31	.25	**.49**	.36	.25	.22
Down Other **31S**	.18	.32	.39	.13	.39	.30	.29	**.44**	.30	.21	.21
Soc.Satis. 32S	.07	−01	.02	.03	−05	.09	.12	−10	−00	.03	.01
Dogmatic **33S**	.24	.32	.31	.24	.32	.27	.25	**.38**	.31	.25	.24
Slf Down **35S**	.31	.40	**.55**	.17	.43	.36	.39	**.52**	.44	.31	.23
Reg.Intol **38S**	.30	.43	**.48**	.17	.44	.39	.39	.44	.42	.37	.28
Effort Str **39S**	.28	.42	**.51**	.14	.46	.34	.33	**.51**	.43	.35	.26
Rgd Habit **41S**	.34	.49	**.57**	.18	.50	.40	.41	**.58**	**.51**	.36	.29
Easy Enjoy 42S	.11	.08	.06	.12	.11	.17	.11	.04	.11	.13	.13
Metab.Dis 43S	.24	.31	.38	.19	.36	.25	.28	.35	.35	.27	.23
Hypoglyc. **45S**	.30	**.44**	**.46**	.18	**.44**	.38	.40	.40	.42	.38	.27
Aff.Avoid **49S**	.28	.38	**.46**	.25	.41	.36	.35	**.48**	.42	.30	.23

	OF1	OF2	OF3	OF4	OF5	OF6	NF1	NF2	NF3	NF4	NF5
Cntrl Sens **50**S	.33	.34	**.45**	<u>.21</u>	.38	.36	.35	**.44**	.39	<u>.28</u>	.32
Guilt Prn **51**S	<u>.27</u>	.35	**.50**	<u>.16</u>	.39	.34	.32	**.49**	.39	.28	.27
Ang/Host. **52**S	.36	.45	.42	<u>.12</u>	.40	.41	.44	.39	.42	.36	<u>.23</u>
Hungr.Hrt **54**S	<u>.28</u>	.41	**.51**	<u>.19</u>	.43	.37	.36	**.50**	.43	.32	.28
Imp.SlfEst **55**S	.29	.38	**.52**	<u>.18</u>	.43	.37	.33	**.55**	.43	.28	.29
Mask Disap **56**S	.30	.33	**.41**	.27	.36	.36	.36	.38	.38	.27	.28
Rejection **57**S	<u>.28</u>	.38	**.51**	<u>.15</u>	.45	.34	.31	**.54**	.42	.29	.27
Comm.Wish 58S	.07	.12	.19	.15	.15	.18	.18	.19	.14	.09	.10
ClmNervNd **59**S	<u>.22</u>	.33	.35	<u>.12</u>	.31	.31	.28	**.38**	.30	.23	.20
Frgt Fail **61**S	<u>.13</u>	.25	.26	.22	.26	.30	.22	.29	.25	.21	.18
Diff.Exper **62**S	.24	.29	.31	<u>.15</u>	.28	.33	.29	.33	.32	.20	.20
Avd Depres **63**S	<u>.27</u>	.30	**.39**	<u>.22</u>	.31	**.37**	.37	.32	.33	.27	.25
Asrt Confd **64**S	.35	.39	.37	<u>.18</u>	.36	.39	**.43**	.33	.38	.31	<u>.26</u>
Avd Attrct **65**S	<u>.21</u>	.28	**.38**	<u>.21</u>	**.35**	.31	.24	**.45**	.30	.21	.28
Imp.Sleep **66**S	.27	.33	**.41**	<u>.10</u>	**.39**	.31	.32	**.46**	.33	.24	.20
Clm/Rel Nd 67S	.12	.12	.10	.13	.10	.15	.13	.16	.10	.07	.09
Subs.Depnd 68S	.17	.19	**.32**	.17	.22	**.29**	.24	.31	.25	<u>.11</u>	.21

Pearson correlation coefficients.

Columns OF1–6 refer to the 'original' STFB factors (referred to throughout this work). Columns NF1–5 refer to the newer STFB factors derived from further study.

In this table, a '–' replaces decimal point for negative correlations.

Variant low values in DAQ rows are underlined.

High point(s) in DAQ rows are in **bold**.

It is clear that our first attempt to discover any possible confounding effects between criminality and addictions mainly discovered that some of the ADDICAUSE axes also provide measures of criminality generally, albeit in ways that differ to some extent from the purer measurement of criminality. However, the same question was also addressed in a second way. Pre- and post-treatment STFB measures were available on the subjects of the ADDICURE treatment programme. Given that the DAQ Axes had already been shown to reveal differential treatment (Tables 1 to 4), if any approximation to differential treatment with the STFB Factors could be shown,

the treatments would have applied differentially to both the DAQ and the STFB variables. If this finding was demonstrated, the two sets of measures would have been found to be conceptually similar, thus measuring equivalent constructs. To the extent that differential treatment is not found on the STFB Factors, to that extent the DAQ and the STFB variables represent different constructs.

Table 29 presents the probabilities of t-tests of residual gain scores' mean differences for each of the nine STFB scales (the original six Factor scales plus Total, Social Desirability Neutral, and Social Undesirability) on each of the nine ADDICURE_treatment programmes. Although the effects that the ADDICURE treatments might have on the criminality measures were a matter of interest rather than prediction, we have assumed (for the sake of statistical comparisons) that all the relationships in Table 10 were predicted. The Table 10 statistically significant probabilities are displayed in **bold**, for ease of recognition.

These results suggest (do not prove) that (1) both the tests of and treatments for criminality and addictions are relatively independent of one another; (2) generic criminality (STFB total score) seems to have been modified by treatments for addictions (among offenders), which might help to account for the significant effects on criminal recidivism found in ADDICURE Study no. 3; (3) STFB Factor 2 (grown-up ADDs) may have a particular affinity for addictions so that it was affected by the ADDICURE treatments – an idea we have implied elsewhere (Quirk, 1976, 1995); and (4) the Values programme, which did not modify criminality measures alone (Reynolds and Quirk, 1996), might be more relevant to criminality as it is mediated by addictions – although this question was not specifically tested since the ADDICAUSE test was not administered to the criminality project subjects (Reynolds and Quirk, 1996).

Table 29: Probabilities of the Effects of each of nine
Addictions Treatments on nine <u>STFB</u> residual gain scores

TREATMENTS STFB Scale	Tx1 SUCC.	Tx2 FLEXI	Tx3 EXCIT	Tx4 SATIS	Tx5 VALUE	Tx6 INNOC	Tx7 HEALT	Tx8 HAPPY	Tx9 INTEG
STFB TOTAL	.31	**.10**	**.02**	**.01**	**.00**	**.00**	**.00**	**.00**	**.00**
SD NEUTRAL	.46	.69	.60	.77	**.06**	.81	.57	.15	.46
S UNDESIRA	**.04**	.13	.64	**.08**	**.03**	.51	.53	.26	.89
F1: GUILT	.34	.36	.34	.49	**.03**	<u>.20</u>	.64	.18	.90
F2: FAILUR	<u>.23</u>	**.10**	**.04**	**.02**	**.00**	**.00**	**.01**	**.00**	**.00**
F3: DISTRE	**.07**	.26	.61	**.10**	**.09**	.91	<u>.88</u>	.36	.77
F4: SENSIT	.33	.66	.68	.75	**.01**	.90	.12	<u>.53</u>	.20
F5: CONFOR	**.00**	**.02**	<u>.16</u>	**.01**	.33	.33	.20	**.07**	.13
F6: DISCIP	**.01**	**.08**	.27	**.09**	.20	.34	.61	.27	<u>.73</u>

Two-tailed tests

The Satisfaction program (Tx <u>no.</u> 4), and the first two of the four treatments targeted mainly at reinforcements, may influence the criminality variables, but they seem mainly to affect those shown in Table 9 to be most closely associated with the <u>ADDICAUSE</u> axes (OF3, OF5, OF6). However, <u>no</u> interactions (differential effects) between treatments and <u>STFB</u> factors are seen in Table 10. For ease of recognition, the most likely axes to be affected by the treatments, conceptually, are marked by <u>underlining</u> their cell probabilities in Table 10.

It is true that we have <u>not</u> been able to definitively show that our measures of addictions (<u>DAQ</u>) and criminality (<u>STFB</u>) are <u>not</u> mutually confounded – perhaps not surprising, since we are dealing with incarcerated addicts, for want of appropriate (noncriminal, nonaddicted) samples in which to examine their relationships. However, at worst, they do appear to be at least minimally confounded. The findings that we have mainly confirm that some of the ADDICAUSE (DAQ) axes, as assumed in the earlier chapters (1 to 8), represent criminality <u>and</u> (or in) addictions. It is particularly reassuring to observe both that the criminality (STFB) factors do <u>not</u> appear to represent addictions well and that some of the ADDICAUSE axes do <u>not</u> seem to reflect the criminality of our offenders.

CHAPTER 17

Prevention of Addictions

Not Holding Out Much Hope of Scientifically-Derived Knowledge Being Used

If a brief treatment has some effects on addictive behaviours, can more extensive treatment have a bigger effect, and can using the treatments for their causes before the addictions emerge have an effect in preventing the development of addictions? The truth is that we don't know. We do have some partial information about the effects of larger amounts of these treatments from the results of the studies reported in the last chapter. But we don't know whether the methods we have suggested to modify the causes in people can work to prevent addictions developing in the first place. For the present, all we can do about this last issue is to use the light we do have to suggest how these questions might be answered in the future.

In what follows, we wish to communicate ideas. We cannot really call them plans since our tentative attempts to implement these ideas in discussions with appropriate authorities have proved less than encouraging. Perhaps these ideas might best be thought of as dreams of what might be. Nevertheless, for whatever they are worth, we shall make so bold as to offer them for your attention.

Many years ago, we were privileged to attend a meeting sponsored by the American Society for Humanistic Education. It brought together a large number of senior educators from all over the United States.

Our task was to collate the opinions expressed concerning *the proper purposes and goals for education.* We were surprised to discover that standard content areas in academic education were virtually ignored by those attending. Indeed, upon inquiry, they had been expressly put aside as being of less than secondary importance. The goals that were conceived to be of primary importance were initiatives that would prepare the person for effective and adaptive social living and for participation in and contribution to the community. The kinds of skills the conference participants imagined to be fostered in a well-designed educational system included things like cooperativeness, assertiveness, self-confidence, courage, diplomacy, friendliness, positive attitudes, serenity, joyfulness, and the like – essentially the sorts of skills fostered in psychotherapy and in the ADDICURE programme.

The authors, although delighted, were inclined to ignore the insistences of the people at that meeting as probably expressing the views of a peripheral or radical group of humanists. However, sometime later, we encountered an observation that, as presently structured, standard academic education *concerns itself almost exclusively with two human skills* (verbal and numerical abilities)[11] out of the more than a hundred human abilities that might as easily have been selected. Quite apart from the purposes <u>and</u> the effects of choosing these two human abilities as predominant in education, the observation did remind the writers of some of the other issues that had been addressed in that earlier conference of educators.

These two experiences drew our attention to some of the other possibilities that might yet be included in conventional education of future citizens. This, in turn, reminded us of two target groups that might be accessed in the attempt to prevent addictions, namely, those not yet addicted and those just beginning addictive acts. That is, we began to think carefully about the very young (say, younger than eleven years of age) and the pre-adults (say, teenagers). We

---

[11]   Reading and mathematics are as prominent as they are in school curricula because most jobs require <u>a little</u> of each and, so far as we can see, for no other reason. – RR

noted that both groups were accessible through the educational system. Might it be possible to introduce content areas into conventional education concerned with precisely the same kinds of issues addressed in the ADDICURE process? This question began to gnaw at our entrails.

Being normal members of contemporary society (more or less), the question we put to ourselves immediately led us to consider several problems in the way of implementing any such idea. A spectre awakened in our heads. If most contemporary citizens (including teachers in particular) were to attempt to address the kinds of issues we had in mind, we felt sure that the following kinds of conversions of concepts would occur almost automatically:

Cooperativeness would be converted to negotiation, compromise, and conciliation.

Assertion would be converted to aggressiveness, nonaggression, and nonviolence.

Confidence would be converted to aggressiveness and avoiding aggrandizement.

Courage would be converted to aggressiveness, competitiveness, and self-defence.

Diplomacy would be converted to debating/political/influence skills.

Friendliness would be converted to sociability, meeting needs, and nonhurting.

Optimism would be converted to confrontation, expectations, and avoiding negatives.

Serenity would be converted to not getting uptight, resting, torpor, and apathy.

Joyfulness would be converted to nondepression, excitement need, and entertainment.

Positive attitudes would be converted to lack of negative attitudes/ avoidances.

As we considered the likelihood of these sorts of conceptual conversions happening, a deep and pervasive shudder of despair

overtook us. Only some of the difficulties associated with such conversions can be remarked upon here.

Conventional Approaches to Addictions

In this section, we are going to do one of the things that we oppose. We are going to mention some of the pitfalls involved in conventional approaches to addictions. Surely, the very first error made by many of us (ourselves included here) is that we are inclined to look for or to notice errors, faults, dangers, and pitfalls first, and perhaps only. Indeed, we often become so engrossed in recognizing and avoiding these kinds of things that we fail to go on to look for or notice the positives. Perhaps this characteristic is a natural result of the human condition. In the jungle, our ANS sympathetic-stress-anxiety reactions supported survival. Consequently, they achieved predominance among our responses. However, they are still triggered by our perceptions, cognitions, and expectations and not by the circumstances in which we find ourselves. And our perceptual and cognitive filters and expectations are probably largely shaped by our values – as we repeatedly pointed out to our subjects in the treatment methods. It may not be really necessary to adopt our kind of approach in addressing addictions. Instead, we might find ways to enhance our lives by moving from negative, conflicted, and avoidant values towards positive, joy-giving, and approach values. We skimmed lightly over methods to achieve this outcome in the synopses.

In addition to looking for and reacting to difficulties first (and perhaps only) that lead to the kinds of conversions listed above and referred to in the last paragraph, we also seem to find it easier to talk in prohibitive and avoidant terms. This trend is particularly noticeable in how most of us approach addictions. Witness the slogans we commonly use: 'If you drink, don't drive', 'Drinking and driving don't mix', 'No smoking', 'You don't need to do drugs to . . .', and 'Drugs aren't cool'. Most people assume that there is no other way to talk about addictions. Heck, we are trying to inhibit or stop addictive

behaviour. Given that kind of thinking, we even justify ourselves in borderline forms of criminal conduct, such as threats: 'Cigarettes can kill you', 'Drugs destroy your life', 'Alcohol kills'. Of course, we justify such statements by remarking that they are necessary to arouse fear to help people prevent addictive behaviour. Our impression is that, far from helping, they are most often counterproductive. But some may counter that they are true. They are NOT true. For example, cigarette <u>smoking</u> may result in illness that may eventuate in death; but <u>cigarettes</u> are merely a commercial commodity that don't even make good and solid bludgeons or bullets.

In what we are now about to say, we do NOT wish in any way to demean or downplay the value of AA or NA. They do a great job! However, once more, they set out to inhibit or suppress the use of addictive substances. Their 'steps' and their use of sponsors to give help and counsel do seem to provide some healing of the pains experienced by addicts. But they and detox centres do focus (at least first) on the undoubtedly necessary process of seeking to ensure that the addict <u>desists</u> from addictive behaviour. We share with others the conviction that abstention is a necessary step in the process of dealing with addictive behaviour. And we admit that we have not yet been able to find the kinds of <u>permissive</u> statements or instructions adequately to express cessation. The closest we have come uses such weak statements as: 'Your doctor knows best what drugs to take' (in spite of the fact that this is often where addiction to opioids starts) and 'Breathe fresh air' (as if anyone can find that commodity any more).

There actually are other ways to express ourselves in slogans and instructions. We have seen a sign offering 'free bracelets for every crime'. In the criminality area, that might work quite well, although we know of no evidence for this statement. However, in the area of addictions, few would challenge the statement that by far the most effective antiaddiction campaign has been the permissively stated program of 'the designated driver'. It tells the designated driver what is expected of him/her, without stating what is <u>not</u> allowed, and it permits others of the party to do as they please without instructed

impediment. Whoever it was that invented this slogan deserves heartfelt congratulations and has earned our love.

Other parts of the traditional approach to addictions have been either (i) to medicate the addict, (ii) to 'educate' the addict, or (iii) to undertake conventional forms of psychotherapy with the addict. We cannot understand any of the logic of these approaches due to the following reasons:

(i) To provide the addict with a <u>substitute chemical</u>, that will work only in so far as it has the same effects on his/her subjective experience, is surely just playing with fire. It simply increases the range of his/her access to and potential uses of addictive substances. Punitive methods, such as Antabuse, will work for a short period of time with a percentage of addicts, just as punitive methods, such as aversive conditioning, work for a time (two to eight years, depending on the method used) with anomalous sexual preferences. The hiatus afforded by punitive methods might be a useful temporary measure, except it is rarely used to permit an interval in which real healing is done.

(ii) To attempt to '<u>educate</u>' the addict, commonly about the effects of addictive substances, seems to us presumptuous and absurd. Although they may attempt to cooperate with, and perhaps even to congratulate, the 'educator', it has been our experience that addicts, as a group, know much more about addictions than most of the 'experts'. Our addicted convicts seem to us to be the superior experts about addictions, and we have found ourselves consulting them often.

(iii) If the <u>psychotherapy</u> used with addicts involves any of the conventional nondirective methods, we suspect it is apt to be interminable and misleading, if not counterproductive. It is a case of 'the blind leading the blind'. Addicts do NOT seem to know what motivates their addictions, for all the reasons implied in chapters 1 through 8. Of course, they know what substances they use and what general effects they obtain from

substance uses. They are not experts in understanding the personality mechanisms and dynamisms operating within them in the nature of causality or in the ways in which chemicals interact with their systems. Even experts in these things, if addicted, cannot find their way through the morass of events that drive them. What the addict knows best is the host of justifications, rationalizations, and other defensive ploys he/she has adopted, along with his/her highly selective memories of his/her childhood and development. If the addict shapes the directions of the psychotherapy, especially if it is focused around his/her addictions, the result can hardly be anything but chaos and misadventure.

But so much for our negativisms and complaints about the problems afflicting traditional approaches to the treatment of addictions. They seemed required as a kind of caveat concerning what we are about to propose for purposes of prevention. We dare not be incautious about how we approach our work and about how we express ourselves about and in our enterprise.

Nevertheless, since addiction is the present topic, and since fostering it is NOT the goal, avoiding or preventing it is an unavoidable aim of this part of the volume. While the negatives in the last sentence create the very problem they aim to avoid, they are used here as a background to illustrate how an alternative way to prevent addiction might be approached. The approach would not be to inhibit vulnerability or enslavement to addictive substances. Rather, it would be to foster freedom, choice, and human strengths. But even that sort of conceptual approach would be premature in seeking to prevent addictions. The first design step (below) would necessarily involve assessment of the stages of development of vulnerability and involvement with addictive causes. How might one proceed with that task?

An Example of Thinking

Before proceeding with an answer to that question, it may help understanding if we digress briefly with a couple of examples contrasting common approaches against the one we have adopted. While we were writing about some of this material, an initiative was started in our local jurisdiction that proposed extended taxation aimed at home brew. The logic involved noted that there is a relationship between cost and consumption. It was argued that consumption might be reduced if costs of home brew were increased by increased taxation.

One of the common views of the motivation underlying addiction is availability and cost. We consider this view to be very weak. In Chapter 3, we showed that the motivations and psychological processes underlying the use of home brew are quite different from those underlying use of beer and other alcoholic beverages. As a consequence, we would argue that raising the costs involved in home brewing (or cigarettes or anything else) is unlikely to affect or prevent addiction to, and thus use of, the substance by very much. Instead, it seems to us most appropriate to modify the real motivations underlying addictive uses if those motivations can be identified and are modifiable.

A parallel observation can be made with respect to crime. Common views of crime (at least from the perspective of lawyers) seem to seek the underlying motivations in (mainly) economic gains on the part of the perpetrator. We are unimpressed with the evidence for such a point of view. Our analysis of the roots underlying crime (Reynolds and Quirk, 1994) suggests that crime is motivated from personality characteristics. Accordingly, in our view, these personality characteristics would best be the targets to address in any attempt to prevent crime.

Having expressed these views, we would hasten to add at least one caveat. There are various ways to reinforce (reward) both addiction and crime. Paying off a kidnapper, affording media attention, acceding to demands of terrorists, or the failure to punish or provide

other consequences to one who defrauds others may very well serve to trivialize and/or reward offenders' unacceptable conduct. Similarly, glorifying (e.g., 'mind-expanding drugs') or trivializing (e.g., 'recreational drugs') use of addictive substances might well interfere with preventive efforts or actually help to reinforce addictive behaviour.

Where to Target Prevention Efforts

I: Ages and Stages. In order to determine the most profitable age(s) at which to introduce preventive measures, the ages at which causative factors in addictions become crystallized (observable) would first need to be determined. This is not entirely a simple task. It would require administration of a quite extensive battery of tests to many (to avoid sample bias) classes of students at each of several grade/age levels – for example, grades 4, 6, 8, 9, 10, 11, and 12. The reason for the battery of tests would be both to acquire information about associated developmental trends (general personality, criminality, addiction, anxiety, depression) and to allow the emergence of addictive trends to be isolated from other general aspects of personality development. In addition to standard statistical procedures used in the analysis of such data, it would likely be necessary to employ methods such as lag-and-lead statistics and path analysis.

II: Demonstration Teaching. Having selected the appropriate grade levels at which the preventive curriculum might properly be introduced, it would be necessary to undertake demonstration teaching for a plurality of purposes. First, it would be necessary to demonstrate that the program package works to accomplish its purposes. This would involve experimental applications of the package (with ample provision for untreated controls) to determine whether modification of target behaviours does occur. For this purpose, demonstrations would be required of effects both on measures of causality and of personality and on future addictive conduct (as seen in the schools and/or afterwards). For example, if addictive behaviour is modified

but not the measures, then the effects achieved would be equivalent to a Hawthorne effect.

Second, if the program works as hoped, it would be necessary to undertake two kinds of demonstration teaching for the teachers to be involved. The first kind of teaching would establish a preparatory sort of orientation in which some of the attitudes and approaches of the teachers would be modified to prevent the kinds of conceptual 'conversions' alluded to above. All our common compensatory assurance that we know all or most of what there is to know about psychology and life, notwithstanding, we are all as green as grass about what makes people tick and about how to teach others. There is ample information available, but nobody we know bothers (or is able) to access the enormous amounts and varieties of information required for the task of interfering with other people's lives.

The second kind of teaching would involve teaching the teachers how to operate the programme. As was implied in the earlier reference to the conference of senior educators, the focus on academic issues would have to be replaced by a focus on the individual human being. Also, errors/failures of student learning would have to be attributed to errors in teaching and/or content and not to the student. To attempt to refocus attention and perspective in this way is no small task.

While the above is admittedly a rather sketchy overview of the task of preparing to consider implementation of a preventive program for addictions (or anything else), it does draw attention to some of the problems that would be encountered. But it also suggests that, with commitment and political will, as well as care in laying the groundwork, it might be possible to prevent the destructive problem of addictions.

III: Curriculum. What has not yet been addressed in the above is the kind of curriculum that would be needed to prevent addictions. Actually, one approach to a curriculum has already been offered both in the references to the ADDICAUSE variables, chapters 1 through 8, and in the synopses of the ADDICURE treatment methods provided in chapters 9 through 17.

Barriers to Implementation

The problem we have yet to consider is how to make the proposed food for the mind *palatable*. It needs to be palatable to parents, teachers, school administrators, and particularly, our youth. And we do have some ideas and information about how to do that.

During our attempts to interest senior educational personnel to undertake the above steps towards prevention of addictions (and/or crime), we encountered some fairly obvious stumbling blocks. We believe these difficulties require some careful attention in planning.

The main stumbling block was the <u>fear</u>. Fear was expressed by many senior educators that parents would object to the idea that their children might be (even potential) addicts or offenders. They feared this might be implied in offering courses to prevent addictions (or crime). It is unfortunate, if inevitable, that in order to justify implementation of a programme, it is necessary to specify its purpose in preventing a calamity. Of course, the kind of curriculum suggested, although aimed at and derived from studies of addictions, is really just a program to address freedom from the development of some of the troublesome personal characteristics that might impair the quality of the person's life.

But to state that runs up against another <u>objection</u>. What young person or parent is going to accept that he/she or his/her child risks developing troublesome personality characteristics or is possessed of any 'mental or emotional' difficulties requiring corrective training? The issue is indeed one of palatability.

Related to this last issue is the whole question of how a preventive program for addictions might be identified or <u>labelled</u> to make it acceptable as a part of a curriculum. Certainly, it cannot be called addictions prevention. That would make the whole program far too specific in purpose and nature. And, in truth, regardless of the sources of the contents to be addressed, such a program would have much wider human applicability than merely one of preventing addictions. But what might it be called?

Also related to this matter is the probability that parents would not be willing to accept that schools undertake to train their children for <u>emotional development</u>. That is something most parents would see as a matter reserved for home learning. They would likely be deeply concerned about delegating this kind of highly individual and personal learning to relative strangers (teachers) and in groups of others (classes). Besides, many parents would be inclined to fear that learning about emotional life in classroom groups might entail their children divulging personal or family secrets or expressing feelings and attitudes towards their family members that might be private, embarrassing, or uncomplimentary. How could those attitudes and fears be assuaged?

But so far, we have only spoken of the reactions of parents. <u>Educators</u> will most certainly react in a hostile way to the kind of program being suggested. Like other people, teachers cherish what they do. They have been trained to teach the conventional curriculum. It is relatively easy for them to teach Language or History or Mathematics. Fear of change and the implicit demand that they learn a whole new body of knowledge, another approach to teaching, and a whole new and very different curriculum must be both threatening and unsettling for them. Even those who see value in what is being proposed or who consider that the curriculum ought to focus on preparation for life (and not just for higher education or work) must necessarily blanch at the actual dimensions of the task involved. How can such a preventive program be made palatable to teachers and the schools?

What is being suggested does amount to general reconstruction of school curricula. And the reconstruction does entail a basic change in the primary purposes of education and in the attitudes adopted by youth, parents, and teachers towards the role of education, its focus, and the means by which it is effected. Indeed, we are suggesting that we need to confirm the views of the educators, referred to at the beginning of this chapter, who met under the auspices of the American Society for Humanistic Education. Perhaps we need to reconsider the roles of education in this increasingly complicated

society. Perhaps education ought to be construed as a preparation for healthy, happy, contributive, and quality human societal living and not just as a preparation for rationality, intellectual problem-solving, and/or work. Perhaps, for the sake of future generations, teachers need to become emotional people fostering the emotional development of their charges.

We don't have the youth and energy needed to advance these initiatives. Nor do we have the answers about how they might be implemented. We must pass the task on to others, if it is ever to be done. We have but one very preliminary key to one door through which entry might be started. That key is this. Addictions pose a huge and escalating problem for humankind and for our societies. This problem might offer some of the incentive to advance towards a broader preparation of our children for life. We have tried to outline at least part of the shape of the key to addictions and, in doing so, have tried to suggest some approaches to education in general that could hold out some hope of addressing addictions too.

APPENDIX A

Addicause Long Form

DIMENSIONAL ADDICAUSE QUESTIONNAIRE (DAQ)

NAME: _____ DATE:_____AGE:____

Instructions: Some of the items in this questionnaire refer to the use of substances. If you have never used that kind of substance, just circle 0 (i.e., "not at all"). Please answer every question. If you have trouble reading the words, please ask someone for help. Take as long as you need to do the questionnaire.

Please circle the number for each statement which most nearly applies to you *right now*. The numbers mean:

0 = "false", "no", "not me at all", "not now"
1 = "occasionally", "once in a while", "maybe sometimes"
2 = "about as often as not", "an average amount", "perhaps"
3 = "most often", "I guess so", "probably", "more than not"
4 = "true", "yes", "definitely", "sure do", "nearly always"

Axis 01

I avoid being noticed in social groups if I can.	0 1 2 3 4
I avoid interacting with others if possible.	0 1 2 3 4
I avoid social groups when I can.	0 1 2 3 4
I try to spend as much time as I can by myself.	0 1 2 3 4
I spend as much time as I can reading and thinking.	0 1 2 3 4
I try to keep myself occupied by myself when I can.	0 1 2 3 4
I am afraid to draw attention to myself in a group.	0 1 2 3 4
I am uncomfortable having to interact with others.	0 1 2 3 4
I am uptight or fearful in groups of people.	0 1 2 3 4
I feel most comfortable being alone.	0 1 2 3 4
I feel most at ease reading or thinking alone.	0 1 2 3 4
I feel least uncomfortable working by myself.	0 1 2 3 4

SocAnx(AvdSoc/ApprSelf)−(A) ....[_][_][_][_][_][_][__][__]

z v a k c e N S

Axis 02

I avoid intimate groups when I can be in large ones.	0 1 2 3 4
I avoid being alone as much as possible.	0 1 2 3 4
I try to avoid working at tasks I have to do alone.	0 1 2 3 4
I seek the excitement and fun of being with others.	0 1 2 3 4
I spend as much time as I can talking with others.	0 1 2 3 4
I feel most comfortable being part of a group.	0 1 2 3 4
I keep from feeling isolated as much as I can.	0 1 2 3 4
I am bored or irritable when I'm by myself.	0 1 2 3 4
I feel a sense of emptiness when I'm alone.	0 1 2 3 4
I enjoy seeing friends and going to parties.	0 1 2 3 4
I am most at ease when I am talking with friends.	0 1 2 3 4
I feel least uptight when I am doing social things.	0 1 2 3 4

GrpEnj(Apprsoc/AvdSlf)+ ....[_][_][_][_][_][_][__][__]

z v a k c e N S

ADDICAUSE Page 2

Axis 03

I give up when too many changes are happening.	0 1 2 3 4
I tune out when too much is going on around me.	0 1 2 3 4
I sometimes feel like there's a fist in my stomach.	0 1 2 3 4
I try to cope when things look reasonably organized.	0 1 2 3 4
I spend time with friends when I am fairly calm.	0 1 2 3 4
I cling on to friends when my life runs smoothly.	0 1 2 3 4
I feel down even when my world looks organized.	0 1 2 3 4
I feel hurt by others even if they say they like me.	0 1 2 3 4
I can't cope well even if things are going OK.	0 1 2 3 4
I try to lift my spirits when I feel I can't cope.	0 1 2 3 4
I seek help when I have too many problems to face.	0 1 2 3 4
I try to find relief when I have too much stress.	0 1 2 3 4

RctDepr(PasDisInt/ActInt)−(C)............[_][_][_][_][_][_][__][__]
                                      z v a k c e N S

Axis 04

I am "cranked up" by changes I have to deal with.	0 1 2 3 4
I want the volume up high when listening to music.	0 1 2 3 4
I am most effective when under heavy pressure.	0 1 2 3 4
I seek out high stress and risk-taking situations.	0 1 2 3 4
I am drawn to active, noisy, exciting situations.	0 1 2 3 4
I get into fast-moving, even if confusing, action.	0 1 2 3 4
I have fun taking calculated risks.	0 1 2 3 4
I enjoy "pulling a fast one" or "conning" somebody.	0 1 2 3 4
I enjoy being in the "fast lane" in daily life.	0 1 2 3 4
I enjoy watching many things going on at once.	0 1 2 3 4
I like listening to more than one thing at a time.	0 1 2 3 4
It's fun to have lots of things happening at once.	0 1 2 3 4

StimHung(ActInt/PasDisint)+(J) ....[_][_][_][_][_][_][__][__]
                                      z v a k c e N S

Axis 05

It's hard work to improve the way I see things.	0 1 2 3 4
I have to think hard to change the way I think.	0 1 2 3 4
Changing myself to a purpose is a hard thing to do.	0 1 2 3 4
I see no purpose to all the learning I have done.	0 1 2 3 4
I think chance guided most of what I've learned.	0 1 2 3 4
I can't make sense out of how we're expected to act.	0 1 2 3 4
I see things the way I see them. That's how it is.	0 1 2 3 4
I feel stuck in the way I think even if it hurts me.	0 1 2 3 4
I've learned to act how I act. I can't change me.	0 1 2 3 4
I see things the way they are. That's the way it is.	0 1 2 3 4
It's a dog-eat-dog world no matter what people say.	0 1 2 3 4
I feel there's no way to change things anyway.	0 1 2 3 4

RgdSlf(RgdPurp/LrnRand)−(cAd) ......[_][_][_][_][_][_][__][__]

z v a k c e N S

ADDICAUSE Page 3

Axis 06

I enjoy going along with the crowd I hang out with.	0 1 2 3 4
I think the attitudes my group has are right.	0 1 2 3 4
Friends are friends regardless of how anyone feels.	0 1 2 3 4
I learn best from watching how others do things.	0 1 2 3 4
I've learned to think the same way my friends do.	0 1 2 3 4
I try to do things to fit in with my group.	0 1 2 3 4
I enjoy seeing myself as acting like my group does.	0 1 2 3 4
I think outsiders don't understand my group's ways.	0 1 2 3 4
I need to feel I'm part of a group.	0 1 2 3 4
I like to see things the way my friends do.	0 1 2 3 4
I really enjoy the sense of sharing in my group.	0 1 2 3 4
I like being influenced to do what my friends do.	0 1 2 3 4

SocInfl(LrnSoc/RgdSlf)+(SRf) ....[_][_][_][_][_][_][__][__]

z v a k c e N S

Axis 07

I see aggression as the worst thing people can do.	0 1 2 3 4
I think people should try not to show their anger.	0 1 2 3 4
I feel that angry feelings should be kept inside.	0 1 2 3 4
I use up my anger by watching TV sports and movies.	0 1 2 3 4
I often won't talk to people I'm irritated with.	0 1 2 3 4
When I feel angry, I often won't do as I'm asked.	0 1 2 3 4
A lot of human interaction is based on anger.	0 1 2 3 4
It is natural to get angry about what others say.	0 1 2 3 4
I feel angry at lots of things a lot of the time.	0 1 2 3 4
I would do anything rather than express my anger.	0 1 2 3 4
When I'm annoyed, it's hard for me to say so.	0 1 2 3 4
I try to find ways to cool myself down when I'm angry.	0 1 2 3 4

AggrInhb(AvdAct/ApprPas)−(T) ....[_][_][_][_][_][_][__][__]
                                     z   v a k c e N S

Axis 08

My family disapproves of using alcohol or drugs.	0 1 2 3 4
Most people disapprove of alcohol and drug use.	0 1 2 3 4
I feel a bit guilty when using alcohol or drugs.	0 1 2 3 4
I often see others as seeing what I do as shameful.	0 1 2 3 4
People often want me to take the blame for things.	0 1 2 3 4
I often feel guilty even when I've done no wrong.	0 1 2 3 4
I feel there are far too many rules to follow.	0 1 2 3 4
I hate having to do what others tell me to do.	0 1 2 3 4
I feel that rules are just made to be broken.	0 1 2 3 4
I often show I disapprove of others' disapproval.	0 1 2 3 4
I often want to find ways to "stick it" to others.	0 1 2 3 4
I enjoy being a rebel.	0 1 2 3 4

GuiIntol(AvdPas/ApprAct:Gui)+(R) ...[_][_][_][_][_][_][__][__]
                                     z v a k c e N S

ADDICAUSE Page 4

Axis 09

I find myself being alone most of the time.	0 1 2 3 4
I do a lot of daydreaming about talking to friends.	0 1 2 3 4
I need desperately to be with people.	0 1 2 3 4
I do a lot of what I do just to be around others.	0 1 2 3 4
I listen to the radio to feel I'm near other people.	0 1 2 3 4
I go for walks to be involved in what others do.	0 1 2 3 4
When I see other people together, I feel like an outsider.	0 1 2 3 4
I hear others talking, and I wish they'd talk to me.	0 1 2 3 4
I feel empty inside unless I am with other people.	0 1 2 3 4
I feel it is my way to be a loner.	0 1 2 3 4
I think a lot to fill up the time when I'm alone.	0 1 2 3 4
I feel lonely most of the time.	0 1 2 3 4

Lonlin(PasSoc/ActAln)−(W) ....[_][_][_][_][_][_][__][__]
　　　　　　　　　　　　　　　z　v　a　k　c　e　N　S

Axis 10

I get out with other people as much as I can.	0 1 2 3 4
I spend as much time as I can talking with others.	0 1 2 3 4
I feel the need to be close to other people.	0 1 2 3 4
I picture myself participating in group activities.	0 1 2 3 4
When alone, I think about what I can say to others.	0 1 2 3 4
I let myself feel lonely to help me want company.	0 1 2 3 4
When alone, I watch TV to see ways people relate.	0 1 2 3 4
I think a lot about how to get along with others.	0 1 2 3 4
I spend time alone to recharge for social contacts.	0 1 2 3 4
I watch groups to see how others relate together.	0 1 2 3 4
I listen to conversations to learn about people.	0 1 2 3 4
I feel the need to be part of a group of friends.	0 1 2 3 4

SocCntct(ActSoc/PasAln)+(SNd) ....[_][_][_][_][_][_][__][__]
　　　　　　　　　　　　　　　z　v　a　k　c　e　N　S

Axis 11

It's better to "be in a fog" than to get to work.	0 1 2 3 4
The demands of reality seem just too much for me.	0 1 2 3 4
The pressure to do things just turns me off.	0 1 2 3 4
It's a lot easier to daydream than to accomplish.	0 1 2 3 4
I don't like being expected to be self-sufficient.	0 1 2 3 4
I try to find ways to "get away from it all".	0 1 2 3 4
I spend a lot of time daydreaming.	0 1 2 3 4
I prefer to put off things I have to do.	0 1 2 3 4
I find a lot of ways to "put in time".	0 1 2 3 4
Tomorrow is a better day to do things than today is.	0 1 2 3 4
I would like best not to have to do anything at all.	0 1 2 3 4
I feel drowned in what others call reality.	0 1 2 3 4

RealDen(AvdReal/ApprUnr)−(U) ......[_][_][_][_][_][_][__][__]

z v a k c e N S

ADDICAUSE Page 5
Axis 12

It annoys me to have to deal with authorities.	0 1 2 3 4
I hate being given orders by anyone.	0 1 2 3 4
I think people older than me are mostly strange.	0 1 2 3 4
I keep others from seeing when I am scared.	0 1 2 3 4
I think of myself as something of a rebel.	0 1 2 3 4
I put up a "tough" front for other people.	0 1 2 3 4
In stores, I always notice the surveillance devices.	0 1 2 3 4
I feel angry at people who try to act too "good".	0 1 2 3 4
I feel as though I've had a raw deal out of life.	0 1 2 3 4
I hate rules and regulations.	0 1 2 3 4
I feel I am criticized too much by others.	0 1 2 3 4
I dislike having to pay sales tax on anything.	0 1 2 3 4

AuthReb(AprUnr/AvdReal)+(ll) ....[_][_][_][_][_][_][__][__]

z v a k c e N S

Axis 13

Picturing the uncertain future just makes me scared.	0 1 2 3 4
Even with planning, you never know what will happen.	0 1 2 3 4
If I'm sure of the future, I will be disappointed.	0 1 2 3 4
When I picture my past, I become weak and depressed.	0 1 2 3 4
I never amounted to much, so there's no hope I will.	0 1 2 3 4
I feel my past left me empty and joyless.	0 1 2 3 4
The future looks just as empty and flat as the past.	0 1 2 3 4
I think life is good only in an imagined future.	0 1 2 3 4
I feel afraid that life will continue as it was.	0 1 2 3 4
Every picture of my past is upsetting or saddening.	0 1 2 3 4
In the past, I can only find rotten memories.	0 1 2 3 4
My life feels like a joyless, empty vacuum.	0 1 2 3 4

FltDepr(ImpFrwd/PwrBck)−(L) ....[_][_][_][_][_][_][__][__]

                                      z v a k c e N S

Axis 14

I can picture lots of resources I got from the past.	0 1 2 3 4
I can remember many things which give me support.	0 1 2 3 4
I can still feel many acts of caring from my past.	0 1 2 3 4
I don't need to see now what the future holds.	0 1 2.3 4
I can't stop all unhappy thoughts of the future.	0 1 2 3 4
I know there will be lots of pain in the future.	0 1 2 3 4
Not all the images from my past are pleasant.	0 1 2 3 4
I likely remember as much hurt in my past as others.	0 1 2 3 4
I can't help feeling sad about losses in my past.	0 1 2 3 4
Picturing what I want will help me to achieve it.	0 1 2 3 4
I can imagine lots of values and good in my future.	0 1 2 3 4
The possibilities of the future make me feel good.	0 1 2 3 4

VivSens(PwrFrwd/ImpBck)+...............[_][_][_][_][_][_][__][__]

                                      z v a k c e N S

ADDICAUSE Page 6

Axis 15

I need to control the sharpness of my mental images.	0 1 2 3 4
I want to empty my mind of its constant thoughts.	0 1 2 3 4
I try to dampen down the strength of my feelings.	0 1 2 3 4
I see my body as being too uptight and too weak.	0 1 2 3 4
I think my mind can't control my body's demands.	0 1 2 3 4
I feel my emotions are often out of control.	0 1 2 3 4
I need to see my life as more settled and slow.	0 1 2 3 4
I want to be less bothered by my too-sharp hearing.	0 1 2 3 4
I feel emotions too strongly for me to bear.	0 1 2 3 4
I need help to reduce the intensity of what I see.	0 1 2 3 4
I need something to help me tune out my thoughts.	0 1 2 3 4
I need some way to make my emotions affect me less.	0 1 2 3 4

CntrlEfft(PwrMnd/ImpBdy)−(CNd) ....[_][_][_][_][_][_][_][__][__]

             z v a k c e N S

Axis 16

I see myself as being physically powerful.	0 1 2 3 4
The way I speak exerts strong influence on others.	0 1 2 3 4
My feelings are strong enough to win over others.	0 1 2 3 4
I look for ways to make my vision of things cleared.	0 1 2 3 4
I try to find ways to grasp life's meaning better.	0 1 2 3 4
I want to increase the strength of my emotions.	0 1 2 3 4
I have very powerful and forceful mental images.	0 1 2 3 4
I impress others with the cleverness of my thoughts.	0 1 2 3 4
I overwhelm others with the force of my emotions.	0 1 2 3 4
I enjoy looking self-confident in whatever I do.	0 1 2 3 4
I can control my body easily with my thoughts.	0 1 2 3 4
My emotions are not strong enough to get in my way.	0 1 2 3 4

SeEnhncCntrl(PwrMnd/ImpBdy)+(M).[_][_][_][_][_][_][_][__][__]

             z v a k c e N S

Axis 17

The grief I feel makes the future look empty.	0 1 2 3 4
I feel helpless as I think about my losses.	0 1 2 3 4
When I think about my losses, I feel weak all over.	0 1 2 3 4
I picture the happiness I had before my loss.	0 1 2 3 4
I think of the fun I had in life before my grief.	0 1 2 3 4
I wish I could get back the energy I used to have.	0 1 2 3 4
As I picture my losses, I only see empty space.	0 1 2 3 4
As I think about the things I've lost, I want to cry.	0 1 2 3 4
I feel my losses are too heavy a burden to carry.	0 1 2 3 4
The picture I have of myself is one of uselessness.	0 1 2 3 4
I keep thinking about how things might have been.	0 1 2 3 4
I feel a great weight of grief on me or inside me.	0 1 2 3 4

Grief(PwrLss/ImpGn)−(Y) ....[_][_][_][_][_][_][__][__]

z v a k c e N S

ADDICAUSE Page 7

Axis 18

I think I look my best when drinking or doing drugs.	0 1 2 3 4
I impress others when drinking or doing drugs.	0 1 2 3 4
I am most self-confident when drinking/doing drugs.	0 1 2 3 4
When drinking/doing drugs, I feel I am not a failure.	0 1 2 3 4
I am accepted by others while drinking/doing drugs.	0 1 2 3 4
I feel most sure of myself drinking or doing drugs.	0 1 2 3 4
I really feel that I am better than other people.	0 1 2 3 4
I feel I am very sensitive to others' motivations.	0 1 2 3 4
I am sure others sense the power of my personality.	0 1 2 3 4
I feel the need to be able to control other people.	0 1 2 3 4
I feel the need to influence others' understanding.	0 1 2 3 4
I feel the need to have power over others.	0 1 2 3 4

SubsSeEnhnc(PwrGn/ImpLss)+(X) .....[_][_][_][_][_][_][__][__]

z v a k c e N S

166

Axis 19

I try to avoid bright light or loud noise.	0 1 2 3 4
I am supersensitive to comments about my health.	0 1 2 3 4
Pain and discomfort "get to me" too much.	0 1 2 3 4
I almost always have pain somewhere in my body.	0 1 2 3 4
I worry about injuring myself any more than I have.	0 1 2 3 4
I am very careful not to strain my neck or back.	0 1 2 3 4
I would like to forget life's pain and suffering.	0 1 2 3 4
I worry about hurting or injuring myself.	0 1 2 3 4
The world seems such a burden I often ignore pain.	0 1 2 3 4
Life would look brighter without the pain I have.	0 1 2 3 4
I'd be out with people more with less aches/pains.	0 1 2 3 4
I'd enjoy being active without the burden of pain.	0 1 2 3 4

PainSens(SensPn/InsnsPls)−(D) ....[_][_][_][_][_][_][__][__]
z v a k c e N S

Axis 20

I see lots of fun situations to get involved in.	0 1 2 3 4
I enjoy talking and laughing a lot with my friends.	0 1 2 3 4
All sorts of things get me excited.	0 1 2 3 4
I can get along OK in almost any situation/setting.	0 1 2 3 4
I don't really care much what other people say.	0 1 2 3 4
The minor injuries and pain I get don't trouble me.	0 1 2 3 4
There are very few situations that bother me.	0 1 2 3 4
Nobody succeeds in conning me or pushing me around.	0 1 2 3 4
I can enjoy activities even when I've been injured.	0 1 2 3 4
The main thing in life is to have a good time.	0 1 2 3 4
I like conning or teasing those of the opposite sex.	0 1 2 3 4
I'm always looking for exciting things to do.	0 1 2 3 4

Hedon(SensPls/InsnsPn)+(JSHun) ......[_][_][_][_][_][_][__][__]
z v a k c e N S

ADDICAUSE Page 8

Axis 21

I seem to see the world better when I'm alone.	0 1 2 3 4
I organize my thoughts best when nobody is around.	0 1 2 3 4
I seem to feel most comfortable when I'm alone.	0 1 2 3 4
When with others, I am distracted by their activity.	0 1 2 3 4
I can't think clearly when others are talking.	0 1 2 3 4
I don't like being part of most groups of people.	0 1 2 3 4
It is easier not to be around where others are.	0 1 2 3 4
I can't seem to find anything to say to others.	0 1 2 3 4
Being with others feels like a burden to bear.	0 1 2 3 4
I enjoy a sense of freedom when I'm alone.	0 1 2 3 4
The conflict of life is not there when I'm alone.	0 1 2 3 4
I feel I would like to be alone most of the time.	0 1 2 3 4

SocWthdrw(BdSoc/GdAln)−(A)(O1)..[_][_][_][_][_][_][__][__]

z v a k c e N S

Axis 22

I like hanging around with the guys in a pub.	0 1 2 3 4
Shooting the bull is a favourite pastime of mine.	0 1 2 3 4
I really like backslapping fun with the guys.	0 1 2 3 4
Most people spend a lot of time drinking in pubs.	0 1 2 3 4
I am proud of my use of alcohol and/or drugs.	0 1 2 3 4
Most people use drugs and/or alcohol.	0 1 2 3 4
I think what happens in life is a matter of luck.	0 1 2 3 4
I think we need unions to protect workers.	0 1 2 3 4
I'm an easy-going person, just out for a good time.	0 1 2 3 4
It feels good to drink someone under the table.	0 1 2 3 4
Telling jokes is the best kind of conversation.	0 1 2 3 4
I am proud of the amount of booze I can drink.	0 1 2 3 4

Subcult(GdSoc/BdAln)+(G) ....[_][_][_][_][_][_][__][__]

z v a k c e N S

Axis 23

I dislike people who use their power over others.	0 1 2 3 4
It's not fair to influence others to think your way.	0 1 2 3 4
It's mean for people to force their will on others.	0 1 2 3 4
I don't have the power to change anything much.	0 1 2 3 4
I can't seem to change my thoughts or attitudes.	0 1 2 3 4
I don't feel tough enough to handle strong feelings.	0 1 2 3 4
I wish I could see how others get power over people.	0 1 2 3 4
I hate others telling me how I should think.	0 1 2 3 4
I don't like feeling always at the mercy of others.	0 1 2 3 4
I usually feel others are pushing me around.	0 1 2 3 4
I often think others influence me too much.	0 1 2 3 4
I sometime feel as though I am always the follower.	0 1 2 3 4

DpndInhib(PwrChg/ImpPrst)−(S+)......[_][_][_][_][_][_][__][__]

           z v a k c e N S

ADDICAUSE Page 9

Axis 24

I believe anybody can influence what happens.	0 1 2 3 4
I think everybody's ideas contribute to any outcome.	0 1 2 3 4
I feel heroes are ordinary people facing challenges.	0 1 2 3 4
I view hanging on to a dream as one way to success.	0 1 2 3 4
I think nothing lasts through time like an idea.	0 1 2 3 4
I feel that sticking at a task is the way to win.	0 1 2 3 4
I see lots in my life that I could usefully change.	0 1 2 3 4
I can think of many ways to improve my joy in life.	0 1 2 3 4
I am comfortable with my ability to change my life.	0 1 2 3 4
I can live quite happily with things I can't change.	0 1 2 3 4
I can make friends and enjoy them as well as anyone.	0 1 2 3 4
I feel happy and content in spite of my limitations.	0 1 2 3 4

NrmlRes(PwrChg/ImpPrst)+(ILoC).....[_][_][_][_][_][_][__][__]

           z v a k c e N S

Axis 25

I watch people's actions to check on what they say.	0 1 2 3 4
I often question the meaning behind what others say.	0 1 2 3 4
I often wonder what others are doing behind my back.	0 1 2 3 4
I'm amazed when people don't notice others' tricks.	0 1 2 3 4
I am surprised at how insensitive people often are.	0 1 2 3 4
I am shocked how unaware people are of intentions.	0 1 2 3 4
I can be less upset staying away from some people.	0 1 2 3 4
I can sometimes forget others' meanness when alone.	0 1 2 3 4
I often don't mind being away by myself.	0 1 2 3 4
I fear I can see how people talk behind my back.	0 1 2 3 4
I worry what others may say about me when I'm away.	0 1 2 3 4
I get upset feeling some people's envy and anger.	0 1 2 3 4

ParSens(SensSoc/InsnsAln)−(ch) ....[_][_][_][_][_][_][_][__][__]
                                       z v a k c e N S

Axis 26

I try to be with people who see things as they are.	0 1 2 3 4
I try to keep those friends who talk reasonably.	0 1 2 3 4
I relate to people who aren't always feeling hurt.	0 1 2 3 4
I nearly always see things clearer when alone.	0 1 2 3 4
I understand things best while thinking in private.	0 1 2 3 4
I think it is best to work out hurt feelings alone.	0 1 2 3 4
I like trying to see the world through others' eyes.	0 1 2 3 4
I really enjoy hearing other people's insights.	0 1 2 3 4
I enjoy feeling others' intensity in discussions.	0 1 2 3 4
I like sitting alone and watching ordinary things.	0 1 2 3 4
I enjoy solving puzzles and problems by myself.	0 1 2 3 4
I like to just sit alone and feel nothing.	0 1 2 3 4

RatnDef(SensSoc/InsnsAln)+(BC) ......[_][_][_][_][_][_][_][__][__]
                                       z v a k c e N S

DDICAUSE Page 10

Axis 27

I wish I didn't have to see every detail in a thing.	0 1 2 3 4
I can't stop thinking until a thought is finished.	0 1 2 3 4
I have to repeat some actions just so many times.	0 1 2 3 4
I wonder if it could ever be OK to make a mistake.	0 1 2 3 4
I think I'd like to say something less accurately.	0 1 2 3 4
I guess some who make mistakes are doing their best.	0 1 2 3 4
I analyse everything to be sure I see it correctly.	0 1 2 3 4
I try hard to reason things out just right.	0 1 2 3 4
I feel good whenever I do something accurately.	0 1 2 3 4
I am annoyed when I see someone doing a job poorly.	0 1 2 3 4
I am afraid of saying the wrong thing.	0 1 2 3 4
I feel relieved when I avoid making an error.	0 1 2 3 4

OppreInhb(PrcGd/ErrBd)−(BO−C) .....[_][_][_][_][_][_][_][__][__]
$$\quad\quad z \quad v \quad a \quad k \quad c \quad e \quad N \quad S$$

Axis 28

I like it when people analyse situations precisely.	0 1 2 3 4
I approve of a person saying exactly what he means.	0 1 2 3 4
I think well of myself when I do a task accurately.	0 1 2 3 4
I try to see that things run well without mistakes.	0 1 2 3 4
I like trying not to hurt other people's feelings.	0 1 2 3 4
I approve of others' efforts to avoid making errors.	0 1 2 3 4
I feel good when a mistake turns out not to be mine.	0 1 2 3 4
I feel some people deserve to be criticized.	0 1 2 3 4
I enjoy making mistakes when I learn from them.	0 1 2 3 4
I am happy when people fail to see mean intentions.	0 1 2 3 4
I am glad when people fail in trying to hurt others.	0 1 2 3 4
I feel good when someone is too happy to feel hurt.	0 1 2 3 4

CmfrtInhb(PrcGd/ErrBd)+(B+)(27) ....[_][_][_][_][_][_][_][__][__]
$$\quad\quad z \quad v \quad a \quad k \quad c \quad e \quad N \quad S$$

Axis 29

I worry I may blush in a group if I am noticed.	0 1 2 3 4
I think I may lose my thought if talking in a group.	0 1 2 3 4
I sense my hand is trembling noticeably in a group.	0 1 2 3 4
I often imagine myself exposed in a group setting.	0 1 2 3 4
I worry that other people know what I'm thinking.	0 1 2 3 4
I feel others can read my feelings from my actions.	0 1 2 3 4
I can see my body sag weakly when my mood is down.	0 1 2 3 4
My voice sounds weak and whining when I'm depressed.	0 1 2 3 4
I feel unable to cope with things when I'm down.	0 1 2 3 4
I get upsetting pictures in my mind of awful events.	0 1 2 3 4
I think of scary situations at times.	0 1 2 3 4
I sometimes fear I will lose control of myself.	0 1 2 3 4

DistrbAff(AnxMnd/DprBdy)−(AC) ....[_][_][_][_][_][_][_][__][__]

z v a k c e N S

ADDICAUSE Page 11

Axis 30

I keep myself from being blue by being very active.	0 1 2 3 4
I don't get down by telling myself I'm the greatest.	0 1 2 3 4
I make myself feel high instead of being depressed.	0 1 2 3 4
When I feel tired, I make mental pictures of success.	0 1 2 3 4
When I start worrying, I mask my thoughts with talk.	0 1 2 3 4
When I feel scared, I energize myself with activity.	0 1 2 3 4
I replace sad images with excited or happy ones.	0 1 2 3 4
I control unhappy thoughts by actively making plans.	0 1 2 3 4
I keep from feeling sad by distracting myself.	0 1 2 3 4
When excited or uptight, I just crank myself up more.	0 1 2 3 4
When worried, I try to solve complicated problems.	0 1 2 3 4
When I feel scared, I try to increase the sensations.	0 1 2 3 4

AffDen(AvdBdy/ApprMnd)+(JCMa)(M) .[_][_][_][_][_][_][_][__][__]

z v a k c e N S

172

Axis 31

I see others as always putting themselves first.	0 1 2 3 4
I don't appreciate other people's nasty remarks.	0 1 2 3 4
I don't like the way people feel towards each other.	0 1 2 3 4
If you spoil others, they become very self-centred.	0 1 2 3 4
I don't say nice things because others get too vain.	0 1 2 3 4
I am disappointed when people laugh at others.	0 1 2 3 4
I am disgusted when people show off or act vain.	0 1 2 3 4
I get angry when someone criticizes me.	0 1 2 3 4
I get annoyed when someone mimics someone else.	0 1 2 3 4
I hate being made a fool of.	0 1 2 3 4
I get angry when someone puts me down.	0 1 2 3 4
I feel disgusted with some kinds of people.	0 1 2 3 4

DwnOth(DsatsOth/SatsSlf)−(ch)(25) ..[_][_][_][_][_][_][_][__][__]
$\qquad\qquad\qquad$ z v a k c e N S

Axis 32

I find seeing my friends a rewarding experience.	0 1 2 3 4
I get a lot of pleasure talking with friends.	0 1 2 3 4
I feel fulfilled being close to the people I like.	0 1 2 3 4
I find myself picking up the habits of my friends.	0 1 2 3 4
I tend to talk and use the same ideas as my group.	0 1 2 3 4
I seem to like doing the same things my group does.	0 1 2 3 4
When my friends go somewhere, I usually go too.	0 1 2 3 4
I have picked up a lot of the phrases my group uses.	0 1 2 3 4
I have a lot of feelings for and about my friends.	0 1 2 3 4
I get a lot of satisfaction from being in my group.	0 1 2 3 4
I enjoy talking things over with my group.	0 1 2 3 4
I like the feeling of closeness among my friends.	0 1 2 3 4

GrpSats(SatsGrp/Hab)+(SRf)(0210) ...[_][_][_][_][_][_][_][__][__]
$\qquad\qquad\qquad$ z v a k c e N S

ADDICAUSE Page 12

Axis 33

It's hard to get others to see things the right way.	0 1 2 3 4
I think most people are pretty ignorant.	0 1 2 3 4
It's frustrating to try to get others to act right.	0 1 2 3 4
I wish others could be made to see things right.	0 1 2 3 4
I try my best to help others understand my position.	0 1 2 3 4
People must learn the way to act in each situation.	0 1 2 3 4
Some jerks want to change how people see things.	0 1 2 3 4
Some people are always trying to change the rules.	0 1 2 3 4
I don't like people trying to change the way I am.	0 1 2 3 4
It surprises me how right I am in how I see things.	0 1 2 3 4
I am proud that my ideas are fixed and clear.	0 1 2 3 4
I feel good that I act as I have always acted.	0 1 2 3 4

Dgmat(GdPrst/BdChng)−(fCnstrcts) ...[_][_][_][_][_][_][__][__]
z v a k c e N S

Axis 34

Other people all seem to see things the same way.	0 1 2 3 4
You can tell how others will think about anything.	0 1 2 3 4
Other people act like rubber stamps of each other.	0 1 2 3 4
I prefer to see myself as "different" from others.	0 1 2 3 4
My ideas are creative, different, and original.	0 1 2 3 4
I try to have unusual or different experiences.	0 1 2 3 4
Most people lead dull, colourless lives.	0 1 2 3 4
Nothing ordinary is interesting enough.	0 1 2 3 4
I feel sorry for "square" or "straight" people.	0 1 2 3 4
I want to be seen by others as being different.	0 1 2 3 4
My beliefs are different from most people's beliefs.	0 1 2 3 4
I am different from the way others learned to be.	0 1 2 3 4

DiffNd(BdPrst/GdChng)+(F) ....[_][_][_][_][_][_][__][__]
z v a k c e N S

Axis 35

I dislike the way I present myself to others.	0 1 2 3 4
I think I am mostly less a human than I should be.	0 1 2 3 4
I lack self-confidence, and I'm never sure of myself.	0 1 2 3 4
I deserve some of the rotten things in my life.	0 1 2 3 4
I am basically a socially undesirable person.	0 1 2 3 4
I expect to fail in most of the things I try to do.	0 1 2 3 4
I think most other people dislike me and how I am.	0 1 2 3 4
I am a failure in achieving society's standards.	0 1 2 3 4
I am less worthwhile than most other people are.	0 1 2 3 4
I have had bad luck in life and am mostly a nobody.	0 1 2 3 4
I would like to get along much better with others.	0 1 2 3 4
I would like to be a much nicer person than I am.	0 1 2 3 4

SlfDeprc(BdSlf/GdOth)−(S) ....[_][_][_][_][_][_][_][__][__]
z v a k c e N S

ADDICAUSE Page 13

Axis 36

I see myself as a particularly good person.	0 1 2 3 4
I only allow myself to think and say proper things.	0 1 2 3 4
I am careful to behave myself always as I should.	0 1 2 3 4
I don't like people who aren't clean and groomed.	0 1 2 3 4
I disapprove of people using foul language.	0 1 2 3 4
I think it's silly for people to make rude gestures.	0 1 2 3 4
Some people don't know how to sit or walk properly.	0 1 2 3 4
I wish people would try to speak better English.	0 1 2 3 4
People should do as they want others to do for them.	0 1 2 3 4
I feel that I follow the straight and narrow path.	0 1 2 3 4
I understand and obey the spiritual and legal laws.	0 1 2 3 4
I feel that those who find fault with me are wrong.	0 1 2 3 4

RgdMrlsm(GdSlf/BdOth)+(ConvPhVi) .[_][_][_][_][_][_][_][__][__]
z v a k c e N S

Axis 37

There is one kind of alcohol that changes how I act.	0 1 2 3 4
I sometimes get drunk on just a couple of drinks.	0 1 2 3 4
I sometimes go into "blind rages".	0 1 2 3 4
Learning to read was harder for me than other kids.	0 1 2 3 4
Doing arithmetic was harder for me than other kids.	0 1 2 3 4
Sometimes I do things I would never intend to do.	0 1 2 3 4
I sometimes suddenly get depressed for no reason.	0 1 2 3 4
I sometimes "lose control" when I'm drinking.	0 1 2 3 4
I tend to be a binge drinker.	0 1 2 3 4
At times I get an odd feeling – a breeze or smell.	0 1 2 3 4
I sometimes think there must be a devil in me.	0 1 2 3 4
I was told I was very "hyperactive" as a child.	0 1 2 3 4

Paroxys(ImpFclt/PwrImpd)−(N) ....[_][_][_][_][_][_][__][__]
z v a k c e N S

Axis 38

I hate losing my freedom almost most of all.	0 1 2 3 4
I feel too restricted by rules and authorities.	0 1 2 3 4
Above all, I just want to be free to be myself.	0 1 2 3 4
I feel I must always be able to see outside.	0 1 2 3 4
It's hard for me to stop attending to my thoughts.	0 1 2 3 4
I like to break rules just for the fun of it.	0 1 2 3 4
I dislike riding in elevators, subways, or planes.	0 1 2 3 4
Others' criticism feels like it restricts/stops me.	0 1 2 3 4
I feel very uncomfortable in a confined space.	0 1 2 3 4
I'd freak out if trapped under a collapsed building.	0 1 2 3 4
I get very upset if someone disagrees with me.	0 1 2 3 4
I often feel that other people control what I do.	0 1 2 3 4

RegIntol(ImpImpd/PwrFclt)+(K:Cls...[_][_][_][_][_][_][__][__]
z v a k c e N S

ADDICAUSE Page 14

Axis 39

I would like to be by myself and away from people.	0 1 2 3 4
I would like to have a good long time just to sleep.	0 1 2 3 4
I have to make heroic efforts just to survive.	0 1 2 3 4
I need some things so badly I almost can't stand it.	0 1 2 3 4
Just too much is expected of me by others.	0 1 2 3 4
I feel cramps and inner aches much too strongly.	0 1 2 3 4
Things are just too upsetting for me to handle.	0 1 2 3 4
I feel that I have to work much too hard.	0 1 2 3 4
Pain and discomfort get to me too much.	0 1 2 3 4
Mostly I feel just plain weak and tired.	0 1 2 3 4
I feel sickly and unable to get myself going.	0 1 2 3 4
I am tired out and exhausted most of the time.	0 1 2 3 4

EffStr(PwrImpd/ImpFclt)−(ECQ)(66) .[_][_][_][_][_][_][__][__]

z v a k c e N S

Axis 40

I look for ways to use ideas that excite me.	0 1 2 3 4
I enjoy thinking lots about things that interest me.	0 1 2 3 4
I get excited when a task I'm doing interests me.	0 1 2 3 4
I don't let myself see difficulties in my way.	0 1 2 3 4
I stop thoughts that might make me want to give up.	0 1 2 3 4
I won't let myself get hopeless/down about anything.	0 1 2 3 4
I look for and solve barriers that are in my way.	0 1 2 3 4
I consider what others say to adjust my actions.	0 1 2 3 4
I may let myself feel down to enjoy cranking back up.	0 1 2 3 4
I may ignore something just to keep myself on edge.	0 1 2 3 4
I stop thinking about a thing to add to anticipation.	0 1 2 3 4
At times I hold back excitement so it gets stronger.	0 1 2 3 4

PepNd(PwrFclt/lmpInfclt)+(JC) ....[_][_][_][_][_][_][__][__]

z v a k c e N S

Axis 41

Once I see a thing one way, I can't see it another.	0 1 2 3 4
It is hard to change my ideas once they are fixed.	0 1 2 3 4
If people hurt me, I forget any good they did before.	0 1 2 3 4
It's hard to teach this "old dog" new tricks.	0 1 2 3 4
I've learned to be careful from lots of hard knocks.	0 1 2 3 4
I've been "burned" often enough not to trust others.	0 1 2 3 4
For me to warm up, I need to be shown that others care.	0 1 2 3 4
I need a lot of evidence to believe what others say.	0 1 2 3 4
I believe you're either for me or against me.	0 1 2 3 4
I learn for myself. Don't teach me how to do a task.	0 1 2 3 4
Once I have my mind made up, don't try to change it.	0 1 2 3 4
People should leave me alone to do things my way.	0 1 2 3 4

RgdHab(HbtPrst/LrnChng)−(chchr) ….[_][_][_][_][_][_][_][__][__]

        z v a k c e N S

ADDICAUSE Page 15

Axis 42

I am ready to try anything that may be fun.	0 1 2 3 4
I like learning all I can about how others think.	0 1 2 3 4
I want to have every experience possible in my life.	0 1 2 3 4
Others seem to want to restrict themselves narrowly.	0 1 2 3 4
I know the way I think is the best way for me.	0 1 2 3 4
I believe I will always feel much as I do now.	0 1 2 3 4
I want my point of view to keep on growing always.	0 1 2 3 4
I keep hearing about new ways to gain enjoyment.	0 1 2 3 4
I attend to how I feel so I can keep myself happy.	0 1 2 3 4
I make sure others see me as cheerful and lively.	0 1 2 3 4
My conversation is always easy-going and positive.	0 1 2 3 4
I won't allow myself to feel down and blue ever.	0 1 2 3 4

EasGoEnj(LrnChng/Rgdprs)+(MaSHu) .[_][_][_][_][_][_][_][__][__]

         z v a k c e N S

Axis 43

I avoid active exercise whenever possible.	0 1 2 3 4
I stay underweight even though I eat too much.	0 1 2 3 4
I tend mostly to breathe in my chest (not diaphragm).	0 1 2 3 4
My muscles don't seem as strong as they should be.	0 1 2 3 4
I am definitely much overweight or underweight.	0 1 2 3 4
Everything I eat seems to go to fat.	0 1 2 3 4
I drink a lot of fluids all the time.	0 1 2 3 4
I tend to eat until I'm stuffed.	0 1 2 3 4
I average more than two bowel movements a day.	0 1 2 3 4
I am tired out unless I eat a lot.	0 1 2 3 4
I am constantly restless, on edge, and active.	0 1 2 3 4
I need to eat the whole time just to keep going.	0 1 2 3 4

MetabDis(AvdPwr/ApprImp)−(P) ....[_][_][_][_][_][_][_][__][__]
                                      z   v   a   k   c   e   N   S

Axis 44

I intend to live in "the fast lane".	0 1 2 3 4
I enjoy keeping lots of projects going at once.	0 1 2 3 4
I keep myself cranked up and high as I can.	0 1 2 3 4
I dislike seeing life going along slowly.	0 1 2 3 4
I hate it when people can't be quick and decisive.	0 1 2 3 4
I won't be slowed down by anyone if I can help it.	0 1 2 3 4
People are mostly just sheep who will buy anything.	0 1 2 3 4
I'll keep conning others as long as they let me.	0 1 2 3 4
I won't slow down and let someone get ahead of me.	0 1 2 3 4
I'll live fast, die young, and be a handsome corpse.	0 1 2 3 4
I don't mind if my life is short if it's exciting.	0 1 2 3 4
I want power and the feeling power gives me.	0 1 2 3 4

FstLnLv(ApprPwr/AvdImp)+(J) ....[_][_][_][_][_][_][_][__][__]
                                      z   v   a   k   c   e   N   S

ADDICAUSE Page 16

Axis 45

I use two or more spoonfuls of sugar in my coffee.	0 1 2 3 4
I have more than 5 colas or 5 cups of coffee a day.	0 1 2 3 4
Normally, I nearly always go without breakfast.	0 1 2 3 4
I feel "on edge" mid-mornings and mid-afternoons.	0 1 2 3 4
I feel excited or restless after coffee or snacks.	0 1 2 3 4
I tend to eat candies or chocolate to get me going.	0 1 2 3 4
An alcoholic beverage or fruit drink will pep me up.	0 1 2 3 4
I usually wake up in the morning drained and weak.	0 1 2 3 4
I'm often just too tired to be able to work hard.	0 1 2 3 4
I tend to feel down and weak before meals.	0 1 2 3 4
I often feel a gnawing pain in my gut before meals.	0 1 2 3 4
I'm mostly pretty tired and "wiped out".	0 1 2 3 4

Hypoglyc(InsBdy/SensMnd)−(O) ....[_][_][_][_][_][_][__][__]

z v a k c e N S

Axis 46

I probably put more strain on my body than I should.	0 1 2 3 4
I guess my lifestyle demands a lot of my body.	0 1 2 3 4
My body seems to tolerate a lot before it wipes out.	0 1 2 3 4
I can visualize things very well in my imagination.	0 1 2 3 4
I think my mind is particularly sensitive to ideas.	0 1 2 3 4
My feelings are very sensitive and react strongly.	0 1 2 3 4
I often forget about looking after my health.	0 1 2 3 4
I do quite a few things I know are not good for me.	0 1 2 3 4
I guess the things I do put a lot of strain on me.	0 1 2 3 4
I'm likely to get sick in the spring and fall.	0 1 2 3 4
I seem often to get sick when I'm on vacation.	0 1 2 3 4
I have rashes, colds, allergies, or bronchitis a lot.	0 1 2 3 4

AllrgStr(SnsBdy/InsnsMnd)+(Q) ....[_][_][_][_][_][_][__][__]

z v a k c e N S

Axis 47

I'm not sure I could deal well with an emergency.	0 1 2 3 4
I lie awake at night worrying.	0 1 2 3 4
Getting things done often uses up lots of my energy.	0 1 2 3 4
I tend to lose interest in things quite quickly.	0 1 2 3 4
I worry about making an embarrassing social mistake.	0 1 2 3 4
I often wake up with a jolt or a big twitch.	0 1 2 3 4
I can get badly shaken up by troubles I meet.	0 1 2 3 4
I can't remain calm if others don't like me.	0 1 2 3 4
I can't calm down easily if something upsets me.	0 1 2 3 4
I am often restless, twitchy, or uncomfortable.	0 1 2 3 4
I often feel jealous or possessive of those I like.	0 1 2 3 4
I tend to tremble or sweat in certain situations.	0 1 2 3 4

PhysAnx(PwrBdy/ImpMnd)−(CQ) .....[_][_][_][_][_][_][_][__][__]
                  z v a k c e N S

ADDICAUSE Page 17

Axis 48

I have received a lot of punishment in my life.	0 1 2 3 4
I believe that most people I know don't like me.	0 1 2 3 4
I seem to get in situations where I get in trouble.	0 1 2 3 4
I believe that life is pretty punishing.	0 1 2 3 4
Criticism is the main kind of attention others give.	0 1 2 3 4
I just expect to have a hangover after drinking.	0 1 2 3 4
A gift makes me wonder what the giver wants back.	0 1 2 3 4
I guess I learn best if my mistakes are pointed out.	0 1 2 3 4
I often try to find ways to "raise a little hell".	0 1 2 3 4
Parents who shout at kids are giving them attention.	0 1 2 3 4
I wonder if punishment is one sign of parents' love.	0 1 2 3 4
When someone finishes giving me hell, I feel better.	0 1 2 3 4

PunRf(BadLrn/GdRgd)+(I) ....[_][_][_][_][_][_][_][__][__]
                  z v a k c e N S

Axis 49

I always find faults even in very beautiful scenes.	0 1 2 3 4
I never seem to hear music, which is perfect enough.	0 1 2 3 4
I know that strong feelings will lead to pain.	0 1 2 3 4
I find ways to ignore ugliness and confusion.	0 1 2 3 4
I don't pay attention to ugliness and chaos in life.	0 1 2 3 4
I control unpleasant feelings so I don't get upset.	0 1 2 3 4
I feel there is too much that is ugly in life.	0 1 2 3 4
I feel the conflict and demands of others too much.	0 1 2 3 4
I am too sensitive to pain and unpleasant feelings.	0 1 2 3 4
I don't allow myself to get excited by beauty.	0 1 2 3 4
I hold back from getting involved in nice music.	0 1 2 3 4
I keep myself from feeling pain or sorrow too much.	0 1 2 3 4

AffAvdnc(SnsUgl/InsnsBty)−(BL) .....[_][_][_][_][_][_][__][__]
z v a k c e N S

Axis 50

I must be conscious of the world's ugliness too.	0 1 2 3 4
I listen to all music, including the awful stuff.	0 1 2 3 4
I let myself feel pain so I can enjoy pleasure more.	0 1 2 3 4
I suppose I miss much of the beauty of life.	0 1 2 3 4
I prefer listening to noisy and not-beautiful music.	0 1 2 3 4
I don't seem to have many nice, pleasant feelings.	0 1 2 3 4
I feel the beauty of nature too strongly.	0 1 2 3 4
I get too involved in listening to classical music.	0 1 2 3 4
I feel used by others because I care too much.	0 1 2 3 4
I don't care if things look ugly or deformed.	0 1 2 3 4
I'm not bothered by hearing harsh or too loud talk.	0 1 2 3 4
I try to prevent unpleasant and disgusted feelings.	0 1 2 3 4

CntrlSns(SnsBty/InsnsUgl)+(BL) ....[_][_][_][_][_][_][__][__]
z v a k c e N S

ADDICAUSE Page 18

Axis 51

I get really upset when things go wrong.	0 1 2 3 4
I can feel guilt or remorse over just little things.	0 1 2 3 4
I get very upset if I can't do something just right.	0 1 2 3 4
If people are hostile to me, I quickly forgive them.	0 1 2 3 4
People say I am a bit too defensive.	0 1 2 3 4
I don't dare tell people what I really feel.	0 1 2 3 4
I often feel worthless when I'm around other people.	0 1 2 3 4
Personal criticism upsets me greatly.	0 1 2 3 4
I feel I need my friends more than they need me.	0 1 2 3 4
I feel I often look like I'd done something wrong.	0 1 2 3 4
If something is expected of me, I feel I must do it.	0 1 2 3 4
I often feel as though I had done something wrong.	0 1 2 3 4

GuiPrn(PasPwr/ActImp)−(R) ....[_][_][_][_][_][_][__][__]

　　　　　　　　　　　　　　z　v　a　k　c　e　N　S

Axis 52

I will come on strong to anybody who challenges me.	0 1 2 3 4
I am always ready to react to any insult I receive.	0 1 2 3 4
I'm on quite a "short fuse," so don't come on to me.	0 1 2 3 4
I may keep from letting go for a while if I have to.	0 1 2 3 4
I do try to talk some annoyances out first.	0 1 2 3 4
I can stay cool for a while, but it's pretty hard.	0 1 2 3 4
I can see that it is sometimes best to be friendly.	0 1 2 3 4
At first I may give someone time to get it right.	0 1 2 3 4
Sometimes I hold back my anger for a while.	0 1 2 3 4
I can't help it if people do things to make me mad.	0 1 2 3 4
I get angry easily at the things people say.	0 1 2 3 4
Although I may not act it out, I often feel angry.	0 1 2 3 4

AngHst(PwrAct/ImpPas)+(AgT) ....[_][_][_][_][_][_][__][__]

　　　　　　　　　　　　　　z　v　a　k　c　e　N　S

Axis 53

My body keeps being weak and without any energy.	0 1 2 3 4
I think that one of these days, I'll wake up healthy.	0 1 2 3 4
I seem to be waiting a long time to feel better.	0 1 2 3 4
My mind is constantly occupied with my being sick.	0 1 2 3 4
I keep wondering, Why me? when others are healthy.	0 1 2 3 4
I seem totally obsessed with my upset feelings.	0 1 2 3 4
Each day, all I see is a bleak and empty day ahead.	0 1 2 3 4
Every thought leads me back to my unhappy state.	0 1 2 3 4
I keep "taking my emotional pulse" to see how I am.	0 1 2 3 4
Whatever I do, I have too little energy to do it.	0 1 2 3 4
I do what my doctors tell me, but it doesn't help.	0 1 2 3 4
No matter what I try, I just can't get going.	0 1 2 3 4

SomDepr(PasBdy/ActMnd)−(QC) ......[_][_][_][_][_][_][__][__]

z v a k c e N S

ADDICAUSE Page 19

Axis 54

I have tried many things to be attractive to others.	0 1 2 3 4
I tell myself I must find ways to shape up my body.	0 1 2 3 4
I go out with friends a lot to feel people care.	0 1 2 3 4
No matter how I look at it, I can't find solutions.	0 1 2 3 4
Everything I find to do turns out to be impossible.	0 1 2 3 4
I feel I need someone else to tell me what to do.	0 1 2 3 4
I see that others' needs are met, but mine aren't.	0 1 2 3 4
I ask for others' advice, but it doesn't help.	0 1 2 3 4
I feel resentful that others get what they want.	0 1 2 3 4
It's just too hard to diet or exercise to firm up.	0 1 2 3 4
I think others should help me more than they do.	0 1 2 3 4
I feel I can't improve things without lots of push.	0 1 2 3 4

HungHrt(ActMnd/PasBdy)+(Dpnd) ....[_][_][_][_][_][_][__][__]

z v a k c e N S

Axis 55

I used to feel attractive to others, but not now.	0 1 2 3 4
My ideas are not creative or interesting enough now.	0 1 2 3 4
Most things I do seem to fall short of acceptance.	0 1 2 3 4
Most people find ways to be attractive to others.	0 1 2 3 4
Others always have interesting things to talk about.	0 1 2 3 4
Others seem to feel good about themselves.	0 1 2 3 4
Whatever I do to please others, it's never enough.	0 1 2 3 4
I don't seem able to make interesting conversation.	0 1 2 3 4
I can't seem to express my feelings well enough.	0 1 2 3 4
I seem often to lose those I feel close to.	0 1 2 3 4
I can't convince others to stay in close contact.	0 1 2 3 4
People won't try to hang on to good relationships.	0 1 2 3 4

ImpSeEst(Lss0th/GnSlf)−(chL) ....[_][_][_][_][_][_][__][__]

z   v   a   k   c   e   N   S

Axis 56

I like people being nearby even if I don't see them.	0 1 2 3 4
Most of my friends seem to find fault with everyone.	0 1 2 3 4
Most of my friends control their feelings well.	0 1 2 3 4
My friends all like to be the centre of attention.	0 1 2 3 4
It's hard to get a word in edgeways with my friends.	0 1 2 3 4
My friends are nice people, but they are hard to like.	0 1 2 3 4
My friends notice me, but mostly when I'm not there.	0 1 2 3 4
When I'm not present, my group likely talks about me.	0 1 2 3 4
I feel my friends miss me when we're not together.	0 1 2 3 4
I miss my friends when we are away from each other.	0 1 2 3 4
Recalling others' criticism is company when alone.	0 1 2 3 4
I miss my friends even though they often let me down.	0 1 2 3 4

MskdDsappt(Lss0th/GnSlf)+(chB) .....[_][_][_][_][_][_][__][__]

z   v   a   k   c   e   N   S

ADDICAUSE Page 20

Axis 57

Others seem not to want my company.	0 1 2 3 4
Other people don't seem to want to talk to me.	0 1 2 3 4
I feel that other people just don't like me.	0 1 2 3 4
I think it is my fate to be alone mostly.	0 1 2 3 4
I spend a lot of time in my own head, thinking.	0 1 2 3 4
I feel that others want to avoid being with me.	0 1 2 3 4
I'm not sure I enjoy other people's company much.	0 1 2 3 4
I feel most comfortable alone with my thoughts.	0 1 2 3 4
I think I don't like other people very much.	0 1 2 3 4
I notice when others are together, they cut me out.	0 1 2 3 4
I'm usually excluded from others' conversations.	0 1 2 3 4
I feel most rejected by those I most care for.	0 1 2 3 4

Rejectn(SepOth/TogSlf)− ....[_][_][_][_][_][_][__][__]
                          z v a k c e N S

Axis 58

I want to spend time together with other people.	0 1 2 3 4
I want to feel I can communicate with others.	0 1 2 3 4
I try to be with people who are on my wavelength.	0 1 2 3 4
I avoid people who see things differently from me.	0 1 2 3 4
I don't need people who think in strange ways.	0 1 2 3 4
I avoid those who don't feel about things as I do.	0 1 2 3 4
I visualize how to share my ideas with my friends.	0 1 2 3 4
I think things out alone and then tell my friends.	0 1 2 3 4
Even when alone, I still feel I'm with my friends.	0 1 2 3 4
My group has a bond of understanding when apart.	0 1 2 3 4
What I need most is to communicate with others.	0 1 2 3 4
I feel empty when I have nobody to talk with.	0 1 2 3 4

CommNd(TogOth/SepSlf)+.................[_][_][_][_][_][_][__][__]
                          z v a k c e N S

Axis 59

I must have some way to calm my nervous tension.	0 1 2 3 4
I can't take my uptight worrying about the future.	0 1 2 3 4
I'd do anything to settle down my nervousness.	0 1 2 3 4
I'd be happy if I could get rid of my uptightness.	0 1 2 3 4
I can talk comfortably when I stop worrying.	0 1 2 3 4
I enjoy everything when I can relax my nerves.	0 1 2 3 4
I feel good when I can stop things bothering me.	0 1 2 3 4
I can think clearly when I finally stop worrying.	0 1 2 3 4
I am confident when I can calm my nerves down.	0 1 2 3 4
I like how I see things when I get settled down.	0 1 2 3 4
I enjoy calming down and talking more slowly.	0 1 2 3 4
I feel good when I'm calm and less hyper or up.	0 1 2 3 4

CalmNerve(AvdPn/ApprPls)−(Q) ....[_][_][_][_][_][_][__][__]

                                z v a k c e N S

ADDICAUSE Page 21

Axis 60

I look for ways to keep cranked up and going.	0 1 2 3 4
I think I need the buzz I get from some things.	0 1 2 3 4
Nothing can replace the high some things give me.	0 1 2 3 4
I don't like feeling down and like an "underdog".	0 1 2 3 4
I don't like to feel my thoughts running slowly.	0 1 2 3 4
I must avoid feeling old and slowed down.	0 1 2 3 4
I like the lift I get from some substances.	0 1 2 3 4
I like to feel my thoughts are sharp and right on.	0 1 2 3 4
I enjoy getting myself active and excited.	0 1 2 3 4
I can't take it when everything is slow and boring.	0 1 2 3 4
Whatever the cost, I need to feel bright and alive.	0 1 2 3 4
I won't stand feeling down, useless, or a nothing.	0 1 2 3 4

SubsUp(AprUp/AvdDwn)+(L−)..........[_][_][_][_][_][_][__][__]

                                z v a k c e N S

Axis 61

I cannot let myself see myself as a failure.	0 1 2 3 4
I want to put any failures out of my mind.	0 1 2 3 4
I will not let myself feel like a failure.	0 1 2 3 4
I can see myself as a success with a little help.	0 1 2 3 4
I think of successes best when I forget the past.	0 1 2 3 4
When I feel confident, I feel like a real success.	0 1 2 3 4
I want to see myself as not failing at anything.	0 1 2 3 4
It feels good to be able to forget some failures.	0 1 2 3 4
I can't feel that I might fail in a relationship.	0 1 2 3 4
Some things help me see myself as a great success.	0 1 2 3 4
I want ways to help me feel especially successful.	0 1 2 3 4
I need to feel that I am totally successful.	0 1 2 3 4

FrgtFail(LssFai/GnSuc)−(SubNd) ....[_][_][_][_][_][_][__][__]
                          z v a k c e N S

Axis 62

I always seek new and different experiences.	0 1 2 3 4
I think of ways to think of things differently.	0 1 2 3 4
I try to do things to change the ways I feel.	0 1 2 3 4
I look for ways to escape the same old routines.	0 1 2 3 4
I'm sick of the same old familiar lines and talk.	0 1 2 3 4
I try to avoid others' "stuck in the mud" ways.	0 1 2 3 4
I want to see and experience success in my life.	0 1 2 3 4
I want to talk smoothly with the other sex.	0 1 2 3 4
I want to succeed and have more fun in sex.	0 1 2 3 4
I must avoid not being sexually attractive.	0 1 2 3 4
I must avoid turning others off by how I relate.	0 1 2 3 4
I must not fail in enjoying sexual experiences.	0 1 2 3 4

DiffExp(GnSucChg/LssFaiPrs)+(F) ....[_][_][_][_][_][_][__][__]
                          z v a k c e N S

ADDICAUSE Page 22

Axis 63

I could easily be depressed and bored if I tried.	0 1 2 3 4
I could think unpleasant thoughts if I let myself.	0 1 2 3 4
I could feel disgusted and down if I let go.	0 1 2 3 4
I would sit and do nothing if I didn't fight it.	0 1 2 3 4
My mind would go blank if I let it.	0 1 2 3 4
I would feel totally bored if I didn't prevent it.	0 1 2 3 4
I keep myself up and active as much as I can.	0 1 2 3 4
I challenge myself to talk in a lively and up way.	0 1 2 3 4
I keep my feelings cranked up as much as I can.	0 1 2 3 4
I try to avoid slipping back into giving up.	0 1 2 3 4
I keep thinking of ways to churn up excitement.	0 1 2 3 4
I avoid letting myself feel depressed or bored.	0 1 2 3 4

AvdDepr(AvdPas/AppAct)−(LMa) (Na) .[_][_][_][_][_][_][_][__][__]

        z v a k c e N S

Axis 64

I always want to look as confident as possible.	0 1 2 3 4
I enjoy being very assertive in what I say.	0 1 2 3 4
I like to take risks that make me feel daring.	0 1 2 3 4
I avoid letting anyone see me as less than competent.	0 1 2 3 4
I don't want to come on in a weak way to anyone.	0 1 2 3 4
I don't want anyone to think that I am scared.	0 1 2 3 4
I like to build myself up to be superconfident.	0 1 2 3 4
I like to come on strongly and aggressively.	0 1 2 3 4
I like to take any risk to feel extra daring.	0 1 2 3 4
I want to be seen by others as strong and great.	0 1 2 3 4
I want to speak with the voice of authority.	0 1 2 3 4
I want to feel up and on top of the world.	0 1 2 3 4

AssrtConf(AprAct/AvdPas)+(MX) .....[_][_][_][_][_][_][_][__][__]

        z v a k c e N S

Axis 65

Others are apt to come on to attractive people.	0 1 2 3 4
It's hard to say no to someone who is special.	0 1 2 3 4
People with power may take advantage of others.	0 1 2 3 4
I can't help my appearance with my skin blemishes.	0 1 2 3 4
It's odd they don't make clothes I like to fit me.	0 1 2 3 4
But for my weight, I might be quite attractive.	0 1 2 3 4
I don't get too much attention not looking my best.	0 1 2 3 4
Not being at my best saves me a lot of hassles.	0 1 2 3 4
I don't mind the things that spoil my appearance.	0 1 2 3 4
I'd rather not have that "come on" look.	0 1 2 3 4
I prefer it when people don't notice me.	0 1 2 3 4
I feel safer not being too attractive/interesting.	0 1 2 3 4

AvdAttr(AvdBty/AppUgl)−(iVAnorx) .[_][_][_][_][_][_][__][__]

z   v   a   k   c   e   N   S

ADDICAUSE Page 23

Axis 66

I find it hard to get to sleep or stay asleep.	0 1 2 3 4
I can't turn my mind off so I can get to sleep.	0 1 2 3 4
It's hard to find a comfortable sleeping position.	0 1 2 3 4
When lying in bed, I often picture things to do.	0 1 2 3 4
My mind keeps going over past events and plans.	0 1 2 3 4
In bed, my body is restless – not ready for sleep.	0 1 2 3 4
I may have vivid dreams when I go to bed at night.	0 1 2 3 4
I worry that I may not wake up if I go to sleep.	0 1 2 3 4
I'm almost afraid to go to sleep at night.	0 1 2 3 4
I prefer to have a night light on when I'm in bed.	0 1 2 3 4
In bed, I worry I won't be able to fall asleep.	0 1 2 3 4
I'm often awakened by a jolt when falling asleep.	0 1 2 3 4

SlpImp(ImpSlp/FacAwk)−(Slp) ....[_][_][_][_][_][_][__][__]

z   v   a   k   c   e   N   S

190

Axis 67

I try to have many places where I can relax.	0 1 2 3 4
I like to get away from noise often to calm down.	0 1 2 3 4
I try to find peaceful times when I can relax.	0 1 2 3 4
I can unwind and relax myself in several settings.	0 1 2 3 4
I have many ways to talk myself down when uptight.	0 1 2 3 4
I try to calm down when I am tense or "hyper".	0 1 2 3 4
I like to see my body's tension being relieved.	0 1 2 3 4
I enjoy telling myself to calm down when I'm tense.	0 1 2 3 4
I enjoy the feeling of calming tension in my body.	0 1 2 3 4
I like to see myself as comfortable and calm.	0 1 2 3 4
I like to talk calmly and comfortably to others.	0 1 2 3 4
I feel good when I'm all relaxed and comfortable.	0 1 2 3 4

ClmRelNd(FacClm/ImpTns)+(Rel) .....[_][_][_][_][_][_][__][__]
z v a k c e N S

Axis 68

I seek other's help to change how I see life.	0 1 2 3 4
I ask others to help me change my thinking.	0 1 2 3 4
I go where others know how to enjoy life more.	0 1 2 3 4
I can't see things differently by myself.	0 1 2 3 4
I ask others to tell me how to enjoy life better.	0 1 2 3 4
I depend on others to help me feel good.	0 1 2 3 4
I can't find exciting experiences on my own.	0 1 2 3 4
I need to be told how to make my life tolerable.	0 1 2 3 4
I need others to find ways to make my life good.	0 1 2 3 4
Others show me exciting ways to colour up life.	0 1 2 3 4
Others help me find enjoyable ways to have fun.	0 1 2 3 4
I learn from others how to make life feel great.	0 1 2 3 4

SubsDep(PasSlf/ActOth)−(Sub) ....[_][_][_][_][_][_][__][__]
z v a k c e N S

C:____ E:____ V:____ A:____ K:____ S:____ N:____ Z:____

ADDICAUSE Page 24

Instructions: For each kind of potentially addictive substance, please thoughtfully write down what you think were the CAUSES **and** the EFFECTS of using each of the substances listed. "Causes" are WHY you started its use, and "effects" are HOW you felt after use.

1. Foods (e.g., coffee, cola, chocolate, sweets, salty things)

CAUSES:_____

EFFECTS:_____

2. Tobacco (e.g., cigarettes, cigars, pipe, chewing tobacco)

CAUSES:_____

EFFECTS:_____

3. Medications (e.g., tranquillizers, antidepressants, pain meds)

CAUSES: []Prescribed, or_____

EFFECTS:_____

4. Alcohol (e.g., beer, wine, hard liquor, others)

CAUSES:_____

EFFECTS:_____

5. Street Drugs (e.g., pot, hash, LSD, cocaine, heroin, mushrooms)

CAUSES: _____

_____

EFFECTS: _____

_____

ADDICAUSE Page 25

VERY IMPORTANT Instructions: PLEASE read this page carefully and understand HOW to do the ratings requested BEFORE you go on to the last page to complete the ratings. The ratings you make need to communicate information to us, and so it is necessary that some standards be used in how people respond to the next page.

For **ANY** and **EVERY** kind of potentially addictive FOOD, MEDICATION, TOBACCO, ALCOHOL, SOLVENT, STREET DRUG, or other substance you have ever used, please mark (a) the NAME of the substance if it not listed, (b) the LENGTH OF TIME YOU USED IT (in YEARS or MONTHS and circle years or months), (c) HOW STRONG YOUR USE WAS (using the rating method shown below), (d) if you stopped, HOW LONG AGO YOU STOPPED USING it, and (e) HOW STRONGLY YOU WOULD **NOW** LIKE TO USE it while you are here (using the same rating method shown below). Just check the N/A box if you NEVER used the named substance.

PLEASE read the instructions for the rating method which follow.

RATINGS: HOW TO ESTIMATE "STRENGTH OF USE" and "PRESENT WANT":

Step **A**: First, we have to define "**ONE USE**" (whether actually used in the past or wanting use now): "**ONE USE**" is defined as **every time** you use a substance (1 to 3 of anything in a row or on one occasion) is "**ONE USE**". (Examples of **ONE USE** might include

193

one to three glasses of wine with a meal or one to three cigarettes in a row or one hit of a drug or one to three pills popped at a time or one to three shots of hard liquor in a row or one or two beers or one can/bottle of cola or one to two cups of coffee at a time or one fill of a pipe or one session of gas or glue sniffing.)

Step **B**: Now, using the above definition of "ONE USE," please rate your **STRENGTH** of **either** past **USE or** present **WANT** for each type of substance, estimated from the following table:

0 = None or No Use or Want = Up to **less than 1 use** per month

1 = Slight Use or Want = from **1** to **less than 2 uses** a month.

2 = Some Use/Want = **2 uses** a month to **less than 1 use** a day.

3 = Considerable Use/Want = **1 use** to **less than 5 uses** a day.

4 = **B** = Binging = any **"binge" use**.

5 = Heavy Use/Want = **5 uses** to **less than 10 uses** a day.

6 = Very Heavy Use/Want = **10 uses** to **less than 15 uses** a day.

7 = Extreme Use/Want = anything **above 15 uses** per day.

PLEASE USE THE ABOVE RATING METHOD TO COMPLETE THE NEXT PAGE.

Kind of Substances		Indicate Years or Months	Use the Above Rating Scale	Indicate Years or Months	Use the Above Rating Scale
		How Long Used	How Strong/ Heavy	Months Off	How Strong Want Now
FOODSTUFFS	N/A	(Never Used Except in Moderation)			
Overeating	N/A	___ Years/Mths	0 1 2 3 B 5 6 7	___ Years/Mths	0 1 2 3 B 5 6 7
Coffee	N/A	___ Years/Mths	0 1 2 3 B 5 6 7	___ Years/Mths	0 1 2 3 B 5 6 7
Cola	N/A	___ Years/Mths	0 1 2 3 B 5 6 7	___ Years/Mths	0 1 2 3 B 5 6 7
Chocolate	N/A	___ Years/Mths	0 1 2 3 B 5 6 7	___ Years/Mths	0 1 2 3 B 5 6 7
Chips/Nuts	N/A	___ Years/Mths	0 1 2 3 B 5 6 7	___ Years/Mths	0 1 2 3 B 5 6 7
TOBACCO	N/A	(Never Used Any At All)			
Cigarettes	N/A	___ Years/Mths	0 1 2 3 B 5 6 7	___ Years/Mths	0 1 2 3 B 5 6 7
Pipe/Cigar	N/A	___ Years/Mths	0 1 2 3 B 5 6 7	___ Years/Mths	0 1 2 3 B 5 6 7
Chewing Tobacco	N/A	___ Years/Mths	0 1 2 3 B 5 6 7	___ Years/Mths	0 1 2 3 B 5 6 7
MEDICATION	N/A	(Never Used Any At All)			
Valium	N/A	___ Years/Mths	0 1 2 3 B 5 6 7	___ Years/Mths	0 1 2 3 B 5 6 7

194

Tranquilizers	N/A	___ Years/Mths	0 1 2 3 B 5 6 7	___ Years/Mths	0 1 2 3 B 5 6 7
Narcotics	N/A	___ Years/Mths	0 1 2 3 B 5 6 7	___ Years/Mths	0 1 2 3 B 5 6 7
Barbiturates	N/A	___ Years/Mths	0 1 2 3 B 5 6 7	___ Years/Mths	0 1 2 3 B 5 6 7
Downers	N/A	___ Years/Mths	0 1 2 3 B 5 6 7	___ Years/Mths	0 1 2 3 B 5 6 7
Uppers	N/A	___ Years/Mths	0 1 2 3 B 5 6 7	___ Years/Mths	0 1 2 3 B 5 6 7
Ritalin	N/A	___ Years/Mths	0 1 2 3 B 5 6 7	___ Years/Mths	0 1 2 3 B 5 6 7
Pain Meds	N/A	___ Years/Mths	0 1 2 3 B 5 6 7	___ Years/Mths	0 1 2 3 B 5 6 7
Seltzers	N/A	___ Years/Mths	0 1 2 3 B 5 6 7	___ Years/Mths	0 1 2 3 B 5 6 7
Antibiotics	N/A	___ Years/Mths	0 1 2 3 B 5 6 7	___ Years/Mths	0 1 2 3 B 5 6 7
ALCOHOL	N/A	(Never Used Any At All)			
Beer/Ale	N/A	___ Years/Mths	0 1 2 3 B 5 6 7	___ Years/Mths	0 1 2 3 B 5 6 7
Rum	N/A	___ Years/Mths	0 1 2 3 B 5 6 7	___ Years/Mths	0 1 2 3 B 5 6 7
Rye	N/A	___ Years/Mths	0 1 2 3 B 5 6 7	___ Years/Mths	0 1 2 3 B 5 6 7
Gin/Vodka	N/A	___ Years/Mths	0 1 2 3 B 5 6 7	___ Years/Mths	0 1 2 3 B 5 6 7
Scotch	N/A	___ Years/Mths	0 1 2 3 B 5 6 7	___ Years/Mths	0 1 2 3 B 5 6 7
Home Brew	N/A	___ Years/Mths	0 1 2 3 B 5 6 7	___ Years/Mths	0 1 2 3 B 5 6 7
Brandy	N/A	___ Years/Mths	0 1 2 3 B 5 6 7	___ Years/Mths	0 1 2 3 B 5 6 7
Wine	N/A	___ Years/Mths	0 1 2 3 B 5 6 7	___ Years/Mths	0 1 2 3 B 5 6 7
Solvents	N/A	___ Years/Mths	0 1 2 3 B 5 6 7	___ Years/Mths	0 1 2 3 B 5 6 7
Other	N/A	___ Years/Mths	0 1 2 3 B 5 6 7	___ Years/Mths	0 1 2 3 B 5 6 7
DRUGS	N/A	(Never Used Any At All)			
Marijuana	N/A	___ Years/Mths	0 1 2 3 B 5 6 7	___ Years/Mths	0 1 2 3 B 5 6 7
Hashish	N/A	___ Years/Mths	0 1 2 3 B 5 6 7	___ Years/Mths	0 1 2 3 B 5 6 7
Opium	N/A	___ Years/Mths	0 1 2 3 B 5 6 7	___ Years/Mths	0 1 2 3 B 5 6 7
Mushrooms	N/A	___ Years/Mths	0 1 2 3 B 5 6 7	___ Years/Mths	0 1 2 3 B 5 6 7
Peyote	N/A	___ Years/Mths	0 1 2 3 B 5 6 7	___ Years/Mths	0 1 2 3 B 5 6 7
PCP	N/A	___ Years/Mths	0 1 2 3 B 5 6 7	___ Years/Mths	0 1 2 3 B 5 6 7
Heroin	N/A	___ Years/Mths	0 1 2 3 B 5 6 7	___ Years/Mths	0 1 2 3 B 5 6 7
Morphine	N/A	___ Years/Mths	0 1 2 3 B 5 6 7	___ Years/Mths	0 1 2 3 B 5 6 7
LSD	N/A	___ Years/Mths	0 1 2 3 B 5 6 7	___ Years/Mths	0 1 2 3 B 5 6 7
Speed	N/A	___ Years/Mths	0 1 2 3 B 5 6 7	___ Years/Mths	0 1 2 3 B 5 6 7
Cocaine	N/A	___ Years/Mths	0 1 2 3 B 5 6 7	___ Years/Mths	0 1 2 3 B 5 6 7
Crack	N/A	___ Years/Mths	0 1 2 3 B 5 6 7	___ Years/Mths	0 1 2 3 B 5 6 7
Other	N/A	___ Years/Mths	0 1 2 3 B 5 6 7	___ Years/Mths	0 1 2 3 B 5 6 7
SOLVENTS	N/A	(Never Used Any At All)			
Gasoline	N/A	___ Years/Mths	0 1 2 3 B 5 6 7	___ Years/Mths	0 1 2 3 B 5 6 7
Glue	N/A	___ Years/Mths	0 1 2 3 B 5 6 7	___ Years/Mths	0 1 2 3 B 5 6 7
Other	N/A	___ Years/Mths	0 1 2 3 B 5 6 7	___ Years/Mths	0 1 2 3 B 5 6 7

APPENDIX B

Addicause Short Form

<u>**DIMENSIONAL ADDICAUSE QUESTIONNAIRE (DAQsf)**</u> **NA ME:**_____

<u>Instructions</u>: There are several parts to this questionnaire. Each part is as necessary as every other. Some of the questions refer to use of addictive substances. If you have <u>never</u> used that kind of substance, just circle 0 or check the N/A box (meaning: does Not Apply to me at all). Please answer <u>every</u> question, giving each one a little thought. If you have any trouble understanding the words, please ask someone for help. Take as long as it takes to do the questionnaire. PLEASE ANSWER EACH QUESTION AS YOU FEEL **<u>NOW</u>**.

<u>Please circle the number for each statement which most nearly applies to you</u> **<u>NOW</u>**. <u>The numbers mean:</u>

    0 = "false", "no", "not now", "doesn't apply to me at all"
    1 = "maybe", "occasionally", "once in a while", "sometimes"
    2 = "perhaps", "about as often as not", "an average amount"
    3 = "probably", "I guess so", "most often", "more than not"
    4 = "true", "yes", "definitely", "sure do", "nearly always"

Axis 02

I avoid intimate groups when I can be in large groups.	0 1 2 3 4
I avoid being alone as much as possible.	0 1 2 3 4
I try to avoid working at tasks I have to do alone.	0 1 2 3 4
I seek the excitement and fun of being with others.	0 1 2 3 4
I spend as much time as I can talking with others.	0 1 2 3 4
I feel most comfortable when I am part of a group.	0 1 2 3 4
I keep from feeling isolated as much as I can.	0 1 2 3 4
I am bored or irritable when I am by myself.	0 1 2 3 4
I feel a sense of emptiness when I am alone.	0 1 2 3 4
I enjoy seeing friends and going to parties.	0 1 2 3 4
I am most at ease when I am talking with friends.	0 1 2 3 4
I feel least uptight when I am doing social things.	0 1 2 3 4

SocEnj[ApprSoc/AvdSlf]+ ....[_][_][_][_][_][_][__][__]
                                    z v k c e N S

Axis 03

I give up when too many changes are happening at once.	0 1 2 3 4
I tune out when too much is going on around me.	0 1 2 3 4
I sometimes feel like there's a fist in my stomach.	0 1 2 3 4
I try to cope when things look reasonably organized.	0 1 2 3 4
I spend time with friends when I am fairly calm.	0 1 2 3 4
I cling on to friends when my life runs smoothly.	0 1 2 3 4
I feel down even when my world looks organized.	0 1 2 3 4
I feel hurt by others even if they say they like me.	0 1 2 3 4
I can't cope well even if things are going OK.	0 1 2 3 4
I try to lift my spirits when I feel I can't cope.	0 1 2 3 4
I seek help when I have too many problems to face.	0 1 2 3 4
I try to find relief when I have too much stress.	0 1 2 3 4

RctDpr[PasDsIn/ActInt]− ....[_][_][_][_][_][_][__][__]
                                    z v k c e N S

ADDICAUSE Page 2

Axis 08

My family disapproves of using alcohol or drugs.	0 1 2 3 4
Most people disapprove of alcohol and drug use.	0 1 2 3 4
I feel a bit guilty when I use alcohol or drugs.	0 1 2 3 4
I often see others as viewing what I do as shameful.	0 1 2 3 4
People often want me to take the blame for things.	0 1 2 3 4
I often feel guilty even when I have done no wrong.	0 1 2 3 4
I feel there are far too many rules to follow.	0 1 2 3 4
I hate having to do what others tell me to do.	0 1 2 3 4
I feel that rules are just made to be broken.	0 1 2 3 4
I often show I disapprove of others' disapproval of me.	0 1 2 3 4
I often want to find ways to "stick it" to others.	0 1 2 3 4
I enjoy being a rebel.	0 1 2 3 4

GuiIntl[AvdPas/ApprAct]+ ....[_][_][_][_][_][_][__][__]

                                   z v a k c e N S

Axis 10

I get out with other people as much as I can.	0 1 2 3 4
I try to spend lots of time talking with other people.	0 1 2 3 4
I feel the need to be close to other people.	0 1 2 3 4
I picture myself participating in group activities.	0 1 2 3 4
When alone, I think about what I can say to others.	0 1 2 3 4
I let myself feel lonely to help me want company.	0 1 2 3 4
When alone, I watch TV to see ways people relate.	0 1 2 3 4
I think a lot about how to get along with others.	0 1 2 3 4
I spend time alone to recharge for social contacts.	0 1 2 3 4
I watch groups to see how others relate together.	0 1 2 3 4
I listen to conversations to learn about people.	0 1 2 3 4
I feel the need to be part of a group of friends.	0 1 2 3 4

SocCntct[ActSoc/PasAln]+ ....[_][_][_][_][_][_][__][__]

                                   z v a k c e N S

Axis 12

It annoys me to have to deal with the authorities.	0 1 2 3 4
I hate being given orders by anyone.	0 1 2 3 4
I think people older than me are mostly strange.	0 1 2 3 4
I keep others from seeing when I am scared.	0 1 2 3 4
I think of myself as something of a rebel.	0 1 2 3 4
I put up a "tough" front for other people.	0 1 2 3 4
In stores I always notice the surveillance devices.	0 1 2 3 4
I feel angry at people who try to act "too good".	0 1 2 3 4
I feel as though I have had a "raw deal" in life.	0 1 2 3 4
I hate rules and regulations.	0 1 2 3 4
I feel I am criticized too much by others.	0 1 2 3 4
I dislike having to pay sales tax on anything.	0 1 2 3 4

AuthReb[AprUnr/AvdReal]+ ....[_][_][_][_][_][_][__][__]

                    z v a k c e N S

ADDICAUSE Page 3

Axis 13

Picturing the uncertain future just makes me scared.	0 1 2 3 4
Even with planning, you never know what will happen.	0 1 2 3 4
If I was sure of the future, I would be disappointed.	0 1 2 3 4
When I picture the past, I become weak and depressed.	0 1 2 3 4
I never amounted to much, so there's no hope I will.	0 1 2 3 4
I feel my past left me empty and joyless.	0 1 2 3 4
The future looks just as empty and flat as the past.	0 1 2 3 4
I think life is good only in an imagined future.	0 1 2 3 4
I feel afraid that life will continue as it was.	0 1 2 3 4
Every picture of my past is upsetting or saddening.	0 1 2 3 4
In the past, I can only find rotten memories.	0 1 2 3 4
My life feels like a joyless, empty vacuum.	0 1 2 3 4

FltDpr[ImpFrwd/PwrBck]− ....[_][_][_][_][_][_][__][__]

                    z v a k c e N   S

Axis <u>20</u>

I picture lots of fun situations to get involved in.	0 1 2 3 4
I enjoy talking and laughing a lot with my friends.	0 1 2 3 4
All sorts of things get me excited.	0 1 2 3 4
I can get along OK in almost any situation or setting.	0 1 2 3 4
What other people say doesn't upset me or "get to me".	0 1 2 3 4
The minor injuries and pain I get don't trouble me.	0 1 2 3 4
There are very few situations that bother me.	0 1 2 3 4
Nobody succeeds in conning me or pushing me around.	0 1 2 3 4
I can enjoy activities even when I have been injured.	0 1 2 3 4
The main thing in life is to have a good time.	0 1 2 3 4
I like conning or teasing those of the opposite sex.	0 1 2 3 4
I'm always looking for exciting things to do.	0 1 2 3 4

Hedon[SensPls/InsnsPn]+ ....[_][_][_][_][_][_][__][__]

z v a k c e N S

Axis <u>22</u>

I like hanging around with the guys in the bar or pub.	0 1 2 3 4
Shooting the bull is a favourite pastime of mine.	0 1 2 3 4
I really like backslapping fun with the guys.	0 1 2 3 4
Most people spend a lot of time drinking in bars.	0 1 2 3 4
I am proud of how much alcohol and/or drugs I use.	0 1 2 3 4
Most people use drugs and/or alcohol.	0 1 2 3 4
I think what happens in life is a matter of your luck.	0 1 2 3 4
I think we need unions to protect workers.	0 1 2 3 4
I'm an easy-going person, just out for a good time.	0 1 2 3 4
It feels good to drink someone "under the table".	0 1 2 3 4
Telling jokes is the best kind of conversation.	0 1 2 3 4
I am proud of the amount of booze I can drink.	0 1 2 3 4

SubClt[GdSoc/BdAln]+ ....[_][_][_][_][_][_][__][__]

z v a k c e N S

ADDICAUSE Page 4

Axis 24

I believe anybody can influence what happens.	0 1 2 3 4
I think that anybody's ideas contribute to any outcome.	0 1 2 3 4
I feel heroes are ordinary people facing challenges.	0 1 2 3 4
I view hanging on to a dream as one way to success.	0 1 2 3 4
I think nothing lasts through time like an idea.	0 1 2 3 4
I feel that sticking to a task is the way to win.	0 1 2 3 4
I see lots in my life that I could usefully change.	0 1 2 3 4
I can think of many ways to improve my joy in life.	0 1 2 3 4
I am comfortable with my ability to change my life.	0 1 2 3 4
I can live quite happily with things I can't change.	0 1 2 3 4
I can make friends and enjoy them as well as anyone.	0 1 2 3 4
I feel happy and content in spite of my limitations.	0 1 2 3 4

PIG/Resil[PwrChg/ImpPrs]+ ....[_][_][_][_][_][_][__][__]

z v a k c e N S

Axis 30

I keep myself from being blue by being very active.	0 1 2 3 4
I don't get down by telling myself I'm the greatest.	0 1 2 3 4
I make myself feel high instead of being depressed.	0 1 2 3 4
When I feel tired, I make mental pictures of success.	0 1 2 3 4
When I start worrying, I mask my thoughts with talk.	0 1 2 3 4
When I feel scared, I energize myself with activity.	0 1 2 3 4
I replace sad images with excited or happy ones.	0 1 2 3 4
I control unhappy thoughts by actively making plans.	0 1 2 3 4
I keep from feeling sad by distracting myself.	0 1 2 3 4
When excited or uptight, I just crank myself up more.	0 1 2 3 4
When worried, I try to solve complicated problems.	0 1 2 3 4
When I feel scared, I try to increase the sensations.	0 1 2 3 4

AffDen[AvdBdy/ApprMnd]+ ....[_][_][_][_][_][_][__][__]

z v a k c e N S

Axis <u>34</u>

Other people all seem to see things the same way.	0 1 2 3 4
You can tell how others will think about anything.	0 1 2 3 4
Other people act like rubber stamps of each other.	0 1 2 3 4
I prefer to see myself as "different" from others.	0 1 2 3 4
My ideas are creative, different, and original.	0 1 2 3 4
I try to have different or unusual experiences.	0 1 2 3 4
Most people lead dull, colourless lives.	0 1 2 3 4
Nothing ordinary is interesting enough.	0 1 2 3 4
I feel sorry for "square" or "straight" people.	0 1 2 3 4
I want to be seen by others as being different.	0 1 2 3 4
My beliefs are different from most people's beliefs.	0 1 2 3 4
I am different from the way others learned to be.	0 1 2 3 4

DiffNd[BdPrst/GdChng]+ ....[_][_][_][_][_][_][__][__]

z v a k c e N S

ADDICAUSE Page 5

Axis <u>36</u>

I see myself as a particularly good person.	0 1 2 3 4
I only allow myself to think and say proper things.	0 1 2 3 4
I am careful to behave myself always as I should.	0 1 2 3 4
I don't like people who are not clean and groomed.	0 1 2 3 4
I disapprove of people using foul language.	0 1 2 3 4
I think it's silly for people to use rude gestures.	0 1 2 3 4
Some people don't know how to sit or walk properly.	0 1 2 3 4
I wish people would try to speak better English.	0 1 2 3 4
People should do as they want others to do for them.	0 1 2 3 4
I feel that I follow the straight and narrow path.	0 1 2 3 4
I understand and obey the spiritual and legal laws.	0 1 2 3 4
I feel that those who find fault with me are wrong.	0 1 2 3 4

RgdMrls[GdSlf/BdOth]+ ....[_][_][_][_][_][_][__][__]

z v a k c e N S

Axis <u>37</u>

There is one kind of alcohol that changes how I act.	0 1 2 3 4
I sometimes get drunk on just a couple of drinks.	0 1 2 3 4
I sometimes go into uncontrolled "blind rages".	0 1 2 3 4
Learning to read was harder for me than for other kids.	0 1 2 3 4
Doing arithmetic was harder for me than for other kids.	0 1 2 3 4
Sometimes I do things I would never intend to do.	0 1 2 3 4
I sometimes suddenly get depressed for no reason.	0 1 2 3 4
I sometimes "lose control" when I'm drinking.	0 1 2 3 4
I tend to be a binge drinker.	0 1 2 3 4
At times I get an odd feeling – a breeze or a smell.	0 1 2 3 4
I sometimes think there must be a devil in me.	0 1 2 3 4
I was told I was very "hyperactive" as a child.	0 1 2 3 4

Paroxys[ImpFclt/PwrImpd]− ....[_][_][_][_][_][_][__][__]

z v a k c e N S

Axis <u>40</u>

I look for ways to use ideas that excite me.	0 1 2 3 4
I enjoy thinking lots about things that interest me.	0 1 2 3 4
I get excited when a task I'm doing interests me.	0 1 2 3 4
I don't let myself see difficulties in my way.	0 1 2 3 4
I stop thoughts that might make me want to give up.	0 1 2 3 4
I won't let myself get hopeless or down about anything.	0 1 2 3 4
I look for and solve barriers that are in my way.	0 1 2 3 4
I consider what others say so I can adjust my actions.	0 1 2 3 4
I may let myself feel down to enjoy cranking back up.	0 1 2 3 4
I may ignore something just to keep myself on edge.	0 1 2 3 4
I stop thinking about a thing to add to anticipation.	0 1 2 3 4
At times I hold back excitement so it gets stronger.	0 1 2 3 4

PepUp[PwrFclt/ImpInfclt]+ ....[_][_][_][_][_][_][__][__]

z v a k c e N S

204

ADDICAUSE Page 6

Axis 44

I intend to live in "the fast lane".	0 1 2 3 4
I enjoy keeping lots of projects going at once.	0 1 2 3 4
I keep myself cranked up and as high as I can.	0 1 2 3 4
I dislike seeing life going along slowly.	0 1 2 3 4
I hate it when people can't be quick and decisive.	0 1 2 3 4
I won't be slowed down by anyone if I can help it.	0 1 2 3 4
People are mostly like sheep. They will buy anything.	0 1 2 3 4
I will keep conning others as long as they let me.	0 1 2 3 4
I won't slow down and let somebody get ahead of me.	0 1 2 3 4
I'll live fast, die young, and be an attractive corpse.	0 1 2 3 4
I don't mind if my life is short if it's exciting.	0 1 2 3 4
I want power and the feeling power gives me.	0 1 2 3 4

FstLnLv[ApprPwr/AvdImp]+ ....[_][_][_][_][_][_][__][__]

z v a k c e N S

Axis 46

I probably put more strain on my body than I should.	0 1 2 3 4
I guess my lifestyle demands a lot of my body.	0 1 2 3 4
My body seems to tolerate a lot before it wipes out.	0 1 2 3 4
I can visualize things very well in my imagination.	0 1 2 3 4
I think my mind is particularly sensitive to ideas.	0 1 2 3 4
My feelings are very sensitive and react strongly.	0 1 2 3 4
I often forget about looking after my health.	0 1 2 3 4
I do quite a few things I know are not good for me.	0 1 2 3 4
I guess the things I do put a lot of strain on me.	0 1 2 3 4
I'm likely to get sick in the spring and fall.	0 1 2 3 4
I seem often to get sick when I'm on vacation.	0 1 2 3 4
I have skin rashes, colds, allergies, or bronchitis.	0 1 2 3 4

AllrgStr[SnsBdy/InsnMnd]+ ....[_][_][_][_][_][_][__][__]

z v a k c e N S

Axis 47

I'm not sure I could deal well with an emergency.	0 1 2 3 4
I lie awake at night worrying.	0 1 2 3 4
Getting things done often uses up most of my energy.	0 1 2 3 4
I tend to lose interest in things quite quickly.	0 1 2 3 4
I worry about making an embarrassing social mistake.	0 1 2 3 4
I often wake up with a jolt or a big twitch.	0 1 2 3 4
I can get badly shaken up by the troubles I meet.	0 1 2 3 4
I can't remain calm if others don't like me.	0 1 2 3 4
I can't calm down easily if something upsets me.	0 1 2 3 4
I am often restless, twitchy, or uncomfortable.	0 1 2 3 4
I often feel jealous or possessive of people I like.	0 1 2 3 4
I tend to tremble or sweat in certain situations.	0 1 2 3 4

PhysAnx[PwrBdy/ImpMnd]− ....[_][_][_][_][_][_][__][__]
z v a k c e N S

ADDICAUSE Page 7

Axis 48

I've received a lot of punishment or abuse in my life.	0 1 2 3 4
I believe that most people I know don't like me.	0 1 2 3 4
I seem to get in situations where I get into trouble.	0 1 2 3 4
I believe that life is pretty punishing.	0 1 2 3 4
Criticism is the main kind of attention others give.	0 1 2 3 4
I just expect to have a hangover after drinking.	0 1 2 3 4
A gift makes me wonder what the giver wants back.	0 1 2 3 4
I guess I learn best if my mistakes are pointed out.	0 1 2 3 4
I often try to find ways to "raise a little hell".	0 1 2 3 4
Parents who shout at kids are giving them attention.	0 1 2 3 4
I wonder if punishment is one sign of parents' love.	0 1 2 3 4
When someone finishes giving me hell, I feel better.	0 1 2 3 4

PunRf[BdLrn/GdRgd]+ ....[_][_][_][_][_][_][__][__]
z v a k c e N S

Axis 53

My body has been feeling weak and without energy.	0 1 2 3 4
I think that one of these days, I may wake up healthy.	0 1 2 3 4
I seem to have waited a long time to feel better.	0 1 2 3 4
My mind is constantly occupied with my being sick.	0 1 2 3 4
I keep wondering, Why me? when others are healthy.	0 1 2 3 4
I seem totally obsessed with my upset feelings.	0 1 2 3 4
Each day, all I see is a bleak and empty day ahead.	0 1 2 3 4
Every thought leads me back to my unhappy state.	0 1 2 3 4
I keep "taking my emotional pulse" to check how I feel.	0 1 2 3 4
Whatever I do, I have too little energy to do it.	0 1 2 3 4
I do what my doctors tell me, but it doesn't help.	0 1 2 3 4
No matter what I try, I just can't get going.	0 1 2 3 4

SomDpr[PasBdy/ActMnd]− ....[_][_][_][_][_][_][__][__]
                                                z v a k c e N S

Axis 60

I look for ways to keep cranked up and going.	0 1 2 3 4
I think I need the rush I get from some things.	0 1 2 3 4
Nothing can replace the high some things give me.	0 1 2 3 4
I don't like feeling down and like an "underdog".	0 1 2 3 4
I don't like to feel my thoughts running slowly.	0 1 2 3 4
I must avoid feeling old and slowed down.	0 1 2 3 4
I want the lift I get from some substances.	0 1 2 3 4
I like to feel my thoughts are sharp and "right on".	0 1 2 3 4
I enjoy getting myself active and excited.	0 1 2 3 4
I can't take it if everything is slow and boring.	0 1 2 3 4
Whatever the cost, I need to feel bright and alive.	0 1 2 3 4
I won't stand feeling down, useless, or a nothing.	0 1 2 3 4

SubsUp[ApprUp/AvdDwn]+ ....[_][_][_][_][_][_][__][__]
                                                z v a k c e N S

Instructions: For each kind of potentially addictive substance, please thoughtfully write down what you think were the CAUSES **and** the EFFECTS of using each of the substances listed. "Causes" are WHY you started its use, and "effects" are HOW you felt after use.

1. **Foods** (e.g., coffee, cola, chocolate, sweets, salty things)

CAUSES:_____

EFFECTS:_____

2. **Tobacco** (e.g., cigarettes, cigars, pipe, chewing tobacco)

CAUSES:_____

EFFECTS:_____

3. **Medications** (e.g., tranquillizers, antidepressants, pain meds)

CAUSES: []Prescribed, or_____

EFFECTS:_____

4. **Alcohol** (e.g., beer, wine, hard liquor, others)

CAUSES:_____

EFFECTS:_____

5. **Street Drugs** (e.g., pot, hash, LSD, cocaine, heroin, mushrooms)

CAUSES:_____

_____

EFFECTS:_____

_____

ADDICAUSE Page 9

VERY IMPORTANT Instructions: PLEASE read this page carefully and understand HOW to do the ratings requested BEFORE you go on to the last page to complete the ratings. The ratings you make need to communicate information to us, and so it is necessary that some standards be used in how people respond to the next page.

For **ANY** and **EVERY** kind of potentially addictive FOOD, MEDICATION, TOBACCO, ALCOHOL, SOLVENT, STREET DRUG, or other substance you have ever used, please mark (a) the NAME of the substance if it not listed, (b) the LENGTH OF TIME YOU USED IT (in YEARS or MONTHS and circle years or months), (c) HOW STRONG YOUR USE WAS (using the rating method shown below), (d) if you stopped, HOW LONG AGO YOU STOPPED USING it, and (e) HOW STRONGLY YOU WOULD NOW LIKE TO USE it while you are here (using the same rating method shown below). Just check the N/A box if you NEVER used the named substance.

PLEASE read the instructions for the rating method which follow.

RATINGS: **HOW TO ESTIMATE "STRENGTH OF USE" and PRESENT WANT"**

Step **A**: First, we have to define "**ONE USE**" (whether actually used in the past or wanting use now): "**ONE USE**" is defined as **every time** you use a substance (1 to 3 of anything in a row or on one occasion) is "**ONE USE**". (Examples of **ONE USE** might include

one to three glasses of wine with a meal <u>or</u> one to three cigarettes in a row <u>or</u> one hit of a drug <u>or</u> one to three pills popped at a time <u>or</u> one to three shots of hard liquor in a row <u>or</u> one or two beers <u>or</u> one can/bottle of cola <u>or</u> one to two cups of coffee at a time <u>or</u> one fill of a pipe <u>or</u> one session of gas or glue sniffing.)

<u>Step **B**</u>: Now, <u>using the above definition of "ONE USE"</u>, please rate your **<u>STRENGTH</u>** of **<u>either</u>** <u>past</u> **<u>USE</u>** **<u>or</u>** <u>present</u> **WANT** for <u>each</u> type of substance, estimated from the following table:

0 = None or No Use or Want = <u>Up to</u> **less than 1 use** <u>per month</u>.

1 = Slight Use or Want = <u>from **1** to</u> **less than 2 uses** <u>a month</u>.

2 = Some Use/Want = **2 uses** <u>a month to</u> **less than 1 use** <u>a day</u>.

3 = Considerable Use/Want = **1 use** <u>to</u> **less than 5 uses** <u>a day</u>.

4 = **B** = Binging = <u>any</u> **"binge" use**.

5 = Heavy Use/Want = **5 uses** <u>to</u> **less than 10 uses** <u>a day</u>.

6 = Very Heavy Use/Want = **10 uses** <u>to</u> **less than 15 uses** <u>a day</u>.

7 = Extreme Use/Want = <u>anything</u> **above 15 uses** <u>per day</u>.

<u>PLEASE USE THE ABOVE RATING METHOD TO COMPLETE THE NEXT PAGE</u>.

		Indicate Years or Months	Use the Above Rating Scale	Indicate Years or Months	Use the Above Rating Scale
Kind of Substances		How Long Used	How Strong/ Heavy	Months Off	How Strong Want Now
FOODSTUFFS	N/A	(Never Used Except in Moderation)			
Overeating	N/A	____ Years/Mths	0 1 2 3 B 5 6 7	____ Years/Mths	0 1 2 3 B 5 6 7
Coffee	N/A	____ Years/Mths	0 1 2 3 B 5 6 7	____ Years/Mths	0 1 2 3 B 5 6 7
Cola	N/A	____ Years/Mths	0 1 2 3 B 5 6 7	____ Years/Mths	0 1 2 3 B 5 6 7
Chocolate	N/A	____ Years/Mths	0 1 2 3 B 5 6 7	____ Years/Mths	0 1 2 3 B 5 6 7
Chips/Nuts	N/A	____ Years/Mths	0 1 2 3 B 5 6 7	____ Years/Mths	0 1 2 3 B 5 6 7
TOBACCO	N/A	(Never Used Any At All)			
Cigarettes	N/A	____ Years/Mths	0 1 2 3 B 5 6 7	____ Years/Mths	0 1 2 3 B 5 6 7
Pipe/Cigar	N/A	____ Years/Mths	0 1 2 3 B 5 6 7	____ Years/Mths	0 1 2 3 B 5 6 7
Chewing Tobacco	N/A	____ Years/Mths	0 1 2 3 B 5 6 7	____ Years/Mths	0 1 2 3 B 5 6 7
MEDICATION	N/A	(Never Used Any At All)			
Valium	N/A	____ Years/Mths	0 1 2 3 B 5 6 7	____ Years/Mths	0 1 2 3 B 5 6 7
Tranquilizers	N/A	____ Years/Mths	0 1 2 3 B 5 6 7	____ Years/Mths	0 1 2 3 B 5 6 7
Narcotics	N/A	____ Years/Mths	0 1 2 3 B 5 6 7	____ Years/Mths	0 1 2 3 B 5 6 7
Barbiturates	N/A	____ Years/Mths	0 1 2 3 B 5 6 7	____ Years/Mths	0 1 2 3 B 5 6 7
Downers	N/A	____ Years/Mths	0 1 2 3 B 5 6 7	____ Years/Mths	0 1 2 3 B 5 6 7
Uppers	N/A	____ Years/Mths	0 1 2 3 B 5 6 7	____ Years/Mths	0 1 2 3 B 5 6 7
Ritalin	N/A	____ Years/Mths	0 1 2 3 B 5 6 7	____ Years/Mths	0 1 2 3 B 5 6 7
Pain Meds	N/A	____ Years/Mths	0 1 2 3 B 5 6 7	____ Years/Mths	0 1 2 3 B 5 6 7
Seltzers	N/A	____ Years/Mths	0 1 2 3 B 5 6 7	____ Years/Mths	0 1 2 3 B 5 6 7
Antibiotics	N/A	____ Years/Mths	0 1 2 3 B 5 6 7	____ Years/Mths	0 1 2 3 B 5 6 7
ALCOHOL	N/A	(Never Used Any At All)			
Beer/Ale	N/A	____ Years/Mths	0 1 2 3 B 5 6 7	____ Years/Mths	0 1 2 3 B 5 6 7
Rum	N/A	____ Years/Mths	0 1 2 3 B 5 6 7	____ Years/Mths	0 1 2 3 B 5 6 7
Rye	N/A	____ Years/Mths	0 1 2 3 B 5 6 7	____ Years/Mths	0 1 2 3 B 5 6 7
Gin/Vodka	N/A	____ Years/Mths	0 1 2 3 B 5 6 7	____ Years/Mths	0 1 2 3 B 5 6 7
Scotch	N/A	____ Years/Mths	0 1 2 3 B 5 6 7	____ Years/Mths	0 1 2 3 B 5 6 7
Home Brew	N/A	____ Years/Mths	0 1 2 3 B 5 6 7	____ Years/Mths	0 1 2 3 B 5 6 7
Brandy	N/A	____ Years/Mths	0 1 2 3 B 5 6 7	____ Years/Mths	0 1 2 3 B 5 6 7
Wine	N/A	____ Years/Mths	0 1 2 3 B 5 6 7	____ Years/Mths	0 1 2 3 B 5 6 7
Solvents	N/A	____ Years/Mths	0 1 2 3 B 5 6 7	____ Years/Mths	0 1 2 3 B 5 6 7
Other	N/A	____ Years/Mths	0 1 2 3 B 5 6 7	____ Years/Mths	0 1 2 3 B 5 6 7
DRUGS	N/A	(Never Used Any At All)			
Marijuana	N/A	____ Years/Mths	0 1 2 3 B 5 6 7	____ Years/Mths	0 1 2 3 B 5 6 7
Hashish	N/A	____ Years/Mths	0 1 2 3 B 5 6 7	____ Years/Mths	0 1 2 3 B 5 6 7
Opium	N/A	____ Years/Mths	0 1 2 3 B 5 6 7	____ Years/Mths	0 1 2 3 B 5 6 7

Mushrooms	N/A	___ Years/Mths	0 1 2 3 B 5 6 7	___ Years/Mths	0 1 2 3 B 5 6 7
Peyote	N/A	___ Years/Mths	0 1 2 3 B 5 6 7	___ Years/Mths	0 1 2 3 B 5 6 7
PCP	N/A	___ Years/Mths	0 1 2 3 B 5 6 7	___ Years/Mths	0 1 2 3 B 5 6 7
Heroin	N/A	___ Years/Mths	0 1 2 3 B 5 6 7	___ Years/Mths	0 1 2 3 B 5 6 7
Morphine	N/A	___ Years/Mths	0 1 2 3 B 5 6 7	___ Years/Mths	0 1 2 3 B 5 6 7
LSD	N/A	___ Years/Mths	0 1 2 3 B 5 6 7	___ Years/Mths	0 1 2 3 B 5 6 7
Speed	N/A	___ Years/Mths	0 1 2 3 B 5 6 7	___ Years/Mths	0 1 2 3 B 5 6 7
Cocaine	N/A	___ Years/Mths	0 1 2 3 B 5 6 7	___ Years/Mths	0 1 2 3 B 5 6 7
Crack	N/A	___ Years/Mths	0 1 2 3 B 5 6 7	___ Years/Mths	0 1 2 3 B 5 6 7
Other	N/A	___ Years/Mths	0 1 2 3 B 5 6 7	___ Years/Mths	0 1 2 3 B 5 6 7
SOLVENTS	N/A	(Never Used Any At All)			
Gasoline	N/A	___ Years/Mths	0 1 2 3 B 5 6 7	___ Years/Mths	0 1 2 3 B 5 6 7
Glue	N/A	___ Years/Mths	0 1 2 3 B 5 6 7	___ Years/Mths	0 1 2 3 B 5 6 7
Other	N/A	___ Years/Mths	0 1 2 3 B 5 6 7	___ Years/Mths	0 1 2 3 B 5 6 7

APPENDIX C

Table 1: Factor structure of Years and Use of Alcohols and Drugs, with factor loadings and possible 'meanings'.

FACTOR 1	LOAD	FACTOR 2	LOAD	FACTOR 3	LOAD	FACTOR 4	LOAD
YEARS Alcohol		YEARS Alcohol					
YCA GinVodka	.85	YCA Brandy	.82				
YCA Rum	.85	YCA Wine	.81				
YCA Scotch	.75						
YCA Rye	.68						
YCA Beer	.45						
YCA Brew	.25						
Drinking		Accompaniment					
% Variance:	34%	% Variance:	18%				
USE Alcohol		USE Alcohol		USE Alcohol			

Use Alcohol

Social Alcohol — % Variance: 54%
- Use GinVodka .84
- Use Rum .83
- Use Rye .71
- Use Wine .55

Solitary — % Variance: 11%
- Use Brew .84
- Use Scotch .77
- Use Brandy .75

Subcultural — % Variance: 9%
- Use Beer .95

Accompaniment — % Variance: 7%

Y & U Alcohol

Heavy Alcoholic — % Variance: 38%
- Use Scotch .82
- Use Brandy .76
- Use Brew .75
- YCA Scotch .60
- Use Wine .54
- YCA Brew .42

Social Alcohol — % Variance: 10%
- YCA Rum .86
- YCA GinVodka .85
- Use Rum .56
- Use GinVodka .52

Canadian — % Variance: 9%
- Use Rye .89
- YCA Rye .78

Subcultural — % Variance: 8%
- YCA Beer .88
- Use Beer .84

Accompaniment — % Variance: 7%
- YCA Wine .82
- YCA Brandy .81

YEARS Drugs

- YCA Heroin .87
- YCA Morphin .78
- YCA Opium .64

- YCA Mushr'm .72
- YCA Cocaine .70
- YCA LSD .69
- YCA PCP .40

- YCA Marijua .90
- YCA Hashish .89

- YCA Peyote .69
- YCA Speed .68
- YCA Crack -.50

Soporific		Dream Making		Mellowers		Brighten	
% Variance: 24%		% Variance: 16%		% Variance: 12%		% Variance: 8%	
USE Drugs		USE Drugs		USE Drugs			
Use Hashish	.80	Use Peyote	.83	Use Heroin	.85		
Use Marijua	.80	Use Opium	.81	Use Morphin	.80		
Use Cocaine	.73			Use Speed	.59		
Use Mushr'm	.66						
Use LSD	.66						
Use Crack	.57						
Use PCP	.50						

Heavy Use		Dream Making		Specialized		Brighten	
% Variance: 40%		% Variance: 14%		% Variance: 12%			
Y & U Drugs		Y & U Drugs		Y & U Drugs		Y & U Drugs	
Use Hashish	.85	Use Peyote	.78	Use Speed	.77	YCA Hashish	.91
Use Marijua	.85	Use Opium	.77	YCA Speed	.60	YCA Marijua	.90
Use Mushr'm	.78	YCA Opium	.61	Use PCP	.50		
Use LSD	.67						

'Common Use		Dream Making		Arousers		Mellowers	
% Variance: 24%		% Variance: 8%		% Variance: 6%		% Variance: 5%	
Y & U Drugs		Y & U Drugs		Y & U Drugs		Y & U Drugs	
YCA Morphin	.83	Use Crack	.84	YCA Cocaine	.83	YCA PCP	.84
YCA Heroin	.79	YCA Crack	.71	YCA Mushr'm	.67	YCA Peyote	.53

215

Use Morphin	.71	Use Cocaine	.65	YCA LSD	.55		
Use Heroin	.62						
Soporific		Heavy Use		Confusers		Specialized	
% Variance:	10%	% Variance:	7%	% Variance:	5%	% Variance:	4%
YRS Alc&Drg		YRS Alc&Drg		YRS Alc&Drg		YRS Alc&Drg	
YCA Rum	.85	YCA Morphin	.82	YCA Peyote	.72	YCA Brandy	.78
YCA Scotch	.74	YCA Heroin	.76	YCA PCP	.61	YCA Wine	.76
YCA Rye	.67	YCA Brew	.63	YCA Mushr'm	.57	YCA Cocaine	.42
YCA Beer	.46	YCA Opium	.57	YCA LSD	.51		
		YCA Speed	.43	DreamMaking		Social	
				% Variance:	11%	% Variance:	8%
				YRS Alc&Drg		YRS Alc&Drg	
				YCA Crack	.80	YCA Marijua	.90
						YCA Hashish	.88
Common Alcohol		Solitary		Fast Response		Mellowers	
% Variance:	17%	% Variance:	13%	% Variance:	6%	% Variance:	6%
USE Alc&Drg		USE Alc&Drg		USE Alc&Drg		USE Alc&Drg	
Use Wine	.78	Use Hashish	.86	Use Heroin	.83	Use Opium	.82
Use Scotch	.78	Use Marijua	.86	Use Morphin	.78	Use Peyote	.79
Use Rum	.77	Use LSD	.71	Use Speed	.67	DreamMaking	
Use GinVodk	.76	Use Mushr'm	.70	Use PCP	.47	% Variance:	7%

Use Brandy	.75	Light Use		Heavy Use		USE Alc&Drg	
Use Rye	.75	% Variance:	14%	% Variance:	9%	Use Crack	.86
Use Brew	.62					Use Cocaine	.67
Use Beer	.46	Y & U Al&Dg		Y & U Al&Dg		Cocaine	
Alcohols		Use Scotch	.79	Use Speed	.74	% Variance:	5%
% Variance:	32%	Use Brandy	.76	Use PCP	.65		
		Use Brew	.71	Use Heroin	.63	Y & U Al&Dg	
Y & U Al&Dg		YCA Scotch	.62			YCA Wine	.77
YCA GinVodk	.89	Use Wine	.58	Specialized		YCA Mushr'm	.75
YCA Rum	.85	Solitary Alcohol		% Variance:	5%	YCA Cocaine	.59
Use GinVodk	.65	% Variance:	7%			YCA Brandy	.47
Use Rum	.61			Y & U Al&Dg		YCA LSD	.41
Uncommon		Y & U Al&Dg		Use Opium	.83	Residual	
% Variance:	21%	YCA Morphin	.85	Use Peyote	.80	% Variance:	4%
		YCA Heroin	.75	Dream Making			
Y & U Al&Dg		Use Morphin	.65	% Variance:	4%	Y & U Al&Dg	
Use Marijua	.86	YCA Brew	.54	Y&U A&D cnt		YCA Crack	.76
Use Hashish	.86	Solitary Drug				Use Crack	.76
Use Mushr'm	.70	% Variance:	5%			Use Cocaine	.54
Use LSD	.61	Y&U A&D cnt				YCA Opium	.53
Youth Use						Effect Need	
% Variance:	10%					% Variance:	4%
Y&U A&D cnt							

217

Use Rye	.74		Use Beer	.86		YCA Speed	.74
YCA Rye	.60		YCA Beer	.83			
Canadian			Subcultural				
% Variance:	3%		% Variance:	3%			
Y&U A&D cnt			Y&U A&D cnt			Arouser	
YCA Hashish	.91		YCA PCP	.71		% Variance:	3%
YCA Marijua	.90		YCA Peyote	.68			
Mellowers			Residual				
% Variance:	3%		% Variance:	3%			

APPENDIX D

Table 2: First and Second Highest Factor Loadings for All 816 Items of the Dimensional Addicause Questionnaire (DAQ), organized by Factors (factored in groups of 120 items, i.e., ten axes at a time).

Note: To conserve table space, the items are presented below in four columnar groups of three columns each.

AXIS ITEM	FACT LOAD	NEXT HIGH	AXIS ITEM	FACT LOAD	NEXT HIGH	AXIS ITEM	FACT LOAD	NEXT HIGH	AXIS ITEM	FACT LOAD	NEXT HIGH
Next	Fact	18%	1302	.40	.29*	3501	.61	.23	5602	.55	.30
1006	.65	.21	Next	Fact	2%	3508	.56	.30	5708	.52	.27
0908	.64	.23	1705	.67	.19	3512	.53	.34	4807	.48	.34*

0906	.63	.23	1704	.64	.17	3509	.52	.38	5604	.46	.33
1010	.63	.29	1711	.52	.47	3502	.51	.36	5705	.39	.39
1007	.62	.16	1706	.49	.34	3511	.51	.42	5006	.38	.35
0909	.62	.30	1507	.46	.23*	3510	.50	.46	4907	.35	.28
0905	.61	.28	Next	Fact	2%	3505	.49	.33	4911	.33	.27
1005	.60	.21	1810	.71	.24	3507	.49	.44	4701	.31	.31
1008	.58	.18	1812	.68	.22	3504	.42	.18	5010	.30	.28*
1009	.57	.20	1811	.55	.32	3706	.30	.28	Next	Fact	7%
0907	.52	.31	1807	.49	.32	Next	Fact	3%	4707	.63	.25
0904	.50	.29	2011	.29	.26*	3111	.58	.33	4702	.61	.31
0902	.48	.23	Next	Fact	2%	3801	.56	.16	4909	.55	.27
1011	.48	.37	1510	.56	.39	3110	.55	.38	5902	.54	.38
0903	.46	.38	1508	.50	.37	3804	.52	.22	4712	.54	.31

0912	.46	.34	1506	.48	.48	3108	.52	.27	4710	.53	.40
1003	.45	.42	1501	.27	.23	3803	.48	.25	5901	.52	.35
1004	.41	.29	Next	Fact	2%	3810	.46	.14	4705	.51	.37
1012	.40	.31	1201	.44	.43	3805	.46	.35	4709	.51	.22
0911	.38	.28	1206	.44	.31	3802	.43	.38	5903	.51	.35*
0806	.38	.21*	1205	.43	.37	3112	.40	.37	5904	.48	.47*
Next	Fact	9%	1208	.38	.29	3809	.35	.31	4703	.48	.27
0104	.72	.18	1212	.36	.23	Next	Fact	2%	4708	.47	.30
0110	.70	.13	1207	.35	.34	3404	.70	.15	4704	.43	.34
0103	.69	.23	Next	Fact	1%	3411	.62	.23	5009	.42	.34
0111	.68	.23	2003	.67	.25	3410	.61	.18	4908	.41	.35
0101	.66	.22	2001	.63	.27	3412	.60	.27	5812	.40	.35*
0102	.66	.27	2002	.62	.20	3406	.55	.27	4706	.40	.32

0109	.66	.22	2012	.59	.22	3405	.55	.20	4711	.39	.33
0108	.63	.27	2010	.51	.23	3407	.44	.34	Next	Fact	3%
0106	.62	.16	2004	.42	.29	3101	.30	.29	5910	.82	.16
0107	.60	.24	Next	Fact	1%	Next	Fact	2%	5909	.82	.18
0901	.51	.23*	2007	.69	.15	3603	.70	.09	5908	.82	.20
0910	.51	.26*	2005	.64	.17	3602	.67	.10	5911	.80	.14
0105	.47	.23	2008	.53	.31	3611	.65	-.21	5907	.78	.18
0112	.45	.18	2006	.51	.20	3610	.62	-.20	5906	.73	.29
Next	Fact	4%	2009	.37	.19	3605	.61	.31	5912	.73	.12
0809	.65	.21	1612	.36	-.26	3606	.53	.32	5905	.64	.32
0808	.63	.23	Next	Fact	18%	3601	.50	.24	Next	Fact	3%
0807	.61	.21	2905	.71	.18	3312	.45	.41	6002	.62	.24
0811	.60	.20	2903	.71	.16	3311	.45	.38	6011	.60	.23

0810	.60	.14	2511	.69	.21*	3712	−.25	.22	6003	.60	.21
0812	.57	.31	2909	.69	.16	Next	Fact	2%	6010	.55	.22
0706	.48	.26	2908	.67	.12	3308	.62	.18	6007	.55	.21
0805	.41	.25	2904	.67	.16	3307	.59	.17	6001	.54	.26
0709	.39	.36	2901	.66	.18	3306	.53	.21	6005	.51	.27
0608	.35	.33	2902	.66	.23	3304	.52	.20	6012	.47	.34
0707	.32	.24	2907	.66	.17	3305	.51	.33	6009	.44	.25
Next	Fact	3%	2906	.64	.15	3303	.38	.32	6006	.39	.31
0207	.65	.18	2510	.64	.29*	3301	.37	.29	6004	.36	.32
0205	.63	.16	2910	.64	.11	Next	Fact	2%	Next	Fact	2%
0204	.62	.13	2310	.64	.16*	3109	.62	.16	4803	.53	.26
0202	.60	.14	2312	.61	.16*	3107	.55	.25	4805	.51	.42
0212	.58	.16	2711	.60	.27	3106	.55	.22	4804	.48	.34

0206	.56	.17	2503	.60	.40*	3102	.39	.34	4903	.48	.34*
0211	.55	.12	2108	.57	.41*	3103	.38	.38	5004	.47	.32
1002	.52	.24*	2109	.55	.43*	3104	.36	.36	4901	.46	.33
1001	.51	.22	2911	.54	.18	3609	.29	.19*	4809	.44	.37
0210	.50	.20	2306	.54	.22*	Next	Fact	2%	4801	.43	.29
0208	.49	.30	2311	.53	.17*	4005	.64	.19	5005	.42	.34
0209	.43	.33	2512	.53	.26*	4007	.57	.26	4811	.34	.24
0203	.40	.33	2912	.52	.23	4003	.56	.30	4808	.33	.33
0201	.27	.22	2105	.51	.37*	4002	.49	.30	4806	.31	.20
Next	Fact	2%	2705	.48	.15	4006	.48	.29	4902	.31	.28
0410	.72	.17	2307	.47	.19	4004	.46	.30	Next	Fact	2%
0412	.68	.15	2305	.47	.21	4008	.44	.32	5610	.72	.18
0406	.66	.23	2703	.45	.19	4001	.37	.30	5609	.65	.18

0405	.64	.19	2207	.43	.26*	Next	Fact	1%	5801	.62	−.25
0407	.64	.30	3012	.42	.33	3708	.76	.19	5810	.55	.24
0404	.62	.15	2701	.41	.21	3709	.75	.11	5807	.49	.26
0409	.60	.33	2704	.38	.21*	3703	.65	.29	5802	.47	.31
0411	.60	.27	2810	.37	.23	3701	.57	.14	5601	.46	.22
0408	.51	.48	Next	Fact	9%	3702	.39	.19	5603	.44	.15
0403	.47	.22	2103	.69	.31	Next	Fact	1%	5809	.44	.42
0402	.40	.32	2604	.65	.23*	3608	.54	.26	5612	.44	.38
Next	Fact	2%	2110	.64	.23	3607	.49	.30	5803	.40	.27
0607	.70	.16	2605	.63	.23	3604	.42	.24	5808	.39	.28
0606	.64	.18	2112	.62	.37	Next	Fact	27%	5811	.36	.28
0610	.63	.26	2101	.60	.29	5508	.71	.15	Next	Fact	2%
0609	.62	.27	2102	.60	.21	5107	.68	.21	4611	.52	.36

0601	.58	.27	2107	.57	.42	5507	.68	.21	5003	.51	.27
0612	.55	.25	2509	.55	.17	5511	.66	.16	4812	.50	.14
0605	.54	.27	2610	.55	.23	5509	.66	.22	4610	.44	.28
0602	.48	.21	2106	.51	.35	5407	.65	.24	4612	.44	.30
0611	.46	.34	2612	.48	.36	5404	.65	.29	5007	.41	.22
0306	.36	.33	2111	.46	.35	5503	.65	.29	5008	.41	.31
0604	.28	.26	2104	.45	.39	5510	.63	.21	5611	.41	.26
Next	Fact	2%	2508	.44	.26*	5406	.62	.35	4810	.33	.33
0502	.58	.25	2606	.43	.31	5405	.62	.39	4910	.31	–.24
0503	.55	.30	2611	.38	.25	5112	.61	.26	5002	.27	.25
0501	.53	.26	2507	.36	.32*	5108	.60	.33	Next	Fact	2%
0711	.43	.23	Next	Fact	4%	5409	.59	.31	4905	.62	.20
0705	.39	.29	2803	.73	.10	5408	.59	.24	4906	.58	.18

0508	.36	.32	2709	.72	.16	5502	.58	.28	4904	.56	.26
0401	.34	.27	2804	.70	.18	5110	.58	.32	4912	.55	.21
0708	.32	.31	2802	.65	.11	5109	.55	.22	5012	.54	.20*
0710	.27	.20	2806	.61	.18	5306	.55	.48	Next	Fact	2%
Next	Fact	2%	2805	.60	.18	5307	.54	.53	4608	.59	.25
0309	.57	.26	2712	.58	.23*	5308	.54	.51	4609	.56	.34
0504	.56	.30	2811	.56	-.26	5411	.53	.27	4607	.48	.26
0308	.50	.38	2706	.53	.16	5412	.52	.22	4602	.43	.31
0506	.45	.33	2801	.50	.31*	5501	.51	.26	4601	.34	.33
0307	.43	.28	2708	.50	.46*	5106	.49	.33	5011	.26	.22*
0303	.41	.27	2602	.45	.26	5102	.49	.23	Next	Fact	2%
0512	.41	.36	2812	.40	.24	4107	.49	.31	4605	.64	.28
0301	.36	.33	2601	.34	.22	5103	.48	.43	4604	.62	.27

.40	.47	4606	.18	.48	5512	.32	.33	2807	.34	.34	0302
.32*	.46	4603	.40	.46	4106	.21	.33	2710	.23	.32	0505
1%	Fact	Next	.40	.43	4109	3%	Fact	Next	2%	Fact	Next
.20	.59	5805	.41	.42	4108	.10	.70	3007	.19	.62	0712
.35*	.46	5806	.38	.39	4504	.16	.69	3008	.24	.61	0312
.34*	.41	5804	.38	.39	5403	.28	.68	3006	.18	.54	0311
1%	Fact	Next	.30	.35	4407	.21	.63	3009	.18	.42	0310
.33	.43	6008	6%	Fact	Next	.23	.60	3001	.19	.38	0304
.26*	.29	5001	.27	.76	5310	.19	.59	3003	.28	.36	0701
25%	Fact	Next	.20	.75	4512	.17	.53	3002	.33	.34	0305
.21	.69	6102	.23	.73	5301	.20	.53	3004	1%	Fact	Next
.29	.64	6106	.24	.67	5304	.36	.51	3005	.28	.59	0510
.28	.62	6107	.34	.65	5312	.34	.49	3010	.28	.59	0507

0509	.52	.38	3011	.44	.19	5303	.60	.42	6108	.60	.26
0511	.43	.41	2809	.29	.22	4509	.60	.24	6105	.59	.23
0603	.35	.29	Next	Fact	2%	5305	.59	.37	6101	.59	.41
Next	Fact	1%	2201	.76	.09	4510	.58	.23	6104	.58	.21
0801	.68	.09	2203	.72	.23	4508	.52	.29	6103	.58	.33
0802	.65	.19	2202	.70	.18	5309	.52	.35	6111	.57	.27
0803	.61	.17	2210	.59	.26	5302	.51	.25	6110	.53	.27
0804	.60	.23	2209	.51	.23	5311	.50	.28	6112	.51	.29
Next	Fact	1%	2211	.45	.36	4511	.39	.32*	6207	.49	.29
0702	.60	.12	2206	.33	.31	4312	.38	.31	6109	.44	.21
0703	.56	.18	Next	Fact	2%	4310	.37	.36	6503	.36	.26
0704	.37	.25	2401	.61	.11	4506	.33	.29	Next	Fact	8%
Next	Fact	23%	2404	.54	.19	4303	.32	.23	6410	.72	.17

229

1312	.75	.22	2608	.53	.41	Next	Fact	4%	6409	.71	.22
1310	.74	.21	2609	.53	.30	5203	.66	.22	6411	.70	.15
1311	.73	.20	2403	.51	.29	5211	.63	.31	6408	.70	.21
1306	.73	.25	2607	.49	.19	5202	.60	.30	6403	.68	.24
1701	.69	.27	2402	.48	.21	4102	.57	.27	6405	.58	.26
1710	.68	.22	2405	.48	.18	5201	.56	.34	6404	.56	.23
1307	.67	.347	2406	.40	.33	4111	.54	.29	6412	.53	.25
1709	.67	.31	Next	Fact	2%	4103	.54	.35	6406	.51	.32
1304	.67	.21	2506	.60	.27	4104	.52	.22	6407	.49	.26
1702	.64	.35	2505	.55	.26	4112	.52	.27	6311	.47	.47*
1305	.61	.40	2502	.53	.21	5205	.51	.26	6402	.41	.36
1712	.60	.43	2504	.51	.33	5212	.51	.44	6501	.36	.29
1309	.60	.33	2501	.43	.29	5206	.50	.37	6502	.27	.26

1703	.59	.35	Next	Fact	2%	4101	.49	.33	Next	Fact	4%
1707	.58	.25	2412	.70	−.23	5101	.47	.44	6601	.83	.12
1308	.58	.42	2410	.64	.22	5210	.41	.28	6606	.81	.16
1504	.55	.28	2409	.61	.23	4110	.38	.35	6603	.79	.18
1301	.55	.24	2411	.53	.21	5104	−.37	.27	6602	.77	.15
1708	.54	.45	Next	Fact	2%	Next	Fact	3%	6611	.69	.15
1502	.53	.30	2302	.71	.17	4203	.63	.19	6605	.67	.23
1511	.52	.38	2303	.68	.22	4202	.62	.16	6604	.64	.20
1209	.52	.37	2301	.62	.19	4208	.56	.16	6612	.60	.22
1512	.51	.41	2304	.43	.40	4210	.53	.36	6607	.55	.19
1509	.51	.47	2308	.36	.25	4207	.52	.20	Next	Fact	3%
1503	.47	.28	2309	.35	.31	4209	.47	.34	6710	.68	.16
1211	.44	.31	Next	Fact	1%	4201	.47	.23	6711	.65	.29

1303	.43	.25	2407	.57	.28	4406	.46	.37	6706	.61	.21
1412	−.40	.39*	2408	.50	.25	4204	.44	.40	6703	.61	.23
1505	.35	.33	2204	.42	.34	4404	.44	.43	6712	.60	.34
1204	.35	.33	2208	.30	.21	5402	.40	.33	6707	.59	.22
Next	Fact	7%	Next	Fact	1%	5401	.39	.38	6704	.58	.22
1110	.66	.23	2603	.41	.31	Next	Fact	3%	6709	.54	.31
1108	.66	.26	2205	.40	.27	4408	.64	.26	6705	.53	.27
1103	.63	.33	2212	.39	.35	4410	.62	.25	6708	.49	.28
1105	.61	.22	Next	Fact	1%	4401	.60	.29	6401	.46	.33*
1102	.59	.46	2707	.60	.34	4403	.55	.38	6701	.44	.25
1111	.57	.24	2702	.38	.31	4411	.53	.22	6702	.39	.30
1107	.56	.35	2808	.26	.25	4412	.50	.35	Next	Fact	3%
1106	.54	.30	Next	Fact	20%	4409	.48	.40	6805	.74	.14

1104	.53	.25	3910	.78	.10	4405	.37	.37	6802	.72	.16
1202	.52	.39*	3911	.78	.12	4302	.27	.22	6801	.72	.19
1112	.51	.49	3909	.76	.15	Next	Fact	2%	6806	.63	.19
1101	.49	.17	3906	.74	.15	5208	.70	.23	6809	.59	.22
1210	.46	.37*	3912	.72	.11	5205	.66	.13	6804	.58	.27
1203	.45	.31	3907	.72	.18	5209	.62	.16	6803	.56	.27
Next	Fact	4%	3908	.66	.16	5207	.61	.26	6808	.56	.25
1602	.70	.22	3905	.56	.25	5204	.54	.31	6811	.54	.21
1603	.70	.17	3903	.54	.32	5111	.39	.31	6810	.54	.18
1608	.68	.21	3812	.51	.22	Next	Fact	2%	6812	.49	.25
1607	.60	.19	3707	.50	.26	4501	.55	.12	6807	.44	.25
1609	.60	.25	3904	.49	.27	4311	.44	.28	Next	Fact	3%
1610	.58	.17	3506	.46	.32	4505	.41	.31	6512	.69	.18

1809	.57	.22	3711	.45	.22	4508	.37	.32	6511	.63	.26
1604	.54	.23	3704	.44	.25	4507	.32	.31	6508	.60	.18
1605	.54	.32	3901	.42	.23	Next	Fact	2%	6505	.56	.22
1601	.54	.18	3710	.41	.22	4306	.72	.22	6510	.52	.21
1611	.40	.21	3808	.40	.28	4305	.69	.16	6509	.48	.23
1606	.38	.18	3705	.40	.19	5410	.47	.43	6504	.47	.22
1808	.36	.14	3811	.40	.35	4304	.44	.33	6507	.45	.28
1109	.20	.18	3902	.39	.29	4307	.43	.32	6506	.37	.22
Next	Fact	3%	3807	.38	.22	4301	.40	.25	Next	Fact	2%
1908	.71	.18	Next	Fact	8%	Next	Fact	2%	6303	.66	.33
1905	.66	.19	3210	.79	.08	4205	.62	.22	6304	.64	.23
1906	.63	.11	3211	.70	.15	4206	.54	.14	6306	.64	.21
1903	.56	.25	3206	.70	.28	4212	.51	.26	6305	.64	.17

1911	.54	.29	3202	.70	.23	4211	.43	.31	6301	.60	.29
1904	.53	.29	3212	.69	.17	Next	Fact	1%	6302	.58	.27
1910	.49	.37	3209	.66	.14	4503	.56	.11	Next	Fact	2%
1912	.46	.16	3201	.65	.16	4502	.48	.40	6309	.68	.27
1901	.45	.18	3203	.62	.19	Next	Fact	1%	6312	.62	.30
1902	.42	.26	3207	.60	.26	5506	.50	.29	6307	.60	.27
1907	.38	.31	3205	.55	.41	5504	.45	.30	6308	.58	.25
1909	.37	.32	3208	.52	.32	5505	.45	.43	6310	.58	.27
Next	Fact	3%	3204	.46	.32	Next	Fact	1%	Next	Fact	1%
1806	.82	.21	Next	Fact	4%	4105	.42	.28	6210	.61	.19
1805	.78	.15	4011	.55	.25	4309	−.26	.25	6209	.60	.22
1803	.77	.20	3401	.51	.25	Next	Fact	25%	6211	.55	27
1804	.74	.19	3409	.50	.30	5702	.83	.24	6212	.55	.30

Item	Fact	1%	Item		1%	Item		1%	Item	Fact	1%
1802	.72	.18	3402	.49	.30	5703	.83	.24	6208	.50	.37
1801	.65	.27	3105	.48	.32	5711	.80	.23	6206	.35	.30
Next	Fact	2%	4009	.47	.23	5710	.79	.21	Next	Fact	1%
1408	.63	.12	4010	.44	.31	5701	.77	.22	6202	.53	.24
1407	.62	.18	3806	.43	.31	5706	.77	.28	6204	.50	.29
1403	.58	-.36	3302	.43	.31	5704	.67	.21	6203	.47	.28
1401	.56	.24	4012	.43	.31	4802	.66	.24	6201	.45	.39
1402	.54	-.42	3309	.42	.25	5707	.65	.25	6205	.37	.32
1405	.53	.16	3403	.37	.35	5608	.65	.17	Next	Fact	1%
1406	.48	.31	3408	.37	.35	5607	.63	.21	6609	.64	.37
1404	.48	.22	3612	.37	.36	5712	.61	.32	6610	.64	.19
1410	.47	.17	3310	.36	.26	5709	.60	.27	6608	.57	.36

<u>1411</u>	.43	-.32	<u>Next</u>	Fact	3%	<u>5605</u>	.59	-.26
<u>1409</u>	.41	.33	<u>3503</u>	.62	.36	<u>5606</u>	.58	.30

* Asterisks identify the secondary factor loadings for items where that loading is on the factor on which the bulk of the other items from its axis load.

237

APPENDIX E

Table 3: Addicause Reliability: Alphas and Means for the sixty scales/axes

AXIS Numb	Axis ALPH	Axis MEAN	AXIS Numb	Axis ALPH	Axis MEAN	AXIS Numb	Axis ALPH	Axis MEAN	AXIS Numb	Axis ALPH	Axis MEAN
01	.90	20.0	18	.87	13.4	35	.89	17.3	52	.83	24.4
02	.82	20.4	19	.84	17.3	36	.77	25.7	53	.92	9.4
03	.67	21.5	20	.77	26.2	37	.82	16.7	54	.90	15.0
04	.86	15.6	21	.90	19.9	38	.79	19.6	55	.88	19.5
05	.85	15.5	22	.80	17.0	39	.90	11.6	56	.85	17.9

ID			ID			ID			ID		
06	.83	18.9	23	.82	22.9	40	.79	22.7	57	.94	14.6
07	.73	21.9	24	.78	32.1	41	.89	17.5	58	.80	24.1
08	.79	18.5	25	.85	23.5	42	.81	24.9	59	.93	27.4
09	.88	14.3	26	.76	26.0	43	.80	14.4	60	.86	23.7
10	.84	18.6	27	.78	25.9	44	.88	14.1	61	.89	31.3
11	.88	12.9	28	.77	33.0	45	.82	13.3	62	.87	28.3
12	.87	15.7	29	.91	16.4	46	.82	22.6	63	.86	24.9
13	.90	15.4	30	.85	18.7	47	.89	18.1	64	.90	25.1
14	.80	31.7	31	.85	26.8	48	.83	18.3	65	.81	20.2
15	.90	16.7	32	.89	28.0	49	.82	16.5	66	.91	15.2
16	.81	21.7	33	.84	24.9	50	.74	17.4	67	.86	31.2
17	.91	19.8	34	.86	17.7	51	.86	21.4	68	.89	17.2

APPENDIX F

Table 4: Test-Retest Stability Indices
(Pearson r) for total $\underline{S}$ and $\underline{N}$ scores and for $\underline{S}$ scores
of Addicure experimental subgroups of subjects

AXIS NUMBER	$\underline{S}$ Tot.Score Retest $\underline{r}$s (N = 143)	$\underline{N}$ Tot.Score Retest $\underline{r}$s (N = 143)	CONTROL Ss Retest $\underline{r}$s (N = 19)	ADDICURE Txs Txs = 1 Txs > 1 N = 81 N = 32
02	.40*	.42*	.41	.34 | .44
03	.29**	.20**	.19	.31 | .39
08	.48*	.41*	.70	.42 | .43
10	.50*	.38*	.67	.51 | .20
12	.61*	.53*	.78	.59 | .65
13	.51*	.38*	.56	.51 | .50
20	.43*	.40*	.61	.50 | .21
22	.61*	.60*	.80	.59 | .50
24	.41*	.41*	.56	.37 | .37
30	.45*	.43*	.66	.60 | −.02
34	.64*	.55*	.71	.67 | .41
36	.43*	.40*	.43	.49 | .31
37	.62*	.53*	.88	.66 | .50

<u>40</u>	.45*	.33*	.76	.55 | −.11
<u>44</u>	.58*	.50*	.76	.62 | .25
<u>46</u>	.60*	.55*	.53	.71 | .34
<u>47</u>	.56*	.44*	.68	.56 | .60
<u>48</u>	.56*	.48*	.84	.54 | .45
<u>53</u>	.59*	.48*	.47	.64 | .56
<u>60</u>	.43*	.38*	.77	.56 | −.18

* $p < 0.000$
** $p < 0.01$

APPENDIX G

Table 5: Factor no. 1 Loadings (order) for analyses of the *S* (<u>sum</u>) and *N* (<u>number</u>) scores and own-factor loadings for *Z* (<u>claimed causes/effects</u>) scores. Underlined *r*s indicate end of factors.

S: AXIS NUMBER AND TITLE	*r*	*N*: AXIS NUMBER AND TITLE	*r*	*Z*: AXIS NUMBER AND TITLE	*r*
29*S*: Disturbed Affect	.85	53*N*: Somatic Depression	.82	34*Z*: Need to Be Different	.74
47*S*: Physiologic Anxiety	.84	39*N*: Effort Strain	.81	28*Z*: Comfortable Inhibitn	.70
39*S*: Effort Strain	.83	45*N*: Hypoglycaemia	.79	44*Z*: Fast-Lane Living	.67
55*S*: Impaired Self-Esteem	.83	47*N*: Physiologic Anxiety	.77	57*Z*: Felt Rejection	.57
57*S*: Felt Rejection	.82	54*N*: Hungry Heart	.76	22*Z*: Subcultural Values	.46
35*S*: Self-Depreciation	.81	35*N*: Self Depreciation	.74	<u>09*Z*: Loneliness</u>	<u>.38</u>
53*S*: Somatic Depression	.81	29*N*: Disturbed Affect	.73	13*Z*: Flat Depression	.61
15*S*: Control Effort	.80	55*N*: Impaired Self-Esteem	.73	63*Z*: Avoid Boredom	.50
09*S*: Loneliness	.80	43*N*: Metabolic Disorder	.73	64*Z*: Assert Confidence Nd	.48
54*S*: Hungry Heart	.80	57*N*: Felt Rejection	.73	17*Z*: Grief Reaction	.46

13S: Flat Depression	.79	15N: Control Effort	.70	26Z: Rationality Defence	.41
51S: Guilt Proneness	.79	51N: Guilt Proneness	.69	46Z: Allergy Stress	.39
17S: Grief Reaction	.79	37N: Paroxysmality	.68	43Z: Metabolic Disorder	.33
66S: Impaired Sleep	.73	48N: Punitive Rewards	.68	60Z: Substance Enhancement	.62
21S: Social Withdrawal	.71	66N: Impaired Sleep	.68	06Z: Social Influence	.51
48S: Punitive Rewards	.70	17N: Grief Reaction	.68	62Z: Novel Experience Need	.48
45S: Hypoglycaemia	.70	13N: Flat Depression	.65	18Z: Self-Enhancement Need	.38
11S: Reality Denial	.68	49N: Affect Avoidance	.65	41Z: Rigid Habits	.35
23S: Inhibit Dependency	.66	50N: Control Sensitivity	.63	05Z: Rigid Self-Image	.33
49S: Affect Avoidance	.66	56N: Masked Disappointment	.62	40Z: Pep-Up Need	--
43S: Metabolic Disorder	.66	09N: Loneliness	.58	32Z: Group Satisfaction	.66
01S: Social Anxiety	.65	38N: Rules Intolerance	.58	04Z: Stimulus Hunger	.65
25S: Paranoid Sensitivity	.65	46N: Allergy Stress	.58	51Z: Guilt Proneness	.56
05S: Rigid Self-Image	.65	41N: Rigid Habits	.57	15Z: Control Effort	--
41S: Rigid Habits	.64	19N: Pain Sensitivity	.56	54Z: Hungry Heart	.58
37S: Paroxysmality	.63	68N: Substance Dependency	.55	29Z: Disturbed Affect	.52
12S: Rebelliousness	.63	11N: Reality Denial	.55	39Z: Effort Strain	.46
19S: Pain Sensitivity	.62	65N: Avoid Attractiveness	.54	35Z: Self-Depreciation	.42

244

07S: Aggression Inhibition	.62	25N: Paranoid Sensitivity	.50	55Z: Impaired Self-Esteem	.42
65S: Avoid Attractiveness	.62	34N: Wish to Be Different	.50	48Z: Punitive Rewards	––
50S: Control Sensitivity	.61	27N: Oppressive Inhibition	.47	01Z: Social Anxiety	.56
68S: Substance Dependency	.61	52N: Anger/Hostility	.47	03Z: Reactive Depression	.51
56S: Masked Disappointment	.61	31N: Demean Others	.40	07Z: Aggression Inhibition	.45
38S: Rules Intolerance	.61	24N: Immed. Gratification	−.14	67Z: Relaxation/Calm Need	.42
03S: Reactive Depression	.57	14N: Vivid Imagery	.02	58Z: Communication Need	.40
46S: Allergy Stress	.55	26N: Rationality Defence	.26	47Z: Physiologic Anxiety	.39
08S: Guilt Intolerance	.54	16N: Control of Others	.05	19Z: Pain Sensitivity	.31
27S: Oppressive Inhibition	.54	28N: Comfortable Inhibitn	.11	56Z: Masked Disappointment	.61
31S: Demean Others	.53	20N: Hedonism	−.03	38Z: Rules Intolerance	.58
34S: Wish to Be Different	.50	42N: Easy-Going Enjoyment	.16	12Z: Rebelliousness	.38
52S: Anger/Hostility	.44	40N: Pep-Up Effect	.29	66Z: Impaired Sleep	.72
04S: Stimulus Hunger	.25	30N: Affect Denial	.27	45Z: Hypoglycaemia	.45
44S: Fast-Lane Living	.42	61N: Forget Failures	.21	11Z: Reality Denial	.41
18S: Self-Enhancement Wish	.46	62N: Novel Experience Wish	.33	59Z: Calm Nerves Need	.39
22S: Subcultural Values	.38	63N: Avoid Boredom	.42	61Z: Forget Failures	.38

20S: Hedonism	−.15	59N: Calm Nerves Need	.47	68Z: Substance Dependency	.61
61S: Forget Failures	.22	64N: Assert Confidence	.31	49Z: Affect Avoidance	.54
62S: Novel Experience Wish	.36	60N: Substance Enhancement	.38	08Z: Guilt Intolerance	.49
63S: Avoid Boredom	.39	67N: Relaxation/Calm Wish	.14	42Z: Easy Going Enjoyment	.34
60S: Substance Enhancement	.37	58N: Communication Need	.34	02Z: Social Enjoyment	.57
67S: Relaxation/Calm Wish	.10	01N: Social Anxiety	.37	25Z: Paranoid Sensitivity	.53
64S: Assert Confidence	.31	21N: Social Withdrawal	.49	20Z: Hedonism	.43
59S: Calm Nerves Need	.51	07N: Aggression Inhibition	.38	10Z: Social Contact Need	.39
58S: Communication Need	.38	23N: Inhibit Dependency	.49	52Z: Anger/Hostility	.35
24S: Immed. Gratification	−.19	05N: Rigid Self-Image	.45		
28S: Comfortable Inhibit'n	.11	03N: Reactive Depression	.36	No Responses on some Axes	
14S: Vivid Imagery	−.05	04N: Stimulus Hunger	.21		
26S: Rationality Defence	.33	44N: Fast-Lane Living	.46		
40S: Pep-Up Effect	.14	18N: Self-Enhancement Wish	.51		
02S: Social Enjoyment	−.05	22N: Subcultural Values	.39		
10S: Social Contact Wish	.36	12N: Rebelliousness	.51		

32*S*: Group Satisfaction	−.02	08*N*: Guilt Intolerance	.40		
06*S*: Social Influence	.28	02*N*: Social Enjoyment	.02		
36*S*: Rigid Moralizations	.06	10*N*: Social Contact Wish	.27		
33*S*: Dogmatism	.33	06*N*: Social Influence	.15		
42*S*: Easy-Going Enjoyment	.11	32*N*: Group Satisfaction	.08		
30*S*: Affect Denial	.25	36*N*: Rigid Moralizations	.08		
16*S*: Control of Others	−.01	33*N*: Dogmatism	.36		

Appendix H

In Tables 6.1 through 6.5, the columns labled **01** to **68** refer to the Addicause axes, as follows:

01-. Social Anxiety	23-. Dependency Inhibition
02+. Group Enjoyment	24+. P.I.G. Effect
03-. Reactive Depression	25-. Paranoid Sensitivity
04+. Stimulus Hunger	26+. Rationality Defence
05-. Rigid Self Image	27-. Oppressive Inhibition
06+. Social Influence	28+. Comfortable Inhibition
07-. Aggression Inhibition	29-. Disturbed Feelings
08+. Guilt Intolerance	30+. Affect Denial
09-. Loneliness	31-. Put Down Others
10+. Social Contact Need	32+. Group Satisfaction
11-. Reality Denial	33-. Dogmatism
12+. Authority Rebellion	34+. Need To Be Different
13-. Joyless Depression	35-. Self Depreciation
14+. Vivid Imagery	36+. Rigid Moralization
15-. Control Effort	37-. Paroxysmal Energy
16+. Control Others	38+. Rules Intolerance
17-. Grief Reaction	39-. Effort Strain
18+. Event Self Enhancement	40+. Pep Up Effect
19-. Pain Sensitivity	41-. Rigid Habits
20+. Hedonism	42+. Easy Going Enjoyment
21-. Social Withdrawal	43-. Metabolic Disorder
22+. Subcultural Values	44+. Fast Lane Living

45-. Hypoglycaemia	57-. Felt Rejection
46+. Allergy Stress	58+. Communication Need
47-. Physiologic Anxiety	59-. Calm Nerves Need
48+. Punitive Rewards	60+. Substance Excitement
49-. Affect Avoidance	61-. Forget Failures
50+. Sensitivity Control	62+. Different Experience
51-. Guilt Proneness	63-. Avoid Depression
52+. Anger, Hostility	64+. Assert Confidence
53-. Somatic Depression	65-. Avoid Attractiveness
54+. Hungry Heart	66-. Impaired Sleep
55-. Impaired Self Esteem	67+. Relaxation Need
56+. Masked Disappointment	68+. Substance Dependency

Table 6.1: Correlation Coefficients between the Addicause axes and ninety-one MMPI Scales (*T* Scores; Raw Omits, and Spy). Some interesting correlations are presented in **bold**.

MMPI SCALES	01	02	03	04	05	06	07	08	09	10	11	12	13	14
ItemsOmit'd	-.04	-.07	-.10	-.07	-.09	-.22	-.01	-.04	-.13	-.06	.02	.01	-.06	.01
Validity: **L**	-.26	.03	-.19	-.33	-.35	-.21	-.25	-.40	-.37	-.12	-.45	-.45	-.32	.02
Validity: **F**	.45	-.06	.34	.39	.53	.30	.40	.51	.49	.18	.52	.56	.51	-.13
Validity: **K**	-.47	.02	-.38	-.29	-.51	-.21	-.50	-.49	-.51	-.20	-.48	-.55	-.48	-.05
Hs (01)	.13	-.12	.12	-.14	.08	-.06	.01	.04	.05	-.06	.01	-.05	.07	-.02
D (02)	.44	-.20	**.24**	.01	.31	-.01	.21	.21	**.35**	-.07	.31	.24	**.44**	-.12
Hy (03)	.11	-.11	.10	-.10	-.02	-.04	-.06	-.01	.01	-.13	-.01	-.07	.09	-.04
Pd (04)	.23	-.14	.10	.19	.28	.11	.10	**.30**	.22	-.03	**.31**	**.37**	.35	-.23
MF (05)	.13	.01	.24	.03	.05	.06	.13	.11	.31	.14	.17	.08	.22	-.08
Pa (06)	**.35**	-.13	.27	.26	**.39**	.19	.25	**.34**	**.40**	.15	**.34**	.36	**.42**	-.07

Pt (07)	**.45**	−.13	**.35**	.22	.39	.19	**.31**	.41	**.50**	.14	**.44**	.40	**.55**	−.09
Sc (08)	.44	−.11	.39	.24	.45	.26	.36	.41	.53	.19	**.49**	.44	.53	−.08
Ma (09)	.04	.17	.23	**.41**	.25	**.28**	.19	**.40**	.17	**.20**	.30	**.36**	.19	.08
Si (00)	**.64**	−**.33**	.27	.02	**.42**	.04	**.38**	.25	**.47**	−.01	**.35**	.37	**.48**	−.07
TSC Fact.I	**.66**	−**.31**	.31	.08	**.44**	.10	**.38**	.29	**.50**	.02	**.38**	.39	**.51**	−.09
TSC Fact.II	.36	−.14	.29	.06	.30	.04	.27	.28	.33	.03	.27	.27	.34	−.05
TSC Fact.III	.33	−.02	.30	.31	.50	.17	.43	**.46**	.40	.19	.42	.52	.37	.06
TSC Fact.IV	.54	−.12	**.39**	.32	**.53**	.23	**.47**	.51	**.61**	.16	**.56**	.56	**.65**	−.10
TSC Fact.V	.42	−.02	.33	.35	.50	.29	.44	.53	.48	.21	.52	.58	.50	−.03
TSC Fact.VI	.44	.01	.45	.35	.53	.29	.47	.55	.60	.26	.56	.55	.53	.03
TSC Fact.VII	.56	−.11	.39	.26	.50	.19	.46	.47	.55	.15	.52	.51	.58	−.02
Plus Gettng	.56	−.13	.43	.34	.55	.25	.49	.52	.60	.18	.56	.59	.59	.01
DY1: **VerySD**	−.56	**.37**	−.21	−.09	−.38	−.03	−.27	−.29	−.42	.07	−.43	−.41	−.46	.22

DY2: **SocDes**	-.36	.29	-.11	.01	-.23	-.00	-.11	-.11	-.23	.11	-.27	-.23	-.30	.19
DY3: SDNeut	.30	.04	.38	.37	.41	.27	.44	.48	.43	.24	.40	.47	.40	.13
DY4: **Undesr**	.48	-.02	.40	.41	**.58**	.31	.51	.56	**.57**	.28	.55	.59	.54	.01
DY5: **VerySU**	.54	-.11	.39	.34	**.58**	.27	.49	.52	**.58**	.18	.57	.58	**.61**	-.05
Primitive D	.28	-.07	.20	.31	.34	.23	.25	.37	.34	.14	.40	.47	.31	-.02
Regression	.31	-.02	.29	.11	.29	.20	.30	.29	.35	.19	.24	.27	.32	.01
Repression	-.17	-.06	-.15	-.38	-.36	-.28	-.22	-.40	-.34	-.08	-.43	-.47	-.33	.02
Denial Def.	**-.51**	.13	-.32	-.31	-.49	-.24	-.42	-.40	-.52	-.12	-.50	-.53	-.50	.04
Projection	.24	-.09	.06	.10	.20	.03	.15	.06	.19	.05	.06	.13	.15	.01
Displacem't	.33	.06	.23	.03	.19	.03	.22	.19	.27	.06	.18	.16	.29	.04
Intellectiz	.04	-.20	-.04	.06	.08	-.13	-.03	-.01	.02	-.03	-.01	.02	-.03	.03
Self-Doubt	.45	-.10	.29	.11	.40	.15	.36	.33	**.46**	.14	.33	.33	**.44**	.01
Reactn Form	**.54**	**-.46**	.18	-.09	.27	-.05	.23	.03	.28	-.11	.16	.14	.27	-.08

253

OvAct.Think	**.43**	.01	**.45**	.35	**.51**	.28	**.46**	**.55**	**.60**	.26	**.56**	**.54**	**.53**	.03
Intell.Effi	-.45	.08	-.32	-.15	-.45	-.23	-.36	-.35	-.46	-.20	-.41	-.42	-.46	.06
Anxiety Aff	**.55**	-.11	**.39**	.26	.50	.19	**.46**	**.47**	**.55**	.15	**.53**	.51	.59	-.02
Depression	.54	-.12	**.39**	.32	**.53**	.23	**.47**	**.50**	**.62**	.16	**.57**	.56	**.65**	-.11
Anger Affct	.42	-.02	.33	.35	**.51**	.29	**.43**	**.53**	.48	.20	.52	**.58**	.50	-.02
Anhedonia A	.48	**-.31**	.23	.09	.36	.02	.23	.29	.41	-.08	.39	.36	.47	-.17
Responsiblt	-.29	.04	-.22	-.37	-.40	**-.25**	-.24	**-.46**	-.29	-.07	-.42	-.53	-.35	.06
Tolerance	-.41	.04	-.32	-.26	**-.50**	-.19	-.46	**-.46**	-.29	-.07	-.42	-.53	-.35	.06
Empathy	.04	.04	.10	.08	-.02	.04	.03	-.00	.12	.07	.02	.00	.06	-.02
Role Play'g	-.49	.13	-.31	-.22	**-.49**	-.18	-.35	-.41	-.43	-.10	-.40	-.47	-.45	.04
Dominance	-.47	.17	-.32	-.14	-.45	-.18	-.39	-.40	-.48	-.08	-.47	-.46	-.53	.09
SocParticip	**-.51**	**.35**	-.16	.03	-.33	-.03	-.24	-.14	-.29	.11	-.26	-.26	-.32	.09
SocPresence	**-.54**	.26	-.31	-.03	-.33	-.02	-.32	-.22	-.44	-.02	-.35	-.31	-.46	.08

Dependency	**.55**	-.04	**.45**	.25	.52	**.27**	.52	.49	**.66**	.27	.53	**.53**	**.61**	-.02
Dom-Submisn	-.44	.22	-.17	-.01	-.25	-.00	-.21	-.15	-.39	.02	-.30	-.23	-.45	.15
Love-Hate	-.50	.06	-.40	-.38	-.58	-.32	-.49	-.54	-.60	-.26	-.58	-.61	-.58	.07
EgoStrength	-.45	.07	-.38	-.09	-.37	-.08	-.36	-.38	-.46	-.16	-.39	-.34	-.46	.05
Resiliency	**-.55**	.18	-.36	-.20	**-.49**	-.15	-.40	**-.46**	-.52	-.08	-.50	-.51	-.54	.10
Self-Control	-.01	-.06	-.06	**-.44**	-.24	-.21	-.09	-.34	-.12	-.04	-.30	-.39	-.15	.09
Impulsivity	.36	-.01	.34	**.45**	.49	.31	.39	**.58**	.48	.15	**.57**	**.64**	.49	-.05
Delinquency	.49	-.09	.36	.32	**.50**	.21	.40	**.48**	**.55**	.14	**.51**	**.53**	.53	-.12
Spy Scale	-.31	.25	-.10	.22	-.06	.18	-.09	.09	-.16	.08	.03	.06	-.10	.05
HabCriminal	.30	-.14	.13	.30	.36	.17	.20	**.41**	.31	-.02	.42	.47	.43	-.22
PrisnMaladj	.01	-.07	-.12	.24	.06	.12	-.02	.13	-.00	-.11	.16	.16	.11	-.18
Escapism	.39	-.08	.26	.36	.44	.20	.27	**.45**	.44	.03	.48	**.54**	.47	-.15
ParoleViola	.44	-.06	.35	.33	.52	.23	.42	**.50**	.47	.15	.46	**.55**	.45	-.02

Recidivism	.18	-.09	.03	.32	.27	.14	.13	.31	.13	-.08	.28	.32	.18	-.11
OvContr.Hos	-.26	.10	-.12	-.30	**-.38**	-.27	**-.32**	-.26	-.31	-.10	-.40	-.42	-.28	.01
Violence	.30	.01	.22	**.43**	**.46**	.29	.28	**.49**	.32	.13	.45	**.55**	.40	-.08
ThreatSuici	.48	-.12	.36	.28	**.53**	.23	**.45**	.50	**.55**	.17	**.51**	.57	**.54**	-.05
UncActOutSx	.40	-.12	.31	.13	.30	.10	.36	.31	.40	.12	.33	.29	.47	-.07
Paedophilia	.45	-.23	.31	-.00	.27	.08	.30	.24	**.43**	.12	.27	.30	.38	-.05
AggravatdSx	-.38	.10	-.24	-.27	-.36	-.10	-.26	**-.42**	**-.43**	-.05	-.44	-.50	-.46	.15
Alcoholism	-.01	.03	.08	.22	.13	.15	.09	.32	.04	-.01	.16	.27	.13	-.00
Drug Abuse	.37	-.12	.29	.36	.40	.14	.28	.40	.42	-.00	.47	.49	.45	-.18
WorkAttitud	.45	-.03	.36	.32	.53	.27	.44	.50	.52	.18	.56	.55	.53	-.07
RehabMotiva	.21	-.13	.03	.08	.20	.02	-.00	.16	.15	-.07	.09	.15	.18	-.12
ChangeMotiv	**.56**	-.18	.39	.27	.50	.17	.41	.45	.58	.12	.55	.53	.60	-.16
ThyroidPath	.06	.01	.05	.07	.13	.12	.03	.05	.08	.12	.04	.07	.10	.02

Caudality	.57	-.16	.38	.21	.53	.18	.46	.49	.55	.12	.52	.51	.56	-.07
LowBackPain	-.06	-.10	-.12	-.04	-.06	-.09	-.09	-.13	-.14	-.12	-.08	-.11	-.05	-.04
ParietFront	.53	-.14	.34	.23	.49	.18	.42	.46	.53	.10	.49	.50	.55	-.07
SocAdjustmt	.65	-.39	.24	-.00	.39	.01	.32	.19	.42	-.06	.29	.31	.42	-.11
DepressCont	.56	-.13	.41	.29	**.55**	.21	.48	.52	**.62**	.18	.56	.57	**.65**	-.10
Poor Morale	.53	-.03	**.41**	.32	**.52**	.30	.49	**.49**	**.59**	**.26**	**.54**	**.54**	**.61**	.01
RelFundam't	-.00	.05	.05	-.15	-.12	-.00	.01	-.03	-.03	.10	-.13	-.15	-.07	.12
AuthConflct	.28	-.03	.19	.28	.43	.15	**.35**	**.40**	.28	.03	.35	**.46**	.33	.03
Psychotic	.41	-.02	.39	.36	.53	.28	.41	.53	.52	.26	.51	.53	.48	.01
Organ.Sympt	.37	-.10	.31	.13	.37	.13	.30	.37	.35	.09	.35	.32	.35	.01
FamilyProbs	.35	-.08	.32	.25	.40	.19	**.35**	.39	**.44**	.12	.41	**.46**	.45	-.14
ManifestHos	.31	-.00	.27	**.44**	**.50**	.31	**.38**	**.53**	.41	.17	**.53**	**.60**	.40	-.01
Phobias	**.44**	-.04	.29	.09	.29	.13	.30	.30	.41	.18	.34	.31	.39	.02

Hypomania	.27	.06	.31	**.37**	.36	**.29**	**.32**	.41	.35	**.24**	.38	.42	.29	.07
Poor Health	.28	-.11	.25	.04	.22	.03	.19	.22	.28	.08	.22	.19	.27	-.09
Phar.Virtue	.44	-.02	.39	.16	**.45**	.21	**.50**	**.41**	**.49**	.26	.38	.40	.49	.05
MAST	.18	-.11	.08	.09	.11	.01	.04	.13	.11	-.13	.09	.18	.15	-.05
DAST	.09	.00	.10	.39	.24	.14	.09	.41	.11	-.04	.33	.36	.29	-.17

Coefficients greater than 0.07 are statistically significant (two-tailed test, $N = 695$)

Table 6.2: Correlation Coefficients between the Addicause axes and 91 MMPI Scales (*T* Scores; Raw Omits, and Spy). Some interesting correlations are presented in **bold**.

MMPI SCALES	15	16	17	18	19	20	21	22	23	24	25	26	27	28
ItemsOmit'd	-.06	-.08	-.06	-.02	.05	-.09	-.06	.00	-.03	-.07	-.03	-.11	-.08	.03
Validity: **L**	-.34	-.03	-.33	-.41	-.21	.02	-.35	-.28	-.29	.01	-.34	-.22	-.26	.00
Validity: **F**	.51	-.02	.47	.45	.33	.00	.45	.42	.42	-.15	.39	.14	.33	.01
Validity: **K**	**-.55**	-.06	-.52	-.41	-.38	.02	-.53	-.38	-.53	.06	-.51	-.32	-.46	-.17
Hs (01)	.19	-.15	.16	-.05	.27	-.22	.09	-.11	.05	-.13	-.02	-.05	-.04	-.18
D (02)	**.44**	-.19	**.45**	.14	.26	**-.32**	**.37**	-.02	.27	**-.31**	.14	-.03	.11	-.15
Hy (03)	.15	-.15	.12	-.05	.16	-.21	.03	-.18	-.04	-.11	-.09	-.06	-.09	-.22
Pd (04)	.28	-.14	.25	.24	.07	-.15	.20	**.16**	.16	-.21	.15	-.01	-.02	-.22
MF (05)	.26	-.03	.19	.08	.12	-.15	.12	-.03	.19	-.09	.17	.10	.10	-.05
Pa (06)	**.46**	-.03	.41	.27	.27	-.10	**.36**	.16	**.29**	-.12	**.29**	.11	**.23**	-.08

Pt (07)	**.59**	-.07	**.58**	.29	.39	-.21	**.43**	.17	**.38**	-.21	.32	.10	**.28**	-.07
Sc (08)	.58	-.03	.52	.32	.37	-.09	**.45**	.27	.40	-.16	.37	.18	.32	-.01
Ma (09)	.25	**.27**	.25	**.34**	.23	**.24**	.13	**.39**	.20	**.18**	.31	.20	.28	.13
Si (00)	**.47**	-.24	.47	.20	.24	-.30	**.60**	.09	**.46**	**-.27**	**.35**	.19	**.28**	**-.00**
TSC Fact.I	**.48**	-.24	.48	.26	.21	-.31	**.61**	.12	**.48**	**-.28**	**.35**	.20	**.30**	**-.00**
TSC Fact.II	.46	-.10	.43	.21	.43	-.21	.38	.10	.32	-.17	.26	.12	.21	-.08
TSC Fact.III	.47	.14	.42	.37	.39	.05	.44	.38	.45	.01	**.51**	**.29**	**.42**	.17
TSC Fact.IV	**.66**	-.04	**.65**	.44	.38	-.14	**.54**	.31	**.50**	-.21	**.45**	.22	.37	.00
TSC Fact.V	.54	.03	.54	.44	.35	-.04	.46	.40	.49	-.07	.46	.23	.39	.05
TSC Fact.VI	**.63**	.05	.60	.41	.48	.02	.49	.38	**.51**	-.09	**.50**	**.28**	.46	.10
TSC Fact.VII	**.67**	-.01	.65	.37	.45	-.14	.57	.28	.52	-.18	.48	.22	.42	.04
Plus Gettng	.64	.01	.65	.44	.42	-.11	.62	.36	.55	-.14	.53	.30	.44	.08
DY1: **VerySD**	-.44	.28	-.42	-.29	-.26	.33	-.52	-.16	-.35	.36	-.30	-.10	-.18	.14

	1	2	3	4	5	6	7	8	9	10	11	12	13	14
DY2: **SocDes**	-.28	.31	-.27	-.09	-.11	.33	-.30	-.02	-.24	.39	-.09	.10	.00	.27
DY3: SDNeut	.50	.20	.46	.40	.43	.09	.40	.33	.42	.10	.45	.40	.45	.23
DY4: **Undesr**	.60	.09	.59	.48	.44	.03	.54	.44	.53	-.05	.56	.34	.47	.14
DY5: **VerySU**	.66	-.01	.63	.46	.42	-.06	.57	.40	.54	-.15	.49	.24	.41	.04
Primitive D	.31	-.00	.31	.38	.11	-.03	.33	.29	.32	-.03	.31	.23	.19	.09
Regression	.44	.06	.34	.23	**.32**	-.09	.35	.23	.30	-.03	.27	.20	.27	.03
Repression	-.33	-.11	-.27	-.41	-.16	-.12	-.27	-.38	-.31	.05	-.30	-.07	-.14	-.07
Denial Def.	**-.48**	.08	-.49	-.41	-.27	.10	-.52	-.35	-.50	.11	**-.46**	-.25	-.34	-.08
Projection	.24	.10	.21	.11	.17	-.01	.24	.00	.10	-.01	**.17**	.17	.23	.01
Displacem't	.40	-.02	.37	.13	.25	-.13	.27	.01	.24	-.08	.15	.11	.20	-.02
Intellectiz	-.07	-.01	-.03	-.07	-.01	.01	.11	-.04	-.08	.08	.05	**.18**	.06	.12
Self-Doubt	.49	-.09	**.51**	.25	**.37**	-.19	.42	.16	**.41**	-.12	.37	.17	**.34**	.02
Reactn Form	.28	-.30	.27	-.01	.09	-.33	**.49**	-.11	.24	-.28	.15	.10	.15	.01

OvAct.Think	.63	.05	.60	.41	.48	.02	.49	.37	.51	-.08	.50	.28	.46	.11
Intell.Effi	-.53	.06	-.49	-.28	-.37	.11	-.47	-.27	-.40	.18	-.31	-.12	-.33	.03
Anxiety Aff	.67	-.00	.65	.37	.46	-.14	.57	.28	.51	-.18	.48	.22	.42	.04
Depression	.66	-.04	.65	.44	.38	-.14	.54	.32	.50	-.22	.45	.22	.37	.00
Anger Affct	.54	.03	.54	.44	.35	-.03	.46	.40	.50	-.07	.46	.24	.39	.05
Anhedonia A	.38	-.23	.37	.22	.17	-.30	.44	.05	.32	-.32	.23	.04	.11	-.09
Responsiblt	-.30	-.02	-.27	-.42	-.21	-.08	-.32	-.41	-.29	-.07	-.26	-.13	-.18	-.03
Tolerance	-.54	-.07	-.51	-.34	-.37	-.01	-.51	-.37	-.46	-.07	-.46	-.23	-.40	-.12
Empathy	.08	-.09	.12	.03	.05	.00	-.05	-.01	.04	-.11	-.07	-.05	-.01	-.12
Role Play'g	-.51	.09	-.45	-.31	-.31	.15	-.50	-.24	-.44	.17	-.37	-.23	-.36	-.05
Dominance	-.50	.15	-.49	-.30	-.31	.20	-.50	-.21	-.41	.23	-.38	-.19	-.28	.07
SocParticip	-.30	.31	-.31	-.15	-.12	.28	-.47	-.05	-.29	.31	-.19	-.03	-.13	.11
SocPresence	-.43	.20	-.44	-.22	-.28	.30	-.52	-.05	-.36	.25	-.26	-.13	-.25	.01

Dependency	.69	-.00	.67	.38	.44	-.15	.56	.29	.58	-.14	.49	.27	.44	.08
Dom-Submisn	-.38	.20	-.40	-.12	-.13	.31	-.36	.04	-.26	.32	-.14	.03	-.12	.09
Love-Hate	-.60	-.04	-.55	-.46	-.38	-.01	-.54	-.45	-.52	.13	-.50	-.25	-.44	-.10
EgoStrength	-.56	.06	-.53	-.23	-.48	.22	-.45	-.14	-.41	.17	-.36	-.13	-.32	.04
Resiliency	-.61	.13	-.59	-.39	-.39	.24	-.57	-.26	-.49	.25	-.40	-.17	-.33	.04
Self-Control	-.09	-.08	-.11	-.43	-.03	-.17	-.07	-.40	-.11	.01	-.20	-.10	-.05	.05
Impulsivity	.53	.05	.49	.50	.34	.01	.44	.45	.47	-.07	.47	.23	.37	.05
Delinquency	.59	.02	.55	.41	.36	-.07	.53	.32	.44	-.14	.44	.22	.35	.04
Spy Scale	-.13	.24	-.10	.09	-.11	.31	-.27	.22	-.14	.19	-.06	-.10	-.10	.01
HabCriminal	.34	-.13	.34	.36	.11	-.09	.29	.27	.24	-.22	.21	.05	.06	-.16
PrisnMaladj	-.05	-.09	-.02	.21	-.12	.09	-.01	.19	-.07	-.12	-.08	-.03	-.13	-.15
Escapism	.44	-.05	.43	.44	.21	-.07	.39	.28	.36	-.17	.30	.14	.21	-.08
ParoleViola	.53	.03	.48	.38	.40	-.04	.49	.38	.45	-.10	.48	.27	.43	.06

Recidivism	.15	-.05	.10	.36	-.05	-.03	.17	.25	.13	-.10	.16	.08	.04	-.06
OvContr.Hos	-.28	.03	-.29	-.36	-.13	-.00	-.37	-.32	-.29	.02	-.33	-.25	-.24	-.07
Violence	.40	.05	.37	.42	.18	.07	.32	**.42**	.32	-.07	.32	.13	.23	.02
ThreatSuici	.60	-.01	**.55**	.41	**.38**	-.05	**.54**	.37	**.52**	-.15	**.45**	**.25**	.44	.08
UncActOutSx	.49	-.03	**.49**	.19	.33	-.20	.38	.12	.34	-.16	.29	.13	.28	-.03
Paedophilia	.43	-.08	.39	.13	.32	-.28	.43	.06	.36	-.16	.27	.19	.23	-.02
AggravatdSx	-.43	.07	-.42	-.34	-.27	.14	-.41	-.24	**-.35**	.22	-.28	-.09	-.18	.05
Alcoholism	.08	.06	.03	.28	-.02	.13	.08	.23	.06	.02	.07	.07	.05	-.02
Drug Abuse	.43	-.10	.42	.42	.24	-.11	.41	.27	.37	-.18	.36	.20	.21	-.04
WorkAttitud	.58	.02	.56	.39	.38	-.04	.52	.37	.46	-.13	.44	.22	.39	.06
RehabMotiva	.12	-.10	.12	.15	.06	-.11	.13	.03	.06	-.14	-.01	-.00	-.03	-.11
ChangeMotiv	.63	-.08	.60	.41	.37	-.20	.58	.26	.49	-.26	.43	.19	.35	-.04
ThyroidPath	.13	.08	.13	.07	.14	.08	.05	.07	.04	.01	.05	.04	.08	.06

264

Caudality	.60	-.12	**.60**	.35	.40	-.20	.56	.28	.51	-.21	.43	.24	.37	.04
LowBackPain	-.07	-.09	-.02	-.07	.00	-.06	-.07	-.10	-.15	-.09	-.16	-.13	-.11	-.12
ParietFront	.61	-.09	.59	.38	.39	-.17	.54	.28	.48	-.20	.38	.19	.34	-.03
SocAdjustmt	.37	**-.29**	.37	.15	.16	-.34	.59	.02	.40	-.29	.28	.17	.23	-.02
DepressCont	.68	-.03	**.67**	.40	**.40**	-.14	**.57**	.30	**.53**	-.23	**.49**	.23	**.40**	.00
Poor Morale	**.64**	-.02	**.64**	.43	**.43**	-.11	**.53**	.33	**.55**	-.12	**.50**	**.27**	**.42**	.08
RelFundam't	.02	.13	-.00	-.15	.01	-.08	-.01	-.14	-.02	.14	-.02	.06	-.02	.09
AuthConflct	.31	.09	.33	.36	.25	.12	.40	**.40**	.32	-.02	.36	.23	**.29**	.12
Psychotic	.57	.09	.52	.39	.41	.05	.48	.38	.45	-.04	.49	.25	.41	.07
Organ.Sympt	.46	-.07	.46	.29	.43	-.13	.38	.23	.34	-.12	.28	.17	.28	-.01
FamilyProbs	.46	.01	.39	.38	.18	-.08	.41	.31	.42	-.06	.37	.22	.28	.11
ManifestHos	.45	.11	.41	**.46**	.28	.11	.39	**.45**	**.40**	-.01	**.43**	.23	**.37**	.09
Phobias	.48	-.05	.47	.22	**.35**	-.18	.41	.14	**.38**	-.15	**.34**	.07	.25	-.00

Hypomania	.43	**.21**	.39	**.42**	.32	.14	.35	**.38**	.32	.04	.37	.31	**.39**	.14
Poor Health	.35	-.13	.33	.16	.35	-.22	.25	.09	.24	-.16	.17	.07	.14	-.12
Phar.Virtue	**.60**	.11	**.57**	.26	.43	-.09	**.47**	.22	.49	-.06	**.45**	**.24**	**.43**	.11
MAST	.10	-.18	.07	.32	-.03	-.14	.17	.16	.07	-.20	.01	-.03	.01	-.09
DAST	.13	.04	.21	.38	.06	.04	.13	.17	.10	-.11	.11	.01	-.00	-.15

Coefficients greater than 0.07 are statistically significant (two-tailed tests, $N = 695$)

Table 6.3: Correlation Coefficients between the Addicause axes and 91 MMPI Scales (T-Scores; Raw Omits & Spy). Some interesting correlations are presented in **bold**

MMPI SCALES	29	30	31	32	33	34	35	36	37	38	39	40	41	42
ItemsOmit'd	-.03	-.03	-.03	-.10	.03	-.12	-.04	.01	-.00	-.07	-.03	.07	-.02	-.05
Validity: L	-.40	-.17	-.29	-.05	-.13	-.31	-.34	.24	-.38	-.34	-.31	-.08	-.40	.00
Validity: F	.55	.13	.37	-.07	.28	.38	.54	-.15	.51	.38	.49	.15	.47	.11
Validity: K	-.59	-.27	-.52	.04	-.35	-.41	-.48	.03	-.49	-.50	-.48	-.22	**-.58**	-.18
Hs (01)	.13	-.16	-.01	-.13	.04	-.07	.08	.01	.19	-.00	**.23**	-.08	-.01	-.18
D (02)	.35	-.18	.16	**-.29**	.03	.10	**.47**	-.19	.32	.12	**.37**	-.18	.17	-.23
Hy (03)	.06	**-.22**	-.06	-.14	-.05	-.10	.08	-.06	.11	-.10	.16	-.17	-.12	-.24
Pd (04)	.23	-.13	.11	-.17	.03	.19	**.43**	**-.33**	**.33**	.14	.27	-.12	**.24**	-.15
MF (05)	.18	.01	.15	.05	.05	.14	.25	-.01	.06	.07	.17	-.07	.05	-.07
Pa (06)	**.44**	.05	**.21**	-.06	.18	**.29**	**.43**	-.09	.31	.27	**.41**	-.00	**.33**	-.03

267

Pt (07)	.58	.00	.27	-.11	.10	.23	.54	-.15	.45	.32	.49	-.08	.34	-.08
Sc (08)	.56	.06	.28	-.05	.21	.35	.53	-.10	.44	.32	.48	.06	.37	.06
Ma (09)	.26	.29	.18	.21	.24	.35	.18	-.06	.36	.35	.28	.28	.34	.27
Si (00)	.56	-.06	.36	-.30	.15	.17	.51	-.07	.36	.26	.36	-.09	.35	-.11
TSC Fact.I	.58	-.03	.37	-.25	.15	.19	.56	-.09	.36	.29	.38	-.06	.36	-.11
TSC Fact.II	.44	-.01	.25	-.14	.16	.16	.35	-.03	.40	.23	.47	.01	.27	-.09
TSC Fact.III	.48	.26	.44	-.05	.36	.39	.37	-.02	.39	.43	.44	.23	.57	.22
TSC Fact.IV	.63	.12	.41	-.11	.21	.38	.66	-.21	.54	.41	.56	.01	.52	.01
TSC Fact.V	.61	.19	.47	.01	.26	.37	.54	-.15	.55	.50	.47	.11	.57	.11
TSC Fact.VI	.65	.23	.47	.03	.28	.41	.51	-.09	.49	.48	.55	.18	.54	.18
TSC Fact.VII	.68	.13	.46	-.10	.23	.33	.55	-.07	.53	.49	.56	.06	.51	.02
Plus Gettng	.70	.17	.49	-.07	.28	.37	.60	-.15	.58	.49	.54	.09	.56	.06
DYI: **VerySD**	-.50	.12	-.27	.31	-.16	-.20	-.55	.19	-.47	-.25	-.47	.11	-.33	.22

DY2: SocDes	-.38	.15	-.16	.27	.03	-.05	-.39	.17	-.31	-.14	-.25	.24	-.15	.29
DY3: SDNeut	.50	.32	.40	.11	.32	.37	.38	-.02	.42	.46	.42	.27	.47	.22
DY4: Undesr	.64	.24	.48	.03	.33	.44	.57	-.10	.55	.56	.56	.24	.62	.20
DY5: VerySU	.67	.14	.46	-.10	.28	.40	.61	-.14	.55	.47	.58	.11	.57	.09
Primitive D	.35	.13	.29	.06	.09	**.28**	.39	-.22	.33	**.38**	**.32**	.08	.37	.10
Regression	**.44**	.16	.29	.01	.27	**.28**	.33	.06	**.41**	.27	**.35**	.09	.30	.04
Repression	-.34	-.17	-.22	-.05	-.18	-.28	-.31	**.19**	-.31	-.32	-.32	-.10	-.38	-.10
Denial Def	**-.58**	-.08	-.43	.04	-.19	-.33	**-.54**	.18	**-.50**	-.43	-.42	-.05	-.48	-.04
Projection	.24	.05	**.13**	-.05	.11	.12	.11	.05	.13	.12	.13	.02	.14	.04
Displacem't	.33	.00	.20	-.04	.14	.06	.26	.02	.21	.21	.27	-.01	.15	-.05
Intellectiz	-.08	-.02	-.05	-.04	-.07	.04	-.05	-.01	-.07	-.05	-.06	.05	-.00	.06
Self-Doubt	**.56**	.06	**.38**	-.10	.16	.22	**.45**	-.05	.37	.31	.36	-.02	.35	-.03
Reactn Form	.33	**-.21**	.13	**-.33**	.03	-.00	.31	-.01	.11	.06	.18	-.13	.13	-.18

OvAct.Think	.65	.23	.47	.03	.27	.41	.51	-.09	.50	.47	.54	.18	.53	.18
Intell.Effi	-.59	-.11	-.35	.17	-.28	-.29	-.48	.04	-.47	-.36	-.46	-.08	-.43	-.02
Anxiety Aff	.68	.14	.46	-.11	.24	.33	.55	-.07	.53	.49	.56	.07	.51	.02
Depression	.63	.12	.41	-.11	.22	.38	.66	-.20	.54	.41	.56	.02	.52	.01
Anger Affct	.61	.18	.47	.02	.27	.37	.54	-.15	.56	.50	.47	.11	.56	.11
Anhedonia A	.39	-.19	.22	-.32	.05	.17	.53	-.25	.36	.15	.36	-.14	.25	-.21
Responsiblt	-.35	-.08	-.28	.07	-.24	-.30	-.37	.21	-.50	-.39	-.39	-.14	-.46	-.07
Tolerance	-.56	-.18	-.43	.09	-.37	-.39	-.45	.03	-.46	-.46	-.47	-.20	-.55	-.17
Empathy	.01	.07	-.00	.02	-.05	.04	.05	-.02	-.03	-.03	.09	.03	-.05	.00
Role Play'g	-.54	-.04	-.39	.17	-.26	-.31	-.47	.13	-.44	-.40	-.43	-.09	-.49	-.04
Dominance	-.53	-.05	-.33	.20	-.21	-.28	-.56	.21	-.45	-.35	-.42	-.01	-.41	.05
SocParticip	-.41	.12	-.20	.34	-.15	-.09	-.38	.11	-.31	-.17	-.28	.10	-.26	.18
SocPresence	-.50	.08	-.27	.27	-.11	-.16	-.49	.09	-.36	-.19	-.38	.05	-.27	.13

Dependency	.71	.18	.50	-.03	.26	.36	.62	-.08	.51	.46	.54	.07	.50	.04
Dom-Submisn	-.35	.16	-.17	.27	.06	-.06	-.47	.18	-.18	-.08	-.25	.25	-.14	.22
Love-Hate	-.64	-.22	-.44	.03	-.32	-.46	-.59	.10	-.53	-.47	-.52	-.20	-.56	-.19
EgoStrength	-.56	-.09	-.36	.16	-.26	-.29	-.48	-.00	-.41	-.31	-.48	-.06	-.36	.03
Resiliency	-.63	-.05	-.41	.17	-.24	-.30	-.60	.17	-.57	-.41	-.56	-.02	-.47	.07
Self-Control	-.10	-.14	-.12	-.14	-.12	-.23	-.21	.30	-.35	-.24	-.21	-.10	-.26	-.06
Impulsivity	.57	.20	.45	.04	.29	.44	.53	-.22	.54	.48	.49	.15	.56	.11
Delinquency	.60	.11	.38	-.10	.25	.37	.51	-.14	.46	.42	.50	.06	.48	.06
Spy Scale	-.19	.13	-.12	.21	-.03	.09	-.11	-.16	.03	.02	-.09	.09	.03	.14
HabCriminal	.31	-.06	.19	-.15	.10	.28	.51	-.36	.46	.25	.36	-.04	.34	-.10
PrisnMaladj	-.06	-.11	-.09	-.03	-.05	.09	.15	-.32	.22	.00	.07	-.05	.02	-.06
Escapism	.43	.02	.26	-.08	.14	.30	.51	-.30	.49	.33	.43	.02	.43	-.07
ParoleViola	.58	.21	.42	-.05	.30	.38	.49	-.15	.51	.45	.49	.16	.54	.14

271

Recidivism	.21	.06	.08	-.00	.06	.23	.29	-.23	.41	.21	.17	.02	.29	.00
OvContr.Hos	-.31	-.12	-.28	-.04	-.11	-.25	-.34	**.16**	-.33	-.33	-.32	-.16	-.41	-.11
Violence	.45	.14	**.33**	.01	.26	**.37**	**.41**	**-.21**	**.50**	**.44**	.38	.12	**.50**	.10
ThreatSuici	**.61**	.16	**.39**	-.08	**.29**	**.40**	**.55**	-.10	**.54**	.45	**.55**	.16	.54	.12
UncActOutSx	.49	.06	.35	-.12	.11	.24	.42	.01	**.33**	.25	.42	-.01	.32	.00
Paedophilia	.43	.08	.26	-.18	.11	.22	.38	.00	.26	.20	.33	-.01	.19	-.03
AggravatdSx	-.38	.01	-.29	.16	-.12	-.27	**-.50**	**.31**	-.47	-.30	-.41	-.00	-.39	.07
Alcoholism	.08	.10	.10	.06	.14	.14	.10	-.14	**.34**	.21	.08	.12	.19	.07
Drug Abuse	.40	.00	.30	-.09	.15	.32	.52	-.26	**.43**	.36	**.45**	.01	**.41**	-.05
WorkAttitud	.59	.17	.39	-.09	.30	.39	.56	-.14	.52	.44	.52	.14	.54	.11
RehabMotiva	.09	-.11	.03	-.13	.04	.03	.21	-.18	.17	.08	.12	-.06	.09	-.16
ChangeMotiv	.64	.06	.41	-.18	.21	.37	.64	-.18	.53	.39	.55	-.01	.49	-.05
ThyroidPath	.05	.09	-.01	.06	.15	.16	.05	.07	.07	.10	.15	**.18**	.12	.19

Caudality	-.03	.50	.03	.52	.43	.53	-.16	.61	.29	.23	-.15	.41	.08	.64
LowBackPain	-.09	-.12	-.13	.01	-.23	-.07	-.04	-.03	-.09	-.06	-.10	-.15	-.17	-.16
ParietFront	-.06	.49	.01	.54	.42	**.52**	-.15	.56	.29	.23	-.16	.37	.08	.63
SocAdjustmt	-.13	.29	-.10	.30	.18	.30	-.06	.48	.12	.10	-.33	.28	-.12	.48
DepressCont	.02	**.54**	.06	**.60**	**.44**	**.53**	-.15	**.66**	**.41**	.26	-.12	**.44**	.13	**.65**
Poor Morale	.06	**.53**	.09	**.53**	**.46**	**.52**	-.13	**.63**	**.36**	.25	-.02	.51	**.19**	**.66**
RelFundam't	.00	-.14	.04	-.11	-.05	-.08	**.18**	-.09	-.08	-.02	.06	.04	.09	.04
AuthConflct	**.18**	**.50**	.16	.37	**.38**	.39	-.09	.30	**.34**	**.28**	-.08	.31	.13	.36
Psychotic	.16	.53	.24	.52	.45	.44	-.05	.48	.44	.34	-.01	.39	.24	.59
Organ.Sympt	-.02	.29	.10	.50	.33	**.46**	-.07	.40	.24	.23	-.06	.30	.05	.48
FamilyProbs	.08	.41	.10	.39	**.38**	**.42**	-.14	.49	.30	.20	-.06	.35	.09	.44
ManifestHos	.16	**.55**	**.19**	**.43**	**.50**	**.51**	-.17	.43	.37	**.30**	.04	.40	**.21**	**.50**
Phobias	-.02	.29	.02	.36	.37	.36	.00	.39	.17	.13	-.10	.38	.13	**.56**

Hypomania	.43	**.30**	.32	.13	.28	**.34**	.28	-.04	.41	**.46**	.36	**.25**	.46	**.28**
Poor Health	.35	.01	.19	-.13	.11	.13	.30	-.03	.36	.18	.35	-.01	.23	-.08
Phar.Virtue	.61	.24	.46	-.03	.27	**.30**	**.45**	**.05**	.38	**.46**	.44	.13	**.46**	.12
MAST	.17	-.08	.05	-.12	.01	.03	.18	-.22	**.43**	.08	.11	-.13	.09	-.13
DAST	.14	-.01	.05	-.05	-.03	.11	.27	-.32	**.28**	.21	.24	.01	.24	-.04

Coefficients greater than 0.07 are statistically significant (two-tailed tests, $N = 695$)

ItemsOmit'd	.06	-.06	-.03	-.02	-.04	-.00	-.05	-.03	-.05	.02	-.00	-.03	-.07	-.14
Validity: **L**	-.20	-.30	-.37	-.27	-.40	-.39	-.31	-.24	-.34	-.28	-.24	-.33	-.33	-.20
Validity: **F**	.36	.40	.51	.38	.49	.56	.41	.37	.44	.34	.43	.51	.51	.37
Validity: **K**	-.44	-.36	-.46	-.39	-.58	-.57	-.55	-.48	-.57	-.47	-.43	-.54	-.56	-.39
Hs (01)	.19	-.11	.12	.08	.14	-.00	.04	-.02	.08	-.12	.17	.03	.10	-.01
D (02)	**.24**	.04	**.27**	.19	**.38**	**.20**	**.22**	.17	**.38**	.01	**.38**	**.30**	**.37**	.11
Hy (03)	.11	-.11	.09	.06	.12	-.07	-.03	-.06	.04	-.17	.15	.01	.04	-.08

Pd (04)	.13	.17	**.29**	**.21**	**.27**	**.34**	**.15**	.17	.22	.12	.21	**.27**	.24	.13
MF (05)	.09	.04	.12	.11	.21	.06	.11	.13	.18	−.03	.18	.21	.14	.13
Pa (06)	**.27**	**.26**	**.32**	**.24**	**.41**	**.37**	**.31**	**.29**	**.37**	.20	**.40**	**.39**	**.45**	.29
Pt (07)	**.36**	.21	**.46**	**.31**	**.55**	**.37**	**.31**	.27	**.45**	.14	**.49**	**.47**	**.50**	.25
Sc (08)	.35	.27	.44	.29	.48	.44	.34	.33	.45	.19	.46	.48	.51	.33
Ma (09)	.25	**.35**	.29	**.33**	.23	**.37**	.27	**.31**	.17	**.30**	.20	**.29**	.20	.26
Si (00)	**.31**	.09	**.31**	.19	**.50**	.32	**.35**	.25	**.51**	.18	**.37**	**.39**	**.53**	.22
TSC Fact.I	**.30**	.13	**.34**	.20	**.52**	**.37**	**.38**	**.30**	**.53**	.22	**.39**	**.42**	**.56**	.26
TSC Fact.II	.37	.12	.39	.28	.46	.30	.30	.21	.35	.09	.41	.34	.39	.19
TSC Fact.III	**.40**	**.38**	**.40**	**.37**	.46	.53	**.47**	**.44**	.45	**.43**	.36	.45	.48	.38
TSC Fact.IV	**.41**	**.33**	**.53**	**.37**	**.63**	**.54**	**.48**	**.46**	**.60**	**.32**	**.55**	**.62**	**.60**	.34
TSC Fact.V	**.39**	**.37**	**.52**	**.36**	.57	**.57**	**.46**	.43	**.56**	**.44**	.42	.53	.53	.36
TSC Fact.VI	**.47**	**.38**	**.53**	**.45**	**.62**	**.56**	**.49**	.44	**.55**	.37	**.50**	**.58**	.54	.41

TSC Fact.VII	**.44**	.32	**.52**	**.39**	**.68**	.50	**.49**	.39	**.61**	.37	.52	.56	**.58**	.36
Plus Gettng	.46	.33	.55	.42	.67	.59	.53	.46	.62	.40	.49	.59	.62	.40
DY1: **VerySD**	-.31	-.19	-.42	-.25	-.52	-.39	-.32	-.22	-.42	-.19	-.40	-.41	-.47	-.19
DY2: **SocDes**	-.19	-.04	-.24	-.09	-.35	-.18	-.14	-.10	-.31	.00	-.24	-.23	-.33	-.09
DY3: SDNeut	.04	.35	.43	.41	.46	.49	.45	.42	.44	.36	.38	.43	.44	.42
DY4: **Undesr**	.47	.43	.54	.48	.62	.63	.56	.50	.59	.45	.48	.61	.59	.44
DY5: **VerySU**	.44	.37	.56	.40	.64	.58	.51	.46	.59	.38	.54	.61	.61	.39
Primitive D	.22	.30	**.35**	.26	**.34**	**.40**	.30	.26	**.34**	**.31**	.24	**.38**	.27	.18
Regression	**.34**	.18	.33	.23	**.39**	**.37**	.28	.20	**.34**	.16	.31	.31	**.34**	.31
Repression	-.21	-.41	-.39	-.28	-.34	-.40	-.26	-.22	-.32	-.31	-.24	-.36	-.30	-.23
Denial Def.	-.33	-.29	-.48	-.32	**-.57**	**-.51**	-.42	-.37	-.49	-.32	-.37	-.50	-.51	-.30
Projection	.11	.08	.13	.08	.19	.06	.15	.14	.20	.15	.19	.09	.16	.14
Displacem't	.25	.06	.15	.20	.32	.17	.21	.12	.29	.10	.27	.21	.23	.15

Intellectiz	-.07	-.06	-.11	-.05	-.14	.00	-.05	-.01	-.03	.05	-.07	-.05	-.05	-.05
Self-Doubt	.34	.10	.39	.25	.52	.35	.34	.30	.50	.18	.36	.41	.48	.28
Reactn Form	.14	-.04	.09	.04	.29	.11	.15	.04	.30	.05	.20	.15	.31	.06
OvAct.Think	.47	.38	.53	.45	.62	.55	.49	.44	.55	.36	.49	.58	.54	.41
Intell.Effi	-.41	-.23	-.41	-.28	-.52	-.45	-.42	-.30	-.49	-.28	-.43	-.42	-.55	-.36
Anxiety Aff	.45	.33	.53	.40	.68	.50	.49	.40	.61	.37	.52	.56	.58	.36
Depression	.41	.34	.54	.38	.63	.54	.49	.46	.60	.32	.56	.62	.60	.35
Anger Affct	.39	.37	.52	.35	.57	.57	.46	.43	.56	.43	.41	.53	.53	.36
Anhedonia A	.21	.12	.35	.15	.39	.34	.25	.21	.39	.12	.32	.33	.42	.14
Responsiblt	-.29	-.38	-.41	-.31	-.37	-.54	-.37	-.32	-.32	-.34	-.26	-.36	-.36	-.24
Tolerance	-.43	-.33	-.42	-.33	-.50	-.53	-.51	-.43	-.47	-.35	-.40	-.46	-.53	-.37
Empathy	.02	.04	.03	.07	.08	.06	.05	.03	.05	-.10	.08	.11	.07	.12
Role Play'g	-.37	-.28	-.40	-.28	-.52	-.44	-.42	-.32	-.50	-.31	-.40	-.43	-.55	-.28

Dominance	-.38	-.20	-.44	-.27	-.53	-.43	-.41	-.36	-.49	-.22	-.43	-.47	-.54	-.31
SocParticip	-.26	-.08	-.24	-.15	-.39	-.25	-.26	-.13	-.37	-.13	-.26	-.23	-.42	-.16
SocPresence	-.31	-.08	-.31	-.17	-.42	-.26	-.31	-.23	-.44	-.12	-.41	-.40	-.50	-.20
Dependency	**.45**	.27	**.51**	**.39**	**.67**	**.51**	**.51**	**.44**	**.62**	.30	**.55**	**.60**	**.64**	**.42**
Dom-Submisn	-.13	-.03	-.23	-.09	-.36	-.15	-.16	-.12	-.37	-.01	-.32	-.29	-.36	-.09
Love-Hate	-.41	-.42	-.53	-.38	-.56	-.62	-.49	-.46	-.54	-.40	-.48	-.59	-.60	-.44
EgoStrength	**-.44**	-.16	-.39	-.31	-.52	-.36	-.40	-.32	-.47	-.17	-.48	-.42	-.50	-.30
Resiliency	-.43	-.26	**-.52**	-.35	**-.62**	**-.52**	-.46	-.38	-.55	-.29	-.49	-.53	-.57	-.31
Self-Control	-.11	**-.35**	-.30	-.28	-.20	-.37	-.21	-.22	-.13	-.31	-.09	-.27	-.14	-.14
Impulsivity	**.40**	**.46**	**.53**	**.38**	**.55**	**.60**	**.43**	**.42**	**.50**	**.41**	.41	**.54**	.49	.38
Delinquency	**.39**	**.32**	**.48**	**.36**	**.56**	**.48**	.41	.36	**.51**	.31	.47	.51	**.55**	.31
Spy Scale	-.06	.14	.05	.06	-.13	.07	-.05	.03	-.16	.12	-.14	-.03	-.16	.02
HabCriminal	.20	**.30**	**.42**	.30	.38	**.47**	.26	.27	.32	.24	.28	**.38**	**.34**	.20

PrisnMaladj	-.04	.17	.19	.05	.02	.16	-.03	.02	-.02	.05	-.00	.08	-.01	-.05
Escapism	.24	**.35**	**.46**	.32	.49	.51	.37	.34	.40	.30	.36	**.48**	.43	.22
ParoleViola	**.37**	**.34**	**.46**	.37	**.50**	**.55**	**.48**	**.41**	**.49**	**.37**	.39	**.49**	**.53**	.37
Recidivism	.07	.30	.25	.19	.23	**.34**	.16	.17	.18	.25	.12	.22	.19	.15
OvContr.Hos	-.25	-.33	-.33	-.27	-.34	-.42	-.36	-.32	-.38	-.37	-.27	-.35	-.32	-.20
Violence	.28	**.41**	**.42**	**.30**	.41	**.53**	.36	.31	**.40**	**.41**	.28	**.45**	**.45**	.28
ThreatSuici	**.44**	.34	**.50**	**.38**	**.58**	**.56**	**.51**	**.46**	**.56**	**.39**	.48	.55	**.60**	.39
UncActOutSx	.27	.15	.32	.24	**.47**	.31	.29	.29	.39	.16	.40	.38	.39	.21
Paedophilia	.26	.06	.24	.23	**.38**	.26	.24	.21	.37	.09	.32	.29	.39	.21
AggravatdSx	-.23	-.23	-.41	-.31	-.44	-.47	-.34	-.37	-.40	-.30	-.33	-.43	-.43	-.17
Alcoholism	.07	.22	.16	.22	.11	**.28**	.16	.13	.05	.24	-.01	.09	.05	.09
Drug Abuse	.28	.31	**.46**	.31	**.46**	**.45**	.29	.31	**.41**	.23	**.38**	**.47**	**.43**	.22
WorkAttitud	.42	.40	.51	.38	.56	.54	.50	.42	.56	.36	.50	.57	.58	.38

FamilyProbs	.28	.27	.43	.32	.44	.50	.36	.34	.41	.29	.33	.43	.45	.31
ManifestHos	.32	.45	.48	.36	.50	.60	.43	.42	.42	.48	.33	.47	.45	.36
Phobias	.29	.16	.33	.27	.48	.31	.35	.23	.42	.16	.34	.35	.37	.27
Hypomania	.30	.37	.38	.40	.42	.44	.40	.35	.41	.46	.32	.42	.39	.31
Poor Health	.40	.07	.33	.23	.38	.22	.26	.20	.27	.08	.36	.29	.34	.16
Phar.Virtue	.43	.23	.39	.35	.54	.42	.43	.36	.55	.30	.46	.46	.52	.38
MAST	.05	.07	.16	.08	.13	.19	.10	.03	.14	.08	.09	.08	.13	−.02
DAST	.12	.26	.27	.20	.20	.24	.21	.16	.12	.18	.13	.27	.11	.05

Table 6.4: Correlation Coefficients between the Addicause axes and ninety-nine MMPI Scales (*T* Scores, Raw Omits, and Spy). Some interesting correlations are presented in **bold**. Coefficients greater than 0.07 are statistically significant (two-tailed tests, *N* = 695).

MMPI SCALES	43	44	45	46	47	48	49	50	51	52	53	54	55	56

Table 6.5: Correlation Coefficients between the Addicause axes and ninety-nine MMPI Scales (*T* Scores, Raw Omits, and Spy). Some interesting correlations are presented in **bold**.

MMPI SCALES	57	58	59	60	61	62	63	64	65	66	67	68	DAST	MAST
ItemsOmit'd	-.05	-.09	-.03	-.05	.02	.00	.01	-.03	-.02	.04	-.02	-.06	.01	.03
Validity: **L**	-.34	-.15	-.22	-.27	-.05	-.25	-.21	-.30	-.25	-.34	-.02	-.27	-.33	-.20
Validity: **F**	.56	.13	.27	.30	.07	.21	.21	.26	.35	.40	.02	.38	.29	.20
Validity: **K**	-.55	-.24	-.43	-.34	-.25	-.38	-.37	-.32	-.48	-.45	-.17	-.37	-.21	-.18
Hs (01)	.05	-.14	.09	-.11	-.08	-.02	-.07	-.15	-.01	.20	-.06	.03	-.00	.06
D (02)	**.37**	-.07	.20	.02	-.04	.05	.04	-.01	.16	**.36**	-.10	**.20**	.13	.16

Hy (03)	.04	−.16	.07	−.12	−.11	−.05	−.07	−.13	−.07	.18	−.07	.03	.04	.08
Pd (04)	.32	−.07	.03	.09	−.11	.03	.00	.06	.06	.20	−.10	.18	.38	.24
MF (05)	.21	.15	.15	−.00	−.03	.08	.05	−.01	.13	.20	−.03	.23	−.06	.04
Pa (06)	.47	.07	.27	.18	−.01	.14	.13	.12	.28	.32	−.02	.39	.15	.06
Pt (07)	.49	.07	.29	.17	.02	.15	.13	.14	.26	.48	.01	.39	.24	.13
Sc (08)	.54	.13	.28	.24	.05	.21	.18	.19	.33	.40	.07	.39	.20	.09
Ma (09)	.14	.21	.17	.32	.22	.25	.27	.31	.21	.17	.21	.29	.37	.12
Si (00)	.58	.03	.28	.10	.06	.15	.11	.03	.35	.38	−.03	.21	−.01	.14
TSC Fact.I	.59	.06	.30	.13	.04	.19	.15	.08	.35	.41	−.02	.25	.04	.20
TSC Fact.II	.36	.00	.30	.09	.05	.17	.12	.05	.24	.42	.01	.27	.13	.17
TSC Fact.III	.48	.18	.30	.32	.23	.35	.29	.28	.43	.35	.18	.31	.18	.07
TSC Fact.IV	.63	.13	.37	.30	.12	.25	.27	.26	.38	.51	.06	.43	.29	.21
TSC Fact.V	.51	.17	.36	.30	.14	.27	.28	.34	.42	.42	.07	.41	.31	.22

282

TSC Fact.VI	**.57**	**.25**	**.40**	**.35**	.18	**.34**	**.33**	**.33**	**.43**	**.54**	.16	**.47**	.23	.12
TSC Fact.VII	**.59**	.16	**.46**	.29	.19	**.28**	**.28**	.23	**.44**	**.59**	.09	**.43**	.21	.17
Plus Gettng	.63	.17	.44	.33	.18	.31	.31	.26	.46	.54	.11	.40	.26	.21
DY1: **VerySD**	-.56	.09	-.26	-.09	-.01	-.16	-.06	-.09	-.28	-.48	.10	-.21	-.20	-.26
DY2: **SocDes**	-.35	.08	-.13	.02	.11	.00	.05	.10	-.12	-.29	.22	-.13	-.06	-.23
DY3: SDNeut	.39	.26	.34	.37	.21	.38	.36	.36	.37	.39	.26	.36	.27	.14
DY4: **Undesr**	.59	.26	.39	.38	.21	.35	.36	.35	.48	.47	.20	.47	.32	.15
DY5: **VerySU**	.65	.16	.40	.34	.14	.28	.30	.26	.44	.52	.09	.44	.26	.21
Primitive D	.35	.16	.18	**.30**	.05	.22	.21	**.30**	.24	.25	.06	.28	.31	.28
Regression	.35	.16	.26	.15	.07	.21	.20	.13	**.29**	**.32**	.10	**.32**	.05	.29
Repression	-.29	-.11	-.10	-.30	-.02	-.18	-.16	-.32	-.24	-.31	.01	-.24	-.26	-.21
Denial Def.	**-.56**	-.15	-.32	-.28	-.11	-.26	-.25	-.26	-.38	-.44	-.06	-.39	-.21	-.28
Projection	.15	.10	.23	.15	.12	.18	.21	.14	.09	.14	.13	.08	.03	.04

283

Displacem't	.21	.08	**.28**	.06	.07	.12	.20	.07	.14	.32	.10	.21	.02	.08
Intellectiz	.03	-.07	-.05	-.04	.08	.06	.00	.04	.04	-.13	.13	-.11	-.01	-.03
Self-Doubt	**.45**	.12	**.33**	.11	.06	.16	.17	.08	**.31**	**.41**	.01	**.30**	.05	.06
Reactn Form	**.37**	-.07	.14	-.04	-.04	.04	-.00	-.08	.17	.23	-.02	.04	-.13	.05
OvAct.Think	**.57**	**.25**	**.40**	**.34**	.18	**.33**	**.33**	**.33**	**.43**	**.55**	.16	**.48**	.23	.12
Intell.Effi	-.50	-.11	-.32	-.20	-.12	-.22	-.18	-.14	-.34	-.43	-.06	-.33	-.11	-.12
Anxiety Aff	**.59**	.16	**.46**	**.30**	.19	**.28**	**.28**	.24	**.44**	**.59**	.09	**.43**	.21	.17
Depression	**.63**	.14	**.37**	**.30**	.12	**.25**	**.27**	**.26**	.38	**.52**	.06	**.43**	.29	.21
Anger Affct	**.51**	.17	.35	**.31**	.14	**.27**	**.28**	**.33**	**.42**	**.42**	.08	**.41**	.31	.23
Anhedonia A	.48	-.08	.18	.07	-.08	.08	.04	.04	.18	**.34**	-.08	.16	.16	.23
Responsiblt	-.36	-.04	-.16	-.30	-.05	-.20	-.17	-.22	-.25	-.31	-.02	-.23	-.45	-.27
Tolerance	-.51	-.17	-.36	-.32	-.20	-.33	-.30	-.26	-.42	-.40	-.18	-.33	-.19	-.11
Empathy	.04	.01	-.01	.01	-.01	-.01	-.01	-.06	.00	.11	-.10	.14	-.03	-.08

Role Play'g	-.52	-.10	-.31	-.22	-.10	-.19	-.17	-.20	-.41	-.35	-.07	-.28	-.15	-.14
Dominance	-.54	-.09	-.29	-.20	-.03	-.19	-.18	-.12	-.35	-.40	.00	-.31	-.20	-.19
SocParticip	-.44	.06	-.18	-.04	.05	-.07	-.02	.04	-.21	-.30	.11	-.07	.02	-.14
SocPresence	-.51	-.04	-.26	-.08	-.01	-.14	-.10	-.03	-.29	-.36	.04	-.24	-.03	-.15
Dependency	**.61**	**.23**	**.45**	**.28**	.18	**.32**	**.31**	.25	**.45**	**.54**	.11	**.48**	.15	.17
Dom-Submisn	-.41	.03	-.16	-.02	.07	-.00	-.01	-.00	-.16	-.31	-.12	-.19	-.03	-.09
Love-Hate	-.63	-.23	-.34	-.36	-.15	-.30	-.29	-.32	-.45	-.43	-.11	-.44	-.26	-.15
EgoStrength	-.50	-.12	-.34	-.15	-.14	-.20	-.21	-.07	-.35	-.45	-.09	-.38	-.08	-.09
Resiliency	-.58	-.08	-.36	-.22	-.08	-.25	-.21	-.19	-.37	-.54	-.01	-.36	-.28	-.27
Self-Control	-.16	-.04	-.10	-.26	-.02	-.18	-.17	-.31	-.10	-.23	-.01	-.18	-.49	-.34
Impulsivity	**.53**	.16	.30	**.34**	.10	**.31**	.28	**.36**	.40	**.46**	.07	**.40**	.35	.23
Delinquency	**.56**	.14	.34	.27	.12	.25	.20	.24	.36	**.45**	.08	**.40**	.24	.16
Spy Scale	-.18	.01	-.09	.11	.03	-.01	.06	.17	-.10	-.12	.03	.01	.28	-.01

HabCriminal	.39	-.02	.12	.20	-.04	.11	.12	.17	.15	.31	-.07	.25	.48	.32
PrisnMaladj	.03	-.09	-.11	.08	-.13	-.07	.02	.09	-.09	.04	-.13	-.00	.43	.24
Escapism	**.48**	.03	.24	**.30**	.04	.26	.21	.29	.28	**.42**	-.00	**.36**	.45	.28
ParoleViola	**.51**	.14	.29	.28	.14	**.30**	.25	.26	**.43**	.39	.12	**.36**	.26	.24
Recidivism	.22	.01	.10	.24	-.01	.13	.14	.19	.19	.16	.01	.15	.42	.41
OvContr.Hos	-.33	-.15	-.21	-.26	-.08	-.21	-.24	-.28	-.30	-.23	-.04	-.23	-.29	-.15
Violence	**.40**	.07	.22	**.31**	.04	.22	.23	**.30**	.31	.32	.03	.30	.39	.20
ThreatSuici	**.59**	.17	.35	**.30**	.14	.31	.26	.26	.41	**.49**	.11	**.38**	.27	.18
UncActOutSx	.44	.10	.30	.15	.14	.18	.19	.13	.21	.36	.02	.29	.11	.04
Paedophilia	.41	.09	.24	.08	-.04	.09	.05	-.02	.22	.25	-.02	.26	-.06	.05
AggravatdSx	-.44	-.01	-.22	-.18	-.05	-.20	-.19	-.23	-.25	-.43	.01	-.29	-.46	-.22
Alcoholism	.04	.03	.05	.20	.08	.12	.16	.19	.08	.12	.11	.06	.41	.42
Drug Abuse	**.51**	.03	.21	.23	-.00	.21	.19	.22	**.30**	**.40**	-.04	.31	.34	.25

286

WorkAttitud	.55	.13	.35	.33	.18	.30	.29	.30	.43	.46	.11	.41	.31	.19
RehabMotiva	.15	-.11	.04	-.00	-.08	.04	.00	.03	.01	.16	-.07	.12	.17	.14
ChangeMotiv	.64	.10	.36	.24	.07	.22	.22	.20	.39	.54	-.01	.40	.26	.21
ThyroidPath	.12	.12	.12	.10	.03	.16	.04	.10	.05	.07	.10	.15	.01	-.07
Caudality	.57	.10	.39	.26	.13	.26	.24	.19	.40	.47	.06	.36	.25	.22
LowBackPain	-.06	-.15	-.03	-.09	-.03	-.07	-.10	-.05	-.08	.05	-.06	-.11	-.04	-.08
ParietFront	.56	.09	.40	.26	.11	.24	.22	.20	.35	.52	.02	.36	.23	.23
SocAdjustmt	.53	-.01	.23	.06	.02	.11	.09	.01	.31	.34	-.03	.15	-.01	.15
DepressCont	.65	.15	.41	.28	.11	.25	.27	.25	.43	.55	.06	.44	.26	.18
Poor Morale	.59	.21	.40	.29	.15	.29	.31	.25	.45	.51	.07	.47	.22	.15
RelFundam't	-.12	.07	-.08	-.12	-.00	-.05	-.01	-.08	-.10	-.12	.02	.01	-.17	-.05
AuthConflct	.36	.09	.26	.36	.23	.31	.28	.30	.32	.27	.19	.17	.35	.22
Psychotic	.54	.22	.35	.35	.16	.30	.26	.26	.40	.39	.13	.43	.22	.07

287

Organ.Sympt	.37	.06	.29	.15	.10	.23	.15	.12	.28	.41	.05	.28	.20	.18
FamilyProbs	**.47**	.13	.21	.20	.05	.23	.21	.24	**.30**	**.31**	.05	.30	.27	.22
ManifestHos	**.46**	.14	.29	**.35**	.16	**.29**	.28	**.38**	**.39**	**.38**	.13	**.35**	.36	.24
Phobias	**.42**	.18	**.33**	.19	.15	.21	.19	.10	.29	**.39**	.04	**.34**	.12	.11
Hypomania	.33	**.24**	.33	**.36**	**.23**	**.32**	**.33**	**.34**	**.36**	.33	.20	.30	.29	.14
Poor Health	.29	.03	.26	.08	.05	.12	.11	.01	.20	**.34**	.00	.26	.14	.17
Phar.Virtue	**.48**	.24	**.39**	.26	**.22**	**.29**	**.33**	.25	**.44**	**.40**	.16	**.38**	.07	.05
MAST	.14	-.05	.09	.11	-.03	.09	.04	.07	.08	.19	-.09	.08	.18	
DAST	.18	.01	-.03	.25	-.03	.03	.15	.18	.02	.14	-.08	.19		

Coefficients greater than 0.07 are statistically significant (two-tailed tests, $N = 695$)

APPENDIX I

Table 7.1: Discriminant Function % Correct Classifications and Correlation Coefficients between the Addicause axes and ninety-one MMPI Scales, Probabilities are rounded to the nearest two decimal places.

AXIS LABELS AND VARIABLES	BEER USE	BEER YRS	BRND USE	BRND YRS	BREW USE	BREW YRS	GINV USE	GINV YRS	RUM USE	RUM YRS	RYE USE	RYE YRS	SCOT USE	SCOT YRS
DAQ Discrim *S*	47%	64%	46%	67%	80%	70%	58%	54%	58%	55%	50%	51%	65%	57%
% Correct *N*	43%	64%	44%	62%	68%	64%	62%	52%	63%	56%	45%	50%	60%	61%
01: Social *S*	.00	.20	.09	.13	.04	.12	.01	.43	.05	.24	.00	.06	.36	.57
Anxiety *N*	.01	.06	.09	.18	.03	.11	.01	.42	.17	.85	.01	.25	.30	.44
02: Social *S*	.10	.01	.30	.19	.22	.01*	.18	.06	.29	.00	.05	.00	.35	.13
Enjoyment *N*	.05	.01	.67	.43*	.14*	.06*	.13	.17	.53	.07	.01*	.08	.54	.57

289

03: Reactive S	.04	.01	.13	.12	.15	.05	.01	.01	.13	.03	.00	.00	.84	.17
Depression N	.02	.00	.58	.61	.58	.10	.02	.01	.53	.05	.01	.00	.80	.47
04: Stimulus S	.00*	.00	.76	.20	.54	.38*	.02	.04	.48	.00	.22	.00	.59	.03
Hunger N	.00*	.00	.79	.33	.50*	.45	.05	.06	.63	.00	.24	.00	.83	.03
05: Rigid S	.00	.00	.10	.02	.21	.00	.01	.06	.03	.00	.00	.01	.55	.65
Self-Image N	.00	.00	.15	.06	.26	.01	.01	.03	.03	.00	.00	.00	.45	.69
06: Social S	.09	.00	.87	.15	.83*	.22	.18	.02	.30*	.00	.00	.00	.58	.57
Influence N	.06	.00	.87	.30	.78	.33	.09	.02	.56	.01	.01	.01	.69	.80
07: Aggressn S	.01	.04	.08	.01	.06	.01	.51	.13	.91	.06	.20	.02	.98	.36
Inhibition N	.03	.02	.18	.08	.11	.02	.44	.10	.64	.03	.15	.00	.99	.42
08: Guilt S	.00	.00	.05	.02	.03	.02	.01	.32	.05	.01	.00	.07	.95	.18
Intolerance N	.00	.00	.02	.01	.00	.01	.00	.18	.03	.00	.00	.02	.87	.19
09: Loneliness S	.01	.01	.07	.03	.04	.01	.02	.03	.06	.00	.00	.00	.70	.38
N	.04	.02	.07	.03	.03	.01	.03	.02	.19	.00	.01	.00	.65	.53
10: Social S	.99	.01	.30	.10*	.28	.06	.30	.27	.46	.04	.73	.00	.53	.68
Contact Wsh N	.99	.01*	.26	.17	.24*	.13	.38	.32	.54	.08	.75	.02	.47	.82
11: Reality S	.00	.00	.06	.01	.03	.01	.00	.06	.02	.01	.00	.00	.36	.28
Denial N	.00	.00	.03	.01	.04	.01	.01	.05	.06	.01	.00	.00	.21	.38

12: Authorit *S*	.18	.80	.01	.00	.00	.04	.07	.01	.08	.02	.04	.06	.00	.00
Rebellion *N*	.25	.66	.01	.00	.01	.07	.05	.00	.07	.01	.07	.04	.00	.00
13: Flat *S*	.30	.32	.02	.00	.08	.01	.03	.00	.04	.02	.02	.05	.01	.00
Depression *N*	.21	.28*	.04	.00	.11	.02	.03	.00	.03	.01	.04	.03	.01	.00
14: Vivid *S*	.35	75	.06	.66	.12	.72	.48	.64	.06	.11	.49	.43	.34*	.53
Imagery *N*	.07	.25	.35	.84	.71	.96	.61	.42	.09	.11*	.25	.19	.34	.50
15: Control *S*	.34	.89	.15	.01	.22	.25	.11	.04	.02	.13*	.09	.11	.04	.00
Effort *N*	.51	.99*	.04	.01	.10	.25	.06	.02	.02	.13	.13	.12	.01	.00
16: Control *S*	.32	.64	.02	.37	.07	.17	.93	.91	.26	.57	.09	.08	.03	.07
of Others *N*	.50	.48	.03	.16	.13	.31	.91	.86	.45	.76	.22	.14	.02	.07
17: Grief *S*	.54	.89	.02	.02*	.10	.37	.18*	.20	.09	.07*	.13	.13	.02	.05*
Reaction *N*	.73	.86	.03	.03	.21	.50	.19	.16	.13	.05	.24	.18	.02	.02
18: Substanc *S*	.35	.37	.00	.00	.00	.00	.00	.00*	.13	.06	.08	.08	.00*	.00*
Enhancement *N*	.72	.51	.00	.00	.01	.00	.01	.00*	.22	.11	.19	.18	.00*	.00*
19: Pain *S*	.89	.63	.41	.19	.06	.36	.88	.93	.09	.07	.44	.51	.48*	.37
Sensitivity *N*	.97	.50	.35	.16	.13	.69	.86	.80	.25	.08	.52	.55	.29	.06
20: Hedonism *S*	.04	.44	.00	.51	.00	.24	.41	.44	.33	.90	.36	.09	.00*	.14
N	.03	.09	.00	.24	.03	.18	.76	.46	.34*	.55	.47*	.06	.00*	.07

		1	2	3	4	5	6	7	8	9	10	11	12	13	14
21: Social Withdrawal	S	.00	.22	.08	.10	.02	.07	.01	.58	.38	.36	.00	.11	.85	.45
	N	.01	.10	.12	.16	.06	.09	.02	.64	.47	.42	.00	.16	.91	.53
22: SubCult. Values	S	.00	.00	.00	.00*	.00*	.00*	.00	.00*	.01*	.00*	.00	.00*	.18	.00
	N	.00	.00	.00	.00*	.00*	.00*	.00	.00*	.01*	.00*	.00	.00*	.20	.01
23: Inhibit Dependency	S	.03	.04	.10	.22	.15	.12	.02	.14	.19	.11	.00	.03	.54	.30
	N	.04	.02	.12	.22	.06	.17	.01	.28	.32	.19	.01	.05	.83	.48
24: Immediat Gratificatn	S	.24	.86	.00	.33	.70	.21	.01*	.01	.14	.46	.18	.69	.03	.07*
	N	.22	.83	.00	.06	.12	.02	.00*	.00*	.01	.06*	.02*	.28	.01	.01
25: Paranoid Sensitivity	S	.20	.02	.08	.07	.08	.06	.22	.39	.29	.05	.03	.02	.99	.39
	N	.13	.07	.17	.18	.06	.15	.05	.25	.39	.08	.01	.05	.97	.55
26: Rationality Defence	S	.42	.35	.08	.78	.93	.72	.60	.81	.14	.97	.51	.25	.09*	.96
	N	.69	.53	.11	.89	.72	.78	.76	.88	.24	.99	.35	.40	.05*	.88
27: Oppressive Inhibit	S	.15	.14	.29	.25	.21	.11	.46	.43	.89	.18	.12	.09	.90	.51
	N	.02	.12	.26	.35	.18	.14	.20	.33	.77	.14	.11	.05	.84	.80*
28: Comfortable Inhibit	S	.15	.08	.56	.70	.54	.94	.84	.86	.98	.82	.34	.79	.74	.44
	N	.07	.18	.90	.94	.82	.71	.46	.97	.84	.75	.16	.53	.27	.90
29: Affect Disturbance	S	.00	.01*	.12	.22	.04	.06	.01	.04	.13	.06	.00	.01	.79	.49
	N	.00	.01	.28	.53	.08*	.15	.01	.03	.15*	.05*	.00	.03	.98	.70

30: Affect *S*	.23	.72	.00	.61	.00	.28	.34	.86	.06	.35	.04	.35	.00	.61
Denial *N*	.29	.71	.00	.39	.01	.40	.40	.60	.15	.54	.25	.71	.00	.22
31: Demean *S*	.49	.30	.03	.00	.08	.22	.39	.11	.06	.07	.09	.01	.01	.03
Others *N*	.55	.37	.01	.02	.07	.46	.36	.10	.07	.02	.10	.01	.01	.08
32: Group *S*	.86	.73	.26	.29	.60	.43	.75	.46	.78*	.93	.86*	.95	.08	.06
Satisfact'n *N*	.88	.20	.17	.11	.50	.16*	.85	.54	.84*	.69	.79*	.51	.02	.12
33: Dogmatism *S*	.01	.15	.00*	.21	.00	.46	.90	.24	.00	.01	.00*	.01	.05	.24
N	.02*	.33	.00*	.48	.00	.47	.52	.39	.01	.02	.01*	.03	.07	.26
34: Wish Be *S*	.00*	.22	.00	.09	.00	.46	.13	.20	.01	.00	.00*	.01	.00	.05
Different *N*	.00	.27	.00	.11	.00	.47	.11	.12	.01	.01*	.01*	.05	.00	.02
35: Self- *S*	.09	.60	.12	.00	.10	.03	.01	.00	.02	.01	.03	.02	.09	.00
Depreciat'n *N*	.07	.39	.31	.00	.22	.04	.02	.00	.02	.01	.03*	.02	.03	.00
36: Rigid *S*	.48	.52	.39	.22	.52*	.05	.00*	.03	.77	.50	.73	.62	.27	.04
Moralizat'n *N*	.50	.40	.26	.15	.33	.04	.03	.10	.80	.40	.92	.58	.49*	.34
37: Paroxys- *S*	.00*	.00*	.00*	.00*	.00*	.00*	.00*	.00*	.01	.00*	.02*	.00*	.00*	.00*
mality *N*	.00*	.00*	.00*	.00*	.00*	.00*	.00*	.00*	.01	.00*	.01	.00*	.00*	.00*
38: Rules *S*	.02	.67	.00	.00	.00	.10	.05	.06	.03	.05	.02	.05	.00	.00
Intolerance *N*	.01	.70	.00	.00	.00	.28	.04	.11	.13	.22	.07	.15	.00	.00

	1	2	3	4	5	6	7	8	9	10	11	12	13	14
39: Effort *S*	.01	.02	.35	.29	.16	.09	.53*	.69	.74*	.03*	.06	.10	.97	.66
Strain *N*	.02*	.01	.30	.30	.15	.08	.36*	.54	.56*	.01	.09	.08	.99	.42
40: Pep-Up *S*	.19	.01	.69	.72	.79	.57	.72	.86	.41	.48	.88	.04	.86	.18
Effect *N*	.33	.03	.73	.93	.85	.82	.70	.77	.72	.37	.46	.04	.99	.25
41: Rigid *S*	.00	.00	.01	.02	.01	.02	.08	.65	.20	.01	.00	.05	.95*	.21
Habits *N*	.00	.00	.02	.04	.01	.03	.09	.63	.34	.01	.01	.06	.94	.36
42: Easy Go *S*	.07	.00	.07	.09	.61	.11	.61	.32	.09*	.00	.87	.00	.12	.14
Enjoyment *N*	.08	.00	.21	.60	.93	.62	.55	.61	.09*	.11	.91	.01	.32	.47
43: Metabolic *S*	.01	.00	.63	.69	.10	.60	.09	.08	.05	.00	.00	.00	.95	.43
Disorder *N*	.00	.00	.39	.73	.03	.74	.06	.03	.08	.02	.00	.00	.98	.37
44: Fast-Lane *S*	.00	.00	.03	.02*	.04	.09	.04	.17	.16	.00	.01	.00	.58	.01*
Living *N*	.00	.00	.02	.05	.05	.14	.02	.16	.15	.01	.01	.00	.31	.02
45: Hypo- *S*	.00	.00	.05	.37	.10	.24	.06	.12	.01	.00	.00	.00	.39	.48
glycaemia *N*	.00	.00	.04	.27	.05	.24	.08	.23	.04	.01	.01	.01	.44	.38
46: Allergy *S*	.00	.00	.27	.28	.21	.38	.16	.51	.03	.02*	.01	.02	.31	.08
Stress *N*	.00	.00	.29	.26	.26	.45	.29	.43	.13	.10*	.07	.05	.21	.08
47: Physiolog. *S*	.00	.00	.04	.23*	.01	.11	.00	.07	.01	.06	.00	.03	.57	.28
Anxiety *N*	.00	.00	.06	.45*	.03	.20*	.04	.05*	.04	.01	.00	.11	.51	.47

48: Punitive Reinforcement — S	.01	.01*	.00	.00	.00	.01	.01	.00	.00*	.00	.00*	.00	.00	.00
48: Punitive Reinforcement — N	.01	.03	.08*	.00	.02	.03	.02*	.00	.00*	.00	.01	.00	.00	.00
49: Affect Avoidance — S	.31	.71	.12	.00	.04	.36	.46	.12	.02	.09	.06	.08	.00	.00
49: Affect Avoidance — N	.24	.34	.15	.01	.05	.44	.30	.12	.03	.13	.09	.06	.00	.00
50: Control Sensitivity — S	.09	.39	.03	.02	.11	.24	.54	.23	.02	.01	.01	.03	.00	.00
50: Control Sensitivity — N	.07	.48	.03	.07	.10	.32	.33	.13	.02*	.01	.01*	.03	.00	.00
51: Guilt Proneness — S	.15	.64	.06	.00	.18	.39	.04	.04	.15	.18	.25	.18	.01	.00
51: Guilt Proneness — N	.38	.64	.07	.01	.15	.55	.06	.09	.32	.27	.56	.29	.02	.00
52: Anger/Hostility — S	.01	.47	.00	.00	.00*	.46	.04	.33	.01	.14	.03	.04	.00	.00
52: Anger/Hostility — N	.00*	.56	.00	.00	.00*	.59	.03	.22	.01	.10	.03	.01	.00	.00
53: Somatic Depression — S	.70*	.78*	.07	.03*	.05	.43	.18	.28	.08	.18	.24	.30	.00	.01
53: Somatic Depression — N	.79*	.67*	.09*	.14*	.06	.64	.18	.38	.07	.19	.26	.31	.00	.01
54: Hungry Heart — S	.38	.70	.02*	.00	.01	.12	.04	.04	.07*	.16*	.31*	.41	.00	.00
54: Hungry Heart — N	.20	.74	.01	.01	.00	.13	.01	.02	.04	.22	.24*	.31	.00*	.00
55: Impaired Self-Esteem — S	.39	.65	.04	.00*	.00	.05	.01	.03	.02	.02*	.13	.14	.00*	.00
55: Impaired Self-Esteem — N	.19	.50	.06	.00	.00	.04	.01	.01	.01	.03	.13	.10	.00*	.00
56: Masked Disappointm — S	.09	.77	.00	.02	.00	.19	.30	.28*	.07	.07	.04	.07	.00	.00
56: Masked Disappointm — N	.08	.60	.01	.02	.00	.12	.23	.13*	.10	.08	.11	.13	.00	.00

57: Felt *S*	.00	.01	.03	.06	.01	.02	.02	.06	.09	.01	.00	.03	.38	.23
Rejection *N*	.00	.01	.02	.05	.02	.02	.02	.09	.26	.01	.02	.03	.47	.10
58: Need to *S*	.16	.00	.55	.58	.18*	.51	.60	.70	.80	.13	.46	.09	.73	.96
Communicate *N*	.06	.01	.88	.87	.23	.82	.72	.68	.76	.03	.66	.04	.52	.84
59: NeedCalm *S*	.00	.01	.07	.13	.04	.07	.08	.37	.04	.17	.00	.18	.45	.66
Nerves *N*	.00	.02	.24	.26	.07	.21	.10	.19	.14	.43	.02	.13	.63	.89
60: Substanc *S*	.00	.00	.00	.02	.02	.02	.00	.17	.00*	.00	.00	.00	.30	.09
Enhancement *N*	.00	.00	.01	.05	.05	.04	.01	.19	.01	.00	.00	.00	.50	.14
61: Forget *S*	.01	.00	.01	.05	.01	.00	.04	.03*	.04	.00	.00	.00	.37	.27
Failures *N*	.00	.00	.04	.11	.06	.01	.07	.02	.12	.00	.00	.00	.63	.38
62: WshNovel *S*	.00	.00	.06	.08	.02	.01	.01	.02	.00	.00	.00	.00	.32	.04
Experiences *N*	.00	.00	.25	.32	.10	.12	.07	.10	.01*	.00	.03	.01	.86	.34
63: Avoid *S*	.00	.00*	.10	.06	.03	.03	.04	.00	.05	.00	.00	.00	.31	.19
Boredom *N*	.00	.00*	.26	.17	.10	.05	.05	.03	.18	.04	.02	.00	.67	.46
64: Assert *S*	.00	.00	.10	.10	.38	.05	.00	.00	.07	.00	.00	.00*	.58	.05
Confidence *N*	.00	.00	.21	.37	.63	.20	.01	.03	.21	.00	.00	.00	.73	.18
65: Avoid *S*	.00	.01	.10	.20	.05	.19	.19	.39	.42	.05	.00	.06	.70	.88
Attractiven *N*	.02	.04	.12	.16	.04	.12	.42	.60	.58	.05	.01	.08	.86	.64

Variable	1	2	3	4	5	6	7	8	9	10	11	12	13	14
66: Impaired *S* Sleep *N*	.00 / .00	.00 / .00	.06 / .15	.16 / .27	.01 / .08	.12 / .26	.01 / .02	.11 / .20	.01 / .08	.04 / .08	.00 / .01	.01 / .03	.37 / .66	.19 / .56
67: NeedCalm/ *S* Relaxation *N*	.02 / .04	.11 / .17	.31 / .80	.31 / .71	.30 / .78	.29 / .65	.19 / .60	.62 / .57	.10 / .33	.05 / .18	.15 / .44	.13 / .08	.87 / .29	.40 / .96
68: Substanc *S* Dependency *N*	.02 / .02	.01 / .01	.02 / .03	.07 / .09	.01 / .01	.03* / .03	.00 / .00	.04 / .03	.02 / .04	.02 / .03	.00 / .00	.03 / .06	.36 / .42	.04 / .04
ML: MMPI L	.49	.41	.28	.52	.42	.08	.54	.05	.03	.02	.91	.00	.21	.25
MF: MMPI F	.17	.84	.31	.84	.58	.73	.23	.66	.17	.54	.11	.26	.19	.36
MK: MMPI K	.62	.73	.37	.58	.30	.66	.93	.09	.16	.20	.24	.02	.14	.14
01: MMPI Hs	.11	.80	.61	.56	.04	.03*	.01	.12	.00*	.06	.60	.05	.09	.31
02: MMPI D	.89	.98	.30	.65	.13	.06	.17	.12	.09	.11	.19	.07*	.30	.47
03: MMPI Hy	.18	.92	.67	.73	.08	.71	.08*	.19	.00	.20	.68	.05	.48	.50
04: MMPI Pd	.03	.80	.71	.71	.19	.75	.05	.00	.06	.13	.47	.07	.70	.52
05: MMPI MF	.05*	.25	.36	.14	.26	.21	.99	.03	.63	.59	.36*	.75	.55	.70
06: MMPI Pa	.55	.28	.43	.72	.03	.71	.82	.35	.10	.35	.84	.28	.86	.54

07: MMPI Pt	.40	.30	.52	.05	.05	.34	.34	.95	.92	.10	.63	.23	.39	.76
08: MMPI Sc	.58	.54	.49	.17	.30	.07	.29	.40	.97	.24	.55	.36	.76	.32
09: MMPI Ma	.34	.48	.29	.15	.46	.08	.65	.69*	.03	.87	.56	.01*	.32	.71
00: MMPI Si	.11	.16	.23	.15	.31	.43	.15	.93	.17	.06	.20	.09	.81	.69
MMPI TSC F1	.07	.08	.12	.38	.10	.48	.04	.99	.30	.06	.33	.16	.68	.45
MMPI TSC F2	.06	.04	.06	.12*	.03	.03	.32	.18*	.10	.03	.46	.23	.62	.06
MMPI TSC F3	.37	.49	.05	.21	.75	.12	.08	.63	.60	.32	.97	.29	.82	.26
MMPI TSC F4	.16	.13	.04	.21	.03	.08	.05	.42	.37	.07	.61	.43	.48	.90
MMPI TSC F5	.25	.19	.01	.23	.08	.06	.10	.51	.53	.11	.84	.66	.10	.20
MMPI TSC F6	.29	.26	.05	.07	.04	.02	.14	.70	.52	.50	.72	.18	.52	.44
MMPI TSC F7	.24	.11	.26	.12	.08	.16	.30	.98	.62	.14	.48	.19	.09	.44
Plus Getting	.14	.06	.01	.23	.09	.10	.02	.64	.48	.02*	.67	.31	.21	.57
MMPI DY 1	.16	.01*	.38	.05*	.22	.50	.14	.28	.75	.10	.86	.41	.85	.30

MMPI DY 2	.68	.27	.13	.03*	.09	.22	.98	.45	.91	.74	.20	.37	.04	.10
MMPI DY 3	.44	.55	.67	.93	.41	.36	.51	.19	.02	.07	.49	.04	.29	.14
MMPI DY 4	.15	.51	.29	.89	.27	.73	.53	.10	.02	.04	.09	.02	.12	.14
MMPI DY 5	.18	.40	.31	.73	.32	.99	.85	.33	.20	.42	.04	.07	.20	.23
MMPI PrimDef	.20	.81	.81	.91	.10	.32	.15	.01	.05	.06	.28	.00	.04	.05
MMPI Regress	.02	.78	.19*	.70	.38	.30	.62	.12	.24	.23	.65	.21	.74	.43
MMPI Repress	.28	.10*	.80	.32	.91	.23	.86	.00*	.70	.26	.71	.36	.57	.89
MMPI Denial	.70	.52	.04	.52	.13	.67	.33	.08	.28	.06	.72	.02	.14	.21
MMPI Project	.78	.69	.73	.79	.99	.77	.73	.94	.71	.95	.17	.48	.71	.95
MMPI Displac	.96	.50	.44	.80	.38	.96	.94	.99	.91	.57	.24*	.61	.51	.82
MMPI Intellz	.28	.88	.09	.31	.89	.91	.02*	.15	.49	.82	.60	.80	.24	.38
MMPI S.Doubt	.55	.05	.39	.14	.05	.09	.51*	.38	.18	.14	.20	.12	.01*	.04
MMPI RctForm	.16	.64	.31	.82	.11	.15	.98	.72	.41	.47	.14	.83	.59	.32

MMPI OvAcThk	.28	.26	.04	.08	.03	.02	.14	.76	.60	.51	.73	.15	.58	.44
MMPI IntEffc	.22	.10	.30	.01	.86	.41	.73	.67	.99	.80	.82	.12	.92	.13
MMPI Anxiety	.21	.10	.23	.12	.07	.17	.31	.99	.56	.13	.44	.16	.09	.42
MMPI Depress	.15	.11	.03	.22	.03	.08	.05	.36	.36	.06	.59	.40	.54	.86
MMPI Anger	.23	.20	.01	.27	.08	.06	.11	.50	.58	.14	.82	.62	.10	.20
MMPI Anhedon	.32	.52	.43	.40	.08	.30	.22	.53	.46	.16	.56	.52	.86	.91
MMPI Respons	.06	.04	.01	.08	.40	.12	.03	.35	.07	.66	.53	.54	.96	.04
MMPI Toleran	.12	.07	.02	.06	.14	.04	.11	.55	.72	.66	.66	.39	.78	.12
MMPI Empathy	.64	.63	.15	.61	.71	.09	.12	.07	.85	.08	.24	.68	.77	.37
MMPI RolPlay	.55	.45	.19	.27	.54	.66	.13	.59	.99	.88	.24	.03	.94	.47
MMPI Dominan	.04	.02	.16	.08	.24	.47	.44	.91	.37	.06	.32	.25	.42	.32
MMPI SocPart	.42	.27	.75	.05	.91	.99	.47	.54	.36	.02	.73	.31	.09*	.07
MMPI SocPres	.72	.72	.66	.23	.36	.75	.49	.83	.37	.06	.94	.47	.92	.62

MMPI Dependc	.13	.09	.06	.50	.01	.18	.06	.63	.33	.05	.28	.20	.13	.87
MMPI Dom-Subm	.52	.46	.98	.65	.63	.85	.52	.80	.03	.50	.43	.22	.66	.75
MMPI Lov-Hate	.38	.39	.09	.08	.49	.11	.22	.67	.76	.52	.67	.25	.70	.46
MMPI EgoStrn	.11	.09	.17	.15	.02	.03	.26	.47	.53	.23	.25	.17	.98	.65
MMPI Resilie	.03	.01	.01	.05	.01	.03	.04	.41	.24	.02	.69	.38	.51	.16
MMPI S.Cntrl	.19	.44	.00	.98	.20	.00*	.00	.02*	.00	.78	.40	.88	.94	.00
MMPI Impulsv	.17	.20	.00	.36	.05	.01	.01	.62	.18	.83*	.89	.38	.20	.06
MMPI Delinqu	.19	.26	.03	.06	.04	.13	.15	.55	.73	.29	.45	.30	.27	.57
MMPI Raw Spy	.87	.85	.63	.43	.18	.64	.04*	.89	.30	.30	.35	.60	.62	.30
MMPI HabCrim	.20	.35	.01	.55	.06	.01	.00*	.03	.08	.19	.82	.86	.86	.02
MMPI PrisAdj	.90	.09	.71	.54	.94	.13	.12	.09	.01	.55	.09	.38	.87	.04
MMPI Escapis	.17	.22	.00	.18	.00*	.01	.01	.19	.21	.14	.90	.48	.22	.09
MMPI ParViol	.52	.35	.01	.22	.05	.01	.08	.54	.37	.52	.96	.43	.89	.14

MMPI Recidiv	.00	.67	.52	.64	.48*	.03	.11	.04	.01	.57	.24	.03	.90	.94
MMPI OvCoHos	.48	.77	.94	.84	.14	.47	.22	.02*	.09	.13	.42	.10	.59	.44
MMPI Violenc	.28	.54	.24	.80	.94	.64	.45	.07	.01*	.15	.62	.02	.11	.07
MMPI ThrSuic	.08	.96	.38	.64	.20	.52	.43	.08	.01	.04	.01	.01	.02	.02*
MMPI UncAcSx	.64	.69	.97	.77	.51	.40	.95	.89	.92	.99	.21	.73	.58	.85
MMPI Pedophi	.80	.71	.43	.84	.07	.12	.26	.57	.72	.48	.57	.75	.44	.84
MMPI AggrSex	.84	.73	.62	.87	.77	.20	.38	.02	.03	.00	.05	.00*	.09	.06
MMPI Alcohol	.01	.08*	.28	.02*	.44	.00*	.05	.03	.02	.02	.94	.00*	.37	.28
MMPI DrgAbus	.07	.25	.32	.83	.34	.43	.44	.03	.32	.11	.24	.03	.07	.05
MMPI Work Att	.12	.35	.33	.56*	.10	.30	.60	.02	.02	.05	.05	.01	.04	.08
MMPI RehMotiv	.44	.36	.97	.99	.25	.18	.36	.27	.50	.33	.20	.38	.23	.50
MMPI ChngeMot	.79	.41	.06	.63	.12	.33	.67	.04	.24	.01	.14	.03	.04	.05
MMPI ThyroidP	.19	.59	.84	.43	.30	.03*	.47	.54	.50	.82	.73	.84	.27	.79

MMPI Caudalit	.06	.02	.01	.09	.03	.08	.06	.62	.68	.09	.29	.12	.26	.26
MMPI LowBckPn	.49	48	.13	.59	.40	.06	.65	.23	.60	.35	.04*	.17*	.43	.45
MMPI Par-Fron	.05	.02	.02*	.04	.01	.26	.10	.54	.50	.13	.26	.05	.58	.37
MMPI SoAdjust	.22	.22	.36	.27	.17	.56	.10	.87	.46	.03	.55	.39	.61	.23
MMPI DeprCon	.05	.05	.03	.10	.05	.04	.08	.29	.37	.03	.48	.42	.57	.66
MMPI PMorale	.25	.12	.06	.48	.07	.07	.14	.41	.35	.02	.43	.43	.25	.97
MMPI RelFund	.68	.54	.74	.37	.49	.82	.19	.48	.38	.19	.94	.15	.43	.51
MMPI AuthCnf	.14	.27	.00	.24	.20	.03	.04	.17*	.18	.65	.99	.64	.16	.04
MMPI Psychot	.32	.35	.07	.04	.71	.16	.46	.99	.96	.36	.60	.12*	.49	.61
MMPI OrgSymp	.07	.03	.02	.20	.01	.00	.06	.01*	.13	.04	.15	.02*	.84	.04
MMPI FamProb	.38	.52	.15	.07	.08	.18	.17	.81	.49	.57	.49	.93	.26	.76
MMPI ManHost	.53	.55	.01	.32	.15	.02	.06	.28	.10	.46	.56	.49	.26	.12
MMPI Phobias	.27	.06	.59	.13	.95	.92	.91	.48	.31	.39	.49	.33	.01*	.59

MMPI Hypoman	.80	.93	.43	.37	.56	.07	.77	.31	.09	.13	.33	.03	.68	.70
MMPI PHealth	.17	.81	.25	.28	.06	.55	.35	.54	.07	.02	.11	.04	.03	.08
MMPI PharVir	.87	.12	.52	.98	.15	.47	.99	.56	.26	.73	.21	.42	.45	.57
MAST-Alcohol	.00*	.00*	.00*	.00*	.00*	.01*	.00*	.00*	.13	.18	.01*	.01*	.02*	.02*
DAST-DrugsR2	.25	.03	.02*	.05	.09	.11	.10	.13	.58	.79	.35	.10	.42	.47
STFB TotalY1	.15	.00*	.96	.82	.42	.52	.29	.47	.31	.12	.06	.01*	.79	.87
STFB Fact. 1	.37	.00	.89	.95	.81	.98	.82	.85	.07	.04	.15	.05	.49	.43
STFB Fact. 2	.14	.03	.66	.53	.51	.50	.70	.81	.42	.35	.02*	.10	.72	.51
STFB Fact. 3	.20	.00	.59	.32	.78	.83	.05	.09	.80	.55	.03*	.02	.61	.80
STFB Fact. 4	.55	.05	.64	.66	.56	.85	.54	.36	.46	.25	.01*	.01	.01*	.01*
STFB Fact. 5	.39	.00	.94	.59	.99	.71	.80	.96	.01*	.00*	.27	.03	.99	.77
STFB Fact. 6	.03*	.09	.47	.76	.04	.06	.03	.07	.15*	.44*	.62	.56	.04*	.07
MMPI+ % Corr	54%	54%	63%	69%	85%	55%	82%	62%	64%	63%	83%	65%	67%	64%

Numb.P <.05 *S*	50 74%	56 82%	21 31%	22 32%	29 43%	28 41%	33 49%	23 34%	24 35%	43 63%	47 69%	47 69%	3 4%	13 19%
Numb.P <.05 *N*	50 74%	56 82%	21 31%	16 24%	25 37%	25 37%	29 43%	25 37%	16 24%	39 57%	45 66%	45 66%	4 5%	12 18%
Numb.P <.05 *M*	11 12%	2 2%	5 6%	3 3%	12 13%	8 9%	7 8%	24 27%	27 30%	25 28%	11 12%	40 44%	16 18%	9 10%
Numb.P <.05 *C*	1 14%	6 86%	0 0%	0 0%	1 14%	0 0%	2 29%	0 0%	1 14%	2 29%	3 43%	5 71%	2 29%	1 14%

* Asterisks mark variables that entered into the Discriminant Function analysis for this column.

Table 7.2: Discriminant Function % Correct Classifications and Correlation Coefficients between the Addicause axes and ninety-one MMPI Scales. Probabilities are rounded to the nearest two decimal places.

AXIS LABELS AND VARIABLES	COCA USE	COCA YRS	CRCK USE	CRCK YRS	HASH USE	HASH YRS	HERO USE	HERO YRS	LSD USE	LSD YRS	MARI USE	MARI YRS	MORP USE	MORP YRS
DAQ Discrim S	64%	63%	83%	70%	58%	63%	66%	61%	61%	39%	63%	74%	100%	50%
% Correct N	60%	64%	68%	63%	61%	62%	66%	62%	57%	42%	62%	70%	82%	50%
01: Social S	.02	.02	.36	.31	.00	.07	.00	.98	.00	.24	.00	.11	.05*	.97
Anxiety N	.00	.01	.23	.08	.01	.04	.01	.76	.00*	.56	.01	.05	.07	.56
02: Social S	.12	.03	.92	.92	.05	.04*	.99	.53	.03	.25	.08	.08	.17*	.65
Enjoyment N	.03	.05	.97	.73	.08	.09	.94	.46	.01*	.34	.04	.11	.21	.61
03: Reactive S	.00	.00*	.59	.25	.00	.01	.06	.35	.00*	.86	.01	.01	.16	.76*
Depression N	.00	.00	.91	.72	.01	.01	.15	.84	.00	.76	.01	.01	.41	.66
04: Stimulus S	.00	.00	.09	.02	.00	.00*	.25	.09	.00	.03*	.00	.00*	.10	.77
Hunger N	.00	.00	.25	.07	.00	.00*	.55	.16	.00	.09*	.00	.00*	.20	.91
05: Rigid S	.00	.00*	.25	.36*	.00	.00	.00	.11	.00	.17	.00	.00	.07	.85
Self-Image N	.00	.00	.24	.15	.00	.00	.00	.08	.00*	.43	.00	.00	.07	.91
06: Social S	.02	.03	.35	.96	.02	.01*	.03*	.80	.03	.65	.06	.02	.39	.66
Influence N	.00	.03	.20*	.59	.02	.00	.02	.66	.01	.72	.03	.01	.40	.51

	C1	C2	C3	C4	C5	C6	C7	C8	C9	C10	C11	C12	C13	C14
07: Aggressn *S*	.04	.04	.08	.49	.01	.02	.02	.33	.13	.36	.09	.31	.23	.45
Inhibition *N*	.00	.02	.14	.20	.01	.01	.03	.54	.02	.46	.06	.08	.36	.50
08: Guilt *S*	.00*	.00*	.03	.01*	.00	.00*	.00	.03*	.00	.40	.00	.00*	.10	.57
Intolerance *N*	.00*	.00*	.01*	.01*	.00*	.00*	.00	.02	.00	.30*	.00*	.00*	.06	.49
09: Loneliness *S*	.00	.00	.37*	.91*	.00	.00	.01	.54	.01	.63	.01	.01	.35	.94
N	.00	.01	.39*	.50*	.00	.00	.00*	.37	.03	.87	.01*	.01	.30	.96
10: Social *S*	.33	.11	.42	.87	.37*	.24	.86	.41	.13*	.42	.48	.45	.40*	.34
Contact Wsh *N*	.27	.16	.43	.56	.52	.25	.99	.20	.07	.56	.44	.69	.41	.29
11: Reality *S*	.00	.00	.12	.06	.00	.00	.04	.06	.00	.34	.00	.00	.33	.88
Denial *N*	.00	.01*	.08	.03*	.00	.00*	.05	.12	.00	.62	.00	.00	.22	.93
12: Authorit *S*	.00	.00	.04	.04	.00*	.00*	.01	.14	.00	.37	.00*	.00	.02	.94
Rebellion *N*	.00	.00	.04	.06	.00*	.00	.02	.26	.00	.45	.00*	.00	.01	.83
13: Flat *S*	.00	.00	.05*	.01*	.00	.00*	.00	.11	.00*	.30	.00*	.00	.14	.97
Depression *N*	.00	.00	.03	.01*	.00	.00*	.00	.11	.00	.53	.00	.00	.12	.87
14: Vivid *S*	.42	.81	.03*	.02	.31	.41	.25	.10	.25	.43	.24	.55	.25	.24
Imagery *N*	.67	.29	.02	.39	.43	.47	.18	.01	.46	.45	.46	.73	.25	.21
15: Control *S*	.00	.02	.41	.74	.00*	.02	.00	.66	.02	.42	.05*	.12	.17	.90
Effort *N*	.00	.02	.63	.55	.00*	.02*	.00	.93	.05*	.64	.07*	.11	.19	.91

307

16: Control *S*	.34	.27	.09	.20	.46*	.75	.82	.60	.08	.46	.15	.11	.31	.42
of Others *N*	.08	.40	.07	.25	.21	.67	.71	.92	.10	.56	.24	.49	.35	.26
17: Grief *S*	.99	.18	.03	.01*	.30	.01*	.52	.03	.01*	.00	.08	.22	.01	.00
Reaction *N*	.96	.21	.01	.01	.48	.01	.62	.07*	.00	.00	.07*	.26	.00	.00
18: Substanc *S*	.68	.06	.00	.00	.65	.00	.25	.00	.00	.00	.04	.18*	.00*	.00
Enhancement *N*	.93	.07	.00	.00	.88	.00	.41	.01	.00	.00	.07	.31*	.00	.00
19: Pain *S*	.67	.31	.34*	.20	.35	.36	.73	.05	.43*	.04	.96	.97	.37*	.21
Sensitivity *N*	.82	.36	.31*	.14	.45	.26	.99	.11	.38	.04	.90	.88	.36	.18
20: Hedonism *S*	.62	.87	.58	.73	.93	.53	.26	.11*	.54	.64	.85	.58	.34	.23
N	.28	.52	.31	.48	.44	.19	.14	.20	.24	.47	.94	.54	.24	.27
21: Social *S*	.93	.05	.02	.00	.12	.01	.77	.04	.01	.00	.67	.29	.01	.02
Withdrawal *N*	.99	.03	.01	.00	.30	.00	.75	.05	.01	.00	.42	.26	.00	.01
22: SubCult. *S*	.51	.01	.00	.00	.78	.00	.10	.00*	.00	.00	.00*	.00*	.00*	.00*
Values *N*	.55	.00	.00	.00	.86	.00	.09	.00*	.00	.00	.00*	.00*	.00*	.00*
23: Inhibit *S*	.19	.83	.03	.01	.30	.00	.44	.13	.02	.00	.10	.32	.00	.00
Dependency *N*	.21	.60	.01	.01	.58	.01	.57	.08	.00	.00	.07	.26	.00	.00
24: Immediat *S*	.56	.02	.30	.47	.04	.00	.01	.13	.20	.12	.00*	.21	.12	.02
Gratificatn *N*	.70*	.03	.34	.38	.10	.00*	.01	.04	.18	.09	.00*	.00*	.01*	.00*

	1	2	3	4	5	6	7	8	9	10	11	12	13	14
25: Paranoid *S*	.76	.45	.01	.00	.76	.07	.82	.14	.00	.00	.67	.35	.05	.03
Sensitivity *N*	.75	.43	.02	.01	.86	.04	.88	.14	.01	.00	.47	.42	.04	.00
26: Rationality *S*	.81	.56	.14	.04	.61	.96	.19	.39	.30	.02	.85	.69	.20	.67
Defence *N*	.84	.48	.12	.12	.86	.46	.21	.24	.35	.10	.43	.94	.07	.25
27: Oppressive *S*	.86	.44	.12	.29	.88	.59	.72	.21	.25	.05	.98	.43	.27	.27
Inhibit *N*	.85	.19*	.06	.14	.73	.32	.87	.12*	.08	.03	.85	.73	.22	.09
28: Comfortable *S*	.39	.41	.49	.72	.95	.61	.25	.77	.55	.72	.58	.22	.38	.92
Inhibit *N*	.39	.97	.33	.13	.91	.04*	.33	.84	.34	.05	.99	.71	.12	.30
29: Affect *S*	.67	.28	.02	.00	.16	.00	.73	.02	.01	.00	.62	.79	.01	.00
Disturbance *N*	.36	.37	.04	.00	.22	.01	.88	.03	.02	.00	.65*	.98	.02*	.00
30: Affect *S*	.37	.87	.00*	.31	.48	.86	.60	.33	.02*	.21	.73*	.36	.13	.40
Denial *N*	.42	.92*	.01*	.18	.49	.78	.45	.38	.01*	.13	.70	.44	.20	.18
31: Demean *S*	.72	.35	.01	.01	.93	.12	.47	.02	.00	.00	.44	.12	.00	.00
Others *N*	.90	.35	.00	.01	.96	.16	.82	.04	.00	.00	.40	.16	.00	.00
32: Group *S*	.44	.41	.11	.39	.12*	.20	.48	.65	.09	.40	.14	.79	.26	.57
Satisfact'n *N*	.51	.47	.13	.11	.07*	.23	.37	.74	.05	.10	.19	.76	.22	.59
33: Dogmatism *S*	.65	.10	.03	.26	.99	.59	.86	.13	.01	.06	.35	.02	.01	.12
N	.63	.32	.02	.16	.92	.30	.92	.33	.01	.08	.47	.11	.02	.09

309

34: Wish Be *S*	.83	.05	.00*	.00*	.70	.02	.30	.02*	.00*	.00	.32	.03	.00	.00
Different *N*	.86	.06	.00*	.00*	.85	.01	.43	.03*	.00*	.00	.23	.04	.00	.00
35: Self- *S*	.49	.08	.00	.00	.20	.00	.29	.00	.00	.00	.15	.16	.00	.00
Depreciat'n *N*	.19	.05	.00	.00	.20	.00	.37*	.00	.00	.00	.10	.07	.00	.00
36: Rigid *S*	.33	.85	.00*	.00*	.18	.00*	.02*	.57	.00*	.00*	.01	.96	.18	.00*
Moralizat'n *N*	.62	.57	.01*	.00*	.56	.01*	.01*	.43	.00*	.00*	.00	.58	.11	.02*
37: Paroxys- *S*	.07*	.00*	.00*	.00*	.93	.00*	.01*	.00*	.00	.00	.06	.03	.00*	.00*
mality *N*	.07	.00	.01*	.00*	.82	.00*	.01*	.00*	.00	.00	.06	.02	.00*	.00*
38: Rules *S*	.64	.11	.00	.00	.86	.00	.57	.04	.00	.00	.12	.03*	.00	.00
Intolerance *N*	.54	.13	.00	.00	.84	.00	.66	.18*	.00	.00	.07	.04	.00	.00
39: Effort *S*	.52	.07	.00	.00	.16	.01*	.68	.01	.00	.00	.54	.54	.01	.00
Strain *N*	.26	.03	.00	.01	.14	.04	.58	.01	.00	.00	.23	.17	.02	.01
40: Pep-Up *S*	.84	.98	.22	.76	.94	.33	.89	.70	.16	.63	.95	.20	.45	.72
Effect *N*	.81	.90	.28	.52	.93	.21	.82	.59	.09	.43	.98	.47	.42	.25
41: Rigid *S*	.62	.04	.00	.00	.37	.01	.68	.01*	.00	.00	.44	.06	.00	.00
Habits *N*	.61	.03	.00	.00	.28	.01	.77	.01	.00*	.00	.52	.06	.00	.00
42: Easy Go *S*	.82	.72	.25	.81	.17*	.34	.63	.73	.15	.77	.55*	.42	.56	.51
Enjoyment *N*	.58	.97	.21	.71	.22*	.18	.44	.82	.10	.58	.21*	.96	.82	.23

43: Metabolic *S*	.86	.61	.02	.00	.85	.00	.56	.10*	.01	.00	.67	.27	.01	.02
Disorder *N*	.75	.30*	.01	.00	.97	.01	.59	.07	.00	.00	.71	.15	.02	.02
44: Fast-Lane *S*	.35	.02	.00	.00	.59	.01	.67	.05	.00*	.00	.66	.13	.02*	.02
Living *N*	.17	.01	.00	.00	.39	.00	.33	.04	.00	.00	.60	.11	.03	.02
45: Hypo- *S*	.09	.36	.00	.00	.21	.00	.40	.03	.00	.00	.21	.41	.00	.00*
glycaemia *N*	.08	.18*	.00	.00	.25	.00	.33	.02	.00	.00	.26	.21	.02*	.02*
46: Allergy *S*	.76	.43	.00	.00	.82	.00	.28	.23	.00	.00*	.01*	.06	.00*	.00*
Stress *N*	.29	.47	.00	.00	.82	.01	.30	.21	.00	.00*	.02*	.10	.00*	.00*
47: Physiolog. *S*	.45	.20	.00	.00	.49	.00	.96*	.01	.00	.00	.24	.23	.00	.00
Anxiety *N*	.31*	.16	.00	.00	.54	.00	.84	.02	.00	.00	.37	.23	.01	.00
48: Punitive *S*	.09	.01*	.00	.00	.52	.00	.01*	.00	.00	.00	.03	.00	.00	.00
Reinforcemt *N*	.04*	.00*	.00	.00	.37	.00	.00*	.00*	.00*	.00	.03	.00*	.00	.00
49: Affect *S*	.80	.06	.00	.00	.31	.03	.64	.00*	.00	.00	.23	.14	.01	.00
Avoidance *N*	.80	.02*	.00	.01	.40	.02	.71	.01*	.00	.00	.22	.06*	.02	.01
50: Control *S*	.86	.12	.00	.00	.33	.02	.40	.02	.00	.00	.15	.11	.00	.00
Sensitivity *N*	.70	.05*	.00	.00	.36	.02	.33	.01	.00	.00	.27	.12	.02	.01
51: Guilt *S*	.51	.65	.02	.01	.21	.01	.89	.02	.00	.00	.57	.30	.00	.00
Proneness *N*	.66	.52	.02	.07	.42	.02	.93	.04	.00	.00	.55	.23	.03	.00

52: Anger/ *S*	.01	.00	.06	.13	.00	.00*	.00	.59	.09	.94	.00	.00	.22	.96
Hostility *N*	.01	.01	.10	.17	.00	.00	.00	.52	.16	.93	.00	.01	.16	.85
53: Somatic *S*	.11	.07	.26*	.73	.00	.02	.04	.91	.07	.38	.03	.02	.24	.15
Depression *N*	.14	.17	.40	.82	.01	.02	.04	.94	.09	.37	.04	.02	.12	.10
54: Hungry *S*	.00	.00	.54	.15	.00	.00	.05	.80	.00	.29	.00	.00	.54	.59
Heart *N*	.00	.00	.21	.09	.00	.00	.08	.70	.00	.42	.00	.00	.25	.62
55: Impaired *S*	.00	.00	.28	.38	.00	.00	.01	.64	.00	.24	.00	.00	.13	.72
Self-Esteem *N*	.00	.00	.23	.52	.00	.00*	.01	.41*	.00	.28	.00	.00	.03	.86
56: Masked *S*	.03*	.07*	.18	.77*	.01	.04	.01	.62	.13	.72	.05	.10	.24	.56
Disappointm *N*	.03	.07*	.25	.67*	.01	.02	.02	.63	.09	.68	.04	.04	.19	.70
57: Felt *S*	.00	.00	.18	.26	.00	.00	.01	.53	.00	.65	.00	.00	.04	.79
Rejection *N*	.00	.01	.08	.39	.00	.00	.01	.47	.01	.68	.00	.00	.01	.51
58: Need to *S*	.73	.44	.60	.40	.15	.82	.31	.80	.86	.36	.13	.67	.80	.38
Communicate *N*	.85	.69	.55	.43	.20	.61	.41	.65	.75	.45	.31	.45	.40*	.33
59: NeedCalm *S*	.22	.08	.40	.90	.01	.09	.02	.48	.17	.12	.03	.29	.47*	.43
Nerves *N*	.34	.27	.67	.96	.01	.07	.02	.56	.07	.11*	.02	.18	.33	.30
60: Substanc *S*	.00	.00	.03	.07	.00*	.00*	.02	.27	.00*	.24	.00*	.00	.03*	.93
Enhancement *N*	.00	.00	.11	.24	.00*	.00*	.04	.31	.00	.23	.00*	.00	.02	.89

	1	2	3	4	5	6	7	8	9	10	11	12	13	14
61: Forget S	.02	.01	.04	.19	.01	.05	.03	.98	.49	.58	.04	.10	.27	.29
Failures N	.01	.01	.35	.48	.01	.02	.07	.92	.33	.49	.07	.03	.18	.57
62: WshNovel S	.00	.00	.08	.21	.00	.00	.31	.92	.03	.58	.00	.00	.30	.62
Experiences N	.02	.01	.51	.82	.00	.00	.54	.63	.08	.31	.00	.00	.53	.35
63: Avoid S	.01	.00	.06	.26	.00	.00	.03*	.63	.05	.78	.00	.00	.20	.90
Boredom N	.03	.01	.33	.93	.00	.00	.04	.65	.19	.77	.00	.00	.13	.96
64: Assert S	.03	.00	.08	.03	.00	.00	.38	.41	.02	.53	.00	.00	.45	.78
Confidence N	.04	.01	.17	.09	.00	.00	.68	.58	.04	.44	.00	.00	.38	.59
65: Avoid S	.01	.01	.54	.57	.00	.00	.14	.89	.18	.71	.02	.01	.60	.15
Attractiven N	.04	.02	.40	.89	.00	.00*	.08	.79	.35	.65	.07	.01	.34	.20
66: Impaired S	.00	.00	.09*	.05	.00	.00	.08	.55	.03	.21	.00	.00	.09	.06*
Sleep N	.00	.00	.15	.17	.00	.00	.15	.73	.11	.34	.00	.00	.09	.09
67: NeedCalm/ S	.83	.39	.65	.30*	.09	.89	.76	.23	.51	.64*	.07	.65	.96	.34
Relaxation N	.96	.67	.49	.86	.09	.96	.39	.09	.49	.39	.10	.89	.48	.59
68: Substanc S	.00	.00	.11	.16	.00	.00	.04	.67	.01	.18	.00	.00	.07*	.34
Dependency N	.00	.00*	.09	.18	.00	.00	.07	.76	.01	.31	.00	.00	.02	.58
ML: MMPI L	.10	.16	.53	.00	.08	.07	.38	.00*	.07	.06	.01	.00*	.06	.20
MF: MMPI F	.07	.15	.43	.00	.69	.05	.48	.39	.50	.87	.08	.00	.13	.43

MK: MMPI K	.30	.53	.52	.00	.34	.14	.62	.48	.87	.85	.18	.03*	.58	.38
01: MMPI Hs	.62	.00*	.36	.51	.03	.61	.12	.02*	.25*	.55	.56	.21	.02*	.36
02: MMPI D	.13	.61	.44*	.73	.02	.77	.28	.09*	.60	.59	.40*	.97	.47	.94
03: MMPI Hy	.87	.08	.31	.53	.42	.48	.28	.20	.68	.20	.38	.17	.32	.18
04: MMPI Pd	.43	.21	.88	.00	.11	.03	.92	.00	.04	.00*	.00	.01	.01*	.03
05: MMPI MF	.07	.86	.04	.99	.14	.52	.41	.83	.67	.95	.02	.00*	.94	.29
06: MMPI Pa	.06	.51	.68	.00	.45	.51	.33*	.30	.51	.61	.09	.07	.52	.50
07: MMPI Pt	.28	.45	.59	.00	.24	.64	.40	.99	.18	.39	.45	.40	.30	.79
08: MMPI Sc	.26	.23	.20	.00	.24	.17	.38	.58	.11	.64	.10	.08	.13	.53
09: MMPI Ma	.87	.31	.77	.00	.21	.15	.63	.93	.34	.99	.00	.11	.39	.08
00: MMPI Si	.21	.05	.09	.20	.02	.56	.15	.59	.58	.60	.72	.34	.77	.69
MMPI TSC F1	.19	.07	.16	.08	.02	.95	.27	.76	.34	.43	.87	.66	.74	.23
MMPI TSC F2	.37	.08	.55	.01	.12	.37	.01	.39	.25	.91	.62	.79	.18	.90

MMPI TSC F3	.20	.12	.16	.01*	.26	.04	.59	.82	.77	.38	.03	.11*	.87	.26
MMPI TSC F4	.21	.23	.79	.00	.17	.28	.71	.62	.43	.38	.16	.24	.13	.94
MMPI TSC F5	.41	.16	.66	.00	.21	.01	.85	.20	.09	.38	.02	.02	.05	.23
MMPI TSC F6	.19	.20	.80	.00	.09	.04	.49	.38	.51	.83	.11	.01	.17	.88
MMPI TSC F7	.26	.70	.46	.00	.53	.27	.25	.89	.73	.82	.29	.06	78	.86
Plus Getting	.08	.07	.65	.00	.08	.06	.40	.83	.24	.59	.24	.03	.18	.98
MMPI DY 1	.14	.11*	.06*	.02	.18	.28	.40	.33	.25	.31	.67	.31	.56	.44
MMPI DY 2	.03	.19	.13	.23	.34	.28	.49	.67	.13	.50	.67	.84	.73	.75
MMPI DY 3	.29	.29	.61	.00	.32	.24	.12	.12	.55	.32	.07	.23	.20	.91
MMPI DY 4	.16	.06	.89	.00	.11	.04	.40	.53	.30	.22	.04	.00*	.21	.51
MMPI DY 5	.36	.12	.65	.00	.57	.18	.82	.78	.54	.56	.08	.03	.46	.56
MMPI PrimDef	.04	.00*	.74	.00*	.02	.01	.36	.01*	.02*	.21	.00	.00	.00*	.49
MMPI Regress	.63	.39	.91	.00	.16	.10	.29	.18	.16	.48	.34	.21	.63	.57

MMPI Repress	.21	.31	.51	.00	.07	.02	.90	.70	.66	.86	.03	.00*	.68	.68
MMPI Denial	.06	.03	.19	.00	.01	.03	.14	.09	.25	.67	.33	.01	.16	.84
MMPI Project	.03	.99	.65	.19	.15	.53	.10	.84	.39	.99	.10	.43	.68	.45
MMPI Displac	.08	.79	.05	.62	.12	.87	.06	.25	.81	.86	.47	.17	.47	.14
MMPI Intellz	.43	.15*	.41	.47	.47	.70	.46	.40	.47	.42	.32	.19	.90	.08
MMPI S.Doubt	.06	.18	.26	.01	.17	.85	.02	.31*	.31	.80	.53	.47	.65	.88
MMPI RctForm	.48	.05	.14	.24*	.05	.20	.65	.62	.78	.58	.21	.00*	.82	.31
MMPI OvAcThk	.18	.22	.75	.00	.11	.03	.42	.39	.53	.82	.11	.00	.18	.88
MMPI IntEffc	.17	.52	.44	.01	.66	.94	.24	.87	.54	.79	.76	.05	.99	.57
MMPI Anxiety	.22	.70	.42	.00	.54	.26	.26	.87	.71	.80	.26*	.07	.82	.86
MMPI Depress	.18	.19	.76	.00	.17	.26	.71	.63	.44	.35	.14	.24	.13	.91
MMPI Anger	.48	.16	.55	.00	.20	.01	.93	.20	.10	.36	.02	.02	.06	.23
MMPI Anhedon	.11	.29	.24	.13	.12	.91	.51	.62	.59	.40	.26	.60	.24	.87

316

MMPI Respons	.55	.09	.36	.00	.19	.01	.28	.09	.26	.30	.00	.00	.09	.05
MMPI Toleran	.60	.15	.82	.00	.28	.17	.16*	.82	.35	.89	.09	.01	.37	.15
MMPI Empathy	.24	.99	.72	.01	.28	.21	.39	.92	.84	.28	.62	.89	.07	.41
MMPI RolPlay	.42	.31	.74	.00	.09	.14	.47	.73	.82	.70	.62	.75	.79	.97
MMPI Dominan	.78	.23	.91	.00	.13	.78	.34	.88	.56	.79	.82	.19	.73	.41
MMPI SocPart	.26	.31	.11	.02*	.19	.78	.31	.71	.89	.61	.23	.84	.67	.40
MMPI SocPres	.72	.35	.46	.09	.08	.74	.25	.93	.89	.71	.47*	.51	.85	.70
MMPI Dependc	.25	.17	.61	.00	.05	.30	.63	.75	.44	.48	.95	.34	.30	.94
Dom-Submiss.	.46	.18	.77	.85	.33	.81	.68	.70	.65	.51	.45	.93	.95	.75
Love-Hate	.18	.14	.40	.00	.36	.06	.55	.58	.45	.94	.07	.01	.19	.58
MMPI EgoStrn	.39	.42	.84	.07	.06	.92	.25	.76	.51	.90	.58	.55	.38	.96
MMPI Resilie	.07	.09	.32	.00	.05	.09	.16	.27	.14	.73	.19	.07	.08	.53
MMPI S.Cntrl	.15	.05	.15*	.00	.01	.00	.00	.00*	.04	.44	.00	.00	.01	.11

MMPI Impulsv	.04	.27	.61	.00	.01	.00*	.71	.05	.17	.76	.00	.00*	.04	.62
MMPI Delinqu	.40	.06	.77	.00	.48	.10	.44	.64	.63	.73	.06	.03	.48	.60
MMPI Raw Spy	.15	.72	.04	.13	.01	.06	.38	.99	.99	.69	.02	.00*	.85	.13
MMPI HabCrim	.26	.16	.82	.00	.03	.00	.88	.00	.17	.20	.00*	.01	.00	.03
MMPI PrisAdj	.81	.53	.50	.01	.07	.05	.42	.36	.54	.99	.00	.08	.00	.14
MMPI Escapis	.04	.10	.75	.00	.04	.00	.99	.00	.04	.24	.00	.00	.02	.34
MMPI ParViol	.55	.24	.90	.00	.06	.03	.45	.19	.41	.19	.02	.01	.38	.65
MMPI Recidiv	.71	.30	.82	.00	.03	.00	.79	.03	.54	.78	.00	.01	.05	.22*
MMPI OvCoHos	.05	.81	.09	.14	.37	.18	.63	.06	.91	.07	.01	.27	.13	.43*
MMPI Violenc	.36	.12	.69	.00*	.02*	.00	.37	.11	.15	.78	.00	.00*	.00	.38
MMPI ThrSuic	.39	.03	.85	.00	.19	.11	.67	.51	.20	.85	.06	.03	.28	.41
MMPI UncAcSx	.38	.46	.60	.01*	.84	.51	.52	.55	.88	.81	.17	.82	.85	.93
Paedophilia	.85	.14	.11	.73	.24	.72	.99	.61	.90	.47	.91	.42	.56*	.72

Aggravat.Sex	.11	.06	.82	.00	.22	.00	.95	.06	.15	.58	.00	.04	.00	.07
MMPI Alcohol	.04	.00	.04	.00*	.31	.01	.00	.00	.12	.30	.00	.00*	.01	.06
MMPI DrgAbus	.23	.29	.03*	.00	.32	.00	.88	.10	.17	.92	.01	.06	.04	.29
Work Attitud	.04	.11	.99	.00	.18	.03	.64	.59	.17	.87	.04	.01	.10	.42
Rehab.Motiv.	.18	.04	.87	.02	.31	.05	.98	.10	.04	.88	.90	.31	.09	.52
Change Motiv	.07	.15	.43	.00	.07	.10	.71	.38	.33	.30	.10	.49	.24	.58
Thyroid Path	.58	.49	.57*	.74	.24	.89	.21	.45	.83	.28	.33	.35	.29	.98
Caudality	.17	.08	.51	.00	.06	.09	.19	.66	.35	.39	.36	.57	.39	.93
LowBackPain	.80	.78	.29	.02	.72	.45	.37	.58	.06*	.95	.34	.32	.51	.74
Pariet-Front	.23	.25	.87	.00	.12	.15	.10*	.80	.33	.78	.72	.13	.52	.87
Soc.Adjustmt	.23	.14	.07	.51	.02	.62	.33	.81	.37	.45	.62	.30	.93	.31
MMPI DeprCon	.18	.09	.76	.00	.21	.52	.54	.66	.49	.45	.17	.19	.31	.86
MMPI PMorale	.16	.16	.76	.00	.06	.33	.48	.87	.39	.53	.62	.26	.29	.93

MMPI RelFund	.02	.77	.51	.26	.32	.80	.13*	.91	.07	.72	.32	.67	.99	.07
MMPI AuthCnf	.41	.09	.26	.00	.21	.02	.19	.11	.27	.86	.00	.01	.10	.05
Psychoticism	.24	.38	.07	.00	.48	.08	.74	.25	.76	.99	.03	.05	.75	.57
Organ.Sympt.	.35	.03	.30	.00	.01*	.05	.21	.05	.17	.74	.38	.05	.05	.63
MMPI FamProb	.39	.74	.56	.00	.74	.08	.73	.30	.89	.61	.17	.02	.27	.80
MMPI ManHost	.18	.12	.70	.00	.18	.00	.81	.20	.12	.56	.00	.00	.02	.41
MMPI Phobias	.65	.97	.31	.11	.86	.59	.19	.95	.22	.28	.97	.60	.95	.52
MMPI Hypoman	.13	.93	.44	.00	.86	.05	.51	.82	.95	.97	.03	.03	.18	.60
MMPI PHealth	.56	.10	.60	.06	.13	.99	.45	.03	.12	.50	.83	.25	.04	.33
MMPI PharVir	.40	.39	.81	.02	.28	.83*	.42	.96	.68	.55	.73	.85	.85	.99
MAST-Alcohol	.92	.76	.18*	.05*	.17	.46	.75	.88	.10	.45*	.03	.77	.67	.10
DAST-DrugsR2	.00*	.00*	.00*	.00*	.00*	.00*	.00*	.00*	.00*	.00*	.00*	.00*	.00*	.00*
STFB TotalY1	.20	.00	.16	.01	.00	.01	.83	.04	.01	.04	.00	.06	.03	.08

STFB Fact. 1	.23	.00	.23*	.03	.00	.01	.24	.01	.00	.05	.00	.02	.02	.03
STFB Fact. 2	.65	.00	.51*	.02	.00	.19	.66	.32	.01	.25*	.00	.18	.38	.19
STFB Fact. 3	.11	.04	.37	.01	.01	.07	.95	.02	.09	.17	.00	.31	.07	.24
STFB Fact. 4	.63	.41	.87	.87	.63	.00*	.66	.29	.84	.08*	.05*	.19	.12	.65
STFB Fact. 5	.24	.30	.08	.25	.27	.05*	.34	.71	.30	.12	.00	.04*	.47	.28
STFB Fact. 6	.26	.02	.01*	.00	.00	.03	.56	.14	.00	.03	.00	.02	.08	.02
MMPI+ % Corr	61%	69%	60%	73%	56%	58%	59%	63%	69%	77%	70%	55%	72%	55%
Numb.P < .05 S	50 74%	49 72%	12 18%	13 19%	55 81%	52 76%	41 60%	5 7%	44 65%	2 3%	50 74%	47 69%	12 18%	0 0%
Numb.P < .05 N	51 75%	50 74%	10 15%	8 12%	54 79%	53 78%	36 53%	6 9%	44 65%	0 0%	47 69%	50 74%	16 24%	1 1%
Numb.P < .05 M	9 10%	9 10%	7 8%	67 74%	18 20%	29 32%	4 4%	12 13%	5 6%	1 1%	29 32%	39 43%	17 19%	4 4%
Numb.P < .05 C	0 0%	5 71%	1 14%	5 71%	5 71%	5 71%	0 0%	3 43%	3 43%	3 43%	7 100%	3 43%	2 29%	2 29%

* Asterisks mark variables that entered into the Discriminant Function analysis for this column.

Table 7.3: Discriminant Function % Correct Classifications and Correlation Coefficients between the Addicause axes and ninety-one MMPI Scales. Probabilities are rounded to the nearest two decimal places.

AXIS LABELS AND VARIABLES	MUSH USE	MUSH YRS	OPIU USE	OPIU YRS	PCP USE	PCP YRS	PEYO USE	PEYO YRS	SPEE USE	SPEE YRS	GLUE USE	GLUE Yrs	WINE Use	WINE Yrs
DAQ Discrim S	61%	50%	72%	75%	100%	48%	79%	39%	71%	31%	87%	90%	51%	58%
% Correct N	60%	--	75%	76%	81%	55%	71%	40%	70%	32%	96%	93%	53%	59%
01: Social S	.05	.97	.04	.32	.23	.43	.05	.48	.01	.27	.02	.01	.63	.20
Anxiety N	.02	.78	.02	.23	.07	.43	.03*	.39	.04	.94	.02	.01	.63	.26
02: Social S	.10*	.82	.90	.85	.82	.84	.85	.58	.02	.34	.64	.00*	.09	.12
Enjoyment N	.05*	.53	.95	.68	.79	.83	.94	.66	.04	.36	.64	.00*	.81	.25*
03: Reactive S	.00*	.26	.20	.18	.09	.47	.19	.18	.11*	.08	.32	.31	.38	.07*
Depression N	.01	.22	.76	.81	.49	.46	.61	.11	.30	.06	.59	.59	.45	.05*
04: Stimulus S	.12	.14	.45	.10	.36	.18	.44	.83	.09	.16	.12	.62	.00	.03
Hunger N	.18	.35	.53	.31	.63	.18	.43	.99	.34	.32	.16	.84	.00	.07
05: Rigid S	.07	.61	.03*	.12	.26	.05	.05	.36	.04	.14	.02	.00	.07	.01
Self-Image N	.02	.45	.03	.12	.44	.05	.06	.23	.06	.27	.01	.00	.01	.01
06: Social S	.29	.44	.67	.70	.75	.14	.77	.24	.51	.71	.09	.05	.08	.12
Influence N	.21	.15	.65	.76	.67	.14	.65	.16	.33	.89	.10	.07	.05	.06

07: Aggressn S	.44*	.77	.00	.09	.20	.17	.06	.57	.10	.44	.07	.01	.49	.19
Inhibition N	.19	.65	.02	.22	.27	.17	.09	.58	.22	.54	.19	.03	.24	.20
08: Guilt S	.02	.90	.01	.02	.12	.00*	.04	.65	.04	.59	.02	.02	.07	.03
Intolerance N	.01	.58	.00*	.01	.05	.00*	.01	.64	.03	.51	.02	.01	.08	.05
09: Loneliness S	.33	.71	.08	.70	.56	.05	.18	.34	.57	.43	.04	.00*	.53	.00
N	.33	.46	.08	.70	.63	.06	.13	.33	.60	.58	.03	.00	.63	.00
10: Social S	.23	.71	.05	.35	.53	.90	.46	.17	.03*	.41	.60	.30	.43	.07
Contact Wsh N	.14	.60	.07	.35	.46	.90	.39	.06	.08*	.33	.87	.59	.33	.14
11: Reality S	.06	.25	.08	.12	.09	.16	.17	.81	.13	.72	.05	.00	.01	.00*
Denial N	.11	.48	.06	.32	.16	.18	.13	.90	.29	.89	.11	.00	.03	.00
12: Authorit S	.00	.12	.00	.01	.10	.00	.01	.60	.01	.67	.01	.00	.01	.03
Rebellion N	.00	.10	.00	.04	.09	.00	.01	.54	.05	.83	.02	.00	.03	.07
13: Flat S	.01	.47	.01	.02	.03*	.08*	.02	.77	.02	.56	.01	.00	.04	.02
Depression N	.01	.34	.01	.03	.02	.08*	.01	.86	.02	.79	.02	.00	.06	.02
14: Vivid S	.04	.15*	.01*	.10	.02	.76	.05*	.28	.06	.55	.35	.31	.27	.30
Imagery N	.03	.29	.02	.04	.01*	.76	.07	.18	.02*	.62	.16	.39	.15	.80
15: Control S	.22	.78	.05	.22	.20	.61	.07	.12	.24	.14	.01	.00	.67	.15
Effort N	.39	.84	.05	.38	.32	.61	.10	.10	.31	.18	.04	.01	.47	.08

16: Control of Others	S	.35	.78	.02	.80	.75	.74	.13	.22	.99	.75	.24	.43	.04	.76
	N	.25	.39	.05*	.65	.37	.72	.10*	.04	.99*	.55	.41	.83	.07	.69
17: Grief Reaction	S	.14	.40	.03	.46	.24*	.88	.06	.57	.20	.62	.01	.00	.85*	.10
	N	.13	.43	.02	.59	.28	.87	.08	.67	.35	.73	.02	.00	.69*	.14
18: Substanc Enhancement	S	.01	.21	.06*	.37	.46	.01*	.11*	.55	.05*	.22	.00	.01	.00	.01*
	N	.02	.16	.09	.74	.83*	.01*	.24	.64	.08	.32	.01	.04	.00*	.01
19: Pain Sensitivity	S	.96	.54	.06	.64	.50	.38	.29	.18	.59	.08	.14	.03	.52	.18
	N	.88	.65	.04	.87	.90	.38	.29	.17	.84	.12	.22	.06	.31	.20
20: Hedonism	S	.50	.82	.96	.56	.69	.39	.24	.84	.48	.77	.44	.97	.13	.07*
	N	.21	.58	.40	.19	.07	.39	.06*	.44	.38	.91	.06	.31	.17	.06*
21: Social Withdrawal	S	.28	.56	.03	.27	.17	.22	.05	.45	.04	.21	.04	.00	.55	.14
	N	.21	.50	.03	.17	.19	.22	.04	.35	.05	.61	.03	.00	.47	.07
22: SubCult. Values	S	.00*	.69	.00*	.02	.02	.04	.00*	.61	.05	.66	.00	.00	.00	.02
	N	.00	.32	.00	.03	.03*	.03	.00*	.57	.05	.58	.00	.00	.00	.01
23: Inhibit Dependency	S	.14	.74	.06	.20	.43	.13	.37	.16	.13	.70	.24	.13	.63	.16*
	N	.15	.45	.10	.28	.67	.13	.24	.23	.16	.59	.29	.16	.58	.18
24: Immediat Gratificatn	S	.00	.89	.02	.06	.00	.85	.03	.08	.02	.21	.05	.06	.44	.00*
	N	.00*	.85	.01*	.01	.00*	.85	.01	.44	.01	.52	.00	.01	.25	.01*

	1	2	3	4	5	6	7	8	9	10	11	12	13	14
25: Paranoid *S*	.51	.62	.01	.78	.54	.06	.16	.31	.45	.88	.00	.00	.12	.54
Sensitivity *N*	.44	.45	.05	.80	.80	.08	.12	.30	.36	.98	.01	.00	.21	.34
26: Rationality *S*	.67	.93	.10	.89	.76	.67	.26	.08	.12	.49	.68	.80	.27	.87
Defence *N*	.77	.82	.22	.58	.89	.69	.37	.17	.16*	.52	.71	.97	.33	.97
27: Oppressive *S*	.91	.53	.06	.82	.73	.07*	.28	.04	.22	.58	.24	.06	.76	.35
Inhibit *N*	.98	.76	.08	.74	.85	.09*	.14	.03	.41	.61	.32	.15	.48	.17
28: Comfortable *S*	.33	.79	.13	.43	.74	.99	.39	.43	.33	.97	.52	.99	.49	.41
Inhibit *N*	.85	.19	.51	.88	.50	.99	.51	.22	.70	.99	.36	.82	.23	.90
29: Affect *S*	.09	.86	.15*	.42	.28	.45	.22	.01*	.22	.13	.06	.00	.54	.08
Disturbance *N*	.19*	.58	.29*	.60	.56	.45	.39*	.01*	.37	.19	.26	.01	.42	.05
30: Affect *S*	.71	.48	.11	.88	.98	.04*	.68	.31	.56	.73	.26	.46	.07	.11
Denial *N*	.74	.99	.19*	.99	.63*	.05*	.83	.23	.41	.69	.31	.62	.02	.38
31: Demean *S*	.34	.99	.06	.15	.46	.24	.13	.97	.17	.89	.05	.03	.06	.82
Others *N*	.50	.99	.06	.24	.79	.24	.12	.92	.26	.84	.25	.05	.05	.53
32: Group *S*	.75	.99	.63	.56	.27	.85	.52	.59	.01*	.33	.83	.06	.03	.27
Satisfact'n *N*	.71	.56	.76	.53	.17	.85	.54	.48	.01*	.36	.44	.06*	.02	.68
33: Dogmatism *S*	.84	.12	.00	.02	.15	.31	.02	.67	.19	.82	.02	.00	.10	.18
N	.92	.24	.01	.23	.44	.31	.06	.47	.65	.52	.08	.03	.12	.08

34: Wish Be *S*	.11	.77	.00*	.03	.07	.35	.00*	.89	.07	.71	.00	.00	.01	.04
Different *N*	.06	.80	.00	.03	.10	.35	.00	.81	.13	.73	.00	.01	.04	.02
35: Self- *S*	.03	.44	.02	.18	.12	.03	.01*	.15	.04	.28	.00	.00	.01	.06
Depreciat'n *N*	.04	.65	.01	.11	.07	.04	.01*	.11	.06	.40	.01	.00	.01	.05
36: Rigid *S*	.00*	.04*	.10	.45	.44	.03	.54	.28	.13	.40	.58	.82	.14	.22
Moralizat'n *N*	.01*	.07	.25	.29	.34	.03	.51	.41	.08	.38	.16	.35	.34	.89
37: Paroxys- *S*	.00*	.28	.00*	.00*	.00*	.04	.00*	.06	.00*	.36	.00	.00	.00*	.00*
mality *N*	.00*	.47	.00	.00*	.00	.03	.00	.06	.00*	.19	.00	.00	.00*	.00*
38: Rules *S*	.10	.93	.00	.04	.04	.57	.03	.31	.20	.18	.04	.01	.04	.14
Intolerance *N*	.15	.91	.02	.03	.04	.57	.12	.29	.19	.17	.12	.06	.12	.09
39: Effort *S*	.13	.69	.29	.33	.17	.52	.26	.05	.11	.01*	.16	.08	.25	.02
Strain *N*	.13	.83	.16	.14	.06	.52	.15	.01	.11	.01*	.16	.10*	.44*	.02
40: Pep-Up *S*	.63	.26	.22	.73	.70	.45	.77	.43	.41	.56	.17	.26	.04	.88
Effect *N*	.99	.68	.78	.36	.69	.45	.98	.42	.27	.41	.11	.63*	.02	.48
41: Rigid *S*	.22	.41	.00	.10	.07	.46	.00	.30	.28	.16	.01	.00	.06	.22
Habits *N*	.16	.45	.00	.16	.13	.46	.00	.23	.40	.08	.01	.01	.06	.20*
42: Easy Go *S*	.35	.31	.03	.68	.88	.99	.27	.32	.92	.33	.16	.49	.05	.60
Enjoyment *N*	.19	.61	.11	.94	.65	.99	.33	.34	.72	.41	.16	.99	.06	.95

43: Metabolic *S*	.19	.92	.12	.41	.61*	.60	.36	.26	.37	.20	.54	.12*	.06	.26
Disorder *N*	.17	.82	.17	.29	.35	.60	.33	.40	.42	.24	.50	.07	.04	.26
44: Fast-Lane *S*	.17	.67	.04	.15	.10	.23	.03	.91	.32	.48	.00	.03	.00	.06
Living *N*	.12	.56	.02	.07	.06	.23	.02	.79	.33	.38	.01	.04	.00	.13
45: Hypo- *S*	.01	.91	.10	.19	.35	.81	.17	.21	.32	.12	.14	.14	.02	.06
glycaemia *N*	.01*	.77	.04*	.18	.25	.81	.11	.16	.37	.20	.14	.13	.05	.11
46: Allergy *S*	.03	.65	.01	.02	.22	.39	.11	.80	.07	.89	.04	.06	.03	.78
Stress *N*	.02	.84	.01*	.01	.20	.39	.09	.66	.06	.90	.10	.17	.04	.84
47: Physiolog. *S*	.08	.79	.03	.16	.18	.17	.13	.12	.12	.36	.05	.02	.05	.49*
Anxiety *N*	.08	.69	.02	.08	.18	.17	.11*	.16	.18	.61	.15	.04	.22	.39*
48: Punitive *S*	.00*	.55	.00	.00	.02	.19	.00	.38	.00	.43	.00	.00*	.00	.13
Reinforcemt *N*	.00*	.35	.00*	.00	.01	.19	.00*	.13	.00*	.27	.00	.00*	.00	.23
49: Affect *S*	.31	.65	.05	.24	.47	.30	.16	.29	.14	.33	.01	.00*	.04	.10
Avoidance *N*	.11	.95	.03	.16	.28	.30	.12	.36	.12	.57	.02	.01	.06	.16
50: Control *S*	.37	.68	.01	.08	.44	.27	.08	.37	.06	.19	.01	.00	.01	.22
Sensitivity *N*	.21	.85	.01	.08	.40	.27	.04	.60	.13*	.20	.02	.01	.02	.05*
51: Guilt *S*	.40	.51	.22	.66*	.85*	.58	.52*	.09	.56	.22	.15	.00	.07	.33
Proneness *N*	.33	.34	.33	.54	.68	.58	.68	.10	.64	.31	.54	.03	.05	.29

52: Anger/ *S*	.13	.93	.03	.07	.17	.44	.06*	.39	.10	.47	.00	.04	.02	.14
Hostility *N*	.12	.87	.01	.12	.16*	.44	.03	.52	.36	.70	.00	.04	.01	.18
53: Somatic *S*	.28*	.77	.22*	.78	.96	.47*	.35	.19	.69*	.13	.24	.02	.28	.01*
Depression *N*	.25*	.69	.17	.90*	.94*	.44*	.32	.17*	.50	.13	.24	.02*	.49	.02*
54: Hungry *S*	.08	.65	.15	.21	.41	.14	.25	.42	.51	.24	.10	.10	.06	.00
Heart *N*	.03	.73	.07	.13	.24	.14	.17	.49	.54	.44	.15	.03	.21	.00
55: Impaired *S*	.06	.47	.03	.16	.32	.01	.05	.04	.15	.28	.05	.00	.07	.01*
Self-Esteem *N*	.03	.24	.02	.15	.23	.02	.03	.04	.15	.49	.13	.01	.04	.01
56: Masked *S*	.43	.73	.03	.34	.23	.16	.10	.32	.57	.30	.02	.01	.01	.07
Disappointm *N*	.36	.71	.02	.22	.21	.16	.11	.25	.43	.29	.11	.06	.00	.03
57: Felt *S*	.07	.94	.01	.11	.08	.56	.03	.18	.05	.25	.03	.00	.24	.00
Rejection *N*	.10	.66	.01	.11	.07	.56	.03	.20	.15	.29	.04	.00	.50	.00*
58: Need to *S*	.62	.88	.25	.89	.99	.37	.33	.08	.90	.30	.51	.28	.00	.40
Communicate *N*	.55	.61	.54	.71	.90	.36	.52	.03	.72	.39	.56	.63	.01	.12
59: NeedCalm *S*	.92	.47	.04	.52	.71	.41	.19	.10	.64	.46	.12	.01	.03	.91
Nerves *N*	.81	.41	.05	.50	.76	.41	.29	.14	.57	.44	.25	.06	.04	.46
60: Substanc *S*	.04	.41	.01	.05	.01*	.16	.03	.50	.19	.80	.00	.01	.00*	.04
Enhancement *N*	.02	.51	.02	.10	.02	.16	.06	.21	.29	.55	.02	.06	.00*	.02

61: Forget *S*	.82	.47	.02*	.56	.73	.14	.04	.22	.49	.64	.03	.00	.03	.37
Failures *N*	.57	.38	.03	.58	.76	.14	.05	.55	.52	.68	.08	.03	.00	.08
62: WshNovel *S*	.50	.14*	.01	.09	.34	.17	.02	.38*	.82	.48	.01	.00	.00	.17
Experiences *N*	.78	.16	.09	.22	.81	.10	.12	.44	.88	.48	.07	.04	.00	.12
63: Avoid *S*	.33	.80	.03	.13	.30	.71	.14	.18	.53	.56	.01	.00	.01	.15
Boredom *N*	.48	.83	.04*	.22	.35	.71	.19	.06	.88	.30	.03	.04	.00	.25
64: Assert *S*	.29	.24	.09	.48	.32	.18	.17	.40	.76*	.55	.05	.21	.00	.02
Confidence *N*	.40	.34	.29	.33	.42	.18	.28	.55	.49	.61	.09	.49	.00	.02
65: Avoid *S*	.72	.75	.04	.32	.78	.19	.05	.20	.84	.48	.40	.07*	.01	.26
Attractiven *N*	.80	.89	.03	.27	.58	.19	.06	.24	.57	.39	.40	.13	.07	.13
66: Impaired *S*	.14	.87	.02	.18	.10	.28	.05	.10	.15	.33	.07	.01	.06	.24
Sleep *N*	.30	.89	.06	.26	.25	.28	.12	.02	.26	.32	.12	.05	.18	.17
67: NeedCalm/ *S*	.65	.47	.10	.85	.99	.64	.24	.30	.11*	.63	.77	.61	.10	.45
Relaxation *N*	.26	.55	.19	.17	.26	.64	.30	.37	.06	.38	.64	.83	.21	.28
68: Substanc *S*	.09	.56	.10	.15	.01*	.07	.08	.16	.29	.16	.20	.05	.07	.11
Dependency *N*	.07	.41	.07	.11	.01	.06	.07	.40	.22	.22	.38	.14	.12	.15
ML: MMPI L	.32	.33	.16	.17	.00	.17	.23	.90	.05	.60	.90	.90	.29	.03
MF: MMPI F	.71	.44	.02	.13	.00	.01	.49	.10	.49	.74	.46	.46	.22*	.00

MK: MMPI K	.81	.94	.07	.49	.06	.72	.42	.60	.89	.33	.18	.18	.26	.01
01: MMPI Hs	.10	.71	.08	.15	.08	.19	.16	.17	.04*	.54	.49	.49	.95	.22
02: MMPI D	.27	.60	.11	.25	.02	.10	.52	.56	.02*	.74	.66	.66	.28	.33
03: MMPI Hy	.16	.22	.49	.50	.70	.30	.16	.32	.12	.52	.34	.34	.81	.98
04: MMPI Pd	.24	.05	.03	.04	.00	.02	.22	.35	.38	.03	.22	.22	.14*	.05
05: MMPI MF	.01*	.35	.99	.93	.94	.09	.63	.57	.40	.46	.85	.85	.98	.58
06: MMPI Pa	.82	.28	.08	.25	.02	.10	.04*	.16	.13	.54	.10	.10	.63	.89
07: MMPI Pt	.81	.78	.15	.42	.46	.20	.59	.89	.08	.42	.38	.38	.63	.19
08: MMPI Sc	.73	.16	.01	.03	.01	.01	.18	.30	.06	.58	.53	.53	.42	.27
09: MMPI Ma	.11	.15	.02	.07	.00	.28	.99	.27	.94*	.82	.81	.81	.44	.01
00: MMPI Si	.34	.39	.17	.74	.27	.86	.19	.84	.72	.05	.28	.28	.33	.04
MMPI TSC F1	.48	.51	.17	.58	.18	.74	.29	.81	.42	.02	.10	.10	.15	.30
MMPI TSC F2	.39	.79	.01	.22	.16	.13	.39	.45	.16	.40	.92	.92	.23	.49

MMPI TSC F3	.53	.77	.03	.25	.19	.85	.70	.15	.92	.29	.41	.41	.59	.12
MMPI TSC F4	.81	.61	.04	.28	.02	.20	.23	.56	.22	.16	.56	.56	.63	.04
MMPI TSC F5	.66	.34	.04	.15	.00	.29	.12	.29	.88	.46	.32	.32	.81	.00
MMPI TSC F6	.60	.45	.01	.04	.00	.13	.43	.58	.22	.49	.51	.51	.47	.04
MMPI TSC F7	.94	.68	.01	.58	.18	.19	.75	.84	.19	.38	.99	.99	.55	.14
Plus Getting	.63	.86	.06	.27	.08	.35	.39	.56	.34	.15	.34	.34	.24	.02
MMPI DY 1	.33	.52	.01	.11	.00	.03	.36	.26	.23	.86	.89	.89	.19	.19
MMPI DY 2	.48	.91	.53	.66	.30	.43	.24	.34	.17	.49	.74	.74	.40	.24
MMPI DY 3	.81	.70	.10	.76	.00	.21	.84	.75	.28	.33	.94	.94	.25	.08
MMPI DY 4	.91	.84	.02	.17	.01	.19	.36	.47	.49	.37	.68	.68	.44	.01
MMPI DY 5	.89	.97	.03	.29	.02	.17	.56	.21	.60	.42	.53	.53	.52	.04
MMPI PrimDef	.22	.03	.12	.08	.00*	.04	.10	.02	.01*	.13	.23	.23	.03*	.00
MMPI Regress	.42	.27	.01	.11	.09	.24	.09	.54	.21	.35	.87	.87	.72	.01*

MMPI Repress	.42	.24	.15	.05	.02	.30	.99	.00*	.07	.71	.04*	.04*	.99	.00
MMPI Denial	.75	.73	.01	.35	.01	.04	.08	.54	.43	.12	.51	.51	.22	.01
MMPI Project	.07	.83	.78	.78	.28	.42	.42	.54	.53	.68	.78	.78	.20*	.22
MMPI Displac	.01	.33	.71	.52	.23	.38	.39	.27	.28	.10	.27	.27	.21	.83
MMPI Intellz	.75	.44	.85	.87	.52	.01*	.65	.90	.67	.37	.71	.71	.50	.42
MMPI S.Doubt	.70	.69	.27	.43	.93*	.91	.72	.78	.43	.31	.90	.90	.20	.02
MMPI RctForm	.14	.20	.21	.08*	.09	.70	.52	.97	.88	.42	.29	.29	.56	.00
MMPI OvAcThk	.64	.37	.01	.03	.00	.11	.50	.54	.21	.42	.53	.53	.44	.03
MMPI IntEffc	.51	.18	.38	.62	.46	.16	.22	.98	.61	.30	.35	.35	.74	.24
MMPI Anxiety	.96	.70	.02	.57	.16	.22	.75	.87	.24	.39	.91	.91	.55	.14
MMPI Depress	.77	.56	.03	.25	.02	.19	.18	.49	.20	.15	.63	.63	.62	.04
MMPI Anger	.69	.36	.04	.15	.00	.39	.15	.24	.91	.44	.32	.32	.81	.00
MMPI Anhedon	.36	.84	.05	.55	.01	.07	.76	.58	.41	.26	.48	.48	.44	.07*

MMPI Respons	.64	.49	.03	.13	.00	.15	.67	.26	.45	.49	.05	.05	.65	.00
MMPI Toleran	.54	.97	.05	.09	.15	.31	.59	.17	.64	.24	.92	.92	.51	.04
MMPI Empathy	.98	.55	.57	.57	.20	.74	.36	.98	.88	.77	.23	.23	.37	.56
MMPI RolPlay	.62	.76	.12	.72	.10	.16	.47	.24	.66	.39	.88	.88	.27	.03
MMPI Dominan	.70	.86	.52	.39	.09	.35	.69	.91	.21	.39	.86	.86	.40	.03
MMPI SocPart	.30	.45	.77	.78	.08	.47	.46	.49	.96*	.64	.95	.95	.70	.04
MMPI SocPres	.52	.77	.22	.80	.08	.43	.59	.87	.51	.18	.31	.31	.28	.05
MMPI Dependc	.50	.66	.07	.38	.43	.45	.14	.50	.21	.15	.29	.29	.65	.19
Dom-Submiss.	.57	.97	.94	.62	.55	.55	.67	.76	.09	.44	.77	.77	.70	.11
Love-Hate	.91	.50	.02	.08	.00	.02	.17	.15	.46	.58	.98	.98	.52	.02
MMPI EgoStrn	.49	.85	.04	.14	.52	.39	.54	.82	.03	.31	.85	.85	.87	.16
MMPI Resilie	.45	.81	.00	.13	.00	.04	.19	.29	.07	.55	.60	.60	.68	.03
MMPI S.Cntrl	.01*	.00*	.01	.01	.00	.05	.29	.14	.39	.42	.38	.38	.23	.00

MMPI Delinqu	.92	.83	.04	.15	.02	.13	.46	.13	.30	.47	.38	.38	.70	.17
MMPI Impulsv	.31	.09	.00*	.01*	.00	.05	.25	.17	.24	.93	.76	.76	.94*	.00
MMPI Raw Spy	.01*	.10	.61	.44	.02	.71	.82	.39	.63	.26	.35	.35	.22	.00
MMPI HabCrim	.15	.01	.00	.01	.00*	.01	.39	.32	.33	.49	.22	.22	.23	.00
MMPI PrisAdj	.46	.02	.26	.50	.00	.24	.71	.17	.14	.59	.25	.25	.09	.00
MMPI Escapis	.22	.28	.01	.04	.00	.02	.14	.16	.21	.86	.70	.70	.61*	.04
MMPI ParViol	.85	.68	.00	.10	.00	.24	.29	.17	.63	.20	.72	.72	.82	.00*
MMPI Recidiv	.16	.08	.00	.05	.00	.17	.06	.18	.45	.45	.73	.73	.84	.00*
MMPI OvCoHos	.78	.86	.29	.70	.00	.91	.29	.50	.67	.98	.11*	.11*	.84	.03
MMPI Violenc	.13	.29	.00	.16	.00	.16	.51	.07	.82	.72	.32	.32	.98	.00
MMPI ThrSuic	.99	.90	.01	.05	.01	.24	.27	.09	.22	.70	.93	.93	.69	.05*
MMPI UncAcSx	.43	.78	.25	.28	.72	.77	.87	.98	.69	.58	.47	.47	.58	.64
Paedophilia	.02	.88	.46	.57	.12*	.78	.81	.65	.51	.75	.95	.95	.54	.03*

Aggravatd Sx	.75	.25	.00	.17	.00	.00*	.25	.21	.07	.69	.60	.60	.48	.04
MMPI Alcohol	.30	.20	.05	.18	.00	.77	.43	.43	.23	.26	.21	.21	.41	.00*
MMPI DrgAbus	.08	.08	.04	.26	.00	.12	.36	.02	.17	.88	.80	.80	.51	.01*
Work Attitud	.85	.46	.00	.04	.00	.20	.13	.10	.32	.97	.87	.87	.92	.01
Rehab.Motiv.	.29	.25	.46	.22	.01	.32	.35	.29	.35	.79	.59	.59	.96	.45
Change Motiv	.58	.55	.01	.29	.01	.26	.15	.31	.43	.19	.38	.38	.67	.10
Thyroid Path	.93	.83	.36	.80	.09	.15	.91	.99	.50	.70	.41	.41	.57	.25
Caudality	.37	.98	.01	.26	.03	.44	.31	.40	.31	.25	.72	.72	.44	.02
LowBackPain	.46	.31	.82	.49	.26	.13	.24	.78	.50	.99	.48	.48	.37	.76
Pariet-Front	.77	.86	.02	.40	.12	.27	.37	.39	.66*	.83	.81	.81	.33	.04
Soc.Adjustmt	.55	.51	.14	.58	.15	.78	.33	.93	.60	.02*	.23	.23	.19	.12
MMPI DeprCon	.96	.95	.05	.15	.07	.80	.24	.22	.58	.22	.99	.99	.69	.10
MMPI PMorale	.51	.45	.08	.30	.23	.26	.23	.63	.23	.21	.34	.34	.51	.09

MMPI RelFund	.12	.50	.77	.95	.61*	.53	.24	.13	.67	.50	.83	.83	.38	.29
MMPI AuthCnf	.30	.57	.01	.18	.00	.18	.71	.04	.49	.71	.23	.23	.86	.00
Psychoticism	.68	.69	.11	.09	.01*	.80	.62	.08	.94	.57	.20	.20	.84	.10
Org.Symptoms	.22	.93	.00	.04	.01*	.01	.11	.12	.02*	.57	.27	.27	.73	.14
MMPI FamProb	.62	.65	.16	.69	.00	.01	.76	.39	.22*	.68	.76	.76	.21	.21
MMPI ManHost	.89	.54	.01	.20	.00	.35	.22	.21	.83	.57	.93	.93	.85	.00
MMPI Phobias	.42	.47	.83	.65	.86	.51	.96	.90	.66	.18	.54	.54	.91	.48
MMPI Hypoman	.98	.91	.09	.78*	.13	.34	.22	.81	.82	.52	.53	.53	.69	.02
MMPI PHealth	.17	.75	.02	.48	.06	.43	.29	.16	.09*	.32	.92	.92	.97	.39
MMPI PharVir	.13	.46	.71	.97	.78	.99	.20	.72	.56	.27	.58	.58	.34	.19
MAST-Alcohol	.41	.25	.48	.52	.06	.05	.13	.06	.25	.42	.04*	.04*	.03*	.02*
DAST-DrugsR2	.00*	.00*	.00*	.00*	.00*	.00*	.02	.01*	.00*	.02*	.21	.21	.49	.99
STFB TotalY1	.01	.01	.01	.02	.97	.55	.16	.16	.14	.43	.40	.40	.80	.10

STFB Fact. 1	.33	.87	.70	.70	.46	.01	.18	.09	.53	.83	.00*	.00*	.01	.01
STFB Fact. 2	.32	.50	.48	.48	.71	.60	.40	.12	.20	.40	.11	.17	.01	.02
STFB Fact. 3	.08	.62	.65	.65	.74	.15	.23*	.51	.35	.73	.02	.02	.00	.01
STFB Fact. 4	.06	.10*	.25	.25	.73	.76	.53	.12*	.12*	.12*	.60	.55	.97	.99
STFB Fact. 5	.14	.90	.86	.86	.25	.96	.17	.67	.53	.38	.15	.09	.82*	.91
STFB Fact. 6	.95	.98	.77	.77	.08	.12	.08	.00*	.08	.27	.01	.00	.00	.00
MMPI+ % Corr	58%	49%	81%	81%	43%	92%	43%	66%	68%	69%	69%	70%	70%	65%
Numb.P < .05 S	19 28%	31 46%	44 65%	36 53%	1 1%	16 24%	4 6%	24 35%	11 16%	9 13%	11 16%	39 57%	1 1%	16 24%
Numb.P < .05 N	22 32%	31 46%	38 56%	25 37%	1 1%	12 18%	7 10%	18 26%	10 15%	10 15%	11 16%	37 54%	0 0%	20 29%
Numb.P < .05 M	50 56%	1 1%	2 2%	2 2%	4 4%	6 7%	7 8%	1 1%	16 18%	48 53%	13 14%	46 51%	5 6%	5 6%
Numb.P < .05 C	0 0%	0 0%	0 0%	0 0%	0 0%	1 14%	1 14%	1 14%	0 0%	0 0%	4 57%	4 57%	5 71%	5 71%

* Asterisks mark variables that entered into the Discriminant Function analysis for this column.

337

Table 7.4: Discriminant Function % Correct Classifications and Correlation Coefficients between the Addicause axes and ninety-one MMPI Scales. Probabilities are rounded to the nearest two decimal places.

AXIS LABELS AND VARIABLES	COFF USE	COFF YRS	COLA USE	COLA YRS	CIGS USE	CIGS YRS	VALI USE	VALI YRS	DOWN USE	DOWN YRS	UPPR USE	UPPR YRS	PAIN USE	PAIN YRS
DAQ Discrim S	49%	65%	55%	71%	44%	65%	73%	92%	86%	80%	68%	77%	71%	66%
% Correct N	46%	60%	55%	50%	46%	63%	68%	80%	83%	79%	76%	74%	65%	57%
01: Social *S*	.71*	.27	.77	.96	.02	.32	.09	.00*	.36*	.35	.04	.03	.04	.77
Anxiety *N*	.72	.20	.54	.45	.02	.32	.04	.00	.32	.31	.09	.02	.02	.44
02: Social *S*	.90	.06	.64	.37	.76	.00*	.60	.77	.46	.89	.22*	.87	.41	.62
Enjoyment *N*	.84	.00	.49	.14	.86	.00*	.60	.86*	.74	.60	.57	.57	.78	.49
03: Reactive *S*	.44	.69	.05	.84	.99	.33	.07	.02*	.19	.27	.12	.04	.05	.12
Depression *N*	.50*	.62	.14	.00*	.58	.15	.07	.00	.52	.82	.39	.15	.27	.25
04: Stimulus *S*	.40	.00	.62	.11	.03	.00	.16*	.00	.04	.04	.10	.00	.07	.64
Hunger *N*	.56	.00	.50	.06	.13	.00	.61	.00	.16*	.14	.41	.05	.29	.49
05: Rigid *S*	.90	.16	.63	.90	.07	.10	.06	.00	.11	.21	.10	.06	.01	.67
Self-Image *N*	.70	.05	.78	.00	.16	.05	.05	.00	.14	.30	.16	.04	.01	.57
06: Social *S*	.60	.17	.79	.08	.22*	.05	.73	.05	.40	.46	.28	.34	.22*	.80
Influence *N*	.60	.02	.87	.02	.47*	.02	.45	.03	.34	.48	.29	.40	.28*	.35

07: Aggressn *S*	.90	.53	.61*	.71	.13	.35	.05	.02	.13	.22	.01	.39	.01	.21
Inhibition *N*	.69	.27	.55	.01	.17	.33	.04	.03	.26	.41	.02*	.49	.01	.21
08: Guilt *S*	.62	.03	.80	.56	.08	.01	.04	.00	.02*	.06	.05	.03	.00	.31
Intolerance *N*	.89	.01	.99	.00	.21	.01	.01	.00	.01	.04	.05	.02	.00	.30
09: Loneliness *S*	.72	.28	.84	.67	.01	.17	.14	.00*	.38	.48	.07	.06	.02	.29
N	.75	.09	.90	.01	.03	.11	.09	.00	.36	.52	.11	.13	.02	.10
10: Social *S*	.44	.10	.10	.28	.24	.00	.85	.50	.68*	.32	.11	.45	.36	.26
Contact Wsh *N*	.46	.05	.09	.18	.23	.00	.64	.71	.47*	.24*	.10	.79	.57	.15
11: Reality *S*	.34	.17	.88	.44	.06	.06	.02	.00	.04	.07	.06	.04	.02	.40
Denial *N*	.32	.07	.56	.01	.17	.02	.07	.00	.12	.17	.09	.13	.02	.56
12: Authorit *S*	.66	.02	.83	.53	.02	.00	.01	.00	.01	.01	.01	.00	.01	.41
Rebellion *N*	.45	.01	.43*	.05	.03	.00	.01	.00	.03	.04	.02	.01	.00	.33
13: Flat *S*	.34	.21	.56	.36	.35	.02	.00	.00	.00*	.01*	.01	.00	.00*	.06
Depression *N*	.54	.13	.31	.00	.31	.03	.00*	.00	.00	.00	.01	.00	.00	.01*
14: Vivid *S*	.42	.18*	.29	.10	.94	.12*	.03	.53*	.02	.02	.13	.07	.11*	.16*
Imagery *N*	.58	.22	.18	.59	.92	.23*	.02	.98	.00*	.01*	.02*	.06	.14	.03*
15: Control *S*	.66	.58	.89	.66	.13	.10	.01	.00	.12	.14	.04	.04	.01	.14
Effort *N*	.80	.21	.88	.00	.21	.03	.01	.00	.26	.29	.08	.08	.03	.19

16: Control *S* of Others *N*	.66 .74	.11 .06*	.05 .05	.38 .24	.76 .62	.01 .01	.99 .77	.61 .46	.83 .96	.89 .91	.15 .32	.61 .48	.24 .28	.98 .98
17: Grief *S* Reaction *N*	.55 .39	.10 .12	.83 .86	.44 .00	.45 .55	.07 .14	.01 .02	.00* .00	.08* .14	.11 .22	.02 .03	.06 .09	.00 .01	.08 .10
18: Substanc *S* Enhancement *N*	.97 .98	.00 .00	.78 .83	.37 .02	.03* .07*	.00* .00*	.01 .01	.00 .00	.00 .01	.00 .01	.07 .19	.00 .00	.02* .02*	.55 .44
19: Pain *S* Sensitivity *N*	.59 .56	.87 .66	.29 .40	.89 .00	.93 .72	.27 .16	.24 .16	.29 .11	.39 .70	.70 .91	.35 .54*	.54 .65	.02 .04	.32 .46
20: Hedonism *S* *N*	.01 .06*	.14 .04	.96 .15	.08 .82	.87 .87	.01 .00	.82 .25	.87* .85	.89 .34	.84 .30	.62 .85	.90 .88	.94 .37	.25 .18
21: Social *S* Withdrawal *N*	.93 .79	.59 .36	.84 .84	.89 .05	.19 .28	.08 .08	.11 .03	.00* .00	.20 .18	.14 .12	.02 .02	.07 .07	.03* .03	.65 .21
22: SubCult. *S* Values *N*	.67 .74	.01 .00	.26* .34*	.01 .11	.04 .07	.00* .00*	.00 .00	.01 .00*	.00 .00	.00 .00	.00* .00*	.00 .00	.00 .00	.13 .14
23: Inhibit *S* Dependency *N*	.82 .81	.65 .41	.55 .41	.84 .03	.06 .24	.17 .08	.09 .03	.16* .04*	.25 .24	.33 .31	.14 .05	.09 .16	.19 .10	.48 .25
24: Immediat *S* Gratificatn *N*	.28 .35	.15 .15	.40 .18	.00 .07	.74 .74	.25 .22	.00 .00*	.02 .25	.01 .00	.00 .00	.25 .02	.00 .00	.20 .03	.10 .07

340

25: Paranoid *S*	.68	.65	.82	.06	.42	.18	.29	.12	.54	.57	.05	.13	.03	.59
Sensitivity *N*	.75	.38	.97	.06	.31	.12	.17	.04*	.66	.55	.04	.12	.05	.52
26: Rationality *S*	.63	.17	.17	.50	.06	.64	.29*	.11	.38*	.29	.31	.15	.86	.27
Defence *N*	.98	.39*	.08	.55	.02	.59	.81*	.09	.37*	.26*	.10	.17	.77	.44*
27: Oppressive *S*	.99	.72	.09	.66	.61	.28	.60	.08	.87	.83	.13	.62	.07	.59
Inhibit *N*	.68	.94	.06	.49	.56	.27	.19	.01	.54	.80	.10	.95	.05	.61
28: Comfortable *S*	.17	.04	.01	.14	.51	.10	.58	.84	.48	.24	.69*	.24	.70	.62
Inhibit *N*	.48	.43	.09*	.67	.69	.53	.87	.39	.67	.61	.80	.88	.81	.42
29: Affect *S*	.62	.56	.76	.45	.34	.07	.06	.00	.29	.23	.15	.12	.08*	.36
Disturbance *N*	.34	.27	.60	.00	.49	.03	.09	.00	.46	.30	.22	.23	.20	.52
30: Affect *S*	.98	.28	.42	.44	.90*	.00*	.71	.75	.96	.92	.22	.93	.28	.46
Denial *N*	.92	.20	.25	.09	.98	.00*	.95	.74	.89	.81	.52	.82	.57	.47
31: Demean *S*	.95	.18	.70	.90	.42	.36	.07	.01	.11	.19	.19	.55	.05	.31
Others *N*	.96	.08	.89	.07	.40	.13	.06	.01	.12	.17	.10	.66	.03	.19
32: Group *S*	.66	.23	.51	.07	.75	.00	.66	.18	.53	.23	.59	.26	.49*	.23
Satisfact'n *N*	.48	.09	.52	.26	.92	.00	.35	.84	.95*	.72	.28	.36	.78	.16
33: Dogmatism *S*	.87	.37	.38	.66	.74	.06	.16	.17	.07	.06	.02	.76	.00	.07
N	.82	.24	.30	.64	.56	.02	.15	.15	.21	.25	.04	.99	.01	.33

Item	1	2	3	4	5	6	7	8	9	10	11	12	13	14
34: Wish Be *S* Different *N*	.44 .72	.12 .04	.95 .81	.97 .15	.62 .75	.00 .00	.01 .01	.03 .01	.01 .01	.04 .03	.00* .00	.10 .07	.00 .00	.59 .67
35: Self- *S* Depreciat'n *N*	.09 .26	.16 .10*	.79* .52*	.16 .00	.19 .54	.14 .03	.00 .00	.00* .00	.02 .02	.06 .03	.01 .00	.02 .02	.00* .00	.32 .28
36: Rigid *S* Moralizat'n *N*	.92 .91	.07 .22	.14 .11	.36 .12*	.51* .36*	.00* .00*	.14 .08	.01* .01*	.15 .08	.06 .03	.13 .04	.00 .00*	.75 .21	.15 .27
37: Paroxys- *S* mality *N*	.59 .48	.09 .03	.33* .27*	.87 .02	.25 .26	.00 .00	.00* .00*	.00* .00*	.00* .00*	.00* .00*	.00* .00*	.00* .00*	.00 .00	.06 .06
38: Rules *S* Intolerance *N*	.79 .54	.57 .23	.80 .59	.14 .01	.42 .73	.01 .02	.01 .01	.00 .00	.02 .01	.05 .01	.00 .00	.04 .04	.00 .01	.45 .23
39: Effort *S* Strain *N*	.67 .70	.80 .47	.80 .43	.56 .00	.73 .99	.12 .11	.00 .00	.00 .00	.11 .04	.10 .03	.23 .10	.09 .05	.15 .11	.12 .05*
40: Pep-Up *S* Effect *N*	.38 .45	.98 .76	.42 .21	.70 .26	.08 .17	.01 .05	.25* .12	.40 .32	.57 .91	.33 .79	.84 .68	.10* .41	.71 .83	.94 .61
41: Rigid *S* Habits *N*	.99* .87*	.10 .03	.68 .37	.72 .01	.53 .82	.03 .00*	.03 .02	.00 .00*	.11 .14	.12 .19	.01 .01	.18 .17	.00 .01	.69 .99
42: Easy Go *S* Enjoyment *N*	.29* .41	.21 .34	.07* .01*	.22 .13	.80 .66*	.00 .01	.88 .44	.88 .42	.81 .97	.95 .90	.29 .21	.39 .53	.31 .39	.71 .75

43: Metabolic Disorder	S	.67	.21	.71	.04	.57	.16	.07	.00	.06	.20	.03*	.04	.50	.69
	N	.56	.12	.53	.14	.60	.08	.03	.00	.04	.10	.02*	.02	.36	.37
44: Fast-Lane Living	S	.77	.02	.76*	.45	.32	.00	.01*	.00	.06	.09	.01*	.04	.01	.73
	N	.88	.01	.61*	.09	.48	.00	.01*	.00	.03	.03	.02*	.02	.03	.27
45: Hypo-glycaemia	S	.99*	.01	.54	.07	.18	.00	.00	.00	.06	.11	.01	.00	.12	.62
	N	.97*	.01	.39	.01	.43	.00	.00	.00	.03	.07	.01	.01	.10	.61
46: Allergy Stress	S	.95	.37	.60	.27	.59*	.09	.01	.01	.03	.04	.02	.05	.04*	.14*
	N	.82	.11	.32	.38	.89*	.06	.00	.00	.02	.02	.02	.02	08	.55*
47: Physiolog. Anxiety	S	.67	.31	.77	.82	.31	.20	.04*	.00	.15	.14*	.02	.01	.04	.66
	N	.36	.14	.68	.00	.50	.25	.02*	.00	.10	.08	.01	.00	.06	.40
48: Punitive Reinforcemt	S	.67	.10	.50	.91	.25	.00	.00*	.00	.00	.00	.00	.00	.00*	.06*
	N	.57	.10	.17	.01	.40	.00	.00*	.00	.00	.00	.00	.00	.00	.09
49: Affect Avoidance	S	.31	.27	.72*	.70	.35	.00	.03	.01	.05	.08	.03	.21	.02	.37
	N	.28	.30	.39*	.00	.81	.02	.00	.01	.01	.02	.01	.10	.03	.22
50: Control Sensitivity	S	.34	.71	.73	.80	.90	.00	.01	.01	.06	.08	.01	.06	.02*	.16
	N	.61	.50	.63	.00	.51	.01	.00	.00	.05	.08	.01	.04	.01	.49
51: Guilt Proneness	S	.86	.56	.93	.32	.11	.25	.06	.01*	.30	.41*	.11	.25	.13	.85
	N	.44	.46	.94	.01	.18	.38	.02	.01	.20	.27	.05	.18	.23	.75

		C1	C2	C3	C4	C5	C6	C7	C8	C9	C10	C11	C12	C13	C14
52: Anger/	S	.89	.09	.93	.68	.89	.02	.02	.00*	.01	.02	.03	.06	.06	.16*
Hostility	N	.86	.06	.93	.30	.93	.03	.00	.00	.00	.01	.03	.07	.08	.66*
53: Somatic	S	.19*	.09	.53*	.75	.55	.02	.01	.00	.32	.40	.23	.22	.10	.26
Depression	N	.20*	.09	.52*	.00	.84	.05	.00	.00	.32*	.40	.25	.25	.09	.15
54: Hungry	S	.66	.02	.98	.35	.34	.01	.03	.00	.08	.11	.15	.04	.20	.14*
Heart	N	.55	.00	.62	.00*	.64	.00	.01	.00	.03	.06	.02	.02	.24	.04*
55: Impaired	S	.54	.13	.82	.76	.15	.02	.00	.00	.07	.11	.02	.03	.01	.45
Self-Esteem	N	.39	.05	.63	.01	.34	.00	.00	.00	.03	.06	.00	.01	.02	.34
56: Masked	S	.74	.17	.72	.32	.46	.01	.01	.01	.06	.15	.06	.34	.01	.46
Disappointm	N	.59	.08	.70	.01	.82	.01	.00	.00	.04	.09	.05	.13	.04	.68
57: Felt	S	.71	.06	.83	.87	.52	.03	.01	.00	.06	.04	.02	.01	.02	.64
Rejection	N	.55	.03	.55	.01	.58	.02	.00	.00	.03	.02	.01	.02	.02	.31
58: Need to	S	.90	.16	.18	.88	.26	.24	.68	.63	.60	.96	.22	.79	.44	.83*
Communicate	N	.97	.04	.21	.07	.35	.21	.77	.20	.69	.93	.24	.79	.58	.96
59: NeedCalm	S	.68	.21	.83	.20	.70	.15*	.28	.27	.38	.59	.03	.51	.00*	.57
Nerves	N	.55	.40	.60*	.01	.62	.10	.18	.04	.38	.49	.01	.14	.00	.31
60: Substanc	S	.62	.09	.47*	.88	.37	.05	.05	.01	.00	.00*	.00*	.00	.01	.54
Enhancement	N	.99	.06	.31	.05	.36	.06	.03	.00	.00	.00*	.00	.00	.04	.77

61: Forget	S	.83	.06	.07	.73	.71	.01	.25	.28	.03*	.07	.03	.46	.00	.64
Failures	N	.89	.07	.11	.38	.50	.03	.03	.06	.04*	.09	.04	.38	.00	.38
62: WshNovel	S	.56	.45	.20	.75	.94	.03	.30	.23*	.09	.20	.00	.03	.01	.82
Experiences	N	.85	.32	.09	.04	.86	.03	.14	.05	.21	.29	.00*	.03	.09	.36
63: Avoid	S	.53	.02	.60	.45	.69	.00	.02	.03	.03	.04	.01	.06	.01	.85
Boredom	N	.28	.03	.46	.06	.97	.00	.03	.00	.08	.14	.00	.09	.02	.65
64: Assert	S	.54	.03	.10	.35	.48	.06	.30	.09	.05	.10	.12	.08	.18	.70
Confidence	N	.77	.04	.06	.16	.61	.04	.10	.03	.06	.11	.06	.05	.36	.41
65: Avoid	S	.80	.06	.61	.85	.84	.10	.21	.04	.51	.78	.21	.42	.05	.92
Attractiven	N	.80	.03	.96	.00	.67	.12	.07	.06	.41	.59	.10	.42	.01	.40
66: Impaired	S	.90	.19	.88	.87	.74	.11	.01	.00	.06	.11	.01	.01	.01	.23
Sleep	N	.74	.07	.94	.07	.82	.04	.01	.00	.13	.15	.02	.02	.04	.28
67: NeedCalm/	S	.68	.52	.08	.30	.59	.38	.34	.83	.72	.49	.52	.64	.35	.45
Relaxation	N	.93	.73*	.13	.64	.65	.27	.43	.21	.30	.19	.45	.77	.99	.34
68: Substanc	S	.20	.08	.48	.51	.16	.00	.04	.15	.09	.10	.03	.01	.01	.04*
Dependency	N	.17	.05	.27	.01	.24	.00	.01	.01	.13	.17	.02	.01	.02	.08
ML: MMPI L		.18	.93	.96	.04	.05	.22	.80	.02	.00*	.07*	.02	.23	.29	.00*
MF: MMPI F		.06*	.60	.87	.02	.27	.49	.40	.18	.21	.24	.00	.02	.82	.00

MK: MMPI K	.29	.64	.56*	.01	.13	.38	.60	.05	.48	.08	.00	.14	.14	.01
01: MMPI Hs	.70	.85	.43	.02*	.90	.90	.70	.05*	.38	.84	.46	.04	.38	.15*
02: MMPI D	.32	.87	.84	.09	.65	.19	.88	.14	.78	.26	.08	.76	.49	.77
03: MMPI Hy	.44	.81	.45	.03	.64	.67	.62	.38	.75	.20	.07*	.01*	.55	.53
04: MMPI Pd	.63	.23*	.14	.39	.40	.09	.06	.16	.16	.51	.06	.03*	.21	.00
05: MMPI MF	.08	.02*	.84*	.48	.79	.04	.76	.15	.82	.70	.99	.40	.63	.07
06: MMPI Pa	.11	.69	.39	.26*	.57	.03	.68	.02	.45	.98	.05	.15	.56	.04
07: MMPI Pt	.25	.86	.98	.00	.44	.14	.64	.06*	.59	.44	.02	.17	.81	.30
08: MMPI Sc	.28	.31	.94	.01	.28	.12	.45	.08	.27	.84	.01	.12	.77	.10
09: MMPI Ma	.87	.26	.49	.02	.12	.73	.22	.22	.42	.15	.96	.11	.48	.24
00: MMPI Si	.33	.69	.92	.03	.15	.28	.79	.01	.92	.00	.00	.34	.15	.31
MMPI TSC F1	.11	.47	.56	.02	.12	.20	.19	.02	.67	.00*	.00	.37	.14	.58
MMPI TSC F2	.61	.66	.84	.00	.69	.34	.96	.01	.67	.65	.03	.42	.09	.00

MMPI TSC F3	.89	.14	.36	.00*	.37	.56	.14	.14	.48	.10	.00	.10	.23	.02
MMPI TSC F4	.16	.95	.83	.00	.16	.35	.51	.01	.31	.17	.00	.03	.78	.00
MMPI TSC F5	.44	.37	.75	.00	.11	.54	.31	.03	.22	.20	.00	.02	.84	.13
MMPI TSC F6	.33	.58	.85	.00	.12	.29	.69	.05	.20	.26	.01	.24	.45	.01
MMPI TSC F7	.47	.81	.99	.00	.41	.65	.74	.08	.40	.60	.00	.31	.42	.06
Plus Getting	.30	.89	.93	.00	.12	.26	.84	.00	.08	.14	.00	.05	.38	.65
MMPI DY 1	.65	.85	.79	.38	.75	.52	.29	.27	.17	.09	.00	.42	.24	.32
MMPI DY 2	.24	.60	.60	.31	.41	.13	.69	.07	.57	.49	.14	.43	.12	.01
MMPI DY 3	.79	.39*	.28	.01	.13	.65	.31	.13	.05	.09	.01	.51	.15	.01
MMPI DY 4	.54	.77	.86	.00	.22	.47	.31	.08	.12	.52	.00	.08	.48	.01
MMPI DY 5	.56	.65	.83	.00	.11	.62	.45	.12*	.77	.45	.00	.07	.61	.19
MMPI PrimDef	.30	.53	.62	.00*	.03	.02*	.47	.00*	.01	.56	.03	.06	.67	.20
MMPI Regress	.33	.34	.15	.07	.88	.75	.48	.20	.69	.13	.12	.96	.05	.24

MMPI Repress	.77	.90	.98	.68	.05	.88	.61	.71	.51	.27	.45	.00	.80	.01
MMPI Denial	.09	.63	.71	.01	.08	.16	.69	.00	.22	.19	.00	.02	.13	.24
MMPI Project	.08	.79	.19	.08	.26	.20	.34	.72	.73	.49	.19	.67	.03	.81
MMPI Displac	.03*	.08	.70	.45	.74	.93	.52	.25	.50	.33	.13	.46	.03	.86
MMPI Intellz	.22	.80	.35	.32	.69	.91	.64	.47	.62	.80	.83	.89	.66	.41
MMPI S.Doubt	.29	.74	.79	.00	.69	.12	.44	.00	.10	.05	.01	.73	.18	.71
MMPI RctForm	.57	.39	.95	.85	.19	.86	.46	.40	.01*	.01	.02	.23	.59	.00*
MMPI OvAcThk	.32	.67	.80	.00	.17	.27	.70	.04	.20	.26	.01	.27	.45	.10
MMPI IntEffc	.12	.46	.88	.03	.86	.74	.67	.25	.82	.10	.01	.29	.71	.24
MMPI Anxiety	.48	.81	.97	.00	.41	.64	.76	.07	.39	.58	.00	.32	.39	.01*
MMPI Depress	.14	.94	.81	.00	.18	.28	.55	.01	.34	.18	.00	.03	.82	.02
MMPI Anger	.46	.40	.73	.00	.10	.57	.34	.04	.26	.17	.00	.02	.79	.00
MMPI Anhedon	.11	.87	.97	.03	.56	.40	.59	.06	.89	.24	.00	.55	.22	.15

MMPI Respons	.66	.10	.83*	.06	.03	.51	.05	.84*	.86	.61	.01	.00	.29	.00*
MMPI Toleran	.53	.15	.79	.00	.34	.46	.38	.20	.63	.29	.00	.13	.62	.00
MMPI Empathy	.60	.33*	.74	.29	.06*	.71	.10	.11	.59	.75	.50	.30	49	.32
MMPI RolPlay	.29	.94	.92	.01	.17	.73	.79	.22	.92	.48	.00	.10	.82	.15*
MMPI Dominan	.17	.76	.95	.00*	.21	.29	.28	.11	.46	.10	.01	.18	.50	.30
MMPI SocPart	.24	.85	.81	.25	.56	.82	.93	.06	.17	.06	.06	.83	.16	.10
MMPI SocPres	.54	.67	.82	.02	.15	.16	.64	.05*	.78	.01	.01	.90	.43	.22
MMPI Dependc	.14	.68	.83	.00	.06	.20	.44	.00*	.18	.18	.00	.14	.64	.35
Dom-Submiss.	.24	.98	.48	.46	.25	.13	.78	.13	.92	.01	.25	.26	.75	.10
Love-Hate	.09	.75	.85	.00	.11	.39	.65	.09	.17	.16	.00	.00	.91	.00
MMPI EgoStrn	.07	.90	.92	.00	.70	.19	.47	.17	.94	.30	.18	.60	.12	.85
MMPI Resilie	.25	.84	.96	.00	.18	.20	.60	.01	.58	.36	.00	.22	.4)	.09
MMPI S.Cntrl	.89	.55	.93	.56	.02	.98	.03*	.80	.17	.02	.15	.04	.12	.00

MMPI Impulsv	.52	.79	.99	.00	.14	.26	.83	.08	.02	.35	.01*	.04	.64	.00
MMPI Delinqu	.22	.38	.93	.00	.21	.24	.47	.02	.25	.54	.00	.03	.98	.04
MMPI Raw Spy	.46	.10	.52	.70	.20	.50	.03	.00	.98	.77	.70	.33	.06	.00
MMPI HabCrim	.41	.24	.63	.07	.49	.19	.05	.25	.13	.71	.01	.01	.35	.00
MMPI PrisAdj	.20	.24	.97	.09	.87	.35	.18	.09	.43	.46	.52	.06	.53	.01
MMPI Escapis	.15	.63	.77	.00	.06	.48	.21	.04	.06	.65	.00*	.01	.95	.00
MMPI ParViol	.26	.88	.94	.02	.18	.93	.66	.06	.24	.19	.00*	.09	.73	.02
MMPI Recidiv	.87	.31	.80	.82	.01*	.99	.56	.54	.47	.13	.06	.13	.99	.00
MMPI OvCoHos	.20	.82	.58	.19	.03*	.84	.79	.42	.28	.33	.00	.54	.25	.01
MMPI Violenc	.81	.50	.54	.01	.05	.79	.56	.84	.10	.43	.00	.00	.70	.00
MMPI ThrSuic	.43	.19	.99	.00	.04	.28	.30	.03	.38	.29	.00	.05	.51	.00
MMPI UncAcSx	.34	.88	.82	.01	.16*	.24	.85	.12	.89	.50	.02	.10	.65	.43
Paedophilia	.29	.91	.93	.72	.24	.23	.67	.01	.88	.03	.02	.41	.66	.56

Aggravatd Sx	.24	.42	.90	.00	.20	.14	.24	.31	.25	.94	.00	.00*	.81	.00*
MMPI Alcohol	.58	.23	.40	.48	.20	.08	.06	.74	.28	.01	.06	.48	.01*	.00*
MMPI DrgAbus	.29	.69	.75	.02	.28	.01*	.34	.26	.23	.75	.00	.03	.96	.04
Work Attitud	.29	.56	.94	.00	.30	.66	.21	.05	.12	.59	.00	.03	.89	.01
Rehab.Motiv.	.16	.43	.39	.43	.59	.31	.37	.91	.52	.53	.00	.06	.02*	.68
Change Motiv	.10	.83	.88	.00	.20	.12	.82	.04	.35	.22	.00	.04	.92	.11
Thyroid Path	.82	.13	.55	.52	.74	.74	.76	.45	.88	.99	.56	.73	.92	.95
Caudality	.22	.99	.99	.00	.21	.39	.66	.04	.67	.37	.00	.05	.19	.24
LowBackPain	.47	.69	.55	.13	.39	.63	.73	.36	.63	.03	.12	.02	.59	.59
Pariet-Front	.18	.95	.82	.00	.20	.49	.76	.00	.53	.47	.00	.10	.36	.10
Soc.Adjustmt	.18	.41	.61	.17*	.13	.53	.29	.06	.49	.00	.00	.59	.17	.06
MMPI DeprCon	.13	.94	.83	.00	.13	.24	.66	.01	.39	.13	.00	.03	.83	.03
MMPI PMorale	.18	.98	.88	.00*	.29	.07	.39	.01	.09	.13	.00	.03	.35	.25

MMPI RelFund	.35	.67	.17	.34	.09	.60	.96	.06	.79	.14	.10	.10	.39	.04*
MMPI AuthCnf	.96	.26	.70	.01	.07*	.42	.07	.91	.65	.36	.00	.03	.16	.00
Psychoticism	.25	.36	.98	.00*	.38	.27	.42	.11	.26	.20	.00*	.01	.55	.00
Org.Symptoms	.79	.12	.49	.00	.60	.52	.62*	.06	.47	.64	.02	.80	.29*	.46
MMPI FamProb	.15	.37	.78	.42	.04	.89	.80	.48	.71	.95	.00	.01	.65	.00
MMPI ManHost	.86	.46	.75*	.02	.05	.69	.39	.12	.18	.27	.00	.05	.36	.00
MMPI Phobias	.61	.77	.34	.05	.63	.59	.58	.19	.97	.52	.36	.87	.64	.34
MMPI Hypoman	.43	.50	.51	.01	.40	.10*	.59	.24	.04	.84	.00	.39	.07	.00
MMPI PHealth	.33	.94	.60	.14	.81	.42	.61*	.01	.66	.51	.09	.44	.87	.63
MMPI PharVir	.57	.97	.99	.00	.36	.94	.21	.12	.67	.12	.00	.27	.29	.24
MAST-Alcohol	.79	.35*	.04*	.50	.20*	.00*	.01*	.00*	.01*	.03	.00*	.01*	.84*	.18
DAST-DrugsR2	.66	.51	.18	.37	.14*	.45	.00*	.00*	.00*	.00*	.00*	.00*	.13*	.07
STFB TotalY1	.52	.21*	.55	.61	.03	.03	.02	.02	.09	.06	.10	.07	.45	.25

STFB Fact. 1	.59	.35	.52	.69	.08*	.38	.00	.00	.01	.00	.01	.00*	.19	.50
STFB Fact. 2	.51	.27	.42*	.38	.05*	.10	.24	.32	.06	.03	.09	.05	.61	.45
STFB Fact. 3	.49	.15*	.84	.71	.14	.22	.01	.01	.12	.12	.13	.13	.66	.90
STFB Fact. 4	.95	.37*	.30	.78	.76	.07	.67	.52	.37	.34	.22	.20*	.79	.06
STFB Fact. 5	.21*	.19	.42	.64	.02*	.01*	.09	.08	.44	.34	.16	.13	.78	.14
STFB Fact. 6	.63	.15	.04*	.53	.06	.29	.03	.03	.16	.14	.23	.20	.57	.85
MMPI+ % Corr	43%	43%	43%	63%	50%	62%	89%	84%	67%	63%	68%	68%	63%	56%
Numb.P < .05 *S*	1 1%	11 16%	3 4%	3 4%	6 9%	36 53%	34 50%	45 66%	21 31%	16 24%	34 50%	28 41%	40 59%	1 1%
Numb.P < .05 *N*	0 0%	23 34%	2 3%	3 4%	4 6%	43 63%	40 59%	50 74%	26 38%	20 29%	39 57%	29 43%	38 55%	4 6%
Numb.P < .05 *M*	1 1%	1 1%	0 0%	59 66%	11 12%	4 4%	4 4%	32 36%	6 7%	11 12%	64 71%	32 36%	5 6%	43 48%
Numb.P < .05 *C*	0 0%	0 0%	1 14%	0 0%	3 43%	2 29%	0 0%	4 57%	1 14%	2 29%	1 14%	2 29%	0 0%	0 0%

* Asterisks mark variables that entered into the Discriminant Function analysis for this column.

Table 7.5: Discriminant Function % Correct Classifications for Use and Years of some other substances

AXIS LABELS AND VARIABLES	CHOC USE	CHOC YRS	PIPE USE	PIPE YRS	CHEW USE	CHEW YRS	TRAN USE	TRAN YRS	BARB USE	BARB YRS	NARC USE	NARC YRS	RITA USE	RITA YRS
DAQ Discrim S	58%	67%	83%	100%	90%	79%	67%	60%	89%	79%	65%	65%	93%	95%
% Correct N	60%	70%	83%	96%	71%	41%	74%	35%	91%	82%	63%	64%	93%	93%
Predict'n Z	57%	77%	67%	0NEG	67%	77%	64%	49%	79%	76%	67%	64%	85%	51%
MMPI+ % Corr	47%	34%	0NEG	93%	0NEG	65%	95%	71%	98%	98%	67%	100%	88%	83%

Table 7.6: Discriminant Function % Correct Classifications for Present (in jail) Want of some other substances

AXIS LABELS AND VARIABLES	BRAN WANT	WINE WANT	BEER WANT	BREW WANT	SCOT WANT	RYE WANT	COCA WANT	CRCK WANT	HERO WANT	HASH WANT	MARI WANT	MUSH WANT	LSD WANT	SPEE WANT
DAQ Discrim S	88%	80%	60%	83%	94%	99%	63%	75%	86%	96%	71%	95%	100%	87%
% Correct N	92%	77%	56%	80%	93%	99%	62%	73%	100%	99%	71%	95%	100%	87%
Predict'n Z	60%	59%	49%	81%	57%	0NEG	60%	65%	89%	0NEG	65%	62%	0NEG	77%
MMPI+ % Corr	66%	90%	100%	95%	100%	97%	59%	100%	94%	98%	83%	100%	98%	92%

Table 7.7: Discriminant Function % Correct Classifications for Present (in jail) Want for several substances

AXIS LABELS AND VARIABLES	CIGS WANT	PIPE WANT	CHEW WANT	COLA WANT	COFF WANT	FOOD WANT	VALI WANT	TRAN WANT	NARC WANT	DOWN WANT	UPPR WANT	PAIN WANT	BARB WANT	RITA WANT
DAQ Discrim S	53%	93%	96%	63%	54%	74%	82%	95%	90%	95%	96%	92%	98%	62%
% Correct N	54%	97%	100%	62%	58%	80%	82%	91%	88%	95%	97%	90%	100%	62%
Predict'n Z	51%	83%	91%	53%	53%	68%	54%	53%	66%	84%	81%	62%	0NEG	0neg
MMPI+ % Corr	41%	0NEG	0NEG	44%	55%	100%	97%	0NEG	100%	98%	98%	93%	83%	87%

KEY to Table 7 (Expansions for Table abbreviations)

Substances	MMPI Clinical and Experimental Scales	
Beer: Beer (Use/Years)	Validity Scales:	L: Lie
Bran: Brandy		F: Claiming Symptoms
Brew: Home Brew		K: Unconscious Defensiveness
GinV: Gin-Vodka	Clinical Scales:	01: Hs
Rum: Rum		02: D
Rye: Rye		03: Hy
Scot: Scotch		04: Pd
Wine: Wine		05: MF
MAST: MAST (test score)		06: Pa
		07: Pt
Coca: Cocaine		08: Sc
Crck: Crack		09: Ma
Hash: Hashish		00: Si
Hero: Heroin	TSC Factor Scales:	I: Introversion (Tryon, Stein, and Chu)
LSD: LSD		II: Health Concerns
Mari: Marijuana		III: Criticality/Mistrust
Morp: Morphine		IV: Depression
Mush: Mushrooms		V: Anger
Opiu: Opium		VI: Overactive Thinking
PCP: PCP		VII: Anxiety
Peyo: Peyote	Response Set:	PlusGt: Plus Getting (Hathaway)
Spee: Speed		DY1: Very Social Desirable (Messick)
DAST: DAST (test score)		DY2: Socially Desirable (Messick)
Glue: Glue		DY3: Neutral Social Desirability
		DY4: Socially Undesirable (Messick)
Coff: Coffee		DY5: Very Socially Undesirable (Messick)
Cola: Colas	Defences:	PrimDf: Primitive Defences (Haan)
Cigs: Cigarettes		Regres: Regressive Defenses (Haan)
		Repres: Repression (Haan)
Vali: Valium		Denial: Denial Defence (Haan)
Down: Downers		Projec: Projection (Haan)
Uppr: Uppers		Displa: Displacement Defence (Haan)
Pain: Analgesics		Intelz: Intellectualization Defence (Haan)
Tran: Other Tranquillizer		S.Doub: Self-Doubt Defence (Haan)
Barb: Barbiturates		RctFrm: Reaction Formation Defence (Haan)
Narc: Narcotics	Cognitive:	OvActT: Overactive Thinking (TSC VI)
Rita: Ritalin		IntEff: Intellectual Efficiency

356

Affects:

Choc: Chocolate

Pipe: Pipe/Cigar

Chew: Chewing Tobacco

Addicause axes

01: Social Anxiety

02: Social Enjoyment

03: Reactive Depression

04: Stimulus Hunger

05: Rigid Self-Image

06: Social Influence Need

07: Aggression Inhibition Need

08: Guilt Intolerance (defence)

09: Loneliness

10: Social Contact Need   Criminality:

11: Reality Denial

12: Authority Rebellion

13: Flat Depression

14: Vivid Imagery Need

15: Effort at Self-Control

16: Control of Others

17: Grief Reaction

18: Event/Substance
Self-Enhancement

19: Pain Sensitivity

20: Hedonism

21: Social Withdrawal

22: Subcultural Values

23: Dependency Inhibition Need

24: PIG: Immediate Gratification

25: Paranoid Sensitivity

26: Rationality Defence   Work:

27: Oppressive Inhibitions

28: Comfortable Inhibition

29: Disturbed Affects   Organic Scales:

30: Affect Denial

31: Demean Others

32: Group Satisfaction

Anxiet: Anxiety (TSC VII)

Depres: epression (TSC IV)

Anger: Anger (TSC V)

Responsibility (Gough, et al)

Tolern: Tolerance (Gough)

Empath: Empathy (Hogan)

RolPly: Role Playing

Domina: Dominance (Gough)

SoPart: Social Participation

SoPres: Social Presence

Depend: Dependency (Navrn)

DomSub: Dominance-Submission (Leary)

LovHat: Love-Hate (Leary)

EgoStr: Ego Strength (Barron)

Resili: Resiliency (Welsh: A Reversed)

SCntrl: Self Control (Block: EC-5)

Impuls: Impulsiveness

SDelnq: Social Delinquency

RawSpy: Spy Scale (raw score)

HabCri: Habitual Criminality (Panton)

PriAdj: Maladjustment to Prison (Panton)

Escapi: Escapism (Panton)

ParVio: Parole Violation (Panton)

Recidi: Recidivism (Clarke)

OvCHos: Overcontrolled Hostility

Violen: Violence

ThrSui: Threatened Suicide

UncSex: Unconscious Acting Out of Sex

Pedoph: Paedophilia

AggrSx: Aggravated Sex

Alcoho: Alcoholism (MacAndrew)

DrugAb: Drug Abuse (Panton & Brisson)

WrkAtt: Work Attitude

RehabM: Rehabilitation Motivation

ChngMo: Motivation for Change

Thyroi: Thyroid Pathology

Caudal: Caudality (Williams)

LBckPn: Low Back Pain (Hanvik)

ParFro: Parietal-Frontal Symptoms

357

33: Dogmatism

34: Need to Be Different

35: Self-Depreciation

36: Rigid Moralizations

37: Paroxysmal Energy Release

38: Regulations Intolerance

39: Effort Strain

40: Pep-Up Effect

41: Rigid Habits

42: Easy-Going Enjoyment

43: Metabolic Disorder

44: Fast-Lane Lifestyle Need

45: Hypoglycaemia

46: Allergy Stress

47: Physiological Anxiety

48: Punitive Reinforcement History

49: Affect Avoidance

50: Inhibited Sensitivities

51: Guilt Proneness/Feelings

52: Anger/Hostility

53: Somatic Depression

54: Hungry Heart

55: Impaired Self-Esteem

56: Masked Disappointment

57: Felt Rejection

58: Communication Need

59: Calm Nerves Need

60: Substance Excitement

61: Forget Failures Need

62: Need for Different Experiences

63: Avoid Boredom/Depression

64: Assert Confidence Need

65: Avoid (Personal) Attractiveness

66: Impaired Sleep

67: Calmness/Relaxation Need

68: Substance/Events Dependency

Content Scales:

SocAdj: Social Adjustment (Wiggins)

CDepre: Depressive Content (Wiggins)

PMoral: Poor Morale (Wiggins)

RelFun: Religious Fundamentalism (Wiggins)

AutCnf: Authority Conflict (Wiggins)

Psycho: Psychoticism (Wiggins)

OrgSym: Organic Symptoms (Wiggins)

FamPrb: Family Problems (Wiggins)

ManHos: Manifest Hostility (Wiggins)

Phobia Phobias (Wiggins)

HypMan: Hypomania (Wiggins)

PHealt: Poor Health (Wiggins)

PhVirt: Pharasaic Virtue

STFB (Criminality) Scales

F1: Guilt Intolerance

F2: Failure/Inferiority Intolerance

F3: Distress Intolerance

F4: Sensitivity Intolerance

F5: Conformity Intolerance

F6: Discipline Intolerance

Totl: Total STFB Score

Neut: Neutral Social Desirability

Unde: Social Undesirability

Addictions Scales

MAST: Michigan Alcoholism Screening Test

DAST: Drug Abuse Screening Test

APPENDIX J

Table 8: Summary Table for Significant Fs and Discriminating variables/scales in Substance Classes (distilled from Table 7). Notations (s or n – to be compared with 'main causal function' notations) after Number (no.) included in discriminants column identifies discriminating variables where S or N scores predominate (occurring in the ratio of $25s$:$23n$). Notations about predominance of Years of use (y: Persistence/Rigidity), Strength of Use (u: Motivation Intensity), or of Neither (–) are made for the numbers of significant Fs under Alcohol and Drugs, separately. Relevance notations identify primary relevance of variable to uses of alcohols (A), drugs (D), or both (b), and to possible relevance to common subject subgroup characteristics in the population: Cr = offenders, Ad = addicts, Tx = applicants for treatment.

DAQ, MMPI, and STFB Scores	Alcohol Abuse	Drug Abuse	Relevanc					
Scale/Variable Name Discriminant Identity	Main Func	No. $\underline{S/M}$ p < .05	No. $\underline{N/C}$ p < .05	No. In Disc	No. $\underline{S/M}$ p < .05	No. $\underline{N/C}$ p < .05	No. In Disc	$A/D/b$ See SGp

359

01: Social Anxiety	rf	5u	4u	0	13u	14u	3	D	Tx
02*: Social Enjoyment	Rf	5y	3y	6n	6	7	7	b	Ad
03*: Reactive Depress	sD	8	8	2	8	8	5s	b	Tx
04*: Stimulus Hunger	Nd	9	8	4	9	7	6	b	Cr
05: Rigid Self Image	sD	10	11	0	14u	13u	4s	b	Ad
06: Social Influence	Nd	5y	6y	2s	8	8	3	b	Cr
07: Inhibit Aggressn	Nd	5y	5y	0	7	8	1s	b	Tx
08*: Guilt Intolerant	Rf	11	12	0	19	20	18n	D	Cr*
09: Loneliness	rf	11	11	0	11	10	7	b	Cr
10*: Social Contact	Nd	3y	2y	3	2u	0	5s	b	
11: Reality Denial	Rf	12	13	1	10	10	3n	b	Ad
12*: Authority Rebel	Nd	11	10	0	19	18	5s	D	Cr
13*: Flat Depression	sD	13	12	1	18u	18u	10s	D	Tx

14: Vivid Imagery	Nd	0	0	2	6u	7u	6s	D	Ad
15: Control Effort	Rf	5	6	2	10u	9u	6n	D	Tx
16*: Control of Others	Rf	3y	2y	0	1	2	4n	D	Cr
17: Grief Reaction	sD	4	5	6s	11	10	6s	D	Tx*
18: Subst.Slf Enhance	Nd	10	10	8	14	12	9s	b	Ad*
19: Pain Sensitivity	sD	0	0	1s	3u	2u	4s	D	Tx
20*: Hedonism	Rf	4y	4y	6n	0	0	2	A	Cr
21: Social Withdrawal	rf	4u	3u	0	14u	14u	0	D	
22*: SubcultureValues	sD	15	15	14	20u	20u	15	b	Cr*
23: Inhibit Dependent	Nd	5	5	1s	7	7	0	b	
24*: Immediate Gratif	Rf	5	9	8n	12u	16u	10n	b	Ad*
25: ParanoidSensitive	rf	4u	3u	0	9	10	0	D	Tx
26: Rational Defence	rf	0	1	2	2u	0	1n	b	

27: Oppressiv.Inhibit	*Rf*	0	2	1*n*	2	2	4*n*	*D*	
28: Comfortab.Inhibit	*Rf*	0	0	0	0	2*u*	1*n*	*D*	
29: Disturbed Affect	*rf*	7	8	4*n*	10	10	8*n*	*b*	*Tx*
30*: Affect Denial	*rf*	4*y*	4*y*	0	3*y*	3*y*	10*n*	*D*	*Cr*
31: Demean Others	*Nd*	5*y*	6*y*	0	9	8	0	*b*	
32: Group Satisfact'n	*Rf*	1	2	5*n*	1	2	5*n*	*b*	
33: Dogmatism	*rf*	8*y*	7*y*	5*n*	9	5	0	*A*	
34*: To Be Different	*Nd*	11	11	2	15*u*	14*u*	10*s*	*D*	*Cr*
35: Self-Depreciation	*rf*	10	12	1*n*	15*u*	15*u*	3*n*	*b*	*Tx*
36*: Rigid Morality	*sD*	4*u*	2*u*	3	11	10	17	*D*	*Ad**
37*: Paroxysmality	*sD*	16	16	29	20*u*	20*u*	23*s*	*bA*	*Tx**
38: Rules Intolerance	*rf*	12	7	0	15*u*	11*u*	2	*b*	*Cr*
39: Effort Strain	*rf*	4*y*	4*y*	7	10	11	5*n*	*b*	*Tx*

40*: Pep-Up Effect	Rf	3	3	0	0	0	1n	A	
41: Rigid Habits	sD	9	8	2	13u	13u	2	b	Ad
42: Easy Go Enjoyment	Rf	4y	2	2	1u	0	4	A	
43: Metabolic Disordr	sD	6	8	0	7	7	4s	b	Tx
44*: Fast-Lane Living	Nd	11	11	2s	13u	13u	2s	b	Cr
45: Hypoglycaemia	rf	8	9	0	9u	10u	6n	D	Tx
46*: Allergy Stress	rf	7	4	2	12	11	9	D	Tx
47*: Physiol. Anxiety	rf	9	8	6n	11	10	3	A	Tx
48*: Punitive Rewards	Rf	15	14	6	20u	21u	15n	D	Cr*
49: Affect Avoidance	Nd	6	5	0	11u	12u	5	D	Cr
50: Inhibit Sensitive	Rf	9	9	3n	11u	13u	2n	D	
51: Guilt Proneness	sD	5	4	0	9	8	3s	b	Tx
52: Anger/Hostility	Rf	11y	11y	3n	10	12	3	b	Cr

363

53*: Somatic Depress.	rf	5	3	9n	6	6	11	b	Tx*
54: Hungry Heart	Nd	8y	9y	6s	8	9	0	A	Ad
55: Impair Self-Esteem	rf	11	11	5s	14	15	2n	A	Cr
56: Masked Disappoint	sD	7	7	2	8u	7u	5s	b	
57: Felt Rejection	rf	10	11	1	14u	13u	0	A	Tx
58: Communication Nd	Nd	2	4	1s	0	1y	1n	A	
59: Need Calm Nerves	Nd	6u	4u	0	5u	4u	2	b	Tx
60*: Substance Enhanc	Nd	13	13	3s	17u	13u	9s	b	Ad*
61: Forget Failures	Nd	13	9	1s	11u	8u	1s	b	Ad
62*: Novel Experience	Nd	12	7	1n	11u	7	2s	b	Cr
63: Avoid Boredom	Rf	11	9	2	11u	10	2	b	
64: Assert Confidence	Nd	11	9	1s	9	7	1s	A	
65: Avoid Attractives	rf	6u	5u	0	8	6	2	b	Tx

66: Impaired Sleep	sD	8	5	0	11	8	2s	b	Tx
67: Calm/Relaxation	Nd	2	1	0	0	0	3s	b	
68: Subst. Dependency	Nd	12	11	1s	10u	9u	3	A	Ad
MMPI L (Lie) Scale		5y		0	6		2	b	Cr*
MMPI F (ClaimSymptom)		1y		1	6y		0	b	Tx
MMPI K (Defensiven)		2y		0	2y		1	b	
01 Hs (Hypochondrias)		5		2	5		5	b	Tx*
02 D (Depression)		0		1	3u		4	D	
03 Hy (Hysteria)		2		1	0		0	A	
04 Pd (Psychopathic)		4		1	15y		2	D	Cr*
05 MF (Mascul/Femin)		2		2	4u		2	b	
06 Pa (Paranoidal)		1u		0	3		2	D	
07 Pt (Psychasthenia)		2		0	1y		0	b	

								D->	Hi8
08 Sc (Schizophrenia)		0			0	5		0	
09 Ma ('Mania')		3			2	4u		1	b
00 Si (Introversion)		1y			0	3		0	b
TSC Fact.I (Introvert)		1y			0	2		0	b
TSC Fact.II (HealthPx)		4u			2	3		0	A
TSC Fact.III (Critic)		1y			0	4		2	D
TSC Fact.IV (Depress)		4y			0	3		0	A
TSC Fact.V (Anger)		2y			0	7		0	Cr
TSC Fact.VI (OvThink)		4y			0	6y		0	Tx*
TSC Fact.VII (Anxiet)		0			0	2		0	D
Plus Get (Hathaway)		4y			1	2y		0	A
DY1: V.High Desirable		2u			2	4		2	b	Tx
DY2: Desirab (Messick)		2			1	1u		0	A

DY3: Neutr. Desirable	2		0	4		0	b	
DY4: LowSoc.Desirable	4y		0	3		1	b	Tx*
DY5: V.Low Desirable	2		0	4		0	b	Tx
Primitive Defen (Haan)	7		1	15		7	D	Tx*
Regressive Defences	2		2	2		0	A	
Repressive Defences	2y		2	9y		4	D	Tx*
Denial Defence	3		0	8		0	A	Cr*
Projection Defence	0		1	1u		0	bX	Tx
Displacement Defence	0		1	2u		0	bX	
Intellectualization	1u		1	1y		2	b	
Self-Doubt Defence	5		2	2		2	A	Tx
Reaction Formation	1y		0	3		3	D	
Overactive Thinking	4y		0	6y		0	b	

Intellect Efficiency	1u		0	2y		0	b	
Anxiety Affect	0		0	2		1	D	Tx
Depression Affect	4y		0	3		0	A	Tx
Anger Affect	2y		0	6		0	D	Cr
Anhedonia	0		1	2u		0	bX	
Responsibility (Gough)	5		0	9		0	b	*
Tolerance (Gough)	3		0	3		1	b	
Empathy (Hogan)	0		0	1y		0	DX	
Role Playing	2		0	1y		0	A	
Dominance (Gough)	3		0	1y		0	A	
Social Participation	3		1	1y		2	b	
Social Presence	1y		0	0		1	bX	
Dependency (Navrm)	2		0	2		0	bX	

Dominant-Submit Style	1y	0	0	0	AX	
Love-Hate Styl (Leary)	1y	0	5	0	D	
Ego Strength (Barron)	2	0	2u	0	bX	
Resiliency (Welsh A-)	9	0	5	0	A	*
Self-Control (BlockEC)	7	2	16	4	b	Cr
Impulsiveness	5y	2	12	4	b	Cr*
Social Delinquency	2y	0	4	0	b	Cr
Spy Scale	2y	1	6u	2	b	Cr
Habitual Crim (Panton)	6	1	13y	2	b	Cr*
Prison Maladjustment	3	0	6	0	A	Cr
Escapism (Panton)	5y	2	13	0	b	Cr
Parole Viol.(Panton)	4y	1	6	0	b	Cr*
Recidivism (Clarke)	6y	2	10	1	b	Cr*

Over-Control Hostile	2y	1	3u	3	b	Tx
Violence	3	1	8	3	D	Cr*
Threatened Suicide	7	2	6	0	A	Tx*
Unconscious ActOutSex	0	0	1y	1	DX	
Paedophilia	1y	1	1u	2	b	Cr
Aggravated Sex	6	1	8	1	b	Cr*
Alcoholic (MacAndrew)	9y	5	12	1	A	Ad*
DrgAb (Panton&Brisson)	4y	1	8	1	b	Ad*
Work Attitude	7	1	8	0	A	Cr*
Rehabilit.Motivation	0	0	5	0	D	Tx
Motivation for Change	5y	0	3	0	A	Tx
Thyroid Pathology	1y	1	0	1	AX	
Caudality (Williams)	4y	0	3	0	A	

Low Back Pain (Hanvik)	1y		2	1y	1	b	Tx
Parietal-Frontal Symp	7		1	2	2	A	Tx
Social Adjustment Cont	1u		0	2	1	bX	
Depressive (Wiggins)	6		0	2	0	A	Tx
Poor Morale (Wiggins)	1u		0	1y	0	bX	
Religious Fundamental	0		0	1u	2	D	
Authority Conflict	5		1	8	0	A	Cr*
Psychotic (Wiggins)	1u		1	4	1	b	Tx
Organic Symptoms (")	8u		2	12	3	b	Tx*
Family Prob.(Wiggins)	0		0	4y	1	D	
Manifest Hostility	3		0	7	0	b	Cr
Phobias (Wiggins)	1y		1	0	0	AX	Tx
Hypomania (Wiggins)	2y		0	4y	1	D	

Scale					b	Tx
Poor Health (Wiggins)	3					
Pharasaic Virtue (")	0	0	1y	1	D	
STFB F1: Guilt Intoler	3y	0	16	3	D	Cr*
STFB F2: Fail Intoler	2	1	7	2	D	Cr*
STFB F3: Upset Intol.	4	1	9	1	b	Cr*
STFB F4: Sensit.Intol.	5	4	2	6	b	Cr*
STFB F5: Conform Intol	4y	2	3	3	b	Cr
STFB F6: Discipl Intol	4u	4	15	2	b	Cr*
STFB Total Criminal	2y	2	13	0	D	Cr*

* Noteworthy variables. Axis Number * identify Addicause Short-form scales.

APPENDIX J

Expanded Specification of Addicure Treatments

Treatment 1: Creating SUCCESS

The <u>main target</u> of this treatment program is the sense of <u>failure</u> experienced by many addicts both throughout their histories (as seen in their proneness to report and expect punishment and failure) and in their unsuccessful attempts to stop their addictive behaviours. Failure is a punishing experience for them, and they often seek to forget it. These parameters define the strategy.

It is difficult to set out to reduce the sense of failure as it is often denied; and focusing on it seems mainly to impair involvement or participation. To seek to enhance their unrealistic view of their success and importance, however, is inappropriate too. It affords more practice in avoiding reality. The solution seemed to be to help participants to succeed in various ways.

Block 1: Orientation

We always start with housekeeping considerations about the day's schedule and components. Then we proceed to the orientation. Estimate the percentage of the time you were a failure in things you have done in your life. Guess at the percentage. (Responses typically

vary from 20% to 95%.) The actual percentage for all of us is a flat 0%.

Failure is not a characteristic of how humans do things. It is an idea derived from others' judgements, and the notion that you failed comes from accepting another's judgement. Doing one thing successfully and failing to do another. Others might have thought you ought to be or were doing something different from what you were actually trying to do – that is, to do something they thought you were but you were not trying to do. But simply and flatly, they were wrong.

Judgements of what you ought to have been trying to do are based on values or what seems important to you or to the other person. You will always have been trying to do what <u>you</u> thought it was important to do or what <u>you</u> valued.

You may not know that you know, but you do know what you want to do. And you learn very well to do the things you want to do. Humans are enormously competent learning machines. Sometimes we may end up doing something less well than we might have wished or liked. This may be because weak attention/concentration may get in the way or because we haven't practised it enough or haven't figured out the best strategy for doing it. But it is most likely to be that, <u>after the fact</u>, you see ways of doing it differently or of 'succeeding' in a different (by then viewed as a better) way.

Your imagined or affirmed failures of the past occurred either (a) because you were trying to do something different from what someone else thought you should have been trying to do; (b) because, viewed from after the fact, you picked a poor strategy for what you wanted to do, perhaps because you were already older by the time you judged yourself; or (c) because you hadn't yet learned how to do what you wanted to do as well as you, later, thought you should have. Does that mean there's anything wrong with you or that you were a bad or incompetent person? It does not. In fact, the only people who make no mistakes are those who don't do anything. Feedback from efforts is not failure; it is part of successful learning. It may mean that you need (a) to learn how to share or communicate with yourself or others what you are trying to do at any given time, (b) to get some

(treatment) help in finding new or different strategies by which to do things, or (c) to do some more learning about how to do something.

Now, I might point out that

(a) If you want to learn how to communicate about your intentions better, you might take a values or an assertive training programme, (b) You are currently involved actively in learning new strategies in your various treatment programmes, and (c) Right now, let's think about how learning is done.

In the learning circle (Draw O with arrows and stages: $\rightarrow$ Knowledge/Skill $\rightarrow$ Interest/Motivation $\rightarrow$ Effort $\rightarrow$ Learning $\rightarrow$), the point of entry is <u>effort</u> to learn. But if you think of yourself as a failure, or if you think you can't learn, or if you think that effort expenditure seems like too much work, how can you arouse the effort to learn? So much depends on our attitudes.

Life is activity. If you are inactive, you will feel more or less dead. Waiting for things to happen is an approach leftover from childhood. If you want anything in life, it is up to you to do something about it. As adults, nobody gives us anything. We are responsible to ourselves to get anything we want. The most important thing in life is simply 'doing' or activity. Of course, the strategies we use and how we do things are also important. Today's purpose is to find strategies to succeed.

Block 2: Tools

Here are some simple tools for learning that you could use on your own to help in recognizing your immense successes.

First, your own <u>attitudes or expectations</u> will decide how quickly and easily you learn. (Use flash cards with different numbers of random dots on each.) Quickly now, how many dots on this card? (Response is given.) Right! How many on this card? (Response.) Right! (etc.). That was easy, wasn't it? Just like learning. (This is Slack's Estimate the Number of Dots task.) You need to believe

in yourself, to know how really good you are, and to trust in the wonderful programming and capacity of your marvellous brain.

Second, here are some pictures. (There's overhead of coloured pictures torn from magazines ordered from simple to highly complex.) Please tell us what you see. (Purely descriptive response is given.) Good! (Any inferential quality, e.g., juicy tomato, is challenged gently.) Where do you see the . . . (e.g., juicy)? Only what you actually see, please. (Encourage increasingly refined descriptive detail.) (This is Quirk's Perceptual Discrimination training.) Strange to say, starting with general observations or comments, the more exact and refined the way you proceed to see or describe things, the better the control in what you do and the more will be the success and accuracy of your actions.

Third, it's terribly important that you notice your successes and reward yourself for them. It's amazing how little of this most of us do. Partly, that's because we aren't trained in how to observe our successes or even to know what a success is. (Hand out sample cumulative frequency charts.) Of course, we all rely on our memories to recall what we've done. Then we all forget. The trick is to record your every success and in every area in which you are trying to succeed at the time. If you were to keep a record of each kind of action, marking one more occurrence on the chart as soon as you notice it, you will be shocked and amazed at just how much success you have every day. (This is Lindsley's Precision Learning.) What kinds of things you set out to record is up to you. But pick specific things you can observe yourself doing. If you want to become more sociable, on separate charts, record smiling on seeing someone you know, conversations with others, greeting people you know, each time you express an opinion, and so on.

Fourth, a simple tool for success is Relaxation (Programming). We all use up a whole lot of unnecessary energy in tension – energy that could be devoted to a task. If you relax, you will have more available energy and you will be able to concentrate better on the task you are doing. Relaxation is a skill that you can learn easily. (Use progressive muscle relaxation tape [Jacobson's method or Lazarus' tape] or use a guided imagery method [Schutz's Autogenic Training].)

(If you use the former, add differential relaxation; if the latter, add some mnemonics training, e.g., from Page-a-Minute Memory Book.)

Fifth, planning is essential. (Use the Goal-Finding programme.) Life is a journey, not a destination. If you are going anywhere, you had better know where you are going, or you may end up at the North Pole and freeze to death. If you know where you want to go, you had better know how to get there, or you are likely never to make it. This is true in your life just as it is true in travel. (Hand out materials.) The following are ways on how to always succeed:

(1) Set achievement goals, and work out subgoals for each, objectives for each of them, and action plans for each of them. Suddenly, the unachievable dream becomes eventually achievable reality. Make sure you keep working through the action plans and recording completion of each. The record works as a reward to keep persistence up.

(2) Use Personal Development goals to become the person you want to be – your ideal self. If you like, you could spend years trying to figure out who you are. Or you could define the person you would like to be and the qualities you would like to have as your identity, and then, by a fairly simple (self-reward) procedure, develop those qualities and become the person you would like to be. The following is a practice exercise: Suppose you wanted to become assertive. What behaviours have you seen in assertive people? (Responses might include the following: 'made a definite statement', 'stood erect and tall', 'used a brief affirmative sentence', 'expressed an opinion', 'spoke loudly, slowly, and clearly', etc.) Write down the defining behaviours. Each morning, read over the list of behaviours you are watching for. Reward yourself (e.g., say, 'Good', and pat yourself on the back) every time for every approximation to any action on the list. The behaviours will grow, and you will notice yourself becoming the kind(s) of person you want to be. Becoming your ideal self is easy, and the method involves succeeding 100% of the time. There is no failure in it.

Block 3: Therapeutics

Use the Change History (James and Woodsmall's Timeline) procedure. If you knew, when you picture events from the past, where do you see the pictures? Point at where. (Exercise in sample past pictures, if needed, to locate direction of approach along the person's timeline.) If you knew, when you picture anticipated events of the future, where do you see the images? Point at where. (This is an exercise for future timeline, if needed.) It doesn't matter how your timeline lies; anything that seems right to you is perfect. Where do you see present events? Put a bright red flag there to mark the present so you can find it again. Tie a string to the flag, with the other end tied to your great toe. Drift up above your timeline, way up, until it is just a line running way below you. Now drift down again until you are floating a short distance above your timeline but completely out of it.

Drift slowly back over your past timeline until you are over a time when, if you knew, you feel something went wrong that might have been a root cause of a problem you have had ever since. It doesn't matter for our purposes if you know what the event at the time was or not. Turn around and face the present. Take yourself by the scruff of the neck and dip yourself, just for an instant, into that event, and then pull yourself back up well over your timeline. Notice how you felt in the situation, whether or not you remember what it was. Remember how you felt. If you knew, ask yourself, Was this event before, during, or after your birth? If it was after your birth, if you knew, how old might you have been at the time? Now drift back a short time, up to an hour, before the event in question. Facing the present, drift down into your timeline. Notice how you feel. Where have the negative feelings gone? Have they disappeared? Tell yourself whether you have the same feeling as before or a different feeling or no negative feeling at all. If you have the same feeling as before, drift up again and go back until you are over another such time, and repeat the above until the feeling is different or there is no feeling. If the feeling is a different one, mark that place with a yellow flag, then drift up above your

timeline and back until you are over another time that, if you knew, seems like it might be a cause of another problem. Repeat the above procedure until you find a time in which, just before the event, you have no feeling. Each of these events where you have a different feeling may be a situation that is root cause for a different problem.

When you find a time where you have no feeling when you drift down into your timeline just before the event, facing the present, walk slowly along your timeline until you are in the event. Where are the feelings now? If you find you still have some of the original feelings in the situation, drift up above your timeline and return to the present. Pick up some resources from the present. These might be your mature sense of your strength and resiliency; they might include people who feel like resources or sources of strength for you; they might include accomplishments you have made and the like. When you have surrounded yourself with these resources, drift up again, return to just before the past event, drift down into your timeline, and walk forwards into the problematic event. Where are the feelings now? If need be, back up and re-enter the situation a few times, until the feelings are gone. When that has happened, start walking slowly along your timeline towards the present, passing through all the situations that in the past aroused those feelings, taking whatever time you need to re-evaluate the situations and the learnings from them and being sure to carry along with you any positive learnings from those situations. If any feelings recur in these situations, back up again and then re-enter the situations until they, too, are clear. When you have reached the present, open your eyes.

The past is full of events, most of which we don't remember because they left no unpleasant feelings. It is the situations that left negative feelings that we remember and that become bothersome events in our histories. If the feelings are disengaged or removed, the memories change to neutral ones, and they can be forgotten, or remembered, without importance. If the memories change, the history changes.

Undo some effects of failures (using NLP Phobia Treatment). We can use a wrinkle on the last method to get rid of some of the effects

of past failures. Drift up above your timeline and back until you are over a time when you came to feel you were a failure. Now, construct a theatre up over your timeline at that place. Sit down in the theatre facing the present – the direction of the screen. While you are doing that, be a video maker and make a film of a 'failure' event, starting well before the event, when you were still feeling OK, and ending well after the event when there was nothing happening to make you feel badly.

Leaving your body sitting in the theatre watching the screen, drift up out of your body into the projection booth or control room. Through a window in the room, look down at yourself in the theatre below. Watch yourself down in the theatre to see how the you down there reacts. Flip on the projector and run the film through, fairly quickly in black and white. Stop the film at the end. Then do a fast rewind in colour so that all the action is going backwards. How did the you down in the theatre feel? If you are just as uncomfortable as in the original situation, leave yourself in the projection booth and drift up and out to the front of the theatre into the ticket booth. While you are selling tickets, think about the you in the projection booth watching the you down in the theatre, and rerun the film as above. How did the you in the theatre feel? If better, repeat the same procedure from the same positions a half a dozen or more times.

If the you is improving, step back one step in the process. For example, if you are in the projection booth watching the you in the theatre, drift down into the theatre and sit beside the you in the theatre to watch that you at closer quarters. Repeat the film reruns a few times. Then, drift back into yourself in the theatre and watch the reruns – forwards in black and white then fast rewind in colour. When that is comfortable, drift up into the film on the screen and take your role in the movie for a few more reruns. When you are comfortable, roll up the screen, close the theatre, and return over your timeline to the present. How did that feel to you? (Obtain some experiences from participants.)

Convert <u>failure to success</u> and disapproval to approval (use James and Woodsmall's Visual Squash). Close your eyes and catch the

first visual picture that flashes into your mind when you think of Failure. Open your eyes when you have that picture. Who is willing to describe the picture he/she got? (Respond to pictures given. If too concrete, ask for another picture to pop from the unconscious until the picture makes little or no sense.) That's perfect. Close your eyes and catch the first picture that pops in when you think of Success. Open your eyes when you have it. (Check a sample of these pictures too, looking for ones that make little sense.) That's perfect also. (Repeat for Disapproval then for Approval.)

Do you all talk to yourselves a lot? Sure, we all do. That's what it is to think. What parts of you talk to what other parts? Oh, so you don't know. We want you to talk to a specific part of you in what follows. To talk with it, you had better be able to know what part it is and to look at it. If you knew, on which hand would you put the picture of Failure? Fine, then put the picture of Success on the other hand. Now you have two parts of you – pictures that must be parts of you since they came from within you and those outside of yourself so that you can see them and interact with those two specific parts of you.

First, have a conversation with the picture of Failure. Ask it to tell you what its highest intention is for you. When you get an answer, ask it to tell you why it wants that for you. Take the answer and ask the question why it wants that for you. Repeat this until no other answer is possible. Repeat the same process for the picture of Success on your other hand. Surprise, surprise! The final answer for both pictures will be to support survival and/or happiness. That is the reason for the existence of absolutely every part of every person. That is, these two opposite parts of you have the same purpose. (Confirm at each stage.)

Well, if they have the same purpose, maybe they could talk to each other to work out a way in which they could cooperate to achieve their common purpose, without hurting or upsetting you at all. And perhaps the two pictures, once they have found the way to achieve this cooperation, could find a way to show you that they will work together as one harmonious part to achieve their common purpose.

(This last evidence usually results in the person's two hands coming together in what is called the squash, as the sign of coming together into one part.)

When the hands come together (or the eyes are open), ask the participants to close their eyes and to look at the resulting single harmonious new part. Ask for a sample of descriptions of the new resulting part. If two parts remain, ask the person to try it again on his/her own, forcing answers from each of the parts – since they are parts of you – and forcing the two parts to talk to one another, if necessary. If a compromise solution is found, try again. They both want the same thing, so how can they function as one? If a new picture is reported, say, 'That's perfect.' When a new picture is reported, ask the participants to do the following:

Now imagine an infinite source of power, love, joy, and contentment flowing down through your head and out through your heart to the new part and to all the other parts of you as the new part becomes integrated with the rest of your parts.

Block 4: Consolidation

Design your Future for positive experiences. (Review the Personal Development Goals method and focus on positive attributes and how to achieve them.) The method always succeeds and ends up with successes and the ability to recognize successes. Do it. The problem of succeeding is always a matter of recognizing and being pleased with successes. It also requires that you have achievable indicators of success that can actually be observed. Find them. It helps if you know what you want to achieve. What you want to achieve are called goals or objectives. And it also helps if you know what is important to you or what your values are.

What have you accomplished today? (Answers are likely to include the treatment work done during the day.) That's great. But that's not all you accomplished. You got up to face the day. You made your bed, contributing to tidiness. You contributed to your dental

health by brushing your teeth, to your peers by washing yourself, to your physical health by eating your meals. You added to your happiness and that of others by talking with others. You gave yourself a chance to improve the overall quality of your life by attending this programme. On and on, you accomplished many things that you didn't even notice. It's time you began to notice just how good and successful you are all day every day, and you have been all through your life.

But people keep pointing out your 'failures'. Heck, you keep pointing out your own 'failures' to yourself. You might recall that both they and you are wrong when they or you do that. It's their values leading them to think you were trying to do what they thought you ought to be doing. Let them do what they think ought to be done. It's just your incorporation of other people's notions that leads you to find fault with yourself. Hey, you're an adult, and you can decide for yourself what you want to accomplish and how you want to accomplish it. Freedom is just a state of mind that recognizes your right to choose freely what you want to do. You have that right. Isn't it time you exercise it? You are free.

Do a summary of program and cuing observations.

Treatment 2: Creating FREEDOM

The <u>main target</u> of this program is the <u>resistance</u> of addictions to modification, which is to be seen both in their apparently intractable nature and in the fixity of attitudes ordinarily encountered among addicts. This inflexibility tends to be denied, with addicts typically preferring to assign their intractability to addictive properties of their preferred chemicals. At the same time, flexibility tends to be devalued and routines followed. In this instance, it was felt that setting flexibility or freedom as a target would not serve as an impediment to treatment for present purposes.

Block 1: Orientation

(Describe the nature of the human learning machine.) Unlike animal life, in human life, almost everything is learned. You have even learned how to breathe, how to have sex, and how to look and listen – whether or not the learning you did was ideally adaptive. Let's take breathing as our example. Nearly everyone has learned to breathe in unhealthy ways. What happened was that we wanted to look good – either slim or 'masculine' or 'feminine'. To do so, we sucked in our stomachs and tightened our pectorals to expand our chests. Unfortunately, in doing so, we prevented normal diaphragm breathing – into our stomachs – and we sucked air into our chests to expand them even more. Over time, we started the habit of chest breathing. Now, chest breathing is not only shallow breathing (not using all the lungs), it also is quick breathing. This is because although the rigid ribcage will expand a bit, it will only contract as far as it opened. That shortens the OUT-breath to be equal in duration to the in-breath. That shortens the total breath cycle, increasing the number of breaths per minute and not giving the low-gradient, parasympathetic-controlled out-breath time to neutralize the steep-gradient, sympathetic-stress-anxiety-controlled in-breath. So we get too much oxygen in our bloodstreams and become 'hyper'; we get increasingly stressed out and anxious and our brains don't work as well as they might due to fogginess bred of anoxia resulting from reflexive vasoconstriction of the brain's blood vessels to protect the brain cells from danger from the increased blood oxygen levels.

The experience of fogginess feels as though we are dizzy or faint or not quite clear about what's going on around us. Nobody can stand being uncertain or confused too long. Ambiguity is the most common and intense source of fear. The way all of us deal with being uncertain is to use our habits of understanding and thought from the past. And the result is that we use overlearned or habituated attitudes and beliefs and, by satisfying ourselves they worked, add more habit strength to them. The result is increasing fixity or inflexibility of our

ideas, attitudes, and beliefs. And that's just one part of the effects of only one of our habits – how we learned to breathe maladaptively.

How many of you believe that the cause underlying abuse of chemicals is a chemical cause? Of course you do. Heck, it's obvious that chemicals cause chemical reactions in the body to which the body becomes addicted. The trouble is that this idea is wrong. Believe it if you wish. However, if you believe that, the only way to change addiction is to never again touch an addictive substance, which doesn't change the fact that you are an addict. Also, there is a wonderful big bridge in Brooklyn I'd like to sell you. The trouble with some of our beliefs is that we hang on to them desperately in order to avoid having to feel responsible for the things we do that we don't like the idea of doing, and in believing them, we give up our control and ownership of our lives. Today, we want to look at some of the gains and losses that we have due to ideas, attitudes, and beliefs we hang on to. We hang on to ideas and beliefs not only because they have a lot of habit strength from previous learning. They also give us something that is rewarding, and this strengthens the learning of them. One of the main things they give us is a sense that we 'understand' or 'know' our worlds. Knowing or understanding feels good and is rewarding because uncertainty is, for everyone, the greatest source of fear. At least three great human enterprises are motivated by fear of the unknown, namely, languages, sciences, and philosophy.

Languages and their words structure the uncertain and moving universe around us. Sciences set out to predict events after finding the laws that control the universe. Philosophy bridges gaps in our knowledge by careful reasoning about our universe. When we get a concept, law, prediction, or an idea that seems reasonable, we cling to it to help make sense of our world.

Another way we get a faulty sense of assurance about our ideas and beliefs is that having found a way to understand something, any upset or stress we have been feeling tends to get less. We are inclined to attribute the reduction in stress/upset to the idea or understanding. It is more likely to be due to the fact that the arousal from stress cannot continue forever. The body adapts to the ongoing stress or

stressor no matter what idea we formulate to help in living. That is, the 'feeling better' we experience may have nothing whatever to do with the understanding or idea we achieved.

Still another way we satisfy ourselves that our ideas must be right, and thus reward our ideas, is if other people agree with us. We've all heard the slogan 'If a million people believe something, it is bound to be right'. And we act as though that statement were true. It seems to us more likely that if a million people believe anything, it is bound to be wrong. Still, consensual validation of our ideas by others is a powerfully rewarding experience. And if we get ourselves in 'the right' groups of people, we can quite easily get their agreement with our attitudes and beliefs. First, in a group, where everyone wants to be accepted, any attitude expressed by one of the members is likely to be agreed with by the others, if only to maintain group cohesiveness. Second, other, especially new, members are just as uncertain as you are or were about the accepted mores of the group, and they will 'yea-say' anything for acceptance, perhaps starting a wave of yea-saying in the group. Third, groups exist for a purpose – sometimes for status, sometimes to gain access to something like wealth or drugs, and sometimes to dispel loneliness. The achievement by a member of the group's purpose (which is rewarding) is likely to be enhanced by getting into a leadership position – a position established by offering opinions and having the group agree. These are only some of the rewarding factors involved in a clique or group.

Block 2: Tools

Our question now is one of finding how to allow ourselves increasing degrees of adaptability, variety, freedom, and fun. One way might be to do the adult thing or to take back from others to ourselves the power to reward our actions and ourselves. This is one of the main things that the Goal-Finding group sets out to help you do. Especially in the Personal Development goals, the focus is on taking over your life to be governed by yourself.

All through childhood, we felt we were at the mercy of what other (adult) people wanted, and we waited for what we wanted until others gave it to us. Your parents, your brothers and sisters, your teachers, your maiden aunt, and the cop on the block each wanted you to become something different. Each had his or her own goals for you. So each of them meted out rewards and punishments to you for the kinds of actions he or she wanted of you. Is it any surprise that we are all pretty confused about who we are and what we want out of life? Now you are grown up some, and you can decide for yourself who you want to be and what you want to be like. But it won't happen . . . unless you take on the job of rewarding yourself for being and acting the way you want to be. That's what you learn in the Personal Development part of Goal-Finding.

A second way to help achieve our present purpose is for you to learn a new skill of finding the good in yourself, in those around you, and in everything. And that ain't easy. You see, we all learned to find fault, to see mistakes, and to criticize much better than to do the opposite. We've learned that from our interactions with adult others. Parents and teachers are not just OUR parents and OUR teachers. They are people who have many other things to do than run around after us saying, 'good, good, good, good, good, good'. So being efficient people, they wait for that second and a half out of each hour when we are being roaring hellions, and then they point at us, warn us, point out our errors and the like. Our attention is repeatedly drawn to our failures and errors and only rarely to our successes. Is it any wonder that as we grow up, we get to know more about our mistakes or badness than we do about our successes and goodness? If we could identify and notice our goodnesses, we might be able to reward ourselves for success and flexibility instead of looking for the 'rules' by which others seek to influence and even to run us.

But what about the world around us? You might try, every time you are going anywhere from here to there, when the world is moving past you, to find three new things that you like. You don't have to love the things or to find things that take your breath away. It is enough that you like them OK and that they be different things from things

you noticed before. You might find the world in which you live is really quite nice and full of really quite wonderful things.

A third method is to keep yourself in the Here and Now. If you really did that, you might just live forever. If you really lived only NOW, time would mean very little, and you would just be alive. But that is hard. The whole lifestyle involved in Zen, for example, has to do with just being in the here and now. That is, some people make a life's work out of doing this task. You see, thinking gets in the way. Thought always has to do with unrealistic things. The past is gone and does not exist. The future hasn't come yet and doesn't exist. And the future is pouring into the past through the razor-thin present. By the time you think about the present, it is already in the past.

One way to diminish unrealistic thought is to pay strict attention to the stimulus world around you by paying attention to focusing your eyes and ears on things going on in the world outside you. Of course, if you stop for any interval of time to stare at something, naming it with words and thinking about it will follow. So keep the eyes and ears roving, even if only to explore the microstructure of the things you are attending to. It's an interesting exercise in exploring our incomprehensible and fascinating world. That really doesn't need to be comprehended. It's fun, and it helps to keep you in the here and now.

A fourth thing you might do recognizes that you are bound to do some thinking. Too bad! However, if you must think, you might try thinking in the most outlandish manner possible. Of course, you are a sensible person, so you can't let yourself be too outlandish. OK, how about looking for different ways to understand anything you are thinking about. Doing that might even increase your creativity. One way to think about things differently is called Divergent Thinking. You might have a little fun looking through a Dictionary for Divergent Thinkers – Quirk's *Dictionary for Divergent Thinkers*.

Block 3: Therapeutics

Let's try an exercise. Pick a sound that means nothing at all to you. If you can't get one, use the ultimate abstraction, *one*, or the universal mantra, *om*. Close your eyes and start listening to the sound in your mind. Don't struggle to listen to it, and don't try to push other things out of your mind. If you notice a thought or sensation, you don't have to think about it now, just let it pass on by and go back to listening to your sound. (Allow five minutes of silence for this brief exercise in Transcendental Meditation, or TM.) OK, come on back. How do you feel now? (Allow a variety of responses.) TM is something you could practice for about twenty minutes each day. It is probably the best way to reduce the pressure of thinking from introversion, and it has a number of other healthy life benefits (TM).

A second way to reduce the amount of thinking you do, and thus to participate more fully and adaptably in living, is to focus your attention on each task you do. Of course, we know that you do that. But you have probably learned another faulty habit. You probably start a task and work away at it for long periods of time. After all, that's how we were taught to deal with tasks in school. But that's just plain nuts. A person's normal attention span for anything is under five minutes. If you are highly motivated, you might extend it to ten minutes. You might not even notice it, but as you reach the end of your own personal attention span, your mind starts to wander. You may not even know what you were thinking about, but you may be aware that you can't remember what you were just doing. This is because the nerves involved in the task get tired or fatigued.

If you want to be able to concentrate on anything you are doing, to do the best you can at each task, and to reduce the amount of time-wasting thinking, you might timetable your day in time blocks that are never more than five minutes per task and preferably under three minutes. That's impossible, right? Actually, it isn't. How long does it take you to get up and make your bed? That's one task. How long to brush your teeth? How long to read one or two paragraphs? How long to drive from one landmark to another? If you set yourself to

389

go through a day, changing the focus of what you're doing in under five-minute intervals, you will concentrate better, accomplish more, and think less. (This is the Task Focus method.)

A third way to reduce the amount of internal television watching (i.e., thinking) you do is to include the quality of 'outgoing' among your Personal Development goals. Here's the drill. Write down the heading Outgoing as though it's a goal you want to achieve in yourself. Under it, list a half dozen observable behaviours that define an outgoing person for you. When you meet an outgoing person, what do you see that tells you the person is outgoing? (Write responses on the board. Exclude those that cannot be observed directly.) OK, let's say the behaviours include 'approaches others', 'smiles on approach', 'initiates conversation'. Write down the behaviours that are right for you, but let's use these ones for the present discussion.

You are walking along the corridor. People are coming your way. This also means you are approaching them, so you had better, in your mind, start whacking yourself on the back with pleasure for performing one of your outgoing behaviours. But you may say, that's not being outgoing. Don't worry about it. Let's see what happens. After a while of doing this and being pleased with yourself, you may actually begin to smile. Whoops! You'd better start whacking yourself on the back with both hands. The first person you are approaching sees a crazy person approaching him or her, smiling. He or she passes as far away as possible. Perhaps the tenth person sees a nice person approaching and smiles back. Perhaps the twentieth smiling-back person says Hi. After that happens often enough, you might even be motivated to greet a smiling-back person with a hi. Whoops! You had better grow a third arm with which to whack yourself on the back since you are now approaching others, smiling on approach and initiating a conversation. As the habit strengths to do each of these actions increases, you will notice yourself becoming increasingly outgoing. You will also find yourself increasingly attentive to here and now events and a bit less prone to being turned inward in thought (introversion). You may even notice that your overall social behaviour

becomes a little more flexible and adaptive. (This is the Personal Development Goal-Finding programme.)

A fourth way is to find the good in yourself and in others. Of course, that flies in the face of most of our learning. How can we do that? Think of someone who seems to have only faults and who seems to get everything wrong and to do everything wrong. Hey, I think I know that person too. How long was it after you met that person that you discovered what he or she was like? We know you're smart. You probably figured it out almost at once. Did you like the person when you met him or her? Did you categorize the person right away? Sure you did. You labelled the person as 'parent' or as 'black' or 'whitey' or 'drunk' or 'punk' or 'foreigner' or 'competitor' or, or, or.

The truth seems to be that we do NOT see people's faults first and then conclude we disrespect them. It works in quite the reverse order. We decide not to respect others, and then we confirm our disrespect by finding faults in them. The decision to disrespect comes first. Now we know that it probably feels good to disrespect some people, especially those who differ from us. It helps us to feel superior, special, better than the other. But we usually fail to notice that it also increases our fear, bitterness, resentment, anger, and other unpleasant emotions. Of course, when we were younger and needed to feel extraspecial, we were willing (even wanted) to experience those negative feelings in exchange for feeling better than others. Partly, it had to do with the wish to be 'different' – the primitive way we established our identities. But a funny thing happened. Check this out for yourself. You feel disrespect for the other person, and the angry or other negative feelings simply add to our disrespect – each feeds the other. But try this on for size. Now that you're grown up some, you probably have a better sense of yourself, and you may not need to feel better than other people. After all, it was just a compensatory need when you felt young and put down. Now you may be in a position to ask yourself, Who hurts when I disrespect and/or feel angry (etc.) about another? It doesn't matter all that much to him or her. We suspect that the complex involved in disrespect of others only hurts ourselves.

Strange to say, respect and disrespect are just decisions we make ourselves, and we are the only ones who feel good or hurt for making the decisions. If we simply decided to respect everybody, we would start finding the good in everybody. And respect is not a gift to others. It is a gift to ourselves. We find that we live in a world full of good people doing good things. It is a happy world that we created for ourselves. (This is Respect Training.)

A fifth way to increase flexibility and adaptability is by means of assertiveness. We have an Assertive Training programme. But assertiveness is really quite easy. Mostly, it involves using the energies that our energy-producing bodies produce for us. Standing erect, moving instantly (i.e., decisively, without delay), talking in short affirming sentences (without explanations), using 'I' statements (in place of 'You' statements), increasing volume or clarity in speech, and the like are all ways to be assertive. And they all interfere with and diminish thought and rationalization and increase freedom through the variety of our responses.

Let's do an exercise. Write down on different pages three repeating situations from your life in which you feel inhibited, upset, or irritated. Under each one, write down about sixteen responses you might make in that situation, graded from the most aggressive ones at the top to the most underassertive and passive ones at the bottom. Make sure that most of the responses are somewhere in the middle, neither aggressive nor underassertive. (Get a set of responses for one such situation on the board, making sure the responses are reasonably hierarchized.)

Now here's what we want you to do. First, memorize the entire list of responses for each common or repeating life situation. Second, each time the situation occurs, STOP, run through the memorized list of responses quickly in your mind, pick the one that you would be comfortable using, step DOWN one step in the rank order of responses, and deliver that response.

The purposes of this procedure are to get you to increase the range of your responses in common life situations (i.e., increased freedom), to ensure that you are definitely comfortable with the level

of assertiveness you actually use (by stepping DOWN one step), and to help unlearn the anxieties that keep us stuck in our attitudes and what we do (by pairing comfort with the whole list of responses you have just recited to yourself). It is a simple and useful way to make life better. (This is Wolpe's in vivo procedure for assertive training.)

Block 4: Consolidation

(Summarize the day's proceedings. Try to refocus the presentation to model different approaches.) We talked about assertive training with a view to creating response alternatives in order to increase response freedom. But response freedom is also increased by allowing yourself to dream your own dreams freely, without having to have means to help or to enhance your dreams. In a few words, write down a dream. In doing so, pick the kind of language that most appeals to you. Draw a picture of it, if you like. A picture is often worth a thousand words. If you can't draw well enough, later, find a picture in a magazine that fills the bill or get someone you know who can draw well to draw it for you. Make the dream as far out as you like. Make it really special. It is a goal of yours. Perhaps you can work out on paper the details of how you plan to achieve the dream.

There's another way to expand your alternatives. Think about any problem. Break it down into subproblems that have to be solved to solve the whole problem or into its parts or stages. If you have three subproblems, parts, or stages, there are probably four. Find the fourth. If there are four, there are likely five. Find the fifth, and so on. By doing this, you increase your understanding of the problem, you challenge your own toleration for uncertainty in looking for other options, you reduce the chance of missing something that is important so that you are more likely to succeed, and you reduce the pressure of thinking by writing things down. Thus you put a full stop to the need to think. (Reynolds says, 'If 2 choices, then there are 3.') It also helps you to develop goals you want to achieve and helps you achieve them.

Now, you and I believe that we have to exert control over ourselves or we are apt to make mistakes or worse. The need for control is largely a fiction. You have programmed your brain beautifully across the years to respond instantly to all sorts of life situations. Isn't it about time you learned to trust your brain to do the right things? Chances are that if, in an identical situation, you were to act without thought or to think carefully through how to react, you would end up reacting in exactly the same way. Letting go of control is one big part of achieving Freedom.

Did you ever try this? Laugh, and then find a reason for doing so. Try it now. Have a good belly laugh for no good reason at all. Then find a reason for laughing, if you must. Did you know that it's a crime for a man to laugh? The crime is called Mans-laughter. Speaking of crime, you may wonder why some of us are so fond of crooks. One reason is that if it weren't for pickpockets, some of us would have no sex life at all. Laughter relieves tension and leaves a good feeling about life. Enjoy it.

(The summary should remind participants of all the methods suggested and used and should include cuing observations.)

Treatment 3: Creating EXCITEMENT

The <u>main target</u> of this program is on compensating for the <u>reinforcing effects</u> of chemicals in perpetuating addictive behaviour. Excitement is rewarding. It may sometimes be a need to be pursued, and many addicts consider it to be achievable only through the use of excitant chemicals. There seems to be little point trying to reduce the need or pleasure in excitement. There is some point in reducing the joylessness of depression and/or introversion in order to make excitement-seeking less necessary (see Treatment 8). However, it at least seems appropriate to provide means by which other kinds of excitement and reinforcement can be experienced to replace excitant chemicals.

Block 1: Orientation

The role of buzz or rush in addictions doesn't need to be explained to addicts. The Problem of Immediate Gratification (PIG) coupled with long-term harm, pain, and discomfort does need to be explained, less with the focus on the long-term harm and more with the focus on the optimal time delays (½ to 2 seconds) for reinforcement of habit strength. This fact of life, about the effects on habit strength of differing intervals between action and reward, is less a caveat and more a reminder that the reinforcing effects of chemicals depend on the pre-existing state of the individual. The reminder is that, for a rush or buzz to be rewarding, the person's pre-existing state has to involve learned characteristics such as sensation-seeking need, joylessness, boredom, or depression. The caveat is that if the effect of the excitant properties of some drugs is to be counteracted, it requires that these characteristics have to be alleviated or that alternative means for excitation be learned or that the meaning of time has to be expanded to allow the negative consequences to counteract the excitant ones. These reminders and caveats define the task of the day. Some of the other treatment programs in the series address depression and variables such as sensation-seeking and torpor (e.g., the values treatment). This program is concerned with others of the above issues.

It offers one approach to joylessness by examining one major source of inhibition of the main source of joy – emotions or feelings. (Draw a large test tube on the board.) This is not a penis; it is a test tube. Let's pour into it all your love feelings in order to measure the amount of them up the side. By love feelings, it means all the needs, carings, love for others, and even your attachment to things such as a car or silverware. These bubbly feelings have been with you and developing since birth, and your basic amount of these differs little from anyone else's.

A funny thing happens as you grow up. You are lying in your crib helplessly, and you are hungry. You cry. Your parent is outside and doesn't hear you. You cry louder and get all tensed up – indicating

your ANS-anxiety response has been activated. Repetition of this scene conditions your anxiety arousal to the feelings (of need) you have. Let's show that by adding some anxiety feeling on top of your love feelings in the test tube. You grow older. You feel lovingly towards a parent, and you go running to him or her. He or she is too busy to take the time with you. You feel rejected, and some more anxiety feeling gets learned to be associated with your loving feelings. You tell a friend a secret, and the friend blabs it around to others. And more anxiety feeling gets attached to the loving feelings. You are attracted to another child, but he or she runs off and plays with someone else. And more mistrusting anxiety feeling gets connected to your love feelings. (This is Love Test Tube.)

For those who develop enough anxiety accumulated with their love feelings (which is almost everybody), a strange kind of reverse alchemy happens as the years roll by. When your love feelings are stimulated (i.e., you meet someone you like), so are all the learned anxiety feelings. Now you feel increased feelings of love and anxiety. If you experience this amount of feeling as the loving part, the feeling no longer is one of 'I love' but is one of possessiveness – 'The OTHER must love me more than I love, or it is not safe to love.' If that increased amount of feeling is experienced as the fear part, the feeling is one of jealousy – the OTHER probably loves someone else. If it is experienced as the avoidant or inhibitive 'cork' over the love feelings, which is the function of anxiety, the effect is one of blocking or inhibiting feelings expressed to the OTHER, who has to 'prove he/ she is trustworthy before I will trust'. The focus on how the OTHER feels adds to the inhibitive effect of the anxiety cork, distracting attention from our own feelings. We may feel strong feelings within, but they may not be expressed because we are by focusing on the OTHER'S feelings and the pain of rejection we feel.

We can see the problem another way. Instead of looking at the side of the test tube to measure the amounts of feelings up its sides, we could look down the throat of the test tube. At the greatest distance is a small circle of love feelings. Around that are radiating spines of anxiety. Around them is a bigger circle representing the top of the

anxiety cork. If the centre core is love feeling, then the surrounding inhibitive defences involve 'psychological distancing'. That is, we find ways to keep others away for fear that closeness evokes the anxiety feelings. The ways by which we can keep people away, usually without noticing it, include being very clever and intellectual (who can relate to that?) or being tough or gruff or aggressive or being suspicious (paranoid) or just being cold and mistrusting. From others' perspective, all these actions seem hostile, distancing, and aloof. From our perspective, they are merely reactions to how we think OTHERS are behaving or feeling. From an outside perspective, the result is an inhibition of our feelings. But feelings are the way in which we achieve liveliness and joy. So we make ourselves more or less joyless by means of the distancing defences evoked by the love test tube.

Perhaps it is time to take back control over the contingencies by which we run our lives and, in doing so, take back regulation of our own lives. We can, you know.

But how can we take control over the consequences and the contingencies that govern our lives? Consequences are future events that happen to us because of their causes. That sort of thinking is due to our presumption that causes always predate their effects or consequences. If we plan our lives, the effects or consequences we achieve could be the ones we want, by design. If we were to select first the outcomes we want (i.e., future purposes) and then select those actions that would be followed by the outcomes we wanted, we could control our own destinies. If we were to expand our notion of time forwards into the exciting realm of 'the possible', instead of expanding our (memory) lives into the sad and bemoaned past, the consequences of the future can become events of our present lives, ensured by what we do now.

Block 2: Tools

Strange to say, one of the things that makes our lives more joyless than they might be is the kind of words we use. The problem is that we tend to refer to events and things with nouns. What difference could that possibly make? Nouns are categorizing words. Their effect is to stop action, to make the world around us seem more static, to make the relationships among the world's parts seem easier to see, and to make the world around us appear more predictable. But action and unpredictability, while often stimulating anxiety, are also a major source of excitement and increase the options or possibilities of response to the world. To explain how this works would take too long and would bore you to tears. Still, this strange set of facts offers a way to reduce the boredom, joylessness, and lack of emotion we often feel. The trick is merely one of trying, as much as possible, to use verbs in place of nouns. This task is not as easy as it may sound. It may even take using a dictionary a lot to find the verb forms of words. An easier way is to keep a dictionary of Synonyms and Antonyms, a Thesaurus, handy; and find, when possible, the most action-focused words for ideas you want to express. For example, *Abaft* draws synonyms like *Aft, Sternwards*, and *Behind* – of which *Sternwards* is the most action oriented as direction rather than place. *Abaft* draws antonyms like *Forward, Ahead, Afore*, and *Before* – of which *Forwards* is direction rather than place, although *Advance*, if it fits, might be even better. The more you manage to use verbs in place of nouns, the more you are likely to feel excitement, energy, and fun in your life. Nuts, eh?

An even better, but related, way to increase excitement, fun, and energy in your life would be to find yourself 'at cause' in everything in your life. We tend to attribute the causes in our lives to past events over which we had little control and over which we no longer have any control. Indeed, we have a lot of words to convince us that we have no way of avoiding the pains we find in our lives. Words like *victim* and *abuse, rejection* and *abandonment*, and a host of related concepts paint us as helpless effects of others' actions. You may say

that these kinds of events did (or do) happen. What we all tend to remember are the notably unpleasant events in our lives; we tend to forget, and often simply to overlook, the many, many pleasant and good things that also happened in our lives. By focusing on the unpleasant events, we provide ourselves with explanations for why we feel angry, unhappy, or troubled now. That's fine, but then we become the victims of our own logic. We then think of ourselves and present unhappiness as immutable effects, and we then become the effects of former events. One nice thing about being human is that we control our own destinies by pursuing our own goals and purposes in the future. In pursuing our own goals and purposes, we become the causes of our futures in place of others and past events. What difference does that make? Well, quite apart from giving us back control over our lives and quite apart from the fact that purposive thinking increases the range of possibilities and excitement that our futures might hold, it tends to reduce the passivity and inertia that comes from waiting for others to have effects on us and to increase the vitality and hope that come from pursuit of the possibility of whatever futures we might wish or design for ourselves. You are the cause of your life and what happens to you, and I am the cause of what happens to me. That is scary, in a way, since it puts the whole responsibility for your life squarely on your own shoulders; it is also exciting since it makes possible the futures that you may design and pursue. And it does suggest that we all ought to be actively planning our futures.

Another tool we might use to increase the excitement and fun in our lives is to discover all the ways available to get a high, rush, or buzz. Oh dear, I guess that means we have to list for you all the substances that can be used to get a high. Sadly, we are living in an age when many people seem to think that the way to fix feeling awful is by taking a drug. Surely, any thinking person would conclude that to take an artificial toxin is the second last thing to do. The last thing to do is to cut into the body to change it.

Why not get a bigger, better, easier, cheaper, less harmful, and more exciting high? The only reason that some chemicals can produce

an artificial high is that the body comes equipped in such a way that highs are possible. How about using the way the body has been created to produce whatever kinds of highs you want? Of course, the best way to get a high is to experience emotions fully. We'll get back to that later when we expand on what to do about the love test tube. But if you don't want to have to wait until you feel free enough to experience your emotions fully, you might want to consult the small sample of highs (and add your own thoughts) from this handout. (Hand out *Book of Natural Highs*.)

Block 3: Therapeutics

Values, or the things that are important to us, decide what we will do at any moment, how we will judge what we have done afterwards, and who we think of ourselves as being (our personal 'identities'). Here is a simple test to help you to find out what your values are like. (Hand out Values Questionnaire. Allow time to complete it.) Now, for each page, count and record the number of times you checked a value with a dot (.) beside it. Then, for each page, count and record the number of values you checked with no dot () beside it. Then, count and record the number of values you checked separately for the right- and left-hand columns. In a general way, the four counts for each page give information about characteristics of your values that may have important consequences for your life, for your happiness, and for the fun you could have in life.

Let's just play, for now, with the first page, which is concerned with work. Read through the no-dot values you checked. Close your eyes and imagine yourself having a job that involved only those values. How do you feel? (Get some responses.) Read over the dot items you checked. Close your eyes and imagine yourself having a job that involved only those values. How do you feel? (Get some responses.) Read over the items you checked from the right-hand column. Close your eyes and imagine yourself having a job that involved only those values. How do you feel? (Get responses.) How

many of you noticed quite a difference between the three groups of items? Of those who did, how many felt best with the right-hand column values job? Of those who did, how many felt best with the no-dot-values job? And how many with the dot-values job? Of those who did not notice much difference, how many had nearly all dot values? How many had no-dot values? And how many of you could not imagine a job with no-dot values? How many could not imagine one with right-hand column values?

What does all this mean? Let's take the time to explain just one part of this material. For many (not all) people, most of the no-dot values are a real source of joy and excitement. That should mean that lots of no-dot values should result in enjoyment and fun in a job (or a relationship or feelings). That's because, for the most part, the no-dot values are positively pursued values that give mainly pleasure and fulfilment. They are mostly free from conflict, and they are usually based mainly on positive experiences from the past. They tend to give nice highs.

Next, let's go back to the Love Test Tube. The picture of the test tube suggests three kinds of things that might be done to get rid of some of the inhibiting anxiety 'corking up' our yummy love feelings. First, we might just get rid of the cork. The anxiety was learned; perhaps it could be unlearned. The main method for doing that is called behaviour therapy or systematic desensitization (Wolpe). Second, we might consciously and intentionally 'pull the cork' for short periods of time, under our own control. That is, we might simply decide to trust that person there, to let go feelings, and to take whatever consequences follow from letting go. The psychotherapy method used for that is generally classed under cognitive therapy, using methods such as rational-emotive therapy (Ellis). Third, we might 'drill little holes' in the bottom of the test tube to release tiny quantities of love feeling, not sufficient to arouse the anxiety. This method is generally classed as assertive training. In this instance, it is called Affective Responses training. How might we do that? The first thing to understand is that feelings are expressed to and about things that differ in the strength of the feeling of caring and of anxiety. Look

around you and find a stranger. A stranger is less likely to stimulate fear about caring than a friend. Look around you to notice <u>things</u> that you might like. Saying liking things about them is less likely to arouse fears of closeness than saying caring things <u>about</u> a person; and that is less likely to arouse fear of rejection than saying caring things <u>to</u> the person with whom you're talking. So to make sure you don't arouse 'love test tube' anxiety, (1) grade the strength of the emotion you are expressing (from 'it's OK', 'I like', 'It's wonderful', to 'I love'); (2) grade what/who you're talking about (from 'objects', 'scenes', 'third party people', to 'the person you're talking to'); (3) grade the people you talk to ('strangers', 'acquaintances', 'friends' to 'intimates'). Start off expressing mild feelings to strangers ('it's OK') about things (cars, houses, trees), and move very slowly (over many months) through to strong feelings expressed to an intimate with whom you are talking.

But why go through all that elaborate nonsense? You are perfectly able to talk comfortably about feelings even to friends. That may be true, or it may be that the amount of anxiety involved is too slight for you to notice. It's better not to take chances and to overdo each step along the way. But it would be plain silly to go around telling every stranger that you like cars of certain types or colours. Maybe, but remember that the purpose is not to do that so much as to practice the habit of feeling good and comfortable with your caring or closeness feelings. But people will laugh at you if you go around expressing love for cars or houses, let alone for other (third party) people. If you worry about that, you probably need to do the method. That is just your fear talking. Think of it this way. If someone laughs at you for expressing an emotion, what does it mean? Think about it. All it could ever mean is that the person laughing is afraid of his or her own caring emotions. The laughter hides his/her own fear and is not directed at you – even if it seems clearly to be aimed at you. 'OK', you say, 'so I'll do it occasionally.' Remember, every time you do it is a practice trial in learning comfort or unlearning anxiety. Why not do it all day long often? There are lots of steps to go through in the levels of 'expression', 'objects', and 'people' just described. The

more practice you get, the sooner the new habit is developed and the sooner your feelings can be freed to allow you joy and highs in life.

Take a few risks of this relatively safe kind to enhance your life. Like most people, risk-taking is a little exciting for you. This minor kind of risk is pretty safe and can add its own bit of excitement in your life eventually. It might give you a rush. Now, if you knew, where are your images of your future stored? If you were to look at the pictures you have stored in your mind about possible or expected future events, where would those pictures be? Point in the direction of the pictures of the future you see. Any direction is fine, as long as it seems right to you. Close your eyes and drift way up above your future timeline. Drift down again until you are just above it but not involved in it. Drift along the line of your future events. As you look down, there will be lots of times where you don't know what will happen. They may be represented as blank areas (let your pupils dilate to let in more light in case you can discern any events there) or as clouds behind which events may be hiding (enjoy the soft white fluffy ones and notice the silver lining of the darker ones) or as bushes behind which events are obscured (have fun spreading the branches to peer through or peeking around the bushes to catch glimpses of possible future events). When you have had a little trip over your future timeline, drift back and return to the present. Then open your eyes. What kind of kid's game is that? One nice thing about being a child is that we can, free of responsibilities, enjoy daydreams and fantasies. Now, you have had a peek at your future timeline, letting things happen as they will but being a bit curious about what's there. Let's see if that experience can be enhanced.

In your present, make a plan to achieve a dream of yours. Figure out several steps through which you would have to proceed to realize your dream. Second, think of a series of things you might anticipate in the future – you know, birthdays, trips and vacations, seeing friends or loved ones, buying things you want, and the like. Right now, paint each of these things with bright colours, put motion into each one, and listen for some of the sounds that might go along with each.

Is that done? Now, close your eyes and drift up above your timeline, way up, and then drift down until you're just over it but not in it. Drift forwards over the future. Look down to see what you can see. Notice the orderly progression of events leading up to your dream. Notice the anticipated events, with their colours, sounds, and actions. Enjoy your future. When you are ready, drift back and down into the present and then open your eyes. That's perfect. How was that? Did you notice that it felt less like a kid's game? Did you notice that it felt a whole lot better than the first time? All that happened between the first and second trips over your future timeline was that you made some plans and you enlivened the future with colours, sounds, and motion, which are sensory qualities found in reality. Good for you! (This is James and Woodsmall's Future Pacing.)

Block 4: Consolidation

There are some quite simple methods by which to achieve excitement and joy. For example, you could write down Personal Development goals of excitement or joy or emotionality or spontaneity or happiness. (This is the Goal-Finding programme.) If you wanted to achieve some of these characteristics, under each quality, write down a half dozen observable behaviours that you might see in the actions of those people who you think have the quality. If you like, check the *Behavioural Dictionary* (a handout) to find actions/ behaviours. Then, every morning, read over the list of behaviours to remind yourself what you are looking for. Don't try to perform the actions. Just notice and reward yourself immediately whenever you notice any approximation to any behaviour on your list. The rewards can just be noticing your success, being pleased with yourself, imagining whacking yourself heartily on the back, and the like. You'll be surprised how quickly you'll learn to increase the behaviours. And increasing the behaviours increases the associated experiences. It may surprise you, but it isn't the experiences that instigate the behaviours. It works the other way around. You can

increase your fun in life and your liking for yourself as well, all in the easiest kind of learning you ever tried.

But there is another way to increase your joy in life. In fact, joy is really achieved by a simple, but somewhat slow, process. It is a three-step process, and you need to have lots of practice at each step to succeed fully. Here it is.

Step 1: <u>Respect</u> everything and everybody. That does NOT mean looking up to everything and everybody. It DOES mean seeing everything and everybody as equal to you, important, valuable, and good. 'God don't make no junk.' And it DOES mean repeatedly simply <u>deciding</u> to do this in your mind. You may ask why you would give the gift of respect to others, especially to worthless and horrid others. The answer is that the gift of respect is NOT given to others. It is given to us; we give it to ourselves. The more we respect others, the easier it is to find the good in them and the happier we become with the world around us – so full of good things and people. Most people will say, 'Let others respect me, if I'm to respect them.' That's a mistake. That's not how we come to respect others. And others likely respect you more than you think. It's partly that we expect too much from others and partly that we put ourselves down by expecting them to see our faults. Besides, the gift of respect is given by you to yourself in the happiness you can feel in a good world of your making. Strangely, happiness is far less a result of being respected than of respecting others.

Step 2: <u>Trust</u> everything and everybody. That does NOT mean that others will not let us down from time to time. However, if they do, it is only because we expected them to act wholly out of consideration for us. We all act out of consideration for ourselves and what we want first. We do that, and so do others. It DOES mean that we need simply to <u>decide</u> to trust everything and everyone – at this moment and every other. But why would we give the gift of trusting to others, and especially to the sleazy, treacherous, and untrustworthy? The answer is that the gift of trust is NOT given to others. It is given by us to ourselves. When we trust others with our feelings, whether or not they deserve it, we feel safer. It doesn't work the other way around,

as we might think. When we see good in others, it's easy to trust. When we feel safe, it's easy to go to the next step of joy.

Step 3: Love everything and everybody. This does NOT refer to sexual love, in case that has to be said. It does refer to the kind of emotion that draws people towards things or people. The weakest form of love is liking and enjoying things (cars, homes, trinkets, clothing). The strongest form of love is the feeling we can have for relatives and the dearest of friends. Love feelings arouse all the yummy juices and emotions of the body. They are only possible if we feel safe with others. Hence the need to practice trust first. And trust is really only possible if we see the good in others. Hence the need to practice respect first. When love is comfortable and easy, the experience of life is joy.

(Do a summary of the program and cuing observations.)

Treatment 4: Creating SATISFACTION

The main target of this program is the achievement of full satisfaction of needs to replace immediate gratification needs that reinforce addictive conduct. Seeking absent feelings in bodily experiences leads to enhanced physiological discomfort. Immediate reinforcements do drive habit development. There is no point denying it. Delayed reinforcements do not influence habits very strongly. It seems necessary to alter perception and concepts of time as well as the degree of fulfilment and self-regulation of reinforcers. This program is the last aimed at reinforcers. This means that the program ought to help summarize the last three, ought to be more general and inclusive, and ought to begin to move towards abstract concepts to bridge over to the next ones.

Block 1: Orientation

What is satisfaction or being satisfied, and how is it achieved? We talk about social satisfaction as when we have the satisfaction of

competing successfully with another. Let's ignore that childish kind of satisfaction. We talk about satisfaction of an appetite, as when sex, hunger, or thirst have been satisfied. That's closer to what we want to deal with today. We speak of the kind of satisfaction that follows when we have accomplished something we set out to do. That's closest to the kind of satisfaction we'd like to focus on now. That kind of satisfaction works like a reward to add habit strength to whatever we were doing that led to the accomplishment – whether it's eating, drinking, making love, or taking an addictive substance. That's right. Whenever we take an addictive substance, we are trying to accomplish some state of mind that is comforting or enjoyable. The important things to notice in this are that WE are the active agents who are TRYING to ACCOMPLISH something. It's not the addictive substance that is doing it to you. And if we accomplish what we set out to accomplish, we feel satisfied, at least temporarily.

You may have noticed that, as you used a particular substance, over time, it took more and more of it to satisfy you. How come? I know most of us accept the idea that we habituate to the substance. Of course we do, but that hardly explains how it happens or what to do about it. The term *habituation* refers to the addictive process, and it has little or nothing to do with need for increasing doses. Certainly, the body gets to tolerate ever-increasing doses of anything. That is because the person becomes desensitized to the substance. The body starts off by reacting to the intake of the chemical as a foreign body, and the stress-immune system reacts to it. With repeated exposure, the body gets used to the substance so that the intensity of the ANS-mediated immune response diminishes. But that's just how tolerance increases.

The need for an increase in dosage to achieve satisfaction is based on the person's expectations. Did you ever notice that if you repeatedly are treated a certain way by another person, you start to expect that treatment and you stop noticing it after a while? In order to notice it again, the treatment has to involve more of the same. We tend NOT to notice as much events that occur as we expect them to.

But how are expectations formed? To some extent they come from experience that allows us to predict what is likely to happen. But we often form expectations from other sources. One such other source is attitudes. If I have a pre-existing attitude towards a class of events (e.g., people's race, red noses, red lights), even if I never encountered a particular event before that is an example of a class, my stereotypes are apt to come into play and create my expectations about this event. I may conclude that this red-nosed person is an alcoholic instead of being subject today to the condition called erysipelas, or I might think the red light over a doorway means 'stop' or 'do not enter' instead of 'exit'.

Another source of expectations is beliefs. As a silly example, if I believed the world to be flat, I probably would not venture out on a sea voyage far beyond the horizon. Many of us think that our beliefs are formed from real experiences. Most often, they aren't. For the most part, they are formed as statements made by us or others in groups we valued. If group members do not challenge our statements or seem to accept them, our belief in those statements is validated. Beliefs are largely results of consensual validation of statements. Once formed, beliefs establish stereotypes, from which we derive expectations. So what? So we have expectations. What do they do? They do at least two things. First, they provide contents for thought or for 'self-talk' (Tools). Second, they CREATE expected outcomes. Have you ever noticed how often your beliefs proved to be true? The observation about their correctness adds more validation of the beliefs. What we rarely notice is that we tend to act in ways consistent with our expectations. If I believe or expect that members of the opposite gender aren't going to find me attractive or interesting, I will tend not to look after myself, my appearance, or my presentation; or I will tend to present myself, dress, or say things such that there is some minor element that turns others off, as I expected them to turn off (as though it was their action).

A psychologist tested the intelligence of kids in a class. Then, without referring to the results, identified for the teacher those kids, chosen at random, who were bright and those who were not. The

reading scores of the 'bright' and 'not bright' kids were not different at the time of testing. However, a year later, the 'bright' kids' reading scores had improved by two grade levels, and the 'not bright' kids' reading scores had improved by only one-half of a grade level. How come? Could it have been that the teacher's expectations led the 'bright' kids to do better than the others?

A psychologist had students grow some grain. The students were assigned without their knowledge to two groups. The members of the two groups were assigned plots of ground at random. A bag of grain seed was divided into two separate bags. A sign reading Fast-Growing Grain was put on one bag, and another reading Slow-Growing Grain was put on the other bag. The students came to get their seed, and they were given seed from one bag or the other, depending on the group to which they had been assigned. The 'fast-growing grain' grew faster and produced more grain than the 'slow-growing grain'. How come? Could it have been that the students' expectations, based on seeing the signs, caused them to tend their plots differently in some ways?

The main point of this discourse is that expectations, formed as stated, not only create much of the world in which we live (an angry person lives in an angry world, and a happy person lives in a happy world – the world we see is a reflection of ourselves), they also decide what we will notice and thus the amount of satisfaction we have in our lives. If we expect rejection, that is what we will notice. If we live in a world in which what we think we want (expecting the opposite) rarely happens, we are not likely to be satisfied with much of that world. And the sad thing is that we do it to ourselves.

Block 2: Tools

Our expectations and the beliefs that underlie some of them are maintained by thinking about them. Let's speak of thinking as 'self-talk'. We talk ourselves into the beliefs and expectations we have. Sometimes we don't know what the thoughts are by which we do that.

They pass through our heads too quickly to be noticed. However, if we pay enough attention to our thinking, we might be able to guess what some of our beliefs are. When we find them, they seem self-evident and true. But that's an illusion. Make a true statement, if you can. (For responses, demonstrate limitations of each as an absolute truth.) It's not even true that our beliefs aren't true. We just don't know. But surely, we can find out something about truth. How about science as a way to find truth? Science tests only one kind of truth, called pragmatic truth, or whether something works (most of the time). If you do this, does that follow? That is the kind of question asked by science. If you were willing, you could use that kind of truth in your life.

Do you like being uptight, scared, depressed, or dissatisfied? No? Perhaps you would like to decide how you would like to feel. If you did, you could easily try out all sorts of expectations and beliefs to see what sorts of self-talk results in the kinds of feelings you want. The self-talk that works to create the feelings you want, the feelings that satisfy you, refers to pragmatically true beliefs and expectations. They are true!

So here's a tool for today. First, write down some of the outcomes in feelings and satisfactions you want. Second, try out all sorts of beliefs and expectations (whether you believe them or not or even if you don't believe them) to find out which ones, if believed in, make you feel the way you want to feel (your feelings come from self-talk) and record them. Third, adopt those beliefs and expectations as (pragmatically) true, and practice believing in them. You can decide your own thoughts, and thus your own feelings. Enjoy the true thoughts and good feelings.

But expectations come from another source too. And this source exerts a truly malignant influence on all of us. Most of us expose ourselves to large amounts of media contents – in watching television, listening to radio, reading newspapers and other print. Now, you and I know that we expose ourselves to the media for entertainment. Of course, we pay attention to the news and some articles and documentaries in order to find out the facts about what is

going on in the world. And you and I know that the exposure we have to the media has no important effects on our lives. Well, regardless of the reasons why we expose ourselves to the media, those sorts of things that we all know are just plain false. The scientific evidence about exposure to media contents clearly indicates that (i) the media almost never presents any facts, (ii) the news is almost as fictional as everything else in the media, (iii) most of us are misled into a kind of belief that even the entertainment media represents facts in some way, and (iv) exposure to media contents affects the personalities of everybody exposed to it in many damaging ways. And the effect on us from media contents is not insignificant or relatively slight. It is measurable, major, and it affects many parts of our daily human lives. So what can we do about the effects on us of the media? We could adopt the approach one of us takes and never turn on a radio, buy a newspaper, or connect the TV to an antenna. That may seem extreme to you. You could censor for yourself every media exposure you allow yourself. But that's not too reliable a method. You would likely soon forget what you were doing and why.

The best method is to add some enjoyment to the media to which you expose yourself by discussing with friends every media thing to which you expose yourself. That gives you something to talk about, thus easing any discomfort you may have with others. And it gives you the chance to think objectively about what you have seen, heard, or read. You might even develop a discussion group, as a social support group, in which media contents are critically evaluated not for their aesthetic or entertainment values but for their limitations of fact. (This is Media proofing.)

For example, the media presents the world as a dangerous place, where three-quarters of human interactions involve violence and murder. If true, none of us have experienced our fair share of murder and mayhem. According to the media, murder is most commonly performed between strangers and most commonly for financial gain or sexual or other kinds of excitement. It almost never occurs in those contexts. The media suggest that there are more men in the world than women. The reverse is true. According to the media, most

people in the world are rich and famous, use other people for their own purposes, and have piles of money and lots of members of the opposite sex pursuing them. You and I represent the real expectations of the real world much better than those shown in the media. One of the commonest events in life is two people sharing tea or coffee or having a chat, called small talk. How often do you hear about that in the media? You can quite easily become adept at finding the misleading and untrue contents in the media, if you look for them.

We talked earlier about beliefs and their effects in filtering out some of the nice and normal events in life. You might want to examine some of your beliefs and to challenge a few of them just for the fun of it. Here are some materials that may help you do that. There is little point in talking at length about these materials here since you will either be interested or not in examining your beliefs. If, on your own, you want to examine some of your beliefs critically, you might work your way through these pages. (Hand out Beliefs Inventory and interpretation materials.)

We mentioned attitudes we adopt as part of the means by which we filter out some items of information and experience and become fixated on others. The Beliefs materials contain more pages at the end to help you work through some attitudes as well, if you wish. (Hand out Attitudes Training materials.) We won't spend time going over these materials either just now.

Another tool that can help us to get satisfactions out of life involves finding and using positive feelings, attitudes, and experiences. You know how it goes. For many of us, most of our time is spent noticing and commenting on the horrors, miseries, and despondencies of life. We may think that we need to notice the awful in order to be vigilant for it and to help us prevent it. That's one approach taken in AA and NA. But those of us who use AA and NA know that the most valuable parts of those programs are the positive steps we can take to work our way through pain to a happy and constructive lifestyle. So how can we adopt a positive approach to all living? Here are some ways.

The easy way is, every time you are going anywhere (while the world passing you is changing), find three new things that you like.

You don't have to love them. Things you think are nice or you like will do. But each time, find things that are different from those you noticed in going anywhere in the past. The exercise is pleasant and fun, and it makes the time of going anywhere more pleasant than it otherwise would be.

It's a bit harder to focus your attention and thought all the time on the pleasant, good, and worthwhile. Still, if you can, it also helps the quality of life and the amount of satisfaction you experience. For example, look out and see a day that is bleak, wet, and miserable. You might feel good about the day if you remember that you will enjoy the next bright day more by contrast, that the rain provides us and the birds and animals with fresh drinking water and helps the plants and trees to grow, that the humidity is good for your skin, or that the cloud cover provides shade from the blistering sun. Or when someone makes a nasty crack, you might realize that the reason for it is the way the other feels and not what you did (so you might feel compassion instead of being offended), that the person has suggested a brand-new quality you might want to try out to increase the freedom and variety of your behaviour, or that viewing the world that way might be fun or even funny (in response to 'You rat!', you might picture a great white rat nibbling on a tiny bit of cheese). (Use *Dictionary for Divergent Thinkers*.)

There are still other ways to enhance the satisfactions you get from your life. One way is to delay gratification in all sorts of things you do. Setting out consciously to postpone or delay reaching satisfaction seems to increase the amount of satisfaction we experience in most things. This can apply to things all the way from sexual satisfaction through eating snacks to winning a game or solving a problem. The more we put into something in time and effort, the greater the amount of satisfaction at completion. There is a useful spin-off from delaying satisfaction. It teaches us that it is NOT impossible to tolerate unpleasant feelings. In fact, if we wait out unpleasant feelings such as anxiety, which often underlie addictive behaviour for example, the feelings are likely to pass off and go away. Anxiety about a particular thing cannot be maintained even for a couple of

hours. To maintain it, we have to reprime ourselves with thoughts or more exposure to the upsetting event.

Another way is just to enhance the quality of the experience from which we seek satisfaction. This can be done by learning self-hypnosis or just imagery creation (e.g., <u>Page-A-Minute Memory Book</u>) and increasing the experience with hypnotic or other imagery enhancement. Or you could do it without going to all that trouble by making up your own exciting fantasies or images to call up in any experience. For example, if you want to enjoy a conversation with someone, you might imagine you are in a conversation with a person to whom you particularly like to talk. Or while dining on food you don't really like, you might imagine yourself eating some of your favourite foods. The purpose of such images, of course, would be to increase the amount of satisfaction you are having.

Block 3: Therapeutics

Let's play for a while. Let's do the Beliefs Inventory now. (When it is completed, ask participants to score it themselves. Then refer to the interpretations appended for the ten common thinking errors.) Now, let's suppose that one of the styles of thought you use is to expect things to be fair and to get yourself angry when things are not. The first question is, Who ever said that things are supposed to be fair? Where is that rule carved in stone? The second part is to please ask yourself how you would feel if things were always absolutely fair. In such a world, you and I would receive precisely and only what we deserved. Of course, you wouldn't be alive today. You did nothing as an infant to deserve the care, feeding, and shelter your parenting ones gave you. Like most workers, you probably did the least you could get away with at work to 'earn' your pay. Would you pay your employees well for that? You probably did the minimum amount of homework at school that you could get away with. Wasn't it lucky that the teachers took the time to teach much of the material in class? You probably wanted more back than you gave in most of your relationships. I

know I did, when I'm being honest with myself. What did you do to deserve the company of some of the wonderful people you have known? Hey, maybe we should be grateful and happy that the world is NOT fair. Each of us gets from life far more than any of us give. Thank goodness the world isn't fair. Let's be happy for that.

Let's suppose that one of your styles of thought involves getting yourself upset when things in the world around you don't go exactly as you want them to. First, where is it carved in stone that the world is supposed to be controlled by you? Second, isn't it wonderful that the world is NOT controlled completely by you? Think of it. Suppose the world was completely controlled by you and what you want. Great, eh? Like hell it would be! You would have to devote your whole life all day every day (at night too) to ensure that the zillions of horrors possible didn't happen to others and to yourself. If you controlled the world, everything that happened in it would be your fault. You beast you!

A large part of the satisfaction in life comes from social and intimate relationships with others. That's because we're social animals. When we do not have close relationships with others or when we are unable to feel satisfied in our social relationships, we feel lonely. Loneliness is a motive that a thoughtful nature implanted in us to drive us to interact with others. Some of us feel that our loneliness from weak interactions with others or our lack of friends is due to what other people do. Perhaps they are rejecting or don't like us. So how might we set it up so others like us or are less rejecting or so that we can reach out to others and gain more satisfaction in our social relationships? The answer is quite simple really. Social interactions depend on communications, and communications are not hard to improve. Communications involve two things: receiving and sending messages.

Receiving messages is quite easy. It involves hearing and seeing what the other person is saying, pacing the other, and checking to see whether you understood what the other person intended. There's no better way to be thought of by the other as brilliant, competent, friendly, and nice than to be able to listen and show you understand.

The hardest part is hearing and understanding what the other person is saying. The trouble is that we become preoccupied with our own thoughts and interpretations due to introversion, emotions that interfere, or just not having learned how to listen. If we want to hear what the other says, we need to do some things:

(1) We need to focus our eyes and ears on the other person. You know how to focus your eyes. You find a spot and make it look sharp and clear. But if you keep looking at the same spot, your eyes will quickly go out of focus. So you need to keep changing the spot you're looking at. Look at one eye, the other, the mouth, the creases in the forehead, the creases beneath the eyes, and so on. Let your eyes be drawn from one spot to another by the movements and changes occurring in the speaker's face. Looking in this way gives clues to the nonverbal and emotional communications from the other. But how do you focus your ears? You can, you know. Partly it's done by cocking your head slightly to one side or the other. The slight turn that feels most attentive is the correct one, as it will turn your dominant ear towards the speaker. Partly it's done by an automatic slight opening of the ear's passages, which happens when you accept and want to hear a particular sound – the other's voice. It helps if you allow yourself to like the other person. Partly it's done by wanting to pay attention. Some of us habitually tune out those around us. Partly it's done by pacing. We hope you are all practising these skills right now while we are talking to you. It's a chance to learn how to listen.

(2) We need to 'pace' the other person. Pacing involves the skill of assuming attitudes and gestures like the ones used by the other. This sounds like we're saying to mimic the other person. That's not quite it. What the other person is doing and the attitudes he/she adopts are communicated partly in the assumptions made and in the nonverbal communications and the gestures. Don't interpret the nonverbal language and

gestures in your head. In fact, if you do, you are apt to get it wrong. It's better to try to live inside the other person's body or, as the old saying goes, 'walk a mile in another's shoes'. If the speaker turns the hand up, your head might tell you he/ she is asking for something. But turning your own hand up let's your body feel what it is like to express what is being said with that gesture. It might involve weighing or judging something or accepting something or begging a question or any number of other things. Pacing is not obvious mimicking, but it ought to involve some, at least slight, movement in your body as if to find out what doing that in that context feels like. Pacing ensures that you are 'staying with' the other.

(3) We need to check our understandings of what the other is trying to communicate. All too often, we think we know, when, in fact, we don't. As far as we are aware, nobody has ever read anybody else's mind <u>correctly</u>. We all try, and we all fail. The only person who really knows the other's meaning is the other. To ask the other person to repeat doesn't really help. We will hear the same mistakes again, and the other is apt to think we're not paying attention. The best way is to say briefly in your own words what you think the other person is saying and especially to say what you feel is the feeling underlying the other's communication. Start or end your brief summary by indicating that you are stating your understanding of the other's opinion and by asking for confirmation. "If I get it, you're saying that . . . Is that right?" To get it right is the best known way to reveal to the other how bright, empathic, and wonderful a person you truly are. And getting it wrong is much better for human relationships than not confirming or not getting it.

The other part of communication is sending messages. If we send messages in certain ways, we will almost certainly create conflict with others and fail to get our needs met. If we send messages in other ways, we have the chance to get some of our needs met, to make and

keep friends, and to reduce the conflict in our lives greatly. Let's recognize and use some of the main features of sending messages.

(1) The body is an energy-producing machine. We need to use the energy produced, or it will create problems in our lives. Some of us want to be nice people who are liked. So to keep from seeming pushy or obnoxious, we may try to hold back the energy we use in communications. Holding back our energy and being underassertive tends to have several consequences. We may feel chronically dissatisfied because our needs aren't being met by others; we may become depressed or bitter and angry. That's one of many ways we set ourselves up to have negative feelings. To increase the use of energy in communicating, we can do some quite simple things. Try them out. Talk slightly louder until you can feel an echo from the walls, enunciate clearly and crisply, speak slowly to take more time, talk in brief affirmative sentences without explanations (explanations may convince you, not anyone else), make your gestures expansive with extensor movements, and stand or sit in an erect posture. All these kinds of things will use bodily energy and increase your own sense of empowerment. They may also help to lift your mood. Sending communications provides an opportunity to use your body's energies.

(2) Some of us are overassertive or aggressive. This creates conflicts with others and may prevent satisfaction of needs with others. Aggressiveness is often carried in the way we send our messages. Speaking about the other person or using "you" statements tends to get the other person on guard to be ready to defend him/herself. It is a 'flag' to arouse the other's defences. Even being complimentary in the form of a "you" statement is apt to create uncomfortable defensiveness in the other. A much more effective way to send messages is with "I" statements. Starting with 'I think . . .' or 'I feel . . .' expresses yourself, affirms a state or opinion of yours, and

tends not to get anybody else's hackles up. It helps the other to listen to you rather than listening to his/her own head or getting him/her ready to be defensive. It is most likely to result in getting your own needs met and thus in getting satisfaction for you in social relationships. Even saying 'I think of you as an angry person' may be better than saying 'you are angry'.

Some people would suggest that effective communication can be summarized in the 'three-part statement'. The three-part statement starts with an "I" statement expressing how you understood what the other just said (e.g., 'I gather you think the world is flat') and giving him/her a chance to correct any misunderstanding. It continues with an "I" statement about your own feelings on the subject (e.g., 'I feel annoyed that some people still have that opinion'). And it ends with an "I" statement about your response or intended action (e.g., 'I guess we ought to take a trip around the world some time').

(3) Some of us are afraid or anxious in social situations. We may fear how others will react to us or how we will judge our own actions. It's not a bad idea to get rid of that interfering fear. There are several ways to do this.

On separate sheets, write a one-sentence description of a couple or three repeating situations in your life where you feel scared, uptight, frustrated, or angry. For this exercise, let's take the situation (page) where you feel most upset. Under the descriptive sentence for that situation, write down about sixteen responses you might use to that situation. Take some time with this task, and make sure your responses are graded from the most aggressive ones at the top to the most underassertive (doormat-like) ones at the bottom. Make sure that most of your responses are in the middle, neither aggressive nor underassertive. (Make an illustrative hierarchy on the board from responses offered by participants.)

Now, here's the drill: (a) To prepare yourself for future occurrences of this situation, memorize all the items on your list, in their right order. (b) When the recurring situation occurs in the future, each time, (i) STOP, (ii) quickly, in your mind, run through the whole memorized list of responses, (iii) pick the level of response that you would be comfortable giving, (iv) step <u>down</u> one step, and (v) deliver that response. OK, what's all that about? The main thing that goes wrong to create our psychological problems is that we become fixated on responses, many of which are apt to be maladaptive. Treatment involves increasing the range of available responses and thus freedom. Forcing a list of many (sixteen is ideal) different responses increases the range of possible responses greatly. But you say, 'I couldn't use most of the responses'. It doesn't matter. You choose your own response level each time. Following the steps ensures that you'll be comfortable with not only the response you give but also with the whole list that you have just run over in your mind. That is, each time you go through this exercise, you give yourself another practice trial in reducing your anxiety in that situation, about the whole list of responses (thus increasing the available response range), and about assertiveness in general. This does not mean that you will ever use extreme responses at either end of the list. It is most likely to mean that you will increasingly use mid-range reactions (that is, assertive reactions), that you will likely be less prone to anger and depressions, and that you should become less socially anxious over time. (This is Wolpe's in vivo Assertive training.)

Let's try another exercise. Picture (one of) the other situation(s) you have written down. Picture yourself in it. Notice where the picture seems to be seen in relation to where you are now. Move the picture until you seem to see it squarely in front of you, anywhere from one to four feet away. Now start pushing it away from you. As it moves away, it gets smaller . . . and smaller. Let it drift farther and farther away until finally it is just a little dot on the horizon. Now bring it slowly back again, getting bigger and bigger, until it is just in front of you again. Now push it back again, way back until it is just a dot on the horizon. Notice how you feel when it is close to you

and when it is far away. Move it back and forth a few times from up close to way off on the horizon. Finally, just leave it out there at the horizon. Let's try that a different way. Put the picture on a TV screen in full colour. Down in one corner of the screen, put a tiny black-and-white picture of yourself looking and feeling comfortable and satisfied. When I say go, zoom up the little black-and-white picture of yourself until it fills the whole screen and is in bright colour. Go! Clear the TV screen. Return to the screen the coloured picture of the uncomfortable repeating situation and the tiny black-and-white picture of the comfortable and satisfied you. Repeat the zoom of the little picture until it fills the whole screen in colour. Do that sequence again, say, a dozen times. Tell us what happened. (In the usual case, the person has difficulty getting the uncomfortable situation's pictures back again.) That's perfect. (This is James and Woodsmall's The Swish.)

Block 4: Consolidation

Would it be nice to have lots of joyful, happy, and positive feelings? We know. How would you ever feel important and special if you didn't feel awful and suffer the whole time? Of course, if you were to have lots of positive feelings and expressed them, other people would probably want to be with you more, like you better, and notice you more. That too might help you feel important and special. If you noticed, you could be creating positive feelings for yourself just by finding the self-talk that makes you feel positive, recognizing the honesty of those self-statements as pragmatically true. If you could find such self-talk, you could create positive feelings almost instantly whenever you wanted to. If you could let yourself do that, you could then create positive feelings at will with which to reward yourself for any desired behaviour or characteristic you noticed in yourself or your daily life. Think of it. You could pile satisfying rewards on top of satisfaction for your satisfying actions and characteristics. Goodness, you wouldn't want to do that, would you?

Try this. Close your eyes and drift up and out of your body. Drift yourself away until you find yourself over a hill with a gentle slope on a bright, warm day with a cool breeze. Drift down on to the top of the hill. Start to run slowly down the hill, leaping up and forwards from time to time. Notice that you seem to float through the air with each jump. You leap, and you find that if you tilt your head back a bit, you keep floating up and up. Float away until you are over a place from your childhood where you felt safe and cared for. Tilt your head forwards and drift down at that place. Visit the place and recover the good feelings of that time and place. When you're ready, leap up again and drift off to any place on or off the earth you would like to visit. Float over it, looking down at the passing scenes that your mind knows you will find there. If you want to, tilt your head down and land lightly to look more closely at people, places, or things. Be part of that place and its people for a while. Enjoy it completely. When you are ready, leap up again and glide to another place or time. And when you are ready, leap up again and drift back and down into yourself. How did that feel? It was a trip, wasn't it? You can have that fun, at no cost, any time you like. See how easy life and its dreams are? (This is Autogenic Training.)

But how do you get real satisfactions, right? That's easy too. All you need to do is to discover what you really need. It is always within your power to acquire. You see, what we do all day every day is pursue the things that are important to us – our values. And our satisfactions come from whatever it is that makes us feel fulfilled or 'actualized'. Those needs that actualize us, our self-actualizing needs, have been listed by various people. One list of self-actualizing needs might help us to find some of the means by which we can gain increased satisfaction in our lives. (Hand out a List of Maslow's self-actualizing needs.)

(Do a summary with cuing observations.)

Treatment 5: Creating VALUES

The <u>main target</u> of this program is adaptive and mature <u>values</u> development. Years of investment in values of childhood and then in those of the addictive subculture need to be countered. Some of the common attitudes and values of the subculture need to be challenged; and any void created thereby filled with other values. James and Woodsmall's (1987) work in this area is drawn on heavily in designing this programme.

Block 1: Orientation

Values, or the things we consider to be most important to us, are (1) the most general and abstract feature of ourselves that affect everything about us, (2) the best means by which to define or identify ourselves (who we are), (3) in advance, the means by which we motivate what we do and thus determine what we do, and (4) after the fact, the means by which we evaluate what we have done or how we judge ourselves and our actions. Thus, they are perhaps the most important quality we possess.

And most of what we prize most in ourselves and our lives, including our beliefs and our attitudes, depend on our values. One of the most worthwhile and useful things we can do is to examine our values, find out in detail what they are, and find out if any of them need to be changed or assigned a different importance to us. This may be <u>the</u> most crucial thing we can do to ensure our future joy, happiness, effectiveness, and adjustment. But then, you wouldn't want to go to all that trouble, right?

But perhaps your values are already ideally suited to your optimum future adjustment and well-being. Permit us to question some of the values you may have. There are several ways to do this. First, let's consider some of the attitudes and beliefs that tend to be common among people who exhibit various kinds of addictions. While attitudes and beliefs are not values, they depend on and are

derived largely from our values. Since it's sometimes easier to recognize attitudes and beliefs than to recognize values, it may be best to start with attitudes and beliefs, to see if any problems exist.

Many addicted people believe themselves to be mainly physical entities comprised of anatomy and chemistry. They often act as though they believe that they are controlled by their own chemistry and/or the physical events of the past. Commonly, they act as though they had little or no control over their behaviour, and they seem to have an attitude that immediate relief is needed to correct unpleasant feelings. These are a few of their beliefs and attitudes that are maladaptive and false, and they are based on values by which they deny their ability or right to control their own lives or which involve conflict and avoidances. Would anybody share things he/she KNOWS to be true about him/ herself (beliefs) with us? (Discuss offerings.) We will identify some of the values that create such beliefs and attitudes later. For now, if you recognize any such beliefs or attitudes to be part of your personal make-up, you might want to consider them to be useful indicators of your need to examine your personal values. That is today's task.

Let's play a game. Obviously, we have no basis for knowing what your personal values are. But let's try to read your mind. Please score us on a piece of paper to see how good we are as mind readers. Put a check mark beside the number of each of the values that apply to you out of the ones we are about to suggest, by mind reading, are important values for you and your life. Here we go. Hocus-pocus. You highly value (1) Precision, (2) Power, (3) Strength, (4) Intelligence/ Cleverness, (5) Efficiency, (6) Dependability or Reliability, (7) Size (e.g., tallness) or Amount (e.g., of money), (8) Effectiveness or Success, (9) Acceptance by Others, (10) Recognition/Importance.

OK, out of ten, how did we do? (Obtain scores.) So we did pretty well, huh? Well, here's the kick in the head. None of these are, strictly speaking, values. They are all really 'evaluators' by which we measure how well we are doing in achieving other things, including values. Really, they are the kinds of evaluators used by parents and teachers – by adults dealing with children – as markers of growth and development of children. Precision in performance, power in

influencing other children, physical strength (as in sports), successful use of intelligence, speed in completing or accomplishing tasks, dependability in doing anything, success in anything, being accepted by peers, achieving recognition among peers, and growth in size and amount of earnings are all used by parents as benchmarks to celebrate growth in children towards maturity and independence. These evaluators are leftovers from having been a child. They may make one appear useful to others and may help to us to feel important or useful in work settings. But they do not work too usefully as personal values. If you believe those to be your main values, you really need to join us in sorting out just what your real values are.

Once a value has been developed, it tends to persist. This is partly because it becomes an important part of our attitude-thought (cognitive) system, partly because we commit ourselves to anything we do or think for a while, partly because it is self-reinforcing, and partly because we are usually not all that aware or conscious of our basic values. Besides, values are not easily changed just because we think we ought to, or might like to, change them. We need an effective strategy to change or adjust our values.

We would like to offer a brief warning before we get on with this day's tasks. There is one pervasive and insidious source of values from which we all need to protect ourselves. And part of the problem is that we are mostly unaware of the values the media teach us. Every day, we are all subject to learning media values. The media are commercial enterprises whose primary task is to make money for media people and to inflict their beliefs and attitudes on others. Any business tries to maximize income and minimize costs. Consequently, media contents are characterized by (a) glitz, glamour, and sensationalism (to acquire audiences) and (b) minimized expense in production, especially at the point of writing scripts. Consequently, quick-write scripts are adopted that are weak in characterization and plot (and especially in values) and that are carried in large part by flashy, rich, and colourful action (which best controls attention). Watch out for the effects the media are having every day on your values and thus on your life.

Block 2: Tools

(Hand out Values program package and ask participants to get to work on the materials and exercises.) We would like to take a few standard life experiences (work, relationships, feelings, etc.) and identify your important values in each one. First, put a check mark in front of each of your important values in each area, adding those we have missed at the bottom. Second, rank the order of the importance of the checked off values in each area. Third, do the exercises to find missing important values. Fourth, make a final rank ordering of your important values in each area. Fifth, check to discover how your values make you feel. Sixth, let pictures pop into your mind of the top 6 to 10 values in each area. In all of this, please do NOT try to think reasonably, to choose values you think we or others are looking for, or to select what you think 'ought' to be your values. For present purposes, you need to know what your real values actually are. To find out, go deeply inside yourself and let yourself be guided by whatever pops into your mind or that seems right to you. Trust your unconscious to tell you what you need to know. We trust your unconscious to tell you the right things. This is a voyage of discovery and probably the most useful and worthwhile task you have ever done.

(When that is done, finally, ask participants to list their values in each area as they think they ought to be by whatever rules they want to use for themselves.)

Block 3: Therapeutics

You have developed a notion about what your main values are and pictured images to represent each of your main values. Let's use that information. First, there is some understanding about your values that you need. What do your values do for you? Why is it important to you to hold each value? (Ask these questions about a sample of the values participants offer for discussion. Work through enough offered examples to get one or two in each of the following:)

(i) Some values are <u>reflexive</u> values. To obtain their benefit, we depend on others to give something to us. We may be able to work to achieve the valued feedback from others, but we only gain from these values if others do what we want of them. Recognition, appreciation, respect, and the like, if it is important to us to receive them, depend on others to give them to us. Reflexive values are nice to have, but they put us at the mercy of others, subject to the whims of others, and therefore potentially feeling disappointed and victimized. Also they make us feel dependent on others. Please identify each one of your reflexive values with an *R*. (Give participants the opportunity to discuss their values to identify the reflexive ones correctly.)

(ii) Some values are <u>conflicted</u>. This means that we are most aware of failures to achieve the values. And pursuit of these values involves avoidance of their opposites or getting away from their opposites. For most people (not for all; check each for yourself), values such as trust, respect (*R*), safety, recognition (*R*), and the like, if we want them for ourselves, involve <u>avoiding</u> mistrust, disrespect, danger, being ignored, or imprecision, powerlessness, and the like. All the values you selected where you have expressed the value as a 'not' are conflicted values. 'Not' values are things that are important to you to <u>avoid</u>.

Some people believe that <u>avoidance</u> values are formed from many earlier experiences with the value's opposite pole – that is, with not being trusted or able to trust, not feeling respected, not feeling safe, not receiving recognition, or making mistakes. Each of these unpleasant or uncomfortable <u>experiences</u> is stored in memory with a negative or upsetting 'charge' or feeling. Each of these feelings cumulate with the earlier experiences' feelings to increase the amount of negative feeling attached to the value's negative (opposite) pole. But the personality is always in a state of balance. So as the amount of the negative feeling attached to the opposite pole (mistrust, disrespect,

etc.) increases, so does the need pressure or the importance of the positive pole (trust, respect, etc.). The two poles are conceptual parts of ourselves (mistrust-trust, disrespect-respect) that pull farther apart with each new negative experience, creating an approach-avoidance conflict and increasing the value or importance of the ideas or ways of seeing things that are involved.

If you have many conflicted values, several things will follow. You will NOT enjoy your values or the area of life in which they are important to you (e.g., work, relationships, feelings). You will be fairly constantly on edge, vigilantly watching out for evidences of the negative poles (mistrust, disrespect) and finding them fairly often while failing to notice evidences of the positive pole (trust, respect). You will spend a lot of time putting yourself and the world down (i.e., feeling guilty or being depreciating or critical). You won't have much joy in life. You will worry a good deal. And you may fail to achieve much of what you might have expected yourself to achieve. Mark these values with a C. If you're not sure whether a value of yours is conflicted, ask yourself why it's important to you (many times if need be) or why you want that. If any answer you give yourself involves 'avoiding' anything or a 'not', the value is a conflicted one. Mark it with a C.

(iii) Some values are wonderful, <u>approach</u> values. When you value opportunities, joy, love, and the like, you will likely tend to notice instances of these values, to enjoy the experiences associated with them, and to enhance the quality of your life with them. It is worthwhile to ensure that you maximize the number of positive or approach values you pursue in your life. Mark these values with a P, or just write JOY beside them.

(Spend some time with individual's values, helping them to check on the 'type' of each of their values. For example, say, 'You say Trust is important to you. When you think of Trust, what does it do for you? What do you get from Trust? Why is that important to you? And why is that important to you? What evidence would you accept

that Trust and its associated things are present or absent?' List on the board the responses given. Then examine each to find out what the person notices [approach-positive pole or avoid-negative pole] and how it makes the person feel [happy-positive pole or scared/unhappy/angry-negative pole]. If on negative pole, the value is a C or avoidance value, which is important to addictions.)

Survey your values. Are they as you would want them to be, or would you like to change them? There is no point just deciding to change them and expecting them thereafter to be changed. They won't be. But there are ways to change them. Let's play.

Find a value in your lists that you would like to keep but ought to be lower or higher in the rank order of your values. Let's take a couple of examples. If money is at the top of any area's rank order, you are probably a pretty boring and bored person. You might want to shift it down to second or third place in your rank order. If you have too many reflexive values among the first six to ten top values for any area, you likely feel a bit anxious, helpless, or at the mercy of others. You might want to pick one or more of these reflexive values to move much farther down in your ranking. If you have too many conflicted values towards the top of your list but you are hesitant to get rid of the cautiousness they maintain, you might wish to move some of them a bit farther down in your ranking to get some other more-enjoyment-giving values to higher-rank order places. How is this done?

First, pick a value you want to move, select the level of importance to which you want to move it, and note the value above and below the position into which it will be inserted. Remember that by shifting its position downwards, you automatically increase by one the position of all the values above its new position. Close your eyes and let a picture pop into your mind when you think of the value you're going to move. If the picture you get makes obvious sense or represents a given example or concrete instance of that value, try again to see what picture pops into your mind when you think of that value. Let's have a few examples of your pictures. (Get a few of the participants' images and ask them to try again if the pictures are too concrete. If

they are satisfactory, say the next sentence.) That's perfect. Now close your eyes again, and let pictures pop into your mind for the other two values – those above and below the new location. (Get some examples of these pictures, reacting as above. When it appears that all participants have three different pictures to represent the three values, proceed.)

Bring up the picture representing the value you want to move. Notice whether it is in colour or black and white. Notice its colours or shades. Notice whether it has bright or dark spots. Notice whether it is clear and sharp or cloudy, vague or in pastels. Notice if it's framed or has a background. Notice where it is located, its direction and distance from you. Notice any background, any movement, or any sound. When you have identified its sensory qualities, start moving it around, noticing how you feel as it takes different positions – in front of you, higher, lower, to the side, closer, farther away. What you need to discover is how its different positions affect you and how they make you <u>feel</u>. You're trying to find out where you can locate it to increase, and also to reduce, its impact on your <u>feelings</u>. Once you have found that out, change its other sensory qualities to see how they affect how you feel. Add, remove, and change colours; increase and decrease its clarity and sharpness; add and take away movement; add and reduce its background or surroundings; and add, reduce, and change sounds and movement associated with it. As you do each of these things, note how it makes you feel when the changes are there. Once you know what you can do with the picture to increase <u>and</u> reduce the strength of your feelings about the picture, put it back up on a shelf.

Then, in turn, bring down the other pictures and do the same with them until you know how to increase and decrease your feelings about those pictures. If your feelings don't change as you change the location and sensory qualities of any of the three pictures, put that picture away and let another picture pop into your mind when you think about that value. Keep on finding pictures and testing them, by changing location and sensory qualities, until you have a picture for which you can notice changes in your feelings about it as you change

430

its location and sensory qualities. When you know how to increase or decrease your feelings about the three pictures by moving and changing them, you are ready for the next step. (Allow time.)

Compare the locations and sensory qualities of the three pictures, one for each of the three values. For the picture of the value whose rank order you want to change, move it to different locations and change the sensory qualities of the picture while noticing how you feel with each change you make to the picture. Compared to the feelings aroused by the picture of the value <u>below</u> where you want to locate the to-be-moved value, try to find the location and sensory qualities of the to-be-moved picture that create in you a bit <u>more</u> intense a feeling <u>and</u>, compared to the feelings aroused by the picture for the value <u>above</u> where you want to locate the to-be-moved value, try to find the location and sensory qualities of the to-be-moved picture that create in you a bit <u>less</u> intense a feeling. What you're trying to do is to find, for the to-be-moved value, the <u>feelings</u> the picture arouses that are sandwiched <u>between</u> the <u>feelings</u> aroused by the pictures for the other two values. Don't try to be reasonable or sensible about how you judge the strengths of your feelings. Go inside yourself, and let your unconscious tell you how you <u>feel</u>. When you've found the location and sensory qualities of the to-be-moved value's picture so that it conforms to those feeling intensities, anchor the picture for that value in that location and with those sensory qualities. You can do that by any method that works for you. One way is to put the picture on the screen of a very heavy television set and then nail the television set in just that location with huge spikes or anchor it with a big, heavy anchor. When you have done that, open your eyes and look around you. Then close your eyes again and check to make sure that the to-be-moved value's picture is where and how you wanted it in relation to the other values and their pictures. If things have changed, go back and re-anchor any picture that has moved or that has changed appreciably.

With that done, go back inside yourself and relist your values from that area in the right order as they feel to you now. If the to-be-moved value is not in the place you wanted it, close your eyes and

go back to check out whether the pictures are as and where you left them. If not, review them and re-anchor them as before.

What's all this about? Our values have been formed, and are carried to us, through images we carry in our minds. The images mostly don't make much sense because they combine all sorts of features from many memories from the past involving those values. If we want to change the locations of our values in their rank ordering of importance, we need to make the images associated with the values such that they evoke the right quality and amount of feeling in us – the amount of the associated feeling deciding how strong or important the value is to us. And if we want the value to stay where we put it, its image or picture has to stay as and where we put it – hence the need to anchor it.

Let's play another game. Look down your list of values in the various areas of living and find an avoidance value that you would like to heal so that it no longer drives you to avoid things in your life. Trust or respect or others' acceptance would be good ones, but you choose your own. Whichever conflicted or avoidance value you choose, it will have a positive and a negative pole. For example, the two poles of trust might be trust and mistrust, of respect might be respect and disrespect, and of acceptance might be acceptance and rejection. Find the two poles for you of the conflicted value you chose.

Close your eyes and let a picture pop into your mind for the negative pole of your value. For example, what picture pops into your mind when you think of mistrust or of disrespect or of rejection? Keep letting pictures pop into your mind until the picture makes little sense or seems a bit far out. When you have the picture of the negative pole of your value, put it up on the shelf. Now, let a picture pop into your mind for the positive pole of the value. For example, what picture pops into your mind when you think of trust or of respect or of acceptance? Check the picture for your value's positive pole to make sure it doesn't make too much sense to you. When you have that picture, put it up on the shelf too, and open your eyes. (Check a few examples.)

Great! Now, you all talk to yourselves, right? We know you do. It's called thinking. The trouble with thinking, or with talking to ourselves, is that we don't know which part of ourselves we are talking with. That's no good. We want to talk to some particular parts of ourselves right now – the parts that we have created across the years involving the two poles of this one of our values. One way to talk to those parts of ourselves specifically and separately would be to place those parts outside of ourselves and to talk to the externalized parts. We could put those two pictures of the two poles of our value outside ourselves and talk to them as parts of ourselves. Close your eyes and hold out your two hands, palms up. If you were going to put the negative pole picture (e.g., that for mistrust, disrespect, or rejection) on one of your hands, if you knew, which hand would you put it on? Trust your unconscious to tell you. That's perfect. Put it there. Then put the picture of the positive pole (e.g., that for trust, respect, or acceptance) on the other hand. Now you have a part of yourself resting on each of your hands. Ask those parts some questions and listen carefully for the answers you get.

First, ask the <u>negative</u> pole (e.g., the mistrust, disrespect, rejection) picture to tell you what its highest intention for you is. Get the answer. If necessary, demand that it gives you the answer. After all, it is part of you and subject to your will. When you get the answer, ask it <u>why it</u> wants <u>that</u> (new purpose) for you. When you get the answer to that, ask it <u>why</u> it wants <u>that</u> (next purpose) for you. Keep asking the why question until the answer is always the same. Then open your eyes. What was the final answer? (If a person is stuck, either push for the answer or get him/her to try again with another popped picture.)

Now close your eyes and ask the picture of the positive pole (e.g., trust, respect, acceptance) what its highest intention for you is. When you get the answer, ask it as often as needed <u>why</u> it wants <u>that</u> (next purpose) for you. When you get the final answer, open your eyes.

Strange, isn't it, but the final answer is always the same. It is for your survival and/or happiness. You see, every part of each of us exists always and only to support our survival and happiness. (Most people are surprised to find that even the negative side of any value

or feeling or part exists for that purpose, regardless of its apparent negativity.)

Surprising isn't it that such different pictures of such different poles have the same purpose for you? Since they have the same purpose for you, perhaps they could talk to each other to reach some agreement about how they can each help to achieve their common purpose for you while contributing to your joy. And perhaps they could find a way to express their coming together in agreement so that you and they will know that they will work together as one part of you in the future. So close your eyes and ask them to talk this over with each other and to find a way to show to you that they will cooperate together as one part of you to achieve their common purpose. (The two hands tend to move together as the sign. When that happens, proceed. If some hands do not come together, ask those people if they have experienced a problem in this. The answer may be that the two pictures changed to the same one on both hands or that the pictures no longer contradict each other. If not, the person should be encouraged to demand the two parts reach an agreement and show that they intend to cooperate.)

Now, close your eyes again and look at the picture you now have of that new part. Who is willing to describe the new part? (Get a few examples.) That's perfect. Now, imagine an infinite source of power, love, happiness, and contentment shining and coming down through your head and out through your heart to that new part of yourself and also to all the rest of the parts of yourself as the new part integrates itself with the rest of the parts of you. When you are done, open your eyes. (This is James and Woodsmall's Visual Squash.)

Block 4: Consolidation

Did you feel better after the earlier exercises? (Allow brief discussion and comments.) Do you feel there remains some pain or distress associated with your early experiences related to the conflicted value you changed? Close your eyes and scan back over

all your memories of the past. Get an idea of where they lie in relation to where you are now. Whatever direction they approach you from is perfect, but do get a direction. Drift up, way up, over your timeline and then drift down a bit but staying well out of and above your timeline. Drift back over your past memories until you find a place that you think might have been the root cause of your pain or distress about this value. Drift about twenty minutes back before that time, and drift down into your timeline facing the present. Where are those feelings now? If they are still there, drift up and back to find an earlier time that might have been the root cause. Drift back twenty minutes before that time and drift down into your timeline facing the present. Repeat this until you do not have that feeling of pain or distress. When you have found the time, walk slowly forwards into the root cause situation. If the feelings are still there, drift up and back again to about twenty minutes before and walk into it again. If the feelings are just as strong in the situation, drift up and back to the present. In the present, collect some resources around you, such as your more mature understandings, your relative invulnerability, loved ones with whom you feel safe, some of your accomplishments, and the like. And then return to try again. If that doesn't reduce the feelings in that earlier situation, please drift up and back to the present and raise your hand. When you're done, come back to the present and open your eyes. (If any participants raise their hands, get the group to go back above their timelines and construct a theatre over the critical place. Perform the trauma procedure as described in treatment 1: Creating Success, Therapeutics. Alternatively, try the Swish procedure used in treatment 4: Creating Satisfaction. If need be, the second presenter can take the individual aside and ask about the problem. Some familiarity with other NLP and behavioural methods may be needed in order to find solutions to the problems identified.)

Remember that reflexive values place you at the mercy of others. Let's think of an example. In prison, it is common practice to look up to the 'solids' and down on the 'rats' or 'pigeons'. We all know that the 'solids' are the tough and courageous inmates who do their

own time and don't bother with other people's time. We all also know that the 'rats' and 'pigeons' are the weak, timid, and cowardly inmates who do everybody else's time. That's true, right? Actually, the reverse is more true. The solids are those who are so fearful of others that they have to pump iron to feel strong and safe, who are afraid of being caught and unwilling to live with the consequences of their own behaviour, and who insist that others 'dummy up', thus trying to do other people's time. The rats and pigeons are those who don't worry about the consequences of their behaviour and who are not afraid to come forwards when someone breaks a rule. Maybe we have some of our ideas all scrambled up. Of course, the conventional views of solids and rats are based on <u>beliefs</u> that are adopted in order to feel accepted or part of the inmate culture. They are not values. But beliefs are developed from values. The values involved in these example beliefs are the values of the inmate culture or counterculture that involve rebellion against rules and authorities. Commitment to values such as these ensures that we perpetuate our participation in whatever is involved in crime and its associated subcultures. If we want to change our lifestyle, say, of crime or addiction, it is probably necessary first to change our commitment to their values. That's what we have been trying to do today.

But what's the point of changing our commitment to particular values? Partly the point has to do with acquiring new lifestyles for ourselves that are continually rewarding and enjoyable and thus getting to like and respect ourselves a whole lot more than we do; partly the point is to become useful and contributing members of the community of people that has bred us, kept us alive, and that offers us much more than any of us give. If that seems like a worthwhile goal, one of the better ways to achieve that goal is to know our values, to adjust our values to suit the lifestyle we want, and to get rid of the conflicts within some of our values – conflicts within us that are reflected in the conflict with others in our lives and in the pain and distress that drive us to seek feeling better with the help of our addictive substances.

(Do a summary and cuing observations.)

Treatment 6: Creating INNOCENCE

The <u>main target</u> of this program is <u>guilt feelings</u> and the complications that can develop surrounding them, including those of criminality and addictions. The paradoxical manner in which the treatment of conflict must be approached is nowhere more clear than in the treatment of guilt intolerance. Increasing guilt feelings tends to increase defensive denial (intolerance) of guilt and thus to increase the risk of crime (Reynolds and Quirk, 1996) and the felt need for an addictive. Decreasing guilt feelings directly is almost impossible since they tend to be denied or unacknowledged. Decreasing innocent feelings is tantamount to increasing guilt with its consequences (above). And increasing innocent feelings, if incautiously done, feeds directly into the strategy offenders and addicts already tend to adopt, namely the defensive denial or the suppression of guilt. Paradoxical means need to be adopted to 'get around' this paradoxical state of affairs.

Block 1: Orientation

Who never feels guilty? Who enjoys feeling guilty? Whether or not we deny feeling guilty now, everybody has felt guilty in the past. And we all hated feeling guilty. Guilt feelings imply a sense that we have done wrong or have been bad. At least, we all know what being bad or doing wrong is by other people's standards. What percentage of your life have you been bad or done wrong? (Get estimates of percentages. They tend to vary from 5% to 99%.) OK, let's decide who the worst person who ever lived is. My nominee would be Adolf Hitler. Let's use him as our example. What percentage of his life was he bad or did he do wrong? (Estimates tend to vary from 50% to 100%.) Now here's a kick in the head. It seems likely that Adolf Hitler was a bad person for under 2% of his life. And though we hate to insult you in this way, your badness probably doesn't get anywhere near even 1% of your life. Think of it this way. You and

Adolf slept away about one-third of your lives. Were you bad then? For the first nine or ten years of your life, you were being a kid, just learning how to be good. Were you bad when you didn't know any better? Let's see, that brings your possible bad time down to, let's say, 50%. Of course, you spent a couple of hours each day eating and another hour travelling to and from school and work. Were you bad then? That brings us down to a maximum of 40%. You probably spent four hours a day watching television and talking to friends. Was that bad? Now we're down to a maximum of about 20%. How about the time at school and work? Were you bad then? Whoops, we're now down to under 1%.

Let's do it differently. Add together all the seconds and minutes in your life that you have been bad. Include only the time of doing your bad actions. Does it amount to twenty-four hours' worth? Was it more? How about two weeks' worth, twenty-four hours a day, seven days per week? Let's even give you that excessive an amount. How old are you? Multiply your age by fifty-two weeks. Say you're eighteen. That's 936 weeks of being alive. Your two measly weeks of being bad amounts to a little over 2/1,000 of your life or one-fifth of one percent. What a bad person you are! Sorry, but you just don't hack it as a bad person. You're going to have to try harder if you want to shape up as the bad person you apparently think you are. In fact, poor you, you're really an enormously good person!

But where do we get the idea we might be bad people? There is a very good reason for it. You see, whether or not you know it, you were raised by parenting adults and teachers. Of course, they were YOUR parents and YOUR teachers. So they should have spent all their time looking after and teaching you since that was all they did in their lives. At least, that's what we thought as children. They related to us in those roles, so that's most of what we knew about them. Now, of course, we know they were also workers, cookers, spouses, travellers, entertainers, cleaners, pet owners, gardeners, and had a host of other roles. Strange to say, few of us modify our childhood understandings of these people according to our grown-up understandings. We forget that they were people who happened to be

doing an extra task in raising us. They were busy, and they just didn't have all day long to follow around after us saying, 'good, good, good, good', etc. So they adopted the more efficient procedure of waiting for that ten seconds to half a minute out of each good hour in which we were roaring hellions, and then they warned us, controlled us, pointed out our mistakes, and took us to task. This drew our attention most strongly, clearly and poignantly to our errors, misdeeds, and (presumed) 'badness'; and we mostly ignored or failed to notice our wonderfulnesses.

The notion that we are bad or guilty comes from errors of several different kinds. First, we fail to notice that we are good by failing to notice our goodnesses and by watching out for our badnesses. Second, we fail to understand that the purpose others have for drawing our attention to our mistakes is the loving hope that we will grow into happy people. The purpose is to help us achieve happiness. Third, we fail to notice that adults have other things to do than just to be parents or teachers, so we take their negative input as applying to all our actions and/or ourselves. Fourth, we fail to notice that, like we ourselves, everybody else, including parents and teachers, are always doing the very best we can, at every moment, given the circumstances in which we find ourselves. We or they can be wrong, but all of us do the very best we can at every moment. Fifth, we take into ourselves the judgements made by others around us, especially adult others. This last error needs more comment.

We as children love those great big adults who look after us. And they always seem to be right. Heck, what do we know? Oh, of course, we as children probably think we know everything. However, if they judge us, their judgements must be right. If they, who love us and care for us, seem angry with us, it must be because we are unworthy of their love. So we must be bad. The child mind works in a simpler way than the adult mind. The child mind, however, is a learning mind. It learns very efficiently how to AVOID the dangers of being judged as bad. It learns to pay attention to, or to notice, those acts that will be judged as wicked or lead to loss of love (in child eyes). It remembers the error or bad act and hooks to it an emotional response

as a way to mark or keep it active in memory. The way this is done is to 'incorporate' it as part of the self. That is, the act is taken to be part of the self, but it is a part TO BE AVOIDED. Then when we do the act again, we find that we are judging ourselves and with the negative emotional charge that we have attached to the memory. We feel bad again, but this time by our own incorporated judgement. This experience is called guilt. And the part of us that does the judging is often called conscience.

Now, some of us get to hate our consciences. They keep saying we are bad, making us feel like small vulnerable children once more and making us afraid we are or will be unloved. Quite early in life, we can start to hate this feeling – for which, of course, we blame those we think 'did it to us' for it. If the feeling feels bad enough or we decide that those we think did it to us were themselves the bad and wrong people, then we may come to decide that the bad feeling is the thing that is bad and not we ourselves. There are several ways that we can then deal with the bad feeling about the bad feeling. We can set out to AVOID the bad feeling (1) by trying not to provoke it by being 'good', (2) by means of experiencing the feeling we get from the bad actions as excitement (rather than distress or discomfort), or (3) by finding a way to stop the bad feeling as quickly as possible whenever it happens. The second of these ways to handle the bad feelings tends to result in delinquency and, later, in crime, and the third tends to result in addiction to any substance or action that helps make the bad feelings feel better (however temporarily).

Now we are grown up enough to examine our actions and the bad feelings from our incorporated judgements of ourselves in the light of reason and mature judgement. How much of the time are you, or have you been, a bad person? Under 1%? Just how bad does that make you? OK, then, how good are you? We know what part of your answer will be. How about all that use of addictive substances and the number of times you have tried and failed to quit? And how about all the times you have hurt yourself and others with your addictive behaviour? Just for a moment, forget about the number of times you have failed to quit. Have you tried to quit? Please don't

lie to yourself by saying that you must have wanted not to quit since you kept failing. Even thinking about quitting means you wanted to quit. Failing comes from the fact that it is hard to give up feeling better quickly and from having to live with feeling bad. Every time and all the time that you thought about quitting, no matter what you did about it was time during which you were being, or trying to be, good! You good person you! Please add that to the good part of you. All we need to do to help that good part of you along is to learn ways to succeed – strategies for success.

One way to do that is to notice the huge number of times when you were not doing addictive acts – when you were not smoking or drinking or doing drugs. We tend to ignore those times. But you already know how not to do addictive behaviour since you have done nonaddiction lots of times, including now. You're already good at that. Perhaps you might want to figure out HOW you did that!

Even if that doesn't work completely, all that you would need to do would be to get rid of the bad feelings or to enjoy the bad feelings or have fun with them so you don't need to find relief from them any more. We know, you think that would be a hard thing to do. But that's the main part of today's task.

But before we can get rid of the bad feelings, we need to ask ourselves what purpose they serve in our lives. They do have a purpose, or else they wouldn't be there. What useful thing could such bad feelings ever have in our lives? To figure this out, we have to return to the past to see the world through child's eyes again. As children, we get upset or angry when something hurts us – hurts us physically or hurts our feelings. So when we as children see adults upset or angry, we can only assume that their feelings have been hurt. We love those who love and look after us. We certainly don't want to hurt their feelings. That's why we incorporate into ourselves their judgements of us, along with the associated bad feelings. So the purpose or function of guilt feelings or conscience is mainly to help us keep from hurting the feelings of those we love.

As we grow older, we tend to think of behaviours that hurt other people as angry or aggressive actions. So the purpose or function of

conscience or guilt feelings tends to be to help us AVOID anger or aggressiveness or the hurt it is supposed to cause in others. Now that we are grown up, perhaps we ought to review <u>what</u> happens when we try to AVOID aggression or anger and <u>how</u> hurt is actually caused. That's part of today's task too.

But let's suppose that guilt feelings are necessary, at least some of the time. How will we be able to tolerate them, when they occur, without having to resort to the use of addictive substances? Of course, in the long run, we may have to learn to accept them and to discover that they are not all that awful. That is, expecting the bad feelings and letting them last for a while without having to relieve them can become perfectly possible. But you'd expect people who don't have an addiction to cope with to say that kind of thing. However, there is another thing we could do about guilt feelings. We might even be able to learn to enjoy them. We might even learn to enjoy other people's attempts to lay guilt trips on us. That is nuts, right? Still, it might be possible.

Block 2: Tools

The first tool for today is to find the good in ourselves. Are you predominantly a bad person or a good person? On paper, start adding up the time you have been good to make a realistic estimate of how good you are. One way to do that realistically might be to add up the time you were a good person, doing good things, during the past day. You haven't done anything good during the last day, have you? Oh no? When you got up this morning, did you make your bed, relieve yourself, brush your teeth, bathe, comb your hair, say good morning to somebody, have some breakfast, tidy or clean something up, do some work, smile at somebody and/or walk or travel somewhere? Did you sleep some during the night? Were these healthy, social, helpful, good things to do? Notice how much of our good behaviours and time we simply don't notice? In another column, add the numbers of seconds and moments you did bad things. Remember that even

between the seconds of taking drinks or drugs, we are doing good things like talking to others, watching TV, or just sitting being and feeling good. Let's try to be fair to ourselves as well. What percentage of the time of your life were you bad? Make an estimate.

But other people have been or are being hurt by you, right? Let's take a few moments to look honestly at that idea. Actually, nobody hurts anybody else. We are the ones who hurt ourselves. Nobody has a right to expect anything from anybody else. What happens is that the person who is going to feel hurt THINKS that the hurting person SHOULD NOT act the way he/she is acting. By talking to him/herself that way, he/she makes him/herself angry. The anger he/she has thus created arouses guilt feelings fairly automatically, and the felt component of those guilt feelings is the feeling of being hurt attributed to someone else.

So is it true that you and other people hurt one another? Of course it is, right? Let's use our favourite example of this. You are walking along a sidewalk. Suddenly, you feel a bump on your shoulder. How do you feel? Do you imagine you feel angry or hurt? You do not. All you feel is surprised by a sudden and unexplained event. The orienting response has been activated. It almost demands that you turn around to see what happened. But that's all you feel . . . yet. You turn around. What you see is a twelve-foot-tall man with shoulders three feet wide with a knife in one hand and a club in the other. And he is menacing. How do you feel? You probably feel scared out of your skull. But suppose you are twenty feet tall, with six-foot-wide shoulders and automatic guns in both your hands. How do you feel? You probably would feel scornful of the shrimp. Of course, in actuality, you're not twenty feet tall, and you don't have any automatic weapons in your hands. But then, actually, I was wrong. What you see when you turn around is really a punk little kid who is trying to show off to his punk little friend. How do you feel? You probably feel angry at the punk. Hey, you could beat him/her up, if you wanted to. So it's safe to feel angry. Damn! I was wrong again. It's not a punk kid. It's your boss, and he/she is laughing to a friend about his/her right to upset you. How do you feel? You probably feel hurt by his/her callousness.

Oh, I'm sorry, I was wrong again. It's not your boss; it's a little old person on crutches who stumbled on the sidewalk and bumped into you by accident. How do you feel? Probably, you feel compassion and concern that he/she is OK. But suppose you are also a little elderly person on crutches too. How do you feel? You'd probably chide the person angrily for being so careless about injuring you. You see, in all these scenarios, it's NOT the event – the bump – that makes us angry. It's how we see the situation or what we tell ourselves about the situation.

There are two general ways by which we upset ourselves, and it is always WE who upset OURselves – never other people. One way is the following: an event occurs –> we become aroused –> we talk to ourselves in a certain way –> we become upset or angry. The other way is the following: an event occurs –> we talk to ourselves about it in a certain way –> what we say arouses our feelings –> we become upset or angry. An example of the first way was given in the situation we just described. An example of the second way occurs every time we feel insulted, put down, or our feelings are hurt.

The important question is, <u>What</u> do we say to ourselves or <u>how</u> do we talk to ourselves about events that result in our feeling upset or angry? It's hard to know what we say to ourselves. Many of our thoughts become so habitual that they just flip past us in the twinkling of an eye before we know we had a thought. It might be worthwhile to capture or notice some of these thoughts as they flip past. It's hard to do. So here are a couple of clues for us to use in this exercise to try on your own. Just saying 'that (an event) makes me mad' doesn't do it. Check to see if by itself it does. One way to find what we are saying to ourselves is to see whether saying any particular thing gets us upset. Generally, the kind of idea that works to get us upset is one that tells us that the other person <u>shouldn't</u> have said it or <u>shouldn't</u> be trying to upset us, that it is <u>awful</u> that such a thing occurred, or that some horrible <u>catastrophe</u> is about to happen. Nothing <u>shouldn't</u>, or should, happen. People say and do things for their own purposes and not to upset or hurt us (unless the person's purpose was to upset or hurt another for his or her own reasons and it

444

might have been said or done to anybody else). No event is inherently <u>awful</u>, unless we choose to make it so. And the only real <u>catastrophe</u> that we can do much about is the catastrophe of upsetting ourselves about an unknowable future possibility that hasn't happened. We could all profit by finding out what we say to ourselves to upset ourselves. (This is Ellis's Rational-Emotive Therapy.)

But we have all suffered guilt feelings because we believed we were hurting or had hurt others. The function or purpose of those feelings, if you remember, is to keep us from doing angry or aggressive things that we believed hurt others. Quite apart from the fact that we were wrong in that belief, we have all learned to block our angry or aggressive feelings to keep from hurting others. The way we have done this is to use one of the many means people find to 'control' or stop themselves from doing certain kinds of things. The trouble is that the ways we find to control or stop all sorts of actions also inhibit the use of the body's energies. The body is an energy-producing machine. And inhibiting energy use results in depression or compulsive behaviour such as addictions. That's right. Depression is NOT due to the horrible events of the past nor does it descend upon us without cause. We do it to ourselves. It is not to our advantage to block our energy use. Using the body's energies is one way to help stop depression and compulsive actions like addictions. Does that mean that aerobic exercises and fitness are good for us after all? Yes. But that's not the only way in which to use body energies, and it isn't even a necessary way. It's only one way out of hundreds of ways, many of which can be done without big strong movements of the body. The basic way in which we use the body's energies is by assertiveness. Hold it! Assertiveness is NOT limited to what this author or that one chooses to focus on in teaching assertive skills.

Assertive Training is a wide array of procedures to encourage the use of body energies. Most assertive trainers are social behaviourists. They teach ways to communicate or to send assertive messages to others. The most basic assertive method in social communication is the so-called I statement or, more generally, the Three-part statement. Aggressive <u>and</u> underassertive sentences tend to use the 'You'

statement. In its aggressive form, it attributes to somebody else the source of our own feelings. It takes the following form: 'You make me angry.' In its underassertive form, it attributes power or importance to someone else. It takes the following form: 'You shouldn't have to do that. I'll do it.' In either case, the control over our own lives and feelings is transferred to someone else. We do not acknowledge our own rights and power in our own lives. The 'I' statement expresses our own feelings without attributing the cause of them to anybody or anything else. It asserts our own rights to have feelings of our own, no matter why the feelings are there. It takes the following form: 'I am angry.' Notice that there is no explanation given for the feeling. Any explanation attributes the feeling to another person as its cause (an implicit 'You' statement) or to a general principle that takes over from the speaker responsibility for the feeling, thus making the principle (and not the speaker) the active (energized) agent causing the feeling. A useful motto for assertive 'I' statements is, 'Never explain. Your friends don't need it, and your enemies won't believe it anyway.' Just taking responsibility for our own feelings is assertive and uses bodily energies.

The general form of the 'I' statement is the Three-part statement. The three parts of this statement facilitate assertive communication. The first part expresses in our own words our understanding of what the other person just said. It takes the following form: 'I understand you to have said that . . .' This allows the other person to correct any misunderstanding of what was just said and provides the basis for what is to follow. The second part expresses how we feel about the matter being discussed. It takes the following form: 'I feel upset (or happy, etc.)'. It is the standard 'I' statement. The third part expresses our intention or the position or action we will take. It takes the following form: 'I think/believe that . . .' or 'I will take the position/action that . . .' It makes an assertive, personal affirmation. Assertive sentences such as the 'I' statement or Three-part statement foster good communications; do not arouse defensiveness, competition, enmity, or conflict; and do not challenge other people.

But communications are not the only ways to be assertive. Each action or, if you wish, each element of body language can use the body's energies effectively. Standing or sitting with the body erect, using large and expansive (extensor) gestures, maintaining eye contact, speaking clearly and audibly, using short sentences (without explanatory clauses), enunciating crisply, and a host of other minor aspects of body use are assertive. They use the body's energies, and they expand one in space, if only by reaching out towards the other person (e.g., eye contact) or filling the area (e.g., clear and crisp speech). To some extent, assertive use of bodily energy is accomplished by one's own sense of personal impact on the world around. And such impact need not be destructive. It can even work better if it is constructive. There is one caution that may be needed. No criticism or judgement is ever assertive. It may have an impact on those around, but no matter how cleverly it is hidden, it is always in the form of a 'You' statement.

We suggested above that each of us is almost entirely a good person. Let's remember that the same applies to everyone else as well as to us. It would be to everyone's advantage if we were all able to see ourselves and the world around us as good. But how can that be accomplished? To figure out the answer to that question, we have to start somewhere else.

Your parents and ours were NOT OUR parents. Of course they were OUR parents, but that was not ALL they were or are. They were people, and people never have ONLY one identity. They were also spouses, workers, friends, relatives, entertainers, sleepers, lovers, and a host of other things. They did not have the time to be parents ONLY. It was only through our child eyes that they were parents only. That's mainly what we saw them doing. Because they had other things to do, they could not go around all day long patting us on the head and saying 'Good, good, good, good, good, good'. Instead, they went about their lives watching out of the corners of their eyes and, out of sheer love and the desire to ensure our greatest happiness, shouting out warnings or commands whenever what we were doing might lead to danger of injury, pain, or irritation of others. These reactions occurred in response to those couple of seconds out of each hour when we were

roaring hellions. The rest of the time, we were as 'good as gold'. That's how it comes to be that most adults know more about their errors and mistakes than they do about how truly good they all are.

The way in which our errors and badnesses are drawn to our attention is in the form of 'You' statements or criticisms. Perhaps it's time to grow up and to give up criticisms of ourselves and of others. Perhaps we might even start looking around for the good things in ourselves, everybody else, and the world. They are everywhere and can easily be found once we have adjusted our filter habits to find the good things.

Once we have started to find and comment on the good things in life, two other interesting things tend to follow.

First, we start setting an example for others. Others, too, can learn to notice and find the good around them. That includes the good in you. Suddenly, other people are rewarding you for your goodness by noticing it. Our acts benefit us in the long run.

Second, we find ourselves in the position to make a useful and solid contribution to our communities. We find ourselves in a headspace where we are drawn to positive ways of viewing things. And positive things happen if we look for and see things in positive ways. Let's understand how this works through a rather basic example.

Let's suppose that you concluded that it is important to have peace in this world. We can't do it all by ourselves, and there are lots of pressures acting against it. In fact, our habitual preoccupation with criticism has been formalized in our society in most educational programs and in the practice of the Law. The Law seeks to 'keep the peace' by regulation and maintaining order. It finds instances of actions that contravene and punishes the perpetrators. The Law indicates what not to do and demeans those who do the proscribed acts. This approach, far from fostering peace, fosters warfulness or crime. If we really wanted to create and maintain peace, we might better find principles that state ideals and reward or congratulate those who act in ways consistent with those principles. By way of example, the following peace principles might serve us well in creating and maintaining peace:

1. The Golden Rule. In all things, act towards others as you would have them act towards you.
2. The Inclusion Principle. Draw an inclusive circle around every person to include everyone in as part of your community.
3. The Consistency Principle. Act in ways consistent with your beliefs and principles and how you hope others will act.
4. The Cooperation Principle. Be liberal in cooperating and sharing all of your own with others.
5. The Conservation Principle. Be conservative in the use of all resources and in the production of waste.
6. The Resource Exchange Principle. Use your energies to serve others in communal exchange and accept theirs in return.
7. The Consideration Principle. Accommodate to the rights, joy, and survival needs of others, including all future generations.
8. The Political Principle. Share power equally with all people, keeping no extra power for yourself.
9. The Accomplishment Principle. Achieve the best and most worthwhile person you can be, limited only by others' rights and needs.
10. The Respect Principle. Give respect to each person (and yourself) to foster awareness of the good in all people.
11. The Trust Principle. Trust every person (and yourself) in order to feel safe with everybody.
12. The Love Principle. Exercise love and caring for all others as widely as possible to maximize your own joy.
13. The Positive Reward Principle. Look for the positive in everything and acknowledge and praise it so you feel good.
14. The Agreement Principle. Find common/shared elements in all viewpoints and merge them inclusively to find agreement.
15. The Common Purpose Principle. Seek in all things common purpose to ensure cooperative pursuit of coexistence.
16. The General Principle. All other considerations, means, and approaches are subordinated to these principles in the active pursuit of peace – if peace is our primary purpose in life.

To pick a purpose or two, such as peace, to find positive ways to achieve it/them, and to lead your life according to those ways is the best way to make a solid and worthwhile contribution to the communities in which we live. To make such useful contributions is the best way to counter guilt or to make up for the many times we have all done dumb things. Strangely, as we pursue a positive initiative such as peace, guilt feelings simply vanish.

Block 3: Therapeutics

Change history (James and Woodsmall's Timeline) to modify guilt experiences. (See under Creating Success: Therapeutics.) The purpose of this procedure, which we can do by ourselves any time we wish, is to rid our histories of the gnawing guilt feelings that, built up over the years, have made us angry and unwilling to acknowledge or to tolerate any guilt feelings we have.

Modify guilt-versus-innocence concepts (James and Woodsmall's Visual Squash. See under Creating Success: Therapeutics) to defang guilt feelings. The purpose of this method, which we can use any time we wish on our own, is to undo some of the pain of feeling guilty that has increased our felt need to see ourselves as innocent and to value our innocence.

Who would like to serve as a victim to help us demonstrate another way to get over guilt feelings? (Accept a volunteer to take the 'hot seat' in the middle of the room.) Pick something you feel guilty about. If you can't think of anything other than your addictive behaviour, pick that. What was it you did that was wrong or bad? (Obtain answers.) Who were your victims? Who hurt most because of that? (Query until the person identifies him/herself.) How did you hurt yourself? (Get answers.) Did you ever not hurt yourself? In what ways and how? (Get responses. If the person affirms he/she continuously hurt him/herself, examine the progress of life.) When you were sleeping, while you were having meals, while you were at school or work, while watching TV, etc.? Is it true that for most of

your life you were not hurting yourself in that/those way(s)? How about those you love or care about? Did you hurt them more than you did them good? (If the person affirms more hurt than good, ask, 'Then how come they stayed with you or kept on loving you?') You know as well as we do that most people accept much less 'abuse' than they get in good things. When they feel that abuse exceeds goodness or positive value to them (actually long before that), they simply forget the good and abandon the abuser.

Let's be real. You mean to tell us that you were more good than bad? Of course you were. In fact, as we pointed out earlier, you have always been many times more good than bad. If you're going to assign such importance to your badness that you play it up as greater than your goodness, you might at least have the good grace to enjoy and to be proud of your badness. Heck, you didn't accomplish all that much of it. Of course, you really are a bit proud of it, aren't you? You have been willing to show off your badness to us today. So you must be a bit proud of it. If that's true, it must be something you consider important or something that makes you feel important. Hey, that's OK. But you at least have to be aware that you feel in some conflict about it. On the one hand, you think of it as bad. On the other hand, you're proud of it or think it's important. Conflict is a part of what goes on in all our heads. We fight with ourselves.

But the conflict is the most damaging thing of all. Maybe we could do whatever seems right to us without conflict over it. What purpose does your 'bad' act serve? What does it do for you? (Get responses.) And what does that do for you? And what does that do for you? (These questions seek the most general and the most important purposes or values the person has or those that the badness behaviour is instrumental in achieving.) In this pursuit, although survival and happiness (as in the Squash) are the most general reasons for anything's existence, self-actualizing or meta needs may appear as the perceived bases for survival and happiness. Such meta needs might include things such as power, importance, or even helplessness (as a means to maintain dependency on others). (Keep questioning until the bases for the instrumental conduct are clear.) OK, so you

want to feel (happy, important, powerful, etc.). Are there ways you could achieve those feelings other than the ways you have tried? (Push for alternatives and suggest others.)

It is surprising that once people find what they are trying to achieve (final causes), it is relatively easy to find other ways to achieve their purposes or satisfy their needs. Moreover, once they know what they seek, most people enjoy pursuing their goals, purposes, and needs in prosocial and positive ways. However, the solutions found need to provide real challenges and options and not just do-gooder-mouthed moralistic mumbo jumbo hogwash that sounds conventional and 'proper'.

Block 4: Consolidation

Enjoying life is enhanced by finding the good in every situation and in trusting everyone. Remember to reset your filters that support beliefs, to enjoy receiving (practice the fun of being criticized) and avoid giving criticism, and to find principles for living that have a chance of achieving what we want to achieve – as purposes we choose for our lives and as self-actualizing needs. Remember the example of creating peace by setting that as a primary value or purpose or goal, finding the positive principles to achieve the positive state, and living those principles both to enhance your own life and to set an example for others. Remember that enjoying life is accomplished best in the here and now and by focusing on immediate experiences and events. (This is Perceptual Discrimination/Fair Witness Training.) For everyone, thinking about the past is at least mildly depressing (the unpleasant events stand out much more sharply in memory than the pleasant ones), and thinking about the future is scary (at the very least, it is unknown or uncertain). The present is fun. Remember to be rid of negative or unpleasant feelings or situations by using such methods as Timeline trips, the Swish, or the Visual Squash. But don't just think about doing the exercises. Do them. Remember to use your body's energies to improve your mood and make life feel happier.

Using your energies includes active use of the body's muscles, either in exercise or just in expanding yourself in space by how you talk and how you carry yourself. It also includes communications in the form of 'I' statements or the Three-part statement, minimizing the use of critical 'You' statements. And remember to notice just how really good you really are.

(Do a summary and cuing observations.)

Treatment 7: Creating HEALTH

The <u>main target</u> of this program is on maintaining and valuing <u>health</u>. Psychological and physical health are most commonly impaired by (1) stress and (2) expectations from personal beliefs. If chronic stress can be relieved and personal health beliefs modified, future health can be improved radically. Since many of the discriminants-controlling addictions relate to distress and to general physical malaise, improvement of health should serve to diminish addictive behaviours or self-medications.

Block 1: Orientation

As far back as the 1930s the role of the body's <u>stress</u> response in health and disease was pretty firmly established. The stress response of the body creates most of the chronic and killer diseases afflicting humankind. It is central to nearly all the so-called mental or emotional diseases. And it plays a central role in the body's capacity to recover from physical diseases. However, the body's stress response has been badly misunderstood in everyday ways of talking about it.

The body's stress response is a standard reaction of a very particular kind. There is a major part of the peripheral outflow nervous system called the <u>Autonomic Nervous System</u> or the ANS. The ANS is comprised of two major branches – the Sympathetic and the Parasympathetic branches. Both of these nerve tracts feed almost every organ and part of the body. However, as we will explain later,

there is no parasympathetic feed to the adrenal glands. And the two branches compete with each other so that when one is active, the other becomes inactive. The response of the sympathetic branch of the ANS is an immediate survival response. Consequently, it takes precedence over the parasympathetic and other response systems.

When the sympathetic branch is active, the heart rate is accelerated, breathing shifts from diaphragm to chest breathing, the blood vessels of the gut become narrower and those feeding the muscles become wider, the pupils of the eye dilate, and a host of other arousal responses occur. Also the body's autoimmune system is activated, releasing fluid to target areas and increasing the white blood cell count. The body becomes prepared to deal with an emergency. And the subjective experience is one of arousal, of anxiety or fear (ready for flight), or of anger (ready to fight). This reaction of the body is called the stress response.

When the parasympathetic response is activated, among many other things, the heart rate slows down, breathing tends to return to diaphragm breathing, the pupils become reactive to the amount of light present, the blood vessels in the gut widen and those feeding the muscles become narrower, and the immune response rests. The body becomes calmer and 'veges out'. And the subjective experience is one of calmness or pleasure.

We think it's important that you know at least this much about how an important part of your body works. There is a little bit more that you probably ought to know. We think some knowledge about our bodies is necessary to allow us to understand ourselves. If the sympathetic response of the ANS occurred without any other thing happening, it would occur and vanish almost in the twinkling of an eye. However, the sympathetic response is aroused by emergencies where there might be danger. In a tropical jungle, the fleeting glimpse out of the corner of your eye of something yellow and black moving would arouse a sympathetic response. This is called the Orienting Reflex, since it activates a quick turn of the head to see what might be there that might be dangerous. If the eyes do not detect any danger at once, the sympathetic response subsides. But that might not be

too wise from the point of view of survival. The tiger might have vanished behind rocks or bushes. So the body is constructed to extend the sympathetic arousal for a short period of time after it is activated. This is done by stimulating the adrenal glands to pump out adrenaline. Adrenaline circulates through the body and keeps the arousal going, mimicking the sympathetic response. The absence of parasympathetic feed to the adrenal glands, which we mentioned earlier, means that the maintained arousal cannot be damped down too quickly. This keeps the body vigilant and ready to respond in case the emergency is a real one requiring actions of flight or fight, for which the body has been prepared by the sympathetic-stress response.

There are three more things we need to talk about before we have finished with this lecture on how the body works. Stay with us because this information is important to your life.

The first thing has to do with health. The autoimmune system, by which the body fights off infection and disease, is stimulated and orchestrated by the sympathetic ANS response. It involves release of a wide range of hormones that activate fluid retention and distribution, white blood cell production, and cell growth to repair damage to the body. If the sympathetic-stress-anxiety-immune response is activated too often and the adrenergic extension of it makes arousal more or less continuous, the use of the stress hormones may exceed the rate of their production. This can result in either or both of two consequences. The stress hormones can become depleted so that the body can no longer fight off disease or deal with errors in body maintenance. And the continuous activation of the immune response can create immune diseases such as arthritis and cancer. It is not to anyone's advantage to have too continuous or repeated sympathetic activation going on in the body.

The second thing has to do with personal experience. The activation of the sympathetic response is experienced as arousal. The experience felt by the person depends on the person and how he or she habitually understands life circumstances. The experiences provoked can be felt as unpleasant sensations such as anxiety or anger, or they

455

can be felt as pleasant sensations like excitement or sexual arousal. The physiological response underlying all these experiences is more or less the same. It involves activation of the sympathetic branch of the ANS. That is, a high, whether it is due to activating drugs, sexual arousal, fear, anger, or just plain happy excitement, involves the same basic physiological activation of the ANS. And the high can be produced in all sorts of ways, either voluntarily or involuntarily, intentionally or unintentionally.

The third thing has to do with <u>how</u> the stress response is <u>activated</u>. How does it get going? (Obtain some answers.) There are three kinds of basic experiences that automatically arouse the sympathetic response. These are loss of support, as in falling; sudden and loud noise; and intense local sensory experience usually called pain. That's why you get aroused and excited by loud music. There are three sensory experiences that tend to focus attention and thus support the Orienting Reflex. They are colour, motion, and sound. That's why explosions and riots get people excited. And there is one basic class of events that activates sympathetic arousal. It is change of any kind. Change of any kind in the world around us requires changes in what we do or adaptation. That's why Selye called the stress response the General Adaptation Syndrome. All any of us needs to do to become aroused is to expose him or herself to falling, loud noise, pain, colour, motion, sound, or change. We don't have to go to the expense and loss of freedom of doing drugs to achieve a high.

But while it is easy, even commonplace, to achieve a high or to become aroused, for the sake of health, comfort, and peace in life, we also need to be able to achieve calmness, rest, and a strong parasympathetic response. In fact, if we don't also master the art of achieving a parasympathetic response, we will not feel or enjoy fully the sympathetic arousal. So how can we learn to manage our sympathetic-stress-anxiety reactions? Few of us know how to do this partly because we have never learned how and partly because we have learned erroneous ways to use our body's functions.

The first and easiest way to manage our stress responses is through <u>relearning how to breathe</u>. Breathing patterns are not automatic. We

have learned how to breathe, and most of us have learned how to breathe wrongly. In the attempt to look beautiful while we were young, we all, males and females, have tried sucking in our stomachs to expand the apparent size of our chests. That has made it difficult for us to 'breathe into our stomachs' or to do healthy diaphragm breathing. Instead, we have tended to practice the art of breathing into our chests or chest breathing. This, in turn, has increased the ease and speed with which we become aroused, anxious, angry, or excitable. We ought to explain how breathing works before talking about how to manage breathing better.

Normal diaphragm breathing pulls the air in from the diaphragm muscle at the bottom of the lungs. It involves long, slow breaths. They are slow because the OUT-breath is about two or three times longer than the in-breath. When chest breathing begins, either by the habit of sucking the stomach in or under stress conditions, the expansion of the lung cavity is accomplished by expanding the chest. The rib cage is a rigid structure that will expand to a certain extent. But it will only contract the same amount as it has expanded. The result is that the OUT-breath is shortened to the same duration as the shallow in-breath. That means there are more breath cycles per minute. This, in turn, results in more oxygen getting into the system. In an emergency, the increased oxygen level getting into the bloodstream from the lungs is desirable. It increases the amount of oxygen to be metabolized with nutrients by the muscles to permit the muscles an extra level of energy with which to deal with the emergency. From the point of view of survival, that is helpful in case we need to fight or run away.

But we are seldom in real emergency situations calling for excess supplies of energy to deal with dangers. We now live in an engineered safe society with stout tiger-proof doors, railings to prevent falling from high places, and traffic lights to give all a fair chance at safe travel. There are no dangers other than those we manufacture for ourselves or for others. So if we practice chest breathing, for reasons of aesthetics or imagined danger, we increase the body's available energy without having anything to do with the energy except to 'stew

in our own juices'. The results are characteristic, commonplace, and uncomfortable.

The following are several effects:

(1) The increased oxygen available to the muscles lowers their metabolic threshold, increasing muscle tension and the subjective sense of being uptight.

(2) The increased blood oxygen poses a threat to the survival of brain cells. To protect them, a reflex constriction of the blood vessels in the brain is triggered by an oxygen receptor in the blood vessels. This reflex response results in a lessened volume of the highly oxygenated blood supply to the brain. That actually reduces the brain's oxygen supply. The resulting anoxia is experienced as dizziness, wooziness, or reduced efficiency of brain functioning. This sensation scares some people.

(3) Unlike the indefatigable smooth muscle of the diaphragm, the striate muscles of the chest wall react quickly to yank the chest open for chest breathing, but they also tire out quickly. Before long in chest breathing, the muscles fatigue and the person feels a tightness and/or pain in the chest and/or a sense that he or she cannot breathe easily. These symptoms, although nonsignificant, may be interpreted as heart trouble and may scare the person even more.

(4) The rapid passage of air through the throat tends to add to the natural stress reaction of dry mouth, so the person may start to swallow in the effort to moisten the mouth. But he or she is only swallowing air. A saliva bubble may then grow in the stomach from the swallowed air. At some point, the person may feel he or she can't swallow or breathe – due only to the balloon of air in the throat. This can scare the person even more.

(5) The shortened parasympathetically controlled OUT-breath affords less time for the steeper-gradient sympathetic response (controlling the in-breath) to be neutralized. This means that stress-anxiety grows with each breath. And each increase

in anxiety increases the stress response and increases the tendency to shallow chest breathing.

That's what we do to ourselves by doing shallow chest breathing. Of course, if we want a high, all we need to do is some shallow chest breathing. Why go for any more by way of expense? But if we are to enjoy that high instead of letting it pass by unnoticed, we had better learn how to have periods of calmness in between to permit a contrast experience. So how can we do that?

The simplest answer is to master the art of reinstituting diaphragm breathing from time to time by using long OUT-breaths. Now, we're sure you just heard us asking you to breathe deeply. Right? We did NOT say that. We said the absolute opposite. We have all been taught to breathe deeply. That is exactly the WRONG thing to do just about always. Instead, for about three or four bursts of three or four breath cycles, push the air OUT of your lungs for three or four or five times as long as the preceding in-breath. Do NOT interfere with the in-breath. Let it happen as it wants to. Just time it in your mind. Then make the following OUT-breath three or four or five times longer, to exhaust your lungs completely. Repeat this for three or four breaths, followed by three or four uninfluenced breaths. And repeat that sequence about three of four times. By the end of that time, you will feel a slight but significant reduction in your stress-anxiety-anger intensity, and the symptoms of hyperventilation noted above should disappear.

Incidentally, there are some things you should know about this corrective procedure for hyperventilation and for shallow chest breathing. The reason for not doing a dozen or more long OUT-breaths in a row is merely that the reflexive constriction of the brain's blood vessels is reversed slower than the reduction of the blood oxygen level. If you reduce the blood oxygen level quicker than the reflexive constriction response, you lower the oxygen level to the brain even further, and you may become more dizzy or faint. Next, by doing this corrective long OUT-breath procedure, you reinstate normal and healthy diaphragm breathing to some extent, and this

is all for the good. Next, you may notice you wheeze a bit during long OUT-breaths, which may lead you to feel you shouldn't do them or that you are having more trouble breathing. If it persists, consult a health professional. Mostly, you will notice it goes away and you can actually breathe easier. The wheezing is likely only because you had some bronchial constriction due to the preceding hyperventilation. That constriction should let go as you persist in your long OUT-breaths.

Notice that in what we have just said we are using the opposite (parasympathetically controlled OUT breath) response to compete with the stress-associated (sympathetically controlled in-breath) breathing response. To manage our stress reactions, we need to find various parasympathetic-associated responses to compete with and undo the sympathetic-associated responses involved in stress. There are quite a few of these parasympathetic-associated responses that can be used in addition to correcting the sympathetic chest-breathing response by using long OUT-breaths.

If we are prone to more than one or two bowel movements a day so that the bowel contents are fluid, we are creating stress for ourselves by requiring our rectal sphincters to be held tight closed (a sympathetically controlled response). Reducing the frequency until the bowel contents are firm permits the rectal sphincter to let go or relax (a parasympathetically controlled response). Also, general muscle relaxation is a parasympathetic-associated response that can moderate the sympathetic-stress-anxiety response. Indeed, if deep relaxation is paired repeatedly with images of anxiety stimuli, the result may become habitual nonanxiousness in those situations – systematic desensitization. Assertive (NOT aggressive) behaviour activates a parasympathetic response that can be used to counter anxiety. There are many other competing responses that can be used to manage stress.

Now all this might sound as though we are pushing some kinds of treatments for you to get involved in. We are not. We have a quite specific attitude about treatment. You only fix things that are wrong; and you only seek treatment for something you can't do by yourself.

We believe that the job of looking after you and your health is nobody else's business except your own. You are the only person who has to live with the illnesses you permit to affect you, and you are the only person who has any benefit from whatever you do to improve your health. To turn over the care for your health to anyone else – doctor, lawyer, medicine man, or chief – is both unrealistic and asks for every illness and associated cost you get. Nobody should be allowed to tell you what you ought to do or what ought to be done to you. Get information from experts, and get second and third opinions if you don't like the first information you get. Then go home and decide for yourself what you ought to do about your health. It is yours and only yours. You wouldn't think of letting a stove salesman decide FOR you which stove you ought to buy. Don't let us or any other health salesman, called doctor or nurse, tell you what health services you ought to buy. Make up your own mind. Practice consumerism in the health area too.

Block 2: Tools

We know that you really don't care all that much about your health. You have other more important priorities. So perhaps you would be interested in demonstrating to yourself that you are in good health with only an average amount of stress to undermine your future health. If so, we have an idea for you.

We all feel sick at times, and we all feel a certain amount of stress. Whenever those feelings occur, one way to show yourself how basically healthy and together you are is to graph the growth of improvement in your state. To do this, all you need to do is to make a set of cumulative graphing tables and use them. A graph of this kind just involves a series of vertical lines with markings all the way up to show the number of times something happens. The handout contains some sample graphs. On each graph, mark at the top what you are going to record on it. You could record anything on these graphs. For present purposes, what you might record are any

kinds of indications that you are getting better or any indicators of good health. Temperature coming down, pulse rate getting lower, sweat level getting drier, nausea feeling less, pain getting less – all might be good indicators of feeling better. Calm feelings in you, comfortable breathing, good energy level, good mood, laughing, telling jokes, friendly conversations, absence of pain – all might be good indicators of good health. Pick the indicators you want to use and, perhaps at hourly (or less or more) intervals, if the positive indicator were present during the last interval, put a mark at the next position on that day's vertical line. Each vertical line is for one day. At the end of the week, add together the number of marks for all the days and record that total number. You'll impress yourself with how well you are doing.

INDICATOR to Be Recorded: _____

No	Mon	Tue	Wed	Thu	Fri	Sat	Sun
34	-|	-|	-|	-|	-|	-|	-|
33	-|	-|	-|	-|	-|	-|	-|
32	-|	-|	-|	-|	-|	-|	-|
31	-|	-|	-|	-|	-|	-|	-|
30	-|	-|	-|	-|	-|	-|	-|
29	-|	-|	-|	-|	-|	-|	-|
28	-|	-|	-|	-|	-|	-|	-|
27	-|	-|	-|	-|	-|	-|	-|
26	-|	-|	-|	-|	-|	-|	-|
25	-|	-|	-|	-|	-|	-|	-|
24	-|	-|	-|	-|	-|	-|	-|
23	-|	-|	-|	-|	-|	-|	-|
22	-|	-|	-|	-|	-|	-|	-|
21	-|	-|	-|	-|	-|	-|	-|
20	-|	-|	-|	-|	-|	-|	-|
19	-|	-|	-|	-|	-|	-|	-|
18	-|	-|	-|	-|	-|	-|	-|

17	-|	-|	-|	-|	-|	-|	-|
16	-|	-|	-|	-|	-|	-|	-|
15	-|	-|	-|	-|	-|	-|	-|
14	-|	-|	-|	-|	-|	-|	-|
13	-|	-|	-|	-|	-|	-|	-|
12	-|	-|	-|	-|	-|	-|	-|
11	-|	-|	-|	-|	-|	-|	-|
10	-|	-|	-|	-|	-|	-|	-|
9	-|	-|	-|	-|	-|	-|	-|
8	-|	-|	-|	-|	-|	-|	-|
7	-|	-|	-|	-|	-|	-|	-|
6	-|	-|	-|	-|	-|	-|	-|
5	-|	-|	-|	-|	-|	-|	-|
4	-|	-|	-|	-|	-|	-|	-|
3	-|	-|	-|	-|	-|	-|	-|
2	-|	-|	-|	-|	-|	-|	-|
1	-|	-|	-|	-|	-|	-|	-|

TOTALS FOR EACH

DAY:____ ____ ____ ____ ____ ____ ____

WEEK: _____

What is this graphing procedure all about? The purpose is to help yourself to encourage your body to improve and maintain its health. There was a physician once who made a lot of money just teaching his patients to repeat to themselves, 'Every day, in every way, I'm getting better and better'. Do it.

Make as many different graphs for as many different indicators as you like. You can use this method to improve your school or work performance, your social skills, and anything else too. (Ogden Lindsley's Precision Learning method is adapted here.)

The next tool is going to make you think you are back in grammar school. It has to do with the body's need to use the energy is produces. Don't worry; we're not about to recommend an active exercise programme. At least one of us is opposed to any kind of exercise, considering it bad for one's health. However, you can still use the body's energies without actually doing anything very much. The founder of the Fitness Institutes in Toronto is reputed to have performed an experiment in physical fitness. People who wanted to take off weight and to increase their muscle development were assigned at random to two groups. One group practised an active exercise program every day. The other group stood for the same length of time as the exercise program each day, but all they did was actively imagine themselves doing the exercises. Both groups took off weight and increased their muscle development, and both to the same degree.

This story does not mean that one can expect to get good results by sitting around daydreaming about exercise or muscle use. The imagination needs to be an active imagination of the muscles doing the work. And the body needs to be held upright so the muscles are actually working. Now for the grammar school part. You can get some of the same benefits just from your posture – that is, how you hold yourself as you sit, stand, and walk. The taller you sit, stand, and walk, the more you extend your arms and legs, the more you balance your head in an upright position, the more you use your body's energies. Believe it or not, your teacher was right about your posture. Good posture is good for you. It does use the energy of the muscles, and it feels good.

But there's another side to that coin. Learning how to relax your body fully and using relaxation for one or more periods of time each day is also good for your body. Your ANS sympathetic nervous response is going to occur as you have to adapt to the many changes in what you are doing each day. The excess energy that is produced as a result of this fact needs to be used up for your health. But you also need to exercise the parasympathetic nervous response to give

the body and the immune system a rest. This is accomplished best by relaxation. Let's do an exercise in learning to relax.

Curl your toes up tight until you feel a sort of cramping sensation in the arches of your feet. That sensation locates from inside you the group of muscles we will refer to as the muscles of the arches of your feet. Now, ever so slowly, let your toes uncurl and feel what it feels like for those muscles to <u>be relaxing</u>. Try to remember what that sensation feels like because we are going to use that sensation. Now, raise your toes off the floor to flex your ankle. Keep it up until you can feel a tightness in the front of your shin and a stretching sensation in the calf of your leg. That locates the muscles of the lower leg from inside. Now, ever so slowly, let your toes come back to the floor, and pay attention to the sensations in your lower legs as the muscles relax. Try to retain the memory of those sensations.

Let's try a couple more muscle groups. Raise your shoulders up against the sides of your head. Feel the tightness in the upper surface of your shoulders. When you can feel that, slowly let your shoulders droop down, and pay attention to and remember the sensations of the muscles on the top of your shoulders relaxing. Cross your arms across your chest until you feel a tightness in your pectoral muscles. Then let the arms come back down to your sides, and notice and remember the sensations from the muscles in the front of your shoulders relaxing. Gently, try to touch your elbows together behind you, and note the tightness between your shoulder blades. Then let your arms return to your sides, and notice and remember the sensations of the muscles on the back of your shoulders relaxing. Clench your teeth tight together until you can feel tightness in the muscles of your jaw. These muscles are on your cheek just below your ears. When you have the sensation, let your jaw go, and feel and remember the sensations of your jaw muscles relaxing. All the muscle groups in the body have sensations associated with their tension and their relaxation. And you have felt them all many times in your life. So we will be satisfied for the moment with these brief reminders of where the muscles are and how they feel as they are relaxing.

Lie on your back on the floor. Prop a pillow or the back of a chair under your head in order to stretch the muscles at the back of your neck slightly. Lie with your feet slightly parted and your legs slightly bent out at the knees. Lay your arms at your sides, with the elbows bent just a little and your shoulders drooping.

Think about the muscles of the arches of your feet. Don't tighten anything now; just let the muscles relax. Imagine the sensations of muscle relaxation in the muscles of the arches of your feet occurring and going further and further and further. As you do, the sensations you'll have will be that your arches seem to come down until you feel sort of flat-footed. Let go the muscles of the arches of your feet loosely.

Let go of the muscles of the lower part of your legs. Imagine the sensations of muscle relaxation in the lower part of your legs occurring and going further and further and further. As you do, the sensations you'll have will be that your ankles feel loose and floppy. Let them go loosely.

Let go of the muscles of the upper surface of your upper legs. Imagine the sensations of muscle relaxation in the upper surface of your upper legs occurring and going further and further and further. As you do, the sensations you'll have will be that your seat seems to sink deeply into the floor. Let them go loosely.

Let go of the muscles on the inner surface of your upper legs. Imagine the sensations of the muscles between your legs relaxing. As you do, the sensation you'll have will be that your knees seem to roll apart on their sides. Let them go loosely.

Let go of the muscles on the surface underneath of your upper legs. Imagine the sensations of muscle relaxation in the undersurface of your upper legs occurring and going further and further and further. As you do, the sensations you'll have will be that your legs feel heavy all over, heavy and loose, heavy and limp. Heavy. Let go loosely.

Let go of the muscles of your back. Imagine the sensations of muscle relaxation in the small of your back occurring and going further and further and further. As you do, the sensations you'll have

will be that your back settles deeply down into the floor. Let your back muscles go loosely, sinking deeply, way down.

Give your fingers a stretch. Stretch them out a good one. Then let them go loosely.

Let go of the muscles of your arms. Imagine the sensations of muscle relaxation all up and down your arms occurring and going further and further. Don't do them now, but these include the muscles that bend your wrists in and out and the muscles that bend and straighten your elbows. Let them go loosely. As you do, the sensations you'll have will be that your arms feel loose and limp, resting deeply and heavily into the floor. Let them go loosely, sinking deeply.

Let go of the muscles of your shoulders. Imagine the sensations of muscle relaxation in the top, front, and back of your shoulders occurring and going further and further and further. As you do, the sensations you'll have will be that your shoulders droop down loosely and that your shoulders sink evenly and deeply into the floor. Let go loosely, drooping down loosely, resting back deeply. Let go of the muscles of your forehead. Gently push all thoughts and worries out of your mind for the present. There's lots of time to think later. Concentrate your attention only on the sensations of your body's muscles relaxing. Let your forehead become smooth and calm and relaxed.

Let your eyes rest lightly closed. Let your eyelids relax.

Let go of the muscles of your mouth and lips. Imagine the sensations of muscle relaxation in the muscles of your jaw occurring and going further and further and further. As you do, the sensations you'll have will be that your jaw droops down until there's a gap between your teeth. Let your jaw droop loosely.

Let go of the muscles of your lips. Let your lips become soft and puffy and relaxed.

Let your tongue rest loosely on the floor of your mouth. Let it go loosely, relaxed.

Let your whole body go limp, loose, and relaxed all over. Let yourself feel like a wet rag, limply draped on the floor. Let yourself feel like a great lead statue, resting heavily into the floor. Let yourself go.

(Allow a minute or so of silent relaxation. Then ask the participants to rouse themselves and to report how they felt. A few affirmations of calmness will do. Debrief the participants, since this method of muscle relaxation will be used later for purposes of systematic desensitization.) Notice that we talk in a slow way, paced roughly at the speed of out-breathing. This is NOT hypnosis. It used voluntary relaxation instructions. As you practice this skill, you may notice that relaxation skills advance in three stages. The first level of relaxation involves feeling pretty relaxed, as most of you felt just now. The second stage involves involuntary twitches, you know, of the kind you sometimes have just as you are falling asleep. These happen because your body is used to being fairly tense. It is unused to getting deeply relaxed. So it momentarily reinstates its tense state in a twitch or spasm. It only means you have become more deeply relaxed than you are used to being. The third stage involves loss of awareness of where some of your body parts are. For all you know, your arms are in Timbuktu and your legs are in China. We promise to go fetch them and return them if they take off on such a trip. This loss of awareness of your body parts occurs because you are so relaxed that the kinaesthetic muscle sensations that tell you what your body parts are doing are not working since your muscles are doing nothing. They are fully relaxed. We would be pleased for you if you could reach that third level of muscle relaxation when we use this skill later today.

The last self-help tool we want to talk about today is purpose. Having noticed causality mostly in the physical world, most of us are most familiar with initial or antecedent causes that work in the physical world. Initial causes are the kinds of things we usually think of as <u>the</u> causes of events. They occur before their effects or the things they cause. (Give examples.) But in the world of psychology, or the behavioural universe, which is the real place we all live, initial causes have almost no importance or effect at all. Nearly all the causes that act in our daily lives are final causes or the purposes or needs that we pursue. Final causes don't happen until <u>after</u> the effects they cause. (Give a few examples.) If we want good effects in our lives and in our health, all we need to do is to set out to achieve those purposes.

Purposes are decided on and designed by the person who has the purpose. Almost everything that happened to you in your life, you caused to happen. That does not mean that you set out with the conscious, or unconscious, intention to have everything happen as it did in your life. Everything we do has natural consequences. If you wanted to feel important or special, you did a number of things to achieve those final outcomes. Some of those things would have taken something from others or have made others feel less important or special. The natural consequences of that might well be that others did things to you that you didn't like. That is, we call down on ourselves the costs involved in achieving each of our purposes. Only 'nothing' is free of costs. However, whether or not we intend to acquire the costs we have to pay, we bring them on ourselves by acquiring the benefits we seek from our purposes. We could decide on the purpose of obtaining, having, and maintaining good health if we wanted to. How could we design our future health for ourselves without foregoing other things we might want to do? The answer can be found, the design made, and your future health reasonably assured. But you would have to take on the job of deciding on the purpose and designing your own future health. Only you can know what kinds of health you want and what other things you also want to pursue. All we can do is help you to find how to design that purpose, if you choose it. (Sketch in an overview of James's [1992] *The Secret of Creating Your Future* and reference the availability of his program tapes.)

Block 3: Therapeutics

(Wolpe's systematic desensitization [RIT] is used for standard anxiety stimuli involving health and feeling good. The same relaxation method is used as that outlined above. The relaxation effect is amplified by additional use of lateral eye tracking back and forth across the picture being imagined. A sample of the stimuli employed is shown below.)

Picture yourself feeling as if you had a cold or the flu coming on. Then check your body over, and notice that you feel pretty calm and well.

Picture yourself experiencing some pain in your body. Check your body over, and notice that the pain is slowly subsiding and you are feeling better.

Picture yourself being told by your doctor that you have a disease that can be cured by means of medication. Check your body, and notice that it feels calm and better than it did.

Picture yourself being told by your doctor that you have a disease that cannot be cured. Check your body over, and notice that it feels calm and better than it felt before.

Picture yourself lying in a hospital bed, feeling very ill. Then check your body over, and notice that you feel calm, comfortable, and better than you felt a few moments earlier.

Picture yourself at home on a muggy, humid day. Check yourself over, and notice your body is comfortable, relaxed, and at ease.

Block 4: Consolidation

(This is further exposure to James's health beliefs review from *The Secret of Creating Your Future*. Beliefs concerning personal destiny, genetic inheritance, expected outcomes, longevity, and the like are elicited from participants and subjected to scrutiny and analysis of the linguistics involved. For a sample of beliefs, necessity is challenged. Assumptions concerning the nature of causality adopted by participants are reviewed, and the predominant role of final cause (purpose) in human life is affirmed. The role of the brain in regulating everything in the body (and in life) is stated, followed by instruction in the (verbal and imagery) means by which the brain's activities are regulated. Participants are then asked to design specific health goals for themselves and to use standard planning methods to achieve those goals.)

(Additional relaxation, coupled with further brief systematic desensitization for health-related images is undertaken. In this part of the programme, the stimuli employed include pervasive environmental stimuli commonly associated with malaise [humidity, temperature, social isolation] and proprioceptive sensations [joint pain, headache] as the targets for desensitization.)

(Do a summary and cuing observations for the day's learnings.)

Treatment 8: Creating HAPPINESS

The main target in this program is to counter the various types of depressions that underlie much addictive behaviour. Alcoholism has long been linked to anxieties by virtue of its tranquillizing effects. Depressions are almost more central to addictions, although in much more complicated ways.

Anhedonic depressions (Axis 13, occurring most commonly among introverts and obsessives) create a need for feelings and aliveness that can be generated artificially by the rush or buzz from some chemicals. Reactive depressions (Axis 03, from energizing difficulties arising from depletion of stress resources) create a sense of pressure that can be relieved by soporific and mellowing chemicals. Somatic depressions (Axis 53, activating and reacting to dependent states, panic, or immune problems such as allergies) interact with contemporary reliance on chemical 'treatments' to foster dependency on some chemicals. Temperamental depressions (depressed mood) are almost automatically viewed these days as being most appropriately treated by (self-) medication.

The felt depression provides the motivation to seek relief. And the relief achieved through the chemical functions as the reinforcement to perpetuate both the avoidance activity (seeking relief) and the depression (the response necessary to seek and obtain relief). This program assumes that if a fairly continuous happy, lively, and calm state can be achieved, the felt need for relief from depressions might no longer exist.

Block 1: Orientation

Who has never experienced a period of depression? Congratulations! So you have all had a chance to develop some expertise in today's topic. It is 'How to Become (and Stay) Depressed'. How did you do it? (Allow some affirmations that it happened <u>to</u> them.) OK, so who feels at least moderately depressed right now – that is, other than the natural reaction to hearing us ask such a silly question as, How did you do it? Is anybody willing to expose his/her depression in this group? (If not, play the game between the presenters.)

Where did your depression come from? How do you experience it? It never comes from events of the past. Those events of the past that we ruminate about when we are depressed are not the causes of anything. The first thing we need to know about being depressed is that the depressed mood comes <u>before</u> the thoughts about the past. The thoughts about the depressing past serve three purposes. First, they make us feel better by finding what we think of as the 'causes' of our depressed mood. Actually they are just excuses for it. Hold it! Are we suggesting that the unhappy events of the past didn't happen or don't justify our awful feelings? No, we are not. We'll come back to that. Second, they allow us to feel more depressed for a longer period of time by bringing unpleasant feelings from the past to amplify and, through thought, extend the felt depression. Hold it! Are we suggesting that you want to feel depressed and to amplify and extend the depression? Not exactly. But we'll come back to this. Third, the bitterness, even anger, we feel about those past events allows us to avoid feeling angry (and thus energized) NOW since there is little that we can do now about those past events. Hold it! Are we saying that depression serves a useful purpose? Not entirely. But we'll come to the purposes it serves next.

Our next question is, What do you gain from being depressed?

Not a thing, right? It's an awful experience with no benefits at all to it. Did you ever notice that while you may hate it when they do, you expect other people to notice when you're depressed? In fact,

472

since we feel so helpless when we're depressed, we expect, or at least hope, that someone will do something to help us get undepressed. In fact, don't you sometimes feel just a little bit important when you are depressed? After all, who else has had to put up with the unhappy events of your past and your present nasty feelings? It is interesting that the main gain we get from fear is the justification we get from it for avoiding situations; and the main gain we get from depression is the justification we have for being looked after by others and the sense of importance we get from others' caring for us.

Now let's go back to the things we were not saying before. The thinking about unhappy events of the past is done partly to justify the expectation that others will 'make up' to us for the past. The intensification and extension of the depression that comes from thinking about the past increases the apparent depth of the depression, and that increases the demand on others to help. And the avoidance of anger in the present both prevents anger at those around on whom we depend to make us feel better and provides a distraction to no-longer-existing (or manageable) things to carry the anger helplessly. OK, go ahead and be angry at those awful and outrageous statements we just made. If you can, you might even find your mood lifting right now.

You see, not all, but just about every kind of depression is a result of ways we use to prevent anger from being felt. There are some noteworthy exceptions to this principle, but not many. The behavioural symptoms of depression mostly involve actions that impede the expression of anger or of the body's energies. Let's play a game and make ourselves depressed. All you need to do is to stare downwards and into space (allowing thoughts to take over and keeping you from noticing present events that might arouse feelings or actions), slump your body towards its own centre of gravity (making you feel de-energized, heavy, and having to work just to stand up), wrinkle the forehead heavily (to enhance the occurrences of unhappy thoughts), turn down the corners of the mouth (to communicate sadness), and move very slowly and heavily (to prevent use of much energy). Try it. It's fun. You can probably even increase the depression by tightening the rectal sphincter as though you were trying to be constipated.

473

It's interesting that depression also increases people's impulsiveness. The reason seems to be that they are not as concerned with future thoughts, so future consequences do not control behaviour as much as they ordinarily do. Also, it feels as though nothing can be worse than the feelings right now, so the future seems as though it doesn't matter all that much. The thoughts that occur in depression are mainly unhappy ones from the past. By way of contrast, anxiety focuses us on the future and anticipates the dangers it may hold. That is, in our business, the past is depressing, the future is scary, and the present is fun.

Essentially, the symptoms of depression express a need to depend on other people – a dependency need. In order not to prevent others from allowing dependency on them, the depressed person tends to hold back on anger in the present for fear it will interfere with reliance on others. So the symptoms of depression are merely means by which we prevent energy or anger expression. Fatigue (increased by sleep disorder), lack of energy, depressed mood, increased thought pressure, and a sense of helplessness (and crying for help) are all defensive means to suppress energy use.

But why are we on about depression? Surely the topic was one of creating happiness. It's not a bad idea to know and understand any enemy that stands in our way. If we are to create happiness, we first need to understand how we create unhappiness, sadness, or depression. That's right. We now need to return to our initial question: How do we make ourselves depressed? or How do we do depression? The answer to such a question differs from person to person. So we have to explain briefly some of the ways we do it.

Introverted people think a lot. Thinking competes or interferes with feelings and with actions. The more we think, the less we feel. The more we think, the less active we are. As a result of their thinking, introverted people experience less intense feelings than others, which is comforting in a way, but that leaves the person feeling joyless and empty. As a result of their thinking, introverted people use less of the energy their bodies produce, which may feel efficient, but it then increases depression. The introversion and depression together may

impede use of the body's energies to the point that the person feels constantly frustrated or blocked, so rage may develop as a means to try desperately to get out of the resulting self-imposed inhibitions, rules, and other restraints.

Some people have learned that it's not nice to be angry. They may come to think of anger as a hurtful motivation that ought to be controlled. The controls they develop in themselves inhibit the use of energy, for fear that someone is hurt or harm is done. Such people try to be nice. The pleasant reactions of others to their controls and niceness serve as rewards to increase their reliance on others as a source of pleasure and reassurance. In turn, this enhances their dependency. They are then doubly prone to sadness and depression, as a dependency response and as a means to inhibit the expression of anger.

Some people have learned to fear emotional closeness to others for fear they may be rejected and feel hurt. They may find ways to hold themselves aloof, at a psychological distance from others, so they don't risk emotional commitment. Most of these ways have a kind of hostile flavour to them, which does keep others at an emotional distance. To justify their hostility towards others and their sense of despair about finding friends who 'can be trusted', they often ruminate about the mistreatment they have received in the past from others. Whether imagined or real, the purpose of the ruminations seems to be to remain conscious of the imagined ill-will of others and to perpetuate aloofness. The thinking, coupled with the ruminations about past unhappiness, creates a bitter kind of depression that views the world in hopeless terms.

These are only some of the ways depressions form themselves out of the pre-existing approaches to life that people adopt. And unfortunately, an angry person lives in an angry world; a depressed person lives in a depressing world. The world we live in is a mirror of ourselves. That is, the world we live in is one created by ourselves and not the reverse.

Although we accept as axiomatic that we are always wrong, we have developed the crazy idea that you might prefer to be happy

throughout your life and that you might prefer not to get yourself depressed. If, by some miracle, on this occasion we happened to be right about you, it might be worthwhile for you to learn how to be happy, even joyful, and even all the time.

Block 2: Tools

If you wanted to be happy, the first thing to do might be to discover just how you depress yourself. You see, we're from a temporary employment agency, and you have hired us to take on a job of work for you while you're taking a vacation. In this case, since you surely would not want your depression to go untended while you are taking a holiday from it, you are going to have to teach us how to do your depression thing. And you should know that we are very conscientious employees. We want to be sure that we do our job right while you are on vacation. So who would like to take on the job of teaching us how to be depressed just like you are (or have been)? (If nobody is willing to do the teaching, the presenters play the game of teaching by one of the other. Be very careful and critical of the effects on the learner of doing the various suggested ways of getting depressed. Seek self-talk, actions, images, and the like that might be involved in creating the depressed mood. When techniques work, the learner acknowledges the extent to which they have the desired effects.) So it just may be that you could discover just how you depress yourself. (This is NLP/James's Modelling Behaviour procedure.) We'll return to this later.

The next tool is one you might like to keep using for the rest of your life. Write down some qualities of yourself you might like to have in greater measure. Include *Happy* and *Outgoing* in your list. Two or three qualities will do for now. Under each of these qualities, write down at least a half a dozen behaviours that you can actually observe that you might see in another person who you believe has each quality in large quantity.

476

You might want to notice that happy people tend to smile, to move in a light and quick way, to focus their eyes on people and things around them, to comment on nice things happening or being said, to turn the inflections in their voices upwards at the end of sentences, to express positive feelings about all sorts of things, and the like. You might want to notice that outgoing people tend to approach other people, to smile at others, to talk freely in groups, to start conversations, to ask others about their pleasant recent experiences, to listen attentively to what others say and to reflect the positive feelings in what they hear, and the like. If these are some of the kinds of observable things that you believe happy or outgoing people do, then include them in your list. If you disagree, list your own views of what such people habitually do that demonstrates to you that they are happy or outgoing.

Now, here's how to use your lists to become a happy person fairly continuously. Each morning, take a moment to read over the list of behaviours you have just made. This is to remind you about what you are watching for all day. Go about your life. Don't make any effort to do any of the behaviours on your lists. Just pay attention to what you are doing to ensure that you notice each and every occurrence of any approximation to a behaviour on your lists. As soon as each occurrence happens, reward yourself with praise and a mental pat on the back. (Use the example for *Outgoing* cited under the third method of Therapeutics for Treatment 2: Creating Flexibility to explain how this might be done.) The important thing about this method is that you must be easy about accepting an action of yours as an occurrence of the behaviour from your lists. And you must notice and reward yourself for it by being pleased with yourself. (This is Personal Development Goals procedure.)

How does this work? Surely, I'll only act one of those ways if I am either happy or outgoing. Not true. We know, it sounds right that I act in a certain way because I first feel that way. The reverse is more true. The actions occur first. The brain becomes aware of the actions on its internal proprioceptive senses. Then the brain experiences the feelings. It is more true that I am happy because I laugh than that I

laugh because I'm happy. But each single bit of behaviour, by itself, does not create the feeling or experience. There are many actions involved in each feeling. That's why it was necessary to list several different behaviours for each of the qualities you want to achieve.

Because actions are relatively mutually consistent with one another, all we need to do is to increase the habit strength to do each separate action, and the whole bunch eventually come together to have the desired result. But you don't want to force the actions by acts of conscious will. If you do, you will learn how to force the states you are seeking. They will occur only in parts, and the whole experience will feel rather artificial. Instead, just wait for each separate action to occur, with your awareness primed to notice it, and then reward its automatic occurrence. Although you handle each behaviour separately, they will increasingly occur together with other related behaviours fairly continuously and with a good sense of 'real' experiences.

The next exercise you might want to do every day involves assertiveness. Remember that depression involves inhibiting the use of the body's energies. Similarly, happiness involves the lively use of the body's energies – being perky and alive, as well as doing active things. Assertive training is concerned with using ways to employ the body's energies. There are all sorts of ways to assert yourself. Assertiveness is neither aggressiveness nor underassertiveness. Assertiveness lies somewhere in between those two extremes. Let's think of it this way:

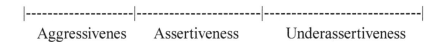

|--------------------|----------------------|----------------------------|
Aggressivenes   Assertiveness   Underassertiveness

Assertiveness involves the comfortable use of the body's energy. Underassertiveness involves a fear of getting too angry or of risking hurting others. To avoid that, the person holds back from expressing feelings, especially angry ones. One of the problems with that is that the person may become depressed. Another problem is that the fear of getting angry increases the person's level of arousal,

perhaps to overwhelm controls, perhaps to result in angry outbursts. That is, aggressiveness is largely a reaction to the arousal of fear of anger, such that the arousal adds to the felt anger, possibly overriding controls. If we could get comfortable with strong feelings such as anger, we might get rid of both underassertiveness (with its risk of depression) and aggressiveness.

But anger is surely universally accepted as a 'bad' thing. Surely it is harmful and ought to be avoided. We would not want to contradict any beliefs you might hold in this matter. However, it may not be anger that is risky, but rather aggressiveness. We would like you to consider this idea for yourself.

Picture a test tube. Into this test tube, we're going to pour all your body's energies to measure their amount up the side of the container. The raw amount of your basic energy probably does not differ too much from that of anybody else.

But a strange thing happened across the years. You were feeling energetic, rushing about the house and having fun. Your parent anxiously warned you to stop running around, to slow down a bit, and to be more careful. You didn't understand that the parent was worried about knocking over precious trinkets and breaking family property. All you knew was that you were feeling energetic and having fun. Is something wrong with energy?

You were feeling energetic, so you raised your voice while talking. Your parent boomed, 'Don't you raise your voice to me!' Is something wrong with energy?

You were sitting class, feeling energetic and restless. The teacher snapped at you, 'Sit still and pay attention!' You still didn't understand that attention was important to learning. Was there something wrong with energy?

You were having fun wrestling with or swinging around one of your friends. Your parent warned you anxiously to simmer down a bit. You didn't understand that your parent was worried about how the friend's parents might react if the friend was hurt. Something must be wrong with energy.

Each of these kinds of repeating experiences aroused some anxiousness in you that, over time, was learned to be associated with the events or circumstances (in this case feeling energetic) of the time. Let's represent that learned increase in anxiety associated with energy as a kind of sticky substance poured into the test tube over the energy, increasing the amount of the experience involved. It is sticky because the fear experience is supposed to help control or inhibit overexuberance and the use of our abundant energies.

Now, later in life, when you feel energetic, you feel the energy and all the other feelings that have habitually come to be associated with it. That increased amount of feeling, comprised of two different kinds of components, produces a new experience. If the experience of the increased feeling is that of the anxiety part, the sensation is one of being uptight or tense. If the experience is that of the sticky 'corking' effect of the anxiety part, the sensation is of control or inhibition (or confinement). If the experience is that of the energy part, the sensation is one of anger – that is, energy with the bitter taste of anxiety.

If we were to view anger in this way, it may just be that we would come to some conclusions about it that are different from those we reached as children. For example, we might even conclude that anger is a good thing – the feeling associated with the evocation of energy modulated by the process of socialization. It might even be worth remarking that what keeps people living together in social groups (society) is the mutual exchange with each other of energy – each doing the kind of thing he or she is best suited to or is willing to contribute to the common good.

The problem is that anger, if overcontrolled, can be released periodically in aggressive behaviour. And aggressiveness may be the problem. If energy is used comfortably in assertive ways, it might serve only the common good. In case you decide to see it that way, it would be well to learn how to be assertive. (Refer to the Tools section of Treatment 6: Creating Innocence for a method to teach Assertiveness. In addition, use Wolpe's method for in vivo Assertive training as appearing in the Therapeutics section of Treatment 4: Creating Satisfaction.)

Block 3: Therapeutics

(Get participants to pair off. Allow about five minutes for each member of each pair to teach the other how to be depressed. Ask for feedback about the success achieved by the teacher in showing how it is done and by the learner in acquiring a depressed mood. Emphasize the fact that different people depress themselves in different ways, and the need for the teacher to know how he/she accomplishes depression – knowledge that needs to be expressed in words so it can be remembered by the teacher. Get each person to make notes as a reminder about how he/she depresses him/herself. Administer a brief Values test for areas of living such as feelings, relationships, and/or work. Our test is constructed such that reflexive values tend to appear in the right-hand column of each page and conflicted or avoidance values are marked with a dot [period]. The test requests that all listed values in each area of living that are viewed as important be checked and then the checked values ranked for their importance. Then respondents count the relative numbers of checks they have made for reflexive [right-column entries], conflicted [dot], and nonconflicted [no-dot] items. This allows them to discover the roles of these three kinds of values in their higher priority [high ranked] values.)

The purpose of the test is to discover if the values to which we subscribe contribute to depression or interfere with happiness. In general, reflexive values, which depend on others for fulfilment (e.g., recognition, appreciation), foster dependency. They thus enhance the risk of depression and/or felt lack of being fulfilled in life. Conflicted values, where one tends to notice, and even be vigilant for, occurrences of the negative or unpleasant pole (e.g., Not in danger, mistrust), even if stated in terms of the positive pole (e.g., security, trust), create and maintain constant stress and strain, focus the person on unpleasant or feared events, and do not contribute to happy or joyful living. In contrast, approach values contribute to happy and joyful living, especially if they are active (as opposed to reflexive) values. (These distinctions are made after participants have completed the test. Participants are asked [with whatever help they

require] to identify one of two conflicted and one or two reflexive values that are of paramount importance to them. Two exercises are undertaken. One seeks to change the relative position of one or two reflexive values in each person's rank order of his/her values. The attempt is made to bring their importance down in the rank order and to elevate the rank order of one or two more active [left-hand column] values. The method is described under Therapeutics in Treatment 5: Creating Values taken from James and Woodsmall, 1987.)

(The other exercise seeks to rid the person of vigilant distress associated with one or two of the conflicted [dot] values, as it were to remove their negative or conflicted effects on the person. The method used is described under Therapeutics in Treatment 5: Creating Values, also from James and Woodsmall, 1987.)

Block 4: Consolidation

(Although focusing particularly on the substance of the present programme's activities, and although referencing happiness as the purpose, the consolidation part of this program is equivalent to the Consolidation section in Treatment 3: Creating Excitement. The methods used are reviewed and summarized with cuing suggestions.)

Treatment 9: Creating INTEGRATION

The main target of this program concerns several aspects of personal integration and consolidation. It is concerned with the consolidation of learning and integration of new habits in the person's habit-family hierarchy that might serve to counter addictions. It is concerned with the person's personal sense of integration or of 'being together'. It is concerned with the person's integration in social groups and in society generally. It is concerned with the individual's personal contribution to him or herself and to others that, in the long run, might be best expected to consolidate any learnings achieved. It is as paradoxical in its message as any of the other treatments. It

seeks to integrate and consolidate a host of factors in the person while at the same time enhancing his/her sense of personal freedom and entrepreneurial initiative. In these ways, it is at once the most general and the most summary of the programmes.

Block 1: Orientation:

Most of you know us from other types of contacts we have shared. You all know that we are crazy. However, you ain't seen nothing yet. If you think you are making any sense out of what we're going to do today, we suggest that you simply assume that you are getting it wrong. Better still, you might explain it to us, since we haven't a clue what we're doing. In fact, today we're going to try to talk to your unconscious. While what we say may sound as though it means something to your conscious awareness, we are probably really talking at another level altogether. But bear with us if you can. We actually have quite a clear idea about what we're trying to do and how to do it. With that hopefully confusing introduction, let's proceed.

What we want to do today is to help your minds to use any kinds of learning or experience to serve you best in daily living. Strangely, this is NOT done best by means of understanding things consciously. It is done best by means of automatic responses that have been built into you over the years of growing up. In fact, conscious understanding of events may actually interfere with the general useability of information and experience. What happens is that our conscious understandings help us to orient ourselves in the particular situations to which conscious experience applies, whether or not the situations involved are specific or general. We have another level of functioning – call it unconscious, unaware, or automatic, or spirit if you like – that is concerned with our survival and happiness. That is the level at which we want to work today, if you will let us.

Unfortunately, for most of us, this other, let's call it unconscious, level has been tuned across the years to force us to AVOID fearsome,

worrisome, or awful events that, as children, we came to believe pervade the world. Actually, we live in a carefully engineered safe society in which there is really nothing at all to fear as long as we abide by some fairly simple and obvious means to regulate our behaviours. If this was a program concerned with criminality, we would call those means to regulate our behaviours rules just to get your backs up. In this programme, we are going to call them guides, just to get your backs up. Actually, they are just ordinary bits of obvious common sense, like walking on sidewalks rather than on roads in front of cars or waiting your turn at stop signs and traffic lights. We know, that sort of thing is offensive to you since you are too special to have to do what everybody else has to do. But we aren't going to bother with that sort of thing today.

The other programs in this treatment series tried to get around or through some of the troubling things of our histories that made our guides feel oppressive or offensive, and that turned our unconscious minds to react to life by AVOIDING it. Today's program assumes that we have come to grips with some of that AVOIDING stuff and that we are ready to advance to broader sunlit pastures, as Sir Winston Churchill expressed it. To do that, we need to address a whole bunch of tiny and important things.

Let's start with our insides. In a way, our brains are like computers. Actually, of course, it's computers that are in some ways like our brains. But let's talk about it the other way around. Computers enter the words and other things we put into them in a kind of temporary buffer memory that we can see on the screen. The experience entered into this temporary buffer can be examined and even changed to suit our conscious ideas and wishes. After a while, when we have had time to examine, check, and change those things on the screen, we may decide that it's OK, and we save the information. When we ask the computer to save the information on the screen, it goes into permanent memory, and it is stored in whatever places on the hard drive that the COMPUTER decides is right for IT. Our brain is constructed even better than that. It decides WHEN, WHERE, and HOW the information we have in our conscious minds ought to be

stored in our unconscious minds. This is important to each of you, so bear with us while we explain.

WHEN is information stored? This is the least important bit of knowledge, partly because we can't do much about it. However, it is stored in two stages. Conscious information waits in consciousness for about forty-two hours or two days. There it can be checked and reviewed. This first forty-eight hours is important because if we let the information we have in recent memory mean or signal danger, fear, unhappiness, anger, or other kinds of negative emotions, when it goes into medium-term memory storage, it gets coded or entered into the unpleasant or danger-signalling parts of memory, where it will later be accessed first and assigned first priority. The trouble is that, AT THE TIME, the danger parts of anything ARE assigned special importance by us. It's lucky that the first stage of storage is delayed for forty-eight hours, allowing us to use good sense after we are out of any given situation while thinking about it to look around and orient ourselves towards the positive and happy and rewarding aspects of each of life's events. Other programs in this series tried to teach how to do that. It is to our advantage to store in memory the positive and happy aspects of any event. And in the forty-eight-hour short-to-medium-term storage, each event will be coded and stored with other events and reactions that have a similar emotional or feeling tone. Let's set up our habits in the ways that serve our lives best. That is, rethink recent events in the most positive light you can find.

Medium-term, forty-eight-hour memory is stored as unintegrated, isolated events, coded mainly for their emotional tone. Such memories wait in medium-term memory, being checked against the rest of our personality and habits WITHOUT OUR BEING AWARE OF IT. About six weeks after the event, experience, or learning, the brain automatically stores the surviving aspects of the event in long-term memory. And it stores it there in such a way as to make it most completely related to and integrated with the rest of our personality. Actually, it doesn't do that all at once. It may take several tries, each about six weeks apart, to reintegrate the new learning with the rest of the learnings in the personality. We may even feel a bit 'shook

up' and troubled during each of these six-week reintegration periods involving important and widespread learnings or experiences. Important ones are likely to include major therapeutic changes or the results of experienced trauma. The main thing to notice about this, since we can't do much about its unconscious operations, is to remember that quite often, when we feel shook up and troubled, even for up to a couple of weeks at a time, it may simply be because our minds are consolidating or integrating important things into our personalities. And that's a great thing to have happening! It means we are growing in important ways that will affect our futures. That is, we are forming important parts of our personalities, so our experiences were NOT unimportant or meaningless after all. In fact, if we do our jobs well today, you may feel shook up and troubled for short periods of time – six weeks, twelve weeks, eighteen weeks, and perhaps twenty-four weeks from today. Wouldn't that be fun!

WHERE and HOW the memories are stored has been implied in what we have already said. And they represent the important parts of what we have already said. The WHERE is given by the emotional or feeling tone we adopt during the first forty-eight hours after an event. If we view the event with sadness or fear or anger, it will be stored in the AVOID area. We try to direct most therapeutic stuff to that area in order to fix that area's memories and images. It was partly for that reason that we started off as we did today. You would be well advised to think about ALL <u>OTHER</u> kinds of experiences in a positive and happy way, at least finding the 'silver lining for each cloud', if only to ensure for yourself a large supply of positive memories and personality elements to help you have a happy and enjoyable life.

The HOW is given by how you handle each experience in life. You have time during the first forty-eight hours to find and focus on the positive aspects of each experience so it is stored in the most rewarding places. You have a chance to make sure that you get perspective on each unpleasant situation to get the best out of it during that first forty-eight hours. And you have a chance to reinterpret unexplained uncomfortable feelings you have, even if they last up

486

to two weeks, as desirable and promising events involving only the healthy integration in your personality of new learnings that are challenging some of the old and painful learnings of your past. Enjoy disruption! It may be GOOD FOR YOU!

Block 2: Tools

Now let's move outside our bodies. Look around you. We live in a social world, don't we, with all sorts of other people around us and interacting with us. When we were infants and children, those around us came to us, brought what we needed to us, and looked after us. Most of us got the idea that we were pretty important with everybody we knew clucking and fawning over us. We liked that way of having things, and we'll be damned if it is going to stop happening that way. Though people have stopped acting that way towards us now that we're grown up, we keep acting as though that was the ONLY right way to have things. And if things aren't the way they are supposed to be, we'll do our best to achieve that happy and comfortable state of helpless dependency as often as we think it ought to exist – that is, all the time. Oops! We've just described the state we all seek in addictive behaviour.

Funny, though! When we were children, we used to think how great it would be to be all grown up, free to choose what to do and how to do it, and in charge of our own lives. Now that we have reached that important and much-to-be-desired state of being, we act as though we want to be children again. Do we? Of course we do! And of course we don't! That's in the nature of conflict – to want and not to want at the same time. Actually, what we want is to have EVERYTHING even if the various things we want are totally incompatible and even if we know it. There's a saying about this: 'I want to eat my cake and have it too.' Too bad! As we are fully aware, it doesn't work like that. So how can we 'eat our cake and have it too'? It ain't all that difficult to do, if we plan it right.

The trouble is that we have tended to plan things in ways that don't work. We do that not because we're stupid but because we set up most of our strategies for doing things when we were children. And children are NOT well known for their experience, wisdom, and understanding of life. If you'll pardon the expression, we got things ass-backwards. We decided to be children who grew up. Unfortunately, it doesn't work that way, and it keeps us forever in conflict within ourselves. What we would suggest as an alternative adult approach is to be grown-up children. Now what the hell does that mean? Who knows? We just made that up.

Let's look at someone sitting near us. Just pick anybody you want to look at, and look at him/her. It doesn't matter what part or aspect of the other you look at since you're not looking at him/her to interact with him/her; just to look at him/her. Hey, get your minds out of the gutter, and rejoin us in this garbage! Think of this. The person you're looking at is IN FACT A GROWN-UP. He/she is NOT a child. You can see that. Somebody is probably, in turn, looking at you. He/she also sees a grown-up person. Keep looking at others around you, and let what you can see of each one impress itself on your mind, showing you definitely that each one is a grown-up person and that each one, in looking at you, sees a grown-up person. OK, so we're all grown-ups. So what? IF that is true, then we had better, for the sake of not-particularly-unpleasant reality, think of ourselves as grown-ups. Of course, you KNOW you're a grown-up. Why make such a thing of it? The reason is because we all have a whole lot of redoing of our habits to do – habits that were formed and strengthened all through our years of growing up. And we're asking you to change those well-entrenched habits in a few moments here and now. Don't worry, we won't forget about our other domain.

So your PRIMARY IDENTITY <u>NOW</u> is as a GROWN-UP, right? Hey, you've arrived where you always wanted to be – a GROWN-UP. But we would all like to be children too. OK, so let's ADD that to our identities. For this purpose, close your eyes and go for a few moments into yourself. Think about it. On the outside, the body you have is grown up, with all the advantages that come from that source. On the

inside, that is your personality and the way you feel, is still that of a child. You still have the wonderment and fascination of the child; you still have the light-hearted, happy, and contented feelings of a child; and you still have the needs for others and for their love that you had as a child. PLEASE try to focus on those parts or aspects of being a child.

We know, you're having a hard time getting past your unsatisfied needs for attention, importance, and recognition; you're having trouble not noticing the helplessness, pain, and mistreatment that you felt as a child; and you just can't seem to stop paying attention to the fears and anger you felt about those big people around you who were supposed (by you) to know better but didn't. Don't try to stop yourself from attention to those things, if you must. We know you can't do a 'not do'. But simply wait through those things and gently try to come back to the other happier things such as the wonderment and fascination; the light-hearted, happy, and content feelings; and the needs for others and for their love that were also a part of childhood. Take your time. You need to find those parts of the child in you too.

If you can be a grown-up first, as you are, but with all those nice parts of being children inside you, you can be a grown-up child. And that was the first part of what we wanted you to experience today so that you could practice that way of being every day, as the first of our self-help tools for a better life for today. But there are others to work on too.

You know, we DO spend a lot of time thinking and reviewing our lives every day. We've just suggested two profitable ways to approach that thinking and self-observation, namely, making sure we find and focus on the positive aspects of each experience (the silver lining to every cloud) at least during the first forty-eight hours after each event and noticing our own and others' grown-up states while focusing within on the positive aspects and values of our childhood lives. The purposes of doing those things are to enhance the happiness and good feelings embedded in our personalities to serve our futures well and to construct for ourselves happy and healthy identities, free

of conflicts. But in both of these aims, our purpose is to learn for ourselves to benefit ourselves.

Learning is something else we could profitably learn to do better than we learned to do it as children. We often even got the strategies of how to learn wrong. Those who taught us didn't teach us how to learn. Most of us think that learning involves getting an idea in memory and understanding it. That's school learning. It has little to do with us or with living. That is learning of things OTHER PEOPLE want us to know. As grown-ups, we ought to be able to choose for ourselves what we will learn and benefit for ourselves from our learning. Let's do that.

If YOU want to learn anything FOR YOU, don't copy the information down for later review. That just tells you what we or someone else thinks you ought to know. Phooey! Write down either (a) the outcome you want to achieve FOR YOU or (b) the things YOU want to DO more of FOR YOU. If you write down the OUTCOME you want for you, the strategy to use to achieve that OUTCOME is a purpose-oriented or goal-oriented strategy. Our Goal-finding program will help you to make that strategy work for you so you can achieve the OUTCOMES you seek at any time in life. We will come back to one kind of outcome later. If you write down what YOU want to DO more of FOR YOU, then the strategy for achieving more of that kind of DOING FOR YOU is for YOU to take on the job of REWARDING YOURSELF for doing it. We're going to look at how to reward yourself in a moment. But first, just a comment about how this relates to the last exercise.

You're grown-up on the outside, right? Grown-ups DO things on the outside. That's part of being grown up. Every time you prepare for learning by writing down something you want to DO, you're exercising your grown-up side. But you're making it happen by rewarding yourself with the kinds of things you want – your inner child aspect. Inside we're all children, full of light-hearted happiness, wonderment, and fascination and needs for other people. Children want results or outcomes to happen, right? Every time you prepare for learning by writing down an OUTCOME or goal, you're expressing

your inner child. But you'll find that the only way to make things happen the way we want them to is to DO specifiable kinds of things to make them happen – your outside grown-up aspect. You can be both, but always starting with the realization that you are now grown up.

So how to learn to DO something – a skill or a way of being? First, as we said, you need to write down what it is you want to do. Hey, you can do anything you want to do, right? If so, how come we are all so unsuccessful in making the friends, getting the jobs, and acquiring personal property that we always wanted? Come on, let's be real with ourselves. We know, those are outcomes and not what we DO. Oh yeah? We all know that's not right, we hope. Now, here's a funny thing about that. We actually all do know one kind of thing we have all set out to DO. We all know what we want to do, or have to do, to DO the addictive acts to get a high. The trouble is that most of us don't know what ELSE we might want to DO. How about talking to others comfortably; how about making love better (yes, even better than you do now); how about enjoying the world around you, like sunsets, trees, and the like (yes, that's a doing too); how about reading about the wonders of the world around us and about different ideas (yes, two heads are better than one); how about writing about your experiences and thoughts well enough that somebody else might enjoy reading what you wrote; how about doing sports really well; how about doing and enjoying hobbies of various kinds; how about enjoying the company of other people; how about doing work tasks so well that you are in high demand as a worker; how about making a useful contribution to others and the society that provides so lavishly for you; how about . . .? All these things, and more, you might want to learn how to DO FOR YOU.

Second, after you have written down the things you want to DO more FOR YOU, each on a separate piece of paper, under each thing you want to DO, write down some (or all) of the indications you could observe that you are doing each action WELL. Examples might be these kinds of things. If you want to talk to people more, the indications might be the number of sentences uttered or statements

made to other people, the number of sentences they made that you listened to, and/or the number of people you talked with. If you want to make useful contributions to your community, indications might be the different tasks you can do at the time or in the place where you are at the time that are useful to others, the number of times you help others with their tasks, and/or the number of tasks you can find and start doing that might contribute usefully in your community. The choices are yours about what you want to DO and what indicators of them you will use.

Third, for EACH indicator, make a little table on the page. The tables should have numbers from 1 to any number up the side and days of the week or month along the bottom. You ought to carry the paper(s) with you, along with a pen or pencil. The task is to make a mark beside the next number up the side of the table for that day. In this way, you keep a record of the times you DO each of your indicators. Who needs to go to all that trouble, right? Hey, you can remember well enough what you did. Oh yeah? List all the things you did so far today that contributed to your present community that involved talking to others, that improved your health, that increased the marketability of your job skills. You might get a few, but we guarantee you have only retained a very small percentage of the many things you have already done TODAY towards each one of those things. And that's the problem. We just don't use good strategies for learning just how good we are or to increase our value and worth to ourselves and others. That's what we're trying to show you how to do right now.

Fourth, each week or month, whatever interval you're using along the bottom of your tables, record the total numbers for that interval on master sheets under each indicator for each action you want to DO. Be pleased with yourself for your accomplishments. It doesn't matter precisely what actions you did, as long as they each qualify for one of the indicators. Know that each and every record of an action indicator is another assurance that you are learning the kind of skill or action you are trying to increase. You are just plain great! You'll soon find that in spite of the pain you imagine this unnecessary and

boring task will entail, you are really enjoying having a record of how well you are doing, and you will even, pretty soon, enjoy making the records and rewarding YOURSELF. Besides, you will soon discover something you suspected but never really knew was true, namely, that you are an impressive and worthwhile person who might even get to like him/herself.

There's another thing you might usefully and profitably do for yourself every day, as another kind of self-help. In other treatments, we have asked the question, What is important to you? The purpose of that question was to ask you to examine your own personal VALUES. We'll be coming back to that later. The question might be asked slightly differently as well. It might be asked, What needs or gains in life are important to you? Of course, we all need to survive. For that, we need to gratify our basic survival needs, such as air to breathe, food and fluid to eat and drink, a place to eliminate body wastes, shelter and clothing to keep us warm, activity to use the body's energies, sleep to calm and rejuvenate us, a sexual life to reproduce our species, freedom from life-threatening dangers and severe pain, means by which to acquire basic survival resources (usually called work), and some changes occurring around us to prevent boredom. We all need those things. But that's NOT ALL of life! They might be all of life if we were animals and nothing more. But we are humans as well.

As humans, we are conscious or aware of our selves. We possess a self. And that self needs nourishment too. Most of us continue our old habits of childhood, imagining that what nourishes the self is what OTHERS DO to and for us. But that was the way our child selves got nurtured. Look around you again. We're all grown-ups now. Remind yourself in this way of that fact lots every day. It's easy to forget. How are grown-up selves nurtured? Some of us think we know. It's done by feeling different, important, special, better than others, in control of the world or at least of other people, excited, on top of the world, almost omnipotent and invincible, with other people doing things for us, right? WRONG! That's how children's and adolescents' selves are nurtured. Children get to feel important, special, better

than others, and omnipotent because the adult world around them is looking after them, provides them with security and puts their needs first. Adolescents haven't figured out yet how to establish their own individual identities, and so they do it by the simplest and most obvious means – by seeing themselves as different, excited, and on top of the world (a post-pubertal awakening that becomes ordinary eventually), and invincible (to feel safe, since they are still less powerful than the grown-ups around them). Perhaps there are other ways to nourish the grown-up self. Let's pretend there are. What might they be?

A guy named Maslow tried to figure out answers to that question and came up with what he called self-actualizing needs. He believed that we don't pursue our self-actualizing needs until basic survival needs have been met. They have been met for all of us to a sufficient degree. So what are the next set of needs we might usefully and profitably go after? (Give hand-outs.) Here is a list of the kinds of self-actualizing needs Maslow suggested. As you look over this list, please remember something else. The needs from this list that you appreciate as the ones you want to pursue are likely to be those that are most consistent with your present VALUES. That is, if you have a strong value for money, you are likely to 'see' such self-actualizing needs as richness as meaning 'being rich'. If you have a strong value for controlling others or for sexual gratification, you are apt to understand or 'see' self-actualizing values such as beauty as referring to the 'sexual attractiveness' of others or yourself. Although those might be examples of particular applications of some self-actualizing needs, the NEEDS actually go much broader and deeper than just those limited applications of them.

You might usefully consider, reconsider, and consider again and again over the next months the self-actualizing needs that you have and need to create a reasonably fulfilling satisfaction of your basic human self. (Encourage some discussion of the needs that individuals might select, and examine the INSTRUMENTAL value of each for the self and for personality development.)

Let's come outside ourselves again and realize something about the communities in which we live. What is the purpose or reason why people live together in societies? Is it for self-protection? Is it to give everyone other people to rip off or to make money from? Is it because people want others to talk with? Is it just a dumb habit we follow because as children we were taught that was the way to live? Of course, it is none of these. Protection is easier in a small group than in a large one; money and ripping others off is a relatively recent invention; we really only need one other person, a mate, to talk with; and we were among those who most utterly resisted what we were taught as children.

The reason is that the nature of humankind is such that we have discovered that we can function, get along, and accomplish best in societies. We come equipped with a motive, called loneliness, whose purpose is to drive us to be with others. We come equipped with varying kinds of skills and things that interest us, not being driven by instincts that would make us all the same. This means that we will be able to do one kind of thing better than other things, and we need other people to do the things we need to have done for us for our fulfilment. It is this fact of differences among us that makes social living the kind of lifestyle that works best for humans.

A society works ONLY if everybody in it contributes his/her energies to everybody else to derive his/her needs also from the energies of everybody else. If you want to memorize something today, that is the most worthwhile thing to memorize. Society exists and works only if everybody contributes his/her energies and special talents to do for everybody else what he/she is good at and reciprocally accepts the results of everybody else's energies and talents to help support his/her existence. In the type of society in which humans live, everybody does and contributes something different, and everybody's contribution is equally as good, necessary, and valuable as everybody else's. That's not just political hogwash, moralistic egalitarianism, a personal belief we cherish, or another fairy story or fable. It's the way it works, if it's going to work. That does NOT mean, as some opportunistic power mongers try to say, that we live in

societies to <u>serve</u> other people. We live in societies to serve <u>ourselves</u> best. But there is a kind of moral injunction that goes along with best serving ourselves. It has to do with the CONTRIBUTIONS we make to others.

Look at your neighbours in this room. Try to remember anything you know about any of them. What does he/she do unusually well? What does he/she seem to enjoy doing? What does he/she do that might contribute something that you need to have done? It doesn't matter too much whether you know that he/she is good at, likes doing, or might contribute to you. Think about this. Can you force or make each OTHER person do for you what you need from him/her? We might be able to kid ourselves into believing we can. But we absolutely cannot! The only person anybody has any real power over is him/herself. All the rest of the power over others that people like to think they have is an illusion. While I am standing over any one of you with a stick or any social skill in manipulation I may have, I may be able to enforce from you a grudging and half-hearted acquiescence in doing my will. But as soon as I try to do that with two people, doing different things at the same time, I leave each for half the time to do his/her own thing, and of course to resist me, while I am trying force the other person to work. We all have too many different kinds of needs to enforce contribution from others.

What we can do is only two things to <u>correct</u> our old childhood habits of trying to push others around and manipulate them. First, we can develop and foster our own helpful and contributing social groups. Second, we can find and do those things that we can usefully contribute to others. Let's try to do the second thing first to see how it's done.

How can we find out what we're good at that might contribute usefully to others and to the society that nurtures us? Of course, in the last analysis, if you really don't know what you're good at, you could undertake an aptitudes-and-interests assessment with any psychologist. Don't worry, we're not going to do that now. Anyway, you already know a great deal about what you're good at, if you just paid attention to that – instead of doing what we mostly do, namely,

telling ourselves what we're no good at or the mistakes we've made – or the fact that we're entirely GREAT. Think about that for a short time while we talk away at you about people's abilities.

During the long, boring process of growing up, we were subjected to three kinds of pressures from others that tended to shape some of the ideas we developed about ourselves. We want to remind you of these pressures briefly so you can try, while thinking about what you're good at, to let the effects of those pressures go and to decide for yourself, free from the effects of those other distorting influences.

How many kinds of measurably different abilities do humans have? (Get a few guesses.) There are probably about 120 different abilities that everybody has in varying amounts. (List a few on the blackboard, as suggested by participants and enriched from psychological lore.) You have some of each kind of ability, and nobody has full credit in anything like every one.

The first set of outside influences that acted on us as children came from our parents. Some of you are or have thought about being parents. What kinds of abilities would YOU most like to see in your children? We'll tell you a few of them. You would like your children to do as they are told, to be obedient or to exercise their acquiescence ability, especially when they are acting in ways that risk danger or harm for them or when they are being the roaring hellions kids often are. You would like your children to move around with good muscular coordination ability so they don't harm nice furniture or the precious things you keep in the house. You would like your children to exercise the social skills and graces of getting along easily with others so that they are pleasant to live with and so they can get along well with their friends. And you would use everything in your power and knowledge to make sure your kids exercised these and other skills. But where do parents get their knowledge about child-rearing from? They get it from the silly books by other parents who think they have found the keys; and they get it by having been children themselves, from their parents and their parents' mistakes. You may think you know how to be a good parent, but you don't any more than we do – and we're supposed to be experts in that field. We all learned

faulty parenting skills from others who were using faulty parenting skills. So parents shout at kids, find fault with kids, punish kids, or praise them lavishly. And these are some of the methods they have learned by which to try to influence their children to exercise the kinds of skills they want the kids to develop, learn, and use.

The second set of influences was the schools we attended. Schools, no matter of what kind, mainly emphasize only two of the 120-plus abilities people have. What are those abilities they emphasize? Reading and arithmetic, right? Since their job is basically to prepare kids for constructive work, they forget about nearly all the skills involved in constructive work and focus on the two that are needed in common in nearly every kind of work, namely, reading and arithmetic. Many of us are not particularly good in those two kinds of abilities. If we are not, we will probably have done rather poorly in school, and we will have felt like failures, no-good people, and sources of trouble and annoyance for our teachers. In fact, if we had more than just a little difficulty with these two abilities, we probably got called bad names, like Learning Disabled or Attention Deficit Disorder, by means of which teachers blame the untaught for not having learned. Who cares what skills or abilities you <u>don't</u> have? It's only the ones you <u>do</u> have that matter.

The third set of influences was your friends and peers. What do you want your friends to be good at? That ought to tell you some of the things your friends tried to get from you. You might want your friends to have such abilities as not telling your secrets, liking you, looking up to you, accepting you, agreeing with you, spending time with you, and the like. You learned the skill of being deaf and dumb in talking to others about your friends; you learned to like and respect your friends and to agree with their ideas and beliefs; you learned to accept only your friends and not others' friends; and since no group of people all want to do the same kinds of things, you learned to hang around in your groups doing nothing until everybody was bored enough they had to stir up a little shit somehow or else to get rid of the boredom by getting high. You taught them your skills pretty well, and they taught you these kinds of skills at the same time.

But, quite apart from what you found out about yourself from those influences, what are YOU GOOD AT doing? That's a really important question. But how can we answer it? Ignoring for the present what other people have congratulated you for – for their own reasons or purposes – what kinds of things have you done where YOU regularly felt satisfied, or at least pleased, with the outcomes? What things do you do that YOU think you do well or right? If the outcomes are useful and contribute to something or to someone, the skills involved in achieving them are useful and contributive. If you feel satisfied with the outcomes, or if you think you do the skills well, your own self-satisfaction will tend to reward your efforts in such actions, and you will be able to develop skill in those activities. It's really that simple.

So don't just think about the skills you have found in this way. Don't just sit there feeling smugly superior to the rest of us. You ARE superior in those ways, but please don't just sit and think of these skills of yours. WRITE THEM DOWN! They are gold and precious gems that will sparkle and adorn the rest of your life, but ONLY IF YOU REMEMBER THEM AND USE THEM! And trust us, you may be absolutely certain you won't forget them, but you will. You will forget them because you will fall back again into thinking and fretting about the failures you are reminded of as you think about what OTHER PEOPLE have thought of you. Quite apart from the uselessness of that kind of thinking, you must surely know you will do it in the future. You will do it, UNLESS you write down your wonderful skills on paper and carry it with you for frequent reference, along with your other identification records. PLEASE write down every one you can think of NOW!

Block 3: Therapeutics

The other question we left off earlier was the question of how to develop our own helpful and contributive social groups? Now we all know that it's up to the group of other individuals to decide whether

they will accept or reject us. We can't break into groups, except by purchasing their substances or by having substances to sell to them. We have to have something they want, right? Wrong! We were children too long, feeling at the mercy of others. All we need to do is to learn, now we're adults, how to become part of groups to support us, help us, and allow us to make contributions.

The most obvious way to become part of a group is to form our own group. That is, we can take the initiative to form groups just as well as anybody else. Somebody has to start any group. Of course, to succeed in forming our own groups probably requires the same skills needed to become part of an existing group. So aside from the reminder that somebody has to start a group and it might as well be you, we haven't said anything useful about joining a group yet. And there are several things to learn.

The first skill for group involvement is skill in listening. Most of us listen _for_ put-downs, rejections, insults, and other indicators that we use to confirm for ourselves that others don't like us. You might remember that some of us only insult our friends or those we like. Why bother saying anything to anybody else? But listening _for_ those sorts of things is not a skill of listening; it is a skill to confirm prejudices or prejudgements.

The main skill in listening involves listening _to_ what others say. You don't have to agree or disagree, praise or criticize what another says. In fact, if you do, it may well turn him/her off. What we do need to do is to check our understanding of what the other said. This is called reflection or pacing. It simply involves repeating in your own words a summary of what the other said, especially the feeling part of it and asking for confirmation of your understanding. We might say, 'If I got it right, you believe that . . .' A little practice makes you comfortable with reflection, and amazingly, the other person will quickly consider you highly intelligent, very understanding, terribly interesting, and one with whom he/she wants to have conversations. Heck, you're interested and understanding and preoccupied with the most important things and ideas there are – his/her interests and ideas. You are worthy of being part of a group with him/her.

The second skill for group involvement is to listen <u>for</u> the things that are important to the members of the group – that is, the group's values. What do they talk about a lot? What do they all seem to agree about? What gets them excited or emotional? You don't have to be part of a group to overhear that sort of thing. Just watch what they do. When you have a pretty clear idea about some of the group's values, before you try to join the group, you ought to consider whether YOU agree with their values. If you don't, look around for another group. If you do, this might be a group to try to join. If you're not sure, either you're not too clear about your own real values or you might take some more time listening <u>for</u> the group's values.

The third skill for group involvement is to 'pace' their actions. If they're sitting erect in serious conversation, sit erect and look serious; if they're walking or running in some direction, do so too; if they're slouching around, doing nothing, that's what you might do. Contrary to all the contemporary hype about racism, what marks people as at least potentially in-group or out-group members is what they <u>do</u> and not what they look like. If you <u>act like</u> group members, you are halfway into the group; if you don't, you're out of the group and probably due for some disparagement, perhaps referring you to another group that acts the way you do. Being like others is mainly acting like others.

The fourth skill for group involvement is to find something you can contribute usefully to the group. This may take a little time to figure out, perhaps while you are still hanging out at the periphery of the group – not yet part of the leadership or the core. But it's not too hard a thing to do. Once you have figured out what's important to the group or what its common values are, all you need to do is to use your perfectly fine brain to figure out <u>what</u> the group is NOT doing that it could usefully or enjoyably do <u>as an expression</u> of its values. You would have to do this also if you were forming your own group. The task is one of finding a <u>mission</u> or <u>purpose</u> or <u>outlet</u> for the group members' energies. If you have the group's values, what might you want or like to do as an expression of those values? Answer that, and without expecting immediate agreement or response from the others,

express the idea and tentatively lead off the action. Even let others say the idea as if it was their own. They may not remember you suggested it, but they will feel warmly towards you, if only for letting them seem to have originated the idea. You do this, and you're in.

Please break up into small groups of four. Don't get together with your friends. Pick others you don't know. The exercise is for each person, in turn, each for about three minutes, to serve as the outsider trying to get into a group of two others, where the fourth person takes his/her turn as observer. The two playing the group talk about anything they want, the one outsider tries to use his/her skills to get in with them, and the observer makes brief notes about how the outsider is doing. Change places about every three minutes, timed by the observer, so all four have a chance to play each role. (Allow about fifteen minutes for this exercise, and walk around observing the small groups.)

How did you do? (Allow brief remarks.) Who found he/she could use some of the skills of group involvement? Did they help? Did you discover that FEELING part of a group isn't all that hard if you approach it smoothly and well? Great!

But we expect that each of you felt a bit uncomfortable while playing each kind of role – talking with a stranger, trying to join, and not participating as an observer. The reason is simply that we all feel a certain amount of social anxiety that we have learned over the years. Even the few of you who have well-honed social skills and who feel good at joining others have developed those skills BECAUSE you felt socially anxious. Whether or not you've noticed it, the bodybuilder who has become expert in the martial arts is usually the one who is most afraid of being attacked or hurt; the person who brags about him/herself and his/her accomplishments is usually the one who feels inadequate or inferior; and the outgoing social butterfly is usually pretty scared of other people and of rejection by them. We all feel anxious about some things. And sometimes that anxiety gets in the way of our being able to make the effort to try things, so we avoid them instead. If that's true of you, you might need some means to reduce your anxieties whenever you want to.

You have all tried some methods for relaxation and probably some kinds of special breathing techniques. The trouble is that most of those methods need to be done when you are not in a crisis or emergency or when you are not in need of getting settled down. There is one thing you can do right, along with anything else you are doing, right in the situation and without anybody else needing to know. We all breathe without having to think about it, right? Right! And your body needs oxygen obtained from breathing IN. So let your body breathe IN just exactly as it would without being noticed – only notice it, and time it in your mind. Then, make the OUT-breath following half a dozen natural IN-breaths go on for three to five times longer than the IN-breath. We know, you all thought we just said to practice DEEP BREATHING. We did NOT! We asked you to do the opposite – to make long OUT-breaths for about six breath cycles. (Demonstrate while counting durations out loud.) You don't have to make it obvious as we just did to illustrate the idea. Just sit as you are now and, without making it obvious, make six LONG OUT-breaths. As you're doing that, please notice that you start to feel (i) a bit less anxious, (ii) a bit less breathless, (iii) a bit more relaxed, and (iv) a bit less tight in the chest. It happens automatically that it calms you down a bit. Hey, you've mastered an important bit of psychological First Aid you can use for yourself.

Here's another bit. Did you ever notice that all anxiety is anticipatory anxiety? None of us knows what the future or even the next moment holds for us. What if the group rejects me or insults me? What if my spouse shacks up with somebody else? What if I make a fool of myself or I pass out or he/she hits me? The 'What ifs' we tell ourselves create all the fears that beset us. Every time you are afraid of something, ask yourself what it is you fear and how you made a 'What if' out of it. Then, say the 'What if' statement under your breath, adding only one word to it – the word prefix *So*. Now your statement to yourself is, 'So what if . . .' If that doesn't take away enough of the anxiety, perhaps even with a chuckle, think through the 'What ifs' ALWAYS in terms of pairs of possibilities.

For example, 'What if I'm sick?' 'So what if I'm sick?' 'I might get worse, or I might get better, in which case there was nothing to worry about.' 'If I get worse, the doctor might not find out what's wrong, or he/she might find out what it is and cure me, in which case there was nothing to worry about.' 'If they can't find out what's wrong, I might just get better on my own, in which case there was nothing to worry about, or I might die, in which I case I won't have anything to worry about anyway.' Try it out now on something you are worrying about.

Next, think about something you are or have worried about or that upset you pretty badly. Close your eyes and get a clear picture in your mind of the situation you were upset about. Shove the picture slightly to one side. Push it straight in front of you. Pull it in a bit closer, and notice that it upsets you a bit more. Push it a bit farther away from you, and notice that it seems to bother you somewhat less. Keep pushing it farther and farther away. It gets smaller and smaller as it moves farther off into the distance. Push it back until it is just a tiny dot on the horizon. Hey, it doesn't bother you much way out there. Isn't that fun? You could probably even do that with your eyes open so nobody could tell what you're up to.

There's another way to do this. Close your eyes. Get the picture of the upsetting situation back in front of you. Put it in a television set, filling the whole screen in full glorious colour. Down in one corner of the screen, put a tiny little black-and-white picture of yourself feeling just exactly the way you would like to feel. Got it? When you're ready, with a swish of action, zoom up the tiny black-and-white picture of yourself as you would like to be so it fills the whole screen in full colour. Look at the coloured picture of yourself as you would like to be for a second or two. Clear the screen. Get the coloured picture of the upsetting situation back, filling the screen, with the little black-and-white picture down in the corner. Then when you're ready, zoom up the picture of you as you would like to be to fill the screen in full colour again. Look at it for a couple of seconds. Repeat this a dozen or so times. It only takes a minute to do. What happened? (Get reports

until someone says he/she couldn't get the upsetting picture back on the screen.) Great! That's what happens after a while with the Swish.

Hey, why not use the Swish right now to get rid of some of the qualities you see in yourself that you don't like or that you feel others don't like. Get the picture of you <u>with</u> the quality you don't want covering the screen in full colour. Put the little black-and-white picture of yourself as you would like to be down in one corner. Zoom up the picture of the you you want to be to cover the screen in full colour. Look at it for a few moments. Clear the screen, and repeat the Swish over and over again.

There's another thing you might try. You want things to happen right when you want them to happen, right? Hey, we're all five hundred-pound parrots, and Polly wants a cracker NOW! That too is a leftover from childhood, when we had to wait until parents or teachers thought it was the right time for things to happen. We mostly have not noticed that waiting for things actually increases the joy in having them. Relaxing and holding off sexual climax not only extends the period of enjoyment, it actually increases the strength of the enjoyment, if not the excitement feeling. Waiting until you're really hungry increases the joy of eating. And not buying something you want for a while, increases the anticipation and the fun of finally getting it.

Hold it, but that doesn't work with substance abuse. Oh yes it does. The trouble is that we have given ourselves the message that we just can't tolerate not having the substance NOW. Is there a child crying in that message? Of course, we can tolerate almost anything we set our minds to do. Have you ever been straight or off addictives without wanting them even for ten minutes? Of course you have. You're not using right now. <u>How</u> did you do that? Seriously, how did you do it? The first thing you did was to know perfectly well that you could do without the shit for an hour or two. <u>How</u>? Well you could take that much time off it. Of course you could! It even makes OTHER things you do while off it more pleasant, and more fun. It really does! The second thing you did was use your 'being straight' skills. You didn't know you had any, did you? Well, you do! We spend

so much attention and energy on HOW we do the addictive thing and HOW MUCH we need it that we don't notice that we can do the straight thing or HOW we do it and HOW MUCH we enjoy the rest of life while we are FREE from the addictive thing. It pays off handsomely to figure out in complete detail HOW you do the straight thing. And you can, and you DO!

But how can we possibly deal with the urge, the hunger, the need, or the craving for the addictive thing? That's what gets in the way of doing the straight thing. Let's get back to that after our break.

Block 4: Consolidation

You have already learned a wide array of things you can do to reduce the strength or pain of any craving, feeling, or pain. It's not a bad thing to use any and all of them. You know LONG OUT-breaths calm you down quickly. You know it helps if you add a *So* in front of the 'What ifs' that scare us or that we worry about. You know the Swish can cut down on any unpleasant feeling. You know that you can last for an hour or two through anything and that delaying gratification may add to the fun of the rest of life. You know that really talking to others simply takes away part of the discomforts from other things like cravings. You know at least four skills for joining groups and that you could even form your own support groups. You know what you could do with your time to make it enjoyable for you and contributive and useful to others because you know what some of your skills are and that you are very successful in using the skills you have. You know why we live in societies, that you get much from others, and that you feel best when you are usefully contributing your energies to others. You know what some of your own self-actualizing needs are, as well as some of the values that motivate you and some of those that get your tail in a knot to screw up life for you. You know that there are ways to get rid of those last values that foul up your life. And you know that the only person who can or will help you improve

your life for you is YOU and what YOU DO. (Extend these summary statements to offer reminiscences and reminders.)

Almost most importantly, you know that your life and what you do are NOT governed by the past events of life and that the real causes of what you do and how you feel lie in the PURPOSES and VALUES you SELECT for YOURSELF. They are easy to select to suit the lifestyle you want, and they decide how you will act and live NOW. Your future is entirely in your own hands, and you can make it anything you might want. If you convince yourself that your future is in the hands of Fate or of others, you will be waiting, bored out of your skull for things to happen the way you think they should, and instead things will happen to you exactly as you think they should not. Your choice, and only yours! We know, we're being mean. Remember, we have formed so many of our ideas as children, and we forget they might well be badly formed or ill taken. We can try to be children who grew up, in which case we will remain feeling like children at the mercy of others who are no longer paying much attention to us. Or we can be what we are, grown-up former children, with the emphasis on being grown-up adults. Good luck! Have fun!

APPENDIX K

Table 9: t-test probabilities of treatment effects on the twenty DAQ S axes: S score results

CREATING . . . DAQ AXES	SUCC. Tx1	FLEXI Tx2	EXCIT Tx3	SATIS Tx4	VALUE Tx5	INNOC Tx6	HEALT Tx7	HAPPY Tx8	INTEG Tx9
EnjSoc S02	.47	.25	.39	.92	.11	*.05	.10	*.10	*.03
RctDpr S03	*.67	.86	.26	.70	.24	.27	*.25	*.14	*.001
GuiInt S08	.83	*.49	.19	.17	*.03	*.03	*.01	*.01	.003
SocCnt S10	.62	.14	.39	*.06	.72	.44	.45	*.27	*.19
AutReb S12	*.07	*.24	*.08	*.001	*.10	*.67	.18	*.08	*.01
FltDpr S13	*.38	.89	.73	*.03	*.03	.32	*.03	*.22	.33
Hedoni S20	*.02	.58	*.44	*.04	.28	.83	.34	.26	*.26
SubCul S22	.40	.79	.70	.79	*.01	.39	.16	.14	*.04
PIGRes S24	*.01	.12	*.39	*.01	.99	.31	.99	.38	.28
AffDen S30	.41	.16	*.24	.29	.15	*.80	.76	*.42	*.01
DiffNd S34	.31	.57	.28	.12	*.55	.40	*.06	.12	*.01
RgdMor S36	.17	*.01	.99	*.03	*.48	*.39	.20	*.07	*.001
Paroxy S37	*.02	*.06	*.02	*.003	*.02	*.32	*.50	.35	.16
PepUNd S40	.40	.43	*.15	*.46	*.30	.31	.26	*.04	*.01

509

FstLan $S44$	.71	.73	.75	***.03**	*.23	.50	***.02**	***.10**	***.08**
AllStr $S46$	.59	.51	.80	.46	.35	.25	.41	.07	.09
PhyAnx $S47$	***.01**	***.10**	.29	***.002**	*.07	.53	***.06**	.26	.15
PunRfs $S48$	***.01**	.29	.38	***.08**	***.09**	*.70	.46	*.31	*.97
SomDpr $S53$	.45	.79	.71	***.04**	.58	.62	*.37	*.56	.93
SubExc $S60$	.67	.67	*.40	.87	.34	***.10**	.20	.18	.08

Two-tailed tests

Ratios of Significant Predicted : Non-Signif. Predicted : Signif. Unpredicted in Columns:|6:2:0 | 3:2:0 | 2:5:0|11:1:0 | 7:4:0| 3:5:0 | 5:3:0| 6:6:0 |9:3:1|

Table 10: <u>t-test</u> probabilities of treatment effects on the twenty <u>DAQ</u> N axes: N score results

CREATING . . . DAQ AXES	<u>SUCC.</u> Tx1	<u>FLEXI</u> Tx2	<u>EXCIT</u> Tx3	<u>SATIS</u> Tx4	<u>VALU</u> Tx5	<u>INNOC</u> Tx6	<u>HEALT</u> Tx7	<u>HAPPY</u> Tx8	<u>INTEG</u> Tx9
EnjSoc $N02$	.56	.72	.80	.84	.07	***.02**	.14	***.08**	***.04**
RctDpr $N03$	*.32	.47	.51	.23	.12	.24	*.14	*.13	***.001**
GuiInt $N08$	.45	*.15	.20	**.03**	***.01**	***.01**	***.001**	***.002**	**.001**
SocCnt $N10$	.97	.57	.60	*.47	.15	.18	.07	***.05**	***.03**
AutReb $N12$	***.09**	***.28**	***.10**	***.005**	***.06**	*.42	**.04**	***.03**	***.001**
FltDpr $N13$	*.32	.87	.70	***.09**	***.02**	.10	***.02**	***.05**	.17
Hedoni $N20$	***.07**	.98	***.87**	*.21	.73	.93	.13	.11	***.06**
SubCul $N22$	.41	.60	.92	.83	***.002**	.24	.06	.11	***.06**
PIGRes $N24$	***.22**	.12	*.43	***.07**	.74	.29	.66	.15	.12
AffDen $N30$	.94	.14	*.18	.53	.13	***.64**	.32	*.30	***.003**

510

DiffNd *N*34	.33	.53	.54	.66	*.56	.55	*.16	.25	***.02**
RgdMor *N*36	.49	***.04**	.93	***.04**	*.39	*.85	.58	*.36	***.01**
Paroxy *N*37	***.03**	*.25	*.21	***.02**	***.06**	*.58	*.42	.33	.24
PepUNd *N*40	.90	.69	*.21	*.59	***.10**	.44	.13	***.04**	*.004
FstLan *N*44	.64	.71	.76	*.23	*.24	.54	***.02**	*.21	***.08**
AllStr *N*46	.74	.33	.38	.68	.28	.44	.70	.23	.20
PhyAnx *N*47	***.04**	*.34	.69	***.04**	*.05	.72	***.03**	.19	.16
PunRfs *N*48	***.08**	.81	.98	*.33	***.09**	*.81	.24	*.37	*.67
SomDpr *N*53	.15	.79	.65	*.28	.47	.50	*.42	*.46	.93
SubExc *N*60	.89	.49	***.08**	.76	.37	***.05**	.24	.18	**.05**

Two-tailed tests

Ratios of Significant Predicted : Non-Signif. Predicted : Signif.
Unpredicted in Columns:|5:3:0 | 1:4:0 | 2:5:0| 6:6:1 | 8:3:0| 3:5:0 | 4:4:1|
6:6:0 |11:1:2|

Table 11: Probabilities of Treatment Effects on Most Relevant *S* Axes of <u>DAQ</u>

TREATMENTS: CREATING . . . DAQ AXES: NAME, NUMBER, *SN*	Tx1 SUCCES	Tx2 FLEXIB	Tx3 EXCITE	Tx4 SATISF	Tx5 VALUES	Tx6 INNOCE	Tx7 HEALTH	Tx8 HAPPIN	Tx9 INTEGR
Punitive Rewards Hx 48 *S*	**.01**	.29	.38	.08	.09	.70	.46	.31	.97
Rigid Moralization 36 *S*	.17	**.01**	.99	**.03**	.48	.39	.20	.07	**.001**
Paroxysmal Energy 37 *S*	**.02**	.06	**.02**	**.003**	**.02**	.32	.50	.35	.16
Physiologic Anxiety 47 *S*	**.01**	.10	.29	**.002**	.07	.53	.06	.26	.15
Subcultural Values 22 *S*	.40	.79	.70	.79	**.01**	.39	.16	.14	**.04**
Guilt Intolerance 08 *S*	.83	.49	.19	.17	**.03**	**.03**	**.01**	**.01**	**.003**
Fast-Lane Living 44 *S*	.71	.73	.75	**.03**	.23	.50	**.02**	.10	.08
Pep-Up Need 40 *S*	.40	.43	.15	.46	.30	.31	.26	**.04**	**.01**
Affect Denial 30 *S*	.41	.16	.24	.29	.15	.80	.76	.42	**.01**

Two-tailed tests

Table 12: Probabilities of Treatment Effects on Most Relevant N Axes of DAQ

TREATMENTS: CREATING ... DAQ AXES: NAME, NUMBER, SN	Tx1 SUCCES	Tx2 FLEXIB	Tx3 EXCITE	Tx4 SATISF	Tx5 VALUES	Tx6 INNOCE	Tx7 HEALTH	Tx8 HAPPIN	Tx9 INTEGR
Punitive Rewards Hx 48 N	.08	.81	.98	.33	.09	.81	.24	.37	.67
Rigid Moralization 36 N	.49	.04	.93	.04	.39	.85	.58	.36	.01
Substance Excitement 37 N	.89	.49	.08	.76	.37	.05	.24	.18	.05
Physiologic Anxiety 47 N	.04	.34	.69	.04	.05	.72	.03	.19	.16
Subcultural Values 22 N	.41	.60	.92	.83	.002	.24	.06	.11	.06
Guilt Intolerance 08 N	.45	.15	.20	.03	.01	.01	.001	.002	.001
Fast-Lane Living 44 N	.64	.71	.76	.23	.24	.54	.02	.21	.08
Pep-Up Need 40 N	.90	.69	.21	.59	.10	.44	.13	.04	.004
Affect Denial 30 N	.94	.14	.18	.53	.13	.64	.32	.30	.003

Two-tailed tests

Table 13: <u>t-test</u> probabilities of treatment effects on the twenty DAQ S axes: S score results with one treatment only.

CREATING.. DAQ AXES	SUCC. Tx1	FLEXI Tx2	EXCIT Tx3	SATIS Tx4	VALUE Tx5	INNOC Tx6	HEALT Tx7	HAPPY Tx8	INTEG Tx9
EnjSoc S02	.86	.28	.06	.27	.42	*.46	.06	*.29	*.53
RctDpr S03	*.11	.09	**.03**	.10	.15	**.03**	*.07	*.22	*.69
GuiInt S08	.69	*.58	.66	.32	*.88	*.87	*.35	*.65	.24
SocCnt S10	.78	.20	.40	**.09**	.51	.72	.52	*.50	*.99
AutReb S12	*.85	*.80	*.87	*.09	*.96	**.03**	.73	*.64	*.14
FltDpr S13	*.30	.48	.15	*.52	*.77	.18	*.88	*.59	.62
Hedoni S20	*.12	.39	*.38	*.09	**.01**	.27	.87	.78	*.78
SubCul S22	.67	.91	.30	.80	*.01	.38	.62	.97	*.69
PIGRes S24	**.01**	.13	*.79	*.31	.07	.96	.30	.26	.85
AffDen S30	.52	.18	*.51	.70	.62	*.30	.64	*.55	*.07
DiffNd S34	.48	.09	.94	.16	*.30	.27	*.86	.94	*.11
RgdMor S36	.32	*.15	**.05**	*.97	*.40	*.39	.51	*.88	*.09
Paroxy S37	*.85	*.54	*.91	*.62	*.42	*.49	*.51	.07	.42
PepUNd S40	.76	.22	*.42	*.89	*.44	.28	.28	*.86	*.63
FstLan S44	.80	.55	.98	**.02**	*.49	.10	*.90	*.39	*.87
AllStr S46	.99	.62	.88	.10	.90	.91	.95	.85	.52
PhyAnx S47	*.65	*.57	.79	*.25	*.17	.29	*.24	.91	.64
PunRfs S48	*.65	.69	.45	*.94	*.98	*.28	.60	*.37	*.30
SomDpr S53	.12	.51	.91	**.08**	.25	.73	*.24	*.83	.95
SubExc S60	.43	.37	*.24	.14	.72	*.44	.33	.74	.51

Two-tailed tests
Ratios of Significant Predicted : Non-Signif. Predicted : Signif. Unpredicted in Columns:|1:7:0 | 0:5:0 | 0:7:2 |5:7:0 | 1:10:0| 1:7:1| 1:7:0|0:12:0 |2:10:0|

Table 14: t-test probabilities of treatment effects on the twenty DAQ N axes: N score results with one treatment only

CREATING.. DAQ AXES	SUCC. Tx1	FLEXI Tx2	EXCIT Tx3	SATIS Tx4	VALUE Tx5	INNOC Tx6	HEALT Tx7	HAPPY Tx8	INTEG Tx9
EnjSoc N02	.90	.37	.18	.56	.56	*.50	**.04**	*.07	*.33
RctDpr N03	*.36	.17	**.01**	.20	.21	**.01**	*.05	*.07	*.93
GuiInt N08	.90	*.68	.99	.26	*.86	*.63	*.32	*.52	.19
SocCnt N10	.94	.41	.70	*.15	.82	.45	.54	*.48	*.91
AutReb N12	*.83	*.67	*.49	*.41	*.76	**.05**	.71	*.43	**.04**
FltDpr N13	*.48	.47	.07	*.84	*.93	.42	*.52	*.70	.52
Hedoni N20	**.06**	.44	*.34	**.04**	**.01**	**.04**	.55	.98	*.82
SubCul N22	.71	.99	.45	.38	**.001**	.76	.60	.95	*.94
PIGRes N24	*.18	.21	*.70	*.47	.16	.66	.10	.68	.91
AffDen N30	.30	.21	*.53	.99	.55	*.13	.55	*.32	*.14
DiffNd N34	.50	.33	.77	.91	*.71	.35	*.68	.87	**.02**
RgdMor N36	.28	*.18	.13	*.57	*.87	**.05**	.14	*.45	**.10**
Paroxy N37	*.79	*.75	*.87	*.47	*.37	*.45	*.90	.24	.49
PepUNd N40	.90	.55	*.60	*.87	*.89	.12	.21	*.60	*.34
FstLan N44	.53	.99	.70	**.06**	*.98	.28	*.50	*.31	*.40
AllStr N46	.87	.74	.89	.14	.39	.83	.87	.64	.70

PhyAnx *N*47	*.90	*.41	.74	*.67	*.27	.14	*.34	.96	.84
PunRfs *N*48	*.91	.48	.27	*.77	*.52	*.34	.86	*.27	*.54
SomDpr *N*53	.37	.54	.92	*.14	.09	.93	*.19	*.78	.41
SubExc *N*60	.21	.87	*.94	.39	.46	*.25	.41	.53	.32

Two-tailed tests

Ratios of Significant Predicted : Non-Signif. Predicted : Signif. Unpredicted in Columns:|1:7:0 | 0:5:0 | 0:7:1|2:10:1 |1:10:1| 2:6:2 | 1:7:1| 2:10:0|3:9:0|

Table 15: Probabilities of Treatment Effects on Most Relevant S Axes of DAQ with one treatment only

TREATMENTS: CREATING . . . DAQ AXES: NAME, NUMBER, SN	Tx1 SUCCES	Tx2 FLEXIB	Tx3 EXCITE	Tx4 SATISF	Tx5 VALUES	Tx6 INNOCE	Tx7 HEALTH	Tx8 HAPPIN	Tx9 INTEGR
Punitive Rewards Hx 48 S	.65	.69	.45	.94	.98	.28	.60	.37	.30
Rigid Moralization 36 S	.32	.15	.05	.97	.40	.39	.51	.88	.09
Paroxysmal Energy 37 S	.85	.54	.91	.62	.42	.49	.51	.07	.42
Physiologic Anxiety 47 S	.65	.57	.79	.25	.17	.29	.24	.91	.64
Subcultural Values 22 S	.67	.91	.30	.80	.005	.38	.62	.97	.69
Guilt Intolerance 08 S	.69	.58	.66	.32	.88	.87	.35	.65	.24
Fast-Lane Living 44 S	.80	.55	.98	.02	.49	.10	.90	.39	.87
Pep-Up Need 40 S	.76	.22	.42	.89	.44	.28	.28	.86	.63
Affect Denial 30 S	.52	.18	.51	.70	.62	.30	.64	.55	.07

Two-tailed tests

Table 16: Probabilities of Treatment Effects on Most Relevant *N* Axes of <u>DAQ</u> with one treatment only

TREATMENTS: CREATING....DAQ AXES: NAME, NUMBER, *SN*	Tx1 SUCCES	Tx2 FLEXIB	Tx3 EXCITE	Tx4 SATISF	Tx5 VALUES	Tx6 INNOCE	Tx7 HEALTH	Tx8 HAPPIN	Tx9 INTEGR
Punitive Rewards Hx 48 *N*	<u>.91</u>	.48	.27	.77	.52	.34	.86	.27	.54
Rigid Moralization 36 *N*	.28	<u>.18</u>	.13	.57	.87	**.05**	.14	.45	.10
Substance Excitement 37 *N*	.79	.75	<u>.87</u>	.47	.37	.45	.90	.24	.49
Physiologic Anxiety 47 *N*	.90	.41	.74	<u>.67</u>	.27	.14	.34	.96	.84
Subcultural Values 22 *N*	.71	.99	.45	.38	**<u>.001</u>**	.76	.60	.95	.94
Guilt Intolerance 08 *N*	.90	.68	.99	.26	.86	<u>.63</u>	.32	.52	.19
Fast-Lane Living 44 *N*	.53	.99	.70	.06	.98	.28	<u>.50</u>	.31	.40
Pep-Up Need 40 *N*	.90	.55	.60	.87	.89	.12	.21	<u>.60</u>	.34
Affect Denial 30 *N*	.30	.21	.53	.99	.55	.13	.55	.32	<u>.14</u>

Two-tailed tests

Table 17: ADDICURE "Creating . . ." Treatments' Effects: One Treatment ONLY

AXES	Tx 1	Tx 2	Tx 3	Tx 4	Tx 5	Tx 6	Tx 7	Tx 8	Tx 9

1. Success (2 + 0 = 2s) creates good feeling (24S, 20N).

	Tx 1	Tx 2	Tx 3	Tx 4	Tx 5	Tx 6	Tx 7	Tx 8	Tx 9
S 24	**_*.01_**	.13	*.79	*.31	.07	.96	.30	.26	.85
N 24	*.18	.21	*.70	*.47	.16	.66	.10	.68	.91
S 20	*.12	.39	*.38	*.09	.01	.27	.87	.78	*.78
N 20	**_*.06_**	.44	*.34	*.04	.01	.04	.55	.98	*.82

2. Flexibility (0 + 2 = 2) may lift Need be Different (34S) and Depression (03S).

	Tx 1	Tx 2	Tx 3	Tx 4	Tx 5	Tx 6	Tx 7	Tx 8	Tx 9
S 34	.48	_.09_	.94	.16	*.30	.27	*.86	.94	*.11
N 34	.50	_.33_	.77	.91	*.71	.35	*.68	.87	***.02**
S 03	*.11	_.09_	**.03**	.10	.15	**.03**	**.07**	**.22**	*.69
N 03	*.36	_.17_	**.01**	.20	.21	**.01**	**.05**	**.07**	*.93

3. Excitement (3 + 1 = 4s) lifts Depression (03, 13) and maybe Social Enjoyment (02) and Reduces Rigid Morality (36).

	Tx 1	Tx 2	Tx 3	Tx 4	Tx 5	Tx 6	Tx 7	Tx 8	Tx 9
S 03	*.11	.09	**_.03_**	.10	.15	**.03**	**.07**	**.22**	*.69
N 03	*.36	.17	**_.01_**	.20	.21	**.01**	**.05**	**.07**	*.93
S 13	*.30	.48	_.15_	*.52	*.77	.18	*.88	*.59	.62
N 13	*.48	.47	_.07_	*.84	*.93	.42	*.52	*.70	.52

4. Satisfaction (6 + 1 = 7s) creates Enjoyment (44, 20) and Social Contact (10) and reduces Depression (13).

S 44	.80	.55	.98	***.02**	*.49	.10	*.90	*.39	*.87
N 44	.53	.99	.70	***.06**	*.98	.28	*.50	*.31	*.40
S 20	*.12	.39	*.38	***.09**	**.01**	.27	.87	.78	*.78
N 20	*.06	.44	*.34	***.04**	**.01**	**.04**	.55	.98	*.82
S 10	.78	.20	.40	***.09**	.51	.72	.52	*.50	*.99
N 10	.94	.41	.70	***.15**	.82	.45	.54	*.48	*.91

5. Values $(4 + 2 = 6s)$ reduces Subcultural Values (22) and maybe Somatic Depression (53) and increases Hedonism and Enjoyment (20, 24).

AXES	Tx 1	Tx 2	Tx 3	Tx 4	Tx 5	Tx 6	Tx 7	Tx 8	Tx 9
S 22	.67	.91	.30	.80	***.01**	.38	.62	.97	*.69
N 22	.71	.99	.45	.38	***.01**	.76	.60	.95	*.94
AXES	Tx 1	Tx 2	Tx 3	Tx 4	Tx 5	Tx 6	Tx 7	Tx 8	Tx 9
S 53	.12	.51	.91	***.08**	.25	.73	*.24	*.83	.95
N 53	.37	.54	.92	*.14	.09	.93	*.19	*.78	.41

6. Innocence $(6 + 1 = 7s)$ reduces Rebelliousness (12) and Rigid Morality (36) and Depression (03) and increases Enjoyment (20).

S 12	*.85	*.80	*.87	***.09**	*.96	***.03**	.73	*.64	*.14
N 12	*.83	*.67	*.49	*.41	*.76	***.05**	.71	*.43	***.04**
S 36	.32	*.15	**.05**	*.97	*.40	*.39	.51	*.88	***.09**
N 36	.28	*.18	.13	*.57	*.87	***.05**	.14	*.45	***.10**

7. Health $(3 + 2 = 5s)$ creates Social Enjoyment (02) and reduces Depression (03).

S 02	.86	.28	.06	.27	.42	*.46	<u>.06</u>	*.29	*.53
N 02	.90	.37	.18	.56	.56	*.50	**.04**	***.08**	*.33
S 03	*.11	.09	**.03**	.10	.15	**.03**	**<u>*.07</u>**	*.22	*.69
N 03	*.36	.17	**.01**	.20	.21	**.01**	**<u>*.05</u>**	*.07	*.93

8. Happiness (2 + 1 = 3*s*) creates Enjoyment (02) and reduces Bad Memories (37).

S 37	*.85	*.54	*.91	*.62	*.42	*.49	*.51	<u>.07</u>	.42
N 37	*.79	*.75	*.87	*.47	*.37	*.45	*.90	<u>.24</u>	.49
S 02	.86	.28	.06	.27	.42	*.46	.06	<u>*.29</u>	*.53
N 02	.90	.37	.18	.56	.56	*.50	**.04**	**<u>*.08</u>**	*.33

9. Integration (5 + 1 = 6*s*) increases Difference Need (34) and reduces Affect Denial (30), Rebelliousness (12), and Rigid Morality (36).

S 30	.52	.18	*.51	.70	.62	*.30	.64	*.55	**<u>*.07</u>**
N 30	.30	.21	*.53	.99	.55	*.13	.55	*.32	<u>*.14</u>
S 34	.48	.09	.94	.16	*.30	.27	*.86	.94	<u>*.11</u>
N 34	.50	.33	.77	.91	*.71	.35	*.68	.87	**<u>*.02</u>**
S 12	*.85	*.80	*.87	**.09**	*.96	**.03**	.73	*.64	<u>*.14</u>
N 12	*.83	*.67	*.49	*.41	*.76	**.05**	.71	*.43	**<u>*.04</u>**

Some Axes show no significant relationships.

AXES	Tx 1	Tx 2	Tx 3	Tx 4	Tx 5	Tx 6	Tx 7	Tx 8	Tx 9

No significant effect on Physiological Anxiety (47).

S 47	*.65	*.57	.79	*.25	*.17	.29	*.24	.91	.64
N 47	*.90	*.41	.74	*.67	*.27	.14	*.34	.96	.84

No significant effect on Punitive Reinforcements history (48).

S 48	*.65	.69	.45	*.94	*.98	*.28	.60	*.37	*.30
N 48	*.91	.48	.27	*.77	*.52	*.34	.86	*.27	*.54

No significant effect on Guilt Intolerance (08).

S 08	.69	*.58	.66	.32	*.88	*.87	*.35	*.65	.24
N 08	.90	*.68	.99	.26	*.86	*.63	*.32	*.52	.19

No significant effect on Substance Self-Enhancement (60).

S 60	.43	.37	*.24	.14	.72	*.44	.33	.74	.51
N 60	.21	.87	*.94	.39	.46	*.25	.41	.53	.32

No significant effect on Pep-Up need (40).

S 40	.76	.22	*.42	*.89	*.44	.28	.28	*.86	*.63
N 40	.90	.55	*.60	*.87	*.89	.12	.21	*.60	*.34

No significant effect on Allergy Stress (46).

S 46	.99	.62	.88	.10	.90	.91	.95	.85	.52
N 46	.87	.74	.89	.14	.39	.83	.87	.64	.70

Although there is yet no evidence to support this view, it seems possible that these (unaffected) axes may require more time than other axes for changes in their underlying variables to be noticed or experienced, and thus to be recorded in the test.

Table 18: Results Combining/Double Using some Axes

S 24	***.01**	.13	*.79	*.31	.07	.96	.30	.26	.85
N 20	***.06**	.44	*.34	***.04**	**.01**	**.04**	.55	.98	*.82
S 34	.48	.09	.94	.16	*.30	.27	*.86	.94	*.11
N 34	.50	.33	.77	.91	*.71	.35	*.68	.87	***.02**
S 03	*.11	.09	**.03**	.10	.15	**.03**	*.07	*.22	*.69
N 03	*.36	.17	**.01**	.20	.21	**.01**	*.05	*.07	*.93
S 44	.80	.55	.98	***.02**	*.49	.10	*.90	*.39	*.87
N 44	.53	.99	.70	***.06**	*.98	.28	*.50	*.31	*.40
S 22	.67	.91	.30	.80	***.01**	.38	.62	.97	*.69
N 22	.71	.99	.45	.38	***.01**	.76	.60	.95	*.94
S 12	*.85	*.80	*.87	*.09	*.96	***.03**	.73	*.64	*.14
N 12	*.83	*.67	*.49	*.41	*.76	***.05**	.71	*.43	***.04**
S 03	*.11	.09	**.03**	.10	.15	**.03**	***.07**	*.22	*.69
N 03	*.36	.17	**.01**	.20	.21	**.01**	***.05**	*.07	*.93
S 02	.86	.28	.06	.27	.42	*.46	.06	***.29**	*.53
N 02	.90	.37	.18	.56	.56	*.50	**.04**	***.08**	*.33
S 36	.32	*.15	**.05**	*.97	*.40	*.39	.51	*.88	***.09**
N 36	.28	*.18	.13	*.57	*.87	***.05**	.14	*.45	***.10**
S 30	.52	.18	*.51	.70	.62	*.30	.64	*.55	***.07**
N 34	.50	.33	.77	.91	*.71	.35	*.68	.87	***.02**

APPENDIX L

Table 19: Correlation matrix for <u>DAQ</u> Axes and <u>STFB</u> Factors

STFB Factor Scores DAQ Axis NAMES and Numbers	STFB F1	STFB F2	STFB F3	STFB F4	STFB F5	STFB F6
Social Enjoyment 02S	.03	.07	.10	.12	−.03	.09
Reactive Depression 03S	.14	.18	**.28**	.12	**.20**	.18
Guilt Intolerance 08S	.37	.38	.43	.19	.42	.29
Social Contact Need 10S	.05	.13	.19	.11	.09	.20
Authority Rebellion 12S	.54	.56	.58	.15	.56	.51
Flat Depression 13S	.29	**.38**	**.55**	.12	**.43**	.32
Hedonic Enjoyment 20S	.15	.10	.04	.10	.01	.16
Subcultural Values 22S	.39	.36	.39	.35	.36	.38
PIG/Resiliency 24S	.01	−.08	−.07	−.08	−.02	.10
Affect Denial 30S	.17	.13	.10	.08	.09	.26
Need to Be Different 34S	.38	.37	.36	.18	.40	.32
Rigid Moralizations 36S	−.27	−.16	−.18	−.05	−.15	−.16
Paroxysmality 37S	.27	**.36**	**.39**	.27	**.35**	.32
Pep-Up Need 40S	.17	.03	.04	.10	.02	.17

Fast-Lane Living 44*S*	.47	.38	.38	.17	.40	.41
Allergy Stress 46*S*	.16	.28	.28	.01	.16	.30
Physiological Anxiety 47*S*	.23	**.36**	**.45**	.07	**.40**	.31
Punitive Rewards 48*S*	.43	.47	.52	.25	.47	.47
Somatic Depression 53*S*	.17	**.29**	**.36**	.18	**.28**	.24
Substance Excitement 60*S*	.26	.25	.30	.07	.24	.37

Correlation coefficients

Table 20: Probabilities of the Effects of each of nine Addictions Treatments on Nine <u>STFB</u> residual gain scores.

TREATMENTS <u>STFB</u> Scale	<u>Tx1</u> SUCC.	<u>Tx2</u> FLEXI	<u>Tx3</u> EXCIT	<u>Tx4</u> SATIS	<u>Tx5</u> VALUE	<u>Tx6</u> INNOC	<u>Tx7</u> HEALT	<u>Tx8</u> HAPPY	<u>Tx9</u> INTEG
<u>STFB</u> TOTAL	.31	.10	**.02**	**.007**	**.002**	**.000**	**.001**	**.000**	**.000**
SD NEUTRAL	.46	.69	.60	.77	.06	.81	.57	.15	.46
S UNDESIRA	**.04**	.13	.64	.08	**.03**	.51	.53	.26	.89
F1: GUILT	.34	.36	.34	.49	**.03**	.20	.64	.18	.90
F2: FAILUR	.23	.10	**.04**	**.02**	**.001**	**.000**	**.005**	**.000**	**.001**
F3: DISTRE	.07	.26	.61	.10	.09	.91	.88	.36	.77
F4: SENSIT	.33	.66	.68	.75	**.01**	.90	.12	.53	.20
F5: CONFOR	**.004**	**.02**	.16	**.01**	.33	.33	.20	.07	.13
F6: DISCIP	**.008**	.08	.27	.09	.20	.34	.61	.27	.73

Two-tailed tests

APPENDIX M

Table 21.1: Discriminant Function % Correct Classifications and Probabilities of F (relationship) between Addicause and other scales and Indicators of substance uses. Probabilities are rounded to the nearest two decimal places.

AXIS LABELS AND VARIABLES	DUF1D Use	DUF2 DUse	DUF3 DUse	MAST Alco	AUF1 AUse	AUF2 AUse	AUF3 AUse	AYF1 AYrs	AYF2 AYrs	AUY1 AU AND Y	AUY2 AU AND Y	AUY3 AU AND Y	AUY4 AU AND Y	DAST Drug
DAQ Discrim S	47%	45%	40%	56%	35%	38%	48%	46%	41%	43%	38%	43%	47%	53%
% Correct N	50%	46%	53%	58%	—	39%	56%	46%	45%	43%	38%	44%	44%	58%
01: Social S				.05	.09		.57			.17				.29
Anxiety N				.20	.00		.31			.05				.27

527

	1	2	3	4	5	6	7	8	9	10	11	12	13	14
02: Social Enjoyment S	.36	.62	.13	.94	.41	.25	.06*	.15	.29	.59	.55	.42	.11	.89
02: Social Enjoyment N	.24	.16	.24	.99	.59	.48	.23*	.31	.75	.50	.82	.55	.28	.75
03: Reactive Depression S	.27	.91	.22	.07	.67	.63	.55	.05*	.83	.95	.54	.39	.73	.01*
03: Reactive Depression N	.03	.32	.28	.09	.43	.78	.75	.02*	.80	.87	.53	.47	.80	.01*
04: Stimulus Hunger S				.11	.36		.00			.05				.00*
04: Stimulus Hunger N				.08	.05		.03			.04				.00*
05: Rigid Self-Image S				.02	.04		.00			.00				.00
05: Rigid Self-Image N				.01	.00		.01			.00				.00
06: Social Influence S				.35	.00		.00			.00				.01
06: Social Influence N				.24	.01		.03			.01				.01
07: Aggressn Inhibition S				.31	.14	.41	.70			.60				.22*
07: Aggressn Inhibition N				.28	.23	.16	.14			.13				.16
08: Guilt Intolerance S	.00	.01	.00*	.00	.12		.41	.99	.15	.12	.44	.10*	.25	.00*
08: Guilt Intolerance N	.00	.00	.00*	.00	.15		.62	.95	.11	.18	.33	.10*	.23	.00*
09: Loneliness S				.00	.08		.15			.16				.08
09: Loneliness N				.01	.00		.39			.02				.13
10: Social Contact Wsh S	.33	.67	.02	.53	.17	.80	.04	.42	.13	.34	.44	.48	.06	.62
10: Social Contact Wsh N	.16	.48	.04	.33	.26	.42	.14	.34	.09	.24	.44	.61	.08	.31*

	1	2	3	4	5	6	7	8	9	10	11	12	13	14
11: Reality *S*				.01										.00
Denial *N*				.01										.00
12: Authorit *S*	.00*	.00*	.03	.01	.24	.45	.04	.40	.09	.16	.12	.47	.02	.00
Rebellion *N*	.00*	.00*	.02	.01	.22	.24	.07	.28*	.08	.21	.08	.56	.01	.00
13: Flat *S*	.01	.32	.19	.00	.88	.28	.28	.65	.76	.29*	.71	.99	.18	.00
Depression *N*	.02	.53	.57	.00	.80	.10	.68*	.58	.62	.19*	.82	.98	.27	.00
14: Vivid *S*				.74										.20
Imagery *N*				.66										.45
15: Control *S*				.02										.04
Effort *N*				.01										.08
16: Control *S*				.13*										.18
of Others *N*				.34*										.27
17: Grief *S*				.08										.00
Reaction *N*				.03										.00
18: Substanc *S*				.00*										.00*
Enhancement *N*				.00*										.00*
19: Pain *S*				.71										.21
Sensitivity *N*				.48										.15*

	1	2	3	4	5	6	7	8	9	10	11	12	13	14
20: Hedonism S	.81	.06	.87	.19	.92	.86	.46*	.33	.78	.60	.44	.30	.94	.35
N	.26	.03	.44	.35	.99	.80	.18*	.75	.62	.50	.59	.22	.86	.08
21: Social Withdrawal S		.02												.07
N		.05												.07
22: SubCult. Values S	.03	.01	.12	.00	.79	.58	.17	.89	.24	.53	.04	.04	.08	.00
N	.01	.01	.03	.00	.86	.49	.11	.93	.13	.39	.06	.09	.06	.00
23: Inhibit Dependency S				.29										.17
N				.18										.02
24: Immediat Gratificatn S	.98	.25	.63	.05	.78	.79	.69	.57	.83	.39	.31	.61	.92	.42
N	.76	.35	.29	.07	.92	.76	.74	.95	.86	.66	.53	.70	.81	.70
25: Paranoid Sensitivity S				.62										
N				.58										
26: Rationality Defence S				.83										
N				.97										
27: Oppressive Inhibit S				.40										.19*
N				.19										.09*
28: Comfortable Inhibit S				.56										.27
N				.55										.95

Variable	C1	C2	C3	C4	C5	C6	C7	C8	C9	C10	C11	C12	C13	C14
29: Affect S				.01										.05
Disturbance N				.00										.06
30: Affect S	.98	.82	.42	.99	.44	.52	.31	.95	.28	.24	.39	.18	.11	.55
Denial N	.80	.49	.23	.68	.69	.54	.69	.75	.33	.45	.59	.40	.23	.24
31: Demean S				.11										.12
Others N				.14										.04
32: Group S				.30										.98
Satisfact'n N				.64										.71
33: Dogmatism S				.32										.88
N				.40										.25
34: Wish Be S	.28	.14	.14	.52*	.43	.17	.83	.71	.35	.08*	.26	.54	.35	.01
Different N	.21	.07	.12	.22	.37	.26	.89	.98	.28	.26	.60	.73	.59	.00
35: Self- S				.00										.00
Depreciat'n N				.00										.00
36: Rigid S	.01*	.54	.57	.12	.37	.13	.64	.08	.37	.99	.20	.68	.76	.00*
Moralizat'n N	.01*	.48	.25	.43	.30	.08	.54	.09*	.45	.92	.23	.89	.91	.00*
37: Paroxys- S	.06	.16	.35	.00*	.13	.91	.00*	.43	.02*	.17	.01*	.00*	.00*	.00
mality N	.04	.10	.36	.00*	.17	.78	.00*	.64	.01*	.14	.02*	.01*	.00*	.00

	1	2	3	4	5	6	7	8	9	10	11	12	13	14
38: Rules *S*				.01*										.00
Intolerance *N*				.02*										.00*
39: Effort *S*				.09*										.00
Strain *N*				.05*										.00
40: Pep-Up *S*	.96	.63	.75	.53	.69	.76	.48	.19*	.98	.29	.19	.12	.42	.42
Effect *N*	.81	.36	.49	.98	.34	.82	.28	.13	.93	.18	.19	.09	.54	.19
41: Rigid *S*				.10										.00
Habits *N*				.09										.00
42: Easy Go *S*				.45										.93
Enjoyment *N*				.73										.54
43: Metabolic *S*				.08										.00
Disorder *N*				.09										.00
44: Fast-Lane *S*	.51	.04	.08	.12	.10*	.11	.31	.47	.38	.18	.03	.27	.15	.00
Living *N*	.47	.16	.20	.08	.14	.18	.22	.65	.07*	.10*	.10	.09	.12	.00
45: Hypo- *S*				.00										.00
glycaemia *N*				.00										.00
46: Allergy *S*	.03	.03	.65	.09	.88	.73	.31	.83	.91	.82	.27	.69	.41	.00
Stress *N*	.02	.02	.19	.11	.98	.88	.68	.76	.82	.79	.33	.88	.72	.00

	C1	C2	C3	C4	C5	C6	C7	C8	C9	C10	C11	C12	C13	C14
47: Physiolog. *S*	.00*	.09	.01	.01	.38	.48	.35*	.84	.60	.80	.28	.93	.32*	.00
Anxiety *N*	.00*	.06	.05	.03	.22	.25	.51	.75	.55	.89	.20	.76	.18*	.00
48: Punitive *S*	.00	.02	.11	.00	.38	.74	.00*	.74	.62	.27	.02	.09	.01	.00
Reinforcemt *N*	.00	.03	.03	.00	.42	.57	.00*	.65	.59	.19	.02	.21	.01	.00
49: Affect *S*				.05										.00
Avoidance *N*				.04										.00
50: Control *S*				.33										.00
Sensitivity *N*				.06										.00
51: Guilt *S*				.01										.02
Proneness *N*				.01*										.02
52: Anger/*S*				.01										.00
Hostility *N*				.00										.00
53: Somatic *S*	.01	.04	.06	.02	.41	.88	.50*	.78	.23	.42	.50	.86	.56	.01
Depression *N*	.00	.04	.03	.02	.22	.46	.59*	.55	.10	.23	.43	.74	.34	.01
54: Hungry *S*				.03										.00
Heart *N*				.03										.00*
55: Impaired *S*				.02										.02
Self-Esteem *N*				.01										.01

533

56: Masked *S*	.25			.40										.09
Disappointm *N*	.08			.18										.09
57: Felt *S*				.02										.00
Rejection *N*				.03										.00
58: Need to *S*				.79										.71
Communicate *N*				.72										.86
59: NeedCalm *S*				.11										.63
Nerves *N*				.15										.48
60: Substanc *S*	.25	.04	.55	.01	.45	.11*	.61	.37*	.25*	.11	.63	.55	.63	.00
Enhancement *N*	.08	.09	.25	.01	.13	.07*	.94	.75	.38	.18	.67	.52	.83	.00
61: Forget *S*				.37										.59
Failures *N*				.46										.30
62: WshNovel *S*				.01										.12
Experiences *N*				.01										.17
63: Avoid *S*				.14										.00
Boredom *N*				.02										.00
64: Assert *S*				.04										.00
Confidence *N*				.03										.00

65: Avoid *S* Attractiven *N*				.10 / .07									.11 / .06
66: Impaired *S* Sleep *N*				.00 / .00									.00 / .00
67: NeedCalm/ *S* Relaxation *N*				.36 / .35									.40 / .37*
68: Substanc *S* Dependency *N*				.01 / .02									.00 / .00
ML: MMPI L	.02	.16	.30	.00	.98*	.87	.19	.88	.98	.96	.20	.62	.57
MF: MMPI F	.01	.07	.01	.00	.65	.64	.38	.62	.46	.63	.78	.89	.24
MK: MMPI K	.14	.34	.05	.00	.39	.72	.03	.96	.56	.79	.01	.80	.07
01: MMPI Hs	.72	.33	.60	.92	.17*	.37	.66	.44	.67	.36	.69	.71	.89
02: MMPI D	.47	.40	.44	.20	.43	.83	.19	.97	.43	.19	.31	.84	.17
03: MMPI Hy	.70	.50	.38	.63	.93	.41	.89	.34	.56	.30	.49	.69	.92
04: MMPI Pd	.01	.24	.17	.00	.61	.74	.29	.31	.09	.87	.42	.80	.13

05: MMPI MF	.04	.39	.49	.07	.32	.71	.19*	.86	.72	.47	.10	.62	.24	.92
06: MMPI Pa	.04	.28	.99	.17	.75	.75	.35	.61	.70	.99	.18	.01	.04	.00
07: MMPI Pt	.00	.06	.50	.23	.94	.34	.44	.22	.96	.55*	.07	.00	.17	.00
08: MMPI Sc	.03	.04*	.96	.51	.72	.38	.34	.19	.79	.73	.09	.00	.12	.00
09: MMPI Ma	.01	.34	.91	.48	.08*	.14	.02	.09	.20*	.60	.03	.13	.18	.03
00: MMPI Si	.24*	.01	.73	.38	.11	.18*	.48	.12*	.70	.17*	.05	.61	.75	.68
MMPI TSC F1	.54	.00*	.86	.14	.20	.17	.58	.07	.42	.43	.01	.29	.50	.21
MMPI TSC F2	.01	.79	.81	.56	.74	.95	.37	.70	.49	.41	.10	.20	.38	.26
MMPI TSC F3	.00	.00	.79	.22	.74	.22	.98	.00	.99	.44	.14	.01	.13*	.18
MMPI TSC F4	.00	.06	.88	.09	.79	.09	.96	.07	.58	.60	.00	.08	.23	.00
MMPI TSC F5	.00	.00	.74	.08	.27	.10	.99	.00	.55	.36	.00	.03	.54	.08
MMPI TSC F6	.00	.05	.95	.65	.72	.39	.37	.05	.96	.99	.02	.00*	.01	.00
MMPI TSC F7	.00	.04	.69	.05	.99	.35	.24	.01	.95	.62	.00	.02	.33	.04

Plus Getting	.01	.28	.01	.00	.37*	.78	.00	.99	.18	.84	.06	.74	.00	.00
MMPI DY 1	.04	.09	.09	.00	.99	.59	.17*	.31	.20	.32	.17	.84	.00	.03
MMPI DY 2	.64	.36	.33	.02*	.79	.18	.79	.78	.38	.11*	.26	.67	.05	.66
MMPI DY 3	.04	.07	.00	.00	.61	.26	.02	.46	.78	.12*	.59	.61	.11	.00
MMPI DY 4	.00	.13	.01	.01	.67*	.90	.00	.93	.19	.29	.28	.67	.01	.00
MMPI DY 5	.00	.30	.00	.00	.66	.99	.03	.89	.24	.84	.20	.96	.03	.00
MMPI PrimDef	.00	.02	.17	.00	.59	.55	.06	.06	.67	.86	.21*	.48	.01	.00
MMPI Regress	.43	.03	.00	.00*	.99	.19*	.01	.06	.61	.19	.25	.42	.06*	.28
MMPI Repress	.33	.68	.30	.00	.15	.60	.03	.14	.17	.39	.53	.33	.05	.00
MMPI Denial	.01	.05	.05	.00	.76*	.32*	.02	.49	.23	.23	.11	.57	.01	.00
MMPI Project	.46	.27	.13	.37	.43	.62	.58	.94	.81	.44	.87	.22	.79	.30
MMPI Displac	.22*	.70	.16	.12	.38	.26	.62	.55	.93	.41	.30	.64	.73	.99
MMPI Intellz	.11	.13	.82	.31	.36	.17	.90	.37	.01*	.04	.43	.08	.72	.12

537

MMPI S.Doubt	.26	.39	.05	.11	.47	.63	.05	.79	.40	.92	.38	.82	.05	.05
MMPI RctForm	.76	.78	.78	.12	.40*	.94	.26	.95	.41*	.69	.99	.88	.04	.00
MMPI OvAcThk	.00	.01	.00	.01	.99	.94	.05	.33	.46	.69	.58	.93	.06	.00
MMPI IntEffc	.01	.10	.02	.16	.80	.76	.06	.97	.06	.63	.37	.50	.04	.12
MMPI Anxiety	.04	.33	.02	.01	.67*	.96	.01	.24	.37	.99	.05*	.77	.05	.00
MMPI Depress	.00	.24	.09	.00	.59	.63	.08	.96	.11	.81	.08	.90	.09	.00
MMPI Anger	.06	.47	.03	.00	.34	.62	.00	.97	.14	.34	.10	.82	.01	.00
MMPI Anhedon	.06	.56	.34	.01	.17	.79	.20*	.74	.45	.84	.64	.68	.06	.20*
MMPI Respons	.00*	.00*	.00	.00*	.65	.69	.06	.63	.06	.30	.54	.28	.03	.00*
MMPI Toleran	.00	.05	.00	.04	.51	.88	.12	.82	.15	.55	.28	.94	.09	.00
MMPI Empathy	.19	.17	.56	.02	.52	.76	.40	.35	.00*	.03*	.69	.88	.22	.50
MMPI RolPlay	.07	.14	.22	.15	.00*	.65	.18	.19	.06	.65	.00*	.34	.02	.00
MMPI Dominan	.04	.23	.04	.00	.68	.07*	.43	.95	.07	.71	.28	.43	.13	.00

	1	2	3	4	5	6	7	8	9	10	11	12	13	14
MMPI SocPart	.95	.94	.53	.18	.75*	.25	.86	.88	.18	.28	.33	.83	.07	.25
MMPI SocPres	.21	.88	.03	.25	.63	.85	.30	.84	.31	.37	.07	.83	.01	.64
MMPI Dependc	.04	.56	.06	.00	.38	.82	.00*	.70	.12*	.95	.05	.79	.00	.02
Dom-Submiss.	.36	.96	.83	.17*	.28	.08	.50	.36	.07	.17	.43	.75	.09	.88
Love-Hate	.00	.18	.00	.00	.82	.99	.10	.80	.29	.88	.45	.91	.05	.00
MMPI EgoStrn	.05	.25	.02	.26	.78	.81	.18	.26	.46	.90	.85	.97	.26*	.08
MMPI Resilie	.02	.23	.02	.00	.90	.97	.03	.41	.38	.77	.03	.93	.02	.00
MMPI S.Cntrl	.00	.00	.04	.00	.62	.54	.04	.07*	.02	.29	.13	.67	.09	.00
MMPI Impulsv	.00	.00	.00	.00	.90*	.98	.01	.21	.02	.71	.27	.92	.10	.00
MMPI Delinqu	.00	.11	.01	.01	.43	.54*	.18	.38	.13	.29	.39	.57	.24	.00
MMPI Raw Spy	.01	.05	.86	.07	.77	.95	.05	.60	.07*	.02*	.80	.07*	.01*	.12
MMPI HabCrim	.00	.04	.09	.00	.93	.62*	.08	.21	.02	.94	.41	.97	.06	.00*
MMPI PrisAdj	.00	.01	.83	.00	.13*	.43	.18	.79	.08	.52	.47*	.96	.28	.00

MMPI Escapis	.00*	.00*	.31	.00	.55*	.96	.05	.63	.13	.72	.02*	.55	.01	.00
MMPI ParViol	.12	.43	.01	.00	.95	.99	.01*	.43	.71	.90	.14	.86	.05	.00
MMPI Recidiv	.12	.08	.54	.00*	.17	.27*	.00*	.00*	.01*	.27*	.12	.42*	.04	.00
MMPI OvCoHos	.63*	.28*	.75	.07	.26	.75	.25	.65	.05*	.58	.99	.16*	.09	.00
MMPI Violenc	.00	.01	.05	.00	.38	.26*	.06	.38	.13	.10	.14	.45	.09	.00
MMPI ThrSuic	.00	.10	.00	.00	.81	.86	.01	.44	.17	.96	.13	.95	.02	.00
MMPI UncAcSx	.24	.78	.03	.56	.56	.29	.10	.93	.17*	.70	.42	.49*	.21	.29
Paedophilia	.43	.71	.02	.36	.20*	.89	.10	.87	.85	.72	.31	.84	.17	.25*
Aggravat.Sex	.00	.00	.22	.00	.69	.38	.50	.57*	.25	.54	.33	.47	.02	.00*
MMPI Alcohol	.00	.11	.42	.00*	.11	.48	.05	.32	.53	.27	.92	.69	.02	.00*
MMPI DrgAbus	.01	.04	.53	.00	.25*	.56	.17	.10	.05	.27	.07	.80	.11	.00
Work Attitud	.00	.03	.03	.00	.80	.71	.02	.78	.11	.93	.28	.91	.02	.00
Rehab.Motiv.	.57	.70	.63	.20	.44*	.99	.79	.77	.11	.83	.24*	.84	.79	.02

Change Motiv	.01	.06	.17	.00	.57	.91	.09	.92	.43*	.99	.12	.67	.03	.00
Thyroid Path	.95	.82	.90	.39	.80	.49	.43	.02*	.52	.97	.73	.78	.28	.89
Caudality	.01	.34	.04	.00	.87	.44	.02*	.60	.10	.62	.20	.93	.03	.00*
LowBackPain	.91	.47	.17	.66	.55	.68	.01*	.20	.14*	.45	.30	.93	.08	.93
Pariet-Front	.04	.28	.02	.00	.42	.81	.04	.83	.11	.88	.12	.51	.04	.00
Soc.Adjustmt	.66	.64	.79	.03	.40	.51	.09	.72	.72	.12	.68	.90	.00	.20
MMPI DeprCon	.01	.59	.01	.00	.53	.81	.09*	.49	.20	.85	.04	.80	.12	.00
MMPI PMorale	.01	.46	.02	.03	.13	.46	.01	.52	.05*	.76	.03	.65	.00	.00
MMPI RelFund	.15	.07	.73	.82	.83	.17	.69	.87	.07	.12	.82	.41	.20	.03
MMPI AuthCnf	.03	.14	.11	.00	.98	.90	.07	.74	.39	.69	.53	.94	.12	.00
Psychoticism	.00	.11	.00	.09	.92	.57	.13	.24	.60	.40	.39	.98	.38	.00
Org.Symptoms	.03	.21	.12	.00	.46	.25	.09	.15	.83	.49	.94	.64	.16	.00
MMPI FamProb	.01	.36	.35	.00*	.33	.89	.01	.77	.07	.60	.06	.62	.01	.00

	C1	C2	C3	C4	C5	C6	C7	C8	C9	C10	C11	C12	C13	C14
MMPI ManHost	.00	.01	.65	.21	.25	.16	.99	.00	.95	.63	.00	.01	.58	.09
MMPI Phobias	.30	.29	.75	.64	.86	.50	.92	.13	.53	.54	.55	.01*	.96	.56
MMPI Hypoman	.00	.14	.75	.58	.04*	.64	.63	.03	.48	.32	.00	.25	.19	.25
MMPI PHealth	.02	.65	.69	.19	.69	.97	.92	.58	.80	.52	.16	.41	.36	.44
MMPI PharVir	.12	.15	.45	.28	.54	.26	.53	.09	.52	.08	.75*	.11	.67	.14
MAST-Alcohol	.15										.00*			
DAST-DrugsR2	.00*										.09			
STFB TotalY1	.00										.24			
STFB Fact. 1	.00										.76			
STFB Fact. 2	.00										.13			
STFB Fact. 3	.00										.13			
STFB Fact. 4	.20										.94			
STFB Fact. 5	.01										.50			

STFB Fact. 6	.00										.03			
STFB + DAQ:S and N		49%	45%	38%	40%	47%	56%	57%	42%	45%				
MMPI+ % Corr	96%	51%	46%	52%	48%	60%	45%	53%	53%	65%	100%	53%	54%	55%
Numb.P < .05 *S*	39 / 57%	3/20 / 15%	2/20 / 10%	4/20 / 20%	3/26 / 12%	1/20 / 5%	1/20 / 5%	7/26 / 27%	0/20 / 0%	2/26 / 8%	31 / 46%	34 / 50%	19 / 28%	31 / 46%
Numb.P < .05 *N*	40 / 59%	3/20 / 15%	1/20 / 5%	2/20 / 10%	4/26 / 15%	1/20 / 5%	1/20 / 5%	5/26 / 19%	0/20 / 0%	5/26 / 19%	32 / 47%	15 / 22%	22 / 32%	31 / 46%
Numb.P < .05 *M*	65 / 72%	41 / 46%	0/90 / 0%	9/90 / 10%	3/90 / 3%	9/90 / 10%	3/90 / 3%	34 / 38%	0/90 / 0%	1 / 1%	58 / 64%	61 / 68%	50 / 56%	1 / 1%
Numb.P < .05 *C*	6 / 86%										1 / 14%	0 / 0%	0 / 0%	0 / 0%
M + S M:S Number.		55% / 4:3	47% / 3:2	56% / 6:1	47% / 6:0	64% / 10:3	57% / 10:2	56% / 3:3	53% / 10:3	62% / 12:0				
M + S + N M:S + N Numb.		55% / 4:3	47% / 3:2	56% / 6:1	47% / 6:0	65% / 10:4	61% / 10:2	69% / 14:7	58% / 12:4	70% / 16:5				
M + STFB + S + N M:STFB + S + N.		56% / 4:5	47% / 3:2	55% / 6:1	53% / 8:1	64% / 8:4	53% / 3:3	66% / 10:6	54% / 3:5	69% / 16:8				

543

STFB + S + N	45%	42%	57%	56%	47%	40%	38%	45%	49%
STFB:S + N	1:3	0:2	4:6	3:5	1:3	1:1	1:1	3:0	3:2

* Asterisks mark variables that entered into the Discriminant Function analysis for this column.

Table 21.2: Probabilities of F (relationship) between Addicause and other scales and Indicators of substance uses and Discriminant Function % Correct Classifications

AXIS LABELS AND VARIABLES	DYF1 DYrs	DYC1 DYrs	DYC2 DYrs	DYC3 DYrs	DUY1 DU AND Y	DUY2 DU AND Y	DUY3 DU AND Y	DUY4 DU AND Y	DUY5 DU AND Y	DYC4 DYrs	ADF4 ADUY	ADF1 ADUY	ADF2 ADUY	ADF3 ADUY
DAQ Discrim S	xxx	44%	--	45%	57%	40%	39%	46%	xxx	46%	48%	40%	46%	39%
% Correct N		46%	--	55%	57%	43%	46%	xxx		xxx	xxx	--	42%	--
01: Social S	.38													
Anxiety N	.72													
02: Social S	.83	.15	.53	.88	.97	.45	.15	.60		.76	.72	.63	.79	.94
Enjoyment N	.23	.16	.54	.78	.62	.44	.38					.87	.65	.70
03: Reactive S	.02	.38	.70	.19	.69	.67	.25	.24		.81	.37*	.86	.76	.73
Depression N	.11	.18	.74	.13	.11	.51	.19					.41	.46	.40

	1	2	3	4	5	6	7	8	9	10	11	12
04: Stimulus *S*	.11											
Hunger *N*	.26											
05: Rigid *S*	.57											
Self-Image *N*	.25											
06: Social *S*	.89											
Influence *N*	.96											
07: Aggressn *S*	.13											
Inhibition *N*	.32											
08: Guilt *S*	.19	.71	.03	.00	.05	.02	.00	.01	.02*	.87	.21	.60
Intolerance *N*	.02	.33	.01*	.00	.03	.02				.89	.06	.76
09: Loneliness *S*	.47											
N	.02											
10: Social *S*	.02	.50	.68	.60	.07	.23	.40	.64	.03*	.49	.52	.19
Contact Wsh *N*	.04	.47	.61	.27	.08	.37				.54	.19	.14
11: Reality *S*												
Denial *N*												
12: Authorit *S*	.01	.13	.00*	.00*	.00*	.00*	.00*	.00*	.25	.35	.03	.57
Rebellion *N*	.00*	.16	.01	.00*	.00*	.00				.29	.01*	.64

13: Flat *S* Depression *N*		.22 .38	.48 .92	.02 .07	.02 .01	.21 .49	.19 .16	.08		.02	.89	.64 .85	.25 .24	.51 .70
14: Vivid *S* Imagery *N*														
15: Control *S* Effort *N*														
16: Control *S* of Others *N*														
17: Grief *S* Reaction *N*														
18: Substanc *S* Enhancement *N*														
19: Pain *S* Sensitivity *N*														
20: Hedonism *S* *N*		.97 .54	.58 .85	.84 .49	.33 .42	.18 .13	.03 .02	.12		.33	.16	.29 .35	.31 .36	.98 .87
21: Social *S* Withdrawal *N*														

	C1	C2	C3	C4	C5	C6	C7	C8	C9	C10	C11	C12	C13
22: SubCult. *S* Values / *N*	.02 / .04*	.14 / .22	.83 / .43	.04 / .04	.05 / .04	.01 / .00	.02		.07	.71	.26 / .43	.41 / .27	.35 / .52
23: Inhibit *S* Dependency / *N*													
24: Immediat *S* Gratificatn / *N*	.54 / .99	.31 / .56	.26 / .59	.35 / .36	.36 / .48	.82 / .86	.67		.92	.39	.22 / .50	.68 / .85	.28 / .40
25: Paranoid *S* Sensitivity / *N*													
26: Rationality *S* Defence / *N*													
27: Oppressive *S* Inhibit / *N*													
28: Comfortable *S* Inhibit / *N*													
29: Affect *S* Disturbance / *N*													
30: Affect *S* Denial / *N*	.32 / .54	.79 / .74	.95 / .80	.84 / .99	.68 / .66	.76 / .53	.20		.83	.23	.57 / .79	.87 / .90	.42 / .29

31: Demean S / Others N												
32: Group S / Satisfact'n N												
33: Dogmatism S / N												
34: Wish Be S / Different N	.15 / .14	.84 / .73	.20 / .18	.14 / .06	.10 / .04	.08 / .01	.01	.10	.12	.56 / .76	.38 / .23	.71 / .99
35: Self- S / Depreciat'n N												
36: Rigid S / Moralizat'n N	.37 / .30	.60 / .55	.39 / .60	.00* / .00*	.03 / .02*	.75 / .68	.62	.12	.64	.01* / .05	.01* / .04*	.04* / .14
37: Paroxys- S / mality N	.10 / .07	.55 / .46	.66 / .53	.34 / .13	.20 / .23	.37 / .20	.02	.26	.85	.14 / .15	.95 / .47	.17 / .23
38: Rules S / Intolerance N												
39: Effort S / Strain N												

40: Pep-Up **S**	.93	.73	.89	.95	.40	.11	.43		.47	.19	.16	.86	.50
Effect **N**	.58	.99	.82	.92	.64	.23					.10	.86	.85
41: Rigid **S**													
Habits **N**													
42: Easy Go **S**													
Enjoyment **N**													
43: Metabolic **S**													
Disorder **N**													
44: Fast-Lane **S**	.20	.52	.23	.01	.16	.00	.17		.22	.34	.12	.57	.70
Living **N**	.64	.67	.28	.05	.25	.00					.37	.53	.61
45: Hypo-**S**													
glycaemia **N**													
46: Allergy **S**	.13	.50	.02*	.05	.03	.01	.01		.02	.78	.22	.33	.54
Stress **N**	.09	.75	.06	.05	.08	.02					.46	.28	.85
47: Physiolog. **S**	.09	.19	.02	.06	.09	.05	.00		.00	.35	.20	.02*	.72
Anxiety **N**	.12	.53	.04	.06	.11	.03					.14	.03	.72
48: Punitive **S**	.03	.39	.01	.01	.00	.00	.01		.00	.06	.07	.35	.38
Reinforcemt **N**	.01	.61	.01	.00	.00	.00*					.22	.03	.54

49: Affect S Avoidance N												
50: Control S Sensitivity N												
51: Guilt S Proneness N												
52: Anger/ S Hostility N												
53: Somatic S Depression N	.01* .01	.68 .59	.26 .07	.12 .02	.08 .06	.00 .00*	.01	.00	.30	.34 .31	.15 .06	.92 .98
54: Hungry S Heart N												
55: Impaired S Self-Esteem N												
56: Masked S Disappointm N												
57: Felt S Rejection N												

58: Need to *S* Communicate *N*											
59: NeedCalm *S* Nerves *N*											
60: Substanc *S* Enhancement *N*	.41 .11	.28 .29	.28 .24	.16 .17	.07 .22	.00 .01	.01	.03	.47	.30 .32	.80 .45	.70 .54
61: Forget *S* Failures *N*											
62: WshNovel *S* Experiences *N*											
63: Avoid *S* Boredom *N*											
64: Assert *S* Confidence *N*											
65: Avoid *S* Attractiven *N*											
66: Impaired *S* Sleep *N*											

67: NeedCalm/ *S* Relaxation *N*											
68: Substanc *S* Dependency *N*											
ML: MMPI L	.21	.59	.02	.10	.24	.17				.09	.52	.68
MF: MMPI F	.06	.67	.23	.26	.66	.00				.71	.15	.99
MK: MMPI K	.29	.92	.27	.46	.09	.10				.00	.95	.03*
01: MMPI Hs	.80	.21	.88	.41	.80	.22				.65	.69	.26
02: MMPI D	.78	.59	.64	.67	.49	.49				.26	.53	.51
03: MMPI Hy	.55	.36	.47	.60	.71	.65				.31	.45	.10
04: MMPI Pd	.37	.42	.10	.17	.21	.15				.63	.05	.19
05: MMPI MF	.69	.67	.14	.11	.56	.43				.13	.52	.13
06: MMPI Pa	.01*	.39	.06	.45	.17	.00*				.14	.03	.62
07: MMPI Pt	.06	.10	.23	.45	.36*	.04				.17	.04	.81

08: MMPI Sc	.03	.10	.02	.22	.09	.01				.60	.02	.45
09: MMPI Ma	.01	.99	.01	.06	.17	.00				.11	.45	.31
00: MMPI Si	.70	.83	.91	.50	.39	.84				.02	.48	.89
MMPI TSC F1	.99	.35	.59	.94	.70	.82				.01	.84	.85
MMPI TSC F2	.62	.35	.76	.68	.91	.13				.12	.70	.91
MMPI TSC F3	.70	.67	.15	.23	.54	.06				.05	.63	.33
MMPI TSC F4	.21	.83	.13	.12	.04*	.09				.02	.13	.25
MMPI TSC F5	.81	.65	.30	.78	.91*	.19				.03	.69	.36
MMPI TSC F6	.02	.37	.06	.05	.13	.04				.22	.11	.45
MMPI TSC F7	.14	.87	.38	.11	.56	.15				.00	.35	.71
Plus Getting	.74	.39	.22	.48	.53	.16				.00	.47	.59
MMPI DY 1	.40	.17	.10	.27	.65	.05				.16	.29	.13
MMPI DY 2	.58	.72	.77	.90	.97	.92				.87	.48	.04

MMPI DY 3	.08*	.51	.10	.36	.43	.28					.40	.69	.01
MMPI DY 4	.07	.94	.08	.11	.21	.00					.02	.24	.30
MMPI DY 5	.16	.87	.10	.33	.26	.00					.05	.08	.38
MMPI PrimDef	.20	.11	.04	.03	.05	.07					.07	.05	.97
MMPI Regress	.49	.40	.14	.15	.92	.82					.01	.91	.03*
MMPI Repress	.20	.07	.11	.96	.28	.38					.14	.55	.62
MMPI Denial	.85	.12	.16	.26	.50	.09					.02	.33	.65
MMPI Project	.70	.46	.80	.45	.24	.94					.74	.77	.12
MMPI Displac	.72	.97	.95	.76	.30	.85					.21	.73	.17
MMPI Intellz	.03	.75	.98	.43	.13	.56					.60	.10	.04
MMPI S.Doubt	.11	.88	.61	.53	.64	.60					.10	.74	.61
MMPI RctForm	.82	.45	.31	.63	.28	.80					.37	.43	.38
MMPI OvAcThk	.02	.37	.08	.05	.14	.05					.17	.11	.40

MMPI IntEffc	.28	.37	.18	.19	.27	.05					.11	.31	.59
MMPI Anxiety	.18	.88	.44	.12	.52	.16					.00*	.38	.74
MMPI Depress	.26	.86	.14	.10	.05	.13					.02	.12	.23
MMPI Anger	.78	.67	.24	.64	.82	.13					.02	.69	.30
MMPI Anhedon	.27	.82	.16*	.71	.41	.53					.37	.31	.56
MMPI Respons	.01	.84	.02	.00	.01	.00					.72	.01	.09
MMPI Toleran	.07	.42	.01	.10	.34	.00					.17	.30	.38
MMPI Empathy	.54	.55	.79	.45	.18	.18					.83	.14	.80
MMPI RolPlay	.55	.77	.36	.31	.27	.00					.00*	.21	.41
MMPI Dominan	.20	.96	.45	.04*	.15	.41					.13	.17	.30
MMPI SocPart	.58	.96	.99	.86	.36	.99					.74	.95	.49
MMPI SocPres	.86	.17	.45	.56	.88	.10					.01	.54	.76
MMPI Dependc	.31	.60	.34	.14	.64	.12					.00*	.44	.80

Dom-Submiss.	.96	.67	.73	.23	.68	.26				.50	.54	.63
Love-Hate	.05	.88	.04	.32	.49	.00				.26	.15	.77
MMPI EgoStrn	.06	.41	.45	.10	.90	.15				.06	.20	.49
MMPI Resilie	.24	.45	.13	.25	.61	.05				.00	.37	.95
MMPI S.Cntrl	.00*	.02*	.00*	.02	.00*	.12				.16	.01	.05
MMPI Impulsv	.02	.65	.01	.01	.00*	.01				.05	.06	.36
MMPI Delinqu	.13	.68	.12	.20	.44	.00				.11	.01	.64
MMPI Raw Spy	.18	.34*	.67	.03	.01	.02*				.29	.22	.18
MMPI HabCrim	.06	.71	.05	.02	.00	.05				.54	.01	.14
MMPI PrisAdj	.07	.87	.49	.00*	.00	.13				.22	.01	.00*
MMPI Escapis	.00	.42	.00	.00	.00	.00*				.08	.00*	.67
MMPI ParViol	.47	.57	.29	.65	.96	.26				.04	.99	.16
MMPI Recidiv	.09	.58	.18	.17	.16	.34				.13	.88	.26

	.05*	.28*	.40	.41	.71*	.28				.23	.21*	.25
MMPI OvCoHos												
MMPI Violenc	.04	.98	.01	.05	.04	.00				.26	.09	.38
MMPI ThrSuic	.11	.57	.02	.06	.43	.01				.06	.10	.84
MMPI UncAcSx	.18	.82	.74	.12	.46	.97				.19	.73	.62
Paedophilia	.15	.09	.38	.13	.80	.31				.29	.11	.24
Aggravatd Sx	.01	.69	.06	.11	.00*	.07				.06	.01	.07
MMPI Alcohol	.02	.91	.00*	.00*	.04	.19				.31	.05	.97
MMPI DrgAbus	.01	.77	.08*	.68	.04	.21				.17	.30	.28
Work Attitud	.07	.88	.13	.02	.09	.02				.10	.23	.43
Rehab.Motiv.	.97	.47	.17	.53	.39	.63				.82	.59	.20
Change Motiv	.15	.35	.18	.32	.26*	.12				.00	.15	.96
Thyroid Path	.29	.69	.53	.98	.86	.12				.99	.49	.75
Caudality	.20	.99	.33	.19	.12	.10				.01	.51	.74

LowBackPain	.65	.88	.27	.60	.37	.53					.01	.33	.13
Pariet-Front	.16	.99	.32	.09	.18*	.06					.09	.38	.83
Soc.Adjustmt	.82	.77	.66	.93	.62	.99					.03	.53	.70
MMPI DeprCon	.12	.88	.10	.14	.29	.05					.06	.17	.53
MMPI PMorale	.19	.87	.44	.18	.24	.16					.00	.39	.25
MMPI RelFund	.16	.80	.89	.99	.09	.65					.65	.64	.00*
MMPI AuthCnf	.12	.67	.01	.15	.51	.03					.20	.67	.30
Psychoticism	.04	.38	.03	.15	.42	.00					.10	.11	.38
Org.Symptoms	.06	.25	.14	.12	.35	.01					.29	.13	.62
MMPI FamProb	.29	.68	.07	.34	.08	.09					.11	.09	.46
MMPI ManHost	.73	.63	.07	.42	.75	.07					.41	.90	.12
MMPI Phobias	.29	.94	.32	.54	.02*	.77					.51	.23	.63
MMPI Hypoman	.27	.79	.62	.34	.63	.04					.04	.90	.06

MMPI PHealth	.10	.35	.29	.47	.94	.06					.23	.61	.86
MMPI PharVir	.37	.90	.60	.62	.77	.09					.04	.17	.26
MAST-Alcohol													
DAST-DrugsR2													
STFB TotalY1													
STFB Fact. 1													
STFB Fact. 2													
STFB Fact. 3													
STFB Fact. 4													
STFB Fact. 5													
STFB Fact. 6													
MMPI+ % Corr	55%	42%	54%	70%	61%	45%					52%	46%	48%
Numb.P < .05 *S*													

Numb.P < .05 *N*													
Numb.P < .05 *M*													
Numb.P < .05 *C*													

* Asterisks mark variables that entered into the Discriminant Function analysis for this column.

REFERENCES

Dahlstrom, W. G., Welsh, G. S., and Dahlstrom, L. E. (1972). <u>MMPI Handbook: Volume I, Clinical Interpretation</u>. Minneapolis: University of Minnosota Press.

Dahlstrom, W. G., Welsh, G. S., and Dahlstrom, L. E. (1975). <u>MMPI Handbook: Volume II, Research applications</u>. Minneapolis: University of Minnesota Press.

Dunn, W. L. (Ed.). (1973). <u>Smoking behaviour: Motives and incentives</u>. New York: John Wiley and Sons.

Ellis, A. (1962). <u>Reason and emotion in psychotherapy</u>. Secaucus, N. J.: Lyle Stuart and Citadel Books.

Hunt, W. A. (Ed.). (1970). <u>Learning mechanisms in smoking</u>. Chicago: Aldine.

Jackson, D. N. (1974). The Personality Research Form. Port Huron, Michigan: Research Psychologists Press.

James, T. and Woodsmall, W. (1987). <u>Time-Line Therapy and the basis of personality</u>. Cupertino, CA: Meta Publications.

Leary, T. (1957). <u>Interpersonal diagnosis of personality: a functional theory and methodology for personality evaluation</u>. New York: Ronald Press.

Manson, M. P. (1965). The ALCADD Test: Manual of directions and norms. Beverly Hills, CA: Western Psychological Services.

Manson, M. P. (1965). Manual: The Manson Evaluation. Beverly Hills, CA: Western Psychological Services.

Marlatt, G. A. and Gordon, J. R. (Eds.). (1985). Relapse Prevention: Maintenance strategies in the treatment of addictive behaviours. New York: The Guilford Press.

McDougall, W. (1923). Purposive or mechanical psychology. Psychological Review, 30, 273–288.

Murray, H. A. (1938). Explorations in personality. Boston: Harvard Psychological Clinic.

Osgood, C. E. (1953.) Method and theory in experimental psychology. New York: Oxford University Press.

Peniston, E. G. and Kulkosky, P. J. (1990). Alcoholic personality and alpha-theta brainwave training. Medical Psychotherapy, 3, 37–55.

Quirk, D. A. (1976). Treatment for epileptic alcoholism. The Ontario Psychologist, 7, 36-41.

Quirk, D. A. (1993). The Goal-Finding programme: Trainers' manual. Brampton, Ontario: Ontario Correctional Institute Program Report (PR93-1).

Quirk, D. A. and Reynolds, R. M. (1991). Large-group psychological treatment workshops. Brampton, Ontario: Ontario Correctional Institute Research Report (RR91-1).

Reynolds, R. M. (1994). The Survey of Thoughts, Feelings, and Behaviours: Manual. Champaign, Illinois: IPAT (in press).

Reynolds, R. M. and Quirk, D. A. (1994). <u>Transforming the criminal mind</u>. Oakville, Ontario: Author.

Selye, H. (1976). <u>The stress of life</u>. New York: McGraw-Hill.

Sterman, M. B. (1974). Neurophysiologic and clinical studies of Sensorimotor Rhythm EEG biofeedback training: Some effects on epilepsy. <u>Biofeedback and Self-Control, 1973</u>. Chicago: Aldine.

Welsh, G. S. and Dalhstrom, W. G. (Eds.). (1956). <u>Basic readings on the MMPI in psychology and medicine</u>. Minneapolis: University of Minnesota Press.

Wolpe, J. (1958). <u>Psychotherapy by reciprocal inhibition</u>. Stanford: Stanford University Press.

ABOUT THE AUTHORS

Douglas Arthur Quirk (1931-1997)

Douglas A. Quirk was born in India, the son of missionary parents and, if I remember correctly, spent some time in boarding schools in England. He was educated in the classics, as well as in the classical English music hall ballads.

He received his B.A. and M.A. from the University of Toronto, and completed all of the requirements for his Ph.D. except for his dissertation – and he subsequently taught Psychology for Psychiatrists and Nurses in the U. of T. Department of Psychiatry for many years. He was a Clinical Fellow of the Ontario Society for Clinical Hypnosis, the Behavior Therapy and Research Society, and the American and Ontario Associations of Marriage and Family Counsellors, and he was a Fellow of the Royal Society of Health.

Doug was a prolific writer. His many publications included:

(1966) The Application of Learning Theories to Psychotherapy: Component Therapies and the Psychoses. Paper read at the Canadian Psychological Association Annual Convention

(1968) Former Alcoholics and Social Drinking: An Additional Observation. The Canadian Psychologist, 9, 498-499

(1976) O.P.A.'s Brief to the Royal Commission on Violence in the Communications Industry. The Ontario Psychologist, 8, Supplement

(1980) Nutrition and Crime: a review. Report Prepared for The Solicitor General of Canada

(1982) Biofeedback in Dangerous Offenders: Learning Normal Functioning of the Nervous System. Poster Session Paper, Ontario Psychological Association, Annual Convention

(1986) Nutrition and Violence. Invited Address, John Howard Society of Canada Conference

(1991) A Practical Measure of Offence Seriousness: Sentence Severity. Ontario Correctional Institute Research Report (RR91-1)

(1994) The nature and modification of criminality, Paper presented (with Reg Reynolds) at the Annual Convention of the Ontario Psychological Association.

At various times during his career, he served as consultant to the World Health Organization, (S.E. Asia Region), the Scarboro Foreign Missions Society (Toronto), the Canadian Institute of Stress (Toronto), Toronto Catholic Children's Aid Society, York-Lea Mental Health Project (Toronto), the American Society for Humanistic Education, the Institute for Applied Psychology, Humanitas Systems (New York), Biomedical Engineering Associates (Toronto), North York General Hospital (Toronto), and Green Valley School & Hospital (Florida).

From 1959 to 1967, he was Senior Psychologist at the Ontario Hospital, Toronto and, from 1961 to 1967, Director of the Behaviour Therapy Unit there. From 1967 to 1971, he was Director of Clinical and Research Labs at the Clarke Institute of Psychiatry. Briefly, he was in full-time private practice; and then from 1975 to 1995, he was Senior Psychologist at the Ontario Correctional Institute.

Reg M. Reynolds, Ph.D., C. Psych. (Retired)

Reg Reynolds was born in Grande Prairie, Alberta. He attended London Normal School (for teacher training) before becoming interested in psychology and special education. He received his B.A. and M.A, from the University of Western Ontario, and his Ph.D. from the University of Waterloo.

He was a psychologist for almost sixty years. At various times during his career, he functioned as a counsellor and psychotherapist for individuals, couples, and groups; as Director of Vocational and Recreational Services at Lakeshore Psychiatric Hospital; as Chief Psychologist at the Vanier Centre for Women, the Oakville Reception and Assessment Centre (for juveniles admitted to training school), and the Ontario Correctional Institute; as a consultant regarding the assessment and treatment of sex offenders; as a consultant regarding ethical issues; as Coordinating Psychologist for the Central Region of the Ontario Ministry of the Solicitor General and Correctional Services; as a researcher; as a college lecturer; as an intern in, clinical member of, and board member of the Halton Centre for Childhood Sexual Abuse; as an intern, co-therapist and therapist in the treatment of spousal abuse; as a member of the Council of the College of Psychologists of Ontario; as a developer of biofeedback equipment and as a provider of biofeedback; as a student of education and special education; as a student of Applied Behavioural Analysis (ABA) and its application in the treatment of children with autism; as psychologist and Supervising Clinician in the Ontario Government's Intensive Behavioural Intervention program for children with autism; as an educator of parents of children with autism; and, more recently, as clinical supervisor of ABA-based programs for children with autism.

He is the author and publisher of *Teaching Children with Autism: An ABA Primer*, and has several other books in press.

INDEX

A

AA groups, 42, 45, 48, 59, 148, 412
ABLE reading ability, 108, 123
Addicause, xi, 5, 33, 38, 41–42, 63–
    64, 70–71, 74–79, 82, 84, 108,
    110–11, 121, 123, 136
Addicause scales, 19, 59, 70–71, 73,
    79, 83–84, 118
addictions, ix–xii, 3–7, 9–11, 13–23,
    43–47, 69–71, 81–82, 84–85,
    101–3, 113–16, 119–21, 125–27,
    135–39, 141–45, 147–56
addictive behaviour, ix–xi, 3–4, 10–
    11, 13, 15–17, 32, 45–47, 49–50,
    73, 82–83, 102–4, 118–21,
    147–48, 152, 440–41
addictiveness, x, 44, 57, 70, 86, 115–
    16, 136
addictive personality, 16, 20, 46
addictive substances, x, 14–15, 17, 19,
    22, 32, 38, 43, 45–47, 51, 74–77,
    81–82, 148–50, 152, 407
Addicure, 41–42, 106, 117, 134, 241,
    519
alcohol, 3, 17–18, 38–39, 57–58,
    80–81, 84–87, 106, 116–17,
    168, 192–93, 199, 201, 208–9,
    213–14, 359
ANS (autonomic nervous system),
    11–12, 102, 147, 453–54, 456,
    464

anticipatory avoidance, 12
anxiety, 4, 12, 76, 81, 152, 289, 294,
    306, 356–57, 396, 401–2, 413,
    454–55, 480, 502–3

B

badnesses, 387, 437, 439, 448, 451
blocks
    Consolidation, 97–105, 382, 393,
        404, 421, 434, 452, 470, 482,
        506
    Orientation, 95–96, 98–104, 153,
        373, 384, 395, 406, 423, 437,
        453, 472, 483
    Therapeutics, 95, 97–104, 378, 389,
        400, 414, 426, 435, 450, 469,
        477, 480–82, 499
    Tools, 95, 97–104, 375, 386, 398,
        408–9, 426, 442, 461, 476, 480,
        487

C

causality, 6, 38, 47, 68–69, 150, 152,
    470
causes, kinds of
    final, 2, 7–11, 13, 15–17, 20–21, 33,
        35–37, 53–54, 68–69, 81, 86,
        88–89, 93–94, 107
    initial, 7–11, 15–16, 54–55, 59, 468

perpetuating, 7–11, 16–17, 20, 35–37, 53–54, 68–69, 81, 86, 88–89, 93–94, 98, 116
causes of addiction, xi, 4, 6, 11, 14, 19–20, 46–47, 49, 55, 61, 63, 73, 75, 82, 93
chronic, 2, 6, 9–12
cognitive therapies, 10, 103, 401
criminality, 43–44, 74–75, 79, 101, 114, 116, 128, 131, 136–39, 141–43, 152, 357–58, 437, 484, 566
criminality measures, 44, 114–15, 138, 141–42

D

DAQ (Dimensional Addicause Questionnaire), 21, 23, 26, 29, 38, 56, 108, 114–17, 123–26, 138–39, 142–43, 157, 509–10, 512–15, 517–18
DAQ axes, 89, 91–92, 109–11, 114–15, 117, 119, 124–27, 137–39, 141, 509–10, 512, 514–15, 517
DAST (Drug Abuse Screening Test), 3, 43, 56, 63, 69–70, 73–74, 79, 82, 106, 108, 122–23, 258, 266, 274, 356
decortication, 17–18
depression, 4, 12–13, 16, 18, 76, 81, 103, 290–91, 306–7, 322–23, 338–39, 445, 471–76, 519–20, 528–29
diagnosis, 1–2, 46
differential treatment, 112, 115, 117–19, 127, 141–42

E

energies, body's, 418, 445, 447, 452, 464, 473, 475, 478–79, 493

F

factor analyses, 22, 58–60, 66–68, 86–88, 137
factor loadings, 61, 68, 213

G

goodnesses, 387, 439
group involvement, 500–502
guilt feelings, 101, 437, 441–43, 445, 450

I

inertia, 7, 399
internal consistency, 62, 64
IPAT Anxiety Form, 108
'I' statement, 392, 446, 453

J

joylessness, 19, 90, 99, 395, 398

L

Learned escape, 12, 15
love feelings, 395–97, 401

M

MAST (Michigan Alcoholism Screening Test), 3, 43, 56, 63, 69–70, 73–74, 79, 82, 106, 108, 122–23, 258, 266, 356, 358
MMPI (Minnesota Multiphasic Personality Inventory), 71, 74–79, 81–83, 108, 123, 281, 297, 304, 313–14, 329–30, 345–46, 353–55, 535, 552, 561

N

NA groups, 45, 48, 148, 412
needs, 17, 20–23, 36–37, 63, 68, 86, 94, 107

Needs, 22

needs, self-actualizing, 422, 451–52, 494, 506

N score, 54–55, 68–69, 80–82, 87–88, 108, 110, 112, 123, 125, 127

O

OCI (Ontario Correctional Institute), iii, x, 40–42, 45, 56, 59, 65, 75, 86, 94, 108, 123, 133–34, 566–67

OUT-breath, 384, 457, 460, 503

P

polar concepts, 22–23, 25–26, 29–30

polar words, 22–23

predictions, discriminant, 75–77, 79

R

reflexive values, 427, 481–82

reinforcements, 11, 19, 35, 37, 80–81, 86, 94, 99, 116, 143, 394–95, 406, 471

reinforcers, 9, 11, 15, 20–23, 33, 36–37, 53, 63, 68, 80, 89, 98, 100, 406

response sets, 38, 62–63

RPM (Ravens Progressive Matrices), 108, 123

S

scales, 14, 25–26, 28–33, 35, 37, 51–53, 55, 59–62, 64–67, 69, 71–73, 78, 84–86, 114, 358–59

S score, 52, 54–55, 68–69, 80–82, 87–88, 110, 112, 123–24, 127

statements, three-part, 100, 419, 445–46, 453

STFB (Survey of Thoughts, Feelings, and Behaviours), 74–77, 79,

82–83, 108, 114, 123, 136–39, 142–43, 358, 526, 543–44, 562

street drugs, 18–19, 38, 56, 58, 78, 80–81, 84–85, 116, 138, 193, 209

T

tools for treatment

Autogenic Training, 422

Estimate the Number of Dots task, 97, 375

Future Pacing, 99, 404

Goal-Finding programme, 97–99, 103, 377, 386–87, 391, 404, 490, 562

Love Test Tube, 99, 103, 396–97, 400–401

Media proofing, 101, 411

Modelling Behaviour procedure, 476

Personal Development Goals procedure, 97, 477

Precision Learning, 97, 376, 463

Rational-Emotive Therapy, 100, 103, 401, 445

Swish, 102, 104, 421, 435, 452, 505–6

Task Focus method, 390

timeline, 97, 99, 378–80, 403–4, 435

Visual Squash, 97, 101–2, 434, 450, 452

in vivo procedure for assertive training, 393, 420

treatment component, ADDICURE

treatment 1, 91, 96, 113, 373, 435

treatment 2, *91, 97, 113, 383, 477*

treatment 3, *91, 98, 113, 394, 482*

treatment 4, *91, 99, 113, 119, 406, 435, 480*

treatment 5, *91, 100, 113, 423, 482*

treatment 6, *92, 101, 113, 437, 480*

treatment 8, *92, 98, 103, 113, 471*
treatment 9, *92, 104, 113, 119, 132, 482*
treatment programmes, 44, 64, 84, 86–89, 92–93, 96, 107–8, 112, 122–24, 126–27, 373, 395
types of depressions
anhedonic, 471
reactive, 33, 36, 53, 62, 81, 88, 138, 245–46, 357, 471, 525
somatic, 81, 138, 243, 358, 471, 520, 526
temperamental depressions, 471

U

universe
behavioural, 7–9, 116, 468

physical, 7, 9

V

validity
concurrent, 70, 71–73
construct, 71, 73, 83–84, 93, 111, 117–18, 126
face, 70
predictive, 70, 77
values
avoidance, 427, 429, 432, 481
conflicted, 427–29, 432, 434, 481
personal, 101, 424–25, 493
real, 425–26, 501

Y

'You' statement, 392, 445–47, 453